Russian Nationalism
Since 1856

Russian Nationalism
Since 1856

Ideology and the Making of Foreign Policy

Astrid S. Tuminez

ROWMAN & LITTLEFIELD PUBLISHERS, INC.
Lanham · Boulder · New York · Oxford

ROWMAN & LITTLEFIELD PUBLISHERS, INC.

Published in the United States of America
by Rowman & Littlefield Publishers, Inc.
4720 Boston Way, Lanham, Maryland 20706
http:/www.rowmanlittlefield.com

12 Hid's Copse Road
Cumnor Hill, Oxford OX2 9JJ, England

British Library Cataloguing in Publication Information Available

Library of Congress Cataloging-in-Publication Data
Tuminez, Astrid S.
    Russian nationalism since 1856 : ideology and the making of foreign policy / Astrid S. Tuminez.
        p. cm.
    Includes bibliographical references and index.
    ISBN 0-8476-8883-6 (alk. paper)—ISBN 0-8476-8884-4 (pbk. : alk. paper)
        1. National state. 2. Nationalism—Russian (Federation) 3. Nationalism—Russia. 4.
    Russia (Federation)—Foreign relations. 5. Russia—Foreign relations. I. Title.

JC311.T86 2000
320.54'0947—dc21
                                                                                            99-087952

Printed in the United States of America

♾™ The paper used in this publication meets the minimum requirements of American National
Standard for Information Sciences—Permanence of Paper for Printed Library Materials,
ANSI/NISO Z.39.48-1992.

For Jeffrey and Michal

Contents

Acknowledgments

At the age of five, I attended my first day of formal education at a Catholic school for girls in Iloilo City on the island of Panay in the Philippines. My teacher explained that the smartest girl would sit in the first seat, first row, and the rest of us would be ranked by smartness—with the unfortunate dummy of the group taking the last seat in the last row. Having never learned the ABCs or 123s in my nipa hut home, I was seated in the last seat, last row, and, for a few days, suffered the ignominious distinction of being the least intellectually developed girl in first grade. Thankfully, the rest of my academic career turned out better than those first few bewildering days of school. I'm sure my late teacher would have been pleasantly surprised to hear that I've written a book.

Writing this book took a lot of help and I want to acknowledge the input of many friends and colleagues. I owe a huge debt of gratitude to my former thesis adviser at MIT, Donald L. M. Blackmer, who supported me in my sometimes discouraged attempts to finish this book while keeping other demanding, full-time jobs. Don gave me useful advice, read my draft chapters, and provided inspiration. One can't ask for more from a friend and adviser! I also want to thank Stephen Van Evera, who asked good questions when I wrote the dissertation on which this book is based. The Project on New Approaches to Russian Security, under the direction of Celeste Wallander, gave me helpful comments on chapter 2 at one of its academic conferences. Others surrendered more of their free time to give me comments: Mark Kramer, Stephen Hanson, Ted Hopf, Kim Zisk, Brian Taylor, and Kim Malone. I thank them and hope that I haven't overly taxed their friendship and good humor.

Dr. David Hamburg, Senator Sam Nunn, and Lord David Owen were very kind to review my manuscript and give me comments. I greatly appreciate their support given their extremely busy schedules and hope that I did not hound them too much with notes and phone calls. The Council on Foreign Relations gave me an office to use on weekends when I worked on the book and other Russia-related research and gave me the chance to think further about Russian nationalism as a Council Adjunct Fellow. For this, I am most thankful to Leslie H. Gelb, Lawrence

J. Korb, and Vincent A. Mai. I also want to thank Vlada Tkach, Alfred Alden, and Leonardo Arriola, who gave me valuable research assistance.

I want to thank my editor at Rowman & Littlefield, Susan McEachern, who early on thought my work worth publishing. I am grateful also to Matt Hammon, who answered many questions, and Lynn Gemmell, who patiently and efficiently worked with me on copyediting and production.

I would like to acknowledge two professors who, more than anybody, got me interested in Russia and things Russian: the late Teodosio Lansang of the University of the Philippines and Gary L. Browning of Brigham Young University. I also want to thank the staff in archives and libraries that I used in Moscow, and the Russian politicians and scholars who generously gave me interviews. I want to acknowledge Maurice R. Greenberg, Axel I. Freudmann, and Frank G. Wisner at American International Group, who convinced me to launch a new career on Wall Street without giving up this project.

My late father, Lazaro Tuminez, never prodded me to do anything but was always a gentle, reassuring presence in my life. He would have been delighted to see this book. My mother, Redencion Segovia, was known to be out harvesting in the rice fields when many months pregnant. She has taught me perseverance and the art of juggling multiple tasks and roles. My greatest debt is to Jeffrey, whose wit, intelligence, and love never fail, and Michal, whose gifts to me are endless. With this project done, we can now do some serious work on play-dough and coloring books!

1

A Looming Specter?
The Problem
of Russian Nationalism

For thou art an holy people unto the Lord thy God, and the Lord hath chosen
thee to be a peculiar people unto Himself, above all the nations that are upon
the earth.

—Deuteronomy 14:2

To feel truly and proudly Russian, Russians . . . instinctively strive toward
expansion and its corollary, militarism.

—Richard Pipes, 1995

Russia has never consolidated itself as a nation-state. Because the Russian state
developed as a multinational empire with an autocratic government, its leaders generally demurred from the option, exercised by other western European
rulers in the nineteenth century, to consolidate their rule and unify their states by
(in part) deploying nationalism—an ideology that formed and exalted one
"nation," while also locating the source of political power squarely in the hands of
the "people." Its historical weakness notwithstanding, many observers point to
nationalism as an important factor in post-Soviet Russian domestic politics and
foreign policy. Many take as given the strength of a malevolent Russian nationalist ideology, ascribing such negative developments inside Russia as the extremist
Vladimir Zhirinovsky's electoral victory in 1993, Moscow's wars in Chechnya, the
Russian Duma's refusal in 1997 to return art booty from World War II, and strikes
and other manifestations of discontent in 1998 to the rising power of aggressive
nationalism. In foreign policy, experts warn that ugly strains of nationalism are
fueling Russian hegemonic and expansionist actions in the "near abroad" and are
contributing to ominous unpredictability in Russian behavior. In the United
States, policymakers who support NATO expansion underline the need to hedge
against the possible resurgence of Russian imperialism, chauvinism, and nation-

1

alism. Yet others, alluding to Weimar Germany's experience, warn that economic hardship and national humiliation among a "frustrated and resentful" people could create a nationalist backlash that would renew Russian authoritarianism at home and unleash aggression abroad.[1]

Is widespread concern about the malevolent effects of Russian nationalism—especially in foreign policy—justified? What has been the record of nation-building in Russia, and how did nationalism evolve in the multiethnic, imperial Russian state? What variants of nationalist ideology have been propagated in Russia, and what are their benign or aggressive implications for foreign policy? What triggers the articulation of aggressive nationalism, and what factors facilitate its influence on Russian foreign policy? Do historical precedents imply that Russians are likely in the future to let aggressive nationalism govern their international behavior? What might facilitate the evolution of a benign nationalist ideology in Russia, and what Western policies might help or hinder this possibility? These are the questions this book addresses.

WHAT ARE WE TALKING ABOUT?
NATIONALISM AND NATIONS

Scholars and observers of nationalism tend to disagree on the meaning of the term. For the purposes of this book, nationalism refers to a political ideology[2] that holds that (1) there exists a nation with identifiable members; (2) the nation, as a collective, has characteristics that make it distinct; (3) the individual and the state's highest loyalty must be to the nation's core interests or mission; and (4) the nation is the chief repository of legitimate political authority.[3] Nation is a *concept* or *category* used to connote a community of people who share kinship based on race, culture, language, ethnicity, religion, and/or citizenship. Because the "nation" is the delineated source of political authority, nationalism implies some consensus between rulers (or aspiring rulers) and the purported members of a nation on mutual goals, rights, and obligations.[4] This implies that nationalism has a key role to play in binding state and society effectively in a common sense of identity and purpose. This book deals precisely with nationalism as a consolidating factor in Russian history and politics. It is not concerned with the nationalism of narrow elites, but with nationalism that becomes widely resonant and mobilizes people to action.

The political aspect of nationalism is important because nationalism is a modern phenomenon whose potency and impact are most clearly manifest in the political arena—that is, "nationalism is, above and beyond all else, about politics and . . . politics is about power."[5] This book aims to elucidate, in part, the role that nationalism has played to support, attack, or influence state power in Russia and why, in some cases, particular nationalist ideas succeeded in shaping the state's foreign policy. Other approaches treat nationalism primarily as a general state of mind or style of thought, but such approaches obscure the political processes and ends that are intimately connected with the rise and use of nationalism as a political instrument in the modern state system.[6]

Because "nation" is a concept or category, it follows that nations are often not the real or enduring entities that many take them to be. In Rogers Brubaker's words, the interesting question is not "[What] is a nation?" but "How does nation work as practical category . . . as cognitive frame? What makes the use of that category by or against states more or less resonant or effective? What makes the nation-evoking and nation-invoking efforts of political entrepreneurs more or less likely to succeed?"[7] The conceptual flexibility of a nation makes it a potent force in politics, allowing nationalists or the preachers and practitioners of nationalism to evoke or invoke selectively those ideas that might best serve their aims in a particular political, economic, or cultural context.[8] Finally, the claim that a putative nation or "people" is the repository of legitimate political authority does not imply that nationalism must rise in tandem with mass democracy, although it has been the case that liberalizing political reform does facilitate the rise of nationalism and movements to support it.[9] Unrepresentative and narrow elites may claim that they speak or act on behalf of the nation, even while violating in practice the rights of the population. This was true, for example, of Joseph Stalin's use of Russian nationalism in the Soviet Union, when he claimed to speak for the Russian nation even while his regime slaughtered millions.

But nationalism—confined to a narrow, repressive elite—can work only temporarily as a mobilizing force. In the long term and in the context of diminished use of coercion, the state's ability to harness nationalism for its purposes will depend in part on some devolution of political power from state authorities to the people ruled. Similarly, intellectuals and other unofficial generators and proponents of nationalist ideas must ultimately seek broader support from society in order to increase the political power of their ideas. The more they are able to attract followers, the more likely that their nationalist prescriptions will have an impact on the opinions and actions of the ruling regime. Without broader societal support or consensus between nationalist proponents and larger social groups, nationalism is less likely to influence who exercises state power and how.

Nationalism's content and intensity can change over time and under different political and social circumstances,[10] but in all cases the idea that a purported nation should be the locus of individual and collective loyalty is critical. Also critical is the intensity of belief in the nation and its purposes. It is such belief—and much less the factual or enduring content of nationalist ideology—that moves people to social action. The fact that the content of nationalism can and does change, and that "nation" itself can be a flexible concept, does not mean, however, that nationalist beliefs can be equally and easily manipulated in all circumstances. The particulars of historical experience, ethnic socialization, cultural traditions, and collective memory create a "structure of political discourse"[11] that renders public consciousness more susceptible to some nationalist ideas than others and increases the likelihood that these ideas will shape social attitudes and actions.[12] Those who advocate radically new parameters of nationalism might have a more difficult time finding resonance among potential mass followers whose preexisting shared myths, traditions, symbols, and emotive memories diverge from the new ideas being propagated.[13]

NATIONALISM, THE STATE, AND FOREIGN POLICY

What is the linkage between nationalism and the foreign policy of a state? Every dominating system, especially the state, must establish and cultivate its legitimacy using material, coercive, ideological, or other means. In the modern context, nationalism has become an extremely powerful instrument for those who wield state power and wish to strengthen their legitimacy and stabilize their rule.[14] Nationalism has legitimating effects because it anchors political power in a defined "nation," and those who can successfully claim to represent the nation and defend its alleged interests are likely to strengthen their political appeal, increase their societal support, and secure their power. In other words, nationalism can be an important ideological pillar of the state and can supplant or complement other sources of state legitimacy.

Nation as category delineates boundaries between groups largely for political purposes. It reflects the experience of contact with significant "others" and asserts a specific interpretation of that experience. Thus, it carries important implications for foreign policy. Who is *in* the nation, and who is *out*? What should be the proper relationship between insiders and outsiders? What actions should leaders take to maintain this relationship, and what policies would best serve the putative nation's wellbeing? What critical or transformative events and contacts with outsiders crystallize the way a nation is defined at particular points in time?[15] Do these events and contacts validate particular viewpoints on how the nation should behave toward outsiders or "others"? These questions link nationalism with foreign policy: how a state conducts its international affairs can potentially affirm or contradict nationalism, an ideological source of political legitimacy. By taking certain actions in foreign policy, state elites can either undermine or bolster their own rule.[16] They could become vulnerable to criticism by unofficial groups who might claim to be truer articulators and defenders of the nation's interests. These groups may seek the right to exercise state power, change the direction of foreign policy, or even create their own state. Whatever their claims may be, these groups can undermine the legitimacy of a ruling regime and the integrity of a state, and they can force state authorities to pursue certain actions in foreign policy—all in the name of the nation.

NATIONALISM: BENIGN AND AGGRESSIVE VARIETIES

Widespread concern about nationalism's malevolent effects, especially on a state's international behavior, is not new and prevails in much of the literature on nationalism in general, and Russian nationalism in particular. E. H. Carr, C. J. H. Hayes, and Arnold Toynbee, for example, assert that nationalism inevitably deteriorates into militarism, imperialism, and even fascism. Some scholars on Russia make similar linkages, arguing, in sum, that Russian nationalism is a "malignant and monolithic force that is unreformable and tends inexorably toward extreme forms of racism and authoritarianism."[17]

Although many scholars indeed view nationalism as chiefly malevolent, others seek to distinguish the nuances between nationalism as a benign or constructive force and nationalism as an aggressive or destructive ideology.[18] In the Russian case, scholars debate two sets of issues. First, is the *content* of Russian nationalism, as Liah Greenfeld has argued, "ethnic, collectivist, and authoritarian" and infused with anti-Westernism, exaggerated claims of uniqueness, and an apocalyptic sense of mission?[19] Is Russian nationalism intrinsically malevolent and, therefore, likely to degenerate into aggression or fascism, or does it include a spectrum of benign and malevolent variants? Can certain types of nationalism, in fact, be a positive force for state consolidation, economic development, and the pursuit of collective welfare? Can nationalism be a force for good inside Russia?[20] This book seeks to highlight differences in nationalist ideologies that have been propagated in Russia in the past century and a half and contends that the menu of nationalism in Russia does not contain only aggressive options.

The second issue of debate concerns the effects of Russian nationalism: Are militarism, expansionism, and imperialism inevitable products of nationalism? Adam Ulam and Richard Pipes imply that such effects are continuous and determined and that Russian nationalism or a broadly defined "national culture" has always caused aggression and expansion during both the tsarist and Soviet periods.[21] Rather than supporting these claims of determinism and inevitability, this book seeks more to elucidate the contingent nature of Russian nationalism and its impact. It provides some detail on the conditions under which specific variants of nationalism have, in the past, stimulated Russian expansion and military responses in foreign policy. This book also seeks to differentiate between strategic or imperial state interests that have motivated Russian expansion or military action, versus similar behavior that is propelled primarily by nationalism. This argument is developed further in chapter 2, where the historical weakness of nationalism in Russia is juxtaposed with the growth and strength of the imperial state.

THE CENTRAL ARGUMENT

This book argues that nationalism has been a weak and uneven force in Russia in general and that aggressive variants of nationalism have only *rarely and briefly* shaped Russian foreign policy. Moreover, when aggressive nationalism did influence the foreign policy decisions of Russian officials, it mainly reinforced Russia's traditional foreign policy interests as a "great power," and did not justify or herald maximalist programs of conquest or expansion. There are, to be sure, many other instances in Russian history when the state expanded its territory by conquest as well as less forceful means, but nationalism was not the primary motor behind the majority of these instances.

Russian rulers have never successfully used nationalism as an ideology to bind state and society in a lasting way. Referring to nineteenth-century Russia, the historian Hans Rogger argues that

> [Russian nationalism] could only with difficulty, if at all, view the tsarist state as the embodiment of the national purpose, as the necessary instrument and expression of national goals and values, while the state, for its part, looked upon every autonomous expression of nationalism with fear and suspicion.[22]

Notwithstanding the weakness and difficult path of nationalism in Russia, there have been two instances in the past century and a half when aggressive nationalism did influence Russian decisions to pursue war as an instrument of foreign policy. These two cases are Russian panslavism in 1856–78, culminating in Russia's decision to go to war against Turkey on behalf of "brother Slavs" in 1877–78, and great power nationalism in 1905–14, which influenced Russia's entry into World War I. In contrast, although many thinkers and politicians have propagated aggressive nationalist ideas in the late- and post-Soviet years (1989–98), their ideas have mostly failed to inspire the use of force or war as a preferred option in Russian foreign policy. This state of affairs can change in the future, but why has aggressive nationalist influence been weak in the first decade of post-Soviet Russia?

This book highlights national humiliation, caused by ignominious military or other defeat abroad, as the triggering mechanism for the articulation of aggressive types of nationalism in Russia. It examines the national humiliation that occurred in Russia after its defeat in the Crimean War in 1856, its failure in the Russo-Japanese War in 1905, and the collapse of the Soviet Union in 1991. Humiliation in these three instances roused aggressive nationalist ideas largely because, for centuries, Russian political discourse has been steeped in imperial thinking and great power myths. These myths and the imperial definition of the state provided fertile ground for nationalist entrepreneurs to sow ideas of perfidy and malevolence by outsiders, the ineffable rightness of nationalist revenge, and the irresistible triumph of force to restore the greatness of a humiliated nation.

But if national humiliation stimulates the articulation of aggressive national-ism, it is insufficient to propel such nationalism to center stage in foreign policy. In the two cases in this book where aggressive nationalism influenced Russian for-eign policy, three factors help explain the outcome: (1) the failure of influential individuals and groups who serve as custodians of collective memory and articu-lators of prevailing ideologies to redefine the imperial state as the basis of Russian "greatness"; (2) a deep erosion and breakdown of governance, which (a) facili-tated the efforts of aggressive nationalist entrepreneurs to capture public attention and support, and (b) made a weakened ruling elite vulnerable to the penetration of aggressive nationalist public opinion; and (3) the occurrence of international threats and crises, which intensified nationalist sentiment and augmented pres-sure on weakened policymakers to take decisive action reflecting an aggressive nationalist agenda. Of these variables, threats and crises in the international sys-tem have been the most important precipitating factors in the impact of aggres-sive nationalism on foreign policy.

In the post-Soviet period (1991–98), Russia has undergone severe national humil-iation and the deep erosion of internal governance. Yet the most aggressive variants of nationalism have not stimulated war or expansionism in Russian foreign policy. In particular, aggressive nationalist arguments to reclaim former Soviet territory or defend the interests of "Russians abroad" have not become core Russian interna-tional priorities. This book argues that aggressive nationalism has not markedly influenced Russian foreign policy because, in the first place, a shift has occurred in the structure of Russian political discourse. Leading state officials and others who educate and inform public opinion, especially in the Gorbachev and early Yeltsin years, have articulated and supported a non-imperial definition of the Russian state. Contrary to Richard Pipes's assertion that to "feel truly and proudly Russian, Rus-sians [even today] . . . instinctively strive toward expansion and its corollary, mil-itarism,"[23] many authoritative Russian policymakers, thinkers, and publicists in the late 1980s and early 1990s have condemned the imperial state and sought other cri-teria on which to base Russian "greatness." Their ideas have resonated in part with a citizenry fatigued by the burdens of the imperial past. These citizens accepted a geo-graphically reduced state, rejected forceful means to change the status quo with new neighbors, and believed that internal stability and welfare should be the focus of the state and people. There are, of course, still many voices in Russia in support of empire, but these have been unable to dominate the country's political discourse—at least by the end of 1998. Second, aggressive nationalism has not decisively influ-enced Russian foreign policy because many Russians in the early 1990s perceived the international system as largely benign. Until 1996, dramatic threats and crises had not emerged to mobilize aggressive nationalist sentiments inside Russia. This dynamic has changed with the expansion of NATO to states that were formerly in the Soviet orbit and with NATO's bombing of Serbia over Kosovo in 1999. The implica-tions for Russian nationalism of a perceived, more hostile international environment will be addressed in the last chapter of this book.

THE CONTENT OF RUSSIAN NATIONALISM

This book looks at three case studies of nationalism and foreign policy in Russia. Each case begins with a description of the content of salient variants of nationalism in the period in question and seeks to capture the benign or aggressive implications of different nationalist ideas for foreign policy. Which ideas are most likely to encourage the state to go to war or prefer the use of force in the conduct of its foreign relations? I focus on three aspects of nationalist thought: (1) criteria for membership in the nation; (2) definition of the self- and other-image; and (3) statement of the national mission.

Membership in the Nation

Nationalism claims that a nation exists whose members are identifiable. If ethnic, rather than civic, criteria determine membership in the nation, then nationalism will likely have aggressive implications for foreign policy. Ethnic nationalism is based on claims of common ancestry; may emphasize a common religion, language, or culture; and includes pan-ideologies such as panslavism. Civic nationalism, in contrast, classifies as members of the nation everyone residing within specific territorial boundaries, regardless of their ethnic, racial, religious, or linguistic background, and emphasizes adherence to rules that govern citizenship within a state.[24] Ethnic nationalism can push states toward unification—for example, states whose putative ethnic members are scattered territorially might seek to rescue their irredenta and conquer territory in order to unify all members of the ethnic group in one national state. Ethnic unification can occur peacefully, but it is more often the case that violent methods are used to rescue and unify irredenta. Besides aggressive action to unify irredenta, ethnic nationalism also threatens disenfranchisement, persecution, or forced assimilation of minorities or foreigners who reside within the borders of a state. External allies or kin of these persecuted groups might come to the aid of their beleaguered relatives and violence could escalate. The tragedies of "ethnic cleansing" in Bosnia, Croatia, and Serbia, and the genocide against Tutsis in Rwanda in the 1990s, starkly illustrate the violence that can arise from ethnic nationalism.[25]

Although ethnic nationalism clearly has more dangerous implications than its civic counterpart, it is not the case that ethnic nationalism always leads to malevolent outcomes. In fact, the probability of such outcomes may decrease if ethnic nationalism co-exists with a liberal-constitutional political framework. Within that framework, membership in the nation may still depend on ethnic criteria, but state authorities will extend full political and cultural rights to minorities or other nondominant groups; allow access to economic benefits among a broad range of ethnic groups; and focus the national mission on internal stability and development rather than outward expansion and aggression.[26] One example of benign ethnic nationalism is Quebecois nationalism, which is linguistically based but accepts a liberal-constitutional political framework. Finally, civic nationalism itself need not always be benign, especially if it advocates the coercive assimilation

of groups who want to preserve their distinct national cultures and ethnic traditions. Violent conflict may arise between dominant groups and targets of assimilation, and attempts by assimilatory targets to seek help from kin outside the state
could lead to violence.

Self-Image and Other-Image

Intellectuals who write about and interpret a nation's history and culture play a
key role in the formation of the national self- and other-image. As Miroslav
Hroch points out, the earliest phase of nationalist development usually begins
with an intensive and passionate concern by intellectuals to know more about the
language, history, and culture of the particular group to which they belong. [27]
The greater the claims of uniqueness in a nation's self-image, the more dangerous the implications of nationalism for a state's international behavior. Its proponents might engage in chauvinistic mythmaking that glorifies the nation while
denigrating outsiders.[28] Chauvinism justifies violence against inferior "outsiders"
and can encourage the repetition of past aggression that has not been recognized
as a wrongdoing. It can also justify conquest and slaughter of outsiders on the
grounds that the national group's "special" status endows it with more rights and
privileges than others and ordains it for glorious purposes. The flavor of chauvinism is captured, for example, in an argument by Albert Jeremiah Beveridge,
who favored U.S. imperialist conquests in the nineteenth century: "We are a con-
quering race . . . American law, American order, American civilization and the
American flag will plant themselves on shores hitherto bloody and benighted,
but by those agencies of God henceforth to be made beautiful and bright."[29]
    Even more dangerous foreign policy implications arise when a chauvinist
national self-image is accompanied by an attitude that exalts war and the military
as instruments for asserting the nation's rights and privileges. It is thus important
to ask, How prominent is the military in the national culture? Do people believe
that the nation's greatness lies chiefly in its military strength and prowess? Is there
a belief that war and conquest strengthen the nation, and is there a vigilant effort
to inculcate military values in society? In Germany, where aggressive nationalism
became a powerful force between the world wars of the twentieth century, some
nationalists preached that war nurtured the best qualities of the German people,
ennobled the nation, and led to national rejuvenation.[30]

National Purpose

Nationalism holds that the individual and the state's highest loyalty must be to the
nation's core interests and its articulated mission. But how do nationalists define
the national mission? If the national mission is defensive toward outsiders and
focused on improving collective welfare, maintaining the territorial status quo,
and strengthening internal cohesion and stability, then nationalism is likely to
have benign implications for foreign policy. But, if the mission emphasizes the
creation of a separate state, hegemony, imperial status, or messianism, national-

ism is likely to have aggressive implications for foreign policy. Its proponents might justify war and expansion as legitimate means to serve the nation's interests. They might also deny other groups those rights that they reserve exclusively for themselves.[31] Undoubtedly, objective realities—including the existence of disputed territories, the dispersal of an ethnic population, and the weakness of neighbors—can mitigate or aggravate the messianic or imperialistic components of an articulated national mission.

NATIONAL HUMILIATION AND THE MYTH OF "GREATNESS"

Nationalist ideologies draw on myths, symbols, traditions, memories, and values that are familiar to a specific group of people.[32] In ascertaining how aggressive types of nationalism come to inform state behavior, it is important to examine the preexisting myths and values to which nationalism appeals. In Weimar Germany, for example, proponents of national socialism appealed to the wounded feelings of Germans who had been socialized in the myth that their state and nation was always, and should rightly be, a great power. Germany's defeat in World War I and the imposition of a harsh peace at Versailles stimulated backlash from elite groups (among them, intellectuals, politicians, and military and religious leaders) who began to preach that their nation had been humiliated and "stabbed in the back" by internal and foreign enemies. Weimar, in their eyes, was the "illegitimate child of defeat."[33] These groups reacted to Germany's national humiliation by advancing extremist nationalism. Their ideas fell on fertile ground because "virtually all sections of opinion" agreed on "the restoration of Germany's great power position" as a prime goal of domestic and foreign policy.[34] Although national humiliation, in isolation, did not cause the collapse of the Weimar Republic and the triumph of Nazism, it did create a context in which Hitler's promises of deliverance (i.e., overthrowing Versailles) and of a racially pure and strong nation with an assertive foreign policy became highly attractive and resonant.

If preexisting notions of great power status are strong, as in Weimar Germany, feelings of national humiliation are likely to be intense after a military fiasco or other international defeat. Elites, in particular, because they are the bearers of culture, the beneficiaries of a vibrant state, and the self-perceived representatives of national health and well-being, may react to national humiliation by propagating aggressive nationalist ideas to raise collective morale, to aggrandize themselves at a time of severe stress, and to seek to recapture lost privileges or positions of prestige and power.[35] They may articulate "compensatory illusions" in response to humiliation, emphasizing their people's "great spirituality . . . human sensitivity, warmth, a poetic soul, and spiritual closeness to 'what is really important in life.'" In contrast, they may portray their oppressors as the "embodiment of efficiency, coldness, intellectualism, and human estrangement."[36] Finally, they may predict the recovery of their nation and its impending vengeance on its torturers.

The concept of *ressentiment*, highlighted in Liah Greenfeld's work on Russian nationalism, explains in part why elites articulate aggressive nationalism in response to national humiliation.[37] *Ressentiment,* a "psychological state resulting from suppressed feelings of envy and hatred," stems from crises of identity among elites who become dissatisfied with their status and wish to change it but are unable to do so. What creates *ressentiment* are two conditions: (1) a belief on the part of the subject that it is fundamentally equal with its object of envy and (2) an actual inequality between subject and object of such dimensions that the presupposed equality becomes practically impossible to fulfill. For elites experiencing *ressentiment,* nationalism becomes an adaptive response to "status inconsistency; they use it to advance . . . status-seeking, status aggrandizement, and status preservation."[38] National humiliation may also affect broader segments of society to the extent that they are effectively socialized in great power myths about themselves and their state. Such socialization occurs via public education, popular culture, and traditions. To the degree that this socialization is effective, members of the broader society will thus also express feelings of, and reactions to, national humiliation.

Russia, comparable to Germany, is a state where centuries of history and socialization have created and reinforced a mythic great power identity tied to the imperial state. This theme is developed further in chapter 2, but it is worth noting for the moment that the term for "great" in Russian, *velikii,* is used to connote "giant size or magnitude, magnificence and splendor, nobility, grandness, excellence, majesty and glory."[39] It is reserved for people, places, and events that have left an indelible mark on Russian history and on prevalent interpretations of that history: Peter the Great, Catherine the Great, Lord Novgorod the Great (capital city, greatest trading center, and military bastion against the West in appanage Russia), the Great Northern War (which marked Russia's entry into the realm of European great powers in the eighteenth century), the Great Reforms (marking radical social and political change in the nineteenth century, including the abolition of serfdom), the Great Revolution of 1917, and the Great Fatherland War (marking the Russians' heroic victory over Nazi Germany). Most instances when "greatness" is invoked in Russian history have to do with Russian military power, territorial conquest, and prestige and respect on the world stage. "Greatness," in short, has been associated with empire and imperial rulers who, before the Bolshevik revolution, bore the title of *tsar* or *imperator* (evoking the Roman *Caesar* and the Roman emperor). Since the reign of Peter the Great (1682–1725), Russians have widely accepted and deeply felt the notion that their state is destined to be great and deserves to be a leading actor in the international system. Because of such a traditional belief, it is likely that national humiliation will cause *ressentiment* and lead to the articulation of aggressive nationalism.[40]

In covering three instances of national humiliation (the Crimean War defeat in 1856, the defeat by Japan in 1905, and the Cold War defeat and demise of the Soviet Union in 1991), this book looks at both the objective and psychological components of national humiliation. Objective components include the immensity of military defeat, diplomatic debacles, the waning of economic and military power, and human and territorial losses. Psychological elements include feelings of betrayal, demoralization, wounded pride, shame, and unjust treatment by external enemies. Concomitantly, there are nationalistic assertions of Russian greatness and uniqueness, the perfidy of outsiders, and Russia's right to avenge wrongs visited upon it. If national humiliation is the precondition that stimulates aggressive nationalism, what variables help translate such nationalism from words into actions? What factors increase the salience of aggressive nationalist ideas and make state decision makers susceptible to their influence?

SOME PROPOSITIONS ON RUSSIAN NATIONALISM AND ITS IMPACT ON FOREIGN POLICY

Russian Political Discourse: Primacy of the Imperial State

In every society, there are individuals and groups that play a key role in assessing the validity of ideas, debating their implications, and promoting or rejecting components of the prevalent structure of political discourse.[41] They include political leaders, journalists and publicists, scholars and writers, religious authorities, civic activists, and military authorities. These actors play a key role in shaping ideas that become most valid or legitimate in a given social and political context. In the context of nationalism, these actors function as custodians of collective memory, emphasizing this or that aspect of a "nation's" history, relationship with others, and collective priorities. The more pluralistic and competent these actors are, if they operate in a context where free speech is protected, the more likely that they can help hinder the impact of aggressive variants of nationalism. They do this by, first, exposing and combating chauvinist mythmaking that nationalist entrepreneurs might use to justify aggressive foreign policy prescriptions.[42] Second, they can try to redefine the structure of political discourse by offering alternative ideas and norms to guide the definition, organization, and activity of the state and the nation it purports to represent. The more competent and vigorous they can be, for example, at invalidating an imperial definition of the state, the more likely that they can help prevent the impact of aggressive nationalism on foreign policy.

Throughout most of Russian history, censorship, illiteracy, and authoritarian government have constrained independent and pluralist voices in Russian political discourse. Nonetheless, many actors have engaged at different times in active debate about Russian social and political development. An important and recurring debate in the past century and a half has addressed the organization of the state and the proper way to conduct relations between state and society. There has been a prevalent bias in Russian political discourse toward defining the role of the state and its greatness in imperial terms. This bias is a result of the fact that, in Russia, imperialism and the state developed coterminously.[43] Russia, in other words, evolved as an empire-state rather than a nation-state, and the needs and rights of society have always been subordinated to the demands of the imperial state. This issue is explored further in chapter 2, but suffice it to say that the imperial state has been the product, as well as the cause of, much of Russian expansionary and militarist foreign policy.

If key actors who shape Russian political discourse fail fundamentally to question or revise the imperial definition of the state and its mythic links to Russian "greatness," then aggressive types of nationalism are more likely to influence Russian foreign policy. That is, if the imperial conceptualization of the state combines with ethnic, hyper-distinctive, and messianic components of nationalist ideology, then there is a greater likelihood for a foreign policy favoring war, expansion, and militarism. However, if guardians of discourse successfully discredit the concept of an imperial state, and offer alternative ideas by which to organize the state and measure its "greatness," then aggressive nationalism is less likely to have an impact on the state's international behavior. The explosive blending of aggressive ethnic nationalism and a definition of state power and greatness in imperial terms is illustrated in Adolf Hitler's Germany and Benito Mussolini's Italy, where foreign policies became relentlessly violent and expansionist.

In the struggle to maintain or alter the predominant structure of political discourse, who is best able to exploit or reinterpret symbols that resonate with the articulate public? Are there symbols that political actors can use to advance a non-imperial definition of the state? Are there crucial events that the custodians of collective memory can highlight to affirm or discredit the imperial state? What evidence is there, if any, of the formation in whole or in part of a new consensus on the nature and role of the state? Alternative, non-imperial definitions of the state can help neutralize the impact of national humiliation; diminish the need for compensatory, aggressive nationalism; and legitimize efforts to focus state power and resources on internal reform and stability rather than external power projection. Did the Soviet period, for example, which emphasized nationality-based administration, help legitimize the idea of the nation-state (i.e., the Russian Federation) as a preferable alternative to the empire-state (i.e., the Soviet Union)?[44]

Erosion and Breakdown of Governance

The erosion and breakdown of governance in a state can help advance the influence of aggressive nationalism. Such erosion happens when (1) ruling state elites are divided in opinion and purpose, and cannot rule cohesively; (2) fundamental ideas (e.g., autocracy, communism) on which state power rests are discredited; and (3) internal security breaks down. The breakdown of governance leads to public loss of confidence in the state and undermines its legitimacy. If rulers have weak or low legitimacy, and if their rule partially depends on some popular consent, they can become vulnerable and susceptible to the efforts of aggressive nationalist entrepreneurs. They may resort to extreme nationalist rhetoric to recapture public attention and loyalty, to fight the image of a weak and ineffective state, and to restore some semblance of national consensus and unity. They may also fail to control effectively the activism of aggressive nationalists among their ranks, and thus facilitate the impact of nationalism on state policy.

If ruling elites are not cohesive, official opinions and policies may be unclear on issues or problems that might resonate deeply with society. Thus, a gap may arise for aggressive nationalists to fill, and nationalists could gain a greater role and greater credibility than might otherwise be the case in setting the agenda and formulating options for foreign policy.[45] As the state's priorities become more confused and as discipline in decision-making erodes, ineffective policies could result. This further increases the likely impact of aggressive nationalists. Official attempts to quell the activities of extreme nationalists at one time may be offset by tolerance and assistance to aggressive nationalists at other times. Also, political entrepreneurs within the state bureaucracy may propagate and aid aggressive nationalism contrary to official policy if they know that their superiors would be unable to impose sanctions against them.

Under conditions of eroded governance, state authorities become more open and vulnerable to the impact of aggressive nationalist public opinion on foreign policy.[46] This is so because of the legitimating effects of nationalist ideology. Indeed, in the past two centuries, nationalism has become the chief principle of legitimization for the modern state. Having successfully transferred sovereignty from traditional sources such as God or monarch to the "people" or "nation," state leaders who wish to be seen as legitimate must claim to represent the nation and be loyal to its interests and mission. When internal governance is shaky, ruling authorities become vulnerable to accusations that they no longer represent the nation or defend its interests. In this case, officials become more likely to listen to, and support, aggressive nationalist prescriptions in order to inject legitimacy into their rule and make it more secure.[47] By allying with public opinion that emphasizes the nation's uniqueness, rightness, and superiority, rulers can hope to reclaim their role as the nation's guardians. They may then blame outsiders for the nation's ills, begin preparations for a military campaign, or initiate aggression against alleged saboteurs of the nation's welfare.[48]

Material incentives and parochial interests can also motivate support for aggressive nationalism, especially in the context of eroded state authority and governance. The stronger these incentives are, the more likely that actors will support aggressive nationalism and advance its prescriptions in the hopes of gaining future rewards or restoring privileges from the past when the state was more cohesive and government was more effective. Some institutions, by virtue of their function, are likely to benefit from aggressive nationalism and may promote its prescriptions. One such institution is the army, whose privileged position and war-fighting function may be well served by chauvinistic and hegemonic ideas that promote national morale and strong armed forces.[49] Members of the military elite may thus lobby for, and preach, aggressive nationalism to facilitate the extraction of resources for military needs and to increase the privileges and prestige of military leaders.[50] In Weimar Germany, such institutions as the Colonial Society and the army, whose privileges and clout were sharply diminished by the Treaty of Versailles, became some of the most vociferous proponents of aggressive nationalism and the restoration of the imperial state. Heavy industrialists and representatives of big business, whose interests suffered due to demilitarization and economic depression, also supported ideas of *lebensraum* or national expansion.[51]

Weimar Germany's experience illustrates the linkage between the erosion of governance and the increased salience and impact of aggressive nationalism. The years following Germany's humiliation at the end of World War I were fraught with internal crises, including assassinations of political figures, the Great Depression in the 1920s (which created as many as six million unemployed citizens), the rise of anti-Weimar paramilitary groups, a *putsch* by the army and other acts of military insubordination, arson of government property, and crises in the cohesion of the cabinet. Several historians note that by the early 1930s, Weimar Germany was in "near civil war" condition.[52] Indeed, at that time, German state authority faced serious challenges, the ideas that underpinned the Weimar regime became severely discredited, and public protest multiplied against the government. Under these circumstances, the promises of extreme nationalists to restore order, albeit by authoritarian and violent means, became very attractive to society and came to dominate German domestic and foreign policies.

International Threats and Crises

Foreign policy results from a combination of international and domestic factors, and a substantive body of literature highlights the role of threat perceptions as a variable in policymakers' deliberations and choice of actions. When threats coincide with crises, in particular, the choices of state actors become more constrained and limited by domestic political factors, including such normative beliefs as nationalism.[53] Because nationalism is an ideology that emphasizes the distinctive qualities of a putative nation in relation to other groups and the world at large, and because it focuses on the characteristics, welfare, and needs of the "in-group," it becomes a salient reference point when society and its rulers perceive high levels of external threat to core historical interests. Aggressive nationalist beliefs come to the fore, in particular, because of their potential for consolidating ethnic identity, forging unity, and mobilizing people to serve the supreme good of a nation under threat.

Perceived external threats include not only military or economic dangers, but also losses in honor, reputation, and prestige.[54] Sensitivity to threats will be particularly high if such threats are linked to previous incidents of national humiliation—thereby intensifying feelings of cognitive dissonance (among the official elite and public) between national myths and beliefs of greatness, on one hand, and a harsh reality imposed by outsiders, on the other. In Weimar Germany such coercive measures imposed by the Allied powers as wresting territory from German control, and French and Belgian occupation of the Ruhr, substantiated conservative political groups' propaganda about "threats" to the German nation and people, and the need to counter those threats with aggressive nationalism.[55] While nationalists can sometimes conjure outside perils to benefit their ideology, objective factors such as geography, demography, history, ethnic conflicts with spillover effects, and relative economic and military power can increase or decrease the credibility of their claims.[56]

The impact of external threat perception in empowering aggressive nationalism in foreign policy becomes even more important in the context of crises.[57] Crises push policymakers and institutions to their limits and can threaten the downfall of personalities and the breakdown of ruling institutions. They do this by revealing starkly the discrepancies and contradictions between underlying social forces and demands, on one hand, and existing resources and policies of state, on the other. Crises also give leaders a very limited time window within which to take effective action. Under these conditions, two outcomes are possible. First, state officials may become convinced of the correctness of aggressive nationalist analysis and become more psychologically predisposed to nationalist prescriptions. They may become willing to take great risks in foreign policy—going beyond what may be sober or rational in a given context—in order to avert further and immediate losses or damage to core interests.[58] Second, officials may yield to nationalist pressure and use nationalism as an ideology to span existing and destabilizing disagreements among themselves, and between them and society. International threats and crises heighten the possibility of irreversible internal rupture and make the need more desperate for policymakers to find ideas that might help internal cohesion.[59]

The role of threats and crises in facilitating the impact of aggressive nationalism on foreign policy can be mitigated if the international system offers resources other than self-help to allow a state to defend against security threats and resolve crises.[60] If resources other than self-help are minimal or ineffective, and international diplomatic efforts fail to resolve crises, then state leaders are more likely to exploit, and yield to, aggressive nationalism.

WHAT COMES NEXT

Chapter 2 discusses the history of Russian nation-building and the unevenness of nationalism as a force in Russia, the primacy of the imperial state in Russian political discourse and experience, and the persistent gap between state and society that prevented the evolution of nationalism as a more permanent, binding ideology. Although rulers of tsarist Russia and the Soviet Union engaged in nation-building, none sought effectively to build long-term ties between society and state on the basis of nationalism. Chapters 3 and 4 describe and analyze cases of Russian nationalism and foreign policy. They highlight the fragmented nature of nationalist ideology, as manifested in the menu of competing "nationalisms" at various points in time, and the brief and limited power of aggressive variants of nationalism that did have a decisive impact on foreign policy. These two chapters chronicle the role and impact of panslavism and great power nationalism on foreign policy in 1856–78 and 1905–14. Chapter 5 describes nationalism during the Soviet period, including Stalin's use of Russian nationalism to help sustain Soviet power. It also chronicles Russian national humiliation after the Cold War and examines the impact of humiliation on Russian nationalist discourse. Finally, the chapter recounts the propositions of the main schools of nationalist ideology propagated in the late- and post-Soviet periods, and describes their implications for foreign policy. Chapter 6 examines post–Soviet Russian foreign policy and argues that aggressive nationalism has been a weak influence—at least, until 1998. The evidence used to illustrate the weakness of aggressive nationalism includes the actions and decisions of Russian policymakers vis-à-vis the Russian diaspora in the "near abroad"; conflicts in Georgia, Moldova, and Tajikistan; and the war in former Yugoslavia. Chapter 7 summarizes the book's findings and assesses the implications of the past for the future. Will a benign or aggressive nationalism consolidate in Russia and inform its behavior toward the outside world? What factors will help or hinder the success of a benign nationalist ideology in binding Russian state and society? In the aftermath of NATO expansion and Kosovo in 1999, what actions and policies of the United States and other Western allies will be particularly significant for the further evolution of Russian nationalism?

NOTES

1. The late Galina Starovoitova once warned that "one cannot exclude the possibility [of a fascist period] in Russia. We can see too many parallels between Russia's current situation and that of Germany after the Versailles Treaty. A great nation is humiliated, [and] many of its nationals live outside the country's borders. The disintegration of an empire [has taken place] at a time when many people still have an imperialist mentality. . . ." See *Radio Ekho Moskvy*, 14 October 1992, and notes from a personal conversation at Carnegie Corporation, New York, 16 November 1992. More recently, a U.S. foreign policy commentator has declared that "Since the end of the Cold War, Western policy toward Russia has been a textbook case in how to drive a people to fascism. Almost everything we have done to Russia repeats what the foolish Western Allies did to Germany after World War I. That, plus the Depression, put Hitler in power. Unless something radically changes, or unless we are much luckier than we deserve to be, something similar could happen to Russia." See Walter Russell Mead, "Don't Panic, Panic First," *Esquire*, October 1998, p. 162. See also "The Price of an Icon," *Economist*, 9 July 1998 (electronic version); "Rising Nationalism," *CQ Researcher*, 22 May 1998, pp. 474–75; Tom Raum, "Lawmakers Justify NATO Expansion," Associated Press, 23 March 1998; "Slap at Yeltsin as Legislators Veto Return of Art Booty," *New York Times*, 14 May 1997, p. 3; William Safire, "Clinton's Good Deed," *New York Times*, 7 May 1997, p. A35; Henry Kissinger, "Beware: A Threat Abroad," *Newsweek*, 17 June 1996, pp. 41–43; John B. Dunlop, "The 'Party of War' and Russian Imperial Nationalism," *Problems of Post-Communism* (March/April 1996):29–34; Charles Gati, "Weimar Russia," *Washington Post*, 17 March 1995, p. A27; Bruce Porter, "The Coming Resurgence of Russia," *The National Interest* (Spring 1991):14–23; Dimitri Simes, "Russia Reborn," *Foreign Policy* 85 (Winter 1991/92):41–62; Peter Reddaway, "Russia Comes Apart," *New York Times*, 10 January 1993, p. E23; and Walter Laqueur, "Russian Nationalism," *Foreign Affairs* (Winter 1992/93):102–16.

2. An "ideology" is a set of ideas, beliefs, and concepts (invented, factual, or normative) that purport to explain or justify a specific social order. If that order does not exist, the ideology "may constitute a believed strategy for its attainment." See Eric Carlton, *War and Ideology* (London: Routledge, 1990), pp. 18–21.

3. This definition includes both state-based and stateless nationalisms and draws on the work of John Breuilly, Paul Brass, and Anthony Smith, who emphasize the political aspects

of nationalism. See John Breuilly, *Nationalism and the State*, 2nd ed. (Chicago: University of Chicago Press, 1994), p. 3; Paul R. Brass, *Ethnicity and Nationalism: Theory and Comparison* (New Delhi: Sage, 1991), chaps. 1–3; and Anthony Smith, *Theories of Nationalism*, 2nd ed. (London: Duckworth, 1983).

4. See chapter 2 for further discussion of this idea and how it applies to Russia.

5. Breuilly, *Nationalism and the State*, p. 1, introduction and chapter 1.

6. The most common definition of nationalism is that used by Ernest Gellner and Eric Hobsbawm: a "political principle which holds that the political and national unit should be congruent." Hans Kohn defines nationalism as a "state of mind" in which the individual's supreme loyalty is to her nation-state. Echoing Kohn, Liah Greenfeld asserts that nationalism is a "particular perspective or a style of thought" based on the idea of the "nation"; it "locates the source of individual identity within a 'people,' which is seen as the bearer of sovereignty, the central object of loyalty, and the basis of collective solidarity." See Ernest Gellner, *Nations and Nationalism* (Ithaca: Cornell University Press, 1983), p. 1; Eric J. Hobsbawm, *Nations and Nationalism since 1780* (Cambridge, UK: Cambridge University Press, 1990), p. 9; Hans Kohn, *The Idea of Nationalism* (New York: Collier, 1944), p. 10; and Liah Greenfeld, *Nationalism: Five Roads to Modernity* (Cambridge: Harvard University Press, 1992), p. 3.

7. See Rogers Brubaker, *Nationalism Reframed: Nationhood and the National Question in the New Europe* (New York: Cambridge University Press, 1996), p. 16; Katherine Verdery, "Whither 'Nation' and 'Nationalism'?" *Daedalus* 122 (Summer 1993):37–46; and Craig Calhoun, "Nationalism and Ethnicity," *Annual Review of Sociology* 19 (1993):222–24. A more common definition of nation is a "group of people who believe that they are ancestrally related." See Walker Connor, *Ethnonationalism* (Princeton: Princeton University Press, 1994), pp. xi, 75; and Robert J. Kaiser, *The Geography of Nationalism in Russia and the USSR* (Princeton: Princeton University Press, 1994), p. 6. This definition excludes the nationalism of multiethnic states—e.g., the United States and Switzerland—whose peoples may not subscribe to the idea of common ancestry but nonetheless believe they constitute a "nation."

8. There are, of course, limits to the flexibility of "nation" as a concept. This is argued further below.

9. Examples of the development in tandem of political, economic, and administrative liberalism and nationalism are Germany in 1815–48 and the former Yugoslavia and USSR in more recent history. See Breuilly, *Nationalism and the State*, pp. 99–101; and Michael Mandelbaum, ed., *The Rise of Nations in the Soviet Union* (New York: Council on Foreign Relations, 1991).

10. On the dynamic quality of nationalism, see Kohn, *Idea of Nationalism*; Boyd C. Shafer, *Nationalism: Its Nature and Interpreters* (Washington, D.C.: American Historical Association, 1976); and Verdery, "Whither 'Nation' and 'Nationalism'?" pp. 37–46. This book does not address directly the debate between the "primordialist" and "constructivist" approaches to nationalism. As Brubaker has noted, primordialism—the view "that nations or ethnic groups are primordial, unchanging entities" is a dead subject that many writers on nationalism continue to resuscitate. Although disagreement continues on the relative weight of sources of nationalism (e.g., premodern traditions versus modern transformations), "[everyone] agrees that nations are historically formed constructs. . . ." Brubaker, *Nationalism Reframed*, p. 15, fn. 4.

11. In the political economy literature, the "structure of political discourse" refers to the prevailing set of political ideas in a given country. New economic ideas that are introduced have a greater chance for consolidation and implementation if their proponents frame them "in terms of existing ideologies and by using symbolic appeals to

commonly held beliefs." See Kathryn Sikkink, *Ideas and Institutions: Developmentalism in Brazil and Argentina* (Ithaca: Cornell University Press, 1991), p. 2. In Peter Hall's words, "There is . . . a certain structure to the political discourse of every nation, based on the network of associations that relate common political ideals, familiar concepts, key issues, and collective historical experiences to each other. . . . Over time, each nation builds up a set of politically evocative concepts and collective reference points that define the terms of political debate and provide participants in the political arena with a discursive repertoire to be used there." Peter Hall, *The Political Power of Economic Ideas: Keynesianism across Nations* (Princeton: Princeton University Press, 1989), p. 383.

12. Karl W. Deutsch elaborates on this idea in *Nationalism and Social Communication: An Inquiry into the Foundations of Nationality*, 2nd ed. (Cambridge: MIT Press, 1966), pp. 86–105. See also Ronald Grigor Suny, *The Revenge of the Past: Nationalism, Revolution, and the Collapse of the Soviet Union* (Stanford: Stanford University Press, 1993); Kenneth E. Boulding, "National Images and International Systems," in Wolfram F. Hanrieder, ed., *Comparative Foreign Policy: Theoretical Essays* (New York: David McKay, 1971), pp. 93–94.

13. Anthony D. Smith, *The Ethnic Origins of Nations* (Oxford: Basil Blackwell, 1986), p. 18.

14. See Max Weber, *Economy and Society: An Outline of Interpretive Sociology*, eds. Guenther Roth and Claus Wittich (New York: Bedminster, 1968), pp. 212–13; and Ronald L. Jepperson and John W. Meyer, "The Public Order and Formal Institutions," in Paul J. DiMaggio and Walter W. Powell, eds., *The New Institutionalism in Organizational Analysis* (Chicago: University of Chicago Press, 1991), p. 207.

15. Rogers Brubaker highlights an approach to "nationness as event," or considering nations not as categories that develop from centuries of political, economic, or social change, but as "something that *happens*." For example, how did the collapse of the Soviet Union and Yugoslavia cause sudden shifts in individual and collective definitions of, and commitment to, nation as category? See Brubaker, *Nationalism Reframed*, pp. 18–20.

16. On the linkage between nationalism and foreign policy, including nationalism as a psychological factor in international relations, see Ilya Prizel, *National Identity and Foreign Policy: Nationalism and Leadership in Poland, Russia, and Ukraine* (Cambridge, UK: Cambridge University Press, 1998), pp. 1–21.

17. David G. Rowley, "Russian Nationalism and the Cold War," *American Historical Review* 99 (February 1994):169–70; C. J. H. Hayes, *Essays on Nationalism* (New York: Russell and Russell, 1966); Alexander Yanov, *The Russian New Right* (Berkeley: University of California Institute of International Studies, 1978) and *Posle El'tsina: "Veimarskaia" Rossiia* (Moscow: Moskovskaia gorodskaia tip. A. S. Pushkina, 1995); and Kalevi J. Holsti, *Peace and War: Armed Conflicts and International Order 1648–1989* (New York: Cambridge University Press, 1991), pp. 317–18. Note also the scholarly emphasis on the nexus between nationalism and war, and nationalism and rising fascism and extremism in Russia. See Stephen Van Evera, "Hypotheses on Nationalism and War," in Michael Brown et al., eds., *Nationalism and Ethnic Conflict* (Cambridge: MIT Press, 1996–97), pp. 26–60; Jack Snyder, "Nationalism and the Crisis of the Post-Soviet State," *Survival* 35 (Spring 1993):5–26; Barry Posen, "The Security Dilemma and Ethnic Conflict," *Survival* 35 (Spring 1993):27–47; Mead, "Don't Panic, Panic First," p. 162; Christian Caryl, "Is This Weimar Russia?" *U.S. News and World Report*, 16 November 1998, p. 48; Karl W. Ryavec, "Weimar Russia?" *Demokratizatsiya* (Fall 1998); and Alexander Yanov, "The Rape of Russia," *Moscow News*, 18 June 1998.

18. Leonard W. Doob, *Patriotism and Nationalism: Their Psychological Foundations* (New Haven: Yale University Press, 1964), p. 263; see also Charles A. Kupchan, "Introduc-

tion: Nationalism Resurgent," in Charles A. Kupchan, ed., *Nationalism and Nationalities in the New Europe* (Ithaca: Cornell University Press, 1995), pp. 2–4.

19. Greenfeld, *Nationalism*, chap. 1.

20. For arguments on the positive role, and necessity, of nationalism in the development of post-Soviet Russia, see Nicolai N. Petro, "Toward a New Russian Federation," *The Wilson Quarterly* (Summer 1990):114–22 and "Within Russia, Nationalism is a Force for Good," *Newsday*, 22 May 1990, p. 51; James Billington, "Let Russia be Russian," *New York Times*, 16 June 1998, p. 15; Sergei Kortunov, *Rossiia: Natsional'naia identichnost' na rubezhe vekov* (Moscow: Moskovskii obshchestvennyi nauchnyi fond, 1997); and Geoffrey Hosking, *Russia: People and Empire* (Cambridge: Harvard University Press, 1997).

21. Richard Pipes, *Survival Is Not Enough* (New York: Simon and Schuster, 1984), pp. 1–40; and the following by Adam Ulam: "Russian Nationalism," in Seweryn Bialer, ed., *The Domestic Context of Soviet Foreign Policy* (Boulder: Westview, 1981), pp. 13–18; *Expansion and Coexistence* (New York: Holt, Rinehart & Winston, 1974); and "Nationalism, Panslavism, and Communism," in Ivo Lederer, ed., *Russian Foreign Policy: Essays in Historical Perspective* (New Haven: Yale University Press, 1962), pp. 39–67.

22. Hans Rogger, "Nationalism and the State: A Russian Dilemma," *Comparative Studies of Society and History* 4 (1961/62):253.

23. Richard Pipes, "Introduction," in Heyward Isham, ed., *Remaking Russia: Voices from Within* (Armonk, N.Y.: Sharpe, 1995), p. 5.

24. Greenfeld, *Nationalism*, pp. 1–12.

25. Myron Weiner discusses the potential for conflict over irredenta in "The Macedonian Syndrome," *World Politics* 23 (July 1971):65–83 and in "Peoples and States in a New World Order," *Third World Quarterly* 13 (1992):317–32. On former Yugoslavia and Rwanda, see "CIA Report on Bosnia Blames Serbs for 90% of the War Crimes," *New York Times*, 9 March 1995, pp. A1, A8; "Survivors Tell of Serb Atrocities in Fallen Enclave," *New York Times*, 23 July 1995, p. 8; Philip Gourevitch, *We Wish to Inform You That Tomorrow We Will Be Killed with Our Families: Stories from Rwanda* (New York: Farrar, Straus & Giroux, 1998).

26. See Michael Lind, "In Defense of Liberal Nationalism," *Foreign Affairs* 73 (May/June 1994):87–99.

27. Miroslav Hroch, *Social Conditions of National Revival in Europe*, trans. Ben Fowkes (Cambridge, UK: Cambridge University Press, 1985), pp. 11–13; and Smith, *Theories of Nationalism*, p. 136.

28. In India, for example, the Hindu nationalist Bharatiya Janata Party has selectively used stories of ancient atrocities committed by Muslim rulers in India to illustrate the hostility and vileness of Muslims, and to justify violence against the latter. See Amartya Sen, "The Threats to Secular India," *New York Review of Books*, 8 April 1993, pp. 26–32.

29. Stanley Karnow, *In Our Image: America's Empire in the Philippines* (New York: Ballantine, 1989), p. 109. On other points dealing with the kinds of national self- and other-images conducive to war and aggression, see Van Evera, "Hypotheses on Nationalism and War," pp. 47–53.

30. See Louis Snyder, *German Nationalism: The Tragedy of a People* (Harrisburg, Penn.: Telegraph Press, 1952), chap. 2; Gary D. Stark, *Entrepreneurs of Ideology* (Chapel Hill: University of North Carolina Press, 1981), chap. 5; and Gordon A. Craig, *Germany 1866–1945* (New York: Oxford University Press, 1978), pp. 491–92.

31. For example, Russian panslavism in the nineteenth century argued for the self-determination of Slavs under Austro-Hungarian and Ottoman rule, but denied the same rights to Poles under Russian imperial rule.

32. Smith, *Ethnic Origins of Nations* and *Theories of Nationalism, passim.*

33. See Louis Snyder, *Roots of German Nationalism* (Bloomington: Indiana University Press, 1978), p. 157. Although some scholars debate how materially punitive the Treaty of Versailles was, they agree on the treaty's destructive psychological impact. The vast majority of Germans rejected the treaty, and resentful elites used the war defeat and humiliating peace to argue that the Weimar government was illegitimate and incapable of defending the nation's interests. One scholar notes, for example, that by "keeping the wounds of defeat and national humiliation open, [reparation payments imposed by Versailles] made it virtually impossible to end the virulent nationalist agitation against the republic at any time during its existence. . . . In many German minds their economic sufferings became directly linked with the foreign oppression imposed upon the nation." See E. J. Feuchtwanger, *From Weimar to Hitler: Germany, 1918–33* (London: Macmillan, 1993), p. 316.

34. See L. Snyder, *Roots of German Nationalism*, pp. 157–87; Feuchtwanger, *From Weimar*, pp. 316–25; Fritz Stern, *Dreams and Delusions* (New York: Knopf, 1987), pp. 147–91; Mary Fullbrook, *Germany, 1918–1990: The Divided Nation* (London: Fontana, 1991), pp. 44–89; A. J. Nicholls, *Weimar and the Rise of Hitler*, 2nd ed. (New York: St. Martin's, 1979), pp. 42–48; Craig, *Germany 1866–1945*, pp. 391–433; Warren Morris, *The Weimar Republic and Nazi Germany* (Chicago: Nelson-Hall, 1982), pp. 73–88; Woodruff Smith, *The Ideological Origins of Nazi Imperialism* (New York: Oxford University Press, 1986), pp. 196–230; and Richard Bessel, *Germany after the First World War* (New York: Oxford University Press, 1993), pp. 254–84.

35. On the fundamental clash between German great power identity, on one hand, and elite feelings of being "buffeted" after World War I, on the other, see Stern, *Dreams and Delusions*, p. 153; Smith, *Ideological Origins of Nazi Imperialism*, pp. 195–200; and Nicholls, *Weimar and the Rise of Hitler*, pp. 42–47. Intellectuals who consider themselves bearers of the national culture play a prominent role in promoting extreme nationalism to enhance their own status and strengthen national pride in the wake of national humiliation. See for example, Craig, *Germany 1866–1945*, pp. 478–80, on the role of professors in purveying malevolent German nationalism; and Greenfeld, *Nationalism*, pp. 191–274.

36. Avishai Margalit, "The Moral Psychology of Nationalism," in Robert McKim and Jeff McMahan, eds., *The Morality of Nationalism* (New York: Oxford University Press, 1997), p. 77.

37. I find *ressentiment* of some use in explaining the content but not the impact of Russian nationalism. In her work, Liah Greenfeld (1) cites mainly literary quotations to show *ressentiment* among the Russian elite; (2) does not explain how nationalism that derives from *ressentiment* moves from the cultural to the political realm; and (3) implies a sociological and psychological pathology among Russian elites, while obscuring the political motivations of Russian nationalists and the domestic and international factors that help make their ideas politically effective. See Greenfeld, *Nationalism.*

38. Liah Greenfeld, "The Viability of the Concept of Nation-State," paper presented to the American Sociological Association, Pittsburgh, August 1992, p. 3; and *Nationalism*, pp. 15–16.

39. Fiona Hill, *In Search of Great Russia: Elites, Ideas, Power, the State, and the Pre-Revolutionary Past in the New Russia, 1991–1996*, Doctoral Thesis, History Department, Harvard University, 1998, p. 105.

40. I am not arguing that national humiliation always and inevitably leads to the articulation of aggressive nationalist ideas. In fact, national defeat and humiliation can also lead to domestic soul-searching, retrenchment from expansionist foreign policies, and a reassessment of national goals. This, one can argue, was largely the case in the United States

after its defeat in the Vietnam War. This outcome, however, is less likely in a state like Russia where, historically, imperial thinking about the state has been strong and the space for open debate about the nature of the state and its national interests has traditionally been highly restricted.

41. The author considers these individuals and groups to be part of what Stephen Van Evera calls "evaluative units." Van Evera, however, specifies universities, a free press, and free speech traditions to be the key components of "evaluative units" that function as "truth squads" to fight malevolent nationalist mythmaking. See Van Evera, "Hypotheses on Nationalism and War," pp. 47–54.

42. Van Evera, "Hypotheses on Nationalism and War," pp. 47–54.

43. See, for example, Richard Pipes, "Introduction," in Heyward Isham, ed., *Remaking Russia: Voices from Within* (Armonk, N.Y.: Sharpe, 1995), pp. 4–5; and Margot Light, "Foreign Policy Thinking," in Neil Malcolm et al., *Internal Factors in Russian Foreign Policy* (Oxford: Oxford University Press, 1996), pp. 35–37.

44. Ronald Grigor Suny's work on the development of nation-state identity in the Soviet Union is especially helpful. See his *The Revenge of the Past: Nationalism, Revolution, and the Collapse of the Soviet Union* (Stanford: Stanford University Press, 1993).

45. The fragmentation of the political elite and the resulting incoherence of state policy can open "windows" through which highly motivated nationalists can advance their ideas and seek to influence the directions of foreign policy. See James G. Kellas, *The Politics of Nationalism and Ethnicity* (New York: St. Martin's, 1991), pp. 81, 85. This dynamic has also been documented in American foreign policy; see Ernest May, *American Imperialism: A Speculative Essay* (New York: Atheneum, 1968).

46. Some of the literature on ideas, institutions, and foreign policy underline how difficult it is for ideas to influence strong, centralized, secretive, and cohesive state domestic political structures. When these structures loosen—as would be the case when internal governance erodes or breaks down—the gate opens for ideas from outside to infiltrate the political decision making process. See, e.g., Matthew Evangelista, "The Paradox of State Strength: Transnational Relations, Domestic Structures, and Security Policy in Russia and the Soviet Union," *International Organization* 49 (Winter 1995):1–38.

47. Nationalism of different types has proven highly effective—at least in the past two centuries—in promoting or restoring cohesion, order, and legitimacy to ruling elites seeking legitimacy and power in contexts of transition and instability. This was arguably the case with Napoleon's France, Bismarck's Germany, Hitler's Germany, and with new states formed through decolonization after World War II. See Charles Tilly, ed., *The Formation of National States in Western Europe* (Princeton: Princeton University Press, 1975), *passim*; Hobsbawm, *Nations and Nationalism since 1780, passim*; Breuilly, *Nationalism and the State*, pp. 65–82, 125–65, 250–78; and James Mayall, *Nationalism and International Society* (Cambridge, UK: Cambridge University Press, 1990), pp. 26–34, 145–52.

48. This behavior amounts to "scapegoating" or using foreign conflict as a vehicle to distract attention away from domestic strife and problems of legitimacy. See Bruce Bueno de Mesquita, "Theories of International Conflict: An Analysis and an Appraisal," in Ted Gurr, ed., *Handbook of Political Conflict* (New York: Free Press, 1980), pp. 394–95.

49. See Hayes, *Essays on Nationalism*, pp. 156–95. On the utility of nationalism for the needs of mass warfare and on the impact of social structures on military effectiveness, see Posen, "Nationalism, the Mass Army, and Military Power," pp. 80–124 and Stephen Peter Rosen, "Military Effectiveness: Why Society Matters," *International Security* 19 (Spring 1995):5–31.

50. This hypothesis does not negate the fact that, for various reasons, leaders of military institutions might also favor nonaggressive nationalist ideology. See Samuel E. Finer, "State and Nation-Building in Europe: The Role of the Military," in Tilly, ed., *Formation of National States*, pp. 154-63; Elizabeth Kier, "Culture and Military Doctrine: France between the Wars," *International Security* 19 (Spring 1995):65–93; and Richard Betts, *Soldiers, Statesmen and Cold War Crises* (Cambridge: Harvard University Press, 1977).

51. Members of the Colonial Society argued that Versailles was unjust in eliminating Germany's colonial possessions. When members of the society realized that the Weimar government was not going to make the restoration of German colonies a central priority, they began to explore cooperation with the Nazi party. Versailles also emasculated the German army and roused intense resentment among generals and other officers who, early on, tried to delegitimize the republic and actively sought a nationalist alternative. See Smith, *Ideological Origins of Nazi Imperialism*, pp. 211–16; and Craig, *Germany 1866–1945*, pp. 426–28.

52. Fullbrook, *Germany*, pp. 67, 44–48; Stern, *Dreams and Delusions*, p. 157; Feuchtwanger, *From Weimar*, p. 317; Bessel, *Germany after the First World War*, pp. 283–84; and Craig, *Germany 1866–1945*, pp. 424–33.

53. See, e.g., Robert Jervis, *Perception and Misperception in International Politics* (Princeton: Princeton University Press, 1976); and James L. Richardson, *Crisis Diplomacy: The Great Powers since the Mid-Nineteenth Century* (Cambridge, UK: Cambridge University Press, 1994), pp. 3–24 and 106–326.

54. See Shafer, *Faces of Nationalism, passim*; Hayes, *Essays on Nationalism, passim*; Jonathan L. Mercer, *Reputation and International Politics* (Ithaca: Cornell University Press, 1995), pp. 44–73; Posen, "Security Dilemma and Ethnic Conflict," pp. 27–47; and Donald Kagan, *On the Origins of War and the Preservation of Peace* (New York: Doubleday, 1995).

55. Morris, *Weimar Republic*, pp. 84–87; and Smith, *Ideological Origins of Nazi Imperialism*, p. 208.

56. For example, if a state is situated next to friendly neighbors and borders between them are legitimate and militarily defensible, nationalist elites will find it more difficult to inflate security threats. However, if a state and its neighbors have had clashes in the past, share unstable borders on territory that may be up for grabs, and perceive each other inimically, malevolent nationalist propaganda becomes more credible. In fact, war could result if nationalism assumes the dynamics of a "security dilemma"—i.e., one party's nationalism begins to threaten others, who then respond by heightening their own nationalism. A spiral of action and reaction may ensure, leading to armed confrontation. See Posen, "Security Dilemma and Ethnic Conflict," pp. 27–47; and Robert Jervis, "Cooperation under the Security Dilemma," *World Politics* 2 (1978):167–213. On the impact of nationalism on state military intervention in ethnic conflicts involving the state's own "marooned" minority in another state, see A. Bikash Roy, "Intervention across Bisecting Borders," *Journal of Peace Research* 34 (1997):303–14.

57. A study that shows that the severity of crises makes the international system more salient as a factor in state decisions to use force is Patrick James and John R. Oneal, "The Influence of Domestic and International Politics on the President's Use of Force," *Journal of Conflict Resolution* 35 (June 1991):307–32.

58. It is one thing for state decision makers to pursue relatively easy opportunities for expansion or conquest or other behavior that fit an aggressive nationalist agenda—e.g., unification of the diaspora, military action on behalf of members of the nation who live outside state boundaries, and territorial conquest. Such opportunities include weak neigh-

bors, material and political support from allies, and the lack or weakness of international sanctions against aggressive behavior. But of even more interest is when decision makers pursue an aggressive nationalist agenda in foreign policy when, rationally, the costs seem extremely high.

59. Dietrich Geyer discusses these issues in *Russian Imperialism: The Interaction of Domestic and Foreign Policy in Russia 1860–1914*, trans. Bruce Little (New Haven: Yale University Press, 1987), pp. 49–63. On the impact of crises in empowering new ideas in state policymaking, see Sikkink, *Ideas and Institutions*, p. 368; and G. John Ikenberry, "Conclusion: An Institutional Approach to American Foreign Economic Policy," in G. John Ikenberry et al., eds., *The State and American Foreign Economic Policy* (Ithaca: Cornell University Press, 1988), pp. 223–25; and Evangelista, "Sources of Moderation in Soviet Security Policy," pp. 275–76.

60. In neorealist theory, states rely almost exclusively on self-help to deal with external threats. But liberal theory provides an alternative: current technology, international economic linkages, and the multiplicity and increasing impact of international and transnational institutions show that states increasingly depend on one another and on international norms to preserve their national welfare. See chapters by Kenneth Waltz in Robert Keohane, ed., *Neorealism and Its Critics* (New York: Columbia University Press, 1986); and Robert Keohane and Joseph Nye, *Power and Interdependence* (Glenview, Ill.: Scott, Foresman, 1989).

2

Nation-Building in Russia: Imperial State, Society, and the Nationalist Divide

[For] Russians imperial greatness can be achieved only at the cost of stunted nationhood.

—Geoffrey Hosking, 1997

We don't have the strength for the peripheries either economically or morally. We don't have the strength for sustaining an empire—and it's just as well. Let this burden fall from our shoulders: it is crushing us, sapping our energy, and hastening our demise.

—Aleksandr Solzhenitsyn, 1990

We did not have sufficient will, or consciousness of our state interests. . . . For six years, not one government has explained to people what they are trying to build, to what end we should all suffer.

—Leonid Abalkin, 1998

In chapter 1, nation was defined as a conceptual category that connotes kinship among a group of people and identifies the purported members of a nation as the chief repository of political authority. This definition points to both civic (i.e., the people as source of political legitimacy, endowed with some political rights) and ethnic (i.e., the people as a community of related individuals) aspects of any nation. It also points to an important corollary of nationalism as a political ideology: to effectively bind state and society, with minimum coercion and for the long term, nationalism must go hand-in-hand with some recognition of the rights and prerogatives of society vis-à-vis the state. In Russia, where the state developed as a multiethnic, authoritarian empire, the idea of nation both in ethnic and civic terms never gained widespread influence in theory or practice. Thus, historians such as Geoffrey Hosking, Hans Rogger, and Roman Szporluk write about "stunted nationhood" in Russia, the perennial suspicion of tsarist authorities of all forms of nationalism and attendant risks of mass mobilization from below, and the tension throughout Russian history between "empire-savers" and "nation-builders." Hosking concludes that, until the end of its existence, the imperial Russian state was a

> multi-ethnic service state, not . . . an emerging nation. Social hierarchy and status were shaped by the need to provide the sinews of . . . empire, through taxation, recruitment, administration and military command. The economy was deflected from productive purposes to sustain the army and administrative apparatus. A nobility was maintained in expensive nonproductivity, absorbing an alien culture to guarantee Russia's status as a European great power. . . . [And] the church was compelled to renounce its function as guarantor of the national myth to become the marginalized prop of an activist secular state.[1]

The experience of western European states with nation-building and nationalism provides a sharp contrast to that of Russia. Ruling authorities in these states, unlike their Russian counterparts, undertook measures to integrate state and society, especially in the nineteenth century. Thus, it became possible for nationalism to work as a glue cementing people and state into modern nation-states.

NATIONALISM: THE GLUE OF MODERN STATES

Samuel Finer traces the amorphous origins of modern states in Europe to roughly a thousand years ago.[2] However, he notes that two characteristics of modern states came much later, only in the late eighteenth and nineteenth centuries. These are: (1) in theory and, to a large extent, in practice, the population of the modern state forms a community of feeling based on "self-consciousness of a common *nationality*" and (2) in theory and, to a large extent, in practice, the population forms a community because of mutually distributed and shared duties and benefits.[3] The characteristics Finer describes are linked to the process of nation-building. They highlight the context in which nationalism developed and played a key role in the integration of state and society, particularly the consolidation of popular loyalty and commitment to the state. Nation-building entails two linked and mutually compatible processes: (1) the cultivation of belief in the common origins, destiny, and distinctiveness of a people (the ethnic or nationality aspect of nationalism) and (2) the development of a shared sense of participation in matters affecting the population and of rights and duties among all members of the group (the civic or citizenship aspect of nationalism). Both ethnic and civic aspects of nation-building and nationalism are embodied in the principles of the French Revolution: "Equality" of rights in the state go hand-in-hand with "Fraternity" among people who share a kinship based on distinct characteristics.[4]

Nation-building and the evolution of nationalism as a cementing factor in modern relations between state and society are late features of the transformation of patrimonial and feudal states into modern nation-states.[5] Guiding this transformation was the imperative for state authorities to balance the *"contingencies upon which the legitimacy of a political order rests."*[6] The most critical of contingencies was that of balancing the previously exclusive powers of the state with the rising assertiveness and demands for participation by various sectors of society. In his study of nation-building and citizenship, Reinhard Bendix notes that political order (the opposite of political anarchy) in modern times presumes the existence of "political community"—specifically, a context where some voluntary subordination of private interests and decision to the public realm occurs because "relations between rulers and ruled involve shared understandings" concerning rights and duties. Where there is political community, the state does not have to rely solely or chiefly on coercion to ensure and assert its authority.[7]

Two features of political modernization from feudal and patrimonial orders were especially salient in the eighteenth and nineteenth centuries. One was the rise of society as an autonomous actor and the concomitant growth of constraints on state power. With the advent of commerce and industrialization, new groups and classes emerged that did not accept the rules of the past and sought to change them. Private individuals who accumulated wealth and knowledge in a growing bourgeois configuration, for example, became less willing to tolerate the state's incursions into their activities or accept strictures imposed by state power on property and market. At the same time, dissatisfied workers who challenged "law and order" as laid down by the state (especially in the second half of the nineteenth century) also helped pave the way for liberal reforms, including the creation of space for civil society, social welfare, and the enlarging of the franchise.[8] The overall result was that

> Far from society being treated as an object of political management by a state operating chiefly in the light of interests exclusive to itself and to which those of society had to be subordinated, the state itself had to become an instrumentality of society's autonomous, self-regulating development. The state's very existence, and its mode of operation, would have to seek justification in the extent to which it allowed that development to unfold according to its own logic, rather than imperiously directing it and bending it to the state's own ends.[9]

The redefinition of relations between state and society eventually produced the codification of the rights of citizens, the entry of the lower classes into politics, and the rise and growth of various forms of representative government. In England and France the government granted rights to the people, including the right to form associations, the right to receive formal education, and the right to political participation and representation via the vote. The Law of August 11, 1792, in France, for example, extended the franchise to all males above age twenty-one who were not servants, vagabonds, or paupers. And after the revolution of 1848, the movement for representative democracy spread rapidly throughout Europe, including France, England, Austria, Germany, Sweden, and Norway.[10] Although it was not the case that all members of society simultaneously and equally attained rights vis-à-vis the state (the liberalization of politics being an uneven process), nonetheless, by the nineteenth century most western European states had clearly made adjustments to enhance their voluntary basis of support in society.[11]

A second—and seemingly paradoxical—feature of the rise of modern states was the strengthening of state power even as some prerogatives were granted to society. The extension of general citizenship, for example, enhanced the state's capacity to prosecute war on a more massive and effective scale than ever imagined. It made possible the creation of national, mass armies infused with deep political loyalty to the state, replacing previous armies whose ranks tended to include many of the "scum, or most helpless of Europe's population."[12] Citizenship and the feeling of shared rights and obligations between state and society also enhanced the state's ability to extract resources from the population for war and other purposes. These changes reached a rather grotesque culmination in the two world wars of the twentieth century, which were fought by national armies and backed by the total mobilization of all national resources of the states involved. But even before the apogee of national warfare in the twentieth century, the French Revolution and subsequent conquests by the Napoleonic army—whose members were infused with revolutionary principles of nationalism and citizenship—already heralded profound changes stemming from the process of modernization and the strengthening of the state.[13]

By the nineteenth century, the concept of nation and the ideology of nationalism had become commonplace in the modern states of western Europe. Nationalism intensified not only as a product of state modernization, but also as a political tool for the maintenance of authority in the modern state. State leaders (as well as their rivals) used nationalism to bolster the legitimacy of their claims to power, consolidate the state's territorial and popular domain, and/or strengthen the state's ability to project power abroad. Thus, in Germany and Italy, political authorities used nationalism to legitimate their efforts to unify separate territorial entities under one state and to coordinate disparate elites to run an effective state once unification had been achieved. Elsewhere, claimants of their own states, including the Poles, Czechs, Serbs, and Irish, used nationalism to justify their struggle against imperial ruling powers. And in France and other European states, the processes of state expansion, war, and direct rule (i.e., the direct incursion of state authority into the daily life of citizens) produced and intensified nationalism. Nationalism, in turn, helped mobilize populations to identify strongly with their state's goals and international strategy, especially in time of war.[14]

In the past two centuries, western European and other modern states have expended immense resources to cultivate and intensify nationalism. Modern rulers have nurtured political loyalty to their regimes by promoting a common set of beliefs and myths about the ties that bind the nation, and by extending to society some benefits of participation and "voice" in the political system. The state has resorted increasingly to persuasion over coercion, using such vehicles of socialization and mobilization as the army, the schools, and the bourgeoisie to homogenize society and focus its commitment to the national state. The end result has been the creation and maintenance of modern nation-states, where there exist "an effective government and a reasonably stable consensus on the part of the inhabitants as to ends and means."[15] In these states, rulers rule with a minimum of coercion while society largely and voluntarily complies with the obligations and duties imposed on it by the state.

Was a modern nation-state ever created in Russia? The scholarly consensus is no. Michael Urban notes that although the Russian people constituted the predominant group in the Russian empire and the Soviet state, the "political unit housing [the Russian] people was not a nation-state."[16] James Cracraft concurs: in Russia, "a political entity regarded by its subjects, conscious of a common nationality, as identical with their collective self and hence deserving of their highest loyalty"[17] was never created. Richard Pipes adds that in Russia in premodern times, "state and society lived different existences"; while Russia did begin to Westernize and modernize beginning in the late seventeenth century, Russian rulers never gave up their patrimonial political culture. The Russian monarchy, conflating authority with ownership, always retained its monopoly on power, did not share legislative authority with society, and never created institutions to link society effectively with the state.[18] Hans Rogger states that Russian territorial consolidation took place before nationalism became a major component of Russian life, causing "no interpenetration of state and society, no lasting accommodation between them."[19] Unlike many western European states, Russia never fully modernized by integrating state and society in one unit bound by common beliefs in one nation and a consensus over mutual rights and obligations. Geoffrey Hosking concludes that a weak and fractured nationhood has been the Russians' "principal burden in the last two centuries or so, continuing throughout the period of the Soviet Union and persisting beyond its fall."[20]

RUSSIA'S EXPERIENCE: WEAK NATION-BUILDING, DISTORTED NATIONALISM

To understand the nature of nationalism in Russia, one must recognize that Russian state and society followed separate trajectories of development, especially in the three centuries preceding the Bolshevik revolution. Scholars have often referred to the state as imperial and hypertrophic (overdeveloped), always exercising a preponderance of power and prerogatives vis-à-vis an oppressed, repressed, and politically weak society. In the famous phrase of historian Vasilii Kliuchevskii, "the state grew fat and the people grew thin."[21] What were the central practices and features that made up the legacy of the Russian imperial state? How did the state conduct its relations with society? How did the nature of state–society relations impede nation-building, thereby weakening the potential of nationalism as an integrative force?

The Imperial State: Expansion and Its Effects

The terms "empire" and "imperial" denote Russia's military expansion, exertion of political control over conquered or assimilated territories, and concentration state resources and activity on maintaining international prestige and sustaining rivalry with other great powers. In addition, "empire" and "imperialism" also connote the state's domestic tyranny for the purposes of empire-building and empire maintenance.[22] The external and internal aspects of the Russian imperial state underline the immensity of the historical legacy that has prevented nation-building and the rise of nationalism as a force for cohesion in Russia.

Russia's territorial consolidation occurred largely via imperial expansion. The birth of the Russian state under Ivan III began with the Muscovite "gathering" (via conquest, purchase, inheritance, and other means) of independent principalities in the fifteenth century. Subsequently, and especially in the nineteenth century, Russian historians and intellectuals characterized this "gathering of Russian lands" as the legitimate retrieval of the patrimony of Kievan Rus' that had been taken away during the time of the Tatar yoke. Historians debate whether or not there is any validity to the Muscovite claim of patrimony,[23] but the fact remains that expansion became an early and normal feature of the Russian state. In the sixteenth century, imperial expansion began in earnest, with Ivan IV's 1552 conquest and annexation of the khanate of Kazan', a sovereign, non-Russian state. The practice of imperial expansion continued at a rapid pace in the late sixteenth and early seventeenth centuries, and extended to new territories in northern Europe under Peter the Great. Peter's reign, particularly his victory over Sweden in the Great Northern War, introduced Russia as a great power on the international stage.

Russia's imperial expansion, while less intense than before, continued into the eighteenth and nineteenth centuries.[24] Two effects of expansion impeded nation-building. First, the imperial state came to include within its boundaries a kaleidoscopic collection of ethnic, linguistic, and cultural groups. Centuries of conquest and colonization, as well as more voluntary types of assimilation of other peoples, created a state that, by 1897, had a population of 128.2 million, less than half of whom were ethnic Russians.[25] Although few of the peoples conquered or otherwise assimilated into the empire had strong traditions of independent statehood, they nonetheless had significant linguistic, religious, and cultural differences from the empire's majority ethnic Russian and Orthodox population. And by the late nineteenth century, some of the non-Russian groups had developed their own elites, literary languages, high cultures, and overt nationalism. At the same time, tsarist authority in the eighteenth and nineteenth centuries depended on many of the non-Russian nobility (particularly Germans, Swedes, Poles, and others) to facilitate imperial rule and administration.[26] This multiethnic mix stifled the development of belief in one nation, and restricted the possibility of the state converting its multiethnic population into a cohesive Russian nation. To hold together the multiethnic state, Russian authorities hesitated to propagate and emphasize a specifically *ethnic* Russian nationalism that would alienate non-Russians in the empire.[27]

A second effect of expansion, which also impeded nation-building, was the fact that Russians, as an ethnic group and as the majority population in most parts of the empire, were not treated a priori as the superior group in the multiethnic state. State officials viewed ethnic Russians, like the rest of the population, as but raw material to be used in the service of empire. Moreover, other non-Russian groups benefited more from imperial arrangements than ethnic Russians, who, in the nineteenth century, lagged behind Poles, Finns, Germans, and people in the Baltic provinces in socioeconomic and sociocultural advancement. And before serfdom ended in 1861, Russians also "bore all [its] burdens . . . from which some other peoples were exempted."[28] Among the nobility, ethnic Russians comprised only 4.6 percent in the seventeenth century and, as late as 1897, native Russian speakers were less than half of the noble class or *dvoriane*. Thus, the state's active subjugation and passive neglect of the mass of ethnic Russians resulted in backwardness and shame precisely among the group that might have formed the core of an "imagined community" called the Russian nation.[29]

Sustaining the Imperial State: Great Power Myths

The previous chapter noted briefly how, in Russia, "greatness" (and the adjective, *velikii*) has been invoked to mark those personalities and instances that have left an indelible mark on Russian history. In most cases, greatness connotes military power, territorial conquest, and international prestige and respect, and is thus tightly linked to the Russian imperial state. The linkage between greatness and imperial power emerged as a dominant theme in Russian political pronouncements and in poetic, historical, and popular literature, beginning at the dawn of Russian national consciousness in the eighteenth century and continuing throughout the rest of tsarist rule. The invocation of great power ideas and myths by intellectuals, historians, and political figures created a socialization process by which most educated Russians came to accept and support the imperial organization and status of the state.

Great power myths and ideas that underpinned the imperial state arose during the formative period of Russian national consciousness under Peter the Great (1682–1725) and Catherine the Great (1762–1796). Nationalism as a political ideology had not yet emerged in this period, but national consciousness existed in terms of "a striving for common identity, character, and culture by the articulate members"[30] of Russian society. Under Peter and Catherine, concepts connoting a nation entered Russian political discourse—for example, *otechestvo* (fatherland), *obshchee blago* (public welfare), and *narod* (the people). Coinciding with the emergence of a nationally conscious discourse was Russia's de facto rise as an imperial power, marked by Peter the Great's victory against Sweden in the Great Northern War of 1700–21. This war, and specific incidents such as the Battle of Poltava, during which Russian troops decimated the Swedish army, came to occupy a central place in Russian history. With the signing of the Treaty of Nystadt to end the war, Russia acquired large territories and gained control of the Gulf of Finland. Celebrating the victory, the Russian Senate conferred on Peter the titles of "Emperor" and "Father of the Fatherland," intimating an association between Russia and the Roman Empire and linking the worthiness of the monarch as leader of a rising "nation" (i.e., people with an equal stake and a natural attachment to a collective *patrie* or fatherland) with his ability for imperial conquest.[31]

Peter the Great cultivated national pride among his subjects by emphasizing their residence in a great empire that could resist the hostility of foreign powers intent on humiliating Russia. In one of the most important works he commissioned in 1703, *The Discourse on the Just Reasons of the War between Sweden and Russia* (printed at twenty thousand copies five years after its initial publication— at a time when the usual edition of such works was around 200 copies), the monarch concluded:

> The past times are not like the present, for then the Swedes thought of us differently and considered us blind. . . . And not only the Swedes, but also other and remote peoples, always felt jealousy and hatred toward the Russian people, and have attempted to keep the latter . . . in ignorance, especially in the military and naval arts. . . . [Now] those, who, it seems, were the fear of all Europe, were defeated by us. And I can say, that no one is so feared as we are. For which one should thank God. . . .[32]

Catherine the Great, who preserved Peter's emphasis on Russian imperial greatness, accentuated during her reign Russia's cultural accomplishments along with its military might, territorial expanse, and political power. In the Charter of 1785, which defined the nature and privileges of the Russian nobility, Catherine paid homage to Russian greatness as follows:

> The All-Russian empire in the World is distinguished by the expanse of the lands in its possession . . . comprising within its borders 165 longitudes [and] 32 latitudes. . . . [In] true glory and majesty of the Empire [we] enjoy the fruits, and know the results of the actions of the obedient, courageous, fearless, enterprising, and mighty Russian people . . . [whose] labors and love of Fatherland together tend primarily to the general good.[33]

Besides Russia's monarchs, intellectuals in the eighteenth and nineteenth centuries also perpetuated the themes of Russian greatness based on military power, conquest, and political strength. Beginning in the eighteenth century, and especially after their emancipation from compulsory service in 1762, many Russian nobles traveled to the West and returned to their homeland with an earnest desire to define those qualities that made Russia distinct. In their writings, they extolled Russian greatness based on battlefield victories and on Russian potential to equal and surpass the West. For example, Mikhail Lomonosov (1711–1765), Russian poet, scientist, and founder of Moscow University, declared that the "Russian empire, by the wealth of its internal resources and its great victories is the equal of the first European states and even exceeds some of them." He and other intellectuals emphasized Russian victory over the Turks, Swedes, and Prussians and the extension of Russian power as far as Japan and China. In their view, even Russian backwardness was a sign of greatness because it constituted "evidence of originality and freshness of mind as yet undamaged and unrestrained by rule and repetition."[34]

Native historiographic development also occurred in the eighteenth and nineteenth centuries, partly in response to denigrating Russian histories written by foreigners and provoking the ire of Russian intellectuals.[35] A widely approved work was Nikolai Karamzin's *History*, on which the author labored from 1803 until his death in 1806. Karamzin's *History* clarified Russian political tradition; accepted autocracy as the key to Russian order and progress; criticized rulers who strayed from Russian national tradition and borrowed too much from the West; emphasized Russia's superb cultural heritage; and justified Russia's wars, which brought palpable gains to the imperial state. The theme of Russian greatness and imperial might suffused Karamzin's work, which enjoyed wide popularity and became a classic from its publication. Although Karamzin's *History* condemned Peter the Great's tyranny and absolutism, it nonetheless praised the monarch for winning "for Russia a position of eminence in the political system of Europe."[36] And, while noting that domestic morals deteriorated under Catherine the Great, he characterized her reign as the happiest because Russia occupied a position of glory in Europe and accustomed Europeans to its many military victories.

In addition to historical writing, popular literature and literary criticism also perpetuated myths of Russian greatness based on imperial state power. In the second half of the nineteenth century, for example, such popular writings as serialized novels, newspaper stories, and detective fiction emphasized the greatness of the Russian empire territorially. Jeffrey Brooks notes that this popular literature showed the evolution of a national identity that was more individualistic and independent of earlier loyalty to the tsar and Orthodox Church.[37] Yet this "new" national awareness was "old" in that it remained wedded to myths of greatness based on the beauty, exoticism, expanse, and might of Russian *imperial* territory. Many great Russian writers, critics, and other literary figures of the nineteenth century, while criticizing the inequities of Russian life, nonetheless affirmed Russian great power myths and defended imperial statehood. Among these were such illustrious writers as Fedor Dostoevskii and Fedor Tiutchev. N. I. Nadezhdin, publisher of Petr Chaadaev's letters (which sparked the Slavophile–Westernizer controversy in the nineteenth century), reflected the views of other literary figures when he defended the autocrat, symbol and ruler of the imperial state. He argued that even if Russia had no civilization and no history of its own, at least it had the autocrat, a supreme and wise leader. "Everything that Russia achieved, everything that Russia was, was due to the ruler. This was cause for Russian pride and for Russian joy, and this was the supreme guarantee for the Russian future."[38]

The preceding account indicates that in Russia, political, historical, and intellectual figures shaped a tradition or structure of political discourse in favor of imperial state power. Guardians of Russian collective memory developed a discourse that gauged the state and its rulers' greatness and legitimacy not on the broad acceptance of a compact balancing rights and duties between state and people, but mainly on the state's might as expressed in its imperial domain, external power projection, international prestige, and accomplishments in the realm of great power competition.[39] This discourse advanced nation-building in a distorted or imbalanced way. It helped formulate the idea of Russian kinship based on belonging to a powerful, imperial state, but neglected the other half of nation-building, which dealt with the acknowledgment and evolution of the people as the repository of political authority and as a relatively autonomous actor.

The Primacy of Great Power Status:
Society and the Burdens of Empire

The expansionist beginnings of the Russian state and the consolidation of Russian imperial and great power status under Peter the Great created a legacy that Russian rulers in the nineteenth and early twentieth centuries largely maintained, to the detriment of nation-building. Although political reform and a very slow trickle of political power to the people did occur during the reforms of Alexander II and after the October Manifesto of 1905, nonetheless tsarist authorities never accepted the nation or people, in idea or practice, as the ultimate source of state power and legitimacy. Instead, what was always paramount to state authorities was the survival and maintenance of empire—specifically, internal control over a massive territory and a multiethnic population and the ability to maintain Russian status among the great powers of the world.

The maintenance of empire, especially its military requirements, necessitated tremendous sacrifice and resources from society, including the nobility and masses. In Muscovite Russia, the state required service of all nobles (through the army or bureaucracy), while it taxed peasants and ordinary townsmen. Under Peter the Great, the requirement of state service became institutionalized in the Table of Ranks, which made state service the only path whereby those with merit or inherited nobility could enjoy a modicum of security and legal protection of their life and property. Although Peter III subsequently revoked the Table of Ranks in 1762 and other monarchs lessened restrictions in the lives of the nobility in the late eighteenth and nineteenth centuries, the tradition of service to the state remained. In key ways, the state retained tremendous power to determine the lives and fortunes of the people.[40] It also retained its prerogative to give or take away privileges granted to the nobility. This happened, for example, during Nicholas I's rule (1825–1855), when, in the name of state security, the monarch curtailed such privileges as travel, previously granted to the nobility and other members of a growing civil society.[41]

Peasants, ordinary workers, and the rest of the mass of Russian people suffered the bulk of the burdens of taxation, military conscription, and serfdom to support the imperial state. Under Peter the Great, Russia became the first country to institute conscription as a permanent method of raising an army. The needs of the army and state administration created obligations and heavy taxation that dominated the lives of ordinary Russians. During Peter's reign, military expenditure routinely absorbed 80–85 percent of Russian revenues. And throughout the eighteenth century and until the second half of the nineteenth, Russia's finances continued to be strained because of the needs of empire and the fiscal requirements of military power. To raise revenues, the state relied heavily on its monopoly on alcohol, creating a situation where Russia's rulers directly contributed to the debauching of their own people for the sake of imperial state requirements. Revenues from the state's liquor monopoly rose from 11 to 21 percent of the state's income from 1724 to 1759, reaching 40 percent by the 1850s and declining to about 33 percent in the 1880s. In the words of one nineteenth-century observer,

> Shocking instances of the deliberate drowning of intellect and conscience in brutish debauch and intoxication for political purposes have been known to occur on a small scale . . . But Russia is the only country in which it has been tried on . . . over one hundred million human beings.[42]

Serfdom was yet another burden imposed on society by, and for, the imperial state. Richard Hellie cogently shows that the formalization of serfdom through the *Ulozhenie* (decree) of 1649, and its persistence thereafter, was due chiefly to the state's need to meet the demands of the army. In particular, the state instituted serfdom to respond to the clamor and demands of an obsolescent middle service class, the Muscovite cavalry, whose members were highly dependent on peasants for the maintenance of their landholdings. Further, economic and psychological insecurity among the cavalry in the late seventeenth century led them to pressure a reluctant government to repeal permanently the right of peasants to move. Although not all of Russia's peasants were enserfed,[43] nonetheless the institution took its economic and social toll. It undermined capital accumulation, entrepreneurship, and internal demand among a substantial part of Russia's population (serfs were estimated at 37.7 percent of the empire in the census of 1858–59), and made land hunger a permanent feature of the social landscape, fueling revolutions that would wrack Russia in the early twentieth century. The landlords' caprice and the serfs' utter lack of legal rights also created a source of mass discontent. Even after the state formally abolished serfdom in 1861, former serfs continued to suffer injustice, bearing more of the financial and other costs of emancipation than either the state or former landlords.[44]

The imperial state relied on a pervasive bureaucracy as its key instrument for extracting needed revenues from an uncommercialized economy at the time of Peter the Great. This bureaucracy grew over time, extending its powers by the nineteenth century to the cultural activities of an increasingly restive society. Although some scholarship highlights positive and progressive aspects of the bureaucracy (especially in the nineteenth century), the Russian civil service remained largely "corrupt, inefficient, arbitrary and concerned with its own welfare rather than the communal interest."[45] It contributed immensely to the alienation of a people that felt abused, humiliated, and exploited at the hands of the state.[46] Taxation, conscription, serfdom, and bureaucracy in the imperial state created and exacerbated the divide between state and people and heightened the reality that the state focused on its exclusive interests to the detriment of society. In response, most of Russia's people could not see the state as the embodiment of their own values and welfare, and society failed to evolve effectively as an autonomous entity. In this setting, nationalism that might cement state–society relations could hardly thrive. Nation-building, as it occurred in western Europe, did not take place in Russia; state authorities strengthened the state *without* yielding substantive prerogatives to society or redistributing some political power to the people. This undermined the chances that nationalism could develop to help create a modern nation-state.

Autocracy, Authoritarian Politics, and the Repression of Civic Autonomy

Scholars have debated the nature of Russian autocracy and broader political culture, with various emphases placed on absolute and personal rule by a strong, supreme ruler, on one hand, or collective rule by an oligarchy or a "pluralist" patrimonial court, on the other.[47] Whichever aspect one might emphasize in patterns of authority in Russia, Archie Brown rightly observes that there is "no getting away from the predominantly authoritarian political nature of . . . Russian political experience."[48] Acknowledging the primacy of authoritarian politics in Russian experience is not to deny the existence of other, more democratic currents in Russian political culture, nor does it imply authoritarianism as an immutable strain of Russian politics.[49] Rather, the purpose of focusing on Russia's authoritarian legacy is to underline the state's vastly stronger position vis-à-vis civil society, and the narrowness throughout modern Russian history of the civic space within which societal voices might be heard and initiatives exercised.

The tradition of Russian autocracy entailed a norm locating all political and legal authority ultimately in the hand of the monarch or tsar.[50] Though not always well executed or effective, the tsar's authority was largely unchallenged by other institutions or organized groups of social elites. Throughout Russian history, various myths have evolved to underline the power and authority of the Russian autocracy. Michael Cherniavsky describes, for example, the myths of prince as saint, theocratic tsar, tsar as heir of the Roman emperors, tsar as sovereign emperor (ruler over church and state), and tsar as "most-gentle ruler" (*tsar batiushka*). The most persistent of these myths—at least since Peter the Great—was the ruler as sovereign emperor, "the new god on earth," who "ruled Russia as his private property, for which he was responsible to no one; the source of his power lay in itself, in its ability to conquer, rather than in any unique quality of myth of Russia itself."[51] The rule of Peter the Great consolidated the myth of sovereign emperor, with Peter's image subsuming both fatherland and the state; in fact, all references to "the fatherland" or "the land" disappeared from military and civil oaths, leaving only Peter, the autocrat, as the embodiment of statehood. The state's usurpation of authority over the Orthodox Church, initiated by Peter and maintained by his successors, further consolidated the myth of the sovereign emperor.[52]

There are no countervailing myths of the people or nation in Russia to juxtapose with myths of autocracy and tsarist power. The myth of the people as "Holy Russia" in some ways counterposed itself to the all-powerful tsar and the state, but it never achieved the same salience as images reflecting the power of the Russian ruler.[53] Power was always located in the sovereign, emanated from him, and did not come from the people. In the realm of politics, this unequal relationship between tsar and people manifested itself in three ways. First, major social initiatives in Russia tended to come from above, and the autocratic monarchy tended to be the driving force behind reforms conducted in Russian politics. A few outstanding examples are Peter the Great's drive for Westernization and empire, Catherine the Great's effort to create a civil society, Alexander II's emancipation of the serfs and other "great reforms," and political and economic reform under Petr Stolypin in the last days of the empire.[54] These reforms from above, to varying extents, elicited public debate, bureaucratic infighting, and uncertain support from those in society who had to implement, or live by, them.

Second, the ruling regime always considered suspect, and sought to repress, autonomous civic ideas and initiatives and the public expression of lofty sentiments about the people. Enterprising and well-intentioned individuals and groups who were fundamentally loyal to the regime, but undertook independent civic activity, fell into disfavor with state officials. A prominent example in the eighteenth century was Nikolai Novikov, who, along with his associates in the Freemasonry movement, took to heart Catherine the Great's injunctions to perform community service. Novikov used his resources to publish books and journals, launch charitable schools, and engage in social debate in his circle of Freemasons. Instead of harnessing his earnest devotion to causes that she herself had recommended for those wanting to serve the state, Catherine accused Novikov of treason and heresy, and sentenced him to fifteen years of imprisonment.[55]

Others who advocated modernizing the Russian state, imposing some limits on autocratic power (and the arbitrariness that accompanied it), and institutionalizing laws that would serve the public welfare could not articulate or implement their ideas fully as they came up against the preferences and prerogatives of autocratic government. Such was the case, for example, with Mikhail Speranskii and his proposals for governmental reforms in 1809, which would have separated the executive, legislative, and judicial functions of government while channeling power through publicly elected institutions. Speranskii failed to have elective institutions introduced. Instead, the tsar's personal agents carried out the intended role of these institutions. The tsar also maintained supreme power over the budget (until 1862) and continued the handling of Russia's finances by patronage rather than transparency and fiscal responsibility.[56]

In yet other cases, those who undertook autonomous civic activity, criticized the empire's ills, or took up the cause of reform were punished. Such was the case with Aleksandr Radishchev, whose *A Journey from St. Petersburg to Moscow* (which condemned the evils of Russian society, including serfdom and conscription) led to his arrest and imprisonment. Similarly, members of the Decembrist revolt of 1825, fired by patriotism and a newfound respect for, and linkage with, the common people (though not necessarily enjoying broad public support), were executed or otherwise punished for treason and rebellion. Admittedly, the Decembrist rebellion was seditious and went beyond merely advocating reform of the state; but Alexander I himself acknowledged that he had "shared and encouraged" the Decembrists' agenda of bringing "enlightenment and the amenities of a civil society more broadly to Russia."[57] Underneath the Decembrists' (mild) revolt against the state was a longing for civil society to be given room for its autonomous expression. As one of the Decembrists, P. G. Kakhovskii, wrote to Tsar Nicholas I from prison: "It is a bitter thing for a Russian not to have a nation, and to terminate everything in the Sovereign alone."[58]

The suspicion of tsarist authority toward independent civic activity and lofty ideals of civil society or the nation stunted the development of normal channels of communication, mediation, and mutual influence between state and people. Representative and communal bodies (e.g., the *zemskii sobor* in the seventeenth century, the peasant *mir*, the *zemstvos* in the second half of the nineteenth century, and the Duma in the early twentieth century) that might have served as conduits between state and society, and the foundation of a more integrated national state, neither took root nor flourished. Interest groups remained too underdeveloped and fragmented to extract genuine concessions from the tsarist government on behalf of the people. All this led to yet a third phenomenon manifesting the unequal relationship between state and society: to make their voices heard and their grievances known to the ruler, the Russian masses (peasants and urban workers) resorted occasionally to violent revolts and rebellions. These included the revolt led by Sten'ka Razin in 1670–71; city uprisings in Russia in 1648, 1662, and 1682; the Bulavin rebellion in 1707–8, which protested fiscal burdens on the peasantry; and the Pugachev rebellion in 1773–75, whose leader promised land for the peasants, the abolition of the poll tax, and a more personal and service-oriented state to replace the impersonal bureaucracy.[59] Until the early twentieth century, Russia lacked institutionalized civic access to state authority and did not have robust channels of mediation between state and society. This explains in part the potent manifestations of societal discontent and fury against the state expressed by the revolutions of 1905 and 1917, which forever swept away the tsarist regime.[60]

THE NATIONALIST DIVIDE

The Russian imperial state and its relationship with society accentuate the distortion of nation-building and the dilemma of nationalism in Russia. In the three centuries preceding the 1917 Bolshevik revolution, a critical mass consciousness based on nation or nationality did not develop in Russia. Neither did a widespread consensus evolve on mutual duties and obligations between state and society. The state itself did not "nationalize" on a massive scale; unlike its western European counterparts, which used nation-building and nationalism to unify and strengthen the state, the tsarist monarchy failed to cultivate an "imagined community" of Russians. But this does not mean that the state was wholly inactive in nation-building. Especially after the Polish revolt of 1863, tsarist authorities became very sensitive to the threat of imperial disintegration, and, as a result, tsars Alexander II, Alexander III, and Nicholas II vigorously applied a policy of russification from the 1860s until 1914. Whereas russification tended to be primarily administrative in the past—focused on "the centralization and unification of the empire's administrative and legal structure in order to promote the interests of the Russian state and to assure government control of society and the welfare of the [ruler's] subjects"[61]—officials introduced a new emphasis on cultural russification. Cultural russification presumed the primacy of Russian language, culture, and religion and created a temporary alliance between tsarist authority and chauvinist nationalist groups in Russia.

Russification: Nation-Building under the Tsars?

Russification, though characterized by some as a relentless policy to transform imperial Russia's multiethnic population into homogenized Russians, was largely a policy to serve the security and integrity of the multiethnic imperial state. As such, it had limited utility for effective nation-building.[62] The chief goal of russification for the tsarist monarchy was to preserve the Russian empire and its own prerogatives within it, rather than nurture a sense of nation in the way that French and German nationalizing rulers did. Indeed, the policy of russification never made "Russians" out of Poles, Jews, Germans, Ukrainians, Georgians, Armenians, Balts, Chuvashes, Bashkirs, and other peoples in the empire. And though conservative segments of Russian society (especially Rightist Nationalists, who are described in greater detail in chapter 4) supported a more cultural version of russification, such support did not last long enough or have a wide enough reach to produce a nation and promote cohesive nationalism. In the aftermath of russification, Russia remained a state where the sense of nation (both ethnic and civic) was weak, and nationalism that effectively bound state and society did not exist.[63]

Russification was not an effective nation-building tool in Russia for three reasons: (1) it was more focused on administrative rather than cultural ends, (2) it faced strong resistance from Russia's multiethnic population, and (3) it was hampered by Russia's limited administrative resources. State authorities sought to unify the empire's borderlands with the center through the "gradual introduction of Russian institutions and laws and extension of the use of Russian in the local bureaucracy and as a subject of instruction in the schools."[64] Thus, policies were implemented to establish a unified legal code for the empire, increase the use of Russian in all regions, remove local political privileges, and eliminate other administrative discrepancies between center and regions. A study of original government documents on russification concludes that nationhood and ethnicity, and their modification, were never at the center of attention of state officials. Tsarist authorities wanted, first and foremost, to create an infrastructure for imperial management and administration, and took varied regional approaches to russification depending on what they thought would best serve the consolidation of imperial rule in areas and regions with large non-Russian populations.[65]

Russification, in its cultural aspect, did favor the Russian ethnic group through such measures as the granting of special status to the Russian language and financing of the Orthodox Church's missionary efforts. Simultaneously, state authorities implemented disadvantageous policies toward non-Russians. For example, officials suppressed the use of Ukrainian in Ukraine from 1847 to 1905; dismantled the Polish university in Vilna; closed the German university of Dorpat in 1893, subsequently reopening it as a Russian university; and imposed "temporary rules" upon Jews in 1882, prohibiting them from resettling or acquiring property in rural areas, and later denying them the right to vote in municipal elections.[66] But russification did not have exclusively negative effects on the non-Russians. The introduction of Russian courts and municipal and police institutions in the Baltic provinces in the 1870s and 1880s, for instance, helped the position of Latvians and Estonians, who were underprivileged compared to the region's German minority. Russification also did not preclude the development of other cultures—for example, Latvian and Estonian—which progressed rapidly even during the policy of active russification.[67] Thus, while russification did advance some aspects of Russian culture, it did not eradicate other cultures in favor of a more homogeneous, ethnically Russian nation.

Russification did not elicit great enthusiasm among Russians—even those who were ethnic nationalists. While partially restricting or eliminating the privileges, amenities, and national rights of non-Russian groups (and taking the most strident measures in Poland and Finland), it did not seek to eradicate the particular national consciousness of these groups and create "Russians" out of them. Imperial authorities did not focus on the forces of nation, nationality, or nationalism, but on integrating the ethnically disparate parts of the empire into one administrative whole.

But even had tsarist authorities wanted to create a more culturally homogeneous "imagined community" of Russians, they would have faced serious impediments, including some among ethnic Russians themselves—in particular, the peasantry. Experts on the culture of Russian peasants underline the wide gulf that divided these masses from their Europeanized, "Russian" brethren. Since the reign of Peter the Great and until the last days of the Russian empire, civilization in Russia meant Europeanization, and peasants did not share the Europeanized "Russian" culture of their more privileged kin. Peasants perceived the urbanized, educated elite as outsiders to their culture, while the Europeanized gentry throughout most of the nineteenth century often perceived the peasants as "dark masses" or "toys to be manipulated at will."[68]

Peasant feelings of separateness targeted not only the gentry and nobles, but also tsarist authority, which time and again had dashed their hopes of land ownership, emancipation from serfdom (before 1861), and certain rights of citizenship. In addition, the vast population of rural Russia before 1917 could not easily assimilate the nation-building component of russification; widespread illiteracy (only about a quarter of the rural ethnic Russian population in 1897 was literate), economic backwardness, and the speaking of hundreds of local patois ensured the predominance of localist over nationalist mentality among the peasantry.[69]

A second reason for russification's limited contribution to nation-building was the strong resistance it faced among the empire's multiethnic population. Resistance among non-Russians came in passive and active varieties. In the passive sense, russification (combined with changes in communication, education, and social mobility in the nineteenth century) stimulated national consciousness among non-Russians. This was true, for example, of Georgian, Baltic, and other non-Russian students in St. Petersburg who, in reaction to russification, developed and diffused their own variants of nationalist ideas when they returned to their home territories.[70] In the more active sense, intensive russification in Poland beginning in 1863 helped stimulate Polish mobilization for insurrection and complete independence from Russia. In Finland, attempts to subject Finnish legislation to Russian authority at the close of the nineteenth century led to widespread protest from the Finns and their boycott of Russian institutions, including the army. And in Armenia, overbearing russification and Russian imperial policies led to assassinations and other terrorist actions against Russian officials and the creation of Armenian institutions directed against Russia (e.g., the *Dashnak* movement).[71]

Third, limited administrative resources—human and otherwise—also curbed russification's potential benefit for nation-building. The army, for example, which in other west European states became a key institution for nation-building, did not serve as an asset. Hampered by illiteracy and expected to be self-sufficient in a state with constant budgetary problems, peasant soldiers spent their time growing food, making clothing, or being hired out as wage laborers.[72] The imperial government could barely afford to feed its soldiers, let alone educate them and inculcate them with nationalist ideas. The imperial government also could not offer sufficient incentives to convince non-Russians of the benefits of russification, especially in its cultural aspect, given that non-Russian groups had done rather well without russification. In the western borderlands, for example, Russian imperial authority depended on the German landowning nobility to maintain social order. Thus Russian authorities abandoned russification in the wake of the 1848 revolutionary outbreak in Europe, and again in 1905, in favor of cooperation with the German nobility to keep restive Estonians and Latvians in the Baltic provinces under control. And in keeping with the old imperial tradition of co-opting elite non-Russians into the imperial nobility, non-Russians occupied numerous positions in the higher professions until late in the nineteenth century, retained their social and economic dominance in various regions, and were in a position to thwart russification. Andreas Kappeler concludes that, in the late imperial period,

> the Russian state . . . could not function without the nobility's cooperation. Thus Baltic-Germans, Germans, Finns, Poles, and Caucasians continued to fill important posts not only in local government, but in the military and administrative elites of the center. The especially numerous Polish nobility took on new tasks in scholarship, technology, and culture.[73]

The foregoing narrative suggests that serious structural impediments against nation-building existed in the tsarist empire. Perhaps some of these impediments could have been overcome had tsarist authorities genuinely made nation-building a supreme state priority. But, until 1917, the policy of Russia's rulers remained, in the words of Theodore Weeks, "pre-nationalist": the ruling echelon defined themselves first as aristocrats, second only as Russians; Poles and Baltic Germans held high positions in government; the empress was German; and the tsar held on to the idea that he ruled by divine sanction and did not need the approval of the "nation." Officials and those among Russia's politically articulate public clearly underestimated "the power and importance of the national question."[74] While ethnic or cultural homogenization as the single tool for nation-building would have been highly problematic for the multiethnic Russian state, some portion of this approach (for example, linguistic homogenization) combined with political liberalization and economic modernization could have worked more effectively. Russian authorities did not deploy the civic aspect of nation-building and thus failed to bind society more effectively to the state based on a consensus on mutual rights and obligations. Russification was only a half-hearted measure, and it failed to build a nation to support the state and, by 1917, failed to preserve even the state itself.

Nation-Building under Soviet Rule: Soviet Nation versus Institutionalized Ethnic Nations

The tsarist empire expired in a bloody and difficult struggle, paving the way for three-quarters of a century of Soviet rule in Russia. When the Soviet Union (USSR) collapsed in 1991, many scholars and analysts immediately pointed to nationalism as the leading cause of its death. In the words of one scholar, the "collapse of the Soviet Union was caused in good measure by nationalism. . . . Nationalism reigned supreme."[75] This statement implies that nation-building and nationalism in the Soviet Union were directed strongly toward challenging state power and cohesion, but this was not entirely the case. Under communism, two processes of modern nation-building occurred in the USSR, both sponsored by the state and intended to increase state cohesion: one emphasized the creation of a supranational "Soviet" nation, while the other focused on the institutionalization of ethnically based nations. The first process succeeded only partially, while the second became the basis for mobilization against the state once it removed its most repressive features.[76]

Efforts to build a multiethnic "Soviet" nation included policies of political, economic, and social advancement for non-Russians in the Soviet Union. The policy of indigenization (*korenizatsiia*), for example, especially during Leonid Brezhnev's rule, gave non-Russians the top position (i.e., first secretary) in republican party hierarchies, while ethnic Russians occupied the second position (i.e., second secretary). Indigenization also made possible entrenched nepotism, corruption, cronyism, illegal activity, and the virtual creation of fiefdoms in Soviet republics where local leaders had long tenures and ruled as they pleased, so long as they observed requisite aspects of obedience and tribute to the communist regime in Moscow.[77] Besides leadership positions in the Soviet Union's ethnonational territories, non-Russian cadres also made it to the highest bodies of Soviet power. Under Brezhnev, in fact, as many as six non-Russians from the republics at one point sat on the Politburo. In the Central Committee of the Communist Party, Ukrainians and

Kazakhs also established a significant presence.[78] Thus, a Soviet elite was forged, consisting of Russians and co-opted non-Russians in the periphery.

Policies that modernized the lives of national groups in the periphery and created opportunities for economic, political, social, and intellectual mobility also contributed to Soviet nation-building. The Soviet government transformed the social landscape of the former Russian empire through education, industrialization, and urbanization. Many elites came to favor the maintenance of the Soviet Union, while the larger population derived relative satisfaction from improvements in their lives. At the same time, among Russians (and russified Slavs and non-Slavs who supported Russian hegemony), a consensus developed for the maintenance of the Soviet state. Most Russians came to view the entire Soviet Union as their homeland; for example, to an early 1980s poll of Russians in the Russian Federation on what they considered as their motherland (*rodina*), 70 percent responded, "the Soviet Union."[79]

Ironically, the forging of a Soviet nation went in tandem with official policies that amounted to the institutionalization of ethnic-based nations in the USSR. In the words of Rogers Brubaker,

> The Soviet state not only passively tolerated but actively institutionalized the existence of multiple nations and nationalities as fundamental constituents of the state and its citizenry. It established nationhood and nationality as fundamental social categories sharply distinct from the overarching categories of statehood and citizenship. . . . The Soviet institutions of territorial nationhood and personal nationality comprised a pervasive system of social classification . . . an interpretative grid for public discussion . . . a legitimate form for public and private identities. . . .[80]

How did the Soviet state institutionalize ethnic nations? Shortly after coming to power in 1917, the Bolsheviks recognized the importance of concessions to groups with highly developed nationalist sentiments and some experience of independence between 1917 and 1921. Without these concessions, they reasoned, the likely outcome would be the unraveling of Soviet power on the territory that constituted the former Russian empire. Early disagreement between Vladimir Lenin and Joseph Stalin on the political and legal framework of the Bolshevik-ruled state yielded to a consensus on a structure that would be sensitive to the concerns of non-Russian groups. Thus, in 1922, a Union Treaty was signed by the Russian Republic, Ukraine, Belorussia, and the Transcaucasus Republic. Two years later, the state adopted a constitution that declared, among other things, that the USSR was a "federal, multinational state formed on the principle of socialist federalism as a result of the free self-determination of nations. . . ."[81]

Having declared its formal position on the self-determination of nations, Soviet nationality policy between 1918 and the early 1920s proceeded to conduct a version of "ethnic affirmative action run amuck."[82] Fifteen union republics were created, each organized along ethno-territorial lines, with a titular nationality or ethnic group representing the population that had nominal control over a homeland territory. In addition, nearly all nationalities, differentiated mainly by language, established their own administrative and territorial units. Between 1918 and 1922 the self-governing republics and administrations of Bashkiria, Tatarstan, Kyrgyzia, Dagestan, Karelia, and Yakutia were created. By 1928, union republics contained national *okrugs*, national *raions*, national soviets, native executive committees, native soviets, *aul* soviets, clan soviets, and nomadic soviets. The Communist Party also decreed ethnic quotas at all levels of administration and fostered the development of distinct and written languages for all ethnic groups, even when this did not seem entirely efficient or rational (as in cases where a written language did not previously exist). By 1938, newspapers were published in sixty-six languages in the Soviet Union.[83]

Besides the creation of ethno-territorial administrative units, Soviet leaders further institutionalized ethnic nations through the policy of indigenization and the introduction of internal passports. Indigenization combined the use of local languages in government, education, literature, and other social communication with the recruitment and training of non-Russians to work in the government, Communist Party, and local Soviet organs. Lenin announced that this policy would assist nations that had been "stateless" under tsarism. As a result, titular nationalities not only increased their numbers in the communist hierarchy in the 1920s but, as previously mentioned, came to occupy the top position in republican party organizations and enjoyed long tenures in power. In 1932, the Soviet regime introduced individual passports, irrevocably demarcating every citizen's nationality at birth and invoking a national and ethnic identity from birth until death.

Modernization policies—including education and mass literacy, urbanization, economic welfare, and security—also facilitated the institutionalization of ethnic nations. Whereas four out of five people in the Russian empire were illiterate, literacy rates in the Soviet Union (in at least two languages, for many) reached 81.2 percent by 1939. Between 1939 and 1984, the percentage of manual workers and peasants who had only elementary education or four years of primary school dropped from being an overwhelming majority to only 18.5 percent. Urbanization also proceeded at a very rapid pace, with the urban population growing at an annual rate of 6.5 percent between 1926 and 1939. In 1960, the USSR's urban population was 49 percent of the total, and rose to 65–70 percent between 1972 and 1985. In the economic sphere, the Soviet state subsidized incomes in underdeveloped regions and implemented comprehensive regional development projects. National income and industrial production grew consistently between 1961 and 1985, along with per capita consumption. Despite uneven rates of growth in different parts of the USSR, living standards as a whole "improved markedly in all republics" from the 1960s to 1985.[84] And after World War II, the USSR became one of the world's two superpowers, whose military capability and international status gave its citizens reason to feel pride in the state and security from potential foreign aggressors.

The institutionalization of nations legitimized the idea of national identity rooted in ethnic particularities, justified collective action based on the interests of putative nations, and gave ethnic groups an organizational context for mobilization. Modernization, at the same time, gave some substance to the idea of citizenship (or the civic aspect of nationalism)—the people cooperated with authoritarian politics in exchange for various goods that the state delivered to them (security, order, economic welfare, education, and so on). Modernization, as some would argue, gave many citizens a stake in the Soviet state and promoted a feeling among the people that the system was "theirs" and worthy of their participation and cooperation.[85] It helped keep centrifugal forces at bay and nurtured the identification of the most important ethnic group, the Russians, with the Soviet Union as their homeland. Most important, it consolidated expectations among the people regarding the state's obligations toward their security and welfare, implying that if the state ever became too weak or incapacitated to fulfill these obligations, it could become unworthy of the support and participation of its citizenry.

Modernization and the institutionalization of nations in the Soviet Union, while facilitating the rise of nations and nationalism, did not mean a consistently tolerant or benevolent official stance toward society or ethnic groups within the state. For example, the social and human costs of Soviet collectivization and industrialization are well known, as are other forms of repression, oppression, and violence inflicted on millions by the Soviet state.[86] Nonetheless, Soviet policies of modernization and institutionalization of nations did whittle away at the strong legacy of the Russian imperial state. Although official intent was for these policies to help overcome fissiparous tendencies along lines of nationality and cultivate public loyalty to the Soviet state, the eventual outcome proved to be the opposite. Soviet rulers legitimized the concept of ethnic "nations" as the basis of political legitimacy, authority, and organization. They also provided sufficient public security and welfare to allow and encourage society to think about its rights vis-à-vis the state. When, under Mikhail Gorbachev, state authorities not only liberalized political space but simultaneously allowed their own weakness to be exposed, nationalism in different forms readily surfaced to challenge state cohesion.

If, to repeat Kliuchevskii's aphorism, in the Russian empire "the state grew fat while the people grew thin," in the Soviet Union the state, despite Stalinist excesses, paradoxically allowed the people (or those who survived the regime's excesses) a greater measure of social and political "nourishment and growth." In particular, by institutionalizing nations and nationalities, the Soviet regime, unlike its tsarist predecessor, created a structure and platform from which the most potent attacks yet against the imperial state could be launched.[87] The breakup of the Soviet Union in 1991 showed the Soviet leaders' incapacity to deal with "nations" that the state itself had helped to nurture and institutionalize, their inability to act decisively in the early phase of challenge from assertive "nations," and their failure to cultivate and maintain "Soviet" nationalism for the purpose of state preservation. Do the demise of the Soviet Union and the existence of a new Russian state that is 80 percent ethnic Russian constitute a qualitatively new opportunity for stronger nationalism to develop in Russia? As in nineteenth-century western Europe, can nationalism become a force for integrating Russian state and society based on belief in a commonly constituted nation and the consensual delineation of rights, duties, and privileges between state and people? These questions will be part of the discussion in this book's concluding chapter.

FOREIGN POLICY AND NATIONALIST CONSIDERATIONS

Richard Pipes argues that the coterminous development of the Russian national state with the Russian empire conflated the processes of state-building and empire-building in Russia. As a result,

> For Russians, national identity [became] . . . indissolubly coupled to the notion of a boundless state. . . . To feel truly and proudly Russian, Russians, therefore, instinctively strive toward expansion and its corollary, militarism.[88]

While Pipes correctly notes the conflation of state and empire in Russia, his implication that an intrinsically expansionist "national identity" has always undergirded Russian expansionist foreign policy goes too far. The contention of this chapter is that nation-building was always weak in Russia. It did not flourish in either its ethnic or civic sense, and worked in a distorted manner to maintain the state rather than bring about a nationalism to bind state and society together. The people served the state's foreign policy and exploits abroad, but nationalism was hardly the motor behind society's adherence to the imperial state's service requirements. Expansion and imperial power may have perpetuated the myth of state authority and greatness, but the mass of Russians hardly viewed imperial expansion as the expression of their deepest values or the supreme measure for preserving and protecting their welfare and aspirations. Despite support for the power and foreign policy of the empire among sections of the Russian nobility and intellectual class, the last century and a half of tsarist rule actually witnessed a widening gulf between the imperial state and the larger society. This was a gulf that narrow "common interest" in imperial expansion failed to bridge.

The decisive factor for Russian expansion was always the aggrandizement and maintenance of the imperial state and the perpetuation of power of those who ruled it. Russian rulers treated people or society as but a resource for narrowly defined state purposes; in the nineteenth and early twentieth centuries, these purposes appeared increasingly remote from the interests, welfare, and aspirations of society. The state did little to cultivate public loyalty and commitment based on common belief in a nation on whom state power rested; neither did it solicit or include the nation's input into its foreign policy decisions. As one scholar has noted with regard to Russian expansion in the Far East,

> Perhaps the most distinctive characteristic of Russian imperialism . . . was that it did not benefit from . . . nationalism. . . . With its multinational composition and its dynastic regime, tsarist Russia was not a nation-state; indeed, nationalism would only have led to the destruction of the empire.[89]

Some might pose Russian expansion in Central Asia as an example of foreign policy undergirded by Russian nationalism. But nationalism in this context was limited to small groups of official elites and reflected the state–society divide. In the name of Russia or Russian glory, a few military leaders—hungry for medals, promotions, and opportunities to rule over new territories—brought the Russian flag to Central Asian territory. Others, in the style of classic colonial imperialism, pursued economic interest and a "civilizing mission" in the Asian lands. For example, the conquest of Khiva in 1872–73 was partially motivated by the interest of Russian trade and industry to have access to the shortest land track possible to Central Asia and open markets where their products might prove more competitive than in western Europe. Leaders such as Foreign Minister Aleksandr M. Gorchakov also declared a civilizing mission: "Russia in Central Asia [was in the position] of that of all civilized states which are brought into contact with half-savage nomad populations" and where the civilized state had the right "to exercise a certain ascendancy over their turbulent and undesirable neighbors."[90]

The nationalist element in Russian imperial expansion in Central Asia did not ignite the imagination of Russian society, and politically significant sections of the Russian public were never very interested in Russia's new eastern conquests. Dietrich Geyer notes that the dominant public opinion was captured in Mikhail Katkov's commentary just weeks prior to Russia's conquest of Tashkent in 1865: "Whatever makes Russia great there [in Asia], weakens her in Europe. Russia's role as a great power is not based there but on her rule over the western marchlands and in her position on the Black Sea. Our history is played out in Europe and not in Asia."[91] The aims of individuals and narrow interest groups (e.g., generals in the military and the Society for the Promotion of Russian Trade and Industry), and considerations of larger imperial strategy, guided Russian policy in the region. Like most of Russian foreign policy, expansion in Central Asia did not reflect the interests or concerns of a larger nation, or embody the values and ideals of an increasingly vocal and politically conscious society.

Russian expansion in Central Asia did not resonate with the broader society; contribute to creating ethnic and civic cohesion in Russia; or unite state, elite, and masses in a set of common ideas, values, and goals. In contrast, at least two cases in the past century and a half clearly illustrate how nationalism did undergird Russian foreign policy. The next two chapters describe these: Russian panslavism and foreign policy leading to the Russo-Turkish War of 1877–78, and great power nationalism and the Russian decision to enter World War I in 1914. The maintenance of imperial state power remained an important input to these foreign policy cases, but, more interestingly, state and society briefly joined together in a common definition of the nation, its interests, and the actions needed to fulfill the nation's aims. In these two cases, a particular conceptualization of the nation and its interests, promoted and supported by individuals and groups from a growing Russian civic space, had a real impact on state decision making.

NOTES

1. Geoffrey Hosking, *Russia: People and Empire 1552–1917* (Cambridge: Harvard University Press, 1997), p. 478; Hans Rogger, "Nationalism and the State: A Russian Dilemma," *Comparative Studies in Society and History* 4 (1962):260–62; and Roman Szporluk, "Dilem-

mas of Russian Nationalism," *Problems of Communism* (July–August 1989):15–35. See also Hugh Seton-Watson, *The Russian Empire 1801–1917* (Oxford: Clarendon Press, 1967), pp. 1–21. Hosking's book is the best articulation I have found of the historical divide between the Russian imperial state and the Russian people that led to the weakness of nationalism throughout Russian history.

2. Other scholars put the genesis of the modern state at a much later date—the sixteenth century. See James Anderson, "The Modernity of Modern States," in James Anderson, ed., *The Rise of the Modern State* (Brighton, Sussex, UK: Wheatsheaf, 1986), pp. 1–20.

3. Samuel E. Finer, "State and Nation-Building in Europe: The Role of the Military," in Charles Tilly, ed., *The Formation of National States in Western Europe* (Princeton: Princeton University Press, 1975), p. 86.

4. Finer, "State and Nation-Building in Europe," pp. 88–89.

5. Liah Greenfeld disagrees with the notion that modernity preceded nationalism but notes instead that nationalism is a pillar of modernity. See Liah Greenfeld, *Nationalism: Five Roads to Modernity* (Cambridge: Harvard University Press, 1992).

6. Reinhard Bendix, *Nation-Building and Citizenship* (New Brunswick, N.J.: Transaction, 1996), p. 23. Charles Tilly echoes this point and notes that various crises of state-building and the search for their resolution were what prompted state–society collaboration and therefore the modernization of states in western Europe. See Charles Tilly, "Western State-Making and Theories of Political Transformation," in Tilly, ed., *The Formation of National States*, pp. 601–38.

7. Bendix, *Nation-Building and Citizenship*, pp. 23, 24–27.

8. Gianfranco Poggi, *The State: Its Nature, Development, and Prospects* (Cambridge, UK: Polity, 1990), p. 53; and Allan Cochrane, "Industrialisation and Nineteenth-Century States," in Anderson, ed., *The Rise of the Modern State*, pp. 64–90. On industrialization and the rise of industrial society as prerequisites of nationalism, implying the growth of ties between a homogenized society and an effective state, see Ernest Gellner, *Nations and Nationalism* (Ithaca: Cornell University, 1983). Gellner argues that the rise of industrial society—with its attendant need for perpetual growth and a flexible, mobile division of labor—stimulated state-sponsored mass education, literacy, and cultural homogeneity and, ultimately, made possible the rise of nationalism.

9. Poggi, *The State*, p. 53. See also his chapters 3 and 4 for a more detailed assessment of the development of the modern state.

10. Bendix, *Nation-Building and Citizenship*, pp. 96–114; and Poggi, *The State*, pp. 53–68.

11. The theme of unevenness in the development of modern state *processes* stands out in Anderson, ed., *The Rise of the Modern State*.

12. Finer, "State and Nation-Building in Europe," p. 142.

13. The Napoleonic army, embodying the ideas of nationality and citizenship, elicited hostile, nationalist reaction in places where it fought and thus helped advance state and nation-building throughout Europe. See Finer, "State and Nation-Building in Europe," pp. 144–47.

14. John Breuilly underplays the central role of nationalism in the unification of Germany and Italy, but concedes that nationalism was important in legitimating to outside powers and their public opinion the claims to national unity by Germany (Prussia under Otto von Bismarck) and Italy (Piedmont led by the Count de Cavour). Nationalism was also important in coordinating the action of disparate elites to run the new states after unification. See John Breuilly, *Nationalism and the State* (Manchester: Manchester University Press, 1982), pp. 96–114. See also James Anderson, "Nationalism and Geography," in

Anderson, ed., *The Rise of the Modern State,* pp. 127–35; and Charles Tilly, *Coercion, Capital, and European States AD 990–1992* (Cambridge, UK: Blackwell, 1992), pp. 114–17.

15. C. E. Black, *The Dynamics of Modernization: A Study in Comparative History* (New York: Harper and Row, 1966), pp. 74–75; Stein Rokkan, "Dimensions of State Formation and Nation-Building: A Possible Paradigm for Research on Variations within Europe," in Tilly, ed., *The Formation of National States,* pp. 562–99.

16. Michael Urban, "The Politics of Identity in Russia's Postcommunist Transition: The Nation against Itself," *Slavic Review* 53 (Fall 1994):740.

17. James Cracraft, "Empire versus Nation: Russian Political Theory under Peter I," in James Cracraft, ed., *Major Problems in the History of Imperial Russia* (Lexington, Mass.: Heath, 1994), p. 226.

18. Richard Pipes, "The Communist System," in Alexander Dallin and Gail W. Lapidus, *The Soviet System in Crisis* (Boulder: Westview, 1991), pp. 16, 18.

19. Rogger, "Nationalism and the State," p. 255.

20. Hosking, *Russia: People and Empire,* p. xx.

21. Hugh Ragsdale, *The Russian Tragedy: The Burden of History* (Armonk, N.Y.: Sharpe, 1996), p. 31. This quote is translated as "The state swelled up, the people languished," in Hosking, *Russia: People and Empire,* p. xxiv.

22. As Michael Doyle notes, the concept of empire carried the connotation of domestic tyranny until the early nineteenth century; subsequently, in the age of imperialism in the late nineteenth century, empire came to be understood chiefly in the external sense of ruling peoples outside of one's own state. See Michael Doyle, *Empires* (Ithaca: Cornell University Press, 1986), pp. 30–32.

23. Edward Keenan argues, for example, that the historical evidence does not indicate that the Muscovite "warrior class" (*dvor*) in the fifteenth century ever claimed succession to Ancient Kiev to justify their efforts to transform their principality into a "lumbering empire." See his "On Certain Mythical Beliefs and Russian Behaviors," in Frederick S. Starr, ed., *The Legacy of History in Russia and the New States of Eurasia* (Armonk, N.Y.: Sharpe, 1994), pp. 19–22; and Karen Dawisha and Bruce Parrott, *Russia and the New States of Eurasia: The Politics of Upheaval* (Cambridge, UK: Cambridge University Press, 1994), pp. 28–30. The benign view of Russian imperial expansion remains a dominant theme among Russian social scientists in the post–Soviet period. See, e.g., *Politologiia na rossiiskom fone* (Moscow: Luch, 1993), pp. 112–22.

24. Seton-Watson, *The Russian Empire,* pp. 1–118; and Aleksandr B. Kamenskii, *The Russian Empire in the Eighteenth Century: Searching for a Place in the World,* trans. and ed. David Griffiths (New York: Sharpe, Inc., 1997).

25. Valery Tishkov, *Ethnicity, Nationalism and Conflict in and after the Soviet Union* (London: Sage, 1997), p. 27. See also Seton-Watson, *The Russian Empire,* pp. 51–61, for a description of the ethnic diversity of the Russian empire at the end of the eighteenth century. Richard Pipes argues that Russia's mode of expansion has been particularly violent and that, for the past three hundred years, it has exhibited "single-minded determination in aggressive wars." Indeed, he states that expansion and imperialism are in the Russian "bloodstream." Other scholars take a less mythic approach to Russian imperial expansion, highlighting its similarity to the activities of other imperial powers; the role that internal interest groups played in the development of imperialist strategies; the role played by permeable frontiers all along the periphery of the Russian state; the absence of unlimited imperial ambitions that other powers have, on occasion, ascribed to Russia (e.g., prior to the Crimean War in 1854); and the opportunities accorded to Russia by weaker neighbors that sought its protection (e.g., Georgia's voluntary accession to the Russian empire). See

Pipes, "The Communist System," pp. 22–23; N. S. Timasheff, "Russian Imperialism or Communist Aggression," in Waldemar Gurian, ed., *Soviet Imperialism: Its Origins and Tactics* (Notre Dame: University of Notre Dame Press, 1953), pp. 17–42; Hugh Ragsdale, ed., *Imperial Russian Foreign Policy* (Cambridge, UK: Cambridge University Press, 1993) (see chapters by Alfred Rieber and Hugh Ragsdale); Dietrich Geyer, *Russian Imperialism: The Interaction of Domestic and Foreign Policy in Russia, 1860–1914,* trans. Bruce Little (New Haven: Yale University Press, 1987), pp. 5–31; and A. N. Sakharov, "The Main Phases and Distinctive Features of Russian Nationalism," in Geoffrey Hosking and Robert Service, eds., *Russian Nationalism Past and Present* (New York: St. Martin's, 1998), pp. 7–18 .

26. Non-Russians in the eighteenth century, for example, occupied many of the highest positions in court, the army, and the civil service. Although tsarist dependence on the non-Russian nobility lessened in the nineteenth century, one scholar concludes that the Russian state "still could not function without the [non-Russian] nobility's cooperation." See Andreas Kappeler, "The Multi-Ethnic Empire," in Cracraft, ed., *Major Problems in the History of Imperial Russia,* pp. 399–401; Hans Rogger, *National Consciousness in Eighteenth-Century Russia* (Cambridge: Harvard University Press, 1960), chapter 1; and Hosking, *Russia: People and Empire,* pp. 146–47, 160–61.

27. I am not implying that the state never sponsored Russian chauvinism to the detriment of non-Russian groups. There was a particularly strong orientation by the tsar and his supporters during the reigns of Alexander III (1881–1894) and Nicholas II (1894–1917) to use ethnic Russian nationalism as a basis of support for the imperial state. See Theodore R. Weeks, *Nation and State in Late Imperial Russia: Nationalism and Russification on the Western Frontier, 1863–1914* (DeKalb: Northern Illinois University Press, 1996); Roman Szporluk, "The Russian Question and Imperial Overextension," in Karen Dawisha and Bruce Parrott, eds., *The End of Empire? The Transformation of the USSR in Comparative Perspective* (New York: Sharpe, 1997), pp. 72–73; and Mark von Hagen, "The Russian Empire," in Karen Barkey and Mark von Hagen, eds., *After Empire: Multiethnic Societies and Nation-Building* (Boulder: Westview, 1997), pp. 62–63.

28. Hosking, *Russia: People and Empire,* p. 39.

29. Kappeler, "The Multi-Ethnic Empire," pp. 400–2; Szporluk, "The Russian Question," pp. 74–75; Richard Pipes, *Russia under the Old Regime* (New York: Scribner, 1974), p. 182; and Richard Pipes, *The Russian Revolution* (New York: Knopf, 1990), p. 84. On nations as imagined communities, see Benedict Anderson, *Imagined Communities: Reflections on the Origins and Spread of Nationalism* (London: Verso, 1983).

30. Rogger, *National Consciousness in Eighteenth-Century Russia,* p. 3.

31. Greenfeld, *Nationalism,* pp. 191–203.

32. Quoted in Greenfeld, *Nationalism,* pp. 197–98.

33. Quoted in Greenfeld, *Nationalism,* p. 203.

34. Rogger, *National Consciousness in Eighteenth-Century Russia,* pp. 258–59, 272. See also pp. 253–75; Greenfeld, *Nationalism,* pp. 225–45, on poetic and intellectual writings emphasizing Russian greatness in relation to the West; and "M. V. Lomonosov Extolls Russian Greatness, 1755," in Cracraft, ed., *Major Problems in the History of Imperial Russia,* pp. 248–49. On the support for empire among Russia's cultural elite, see also Ilya Prizel, *National Identity and Foreign Policy: Nationalism and Leadership in Poland, Russia, and Ukraine* (Cambridge, UK: Cambridge University Press, 1998), pp. 170–72; and Susan Layton, *Russian Literature and Empire: Conquest of Caucasus from Pushkin to Tolstoy* (New York: Cambridge University Press, 1994).

35. For example, German historians residing in Moscow published deprecatory versions of Russian history in the late 1700s. One of them, August Ludwig Schloezer, wrote of Russian origins: "[Russian] history does not go back to the Tower of Babel; it is not as old as that

of Greece and Rome; it is younger even than that of Germany and Sweden. Before . . . [the calling of the Varangians] all was darkness, in Russia and in adjacent regions. Of course there were human beings there, but God alone knows whence and when they came. They were a people without a government, living like the beasts and the birds of their forests, undistinguished in any way, having no contact with the Southern nations, which is why they could be neither noticed nor described by a single enlightened South European." Quoted in Rogger, *Nationalist Consciousness in Eighteenth-Century Russia*, p. 220.

36. See *Karamzin's Memoir on Ancient and Modern Russia*, trans. Richard Pipes (New York: Atheneum, 1974), pp. 120–21 and 54–57.

37. Jeffrey Brooks, *When Russia Learned to Read: Literacy and Popular Literature, 1861–1917* (Princeton: Princeton University Press, 1985), pp. 241–45.

38. Michael Cherniavsky, *Tsar and People: Studies in Russian Myths* (New Haven: Yale University Press, 1961), p. 158.

39. Wright Miller observes that government in Russia "is not traditionally expected to derive its sanction from the governed, from which it follows that government, though unloved, is respected according to its efficiency and even sometimes according to its ruthlessness." Efficiency, as traditionally defined by state authorities in Russia, has less to do with internal welfare than with international status and respect based on Russian military power. See Wright Miller, *Russians as People* (New York: Dutton, 1960), p. 114.

40. The service state tradition meant that social hierarchy and status, economic resources, and human potential were shaped by what the imperial state needed. See Hosking, *Russia: People and Empire*, pp. 478, 246–62; and Pipes, *Russia under the Old Regime*, pp. 191–220.

41. Marc Raeff, *Understanding Imperial Russia: State and Society in the Old Regime* (New York: Columbia University Press, 1984), pp. 35–55, 101–23, 139–50.

42. E. B. Lanin, *Russian Characteristics* (London: Chapman and Hall, 1892), p. 37; S. M. Troitskii, *Finansovaia politika russkogo absoliutizma v XVIII veke* (Moscow: Nauka, 1966), pp. 221–24; David Christian, *Living Water: Vodka and Russian Society on the Eve of Emancipation* (Oxford: Clarendon, 1990), pp. 42–43; and A. P. Pogrebinskii, *Ocherki istorii finansov dorevoliutsionnoi Rossii* (Moscow: Gosfinizdat, 1954), p. 99. On taxation and military conscription as burdens on the Russian people, and on the state of Russian finances, see John Keep, *Soldiers and the Tsar: Army and Society in Russia 1462–1874* (Oxford: Clarendon, 1985), pp. 143–74; Pipes, *Russia under the Old Regime*, pp. 120–22; E. V. Anisimov, "Peter I: Birth of the Empire," in Cracraft, ed., *Major Problems in the History of the Russian Empire*, p. 85; Hosking, *Russia: People and Empire*, pp. 80–104; and Larisa F. Zakharova, "From Reform 'from Above' to Revolution 'From Below'," in Theodore Taranovski, ed. and trans., *Reform in Modern Russian History* (New York: Cambridge University Press, 1995), pp. 99, 120. The practice of extortionary taxation, especially on the peasantry, continued even at the height of industrialization in the last few decades of the nineteenth century. See, e.g., M. E. Falkus, *The Industrialisation of Russia 1700–1914* (London: Macmillan, 1972), p. 63.

43. Richard Pipes estimates that, on the eve of emancipation in 1858–59, roughly 12–15 percent of the Russian empire's population were "classical" serfs—i.e., "bound to the land, subject to the direct authority of their landlords, forced to perform for him any services demanded." He also notes, however, that in the census of 1858–59 37.7 percent of the population were "serfs in the proper sense of the word." Pipes, *Russia under the Old Regime*, pp. 151, 144.

44. Richard Hellie, *Enserfment and Military Change in Muscovy* (Chicago: University of Chicago Press, 1971); Peter Gatrell, "The Meaning of the Great Reforms in Russian Economic History," in Ben Eklof, John Bushnell, and Larisa Zakharova, eds., *Russia's Great*

Reforms, 1855–1881 (Bloomington: Indiana University Press, 1994), pp. 91–93; Zakharova, "From Reform 'from Above,'" pp. 108–16; Falkus, *The Industrialisation of Russia*, pp. 33, 39, 63; and Pipes, *Russia under the Old Regime*, pp. 153–65.

45. Dominic Lieven, *Russia's Rulers under the Old Regime* (New Haven: Yale University Press, 1989), p. 24.

46. The bureaucracy, to be sure, was not a homogeneous entity. It contained, for example, a liberal element that contributed substantively to the social reforms of Alexander II. See Zakharova, "From Reform 'from Above,'" pp. 97–124. On the impact of bureaucracy in separating state and society, see Rogger, "Nationalism and the State," p. 256; and Lanin, *Russian Characteristics*, pp. 8–11. Charles Tilly observes that, under Peter the Great, from "top to bottom, the emerging structure of social relations depended on coercion. . . . [The] effort to extract essential revenues from an uncommercialized economy multiplied the state structure. . . . [and] built up the imperial bureaucracy to its full, ponderous form." See Tilly, *Coercion, Capital, and European States*, p. 141.

47. See, e.g., Russell Bova, "Political Culture, Authority Patterns, and the Architecture of the New Russian Democracy," in Harry Eckstein, et al., *Can Democracy Take Root in Post–Soviet Russia?* (Lanham, Md.: Rowman & Littlefield, 1998), pp. 182–85; and Nancy Shields Kollman, "Muscovite Patrimonialism," in Cracraft, ed., *Major Problems in the History of Imperial Russia*, pp. 37–46.

48. Archie Brown, "Ideology and Political Culture," in Seweryn Bialer, ed., *Politics, Society, and Nationality inside Gorbachev's Russia* (Boulder: Westview, 1989), p. 18.

49. Richard Pipes is the best known among those who subscribe to a view that implies immutability in Russian political culture, arguing that it is in the Russian "bloodstream and changes as slowly and reluctantly as does language and customs." He also ascribes Bolshevism to Russia's fundamentally undemocratic environment and political culture. See Pipes, "The Communist System," pp. 18, 20. On the more democratic aspect of Russian political culture, see Nicolai N. Petro, *The Rebirth of Russian Democracy* (Cambridge: Harvard University Press, 1995); and Theodore Taranovski, "The Return to Normalcy: Commentary," in Taranovski, ed., *Reform in Modern Russian History*, pp. 419–23.

50. See Wayne Dowler, *Dostoevsky, Grigor'ev, and Native Soil Conservatism* (Toronto: University of Toronto Press, 1982), p. 4.

51. Cherniavsky, *Tsar and People*, pp. 83, 89.

52. Cherniavsky, *Tsar and People*, pp. 1–150; Anisimov, "Peter I," pp. 91–92; and James Cracraft, *The Church Reform of Peter the Great* (London: Macmillan, 1971).

53. On the antistate connotation of "Holy Russia" and its impact on antistate sentiments among the gentry after 1812, see Michael Cherniavsky, "'Holy Russia': A Study in the History of an Idea," *American Historical Review* 63 (April 1958):617–37; and Cherniavsky, *Tsar and People*, pp. 128–61.

54. Alfred Rieber accentuates initiatives from above as an enduring element of the Russian reforming tradition in "The Reforming Tradition in Russian and Soviet History: Commentary," in Taranovski, ed., *Reform in Modern Russian History*, pp. 237–38. More recent illustrations of this tradition include Stalin's industrialization drive and Gorbachev's *glasnost'* and *perestroika*.

55. Gareth W. Jones, *Nikolay Novikov, Enlightener of Russia* (Cambridge, UK: Cambridge University Press, 1984), pp. 145–215; and K. A. Papmehl, "The Empress and '*Un Fanatique*': A Review of the Circumstances Leading to the Government Action against Novikov in 1792," *Slavonic and East European Review* 68 (1990):665–91.

56. Marc Raeff, *Michael Speransky, Statesman of Imperial Russia, 1772–1839*, 2nd ed. (The Hague: Nijhoff, 1969); and Hosking, *Russia: People and Empire*, pp. 168–69.

57. Hosking, *Russia: People and Empire*, pp. 143–44; Raeff, *Understanding Imperial Russia*, pp. 136–50; Allen McConnell, *A Russian Philosophe: Alexander Radishchev, 1749–1802* (The Hague: Nijhoff, 1964), pp. 14–16, 106–22.

58. Quoted in Cherniavsky, *Tsar and People*, p. 136.

59. Larisa Zakharova, "Autocracy and the Reforms of 1861–1874 in Russia," trans. Daniel Field, pp. 19–39; and Alfred J. Rieber, "Interest-Group Politics in the Era of the Great Reforms, pp. 58–83, both in Eklof, Bushnell, and Zakharova, eds., *Russia's Great Reforms*; Hosking, *Russia: People and Empire*, pp. 109–111; Raeff, *Understanding Imperial Russia*, pp. 14–17; Anisimov, "Peter I," p. 85; Philip Longworth, "The Pugachev Revolt: The Last Great Cossack–Peasant Rising," in H. A. Landsberger, ed., *Rural Protest: Peasant Movements and Social Change* (London: Macmillan, 1974), pp. 194–256.

60. Some statistics indicate the miserable lot of the Russian people in the last three decades of the tsarist regime and some reasons for societal discontent against the state. In 1887, 103,842 recruits to the tsarist army were sent back because they were physically unfit. The city of Nizhnyi Novgorod recorded 2,200 deaths versus 1,900 births. The death rates in 203 Russian cities ranged from 35 to 171 per thousand, and a provincial famine was a common yearly event in the empire. In 1883, some four-fifths of army recruits from southern districts could neither read nor write, and the level of illiteracy in Russia as late as 1913 was estimated at 60–65 percent. See Lanin, *Russian Characteristics*, p. 15; and Falkus, *The Industrialisation of Russia*, p. 11.

61. Edward C. Thaden, "Russification," in Cracraft, ed., *Major Problems in the History of Imperial Russia*, p. 403.

62. Weeks, *Nation and State in Late Imperial Russia*, pp. 3–14.

63. Rogger notes that the state was always suspicious of nationalism, "not only when the state was confronted by versions . . . formulated by radicals or liberals, but even . . . when it was defined by those who were most vocal in their support of the established order." See Rogger, "Nationalism and the State," p. 256. Weeks adds that neither the tsarist regime nor the mass population was fully enthusiastic about russification; the policy put official Russia in a bind between strong claims not to be destroying local cultures and policies that sought a hegemonic role for the Russian language, Russian culture, and the Orthodox Church. Weeks, *Nation and State in Late Imperial Russia*, pp. 192–96.

64. Edward C. Thaden, ed., *Russification in the Baltic Provinces and Finland, 1855–1914* (Princeton: Princeton University Press, 1981), pp. 8–9.

65. Iu. I. Semenov, ed., *Natsional'naia politika v imperatorskoi Rossii* (Moscow: Staryi sad, 1997), pp. 68–97.

66. See Hans Rogger, *Russia in the Age of Modernisation and Revolution, 1881–1917* (New York: Longman, 1983), pp. 182–207; C. Leonard Lundin, "Finland," in Thaden, ed., *Russification in the Baltic Provinces and Finland*, pp. 357–458; Weeks, *Nation and State*, pp. 13–16; Hugh Seton-Watson, *The New Imperialism* (Chester Springs, Penn.: Dufour, 1961), pp. 30–31; and Louis Greenberg, *The Jews in Russia: The Struggle for Emancipation*, vol. 2 (New York: Schocken, 1976), pp. 30–47. Thaden's book is one of the first to focus on the administrative, cultural, and voluntary aspects of russification.

67. Thaden, "Russification," p. 408.

68. Ben Eklof, *Russian Peasant Schools: Officialdom, Village Culture, and Popular Pedagogy, 1861–1914* (Berkeley: University of California Press, 1986), p. 1; and Robert J. Kaiser, *The Geography of Nationalism in Russia and the USSR* (Princeton: Princeton University Press, 1994), pp. 43–47. The perception of peasants as "dark masses" was not unique to the Russian gentry but observed in other places as well. For example, until the 1870s, urbanized and educated Frenchmen perceived their peasant brethren in a similar way. See Eugen

J. Weber, *Peasants into Frenchmen: The Modernization of Rural France, 1870–1914* (Stanford: Stanford University Press, 1976), p. 5.

69. Thaden, "Russification," pp. 403–10; Weeks, *Nation and State*, p. 13; Eklof, *Russian Peasant Schools*, pp. 403–7; Kaiser, *The Geography of Nationalism*, pp. 69–71; Hosking, *Russia: People and Empire*, pp. 137, 206–24; I. M. Bogdanov, *Gramotnost' i obrazovanie v dorevoliutsionnoi Rossii i v SSSR* (Moscow: Statistika, 1964), pp. 20–29; and Raeff, *Understanding Imperial Russia*, pp. 35–55, 136–37, 193–96. Localist mentality also included relative ethnic tolerance, equality, and ethnic mixing between Russians and their non-Russian neighbors. See Sakharov, "The Main Phases and Distinctive Features of Russian Nationalism," pp. 9–13.

70. See, e.g., Kaiser, *The Geography of Nationalism*, pp. 63, 65; and Ronald Grigor Suny, *The Making of the Georgian Nation* (Bloomington: Indiana University Press, 1989), pp. 126–30.

71. Hosking, *Russia: People and Empire*, pp. 377–87; Thaden, *Russification in the Baltic Provinces and Finland*, pp. 30–32, 76–83; and Ronald Grigor Suny, *Looking toward Ararat: Armenia in Modern History* (Bloomington: Indiana University Press, 1993), pp. 39–45; and "Populism, Nationalism, and Marxism: The Origins of Revolutionary Parties among the Armenians of the Caucasus," *Armenian Review* 32 (June 1979):134–51.

72. See John Bushnell, "Peasants in Uniform: The Tsarist Army as a Peasant Society," in Ben Eklof and Stephen Frank, eds., *The World of the Russian Peasant: Post-Emancipation Culture and Society* (Boston: Unwin Hyman, 1990), pp. 101–14; and Falkus, *The Industrialisation of Russia*, p. 11.

73. Kappeler, "The Multi-Ethnic Empire," p. 400. See also Rogger, *Russia in the Age of Modernisation*, pp. 192–93; and Thaden, "Russification," pp. 403–6.

74. Weeks, *Nation and State*, pp. 195–96.

75. See Norman Naimark's foreword in Ronald Grigor Suny, *The Revenge of the Past: Nationalism, Revolution, and the Collapse of the Soviet Union* (Stanford: Stanford University Press, 1993), p. ix. For a view that focuses more on the weakness of the state than nationalism per se as the primary reason for the collapse of the Soviet Union, see Astrid S. Tuminez, "Nationalism, Ethnic Pressures, and the Collapse of the USSR," in Mark Kramer, ed., *The Collapse of the Soviet Union* (Boulder: Westview, 2000).

76. A good overview on this question is Kaiser, *The Geography of Nationalism*, pp. 94–147.

77. One measure of obedience to Moscow was suppression of anti-Soviet ethnic nationalism. Those who failed to suppress ethnic nationalism were punished—for example, Ukrainian Communist Party First Secretary Petro Shelest' who, in 1972, was removed from his position because he tolerated manifestations of ethnic Ukrainian nationalism. On long tenures, some first secretaries in the Central Asian republics, Georgia, Moldavia, Belorussia, and the Baltics ruled from thirteen to twenty-eight years! See *Dnevnik P. E. Shelesta*, Rossiiskii Tsentr Khraneniia i Izucheniia Dokumentov Noveishei Istorii, Fond 666, Delo 2, listy 333–48 (this citation provided by Mark Kramer); Shelest's interview in *Argumenty i fakty* 2 (1989), p. 14; Bohdan Nahaylo and Victor Swoboda, *Soviet Disunion: A History of the Nationalities Problem in the USSR* (New York: Free Press, 1989), pp. 177–79; Ronald Suny, "State, Civil Society, and Ethnic Cultural Consolidation in the USSR—Roots of the National Question," in Gail Lapidus, et al., eds. *From Union to Commonwealth: Nationalism and Separatism in the Soviet Republics* (Cambridge, UK: Cambridge University Press, 1992), p. 43, fn. 12.

78. Steven Burg, "Nationality Elites and Political Change in the Soviet Union," in Lubomyr Hajda and Mark Beissinger, eds., *The Nationalities Factor in Soviet Politics and*

Society (Boulder: Westview, 1990), pp. 25–26; and Roman Laba, "How Yeltsin's Exploitation of Ethnic Nationalism Brought Down an Empire," *Transition*, 12 January 1996, p. 9. For an account of the extensive corruption led by the highest leaders in Uzbekistan and tolerated by Moscow authorities, see T. Gdlian and N. Ivanov, *Kremlevskoe delo* (Moscow: Gramota, 1996).

79. In Tallinn, Estonia, a comparatively lower percentage of Russians (53 percent) claimed the Soviet Union as their motherland. See Leokadia Drobyzheva, "Perestroika and the Ethnic Consciousness of Russians," in Lapidus, et al., eds., *From Union to Commonwealth*, pp. 101 and 112, fn. 8.

80. Rogers Brubaker, *Nationalism Reframed: Nationhood and the National Question in the New Europe* (Cambridge, UK: Cambridge University Press, 1996), pp. 23–24.

81. "The Constitution of the USSR," in Martha Brill Olcott, ed., *The Soviet Multinational State: Readings and Documents* (Armonk, N.Y.: Sharpe, 1990), p. 8. See also Richard Pipes, *The Formation of the Soviet Union*, rev. ed., (Cambridge: Harvard University Press, 1964); Yuri Slezkine, "The USSR as a Communal Apartment, or How a Socialist State Promoted Ethnic Particularism," *Slavic Review* 53 (Summer 1994):425; Hélène Carrère d'Encausse, *Decline of an Empire* (New York: Harper and Row, 1979), pp. 13–46; and Vladimir Ilyich Lenin, "The Right of Nations to Self-Determination," in Omar Dahbour and Micheline R. Ishay, eds., *The Nationalism Reader* (Atlantic Highlands, N.J.: Humanities Press, 1995), pp. 208–14.

82. I first used this phrase in Tuminez, "Nationalism, Ethnic Pressures, and the Breakup of the USSR."

83. Isaac Deutscher, *Stalin: A Political Biography*, 2nd ed. (New York: Oxford University Press, 1949); Suny, "State, Civil Society," p. 29; Ben Fowkes, *The Disintegration of the Soviet Union: The Triumph of Nationalism* (London: Macmillan, 1997), pp. 35–52, 55–59; Slezkine, "The USSR as a Communal Apartment," pp. 426–39; and S.V. Cheshko, *Raspad Sovetskogo Soiuza* (Moscow: Rossiiskaia Akademiia Nauk, 1996), pp. 142–65.

84. Gertrude Schroeder, "Nationalities and the Soviet Economy," in Lubomyr Hajda and Mark Beissinger, eds., *The Nationalities Factor*, pp. 50, 45–51. See also Moshe Lewin, *The Gorbachev Phenomenon: A Historical Interpretation* (Berkeley: University of California Press, 1989), pp. 30–31, 47; Zvi Gitelman, "Development and Ethnicity in the Soviet Union," in Alexander J. Motyl, ed., *The Post–Soviet Nations* (New York: Columbia University Press, 1992), p. 228; Viktor Zaslavsky, "The Soviet Union," in Barkey and von Hagen, eds., *After Empire*, p. 86; Fowkes, *The Disintegration of the Soviet Union*, pp. 70–82, 100–104; Seweryn Bialer, *Stalin's Successors: Leadership, Stability, and Change in the Soviet Union* (Cambridge, UK: Cambridge University Press, 1980), pp. 214–16; Philip G. Roeder, "Soviet Federalism and Ethnic Mobilization," *World Politics* 43 (January 1991):196–232; and D. A. Dyker, *The Process of Investment in the Soviet Union* (Cambridge, UK: Cambridge University Press, 1983).

85. Hans Rogger conjectures that "the Soviet regime, by reducing this diversity [of interests between various sectors of Russian society] and by its ruthless policy of industrialization and modernization has gone further in bridging the gulf between itself and the nation than the more easy-going autocracy of tsarist days." Rogger, "Nationalism and the State," p. 264. Another argument that the Soviet state "gave everyone a stake in the system" is Tim McDaniel, *The Agony of the Russian Idea* (Princeton: Princeton University Press, 1996), p. 141; see also pp. 137–47.

86. See, for example, Tuminez, "Nationalism, Ethnic Pressures, and the Breakup of the USSR"; Robert Conquest, *The Harvest of Sorrow: Soviet Collectivization and the Terror-Famine* (London: Hutchinson, 1986); and Aleksandr M. Nekrich, *The Punished Peoples: The*

Deportation and Fate of Soviet Minorities at the End of the Second World War (New York: Norton, 1978).

87. Brubaker underlines institutionalized multinationality as the key difference between the tsarist and Soviet states. See Brubaker, *Nationalism Reframed*, p. 27, fn. 12.

88. Richard Pipes, "Introduction," in Heyward Isham, ed., *Remaking Russia: Voices from Within* (Armonk, N.Y.: Sharpe, 1995), pp. 4–5.

89. Sung-Hwan Chang, "Russian Designs on the Far East," in Taras Hunczak, ed., *Russian Imperialism from Ivan the Great to the Revolution* (New Brunswick: Rutgers University Press, 1974), p. 321.

90. See "The Gorchakov Circular on Russia's Mission in Central Asia, 1864," in Cracraft, ed., *Major Problems in the History of Imperial Russia*, p. 410. General Konstantin von Kaufman, colonializing military officer in Central Asia, also echoed Gorchakov's sentiments by asserting that Russia's "unruly neighbors" must submit to the "beneficial, peaceful views of the White tsar." See Karel Durman, *The Time of the Thunderer: Mikhail Katkov, Russian National Extremism and the Failure of the Bismarckian System, 1871–1887* (Boulder: East European Monographs, 1988), p. 144. On the purposes and dynamics of Russian expansion in Central Asia, see Geyer, *Russian Imperialism*, pp. 86–98; Barbara Jelavich, *St. Petersburg and Moscow: Tsarist and Soviet Foreign Policy 1814–1974* (Bloomington: Indiana University Press, 1983), pp. 168–72; *Mission of N.P. Ignat'ev to Khiva and Bukhara in 1858*, ed. and trans. John L. Evans (Newtonville, Mass.: Oriental Research Partners, 1984), pp. 8–27, 74–79; and Mohammad Anwar Khan, *England, Russia, and Central Asia (A Study in Diplomacy) 1857–1878* (Khyber Bazar-Peshawar: University Book Agency, 1963), pp. 49–50, 189–209.

91. Geyer, *Russian Imperialism*, p. 94. See also Jelavich, *St. Petersburg and Moscow*, pp. 171–72.

3

Long Struggle, Short-Lived Triumph: Panslavism, 1856–1878

Russia never had anything in common with the rest of Europe. . . . [Its] history demands a different thought and formula than the thought and formula . . . of the Christian West.

—Aleksandr Pushkin, 1830

Man does not live by bread alone, and nations do not live and define themselves in history merely by their material welfare. We must be concerned not only with the daily lives of the Balkan Slavs, and we must protect them not only from the Turks but also from Western encroachments on their land and from [Western] spiritual seduction and deprivation. The trials of our brothers by faith and ancestry . . . trials that Russia has been called to remove, are not only physical but also moral. . . .

—Ivan Aksakov, 1877

Russia is the propeller and commander of our entire Slavic family: let us go forward all as one in the spirit of our people, under the guidance of our historically affirmed tribal elder, [Russia].

—Ludovit Štur, 1850s

PANSLAVISM AND TSARIST FOREIGN POLICYMAKING

The Slavs and Russia

Russian panslavism is a variant of nationalism that developed in the early nineteenth century. Originally, panslavs highlighted the cultural and linguistic similarities between Russians and other Slavs who comprised minorities in the

57

Austrian, Turkish, and Prussian empires of the late eighteenth century. The minority Slavs included Serbs, Croats, Montenegrins, Czechs, Slovaks, Bulgarians, and even Greeks (whom panslavs linked to slavdom because of their Orthodox religion). These Slavs became interested in panslavism in the first half of the nineteenth century, as they sought to alleviate their oppressed status as imperial subjects, and viewed Russia as a potential protector.

The German philosopher Johann Gottfried Herder was a major influence on the early evolution of ideas on slavdom. Herder wrote that different societies and nations had a distinct character and value in the particular age in which they existed. He identified the Slavs as a race representing peace, humanitarianism, and democracy, as opposed to the bellicose and autocratic Latin and German races. He further praised Slavs as an ascendant and unique people, filled with a strong sense of freedom, youthfulness, modesty, obedience, a peaceful nature, and honesty. They were the heroes of the future. Herder encouraged Slav scholars to study Slavic languages, folklore, and folk culture to ensure that their people always remembered their heroic past and prepared for new glories in the future. Early proponents of panslavism among Slovak and Czech intellectuals (mainly scholars and poets), including Jan Kollar, Pavel Josef Šafarik, Ludovit Štur, and František Palacký, all echoed Herder's ideas of Slav superiority versus the decaying, declining West.[1]

Beginning in the 1850s, panslavism, especially in Russia, evolved from a culturally oriented set of ideas to a political ideology that "confirmed the superiority of Slavs over other nations and Russia's calling as a hegemon in the Slavic world."[2] Reacting to Russia's defeat at the hands of Western foes who allied with the Ottoman Empire in the Crimean War, Russian panslavs looked to the Slavs as their state's potential great allies. They preached that the Slavs, under Russian leadership, would form a powerful national and political entity to surpass the Western world in its power, brilliance, and accomplishments. The ideas of panslavism, although popular among some circles at specific points in time, neither created a sustained mass movement nor enjoyed enduring official support in tsarist Russia. But in 1875–78 these ideas penetrated Russia's highest policymaking circles and enjoyed support from Russian society. In 1875–76, for example, panslav propaganda roused thousands of ordinary Russians and military personnel to volunteer, without official sanction, in the Serbian army to help fight a war of liberation against Turkey. The widespread popularity of panslavism during these years ultimately influenced the tsarist government's decision to go to war against Turkey in 1877 to free Slav "brothers" suffering under imperial Ottoman rule. As many as two hundred thousand Russians gave up their lives in the bloodshed that followed.[3]

Russian panslavism meets the criteria outlined in chapter 1 of a nationalism with aggressive implications for foreign policy. It favored (albeit not exclusively) ethnic criteria for membership in the nation and implied the need to unite all members of the nation—that is, Slavs—under Russia. It also preached a chauvinistic and imperialistic self-image that positioned Slavs above other nations; justified Russian hegemony; and maligned outsiders, especially the "West." The panslav self- and other-image pitted Russia and its Slav allies against western European and other foes and justified aggressive action toward outsiders, who were portrayed as obstacles to the fulfillment of Slavic historical destiny and national potential. The panslav national mission, too, had aggressive implications: it aimed to unite all Slavs in one political entity under Russia, thereby putting Russia in direct conflict with other imperial rulers, particularly Austria-Hungary and Turkey, both of which ruled over large numbers of Slav subjects.

Russian panslavism is only one expression of panslav ideology, and notably the most aggressive in orientation. It preached Russia's holy calling as the liberator of all Slavs and the rightful leader of a united Slav federation.[4] Preachers of this ideology were primarily Russians. With few exceptions, non-Russian panslavs, concerned with liberating themselves from imperial rule, advocated more liberal and non-chauvinistic versions of panslav ideology. These included:

1. Jan Kollar's cultural panslavism based on literary and intellectual reciprocity among the Slavs
2. František Palacký's austroslavism, which advocated territorial integrity for Austria-Hungary so long as Slavs could enjoy the same rights as the empire's dominant German and Hungarian nationalities
3. Democratic panslavism, preached by the Society of United Slavs and the Brotherhood of Saints Cyril and Methodius in early nineteenth-century Russia, which favored an egalitarian Slav federation among Russians, Ukrainians, Poles, and other Slavs
4. Karel Kramar's neoslavism, prominent in 1908–10, which preached democracy, equality, justice, and religious freedom for all Slavs and reconciliation between Russia and Poland.[5]

In Russia itself, hegemonic panslavism emerged and matured in 1856–75. However, Russian interest in the Slavs of the Ottoman Empire dated back to the reigns of Peter the Great (1682–1725) and Catherine the Great (1762–1796). These monarchs took an interest in Orthodox Slavs outside Russia primarily for geopolitical reasons, viewing the Slavs as an asset to Russia in its dynastic competition with nearby empires.[6] Many ordinary Russians also gained firsthand exposure to their Slav neighbors in the course of Russia's numerous wars with Turkey, beginning in the seventeenth century.[7] In 1774, after winning a war with Turkey, Russia gained diplomatic status as protector of the Orthodox Christian subjects of the Porte (the governing center of the Ottoman Empire) and received the right to establish consulates in the Ottoman Empire and build a church in Constantinople. These provisions, which gave Russia a foothold in the Ottoman Empire, were contained in the Treaty of Kuchuk Kainardji. Many Russian publicists and policymakers in subsequent years interpreted this treaty as having given Russia the *judicial* right to intervene in the internal affairs of the Ottoman Empire. Over time, a myth evolved regarding Russia's judicial right—and even divine calling—to protect southern Slavs.[8] In 1812–13, panslav political sympathies in Russia became apparent as the press celebrated Slav successes in the Balkan League War against Turkey.

Slavic cultural societies solicited money and medicine to aid the southern Slavs and held Slavic banquets in Moscow and St. Petersburg, in which participants sang patriotic songs and gave fiery speeches favoring the Slavic struggle for liberation. But the tsarist government, in sympathy with its fellow monarchy, the ruling Habsburgs of Austria (who feared rebellion from their own restive Slav subjects), curtailed what were essentially limited public manifestations of support for Slavic liberation in Russia.[9]

Other than the events of 1812–13, no other remarkable demonstrations of political support for Slavic liberation took place in Russia in the first half of the nineteenth century. But while overt political panslavism was quiescent, panslavism as an academic and cultural program to increase knowledge and understanding between Russia and its Slav neighbors continued to develop.[10] Russians went to Slav lands to study, and Slav students, especially Bulgarians, received scholarships to study in Russia. Slavic studies chairs were established at Moscow University, and newspapers and journals published articles on the Slavs, their lands, and their culture. Official institutions, such as the Ministry of Foreign Affairs and War Ministry, sponsored historical, military-strategic, and other studies of the Balkan Slavs and Russia's wars with Turkey.[11] These efforts helped spread knowledge of the Slavs in Russia, but did not advance panslavism as an official ideology. The tsarist government, especially during Nicholas I's reign (1825–1855), deemed panslavism subversive. Because it preached the liberation of small nations from tyrannical rulers, the tsar feared that panslavism could undermine the legitimacy of all of Europe's imperial regimes, including Russia. Indeed, Nicholas I correctly assessed the danger of panslav ideology; some panslav societies rejected autocratic rule; favored the abolition of serfdom; and advocated autonomy for all Slavs, including Poles, in the Russian empire.[12]

The literature on Russian panslavism, written primarily by historians, offers some explanations for its rise and impact. One argument, articulated by the historian Hans Kohn and others, focuses on the role of Russia's small educated class in the nineteenth century. Kohn notes that these intellectuals, coming "face-to-face" with Russian backwardness relative to European states, sought and propagated panslavism as an ideology that asserted Russia's unique identity, spiritual greatness, and immense material and political potential. This explanation echoes the concept of *ressentiment*, described in chapter 2. Elites experience *ressentiment* when they compare themselves with outsiders, determine that their relative status is inferior, and conclude that they are unable to catch up with their rivals. They promote aggressive nationalism to correct the dissonance they feel between their actual status and what they think it should be. *Ressentiment* helps to explain the chauvinistic and imperialistic content of panslavism and why educated elites supported it, but it does not explain how or why panslavism eventually had an impact on the actions of political decision makers. As Kohn notes, many members of the tsarist court and government in the nineteenth century were not drawn to ideas of panslav solidarity; they tended to be Europeanized and favored modernization and closer contacts with Europe.[13]

A second explanation of the rise of panslavism focuses on the international system. First, scholars note that the Crimean War in 1853–56 caused many Russian intellectual and political elites to feel that the Western powers (particularly Austria) were unreliable allies and that Russia faced an "unreasoning European hatred." Russia must find true allies, and the only credible candidates were the Slavs. Second, Russians who supported panslavism did so because they were imitating the successful nineteenth-century unification of Germany and Italy. Indeed, Russian panslavs pointed to the racial–linguistic basis of both German and Italian unifications as an example for Slavs to emulate. They argued that only when Russia was able to unify the numerous Slavic peoples of Europe under its wing could it hope to generate strength on a par with other European powers. This argument became even more compelling in light of problems of internal instability triggered by the Polish uprising of 1863 in Russia. The threat that Russia might disintegrate when other powers were consolidating on a national basis created a strong rationale in support of panslav nationalism.[14]

This chapter incorporates aspects of the above explanations for the rise and impact of panslavism in Russia. But beyond the *ressentiment* experienced by a small, educated class exposed to European culture, this analysis focuses on broader national humiliation from the Crimean War defeat in 1856 as the key stimulant of panslav ideas and activism. National humiliation had an impact not only on the educated elite, but also on broader sectors of society. This chapter also examines the evolution of political discourse inside Russia in the years following the Crimean defeat and underlines the absence of fundamental and effective criticism of imperial statehood. Despite the fact that international defeat heightened the need and clamor for reform at home, few and feeble voices questioned the imperial organization of the state and its expansionist foreign policy. Russian political discourse reaffirmed tradition and confirmed the validity of great power statehood based on the imperial state. The years after the Crimean defeat also entailed growing erosion of internal governance: many voices questioned the legitimacy of autocracy, the ruling elite exhibited deep fragmentation on key policy issues, and internal reform and terror challenged government competency. Under conditions of internal instability and the continuing predominance of the imperial idea in Russian political discourse, panslavism became a ready and attractive response when threats and crises converged in Russia's international environment in the 1870s. Society responded enthusiastically to panslav propaganda, and pressure intensified on Russian rulers to adopt panslav prescriptions to protect Russian interests. As a result, the tsarist monarchy supported panslavism in foreign policy in 1877–78. But this was to be a temporary shift in the regime's orientation; subsequent events would prove the Russian monarchy unable and unwilling to adopt panslav nationalism as a basis for cementing state–society relations in the long term and as a pillar of foreign policy. Panslavism's negative implications for autocratic rule, for the monarchical principle, and for potential conflict inside Russia were elements that the tsarist regime did not welcome and could not accept.

PATHWAYS OF INFLUENCE IN TSARIST
FOREIGN POLICYMAKING

This chapter explores the rise of panslavism and the factors that helped it briefly influence tsarist foreign policy. Before proceeding, a few words are warranted on the making of tsarist foreign policy. In autocratic Russia, foreign policy tended to be the exclusive domain of the tsar and his close circle of advisers and ministers. Rarely did public opinion or nontraditional actors have an impact on foreign policy decisions and implementation. But as Dietrich Geyer points out in his work on Russian imperialism, tsarist policymaking was not entirely immune to outside influences.[15] Especially in the nineteenth century, sources outside the narrow and official tsarist circle exerted influence on Russian foreign policy. One was special interest groups, whose members developed or pushed policies that served parochial ends. This was best exemplified in Russian expansion in the Caucasus and Central Asia. In Central Asia, Russian generals pursued expansionism even against the tsar's official orders. These generals vied with one another for very lucrative political and material rewards that accompanied the conquest of new territories, and the tsar and his ministers blessed and followed their successful lead in foreign policy.[16]

A second source of influence was individuals with access to the tsar, regardless of whether or not they held any official responsibility for foreign policy. These included members of the royal family, ministers who reported directly to the tsar, and friends of the tsar and his court. Third, the press and politicized society also played a role in foreign policy, especially with the growth of literacy and political journalism in the second half of the nineteenth century. The press served as judge and critic of autocratic government, and its criticism at times resonated with the educated public and Russian decision makers. The press and those in society mobilized by political ideas and opinion formed part of those social sectors on which tsarism partially depended for its existence. Hence, their opinion on foreign policy (depending on the intensity of belief and the extent of public mobilization) mattered to the tsarist government. Finally, as autocracy became an ever less popular and effective form of government in the nineteenth century and mass circulation newspapers brought political discourse directly to a widening literate public, the opinion of the masses also emerged as a source of influence on foreign policy. Ordinary citizens, while not following their government's international relations in detail, had some notion of Russia's place in the world and Russia's role vis-à-vis other states. They also had traditional conceptions of what was important in Russia's foreign relations—for example, Russia's centuries-old position as protector of Orthodox Slavs in other empires. Thus, the tsarist regime, at the risk of losing internal control, could not be entirely immune to strong public feelings and mass mobilization on particular foreign policy issues.[17]

SLAVOPHILISM: PRECURSOR TO PANSLAVISM

Slavophilism was a set of relatively benign nationalist ideas that gained prominence among a coterie of Russian intellectuals in the 1830s and 1840s.[18] The slavophiles did not create a coherent or practical political program, but articulated ideas that later informed panslav ideology. Among the most prominent slavophile thinkers were Ivan Kireevskii (1806–1856), Aleksei Khomiakov (1804–1860), Konstantin Aksakov (1817–1860), and Yurii Samarin (1819–1876).[19] These men came from Russia's conservative upper and petty nobility; all were educated, though not thoroughly Europeanized like the majority of the upper Russian aristocracy. The slavophiles shared an affinity for Moscow and the countryside, where their family estates were located. They saw Moscow as more thoroughly "Russian" compared to the "European" St. Petersburg. Moscow represented old Russia; old noble families; mysticism; conservatism; the capital of religious life; and the bastion of resistance against rationalist, revolutionary, and liberal thought. In contrast, St. Petersburg was the new, Westernized Russia of Peter the Great; a modern city without a past; the cradle of *raznochintsy*, or newcomers to the noble class; and the center of dangerous liberal and socialist thought. Many slavophiles were veterans of the literary and philosophical salons that proliferated in Russia in the early nineteenth century. Among the most prominent was the Society of Wisdom-Lovers, whose members (some of whom became leading slavophiles) subscribed to romantic nationalism and believed that Russia had a distinctive and organic national culture and mission.[20]

Slavophilism emerged primarily in response to a strand of Russian thought known as Westernism. Westernism (a label the slavophiles coined to denote the national apostasy of their ideological opponents) originated from Petr Chaadaev's (1794–1856) *Lettre philosophique écrite a une dame*, published in 1836 in the Russian journal *Teleskop (Telescope)*.[21] In his letter, Chaadaev stressed that Russia was an isolated, rootless entity. It belonged to neither East nor West and had no historical continuity. Russia was isolated from the rest of the world because it chose Orthodoxy rather than what Chaadaev characterized as the universal church of Europe, Catholicism. For Russia to progress, it must repeat the entire European path of development from the beginning. In short, Chaadaev criticized Russia's past and attacked the notion of superiority of the Orthodox Church and the traditional *narod* or "Russian folk." He summed up:

> We, Russians, like illegitimate children, come to this world without patrimony, without any links with people who lived on the earth before us. . . . This is a natural result of a culture based wholly on borrowing and imitation. There is among us no inward development, no natural progress. . . . We grow, but we do not mature; we advance, but obliquely, that is in a direction which does not lead to the goal. . . .

Isolated in the world, we have given nothing to the world, we have taken nothing from the world; we have not added a single idea to the mass of human ideas; we have contributed nothing to the progress of the human spirit. And we have disfigured everything we have touched of that progress.[22]

The slavophiles agreed with Chaadaev that Russia was fundamentally different from the West—even isolated from it. However, from the slavophiles' perspective, isolation was not Russia's bane but its blessing. Because Russia did not share the legacy of Western development, it maintained its wholeness as an organic entity, its harmonious model of social development, and the true Christian faith. It remained loyal to *sobornost'* (communality), the organizing principle of the Russian peasant commune, based on brotherhood, general accord, and harmonious coexistence. Russia was an "organic" entity, suffused with the feeling of unity and free from the internal strife caused by race and class in the West. The West was too rationalistic, juridical, atomistic, decadent, and violent. In the individualistic West, people did not live in harmony and faith; their social contracts reflected the soullessness and selfish calculations of a technological civilization.[23] Denying the more violent aspects of the formation of the Russian imperial state, slavophiles portrayed Russia as fundamentally peaceful and the West as aggressive. In the words of K. Aksakov:

All European states are formed through conquest. Enmity is their fundamental principle. Government came there as an armed enemy and established itself *by force* among the conquered peoples. . . . The Russian state, on the contrary, was founded not by conquest, but by a *voluntary invitation* of the government. . . . Thus in the foundation of the Western state: *violence, slavery, and hostility*. In the foundation of the Russian state: *free will, liberty, and peace*. [Emphasis in original][24]

To slavophiles, the Orthodox religion was a pillar of Russian uniqueness. Russia was the defender of Orthodoxy, the only religion that preserved collective or supraindividual Christian consciousness in its purity. All other religions, including Roman Catholicism and Protestantism, were tainted by the virus of rationalism. In Khomiakov's assessment, Catholicism had replaced *sobornost'* with utilitarian calculations and blind submission to authority (i.e., the pope). Protestantism, on the other hand, was a splintered faith and the "religion of lonely individuals lost in an atomized society."[25] Religion, faith, and spirituality occupied a central place in slavophile thought and superseded the importance of concrete political programs or actions. Slavophiles like Khomiakov postulated that Orthodoxy could save Europe by bringing about the transformation of European intellectual life. Russia did not need to conquer the West militarily because its spiritual faith was sufficient to bring the errant West back to the true Christian fold.

An important area of slavophile interest was Russian internal politics. This, arguably, was the greatest distinction between them and panslavs, whose prescriptions dealt more with Russian great power foreign policy than internal reform. Slavophiles supported autocracy as the legitimate expression of political power in Russia because it was founded on mutual trust between the sovereign and his subjects. Religious faith also underpinned support for the tsar, who was seen as defender of the Orthodox faith and divinely sanctioned ruler. Slavophiles believed that autocracy was the most appropriate system for Russia, whose citizens did not seek Western freedom to participate in politics, but freedom from politics. This meant the right to live according to unwritten rules of faith and tradition, and to pursue full self-realization in a social sphere in which government or the monarch did not intervene. Moral convictions, rather than Western-style legal guarantees or representative institutions, were the best insurance for fair and harmonious relations between monarch and people. At the same time, slavophiles acknowledged the difficult internal social conditions under which Russians lived. They highlighted Russia's social ills, deplored government censorship, and advocated the abolition of serfdom. Some slavophiles became active participants in Russian politics during the reign of Alexander II (1855–1881), when the government eliminated serfdom and implemented internal reforms. The slavophiles were inward-looking to a great degree and believed that reform at home was a priority over foreign messianic ventures on behalf of Russia's Slavic brethren.[26]

To summarize, classical slavophilism focused on the internal spiritual life of Russians, emphasized religion over race or politics as the basis of Slav commonality, claimed that Russia was inherently unique and superior to the West, and advocated internal change rather than imperial or hegemonic politics abroad as Russia's highest priority. Although the slavophile self-image contained chauvinistic elements, slavophilism as a set of nationalist ideas remained benign because its proponents' chief recommendations focused on improvements *inside* the Russian state. On international matters, slavophiles were quiet or restrained; they neither proposed aggressive action on behalf of oppressed Slavs in other empires, nor were they enamored with the idea of a panslav federation led by Russia. The slavophiles' emphasis on religion and spirituality, as well as their attitude of separating the realms of government and society (underlined by the idea that a full life was one in which the civic sphere was untouched by government), made them a weak political force in Russia. It was only after most of the original slavophiles had died that some of their ideas became politicized and formed part of panslav ideology.

By 1860, most of the slavophile leaders were dead, including Khomiakov, the Kireevskii brothers, and Konstantin Aksakov. Their co-thinkers and sympathizers who remained—particularly Yurii Samarin and Ivan Aksakov—shifted emphasis from philosophy and religion to politics and race. Taking an openly panslav approach, they advocated Russian support for freedom-fighting Slavs in Europe and the Ottoman Empire. They argued that Russian foreign policy should emphasize assistance to the Slavs in their struggle for freedom. They also maintained that Slavic groups must submit to Russian leadership. They did not favor equal relations between Russians and other Slavs and censured Poles and Czechs who wanted to pursue independent agendas. Especially after the Polish uprising in Russia in 1863, slavophilism receded while Russocentric panslavism advanced in Russian political discourse.[27]

NATIONAL HUMILIATION AND THE RISE OF PANSLAVISM

The Crimean Defeat, 1856

There is no room here for a detailed history of the Crimean War, but briefly, the war was a culmination of a long series of events surrounding the "Eastern question," or the future of the declining Ottoman Empire. Both Russia and Great Britain wanted to prevent each other from gaining control of Turkey because it could give one side undue advantage in their ongoing imperial competition. In 1844, after Tsar Nicholas I visited Britain, Russian leaders believed they had an agreement with Great Britain to preserve the status quo in case a crisis arose in the Ottoman Empire. If the status quo could not be maintained, then Russia and Great Britain would divide the crumbling empire between them. Russian leaders also believed they had Austrian and Prussian support for the arrangement reached.

In 1850, a dispute in the Holy Land (Palestine) broke out between Orthodox and Catholics over the rights of each group to some of the most sacred shrines of Christendom. In February 1853, Russia issued Turkey an ultimatum to settle the dispute in favor of Orthodoxy and to recognize openly the rights of Orthodox subjects within the empire. The Porte yielded on the first point, but not on the second. A series of diplomatic actions followed, but these failed to resolve the conflict between Russia and Turkey. In October 1853, hostilities broke out between the two countries. Great Britain and France joined the war on behalf of the Porte in March 1854, while Austria exerted strong diplomatic pressures on behalf of the allies against Russia.

During the Crimean War, Russia found itself fighting alone against a formidable European coalition. Although the war was fought in part in the Caucasus and the Danubian principalities, its main front was the Crimean peninsula, where the allies sought to capture the Russian naval base at Sevastopol. For almost a year, Russian soldiers fought heroically to defend Sevastopol against the allies' unrelenting bombardment with superior weapons. Russian heroism notwithstanding, Sevastopol fell in September 1855. The war officially terminated in March 1856, when an international congress met and signed the Treaty of Paris.[28]

Russia's ignominious defeat at the hands of France and Great Britain undermined the idea of Russian solidarity and cooperation with the great powers of Europe, which, up to then, had been the crux of tsarist foreign policy. Nicholas I believed that only such a policy could avert the threat of general anarchy and revolution. But, as the war clearly demonstrated, the other great powers did not reciprocate tsarist Russia's approach. Russia's performance in the war and its subsequent defeat led to national humiliation. First, the war exposed Russian military backwardness and unpreparedness, particularly in military technology, human resources, transportation and other logistics, and financing. D. A. Miliutin, Russian war minister, wrote in 1856 that "despite the fully intensified production of our military factories, there was no possibility whatsoever for us to supply the entire army within a short time with similarly modern weapons as those in the hands of the opposing [British and French] armies."[29] The Russian army fought with obsolete muskets, while the allies used modern rifles; Russia had thirty-five thousand men in the Crimea at the start of the war, while the allies had sixty thousand; Russian soldiers were not adequately clothed or sheltered, and thousands died of cold, exhaustion, typhus and other epidemics. In addition, many Russian officers were ignorant, corrupt, and unprepared to conduct a successful military campaign.[30]

Second, national humiliation stemmed from Russian losses in the war and subsequent conditions imposed by the victors. As many as three hundred and forty thousand Russians died in the last two years of the war alone—a figure equal to the number of Russian fatalities in all wars in the entire second half of the eighteenth century. The defense of Sevastopol, by itself, claimed over one hundred thousand lives. In addition, the war almost brought Russian external trade to a halt and pushed Russia to the verge of bankruptcy. The Treaty of Paris, while not imposing foreign occupation of Russian territory, was nonetheless a "disaster for Russian interests and a defeat for the major policies adopted in Eastern affairs during the century."[31] Russia ceded to Turkey the mouth of the Danube and part of Bessarabia, accepted neutralization of the Black Sea (i.e., Russia could no longer maintain a navy or build coastal fortifications on its own territory!), lost the diplomatic position it had held since 1774 as protector of the Porte's Orthodox subjects, and accepted international control over the Danubian principalities and over navigation on the Danube. In essence, Russia bowed to French and British control in the internal affairs of the Ottoman Empire and to French, British, and Austrian influence over Wallachia, Moldavia, and Serbia. An anonymous note, heavily marked in the margins by Tsar Alexander II and Foreign Minister K. Nesselrode in 1856, noted that the Paris Treaty meant "the diminution of Russian possessions and Russian prestige as a Great Power . . . Russia . . . has emerged from the struggle belittled in the eyes of public opinion and weakened in its political capability."[32]

Third, Russian elites felt humiliated by the betrayal of the European powers, especially Great Britain, France, Austria, and Prussia. Although Austria and Prussia did not join the alliance against Russia, they nonetheless showed signs of preparing to join the allies, even as Russia's position in the war worsened. There was a pervasive feeling in Russia that France and Great Britain had betrayed and abandoned it, and even fueled Russo-Turkish hostilities while feigning to work on regulating the conflict at its early stage. Writers, publicists, and other purveyors of ideas and public opinion generated a tremendous amount of anti-Western rhetoric, highlighting the perfidy of the European powers and the West's "instinctive hatred" for Russia.[33]

Reaction to National Humiliation

National humiliation stimulated an aggressive nationalist reaction from Russian intellectuals, publicists, and ordinary citizens. The highest government officials themselves desisted from fiery nationalist rhetoric because they knew the extent of damage the war had caused, were concerned about internal disorder, and concluded that state interests required retrenchment rather than aggressive nationalist posturing. Tsar Alexander II, who succeeded Nicholas I in 1855, wrote to his friend Prince Bariatinskii in May 1857,

> I must direct your attention again to the *absolute need* to diminish, at any cost, our expenses and *even restrain our military operations for a year or two.* The last three years of the [Crimean] war have had such a deplorable effect on our finances and it is of utmost urgency that we think of wise savings in order to get out of our current difficult situation, whose end may well be a crisis with consequences that we cannot foresee—and God help us![34]

Slavophile intellectuals were some of the first to articulate panslav nationalism in response to the Crimean defeat. Slavophilism became highly politicized even before Russia's defeat,[35] but its transformation into an anti-Western, hegemonic panslav ideology intensified in the wake of national humiliation. The Aksakov brothers and Mikhail Pogodin expressed extremist views against the West and argued that Russian foreign policy should focus on the formation of a panslav federation with a formidable thirty million Slavs in Europe and the Balkans. As the Crimean War proved, traitorous nations surrounded Russia; to defend itself, it must gain the sympathy of its Slav kindred by championing their revolts against their imperial rulers. If necessary, Russia should go to war on behalf of the Slavs. In Pogodin's opinion, war was inevitable and adequate preparation for it required a "permanent Slavic policy" in Russian foreign relations. Commenting on the Crimean War, he declared that Russia pursued the chimera of Austrian moderation, generosity, and neutrality, only to give the West time to force Russia dishonorably from its areas of traditional influence:

> oh, the pinnacle of shame! [We allowed the West] to attack the Crimea, threaten Sevastopol, and hang by a hair the peace of our whole empire. . . . Pursuing the shadow of Austrian neutrality, we alienated our only allies—the Slavs—and stabbed them in the heart and took away the hope they lived by. . . . The plan [of the West] against Russia is colossal. . . . and the question that is being addressed concerns the whole world: Will Russia be or not be?[36]

Yurii Samarin, like Pogodin, also decried Russia's endurance of "every humiliation" at the conclusion of the Crimean War. He noted the "banal accusations and shameless slander" leveled by Western journals and officials against Russia and the pitiful performance of tsarist officials who stood like "indicted criminals . . . anxiously looking around for defenders, trying to find timid excuses. . . ." But, he continued, Russians did not spill their blood in vain because the Serbs, Bulgarians, and Greeks knew that Russia suffered for their good. Europe might celebrate "the victory of its material forces" but Russia will be the ultimate victor. It alone continued to have moral authority over the "young [Slav] tribes . . . to whom sooner or later the East will belong; the victory will be ours."[37]

Chauvinism featured prominently in ascendant panslav rhetoric after the Crimean War. Panslav nationalists condemned Poles and western Slavs who were "contaminated" by the West. It was such contamination that prevented some of these Slavs from accepting Russian superiority and leadership; they failed to grasp that, as the preserver of the true Slavic way of life, Russia's security superseded the rights of other Slav peoples.[38]

Ordinary citizens themselves reacted to national humiliation by supporting nationalist publicists and intellectuals who reasserted Russian greatness in the face of defeat. The public accorded returning military personnel a hero's welcome and joined in fiery speeches and patriotic entertainment. Commentators character-ized the defenders of Sevastopol as Herculean, mythic warriors (*bogatyry*), whose actions embodied the "life-giving" forces of the people or *narod*. Many ignored Russia's dismal military performance and instead extolled the greatness and moral superiority of the Russian army and navy, whose actions, allegedly, so impressed the European powers that they were compelled to impose moderate conditions on Russia in the Treaty of Paris. Yet others considered Russian defeat temporary and insisted that present misfortunes would awaken Russia's "sleeping forces" and lead it to "purification and exaltation." Numerous voices representing Slavophile, panslav, and Westernizing public opinion joined in the chorus asserting that the people would lead Russia's resurrection; only by heeding their voice would the regime regain its moral authority and restore Russia to greatness.[39]

Other public reaction to Russian national humiliation was flavored less with assertive nationalism than with shame and a call for reform in Russia's internal political and economic life. To many, Russia's defeat exposed helplessness, decay, and rottenness (*bespomoshchnost', gnilost'*) inside Russia itself. Critics of tsarism called the war "degrading," and many reacted to Russia's dismal performance with disillusionment and anger. The articulate public felt that the nation (*narod*), despite its sacrifices of money and blood in the war, had been betrayed by its own government. The fall of Sevastopol, in particular, elicited public shame, shock, and outrage. In the words of two citizens:

> The news of the fall of Sevastopol made me weep. If I were in good health I would have joined the militia, without wishing victory for Russia, but with a desire to die for it. My soul was sick at this time. Here all honorable people, no matter what their opin-ions, hung their heads. . . . The people crowded into bars by the hundreds, in the city they moaned and crossed themselves in horror. The shock was terrible . . . as all had trusted the [official] printed statements about the impregnability of Sevastopol.[40]

Society's feelings of betrayal by the government during, and in the wake of, the Crimean defeat led in part to peasant uprisings and other actions expressing the desperation of Russia's serfs, many of whom thought they would be freed after service in the war. Loud and strident criticism of the war came from intellectuals, journalists, educators, bureaucrats, and members of the nobility, many of whom demanded internal political and social reform. Subversive political tracts and verses circulated, condemning "stupid, ignorant officials," and calling on the people to rise against oppressive internal conditions in Russia.[41] Clearly, national humiliation stemming from the war and its aftermath elicited not only the assertion of aggressive, anti-Western nationalism but also a general demand for the state to recognize society or an awakening nation. In this sense, nationalism began to pose a challenge to the traditional Russian imperial state.

CONTENT OF RUSSIAN PANSLAVISM

Chief proponents of panslavism in the nineteenth century included Mikhail Pogodin (1800–1875), a publicist, professor of Russian history, and contemporary of the slavophiles; Ivan Aksakov (1823–1886), panslavism's most ardent political agitator; Nikolai Danilevskii (1822–1885), a botanist, ichthyologist, and philosopher; Rostislav Fadeev (1824–1883), a major general in the Russian army; Mikhail Katkov (1818–1887), an early liberal who turned into a reactionary publicist; V. I. Lamanskii (1833–1914), a scholar in Slavic studies; Nikolai P. Ignatev (1832–1908), diplomat and Russian ambassador to Constantinople; Mikhail Cherniaev, a Russian general who led the Serb army against Turkey in 1876; and M. D. Skobelev (1843–1882), another general who led Russian troops in the war with Turkey in 1877. The next section summarizes the key ideas that these men and their supporters shared.[42]

Membership in the Nation

To panslavs, the key criteria for membership in the nation were ethnic and political: race, language, shared culture, and submission to Russian authority and leadership. Religion was also important, but it did not play as central a role as it did in slavophile ideology. In an 1838 letter to the tsarevich Alexander (the future Alexander II), Pogodin referred to

> our brothers and cousins, the Slavs, who are scattered over the whole of Europe from Constantinople to Venice, from Morea to the Baltic and the North Sea; the Slavs in whose veins the same blood flows as in ours, who speak the same language as we do, and who therefore, according to the law of nature, sympathize with us; the Slavs who, in spite of geographic and political separation, form by origin and language one spiritual entity with us.[43]

Panslavs spread the myth (questioned by later historians)[44] of common geographic and linguistic origin for all Slavs, and argued that Russia was a remnant of a once unified Slav people. They also lobbied, at the 1867 Slav congress in Russia for instance, that Russian be made the official language of all Slavs.[45]

Although there were multiple criteria for membership in the Slavic nation, panslav writings indicate that most decisive was acceptance of Russia's hegemonic authority. Thus, Russian panslavs rallied at different times behind different Slav groups, depending on who adhered most closely to Russian interests and preferences.[46] They included in the Slavic nation the Greeks—who were not Slavic by race, but Orthodox in religion and an ally of Russia; simultaneously, they excluded the Poles—who were Slavic in race but Catholic in religion and were also the Russian empire's most mutinous and ungovernable subjects. Indeed, Russia had a big headache in Poland. Until 1918, Poland and Finland were the only two subject nations of the Russian empire to ever demand separation from the Russian state. Panslavs harshly and uniformly condemned Poland as a state that had betrayed and lost its Slavic essence. They portrayed Poles as traitors whom Rome had fed with its "mother's milk of hate" for Russia and Orthodoxy, and who would catholicize Russia. Panslav vilification of Poland intensified, especially after the Polish uprising of 1863, when some declared Poland "an adopted son of the West . . . which took Latinism into its flesh, blood, and spirit; severed itself from the Slav brotherhood; and became the vanguard army of the latinized West against the Orthodox Slavic world."[47] Katkov portrayed Russians and Poles as two nations engaged in a fatal struggle; one would live and the other would die.[48]

Self-Image and Other-Image

Russian panslavs formulated their self-image in contrast to the "other," which was the collective West or great powers of Europe. They claimed uniqueness and superiority, asserting that the Slavs were unique and superior because they were peaceful, liberal, tolerant, democratic, and never guilty of the forceful conquest of other nations. If religious or political intolerance existed in Russia, it was caused chiefly by Westernized clergy and elites, and by imported Western institutions including censorship or bureaucracy. Moreover, intolerance in Russia was minor compared to the West. Russia epitomized the strength and superiority of slavdom. It was rich physically and spiritually; it encompassed all soils and climates and had plenty of natural resources. In Pogodin's words,

> we have mountains of gold and silver, which have become almost extinct in Europe; we have bread to feed all of Europe in a year of famine; we have forests to rebuild Russia if, heaven forbid, it is burnt to the ground. . . . But the physical assets of Russia are nothing compared with its spiritual strengths. These include intelligence, daring, understanding, patience, and the military features of the Russian nation. All these assets form one gigantic tool, set most purposefully and successfully in the hands of one man—the Russian tsar—who, at any moment, can put this instrument into action by a single motion, give it direction, and set the appropriate speed. . . . I ask, who can compare with us? Whom will we not force into submission? Is not the political fate of Europe in our hands, and the fate of the whole world, if we will only decide one way or the other?[49]

Because Russia was strong and whole—indeed, it was the only free nation among the Slavs and the "truest repository of the Slavic ideal"—it was slavdom's legitimate leader, protector, and ruler.[50]

Danilevskii, perhaps panslavism's most systematic theorist, published a book in 1869 called *Russia and Europe*. In it, he devised a pseudoscientific theory to justify the Slavic nation's special position above other civilizations. He argued that every civilization constituted a distinct "historical-cultural type," which, like botanical organisms, undergoes a long period of development according to species-defined laws of nature, blooms momentarily, then dies. Some nations did not constitute civilizations but were only "ethnographic material" whose purpose was to be absorbed by, or become an adjunct to, the main players on the historical stage. Western civilization was an impressive "historical-cultural" type that developed politically and culturally, but was rotting and soon to die. The Slav type, in contrast, was young and ascendant, and its full development entailed the unprecedented synthesis of political, cultural, socioeconomic, and military achievements in one civilization.[51]

Two other aspects of the panslav self-image dealt with the role and organization of the state and the role of war in national development. Unlike their slavophile predecessors who tolerated the state as a necessary evil, Russian panslavs characterized the state as a sine qua non of national progress and development. Indeed, without the state, an economically and militarily united slavdom would be impossible. A strong, centralized, and autocratic Russian state, specifically, was the best solution for the chaos and disunity that plagued slavdom, and Russia could fulfill its highest potential as the leader of Slavs by shunning all forms of Western parliamentarism and unruly democracy. As I. Aksakov argued,

> The *Slav* races have aspirations that are completely *democratic*, in the *real* sense of the word and not in the theoretical revolutionary sense so popular in Europe. . . . The *ideal*, which is more or less common to all Slav races, is local *self-government*, without any political bearing, sustained and crowned by a superior and central authority which is completely frank and free in the governmental sphere. . . . The people . . . do not seek to govern the state, but they definitely desire a government which can inspire confidence in them through its energy, force, and *impartial and national character*. The reason why the Russian people support the tsar is because the tsar . . . does not belong to any party or any social category. He is above and beyond everything, the first man of the country and, for the people, the personification of the nation. Supreme authority in Russia is not . . . a juridical and abstract issue as it is in constitutional states; what the Russian people want is an authority endowed with a *human* heart, a vital *being*, whose spirit and soul are authorized to supplement the formalism of bureaucracy and the dead letter of the law. [Emphasis in original][52]

While strongly supporting the autocratic state, panslavs also argued for internal reform to eliminate such corrupt Western influences as censorship, bureaucracy, and nihilism.

Panslavs characterized Russian imperialism as generally benign. Russia absorbed other groups not by violent conquest, but by advancing these groups' interests and thereby obeying higher laws toward the establishment of the ultimate civilization. They argued that the state, unlike individuals, was not subject to moral laws. States were secular and temporary entities, whose priority was to meet their greatest potential, whereas individuals were eternal beings who must abide by divine laws as they prepared to face God's judgment. The inapplicability of moral law to the state implied that the state was justified in defending panslav interests, even if it meant harsh and aggressive policies toward Poland, Europe, and other enemies of slavdom. As Danilevskii argued, "An eye for an eye and a tooth for a tooth . . . the Benthamite principle of utilitarianism, or the commonsensical understanding of what is in one's advantage—this is the law of foreign policy, the law of all interstate relations. There is no place here for the law of love or sacrifice."[53]

Panslavs characterized conflict and war as endemic in the struggle between Russia and its foes, and between civilizations. They saw war between Russia and Europe, and between Russia and Turkey, as inevitable. Armed conflicts would bring about the liberation of Slavs and the creation of a united slavdom led by Russia. Panslavs argued that war could have salutary effects on the nation: it would forge panslav solidarity and cleanse Slavs of their subservience to Western ideas and institutions. Danilevskii claimed that although war was evil, there was "something far worse than war, something for which war can also serve as a cure, for 'man shall not live by bread alone.'" I. Aksakov, similarly, stressed that if war were so terrible, Prussia should have emerged tired and weak from its war with Austria in 1866. Instead, war infused Prussia with "living water, [and it] became younger, rejuvenated, and healthier from activity." In three years Prussia fought another war with France and again emerged "greater in strength and glory, renewed, transformed. . . ."[54] By avoiding war, Russia would turn away from greatness and risk becoming a secondary state like Holland or Belgium.

In depicting outsiders, panslavs emphasized Europe's intrinsic inferiority to, and enmity for, Russia and all Slavs. They insisted that European civilization was not a universal civilization, and condemned Russian Westernizers who deformed the true Slav spirit by importing Western ideas and institutions. They described the West as a chaotic, atomized, and divided entity, whereas Russia was an organic entity ruled by order and authority. The West hated Russia because it was waning in vitality, whereas Russia was still to bloom. I. Aksakov claimed that Western instinctive hatred for Russia stemmed from the deep "antagonism of two opposing spiritual and cultural systems, and the envy of a decrepit world toward the new."[55] Similarly, Pogodin denigrated Austria as a "whitened sepulchre, an old tree that [was] rotting inside" and would be uprooted from its roots by "one blow of the wind." His colleague, Petr Shevyrev, added that the West carried "a terrible and contagious disease" that endangered the "true governmental and social health of Russia." Panslav denigration of the West sometimes reached hysterical proportions, as when Danilevskii discovered vinicultural lice during one of his botanical expeditions and asked Alexander II to ban foreign grapes from Russia because they were a sign of insidious Western influence. In another incident, a Russian woman asked Pogodin to comment on Western clothing, and the latter wrote that "[W]estern clothing was the beginning of foreign influence on Russia. By discarding it, we might begin to liberate ourselves from deadly foreign influences. . . ."[56] Viewing the West in highly sinister terms, panslavs preached that conflict between Russia and Europe was natural, inevitable, and the sole means of resolving the "Eastern question" in Russian foreign policy; Russia need not fear because it was divinely ordained to win this struggle and to create a Slavic union to succeed Western civilization.[57]

The panslav other-image targeted Poland (and, on occasion, Jews and other foreigners) as enemies of Russia and the Slav nation. While Russia was the bearer of Christ, Poland was Judas—corrupted by the Western kiss. Without mentioning any of the horrors that Russia had inflicted on the Poles from the time of Catherine the Great onward, panslavs condemned Poles for their disloyalty to Russia and slavdom. Whitewashing Russia's behavior toward Poland, one panslav argued,

> History has proven that the Poles are not capable of defending their statehood. They have never tried to protect their motherland, which no one has attempted to take from them. Instead, they have always tried to seize foreign lands and, as the most faithful servants of Rome, catholicize them. This provoked revolts everywhere and brought Poland to the edge of death. [Poland obstructed the Slav unification process and was a] criminal before the entire Slav world.[58]

Panslavs accused Poles, who were numerous and prosperous in the western region of the empire, as guilty of stealing Russian land; catholicizing a million Russians; and, together with their Jewish co-conspirators, consuming the bread of Russian welfare.[59]

National Purpose or Mission

Russian panslavs defined the national purpose in terms of strengthening the Russian state and enhancing its power on the international stage. Especially in the short term, they advocated the need to strengthen cohesion among the Slavic peoples. As cohesion was reinforced, Russia could then fulfill its divinely foreordained task of liberating the Slavs and establishing a Slavic federation. Danilevskii stressed that the national mission was not to defend such universal ideals as Christianity or traditional social bonds. Instead, it was to create a powerful state, an organism whose expansion would be limited only by the natural laws of evolution. He declared that slavdom ought to be, "after God, the supreme ideal of every Slav"; it should be "higher than freedom . . . science . . . education . . . [and] all worldly goods."[60]

Some panslavs tried to work out concretely how Russia might fulfill its divinely ordained task of liberating other Slavs. But in their rhetoric, it was clear that liberating the Slavs was not the end goal; rather, panslavs saw the national mission first and foremost as enhancing the power of the Russian state. In the Russian Ministries of War and Foreign Affairs, Fadeev and Ignatev worked out detailed geopolitical schemes toward the fruition of panslav dreams. Their schemes emphasized panslavism as a means to expand Russian territory, increase Russian state power, and attain Russian supremacy in Europe. Further, when the Russian general Mikhail Cherniaev unofficially went to lead the Serbian army against Turkey in 1876, I. Aksakov heralded the event not as a step toward Serbian liberation, but as a move favoring Russian interests. "What is most important," he noted, was "that the chief of the Serbs is a Russian, a representative of the Russian idea and the Russian viewpoint on the Slav question. . . . [It] is clear that Cherniaev . . . will augment the honor and grace of the Russian name among the Slavs."[61]

In the longer term, panslavs described the national mission in terms of realizing the evangelical vision of a great Slavic civilization leading and filling the whole earth. This civilization would move Europe's borders to their natural limits (naturally, allowing Russia to expand) and plant genuine Christian enlightenment in all the "wild and barren places of Asia." The Slavic state would create a universal empire based on universal order, and thereby fulfill its mission to "consummate, to crown the development of humanity . . . to harmonize ancient and modern civilizations, to reconcile heart with reason, to establish real justice and peace." This mission was so grand that if it failed, Danilevskii lamented that the "world would only be a miserable chain of accidents and not the reflection of supreme reason, right, and goodness."[62]

SPREADING THE WORD: PANSLAV ACTIVISM AND EFFORTS, 1856–1875

For almost two decades after the Crimean defeat, panslavs disseminated their ideas among the Russian public, as well as in official circles. However, their success was slow and limited, and their ideas failed to resonate strongly with society. In addition, despite some support in court and among Russian diplomats and military leaders, panslav nationalism did not become the official ideology or policy of the tsarist monarchy. It would not be until particular international events and crises converged in 1875–77 that panslavism would resonate broadly with society and be supported briefly by the tsarist government. Who were the panslavs and what motivated them? What social and political changes permitted panslavism to be propagated in what was still a predominantly autocratic environment? How powerful was panslavism as an ideological force in Russia by 1875?

Who Were the Panslavs?

The period following the Crimean War was a time of awakening of public opinion in Russia. The most active panslavs were those who felt the shock of Russian defeat and were disconcerted by Russia's unstable internal condition and diminished external role. They were looking for ideas that might provide answers to Russia's dilemma, and allow the more politically conscious and active segments of society to become a base of support for the tsarist regime. Some panslavs seemed to be genuine believers in the ideas they propagated, but they also used panslavism to pursue narrower, personal ends. Still others seemed motivated by a psychological desire to accomplish heroic feats.

Pogodin, a dedicated and consistent proponent of panslavism from his youth to the end of his life, was arguably a true believer in panslav ideas. Inspired as a young man by the historian Nikolai Karamzin's ideas on Russian distinctiveness and greatness, he traveled in the 1830s to the Slavic lands and saw Russia's destiny in the forging of a Slavic union that would be the world's most powerful state. Russia's defeat in the Crimean War temporarily doused his enthusiasm,[63] but he soon resumed his panslav activity in 1857 in the Moscow Slavic Committee and in memoranda and articles addressed to government officials. Pogodin used panslavism to appeal to powerful political figures in Russia, and to gain entry into the world of power and privilege that was denied to him by his birth in a serf family.[64] He consistently preached panslav ideas as a means to revivify Russian greatness abroad, but was careful not to offend the Russian autocratic regime and its policies at home. His biography portrays him as a person eager to use his ideas to gain attention and recognition from the ruling regime, one who lobbied his associates to help him gain a high governmental position, and an intellectual who was jealous of those who had access to the tsar. Pogodin wrote numerous notes to the tsars and various ministers, even though his messages sometimes never reached their targeted audience. When he did gain access to leaders such as Minister of Education Sergei Uvarov, he was overjoyed.[65]

Ivan Aksakov, another ardent panslav, displayed a psychological drive for heroism and strong convictions. He fought in the Crimean War and became a loyal and outspoken proponent of panslavism the rest of his life. While in college, he wrote to his family, "I am full of resolute will and yearning for labor—labor that is difficult, great, and beneficial."[66] Panslav agitation and its accompanying risks and grand goals fit perfectly with the labor Aksakov desired. He devoted himself passionately to promoting panslavism, regardless of the obstacles, and responded with fiery and defiant notes to officials who criticized his work. His many clashes with Russian authorities in the course of his panslav activity led his long-time senior colleague Pogodin to remark that he was "wont to throw [himself] against the knife . . . with his eyes open!"[67]

Danilevskii, like Aksakov, was also motivated by a desire for heroic and utopian solutions to big questions in Russian life. A botanist and ichthyologist, Danilevskii most likely had his first contact with panslavism through the Russian Geographical Society's ethnographers' section, which sponsored many of his fishing and botanical expeditions and included among its membership some prominent panslav professors. Unlike I. Aksakov, however, Danilevskii expressed his desire for heroism through theorizing rather than activism. His panslav writings attempted to devise a utopian and absolute solution to the problem of Russian backwardness relative to the West, and a prescription for how Russia might sustain its great power status. A biographer has argued that *ressentiment* or hatred and envy of the West may have motivated Danilevskii, who wanted to atone for previous Westernized beliefs by formulating an alternative theory of Russia's distinct nature and mission.[68]

Various sources indicate that other panslavs propagandized panslavism for career advancement and potential material gains. Ignatev, reputed for his penchant for lying and an unmitigated desire for self-advancement, seized on panslavism as an ideology to advance his diplomatic career. He came from a highly placed noble family, with a father who served as governor general of St. Petersburg and became president of the Imperial Council of Ministers. He built his initial reputation in Russian diplomacy by gaining territorial advantages for Russia in China in 1860 and by helping undo the Treaty of Paris's restrictions on the movement of Russian vessels in the Black Sea straits in 1870–71. While ambassador to the Ottoman Empire, Ignatev pursued his proven preference for aggressive power projection in Russian foreign policy. In his notes to Alexander II, he emphasized Russian geopolitical interests and competition with the British and Austro-Hungarian empires, and his approach to panslavism was suffused with his consciousness of imperial rivalry. As for the Slavs themselves, he was cynical, writing for instance to Foreign Minister Aleksandr M. Gorchakov in 1876 that Russia's priority was to find "intelligent people" in the Balkans, especially in Serbia, whom "we can use as we wish." Russia should extend financial assistance to Serbia because "in the East, money is the surest vehicle for influence," and Russia ought to focus on creating on the ruins of the Ottoman Empire a foundation strong enough to resist future pressure from the West. Ignatev's diplomacy in 1864–72 in the controversial creation of a Bulgarian exarchate—a church hierarchy separate from the hierarchy of the Orthodox Church in Greece—further showed that he was less concerned about the liberation of the Slavs than in positioning Russia favorably for the impending fall of the Ottoman Empire.[69]

Parochial interests also motivated another panslav, Aleksandr S. Ionin (1837–1900), Russia's official representative in Montenegro. Ionin supported the Herzegovina uprising against Turkey in 1875 and Montenegro's participation in the war against Turkey in 1876. He particularly favored Russian help to Montenegro rather than the other Slav lands because Nikolai, the prince of Montenegro (1841–1921), had promised to make him prime minister in the event of Montenegrin independence. In 1875–78, Ionin flouted policies favored by the Slavic Committees in Russia in order to protect his political ambitions. He disregarded Serbia and other Slavic lands in favor of Montenegro and, in contravention of Committee instructions, channeled all financial donations from Russia—including those earmarked for Herzegovina—to Montenegro, where he hoped to become prime minister.[70]

Many among military officials who supported panslav ideas had served in expansionist campaigns in Central Asia and the Caucasus, and were not pleased with Alexander II's retrenchment policy after the Crimean debacle. Dismayed by the diminishing power of field generals in Russian foreign policy, they sought to restore a more prominent role for themselves. Many of them had fought in the Crimean War and wanted a chance for a military victory in the Balkans to compensate for the Crimean defeat. Among them were General Cherniaev, known for his conquest of Central Asia; Lieutenant General S. A. Khrulev, a Crimean War hero and veteran of Russian campaigns in Central Asia; General Fadeev, who served in the Caucasus; General M. D. Skobelev; and A. V. Rachinskii, who fought in the Crimea and became a founding member of the Moscow Slavic Benevolent Committee. Among these officers, Khrulev showed keen interest in the potential commercial benefits of Russian expansion in the Balkans.[71]

Generals Cherniaev and Fadeev were officers who built their careers on Russian expansion. Cherniaev came from a military family that had served the tsar for
centuries. He earned the sobriquet "Lion of Tashkent" for leading the conquest of
Tashkent in 1865. As a key player in Russian expansion in Central Asia and the
Caucasus, he had a record of self-glorification and paranoia. The zenith of his
career was his appointment as military governor of Central Asia, from which he
was later removed due to his contemptuous disregard for the orders of senior
civilian leaders, including the governor of Orenburg. One scholar calls Cherniaev
a representative of a "failed class"—a military nobleman in an era of rising capitalism—and an expansionist at a time of Russian retrenchment. Cherniaev liked
to brag that Central Asia was conquered primarily at his initiative and that his
removal from power was unfair persecution at the hands of an "ungrateful government and conspiring bureaucrats."[72] From 1867 to 1875, while in semiretire-
ment, he actively opposed Defense Minister Miliutin's policy of retrenchment and
military reform. He denigrated Miliutin as an "armchair general" and along with
older officers resisted innovations that threatened the patriarchal order in the
army—specifically, the abolition of corporal punishment and the introduction of
military education to non-nobles. He joined a group of conservative politicians
and officers who wanted to reverse Miliutin's reforms and restore the predominance of the gentry and field generals in the military. Cherniaev used his period-
ical, *Russkii mir*, to publicize his views in support of an activist, panslav policy.
When the Herzegovina revolt against Turkey broke out in 1875, he hoped that
Miliutin's liberal reforms would end and his services would be required in a
panslav war against Turkey.[73]

Fadeev, like Cherniaev, built his career on Russian expansionism. From an early
time, he was concerned with expanding Russian power in the Caucasus and
beyond[74] and opposed Russian retrenchment after the Crimean War. In 1870, he
was retired from active military service because of his outspoken opposition to
Miliutin's military reforms. Contrary to official foreign policy under Alexander II,
Fadeev advocated a Russo-French alliance against what he saw as a sinister, emerging German threat to Russian predominance in Slavic areas. He promoted
panslavism to gain the attention of Russian officials, particularly the heir to the
throne, Alexander III. When his career came under threat, he wrote notes to the
tsarevich (knowing of the latter's open attitude to panslavism) and noted that any
action taken against him would hurt Russia's image among the Slavs, who liked
him immensely. He also asserted that he was being punished unjustly for patriotic
views that were supported by those higher than he in the hierarchy. From 1870 to
1875, Fadeev continued to lobby the heir to the throne with notes on restoring
Russian military power and strengthening Russia's geostrategic position in the
East. He also worked with Cherniaev on *Russkii mir*, but parted ways with the latter over a rivalry in leading the Bulgarian movement against Turkey in 1876.[75]

Yet one more notable panslav in the military was General M. D. Skobelev, who
also built a stellar career through Russian expansionism. Along with General
Konstantin Kaufman, he became renowned as leader of Russian troops who exe-

cuted "daring military expeditions" and won victories in Central Asia between 1865 and 1876. Like Fadeev and Cherniaev, Skobelev did not welcome Russian military retrenchment and saw great honor in leading the Russian military once more during the Russo-Turkish war of 1877–78. He became the hero of Shipka Pass in 1877, a turning point in the war with Turkey, and at the time became famous for disobeying orders from the top and using the press to propagate his image as a Slavic national hero.[76]

The Rise of Public Opinion

Socioeconomic and political changes in the nineteenth century led to the rise of public opinion and the broadening of political space for civic activity in Russia. It is in this context that panslavism grew and eventually had an impact on Russian foreign policy.[77] Key changes included the reform of Russian censorship, the rise of the mass press, improvements in mass education from 1840 to the 1860s, and the emergence of new social groups with a clear civic agenda. During the reign of Nicholas I (1825–1855), officials imposed heavy censorship on the press and prohibited political commentary. Discussions were limited to philosophy and literature, and many intellectuals developed the use of Aesopian language to express political ideas that officials deemed subversive.[78] Alexander II, however, revised censorship regulations in 1865, reflecting his reign's focus on reform. Publishers gained the right to petition to have their papers removed from prepublication censorship, and the newly reformed legal system became the arbiter of offenses committed by the press. The government also allowed the press to cover state politics, foreign policy, and social life, issues that had largely been taboo. As a result, coverage of politics and economics exploded in newspapers and thick journals, and public opinion on these topics grew. From 1855 to 1875, Russian periodicals increased fourfold in number, and circulation for the most popular ones ranged from six thousand to over twenty thousand by 1877.[79]

Although censorship was not eliminated, and the government reneged on some censorship reform measures, nonetheless in the 1860s and 1870s a civic voice or public opinion was born in Russian politics. As the Russian newspaper *Obshchee delo* reported, Russian society felt for once within itself "the presence of an independent, moral strength."[80] The mass press was especially important to the rise of public opinion, and its position consolidated with the advent of paid advertising and street sales. Notwithstanding the vestiges of Russian censorship, Louise McReynolds concludes that the mass press influenced public

> perspectives and values. . . . [Its] power [was] . . . in its ability to identify specific subjects and present them for public discussion, that is, to set the political agenda. . . . If Russian publishers were forbidden from editorializing against the autocracy, they were still not restricted from offering readers a wide assortment of ideas about what it meant to be Russian and how the many changes they were witnessing might affect them. This would in turn stir discontent among readers coming to want to decide for themselves the terms of policies that governed their lives.[81]

Significant improvements in mass education began in the 1840s, when popular access to education expanded. In the period 1840–48, university enrollment in Russia increased by more than fifty percent, while enrollment in secondary schools rose at an even higher rate. Later, in the years 1860–1914, university enrollment increased ninefold from 4,641 to 35,965. The number of elementary school students also rose from 400,000 in 1856 to approximately 2.2 million by 1885 (a 450 percent increase). By 1880, there were 1.6 million students in Russian schools compared to 800,000 in 1865. Literacy rates in the Moscow *guberniia*, encompassing Moscow and surrounding areas, climbed from 7.5 percent in 1869 to 17.6 percent in 1881. Literacy was almost 50 percent in Moscow in the early 1880s and 64.4 percent in St. Petersburg. Although Russia's overall literacy rate remained at a low 10 percent by the early 1880s, it was much higher in the big cities, where public opinion and political activism were more pronounced.[82]

The period corresponding with the rise of panslavism was also one of socio-economic change, marked especially by the decline of the traditional nobility and gentry. The emancipation of serfs in 1861 eroded the dominance of the landowning nobility and diminished their political power. Legal reform, industrialization, urbanization, the rise of a bourgeois middle class, the decline of the patriarchal and autocratic order, and the decline of religion further reshaped the traditional order. In education, the special treatment of gentry students ended and gentry representation in the universities decreased. In 1855 students in universities were 65.3 percent nobility and gentry, 23.9 percent *raznochintsy* (people of mixed background below the gentry), and 1 percent peasants. By 1875 gentry representation was down to 43.1 percent, clergy 35.2 percent, and other classes 21.7 percent. As the traditional nobility declined, new groups arose, including the middle class, professionals, and merchants, whose most prominent members used their resources to promote education and the arts for common people—namely, Savva Mamontov, Sergei Morozov, and Pavel Tretiakov.[83]

Another new group was the "intelligentsia," whose ranks included the educated gentry and *raznochintsy* who shared a concern about Russia's evolving social and political life. They were not monolithic in ideology, but included liberals, moderates, and reactionaries. As a group, they propagated, analyzed, and criticized social and political issues in Russia.[84] The intelligentsia, *raznochintsy*, civic-minded merchants, and other new social groupings indicate that in the nineteenth century the sector of society that was both politically conscious and not deeply committed to the traditional imperial state had considerably enlarged. Because of newfound resources, new rights, and social mobility, these groups could try to assert their voices in a more forceful and effective way than ever before in Russian politics.

Panslav Activism and Limited Success, 1856–1875

To what extent were panslavs successful in promoting their ideas and cultivating public and official support before 1875?

Dissemination of Ideas

Beginning in the late 1830s to the 1860s, panslavs published their ideas in papers and journals and sought to inform the Russian public about their Slavic kindred outside Russia. Many panslav-oriented publications did not live long, however; some ran short of funds, while others ran afoul of government censorship. And even those that survived were not immune to occasional problems with money and the censors.[85] These publications included *Moskvitianin* (1841–56), *Moskovskii sbornik* (1846–47), *Russkaia beseda* (1859), *Den'* (1861–65), *Moskva* (1867), *Moskvich* (1867–68), and *Zaria* (1869–71). Relatively small audiences paid attention to panslav writings. *Moskvitianin*, for example, which lasted the longest of the early publications sympathetic to panslavism, barely had 200 subscribers in 1846, compared to 3,000 for its liberal, Westernizing counterpart, *Otechestvennye zapiski*.[86] Panslavs also encountered trouble with the government, including the arrest of leaders such as Samarin and I. Aksakov (both were arrested and briefly detained in 1848).

In the late 1860s, panslavs continued to face government opposition. Officials banned I. Aksakov's last two efforts, *Moskva* and *Moskvich*, in 1869. At the same time, other publicists, sympathetic to the panslav agenda and more agile in dealing with officials, continued to publish. One was Mikhail Katkov, a student of Pogodin and supporter of ideas propagandized by I. Aksakov, Pogodin, Samarin, Danilevskii, and others. For most of his career, Katkov promoted Russian imperial nationalism and panslavism. His *Russkii vestnik* (late 1850s), *Moskovskie vedomosti* (1863–87), and *Russkie vedomosti* (1856–87) carried many articles propagandizing the fate of the Balkan Slavs and rousing panslav nationalism. *Moskovskie vedomosti* was quite successful, with 12,000 subscribers in the 1860s (one of the highest at the time).[87] Panslavs also published such books as Danilevskii's *Russia and Europe* (first serialized in 1869) and Fadeev's *Opinion on the Eastern Question*, but these did not receive wide public attention. Danilevskii's book was not even uniformly popular among Russian panslav sympathizers. The St. Petersburg Slavic Benevolent Committee refused to fund its publication because, in the opinion of one committee official, the book neglected Russian internal reform, without which a panslav dream was impossible. Some circles, however, did value Danilevskii's treatise. The editorial board of *Zaria* endorsed Danilevskii's ideas unequivocally, but the journal itself failed after only two years.[88]

Slavic congresses were another forum for disseminating panslav ideas. The 1867 Slav congress in St. Petersburg, in particular, briefly turned the Slavic question into a headline item for nearly all publications in Russia and sparked a debate among the reading public on Russia's role and responsibilities toward its persecuted Slavic relatives. Before the congress started, the Russian press heavily advertised the upcoming events, the biographies of non-Russian participants, and such issues as Slavic political and cultural unity and the fate of Slavs under Ottoman and Austrian rule. Vladimir Lamanskii, a professor and member of the Slavic Committee, also translated and disseminated widely for the first time in Russia the work of the deceased Slovak panslav Ludovit Štur, who preached that a political union with Russia was the only means by which his fellow Slavs could throw off the foreign yoke and realize their full national potential in an independent state.[89] The 1867 congress moved the panslav idea from "the realm of the book into life," as Russians witnessed a microcosmic image in the flesh of a united slavdom whose potential membership could include sixty million Russians and at least seventeen million western Slavs. But the success of the congress was short-lived and did not lead to official Russian support. Another congress followed the next year in Prague, but the Russian delegation, led by Professor Lamanskii, were minor players. The Prague gathering showed the weakness of the idea of Slavic solidarity led by Russia; non-Russian Slavs dominated the forum and expressed their yearning for equal status with other nations of Europe, including Russia.[90]

Resonance with Public Opinion

Panslav ideas occasionally resonated with the Russian articulate public. In 1857, for example, slavophiles and panslavs formed the Moscow Slavic Benevolent Committee. Confirmed by Tsar Alexander II in 1858, the committee's overt *raison d'être* was to render assistance to Russia's Slavic brothers, particularly the Bulgarians, in educational and religious matters. Although its avowed purpose was apolitical, the committee reported directly to the Foreign Ministry's Asiatic department and used panslavs in the department as a liaison with Slav lands. Further, prominent panslavs in the committee began to use the organization to propagate the political agenda of panslavism.[91] After the 1867 Slav congress, branches of the Slavic Committee were organized in St. Petersburg in 1868, Kiev in 1869, and Odessa in 1870, and a Ladies Section of the Moscow Committee was organized in 1870. The Moscow and St. Petersburg branches became the most politically active of these organizations.[92]

The 1867 panslav congress, organized by the Moscow Slavic Committee, stimulated interest and sympathy among the Russian public. Although the initial and formal occasion was a Slavic ethnographic exhibition, the congress became a political event. In the period 1863–67, while planning for the exhibition, the Slavic Committee found itself in difficult straits, with its budget down to an all-time low of 436 rubles. It did not have sufficient means to advertise the exhibition, and members solicited outside sponsorship. Panslav activism was rewarded when, in May 1867, sixty-two Slav delegates (the majority of whom were Czechs) arrived at the Slav congress. Official Russia did not initially welcome the idea of a Slav congress, but the government changed its mind upon witnessing the warm and energetic public response to the event. Thousands of Russians welcomed the arriving Slavic delegates at the train station, and approximately thirty thousand people attended the Slavic ethnographic exhibition itself. The government extended its hospitality to Russia's Slavic guests by hosting an official reception with the tsar and tsaritsa; in attendance were such prominent figures as Grand Duke Konstantin Nikolaevich,

Foreign Minister Aleksandr M. Gorchakov, and head of the Asiatic department, Mikhail Stremoukhov. The Russian minister of education, Dmitrii A. Tolstoi, also hosted a luncheon for the Slavs and, in what he called "unofficial" comments, expressed sympathy for his guests, underlined the strength of ties between Russia and slavdom, and mentioned the grand future of the Slavic tribe.[93] During the congress itself, participants discussed prospects for Slavic political and linguistic unity, but there was discord on key issues. In particular, Pogodin's denunciation of Poland roused a call for Slavic reconciliation from the non-Russian Slavs. In the end, the Slavic delegates left without forging a strong base of cooperation with their Russian colleagues and with the fear that Russian hegemony would ultimately destroy their dream of independence and equality.[94]

After 1867, membership in the Slavic Committees increased. The St. Petersburg branch had sixty-three new members in 1868 and recruited 324 more in 1869 and 228 in 1870. The payment of dues to the Moscow branch also gained momentum, with the committee's budget increasing from 436 rubles in 1867 to 9,000 rubles by 1868, just one year after the congress, and reaching a high of 12,000 rubles in 1870. But public enthusiasm for the Slavic Committees waned in the early 1870s, and only one third of the Moscow Slavic Committee's 704 members continued to pay their dues by 1874. As a result, the organization's budget fell to 500 rubles in 1875.[95]

Official Support

Some Russian government officials and members of the imperial court sympathized with panslav ideas before 1875, but this did not result in official adoption of panslav ideology. In the late 1830s and early 1840s, Pogodin had access to high officials, especially Minister of Education Uvarov, to whom he addressed a series of memoranda. Uvarov subsequently led a search for Russians to supervise Slavonic studies at Russian universities, shifting from earlier Slavic reciprocity, which entailed the appointment of non-Russian Slavic scholars to lead Slavonic studies in Russia. Other officials who supported panslavism were A. N. Bakhmetev, superintendent of the Moscow school district and first president of the Moscow Slavic Committee, and various heads of the Asiatic department of the Foreign Ministry. The Asiatic department oversaw Russian relations with the Ottoman Empire, and several of its chiefs gave moral and financial support to panslav publications and acted as a conduit for communications between the Slavic Committees and Slavs outside Russia. In 1859, for example, Asiatic department head E. Kovalevskii supported and encouraged the publication of I. Aksakov's *Parus*. Ignatev, chief of the department (1861–64), was also one of the most ardent supporters of panslavism.[96] In court, the tsaritsa and Grand Prince Konstantin Nikolaevich, brother to Alexander II, regularly read I. Aksakov's *Russkaia beseda*. Countess Antonina Bludova, lady-in-waiting to the tsaritsa, was also sympathetic to panslavism, and Alexander II's close friend and adviser, Prince Aleksandr Bariatinskii, urged the tsar to pursue a policy that would put Russia at the head of all Slavic movements for independence.[97] Although panslavism had sympathizers in official circles, their support was sporadic and fragmented before 1875.

TOWARD THE DECISIVE MOMENTS OF 1877–1878

The greatest resonance of panslavism in official and societal circles came in the period 1875–78, culminating in Russia's war with Turkey on behalf of the Ottoman Empire's Slav subjects in 1877–78. Several factors facilitated the resonance and impact of panslavism, including the persistence of the imperial state in domestic political discourse; the deep erosion of internal governance; and, most important, the convergence of threats and crises in the international environment.

Domestic Political Discourse: The Persistence of the Imperial State

The period of reform and lively discussion of social and political issues inside Russia following the Crimean defeat in 1856 heralded a new openness in Russia's political system. However, this openness did not entail a realistic or effective assessment of the problems and burdens created by the imperial state internally or externally. The government remained sensitive to certain types of criticism and continued to exert control where it wanted. Those actors and institutions that guarded and shaped collective memory and validated ideas in Russian society continued to conduct their discourse in terms of old symbols and ideas. Broad affinity and commitment to Russian greatness as an imperial power remained intact. No thorough examination or critique of Russian "duty" toward Slavic subjects of other empires took place. With minor variation, publications from different parts of the Russian political spectrum affirmed common sympathy for the plight of the Balkan Slavs and accepted the notion that the Russian state had to act on their behalf or lose its status as a great power. The tsarist government, as a major socializing institution, did not disavow its imperial character or openly acknowledge the limits and perils of past imperial behavior and foreign policy. Military officials also did not question Russian imperialism. And some who had benefited from past imperial expansion, as illustrated by Cherniaev, Fadeev, and Skobelev, clearly welcomed panslavism and supported its imperial policy prescriptions.

Panslavism was an ideology that affirmed the Russian imperial state and its policies abroad. Thus, it benefited from the predominantly pro-imperial structure of political discourse inside Russia. Its incitement to expand Russian prestige and influence as a great power appealed to a collective memory nurtured by years of imperial history. In contrast, ideas of Russian retrenchment, condemnation of past imperial actions, or arguments regarding the perils of imperial policy were weak in Russian political discourse. However, they did surface in liberal and socialist writings (e.g., in *Nash sovremennik, Delo, Russkii vestnik, Russkoe slovo,* and *Otechestvennye zapiski*), which, in part, highlighted universal rights as the solution to Russia's "Eastern question," minimized Russia's role as protector of the

Slavs, emphasized the danger of panslavism to the integrity of tsarism, and linked the Slavic question with internal Russian reform. Some critics of panslavism declared that if Russia were to fight for the rights of minorities in empires abroad, it must first deliver those same rights to its subjects.[98] But these voices ultimately proved too weak to reorient the imperial bias of Russian political discourse.

The symbols and rhetoric of panslavism fit well with the imperial paradigm. Panslavs touted the imminent millennial triumph of slavdom and heralded the idea that Slavs, under Russian leadership, would vanquish all enemies and bring true civilization to humankind. Panslavs linked their triumphalist imagery with Orthodox symbolism, asserting a "holy calling" for Russia and an "apostasy" that needed to be corrected through the cultural, spiritual, and political reunification of all Slavs. They worked with Orthodox clergy to highlight holy figures in Slavic history such as Cyril and Methodius, creators of the Cyrillic alphabet and God's "own apostles to the Slavs." By infusing their cause with divine meaning, touching on the salvation of individuals and Russia itself, panslavs tied their ideas to Russia's deep and vibrant religious roots and traditions and cast Russian imperialism in a benign light. In the years 1875–78, when mass voluntarism on behalf of panslavism occurred, police records showed that many of Russia's common citizens equated the suffering of the Balkan Slavs with suffering Christian martyrs and saints, and were thus prepared for self-sacrifice on their behalf.[99]

Unstable Autocracy: Challenges to the Old Order

The erosion of internal governance also facilitated the impact of panslavism on Russian foreign policy in 1875–78. Such erosion stemmed from (1) the development of the concept of *narod* or people as the source of political legitimacy, challenging autocracy; (2) the fragmentation of the political elite on key policy issues; and (3) the difficulties of domestic reform and the beginnings of terror in Russia.

People and Nation (Narod) in Russian Politics

After the Crimean War, the concept that political legitimacy rested with the people, rather than a divinely sanctioned autocrat, gained widespread acceptance in Russia. After all, it was the people who sacrificed everything during the war. Many preached the idea that the autocrat should heed the voice and needs of the people to remain a legitimate ruler. This "politicization of society" or the rise of political mass consciousness and movement (*obshchestvennoe dvizhenie*) became increasingly powerful in the 1860s and 1870s. And though mass democracy or political participation did not replace Russian autocratic politics, there were strong signals of diluted monarchical power by the 1870s. Political journalism flourished to replace the "traditional voicelessness of Russian society"; the government abolished serfdom; and the state instituted organs of local government (*zemstvos*) in Russian districts and provinces, covering thirty-four out of seventy provinces by 1875. Members of the *zemstvos* were elected by gentry, townspeople, and peasants, thus indicating a broader apportionment of political power in society.[100]

Radical populism also developed as a challenge to autocracy. Universities became fertile breeding grounds for populists who exalted the common people, over autocracy, as the source of political authority. The power of populism among the educated and politically conscious sectors of society led to the "mad summer" of 1874, when thousands of populists from the big cities (many of them students) donned Russian garb and launched a "movement to the people." They approached discontented peasants in thirty-seven provinces to teach them about politics and revolution. While the peasants did not join the populists en masse, this largely peaceful event sufficiently threatened Russia's autocratic government that the police arrested 770 participants.[101] The "movement to the people" of 1874 marked the rising importance of the "people" in the consciousness of the Russian educated elite and among some of the nobility. This process echoed other instances in the nineteenth century when members of the elite were exposed to the masses and subsequently embarked on actions to unify themselves (albeit with little real success) with the people—in a manner of speaking—to form a community or nation. This was true of the war against Napoleon in 1812, when nobles and peasants fought together for Russia; after the war, the Decembrist revolt occurred as an expression of desire for reform among the nobility. Again during the Crimean War, elites and masses fought side by side, and elite support for reforms in the lives of the peasantry became evident after the war.

Fragmentation of the Political Elite

In the two decades prior to the Russo-Turkish war of 1877, the highest levels of Russian government did not have a consistent policy toward panslavism at home and the "Eastern question" abroad. Official fragmentation on these issues opened the way for unofficial actors—especially panslav nationalists—to take the lead on debates regarding the Balkan Slavs, especially when international crises arose in 1875–78. It also led to policies that gave room for panslavism to influence the actions of official Russia.

Division among ruling officials and the ambiguity of policy stemmed in large part from the nature of autocracy. Although in theory the autocrat was supposed to be omnipotent, in reality the tsar depended on his advisers and ministers for policy proposals and on the large Russian bureaucracy for policy implementation. Ministers, representing different branches of government and subscribing to divergent opinions, competed intensively for the tsar's ear and favor. Members of the royal family with "vastly differing political views [also] sought to sway their most illustrious relative."[102] Under these conditions, panslav proponents were able to make some headway into official institutions and decision making. In the 1850s, for example, Bulgarians in Moscow used Pogodin and others to lobby the education minister, the foreign minister, the head of the Asiatic department, and members of the royal family to support their studies in Moscow. Many of these Bulgarians later became active in the Slavic national liberation movement upon their return home. In the area of panslav propaganda, some officials censored and closed down panslav publications, while other officials rendered financial and other support to such publications.[103]

Within the court and royal family, some members became sympathetic to panslavism and tried to influence the tsar's opinion at a time when the tsar was not disposed to think of new Russian Slavic activism. Indeed, in 1862, the tsar declared that panslavism was "extremely dangerous for Russia and for the monarchical principle. . . . The union of all Slavs under one head is a utopia unlikely ever to become a reality."[104] But others in court did not share his view. Alexander II's wife, "ailing, devout, and suffering" after the death of her eldest son and in light of her husband's philandering with the eighteen-year-old Princess Ekaterina Dolgorukaia, was swayed toward the panslav cause by her confessor and ladies-in-waiting. One of the latter, Countess Bludova, described as an "intelligent and sly" woman and "sworn enemy" of western European culture, was a close and long-term friend and supporter of Pogodin; she dreamed of the Slavs one day ruling all of Europe and spreading Orthodoxy worldwide. She interceded with the court on behalf of panslav causes and influenced not only the tsaritsa but also the tsar. The tsarevich Alexander himself eagerly read panslav materials and in 1877 wrote that he favored a "final resolution"—specifically, war with Turkey—to the "Eastern question" and supported I. Aksakov's stand on the issue.[105] Over time, supporters of panslavism with access to the corridors of power managed to propagandize their ideas among important decision makers.

Another division within the Russian government that helped panslavism was that between Foreign Minister Gorchakov and head of the Asiatic department Ignatev. Gorchakov, foreign minister since 1855, was a mild and conciliatory man who subscribed to the "balance of power" in Russian foreign policy; he believed that consultation and conferences among the great powers were the best ways to pursue Russia's national interest in the "Eastern question." Although he shared the panslav goal of undoing the disadvantageous and humiliating conditions imposed by the 1856 Treaty of Paris, particularly the demilitarization of Russia's southern coastline, he wanted to attain this goal through great power negotiation and consensus. Gorchakov's official policy, however, was dual and contradictory. While wanting to cooperate with the great powers in regulating the Balkan situation, he also rejected European intervention to suppress national movements in the Balkans and encouraged the Balkan Slavs to view Russia as their protector. Gorchakov also favored strengthening Russian ties with Christian Slavs in Turkey and Austria-Hungary but wanted to avoid entanglements that might set a new European coalition against Russia.[106]

In contrast, Ignatev, Gorchakov's subordinate, consistently favored a clear and assertive Russian foreign policy unconstrained by great power agreements. He was not reckless about great power relations but urged Russia's rulers to take every opportunity to improve Russia's relative position among Slavs under Turkish rule. He argued that whatever space Russia failed to occupy would be usurped by other powers. He lobbied intensively for Russian assistance to Serbia, in particular, noting that Serbia was the "pivotal point of the liberation movement" in the Balkans.[107] Those who supported Gorchakov's position included the tsar, War Minister Miliutin, Finance Minister Mikhail Reutern (who argued that Russia's priority was to modernize its economy), and the Russian ambassadors to London (P. A. Shuvalov) and Vienna (N. P. Novikov). The tsar, though supportive of Gorchakov, did not insist on full official support for Gorchakov's policy. Instead, he gave Ignatev (who came with the highest recommendations from one of the tsar's closest friends, Prince Bariatinskii) room to maneuver by allowing the latter to report directly to him and not to the foreign minister. And, in 1864, the tsar rewarded Ignatev with an ambassadorial appointment to Constantinople.[108]

Internal Reform and the Beginnings of Terror

The difficulties of internal reform and the advent of terrorism also eroded internal governance and made the tsarist regime vulnerable to panslav pressure. Alexander II's reforms in 1861–66 had the unfortunate effect of raising popular expectations that the regime could not ultimately deliver. Reforms included the abolition of serfdom; the institution of local self-government organs or *zemstvos*; legal reforms, including trial by jury; economic modernization; and military reform, including the move to make military privileges dependent on educational qualifications, not class origin. Many among the traditionally privileged did not welcome these reforms, while those who were supposed to benefit from them felt deeply dissatisfied. Serf emancipation, for example, did not dramatically improve the lives of peasants, but imposed on them unfair financial burdens.[109]

Alexander II's reforms did not lead to a much-needed social consensus between state and society after the Crimean War, yet the government neither had the will nor resources to grant more concessions and feared losing its authority entirely. From below, a radical opposition of populists and revolutionaries demanded maximal change in Russian internal politics and began a campaign of terror to bring it about. The worst terrorism was to come in the years 1894–1917, but two unsuccessful assassination attempts were made on the tsar in 1866 and 1867, with a third attempt succeeding in 1881. The government responded by limiting the reforms it had begun. It increased censorship, curtailed the influence of local *zemstvos* and the liberal and radical press, and increased public education on Russian religious and national ideas. These measures did not restore the authority of the state, however. As Miliutin wrote, describing the years 1866–75:

> [During those years] of stagnation and reaction, all the strictures of the police not only failed to suppress sedition but, instead, created masses of the discontented, many of whom became new recruits of evil-minded people. . . . It proved . . . that the unfinished reforms and the absence of a comprehensive plan led to a sense of full chaos in all parts of the government.[110]

With the autocratic government besieged from many quarters—and its incompetence and vulnerability exposed—it turned a tolerant eye to the panslavs who were fundamentally supportive of autocracy and a strong, imperial state. The tsar felt that panslav proponents, unlike radicals in Russian society, could be counted among the "loyal" segments of the population and should not be treated harshly. This was his recommendation to Prime Minister Petr Valuev and War Minister Miliutin who, in 1866, expressed their concern regarding the aggressive ideology of panslavism. Valuev noted that the tsar's attitude revealed the "weakness of the government, and essentially [his and Miliutin's] retreat."[111] By the period 1875–78, a weakened and delegitimized tsarist government had extreme difficulty ignoring panslav public opinion and was predisposed to implement its prescriptions.

The Decisive Moments: Threats and Crises in the International System

A convergence of international factors, especially threats and crises related to Russia's great power status and its special role among the Balkan Slavs, was the most important catalyst to the brief influence of panslavism on foreign policy in the years 1875–78. The Crimean War (1853–1856) dealt a heavy blow to the idea that Russia could rely on traditional great power politics to preserve its interests, particularly in the Balkans and Black Sea straits.[112] After the war, Russian foreign policy focused on abrogating the most humiliating provisions of the 1856 Treaty of Paris, particularly the restoration of navigation rights for Russian military vessels in the Black Sea straits and the recovery of Russia's traditional status as protector of Christian Slavs in the Ottoman Empire. The tsarist government and panslavs agreed on these goals, but differed on tactics and strategies for attaining them.

In 1870–71, while Prussia and France were at war with each other, Russia unilaterally abrogated the Treaty of Paris provisions on the Black Sea straits. Prussia supported this action, while Great Britain protested. In March 1871, the great powers convened in London and decided to let the Russian declaration stand. Russia thus was free again to build arsenals and maintain a fleet on the Black Sea.[113] This development satisfied one of Russia's central foreign policy goals, but the problem of how to restore Russian influence and leadership among the Balkan Slavs remained. This pillar of Russian interest played well to the panslav cause. It was the panslavs who, right after the Crimean War, argued vigorously that Russia had no reliable friends but the Slavs.[114] In the interest of maintaining influence among the Balkan Slavs, the Russian government allowed and assisted such activities as the establishment of the Moscow Slavic Committee in 1857, the holding of the panslav congress in 1867, and the formation of other Slavic Committees (1868–70). Russia could not count on great power diplomacy to help improve its stature among the Balkan Slavs; the Western powers were reluctant to see Russian influence expand, and by the late 1860s and early 1870s, Austria-Hungary was competing intensively with Russia for influence in the Balkans.[115]

A series of crises in the 1860s and in 1875–77, coupled with failed attempts at international solutions, helped propel panslavism forward in Russia.[116] First, in 1867, Greek nationalism led to a revolt against Turkey. This crisis gave Russian panslavs an opportunity to publicize the prospect of an impending war in the Balkans and the need for Russia to prepare to help its Orthodox brothers. Second, in the same year, after the dual monarchy of Austria-Hungary was created, the Magyars launched abusive policies against their Slavic (mostly Czech) subjects. This led Czech leaders and national liberation activists to turn to Russia, having lost hope that they could gain autonomy and rights within the Austro-Hungarian Empire. These events lent an air of urgency and vitality to the panslav congress of 1867 and inspired the unprecedented outpouring of financial support to the Moscow Slavic Committee.[117]

Third, in 1875, Christian peasants, reacting to increasing taxation, intolerable agrarian conditions, and oppressive rule, revolted against their Muslim overlords in Bosnia-Herzegovina. The initial Turkish attempt to quell the revolt failed and a crisis ensued. Other Slavs from Austria-Hungary and the Ottoman Empire empathized with the Herzegovinian struggle and collected assistance for the insurgents. In Bulgaria, a small uprising occurred in April and May 1876, to which the Turks responded brutally. Turkish paramilitary units destroyed up to sixty villages and raped, massacred, and butchered between fifteen and thirty thousand men, women, and children. The governments of Serbia and Montenegro at this time hesitated to intervene in the Slavic revolts, but overwhelming public opinion in both countries pushed their leaders to act. The press in Serbia, in particular, incited such passions for war that Serbia's rulers feared they would lose their lives or throne, or both, if they failed to act. In June 1876, Serbia declared war on Turkey and its army began military operations under the leadership of Cherniaev, the Russian general.[118]

The great powers, including Russia, did attempt diplomacy to resolve the Balkan crisis in 1875–77, but failed. The Austrian government in December 1875 sent a note to the six signatories of the Treaty of Paris, outlining proposals for reform in Ottoman governance of Christian subjects. The Andrassy Note, as these proposals were known, called for religious freedom and equality before the law for Christians, fairer taxation practices, agricultural reform, and the creation of a Muslim–Christian commission to implement these measures. The great powers and Turkey accepted these proposals, but the Slavs rejected them. Shortly before Serbia and Montenegro's entry into the war with Turkey, in May 1876, the Three Emperors' League (Russia, Prussia, and Austria) again attempted to resolve the crisis through the Berlin Memorandum, which reiterated the Andrassy Note's provisions and suggested a two-month armistice between Turkey and the Slavs. Italy and France supported this memorandum, but Great Britain rejected it. Turkey interpreted Great Britain's action as a sign that the latter would support the Porte's intransigent stance in dealing with its discontented Slav subjects.[119]

The Serbian army performed dismally against Turkey and, by October 1876, was on the verge of collapse. Russia then demanded an armistice to avoid an outcome that would be utterly humiliating for itself, as self-declared protector of the Slavs, and for Serbia. At the same time, as the correspondence of Foreign Minister Gorchakov and his chief adviser A. G. Jomini show, official tsarist diplomacy still preferred a European solution, not war.[120] If such a solution could not be found, Russian officials knew they must consider other actions or lose international honor and their credibility among the Slavs, as well as risk severe instability at home where panslav public opinion had become highly mobilized.

As the Balkan war became desperate for the Serbs, panslav propaganda increased in Russia and war fever spread, engulfing officials from the War Ministry and Foreign Ministry (including those who initially preferred caution). In November, after Russia had issued its ultimatum to Turkey for an armistice, the tsar ordered partial mobilization of the Russian army in response to Turkish recalcitrance and to internal pressure. Even at this late stage, when war seemed all but inevitable, tsarist diplomats made yet one more attempt to find a peaceful resolution. The Russian government convened a conference of the great powers in Constantinople in December 1876, with a plan to ask Turkey to grant autonomy to Bosnia, Herzegovina, and Bulgaria. At this point, Russia had given up its maximalist claims on behalf of Serbia. When the conference opened, however, the Turks delivered a surprise by announcing that they had granted a constitution to their subjects; the conference, therefore, was superfluous because the new constitution contained all necessary reforms for the Balkan Slavs. A last attempt at an international solution transpired in January 1877. Russia sent Ignatev as an envoy to the great power capitals, and, in March 1877, the London Protocol was signed. This document asked Turkey to conduct reform in the near term to appease its Christian population. Turkey rejected the Protocol as interference in its internal affairs.[121] Thus ended the last effort at great power diplomacy, and, in April 1877, with a panslav rally in full force in Russia, the tsar declared war on Turkey. Serbia, Montenegro, Bulgaria, and Romania soon joined forces with Russia, and the Russo-Turkish War "assumed aspects of an Orthodox war against Islam and a Slavic war of national liberation against the Porte."[122]

PANSLAVISM BRIEFLY TRIUMPHANT, 1875–1878

Although the rise of panslavism was not a straight incline upward, the efforts of panslavs and organizations such as the Slavic Committees did promote knowledge of, and sympathy for, Slavic brothers in the years before 1875. This knowledge and sympathy became politically mobilized when crises broke out in 1875 and 1876. Panslavs relentlessly urged the Russian population and government not to desert the heroic Slavs, urging, in the words of I. Aksakov, that it was "Russia's historical calling, moral right, and duty" to "free the Slav peoples from their material and spiritual yoke and give them the gift of independent spiritual and . . . political life under the shade of the powerful wings of the Russian eagle." Russia ought to be ashamed for leaving its brothers "in faith and ancestry" to cope on their own against the Muslim yoke. He asked, "are we not Christians, are we not Orthodox, are we not Russians, Slavs?"[123]

During the crises of 1875–76, various sectors of Russian society, including nobles, intellectuals, Orthodox clergy, and peasants, displayed a unified outpouring of support for the Slavs. The Slavic Committees solicited material and financial donations on behalf of Bosnia-Herzegovina, Serbia, Bulgaria, and Montenegro and responded to requests from ordinary citizens who wanted to volunteer in the Serbian army. In 1876, an estimated five thousand[124] Russians volunteered to fight in the Serbian army against Turkey. Many of them were common people, including peasants, workers, low-ranked bureaucrats, and noncommissioned officers from big cities as well as the provinces. Reports from the tsarist secret police confirmed the sympathy of ordinary Russians for the Slavic struggle. During Russia's war with Turkey, draft evasion was low and morale high among the mass of peasant army recruits. These recruits were heroic, sometimes walking long distances to reach their mobilization depots. They were fired with great enthusiasm for a war that became a "quasi-holy struggle, almost a crusade, to rescue fellow Christians from the heathen Turk."[125]

Original documents from the Russo-Turkish War show that the government decided to launch military action largely in response to the pressing "voice of the people," which, in 1875–78, was rife with panslav content and emotion.[126] Panslavs influenced the decision to go to war in three ways. First, through their propaganda in the press and other civic activities, they incited such public passion for war that Alexander II's government was compelled to respond to it or risk even greater domestic instability. Second, panslavs co-opted the role of official policymakers and publicly committed Russian prestige and authority to intervention in the Balkans. The existence of a public commitment to the Slavs created the risk that Russia's government would look impotent internationally if it did not go to war. Third, individual panslavs in official positions used their positions and resources to make sure that war happened.

Panslav Incitement for War

Panslav reaction to the Balkan crisis was slow in 1875, but intensified dramatically in 1876 and 1877. The most prominent panslavs zealously argued in speeches and articles that war was the only honorable and viable option for Russian foreign policy. I. Aksakov, in his speeches, made absolutist statements depicting the fight between Slavs and Turks as one between good and evil, and argued that Russia must get involved in the "terrible, bloody, last war of Slavdom with Islam. For the Slavs, this is a fight for life or death." He characterized the Slavs as victims who were undergoing torment "for the sin of Orthodoxy, for the sin of sharing one faith and one thought with [the Russians]."[127] Aksakov recalled Russia's humiliation in the Crimean War and accused the Russian government of "deceiving the enslaved" who were counting on Russian help. He also capitalized on spilled Russian blood (Russian volunteers died while fighting unofficially in the Serbian army in 1876) and urged Russia to go to battle against Turkey, the "enemy of Christ." In a speech to the Moscow Slavic Committee in March 1877, he pronounced,

> The entire responsibility rests with us and with us alone. It is no use to cast blame on others, to be angry at Turkey or Europe. Turkey cannot so easily and simply cease to be, no matter how much we might desire this. Turkey is doomed to fall, but it is right

in fighting for survival. Western Europe is also right in fighting for its interests—though they may be narrow and egoistic—but they are Europe's *own* interests. We are the only ones who are wrong because we deny and destroy our very vital interests.[128]

In *Moskovskie vedomosti*, Katkov initially advocated autonomy for Bosnia-Herzegovina in 1875; but by 1876 he, too, began to issue calls for war. He condemned the Foreign Ministry's reticence and used his paper to encourage the Serbs to go to war against Turkey. He urged Romania to join Serbia's war and, in covering the war for the Russian press, deliberately minimized Turkish victories while hiding the failures of the Serbian army under Cherniaev. Katkov worked with Aksakov to manipulate press reports in order to pressure St. Petersburg policymakers to intervene in the Balkans. When Alexander II finally ordered partial mobilization of the army in 1877, Katkov openly rejoiced and suggested that Russia conquer and occupy Constantinople. Like Katkov, Fadeev used *Russkii mir* to incite the Serbs to battle against Turkey, exaggerate Serbian prospects for victory, urge Russia to go its own way and abandon cooperation with the great powers, lie about Cherniaev's battles and Russian heroism in Serbia, and hide Serbian reverses in the war against Turkey.[129]

More panslav agitation for war came from the cultural intelligentsia, whose voice was authoritative among the reading public. Fedor Tiutchev, Ivan Turgenev, and Fedor Dostoevskii, for example, expressed support for Russian volunteers who were fighting in Serbia and emphasized that war on behalf of Russia's Christian brothers was a moral action. In Tiutchev's words, regardless of the outcome of war, Russia's "moral victory was certain. The work that we are taking upon ourselves is the holy work of Christendom. The reasons for war are pure and moral. If western European politicians cannot understand this, then objective history will make it clear."[130] Other luminaries in the world of Russian arts and sciences, including Turgenev, sculptor Mark Antokolskii, painter Il'ia Repin, and scientist Dmitrii Mendeleev, joined Dostoevskii and Tiutchev in lobbying official support for the Slavs in the years 1875–77.[131]

The Moscow Slavic Committee, claiming to act "in the name of the Russian people," presented the Serbs with a banner of Dmitrii Donskoi and his troops. Donskoi fought and vanquished the Mongols in 1380, and this banner signaled that war in the Balkans was as noble as Russia's struggle against the Mongol hordes. Finally, panslav coverage of horrors in the Balkans, including eyewitness accounts, was extremely effective in rallying the public for war. An account by a Russian agent emphasized the barbaric treatment of Slavs by Turks, including imprisonment and murder of all Slavs capable of bearing arms. It described an encounter with peasants in Bosnia-Herzegovina who had been homeless for weeks and were starving. An old man, barely conscious, approached the Russian agent and exclaimed, "Ah, it is the Russian tsar who sent you to help us." The account concluded that the "thought of mercy from the Russian tsar, or brotherly help from the Russian people [was] the sole hope that the Slavs [had] not relinquished in their difficult situation."[132] Use of the telegraph and high-speed presses (e.g., by *Novoe vremia*) also facilitated the flow and speed of graphic information on the Balkan crisis and roused Russian public opinion as never before. Newspapers printed numerous telegrams from Serbia and one of them, Odessa's *Novorossiiskii telegraf*, dramatically printed telegrams on blood-red newsprint to go with the paper's war rhetoric.[133] Panslav incitement to war was widespread and intense, and even those publications that initially shunned war began to criticize government diplomacy. This was the case, for example, with *Golos*, a paper subsidized by the Foreign Ministry. Panslav agitation stimulated a prodigious public response; even among children, a popular game called the "Eastern question" evolved, with everyone wanting the role of the warrior Cherniaev![134]

Creating a Public Commitment to War

The tsarist government's divided stance on panslavism and the "Eastern question" helped the panslav agenda. Unable to articulate and implement a clear policy, the government tolerated the activities of the Slavic Committees to assist the Balkan Slav insurrections in 1875 and 1876. These committees de facto implemented foreign policy and created a public commitment to war by sending agents, arms, and money to the Slavs; soliciting donations and volunteers; sponsoring "eyewitness" lectures on the Slavic cause; and assisting General Cherniaev in his illegal flight (using a fake passport) from Russia to lead the Serbian army.[135] In the absence of unequivocal directives, panslavs from the Foreign Ministry contravened official policy by encouraging Serbia to support the Herzegovina uprising against Turkey in 1875, thereby enlarging the war and increasing the chances that Russia would be drawn in on behalf of Serbia. Panslav lobbying in the Foreign Ministry also led to an increase in official assignations for the Slavic Committees, which were subsequently spent on arms and other assistance to the Slavic rebels.[136] Even the tsar and Foreign Minister Gorchakov, who were against panslavism, found themselves swept by the rising tide. As Miliutin recorded in his diary in July 1876:

> I discovered today, in deep secrecy, that the state chancellor [Gorchakov] agreed to look through his fingers at the transport of arms to the Serbs and Bulgarians. The Sovereign [tsar] also permitted the minister of finance to give corresponding secret instructions to our customs officials.[137]

By engaging in public activities to assist the Balkan Slavs in 1875–77, panslavs acted as unofficial policymakers and committed Russian prestige and authority at home and abroad to intervention in the Balkans. The panslavs' chief intent was always to push the government to follow where their public activism led. As I. Aksakov argued, panslav agitation and public activities were useful only to the extent that they could stimulate the government to act.[138] Voluntary assistance to Serbia in 1876—including the thousands who responded to newspaper calls for volunteers—led to a deepening and widening of the Eastern crisis. Russian panslavs solicited support for the Serbs and Montenegrins in the hope that other Slavs would join the war against Turkey. They sent agents to Bulgaria to help organize and arm an uprising there. Most important, Cherniaev's unofficial mission to Serbia stimulated intense Russian military fervor. Archival documents reveal deep sentiment among ordinary people, who were extremely eager to pro vide their services to the Serbian army. Cherniaev reportedly received as many as three hundred letters of support a day from peasants, soldiers, musicians, hunters, doctors, nurses, and others. One volunteer apologized for his poverty and the fact that he could offer only moral, not financial, support; a sixteen-year-old boy, swearing that at age thirteen he made a trip of 950 *versts* (about 630 miles) alone, begged the Moscow Slavic Committee to finance his trip to Serbia so he could fight. Poor Russian villages also literally collected kopecks to be sent to the Slavs under Cherniaev's leadership. Ten villages in one *oblast'*, for example, sent a total of 110 rubles to the Moscow Slavic Committee.[139] From the eruption of the Herze-govina uprising in September 1875 to October 1876, the Slavic Committees col-lected between 1.5 and three million rubles for the Slavs, with donations increas-ing as panslav sentiment intensified. Russian Orthodox clergy comforted Orthodox Slavs in Herzegovina and urged them to keep their faith.[140]

The public response to panslav solicitation of donations and assistance to the Balkans revealed a powerful force in Russian society. Public commitment to the Slavic cause was clear and contrasted with official hesitation. Sympathy for the Slavs' plight grew stronger as Russians themselves died in the Serbo-Turkish War in 1876. As the paper *Peterburgskaia gazeta* argued, Russia must fight against Turkey for Russia's own sake and avenge Russian blood: "There are no great rivers in Turkey, only wide bloody streams, created from Christian blood."[141] The tsarist government, fearing the consequences of unprecedented public activism, tried feebly to stem the tide of popular response to panslav agitation. At first it prohib-ited the official retirement of army officers who wanted to fight with Cherniaev, and instructed the police to let volunteers for the Balkan war come into Moscow only by day so that few would see them since most people would be at work. Before long, however, the government yielded to public clamor and stopped try-ing to prevent soldiers and officers from joining Cherniaev; it even paid for the return of some volunteers to Russia when the need arose. The military also allowed doctors to volunteer in Serbia and return to their state jobs later, and no officials objected when railroad authorities granted free passage for volunteers and supplies to Serbia. This change in governmental action reflected the desire of officials to avoid the image of an inactive and paralyzed government at a time when the people or *narod* themselves were making enormous sacrifices to defend Russian honor and prestige.[142]

In the end, panslav agitation helped persuade the tsarist monarchy to declare war against Turkey in April 1877. Shortly thereafter, the government put all Slavic Committee activities under the jurisdiction of the Ministry of Internal Affairs, especially the work of panslav agents in Turkish lands and in Serbia. The govern-ment ostensibly wanted to keep panslav activism under its control, but, at the same time, an obvious (albeit temporary) alliance and sharing of goals had formed between the government and a society fired by panslav ideals. One histo-rian notes that

> The government, because of its murky program and unsuccessful diplomatic game, lost its authority over the mass population, for whom the calls to help [Slav] broth-ers had become clearer and closer. They heard this call from everywhere. All the news-papers wrote about it. And the authority of the Slavic Committees, which were

implementing the popular call, naturally grew. As a result, not only did the activities of the Slavic Committees (which the police deemed dangerous!) proceed without obstruction, but governmental organs and official figures even moved them forward. Generals assisted in recruiting volunteers [for the Slav war against Turkey], the military donated cloth for uniforms, the railroads transported volunteers for free or with a major discount, and so on.[143]

Individual "Diplomacy" for War

Russian officials who supported panslavism contributed to its impact by using their positions to lobby their superiors and fuel the fires of war on the ground. Ignatev, for example, immediately urged the Russian government to send 200,000 troops to help Serbia when the Serbo-Turkish War broke out. He kept Serbia informed of Turkish troop positions, even though this contradicted the policy of the tsar, Gorchakov, and Miliutin. Before the war, he also informed the Serbian military representative in Russia that the tsarist government's urging for Serbia to avoid war did not reflect the tsar's "secret desire"; just as soon as Serbia declared war, Russia would be right behind it.[144] But Ignatev's decisive moment of influence was likely his visit with the tsar while the latter was resting in Livadia in October 1876. The tsar convened a meeting of his closest advisers, and Ignatev was invited despite Gorchakov's protest. The tsarevich wrote frustratedly about his father's indecisiveness at this stage and noted how "even here, from where all orders and decisions originate, there are days when nobody knows or understands anything." Thankfully, the tsarevich continued, Ignatev "opened everyone's eyes," and convinced the tsar to declare war against Turkey even though he and others remained unclear about the reasons why.[145] Although the tsar did not immediately declare war after Livadia, he did ask Finance Minister Reutern to find the means for it. When Reutern sent a note saying that war would jeopardize Russian reforms and economic stabilization, an irritated Alexander II refused to discuss the note with his other ministers, accusing Reutern of wanting to "humiliate" Russia and swearing that neither he nor the heir to the throne would allow it.[146]

Cherniaev was even more notorious than Ignatev in his individual role in pushing for war. In 1875 he used the pages of *Russkii mir* to publicize the Slavic uprisings and urge the Russian government to intervene. Then, in 1876, he encouraged Serbia to go to war by claiming (falsely) that the Russian government supported his leadership of the Serbian army and that he was in correspondence with an aide to the tsarevich. When Serbia suffered heavy losses, Cherniaev refused to think of retreat or negotiation. He cautioned Prince Milan of Serbia that ending the war was an act that Russia and the Slavs would never forgive.[147] Cherniaev's role as commander of the Serb army raised Serbian expectations of Russian help and put Russian prestige on the line. Indeed, when the Serbian army was on the verge of defeat in late 1876, the Serbs became deeply disappointed with the delay in official Russian intervention, and their enthusiasm for their Russian "ally" plummeted. The threat that Russia would appear completely weak and lose all prestige in Europe was clear and became unacceptable to the Russian government. Even Miliutin, who largely remained cautious, modified his position after receiving some assurance that another European coalition would not form against Russia. He urged Alexander II that the time had come for Russia to prove itself once more as a great power and raise itself from the 1856 Crimean defeat.[148]

Members of the royal family and court also contributed to the Russian decision to go to war. The tsaritsa and tsarevich urged war against Turkey to preserve Russian prestige. Together with some of the grand dukes swept up in the tide of panslav nationalism, they urged the tsar to take more decisive steps on behalf of the Balkan Slavs. The empress became actively involved with Russian quasi-official support for the Slavs, particularly through the Society for the Care of Sick and Wounded Fighters (later, the Russian Red Cross).[149] Other Russian officials in the Balkans, including the representative to Montenegro and the consul to Serbia, also conveyed to Serbs and Montenegrins unauthorized promises of Russian support.[150] Such promises fed the war in the Balkans, obstructed the possibility of early resolution, and helped compel Russia to go to war.

CONCLUSION

The story of panslavism illustrates how nationalism with aggressive foreign policy implications briefly united state and various segments of society in Russia and had an impact on Russian foreign policy. The political agenda and prescriptions of panslavs arose as reactions to national humiliation, stemming from Russian defeat in the Crimean War. In the early stage of panslavism, the majority of Russian political elites—and the tsar and his key ministers—did not adhere to panslav ideology. They gauged accurately and wisely that Russia could not espouse and implement a nationalist program that prescribed militant action on behalf of scattered and persecuted members of the Slavic nation abroad. They preferred stability and peace in the wake of a previously disastrous war against a European coalition. In contrast, articulators of panslav ideas were concerned about bruised Russian national pride and sought to salve that pride by reaffirming Russia's predestination to greatness (in this case, as leader of the Slavs and future beacon of world civilization). They also advocated an activist and aggressive foreign policy as a means to fulfill Russia's great mission.

Tsarist authorities and panslavs actually agreed on foreign policy goals that included the restoration of Russian influence and leadership among the Balkan Slavs and the dismantling of provisions imposed by the great powers to restrict Russian movement and military leverage in the Black Sea. Overlapping goals explain in part why some figures in the highest government circles sympathized with panslavism, but they do not explain why the government—stricken by financial woes, domestic instability, weak industrial development, the need for military modernization, and shaky creditworthiness on foreign markets[151]—went to war on behalf of the Slavs in 1877. Two variables conditioned Russian state authorities

to become predisposed to the influence of panslavism, while a third variable—
international threats and crises—became the precipitating factor for the actual
implementation of panslav ideas.

First, the preponderance of the value and desirability of the imperial state in
Russian political discourse made panslavism acceptable and resonant to both
tsarist authorities and the politically articulate public. The main measure for
Russian greatness, in the minds of many, remained the state's ability to sustain its
status as an imperial power and project military power abroad. As Konstantin P.
Pobedonostsev wrote to the tsarevich Alexander, without war, it "would be impossible to clarify the position which rightfully belongs to Russia," for other states
were "ready to drop [Russia] at that very minute [when] they feel [its] weakness."[152] Although political discourse had opened up in unprecedented ways as a
result of Alexander II's "great reforms" in the 1860s, its parameters had not shifted
significantly from traditional, pro-imperial ideas. The guardians of discourse did
not engage widely and deeply in a critical examination of Russia's imperial past
and ongoing aspiration to imperial status. It may have been too early in the
process of autocratic reform to expect the structure of Russian political discourse
to change fundamentally. But clearly, the absence or weakness of such change
helped predispose state and society to panslavism's appeal.

Second, the erosion of internal governance in Russia made tsarist authorities
highly vulnerable to the influence of public opinion, which, in the 1870s, became
suffused with panslav ideas. This chapter has chronicled the role of the mass press
and civic activism in cultivating and mobilizing panslav public opinion. Faced
with numerous challenges to its authority, hampered by division and rivalry
among officials, and sensing that its longevity depended in part on a measure of
popular support, the tsarist monarchy found that it could not ignore panslav public opinion.

Third, and most important, international crises and threats of further humiliation, loss of prestige, and loss of credibility compelled Russian policymakers to
act in support of panslav ideas. If crises did not occur among the Balkan Slavs in
1875–77, and if international attempts to resolve them had not failed, panslav
ideas and policies would not have achieved the prominence and impact that they
did. In the face of crises—connoting the need for decisive action within a relatively short space of time—tsarist authorities yielded to widespread and mobilized panslav public opinion. Without crises in the past (e.g., during and after the
Slavic congress of 1867), panslav public opinion also grew but definitely did not
have a critical input in Russian foreign policy actions.

There were, of course, other contingencies in the international system that
facilitated the influence of panslavism. One was the weakening of the Ottoman
Empire. In the second half of the nineteenth century, the Ottoman Empire was
undergoing its twilight years. British and French intervention in the Crimean War
did not strengthen the Turkish empire for the long-term, but only gave it tempo-

rary respite. This imperial weakness, coupled with severe socioeconomic gaps between the empire's Muslim rulers and Christian peasants, led to a second development that worked favorably for panslavism: the rise of national liberation movements among the Orthodox and Slavic subjects of the Porte. These movements advanced faster in some states than others, but by the period 1866–76, they had strong followings in Serbia, Bosnia-Herzegovina, Greece, and Bulgaria. Russia, as the most powerful Orthodox and Slavic state in Europe, with a long tradition dating back to the eighteenth century of sympathizing with, and intervening for, the Christian subjects of the Porte, naturally became the favored and much sought-after patron of the Slavs. A tradition of russophilism among Bulgars and Serbs added further impetus to potential cohesion between Russians and discontented Slavs.[153]

Nationalism among Slavs helped the advancement of Russian panslavism, as evident in the crises of 1875–78, which originated independently of Russian effort and policy. In the 1860s, Slavic nationalism also helped the Russian panslav program. In Serbia, for example, the ruling prince from 1860 to 1868, Michael Obrenović (and his father before him), worked to remove the Porte's remaining rights in Serbia and expand Serb territory. Serbia—encouraged by support from Ignatev in the Asiatic department of the Russian Foreign Ministry, by the continuing weakness of Turkey, and by Austria's defeat to Prussia in 1866—began to organize a Balkan union against Turkey in 1866–68; it signed treaties with Montenegro, with Bulgarian revolutionaries, Greece, and Romania. The murder of Michael Obrenović in 1868, however, caused the fragile Balkan coalition to splinter. While it is doubtful that the coalition could have fought Turkey successfully, its mere existence constituted an opportunity, eventually favorable to panslavism, which Russia took when, in 1867–68, the War Ministry sent Russian officers to help train the Serbian army.[154]

A final point emerges from this case study: although the tremendous emotional power of nationalist ideology became visible, the tsarist monarchy was unable to understand this power or find ways to use it for the longer-term consolidation, modernization, and unification (in terms of state–society relations) of Russia. Panslavism in the period 1875–78 mobilized the Russian public in unprecedented ways and exerted a remarkable influence on all sectors of society. During these years, state and society briefly united in a common sense of purpose. Yet, as Geoffrey Hosking points out, the tsarist regime feared the elements of democracy and overt social protest contained in panslavism.[155] Thus, panslavism as a uniting nationalist ideology did not last for long. The government recognized the dangers of overt societal intervention in foreign policy and took measures to limit panslav influence. After the assassination of Alexander II in 1881, his son Alexander III launched a reign of reaction, when the articulation and propagation of ideas were again controlled heavily by the state. These issues will be discussed in the following chapter, which chronicles the return of panslavism as an element of great power nationalism in Russia in the early twentieth century.

NOTES

1. Hans Kohn, *Panslavism: Its History and Ideology* (Notre Dame: University of Notre Dame Press, 1953), pp. 1–25; and "Herder, Johann Gottfried (1744–1803)," *The Encyclopedia of Philosophy*, vol. 3 (New York: Macmillan, 1967), pp. 486–89. See also the sources in note 5.

2. *Sovetskaia istoricheskaia entsiklopediia* (Moscow: Sovetskaia entsiklopediia, 1967), p. 793; and Frank J. Fadner, *Seventy Years of Pan-Slavism in Russia: Karazin to Danilevsky 1800–1870* (Washington, D.C.: Georgetown University Press, 1962), pp. 11–72.

3. *Dvadtsatipiatiletie velikoi osvoboditel'noi voiny 1877–1902* (Moscow: Tip. T-va I. D. Sytina, 1902), p. 133.

4. Russian panslavism is a type of "hegemony nationalism," or a motivation for action by a national group that believes it can derive advantage from consolidating smaller units into larger and more dynamic entities. See Louis L. Snyder, *Encyclopedia of Nationalism* (New York: Paragon, 1990), p. 241.

5. The Slovak Ludovit Štur did support Russian hegemonic panslavism. A publicist and politician, Štur became famous as a panslav theorist only posthumously in Russia. Panslav professors in St. Petersburg and Moscow published and disseminated his writings and featured them prominently at the 1867 Slav Congress in Moscow. See Snyder, *Encyclopedia of Nationalism*, pp. 309–10; Michael Boro Petrovich, *The Emergence of Russian Panslavism 1856–1870* (Westport, Conn.: Greenwood, 1956), pp. 18–19; Georges Luciani, *La société des slaves unis 1823–25* (France: Université de Bordeaux, 1963), pp. 1–7; Alexander Joseph Michaels, *Neoslavism and Its Attempt at Russo-Polish Rapprochement 1908–1910*, Master's Thesis, American University, 1956, pp. 1–23; A. N. Pypin, *Panslavizm v proshlom i nastoiashchem* (St. Petersburg: knigo-izd. "Kolos," 1913), p. 65; M. V. Nechkina, *Obshchestvo soedinennykh slavian* (Moscow: Gosudarstvennoe izd., 1927); and Cyprien Robert, "Les deux panslavismes: Situation actuelle des peuples slaves vis-à-vis de la Russie," *Revue des deux mondes*, 1 November 1846, pp. 453–83.

6. On the earliest evolution of panslav consciousness in Russia and on Russian official interest in the Slavs within the context of imperial competition, see I. S. Dostoian, *Russkaia obshchestvennaia mysl' i balkanskie narody: Ot Radishcheva do dekabristov* (Moscow: Nauka, 1980), esp. pp. 23–38, 186–310; and Emanuel Sarkisyanz, "Russian Imperialism Reconsidered," in Taras Hunczak, ed., *Russian Imperialism from Ivan the Great to the Revolution* (New Brunswick: Rutgers University Press, 1974), p. 52.

7. One of Peter the Great's first major acts as sovereign was to fight Turkey in 1695, winning the fortress of Azov by 1696. Other Russian wars with Turkey (before the Crimean War) occurred in 1676–81, 1686–1700, 1710–13, 1736–39, 1768–74, 1787–92, 1806–12, and 1828–29. See John Keep, *Soldiers of the Tsar: Army and Society in Russia 1462–1874* (Oxford: Clarendon, 1985), *passim*.

8. Historians point out that the Treaty of Kuchuk Kainardji did not explicitly give Russia the judicial right to be the protector of Slav subjects of the Ottoman Empire. It did, however, grant territorial, commercial, and religious concessions to Russia. The Russian side interpreted the religious provisions freely to include the right to intervene in the internal affairs of the Ottoman Empire whenever the interests of Orthodox Slavs were at stake.

For more on the treaty, see Albert Sorel, *The Eastern Question in the Eighteenth Century* (New York: Howard Fertig, 1969), pp. 247–51; and Barbara Jelavich, *History of the Balkans: Eighteenth and Nineteenth Centuries*, vol. 1 (Cambridge, UK: Cambridge University Press, 1983), pp. 69–72.

9. Paul Vyšný, *Neo-Slavism and the Czechs 1898–1914* (Cambridge, UK: Cambridge University Press, 1977), pp. 217–19.

10. There were a few activists who did lobby for political panslavism in the early 1800s. Foremost were V. N. Karazin, who lobbied the Foreign Ministry to assist the Slavs in 1804–7; V. B. Bronevskii, a naval officer who wrote two books arguing that Russia should use its military power to free the Slavs and lead a Slavic federation to fight any European coalition that might form against Russia; and M. P. Pogodin, a prominent professor who wrote a series of panslav memoranda to Minister of Education S. Uvarov in 1839–42. See Gosudarstvennyi arkhiv Rossiiskoi Federatsii (State Archive of the Russian Federation; hereafter, GARF), f. 1750, op. 1, d. 32; Pypin, *Panslavizm v proshlom*, pp. 76–80, 84; and Petrovich, *Emergence of Russian Panslavism*, pp. 12–13.

11. Fadner, *Seventy Years of Pan-Slavism*, pp. 12–59; and Dostoian, *Russkaia obshchestvennaia mysl'*, pp. 186–208.

12. Panslav ideas also influenced the Decembrists, whose uprising in 1825 presaged further rupture between Russian gentry society (the stronghold of monarchical support) and tsarist authority. See Dostoian, *Russkaia obshchestvennaia mysl'*, pp. 222–53.

13. Kohn, *Panslavism*, pp. 103–45; and Fadner, *Seventy Years of Pan-Slavism*, pp. 1–59, 232, 293, 337–38.

14. Kohn, *Panslavism*, pp. 103–79; Fadner, *Seventy Years of Pan-Slavism*, pp. 199–239; Dietrich Geyer, *Russian Imperialism: The Interaction of Domestic and Foreign Policy in Russia 1860–1914*, trans. Bruce Little (New Haven: Yale University Press, 1987), pp. 60–62; and Pypin, *Panslavizm v proshlom*, pp. 75–76, 145–51.

15. Geyer rejects the myth that expansion or imperialism is in the Russian "blood" and presents a more rational explanation of sources of influence on Russian imperialism. See Geyer, *Russian Imperialism*, pp. 5–84.

16. Barbara Jelavich, *St. Petersburg and Moscow: Tsarist and Soviet Foreign Policy 1814–1974* (Bloomington: Indiana University Press, 1983), pp. 168–71; and Karel Durman, *The Time of the Thunderer: Mikhail Katkov, Russian National Extremism and the Failure of the Bismarckian System, 1871–1887* (Boulder: East European Monographs, 1988), pp. 44–53, 141–46.

17. Geyer, *Russian Imperialism*, pp. 20–24, 27–31, 70–82; and Durman, *Time of the Thunderer*, pp. 6–7. On the development of the mass circulation press in Russia and its impact on drawing the broader public into Russian political discourse, see Louise McReynolds, *The News under Russia's Old Regime: The Development of a Mass Circulation Press* (Princeton: Princeton University Press, 1991).

18. Slavophilism manifested the romanticism prevailing in Russian philosophical circles in the 1820s to 1840s. Much of Russian romanticism came from Prussia, where many young Russians studied and traveled. The government of Nicholas I deemed it safer to send Russian youth to a respectably despotic Prussia than a chronically revolutionary France, where they might be infected by dangerous ideas. Two aspects of romantic thought attracted Russian intellectuals: (1) the doctrine that "every human being, country, race, and institution has its own unique, individual, inner purpose which is itself an 'organic' element in the wider purpose of all that exists, and that by becoming conscious of that purpose it is, by this very fact, participating in the march towards light and freedom"; and (2) the idea that the West was in decline because of its rationalism, materialism, skepticism, and aban-

donment of traditional spiritual values; as a result, Russia, because of its youthfulness as a nation, its raw and barbaric energy, and its lack of education (its "purity") had the greatest potential for glorious accomplishment and leadership in the future. See Isaiah Berlin, *Russian Thinkers* (New York: Penguin, 1978), pp. 119–20.

19. Some might include on this list Ivan Kireevskii's brother, Petr, and Konstantin Aksakov's brother, Ivan. But Petr Kireevskii did not make important ideological contributions to slavophilism, and Ivan Aksakov was more active as a panslav than a slavophile. See Andrzej Walicki, *A History of Russian Thought: From the Enlightenment to Marxism* (Stanford: Stanford University Press, 1979), pp. 81–111; Nicholas V. Riasanovsky, *Russia and the West in the Teachings of the Slavophiles* (Gloucester, Mass.: Peter Smith, 1965); P. Christoff, *An Introduction to Nineteenth-Century Russian Slavophilism: A Study in Ideas*, vols. 1 and 2 (The Hague: Mouton, 1961 and 1972); and Abbott Gleason, *European and Muscovite: Ivan Kireevsky and the Origins of Slavophilism* (Cambridge: Harvard University Press, 1972).

20. Philosophical and literary circles emerged in Russia in the wake of gentry liberation from compulsory service to the tsar in 1762. The Society of Wisdom-Lovers, in particular, nurtured such future slavophiles as Kireevskii and A. I. Koshelev. The Wisdom-Lovers reacted against eighteenth-century rationalism, searched for a truly "divine" philosophy, and looked to German romanticism for new truths. The society disbanded in 1825, shortly after the tsarist government crushed the Decembrist revolt, but members continued to publish their ideas in *Moskovskii vestnik*, edited by the panslav Pogodin. See Walicki, *History of Russian Thought*, pp. 74–77; Fadner, *Seventy Years of Pan-Slavism*, p. 185; and P. N. Sakulin, *Iz istorii russkogo idealizma. Kniaz' V. F. Odoevskii. Myslitel', pisatel'*, vol. 1 (Moscow: Izd. M. i S. Sabashnikovykh, 1913), pp. 138–39.

21. Chaadaev was a nobleman who served in the tsarist army and sympathized with the Decembrist movement in the 1820s. He did not join the movement but left the army in 1821. In 1823–26, he lived abroad; confirmed his sympathy for Roman Catholicism; and, in 1828–31, wrote eight philosophical letters elaborating his world view.

22. P. Chaadaev, *Philosophical Letters and Apology of a Madman*, trans. Mary-Barbara Zeldin (Knoxville: University of Tennessee Press, 1969), pp. 37, 41; and Taras Hunczak, "Pan-Slavism or Pan-Russianism," in Hunczak, ed., *Russian Imperialism*, pp. 84–85.

23. Konstantin Aksakov, *Polnoe sobranie sochinenii* (Moscow: Tip. P. Bakhmeteva, 1861), pp. 291-92; Nicholas V. Riasanovsky, "Khomiakov on *Sobornost'*," in Ernest J. Simmons, ed., *Continuity and Change in Russian and Soviet Thought* (Cambridge: Harvard University Press, 1955), pp. 185–90.

24. K. Aksakov, *Polnoe sobranie sochinenii*, p. 8. Slavophile aversion to the West came early when, as young men, Petr and Ivan Kireevskii and Aleksei Khomiakov traveled to Europe and expressed severe displeasure and disgust about the West in their notes and letters. See Riasanovsky, *Russia and the West*, pp. 60–156; Walicki, *History of Russian Thought*, pp. 93–99; and Kohn, *Panslavism*, pp. 120–21.

25. Walicki, *History of Russian Thought*, pp. 104, 97–106; and Janko Lavrin, *Russia, Slavdom, and the Western World* (London: Geoffrey Bles, 1969), pp. 71–100.

26. In Khomiakov's opinion, serfdom was the greatest social and moral evil in Russia. See Lavrin, *Russia, Slavdom*, pp. 86–100. See also Richard Wortman, "Koshelev, Samarin, and Cherkassky and the Fate of Liberal Slavophilism," *Slavic Review* 2 (June 1962):261; Fadner, *Seventy Years of Pan-Slavism*, pp. 183–84, 220–22, 236–37; and O. Smal, "The Crimean War and Slavophiles," in J. G. Purves and D. A. West, eds., *War and Society in the Nineteenth-Century Russian Empire* (Toronto: New Review Books, 1972), pp. 122–31.

27. Walicki, *History of Russian Thought*, pp. 92, 111–14; Fadner, *Seventy Years of Pan-Slavism*, pp. 19–38; and Petrovich, *Emergence of Russian Panslavism*, p. 29.

28. For background on the Crimean War, see David M. Goldfrank, *The Origins of the Crimean War* (New York: Longman, 1994) and David Wetzel, *The Crimean War: A Diplomatic History* (Boulder: East European Monographs, 1983). On the war's impact on spurring internal reform, especially the abolition of serfdom in Russia, see E. A. Berkov, *Krymskaia kampaniia* (Moscow: Moskovskii rabochii, 1939), pp. 84–93.

29. I. S. Bestuzhev, *Krymskaia voina 1853–1856 gg.* (Moscow: Izd. Akademiia Nauk SSSR, 1956), p. 160.

30. N. E. Dubrovin, *Istoriia Krymskoi voiny i oborony Sevastopolia* (St. Petersburg: Tip. Tovarishchestva "Obshchestvennaia pol'za," 1900), p. xv; John Shelton Curtiss, *Russia's Crimean War* (Durham: Duke University Press, 1979), p. 558; Berkov, *Krymskaia kampaniia*, pp. 85–87; and S. K. Bushuev, *Krymskaia voina* (Moscow: Izd. Akademiia Nauk SSSR, 1940), pp. 123–24. Russian military backwardness had roots in prevailing socioeconomic conditions. In 1855–59, fifty million of Russia's sixty million inhabitants were peasants; of these, twenty-three million were serfs on noble estates or state lands. Russia also had only 650 miles of rail, built mostly by Americans using American capital. See W. E. Mosse, *Alexander II and the Modernization of Russia*, rev. ed. (New York: Collier, 1962), chap. 1; and Nicholas V. Riasanovsky, *A History of Russia*, 4th ed. (New York: Oxford University Press, 1984), pp. 346–47.

31. Barbara Jelavich, *Russia's Balkan Entanglements 1806–1914* (New York: Cambridge University Press, 1991), p. 140.

32. Berkov, *Krysmskaia kampaniia*, p. 88; Bushuev, *Krymskaia voina*, pp. 124–25; Bestuzhev, *Krymskaia voina*, p. 169; and William C. Fuller, Jr., *Strategy and Power in Russia 1600–1914* (New York: Free Press, 1992), pp. 265–322.

33. P. A. Chikhachev, *Velikie derzhavy i vostochnyi vopros* (Moscow: Nauka, 1970), pp. 9, 50; and Bestuzhev, *Krymskaia voina*, p. 167.

34. Emphasis in original. Translation from French by the author. See Alfred J. Rieber, *The Politics of Autocracy: Letters of Alexander II to Prince A. I. Bariatinskii 1857–1864* (The Hague: Mouton, 1966), p. 105.

35. At the start of the Crimean War, for example, the slavophile Khomiakov praised the government's decision because it reflected official recognition of Russia's duty toward the Christian Slavs of Turkey. He characterized the war as a condemnation of immoral Western policy to suppress the strivings of another people. He also portrayed the war as the beginning of the ultimate triumph of slavdom and the Orthodox cause, and the spread of moral law to guide the future of mankind. He proclaimed that "human blood is precious, war is horrible—but the designs of Providence are inscrutable, and a task must be fulfilled whatever its rigors. Wave, flag! Sound, trumpet of battle! Nations! Forward to battle! God orders mankind to march on!" Quoted in Kohn, *Panslavism*, p. 132.

36. M. P. Pogodin, *Istoriko-politicheskie pis'ma i zapiski v prodolzhenii Krymskoi voiny, 1853–1856* (Moscow: Tip. V. M. Frish', 1874), pp. 279–80, 328–29.

37. All quotes by Samarin are from Iu. F. Samarin, *Stat'i, vospominaniia, pis'ma* (Moscow: Terra, 1997), pp. 74 and 77.

38. Fadner, *Seventy Years of Pan-Slavism*, pp. 195, 211–14, 222-38; Chikhachev, *Velikie derzhavy*, p. 9; and Bestuzhev, *Krymskaia voina*, p. 167.

39. M. A. Rakhmatullin, "Voiny Rossii v krymskoi kampanii," *Voprosy istorii* 8 (1972):117–18; Curtiss, *Russia's Crimean War*, pp. 555–57; Bestuzhev, *Krymskaia voina*, pp. 150, 170–71; Bushuev, *Krymskaia voina*, pp. 132–33; and Berkov, *Krymskaia kampaniia*, pp. 86–91.

40. Curtiss, *Russia's Crimean War*, pp. 552, 550–59; Chikhachev, *Velikie derzhavy*, pp. 10–11; and Rakhmatullin, "Voiny Rossii v krymskoi kampanii," pp. 117–18.

41. Curtiss, *Russia's Crimean War*, pp. 536–49; Bestuzhev, *Krymskaia voina*, pp. 166–67; Bushuev, *Krymskaia voina*, pp. 125–42; and Geoffrey Hosking, *Russia: People and Empire* (Cambridge: Harvard University Press, 1997), pp. 315–16.

42. These ideas represent the most salient elements of panslavism, although panslavs occasionally disagreed on the finer points of their ideology and how best to realize their goals. The panslavs listed here include those who were most visible in activity and influential in theory. Danilevskii was not known initially for his panslavism; he was a member of the Petrashevsky Circle, whose members were arrested in 1849 for their "subversive" socialist ideas. Katkov was a Westernizer before becoming a panslav and great power propagandist. There were other panslav sympathizers such as the writer Fedor Dostoevskii, whose panslavism is described in Hans Kohn, "Dostoevsky and Danilevsky: Nationalist Messianism," in Simmons, ed., *Continuity and Change*, pp. 500–515.

43. Pypin, *Panslavizm v proshlom*, p. 87; and Pogodin, *Istoriko-politicheskie pis'ma i zapiski*, pp. 1–14.

44. See, e.g., Luciani, *La société des slaves*, pp. 1–7; Semon Rapoport, "The Russian Slavophiles and the Polish Question," *Polish Review* 1 (April 1917), pp. 141–42; and W. Lednicki, "Poland and the Slavophil Idea," *Slavonic Review* 7 (March 1929):658.

45. Some Russian panslavs did concede at the 1867 Slavic congress in Moscow that non-Russian Slavs may incorporate into Russian parts of their own languages. See Kohn, *Panslavism*, pp. 142–43; N. P. Barsov, *Slavianskii vopros i ego otnoshenie k Rossii* (Vilnius: Tip. A. Syrkina, 1867), pp. 5–11; and Luciani, *La société des slaves*, pp. 9–29.

46. N. N. Durnovo, *Russkaia panslavistskaia politika na pravoslavnom vostoke i v Rossii* (Moscow: Tip. Russkaia pechatnia, 1908), pp. 90–107.

47. *Sochineniia I. S. Aksakova: Slavianskii vopros 1860–1886* (Moscow: Tip. M.G. Volchaninova, 1886), p. 176. See also Sarkisyanz, "Russian Imperialism," p. 71; Durnovo, *Russkaia panslavistskaia politika*, pp. 3–27; and Nikolai Barsukov, ed., *Pis'ma M. P. Pogodina, S. P. Shevyreva i M. A. Maksimovicha k Kniaz'iu P. A. Viazemskomu 1825–1874 gg.* (St. Petersburg: Tip. M. Stasiulevicha, 1901), p. 101.

48. Mikhail Katkov, "Chto nam delat' s Pol'shei?" *Russkii vestnik* (March 1863):469–76; and Hugh Seton-Watson, *The Decline of Imperial Russia 1855–1914* (London: Methuen, 1952), p. 93.

49. Pypin, *Panslavizm v proshlom*, p. 88.

50. Petrovich, *Emergence of Russian Panslavism*, pp. 103, 82–84, 97–103. Pogodin asked in a secret memorandum to Uvarov, minister of education, "Which of the Slav tribes occupies the first rank today? Which offers the best prospects for future greatness by virtue of its present state and history. . . . My heart trembles with joy. Oh, Russia, my dear fatherland! Is it not you?" See Pypin, *Panslavizm v proshlom*, pp. 88–89; Fadner, *Seventy Years of Pan-Slavism*, pp. 26–27, 319–38; and Kohn, *Panslavism*, pp. 123–28, 159–63.

51. N. Ia. Danilevskii, *Rossiia i Evropa: Vzgliad na kul'turnye i politicheskie otnosheniia slavianskogo mira k germanskomu*, 4th ed. (St. Petersburg: Izd. V. V. Kashpireva, 1895), pp. 109, 253–54, 268; *Russkaia politicheskaia mysl' vtoroi poloviny XIX v.* (Moscow: Akademiia Nauk, 1989), pp. 64–66; Walicki, *History of Russian Thought*, pp. 294–97; Robert E. MacMaster, *Danilevsky: A Russian Totalitarian Philosopher* (Cambridge: Harvard University Press, 1967), pp. 177–250; and Fadner, *Seventy Years of Pan-Slavism*, pp. 319–38.

52. Panslav views on ideal government echoed the slavophile notion of an idealized peasant commune, where there was true freedom in the local sphere and the government itself was unencumbered by people's representatives in the sphere of high politics. See I. Aksakov's letter to the Bulgarian king (in French) in *Sochineniia I. S. Aksakova*, pp. 403–4.

53. *Russkaia politicheskaia mysl'*, p. 64; see also V. K. Tereshchenko, "M. P. Pogodin v obshchestvenno-ideinoi bor'be 30–50kh godov XIX stoletiia." Avtoreferat dissertatsii (Moscow: Gos. universitet im. Lomonosova, 1975), p. 26; Walicki, *History of Russian Thought*, pp. 292–94; Fadner, *Seventy Years of Pan-Slavism*, pp. 305–38; and *Sochineniia I. S. Aksakova*, p. 345.

54. The previous quotes are from Danilevskii, *Rossiia i Evropa*, pp. 474–75; *Sochineniia I. S. Aksakova*, pp. 576–77, 761; Petrovich, *Emergence of Russian Panslavism*, pp. 257–58, 267–71, 281–82; Hunczak, "Pan-Slavism or Pan-Russianism," pp. 101–2; and Smal, "Crimean War and Slavophiles," pp. 123–26.

55. *Sochineniia I. S. Aksakova*, p. 5; Stephen Lukashevich, *Ivan Aksakov 1823–1886: A Study in Russian Thought and Politics* (Cambridge: Harvard University Press, 1965), p. 123; and Smal, "Crimean War and Slavophiles," p. 126. These perceptions of the West became especially salient after the 1848 revolutions in Europe. These disturbances, according to panslavs, symbolized Europe's decay and strengthened the panslav case for preserving centralized, conservative government in Russia.

56. Pypin, *Panslavizm v proshlom*, p. 90; Kohn, *Panslavism*, p. 114; Rossiiskii Gosudarstvennyi Voenno-istoricheskii Arkhiv (Russian State Military Archive; henceforth, RGVIA), f. 213 (Khrulev), op. 1, d. 44, p. 21; and MacMaster, *Danilevsky*, pp. 146–74.

57. Fadner, *Seventy Years of Pan-Slavism*, pp. 337–38; *Russkaia politicheskaia mysl'*, p. 19; MacMaster, *Danilevsky*, pp. 119–31; and Kohn, *Panslavism*, pp. 114, 123–29.

58. Durnovo, *Russkaia panslavistskaia politika*, p. 29. Panslavs may have had some reason to resent and beware Polish elite chauvinism, imperialism, and messianism, but their depiction of Russo-Polish relations was completely one-sided. On the imperial and chauvinistic elements of Polish elite nationalism, see Ilya Prizel, *National Identity and Foreign Policy: Nationalism and Leadership in Poland, Russia and Ukraine* (Cambridge, UK: Cambridge University Press, 1998), pp. 38–74.

59. Barsov, *Slavianskii vopros i ego otnoshenie*, pp. 17–25; and Kohn, *Panslavism*, pp. 123–28. Baltic Germans were also targets of panslav vilification, as exemplified in Samarin's journal, *Okrainy Rossii* (Russian Borderlands). In a letter to the journal in 1868, A. Kruzenshtern, an ethnic German, complained, "We [Germans] are all faithful subjects [of Russia] and not the scoundrels which you have conveniently portrayed." See RGVIA, f. 678, op. 1, d. 628.

60. Danilevskii, *Rossiia i Evropa*, p. 113.

61. *Sochineniia I. S. Aksakova*, p. 21. Panslavs believed that in the context of a crumbling Ottoman Empire, Russia should assist the emergence of friendly states based on the Christian nations that were then "subject to the sultan's sceptre." See GARF, f. 730, op. 1, d. 538, p. 40. See also Pypin, *Panslavizm v proshlom*, p. 87; Fadner, *Seventy Years of Pan-Slavism*, pp. 17 and 344–49; Petrovich, *Emergence of Russian Panslavism*, pp. 260–61; Barsov, *Slavianskii vopros*, p. 16; and Rostislav Fadeev, *Mnenie o vostochnom voprose* (St. Petersburg: Tip. departamenta Udalova, 1870).

62. The quotes in this paragraph are found in Barsov, *Slavianskii vopros*, pp. 4–12; Pypin, *Panslavizm v proshlom*, p. 89; and Kohn, *Panslavism*, pp. 118 and 159.

63. Pogodin was among those Russian intellectuals who, during and after the Crimean War, tried to find common ground at a time of national trial. He declared after the war that he was a "disappointed panslavist" who no longer sought the creation of a panslav federation, but only access for all Slavs, wherever they lived, to the same rights as other peoples of Europe. See Pogodin, *Istoriko-politicheskie pis'ma*, p. 4.

64. Pogodin was born to a serf family in the village of Nikol'skoe Galkino. One biographer records that his father spent most of his life ingratiating himself to the rich and pow-

erful. This trait influenced the young Pogodin, who sought all his life to raise his position in society and become equal with the nobility. See Tereshchenko, *M. P. Pogodin*, pp. 15–26.

65. Upon meeting the minister, he exclaimed, "What can I say about my conversations in the office of the Minister of Education? They gave me this year such gladness as I have not felt in a long time. The minister's attention to my ideas . . . is something that will never be erased from my memory." When Grand Prince Konstantin Nikolaevich commissioned Pogodin to do a short assignment in 1851, Pogodin responded, "The request of your royal highness made me as happy as I could possibly be." See Nikolai Barsukov, *Zhizn' i trudy M. P. Pogodina*, (St. Petersburg: Tip. M. M. Stasiulevicha, 1888), vol. 5, p. 206; vol. 11, pp. 488–89; and vol. 14, pp. 278–82, 341–43; Tereshchenko, *M. P. Pogodin*, pp. 15–26; and Fadner, *Seventy Years of Pan-Slavism*, p. 209.

66. *Sem'ia Aksakovykh* (St. Petersburg: Tip. M. Akinfieva i I. Leonteva, 1904), p. 43.

67. *Sem'ia Aksakovykh*, p. 43; Petrovich, *Emergence of Russian Panslavism*, p. 127; and Russian State Library (hereafter, RGB), Manuscript Division, f. 369, k. 415, ed. 19.

68. This biographer notes that Danilevskii hated the West and was ashamed of his Westernized past as a believer in Fourier and radical socialism. As a radical socialist, Danilevskii suffered four years of incarceration in Russia. Because he could not express his later hatred and anger toward the West through open aggression, he opted for chauvinist, totalitarian theorizing on Russia's relations with the West. See MacMaster, *Danilevsky*, pp. 15–116, 131–45.

69. Thomas Meininger, *Ignatev and the Establishment of the Bulgarian Exarchate 1864–1872: A Study in Personal Diplomacy* (Madison: University of Wisconsin Department of History, 1970), pp. 1–13; Iu. S. Kartsov, "Za kulisami diplomatii," *Russkaia starina* 133 (January 1908), p. 92; Rieber, *Politics of Autocracy*, pp. 106–7; GARF, f. 730, op. 1, d. 538 and f. 730, op. 1, d. 531; RGB, Manuscript Division, f. 230, k. 4389, ed. 10; and M. S. Anderson, *The Eastern Question 1774–1923* (New York: St. Martin's, 1966), pp. 163–64.

70. See the May 1876 letter of N.A. Kireev, Slavic Committee agent in the Balkans, in *Slavianskii sbornik: Slavianskii vopros i russkoe obshchestvo v 1867–1878 godakh* (Moscow: Biblioteka SSSR im. V. I. Lenina, 1948), pp. 105–10.

71. Petrovich, *Emergence of Russian Panslavism*, pp. 129–35, 142–43; Mosse, *Alexander II and Modernization of Russia*, p. 124; David MacKenzie, *The Lion of Tashkent: The Career of General M. G. Cherniaev* (Athens: University of Georgia Press, 1974), pp. xvi–115; S. A. Nikitin, *Slavianskie komitety v Rossii v 1858-1876 godakh* (Moscow: Izd. Moskovskogo Universiteta, 1960), pp. 61–62; Khrulev's correspondence with Ignatev and other notes and articles in RGVIA, f. 213 (Khrulev), op. 1, d. 1, 4, and 6–14; and GARF, f. 730, op. 1, d. 317.

72. MacKenzie, *Lion of Tashkent*, chapter 5.

73. Cherniaev attempted civilian investments while semiretired, but lost most of his assets by 1872. He then assumed a repentant attitude to see if Russian officials might take him back into military service, but they did not. In 1876, he made his final attempt to regain military glory and honor by going to Serbia, against the tsar's wishes, to lead the Serbian army against Turkey. See MacKenzie, *Lion of Tashkent*, pp. xvi–115. In a shorter piece, MacKenzie notes that Cherniaev was motivated also by genuine belief in Russia's mission to unite the Slavs, as evidenced by his declarations. A combination of belief and a desire for adventure and longing for lost military glory seemed the primary motors for Cherniaev's panslavism. See David MacKenzie, "Panslavism in Practice: Cherniaev in Serbia (1876)," *Journal of Modern History* 36 (September 1964):279–97.

74. General Rostislav Fadeev, *Shestdesiat' let kavkazskoi voiny* (Tiflis, 1860).

75. Fadeev made unsuccessful attempts to transport arms to Bulgaria during its revolt against Turkey. See V. A. Cherkasskii's letter to I. Aksakov in *Slavianskii sbornik*, pp. 161–62;

Nikitin, *Slavianskie komitety*, pp. 338–40; GARF, f. 677, op. 1, d. 1023, 1936, 355, and 476; and Fadner, *Seventy Years of Pan-Slavism*, pp. 338–42.

76. See Riasanovsky, *A History of Russia*, p. 389; and Hans Rogger, "The Skobelev Phenomenon," *Oxford Slavonic Papers* 9 (1976):46–78.

77. Richard Pipes argues that public opinion was never an important factor in Russia and the Russian "government conducted foreign policy with little regard for the realities of domestic politics." See Richard Pipes, "Domestic Politics and Foreign Affairs," in Ivo J. Lederer, ed., *Russian Foreign Policy: Essays in Historical Perspective* (New Haven: Yale University Press, 1962), p. 150. This book shows that Pipes's statement does not apply to the case of panslavism in the 1870s. For a discussion of the influence of public opinion on selective Russian foreign policy issues, see Geyer, *Russian Imperialism*, pp. 31–32.

78. Leon Stilman, "Freedom and Repression in Prerevolutionary Russian Literature," in Simmons, ed., *Continuity and Change*, pp. 424–26.

79. McReynolds, *News under Russia's Old Regime*, pp. 21–24 and charts of content analysis of various Russian newspapers on pp. 305–9; L. I. Robniakova, *Bor'ba iuzhnykh slavian za svobodu i russkaia periodicheskaia pechat'* (Leningrad: Nauka, 1986), pp. 83–84, 102; and L. I. Narochnitskaia, *Rossiia i natsional'no-osvoboditel'noe dvizhenie na Balkanakh 1875–1878* (Moscow: Nauka, 1979), pp. 41, 44.

80. MacKenzie, *Serbs and Russian Pan-Slavism*, p. 41, fn 58.

81. McReynolds, *News under Russia's Old Regime*, p. 28.

82. I. M. Bogdanov, *Gramotnost' i obrazovanie v dorevoliutsionnoi Rossii i v SSSR* (Moscow: Izd. Statistika, 1964), pp. 20–29; Reinhard Bendix, *Kings or People: Power and the Mandate to Rule* (Berkeley: University of California Press, 1978), p. 541; Martin McCauley and Peter Waldron, *The Emergence of the Modern Russian State, 1855–1881* (London: Macmillan, 1988), pp. 37–39; and Edward C. Thaden, *Russia since 1801* (New York: Wiley, 1971), p. 244.

83. For narratives and statistics on Russian urbanization, industrialization, and domestic reforms that eroded the privileged position of the gentry, see Thaden, *Russia Since 1801*, pp. 201–2; Riasanovsky, *History of Russia*, pp. 368–84, 422–24; Bendix, *Kings or People*, p. 522; G. I. Shchetinina, "Universitety i obshchestvennoe dvizhenie v Rossii v doreformennyi period," *Istoricheskie zapiski* 84 (1969):166; and V. P. Leikina-Svirskaia, "Formirovanie raznochinskoi intelligentsii v 40–kh godakh XIX v.," *Istoriia SSSR* 1 (1958):83–104.

84. Leikina-Svirskaia, "Formirovanie raznochinskoi intelligentsii," pp. 83–104; and Alan P. Pollard, "The Russian Intelligentsia: The Mind of Russia," *California Slavic Studies* 3 (December 1962):28–29.

85. I. Aksakov tells of his problems with censorship in a letter to Pogodin in November 1858 in RGB, Manuscript Division, f. Pogodin/II, k. 1, ed. 36. See also Anderson, *Eastern Question*, pp. 170–71.

86. *Moskvitianin* did make some sort of a comeback in 1851 when, under the influence of younger editors working with chief editor Pogodin, its readership increased to 1,100. See Petrovich, *Emergence of Russian Panslavism*, pp. 104–28; and Barsukov, *Zhizn' i trudy M. P. Pogodina*, vol. 11, p. 90.

87. Petrovich, *Emergence of Russian Panslavism*, p. 127; Martin Katz, *Mikhail N. Katkov: A Political Biography 1818–1887* (The Hague: Mouton, 1966), pp. 11–14; S. Nevedenskii, *Katkov i ego vremia* (St. Petersburg: A. S. Suvorina, 1888), pp. 334–39; Thaden, *Russia since 1801*, p. 234; and R. I. Sementkovskii, *M. N. Katkov: Ego zhizn' i literaturnaia deiatel'nost'* (St. Petersburg: Izd. F. Pavlenkova, 1892), pp. 33–34.

88. Wayne Dowler, *Dostoevsky, Grigor'ev, and Native Soil Conservatism* (Toronto: University of Toronto Press, 1982), p. 167. *Russia and Europe* was eventually translated into

numerous Slavic and European languages. See Fadner, *Seventy Years of Pan-Slavism*, pp. 340–41; and Thaden, *Russia since 1801*, pp. 266–67.

89. Fadner, *Seventy Years of Pan-Slavism*, pp. 304–314; Nikitin, *Slavianskie komitety*, pp. 189–90; and L. Shtur, *Slavianstvo i mir budushchego* (foreword by V. I. Lamanskii) (Moscow: Imperskoe obshchestvo istorii i drevnosti Rossii pri Mosk. universitete, 1867).

90. Nikitin, *Slavianskie komitety*, pp. 43–44, 56, 156–260; and Stanley Buchholz Kimball, "The Prague 'Slav Congress' of 1868," *Journal of Central European Affairs* 22 (1962):179–80.

91. For a comprehensive, archival account of the activities of the Moscow Slavic Committee and its branches see Nikitin, *Slavianskie komitety*, pp. 39–40; see also pp. 82–90 for an account of the friendly relations between the Moscow Committee and the Asiatic department. Although the majority of committee members were slavophile scholars of modest means, other political and prominent persons were also members—e.g., Pogodin, I. Aksakov, Katkov, Danilevskii, Ignatev, and Fadeev. See *Slavianskii sbornik*, p. 7.

92. An attempt to open a branch in Voronezh failed because of insufficient public support. Nikitin, *Slavianskie komitety*, pp. 51–56.

93. Nikitin, *Slavianskie komitety*, pp. 194–200; and *Sochineniia I. S. Aksakova*, pp. 151–52, 193.

94. Nikitin, *Slavianskie komitety*, pp. 194–209; and Kimball, "The Prague 'Slav Congress' of 1868," pp. 179–80.

95. See Nikitin, *Slavianskie komitety*, pp. 43–56, 156–260; and *Sochineniia I. S. Aksakova*, pp. 151–52, 193.

96. Some of Kovalevskii's colleagues opposed his overt panslav sympathies, leading Aksakov to complain about their attitude in a letter to Countess Antonina Bludova, lady-in-waiting to the empress. See RGB, Manuscript Division, f. 65, k. 8, ed. 1; Petrovich, *Emergence of Russian Panslavism*, pp. 104–28; and Fadner, *Seventy Years of Pan-Slavism*, pp. 1–124, 293–94. Accounts of members of the upper nobility and officials supporting panslav publications are found in *Sochineniia I. S. Aksakova*, pp. 151–52; Barsukov, *Pis'ma M. P. Pogodina*, pp. 72–82, 90; RGB, Manuscript Division, f. Cherkasskii/III, k. 4, ed. 1; and Petrovich, *Emergence of Russian Panslavism*, pp. 136–37.

97. RGB, Manuscript Division, f. Cherkasskii/III, k. 4, ed. 1; RGB, Manuscript Division, f. 120, ed. 21; GARF, f. 730, op. 1, d. 496; and Rieber, *Politics of Autocracy*, pp. 88–90.

98. See Robniakova, *Bor'ba iuzhnykh slavian*, pp. 99, 110–11, 195–96; and articles by Konstantin Leontev (conservative supporter of autocracy) and P. L. Lavrov (a socialist) in Institut Otkrytoe Obshchestvo, *V poiskakh svoego puti: Rossiia mezhdu Evropoi i Aziei* (Moscow: Logos, 1997), pp. 299–301 and 285–87. Criticism of panslavism also came later from Alexander Herzen (who wrote from London) and Vladimir Solovev, who, in the 1880s, condemned Danilevskii's ideas thus: "When one ascribes to any nation a monopoly of absolute truth, then nationality becomes an idol, the worshipping of which . . . leads first to a moral, then a material catastrophe. . . . For a true and farsighted patriotism, the most essential . . . question is not the question of Russia's might but that of Russia's sins." See Kohn, *Panslavism*, p. 178; Fadner, *Seventy Years of Pan-Slavism*, pp. 317–18; Pypin, *Panslavizm v proshlom*, pp. 89–92; Berlin, *Russian Thinkers*, pp. 82–113, 186–209; and V. S. Solovev, *Sobranie sochineniia*, vol. 5 (St. Petersburg: Izd. Tov. "Obshchestvennaia pol'za," 1901), p. 185.

99. RGB, Manuscript Division, f. 231/razd. II, k. 1, ed. 43; Petrovich, *Emergence of Russian Panslavism*, pp. 85–87; *Sochineniia I. S. Aksakova*, p. 13; and Geyer, *Russian Imperialism*, p. 71, fn. 14.

100. Geyer, *Russian Imperialism*, pp. 26–28; Bendix, *Kings or People*, pp. 536–38; and James H. Billington, *The Icon and the Axe: An Interpretive History of Russian Culture* (New York: Vintage, 1970), p. 449.

101. Shchetinina, "Universitety i obshchestvennoe dvizhenie," pp. 164–215; B. S. Intenberg, "Nachalo massovogo 'khozhdeniia v narod,'" *Istoricheskie zapiski* 69 (1961):142–48; and Billington, *Icon and the Axe*, pp. 381–95.

102. Bendix, *Kings or People*, pp. 524–25; and Geyer, *Russian Imperialism*, p. 26.

103. Thaden, *Russia Since 1801*, pp. 265–68; Nikitin, *Slavianskie komitety*, pp. 10–17; and Billington, *Icon and the Axe*, p. 379.

104. Mosse, *Alexander II and Modernization of Russia*, pp. 125–26.

105. See *Aleksandr II: Ego lichnost', intimnaia zhizn' i pravlenie* (Moscow: Galaktika, 1991), pp. 12–27; *Slavianskii sbornik*, pp. 163–66; *Rossiiskie samoderzhtsy 1801–1917*, 2nd ed. (Moscow: Mezhdunarodnye otnosheniia, 1994), p. 195; Nikitin, *Slavianskie komitety*, pp. 150–51, 328; Barsukov, *Zhizn' i trudy M. P. Pogodina*, vol. 11, pp. 239–41 and vol. 13, pp. 80–81; and the tsarevich's notes to his tutor in RGB, Manuscript Division, f. 230, k. 4405, ed. 7–9.

106. *Slaviane i Rossiia* (Moscow: Nauka, 1972), p. 9; and David MacKenzie, "Russia's Balkan Policies under Alexander II 1855–1881," in Hugh Ragsdale, ed., *Imperial Russian Foreign Policy* (New York: Cambridge University Press, 1993), p. 227.

107. See Ignatev's notes (mostly in French) to Defense Minister D. A. Miliutin, Gorchakov, and others from 1862 to 1870 in RGB, Manuscript Division, f. 169, k. 36, ed. 47; f. 169, k. 64, ed. 39; f. 169, k. 66, ed. 38; GARF, f. 730, op. 1, d. 483 and 531; Fadner, *Seventy Years of Pan-Slavism*, pp. 296–97; and Barbara Jelavich and Charles Jelavich, *Russia in the East 1876–1880* (Leiden, Netherlands: Brill, 1959), pp. 4–7.

108. Anderson, *Eastern Question*, p. 182; Petrovich, *Emergence of Russian Panslavism*, pp. 63–65; and S. K. Bushuev, *A. M. Gorchakov* (Moscow: Mezhdunarodnye otnosheniia, 1961), p. 75; Rieber, *Politics of Autocracy*, pp. 77–78.

109. Emancipation actually reduced peasant landholdings, and peasants' redemption payments amounted to three times what the state had paid the gentry for their land. See Larisa G. Zakharova, "From Reform 'from Above' to Revolution 'from Below,'" in Theodore Taranovski, ed., *Reform in Modern Russian History* (New York: Cambridge University Press, 1995), pp. 116–17; McCauley and Waldron, *Emergence of Modern Russian State*, pp. 32–33; and Keep, *Soldiers of the Tsar*, pp. 374–78.

110. *Rossiiskie samoderzhtsy*, p. 198, 194–97; McCauley and Waldron, *Emergence of Modern Russian State*, pp. 149–61; *Aleksandr II: Ego lichnost'*, pp. 20–21; Thaden, *Russia since 1801*, pp. 234–51; and Peter A. Zaionchkovsky, *The Russian Autocracy in Crisis 1878–1882*, trans. Gary M. Hamburg (Gulf Breeze, Fla.: Academic International Press, 1979), p. 48. On the subsequent development of terrorism in Russia, see Anna Geifman, *Thou Shalt Kill: Revolutionary Terrorism in Russia, 1894–1917* (Princeton: Princeton University Press, 1993).

111. Miliutin and Valuev wanted to remove Katkov as editor of *Moskovskie vedomosti* in 1866 because they objected to his panslav nationalist agitation. See *Dnevnik P. A. Valueva*, vol. 2 (Moscow: Akademiia Nauk, 1961), p. 133.

112. The straits were important not only for the defense of Russia's southern borders, but also for Russia's larger military-strategic goals and, in the second half of the nineteenth century, for transportation of Russia's grain export. See Meininger, *Ignatev and the Establishment of Bulgarian Exarchate*, pp. 1–2; and Thaden, *Russia since 1801*, p. 257.

113. For the text of Gorchakov's renunciation of the Treaty of Paris, see *Sbornik dogovorov Rossii s drugimi gosudarstvami 1856–1917* (Moscow: Gos. izd. politicheskoi literatury, 1956), pp. 103–7.

114. As proof of Slavic loyalty to Russia, panslavs touted Bulgaria's secret plan, which was never implemented, to assist Russia during the Crimean War. The journal *Russkaia beseda* declared in 1856, "In those days when all of Europe resounded with cries of frenzied enmity against us, when everyone breathed evil on us, the sole voice of empathy which we heard came from our brothers by blood, the Slavs, and our brothers by faith, the Greeks; and it was not only a voice we heard, but we saw action and acts of love, bravely defying death for their brethren's sake." See Robniakova, *Bor'ba iuzhnykh slavian*, p. 43, fn. 49.

115. Austria had lost its hegemony in Italy and been effectively expelled from German lands. To lessen its internal problems, the Habsburg monarchy, by 1867, came to terms with its most active and powerful minority, the Magyars, and the Austro-Hungarian monarchy was born. In the late 1860s, Austria-Hungary was surrounded by unified national states and, in the words of one historian, had "left only one direction in which [it] could hope to make conquests—southeast toward the Balkans." See B. Jelavich, *St. Petersburg and Moscow*, pp. 152–54.

116. For background, see B. H. Sumner, *Russia and the Balkans 1870–1880* (London: Archon, 1962); Anderson, *Eastern Question*; and David MacKenzie, *The Serbs and Russian Panslavism 1875–1878* (Ithaca: Cornell University Press, 1967).

117. Nikitin, *Slavianskie komitety*, p. 44; Vyšný, *Neoslavism and the Czechs*, pp. 9–10; Kohn, *Panslavism*, pp. 149–51; B. Jelavich, *St. Petersburg and Moscow*, pp. 258–61; and Anderson, *Eastern Question*, pp. 159–66.

118. Prince Milan of Serbia initially favored a resolution of the Herzegovina crisis through a decision by the great powers. But he could not resist the wave of domestic pressure for war against Turkey. The Serbian press agitated for action against Turkey, and even spread false reports that Russia had abandoned its alliance with Austria and was prepared to side with Slavic insurgents in a general war against Turkey. See MacKenzie, *Serbs and Russian Panslavism*, pp. 30–60; Anderson, *Eastern Question*, pp. 174–79, 184–85; Thaden, *Russia since 1801*, pp. 268–69; and B. Jelavich, *St. Petersburg and Moscow*, pp. 175–80.

119. C. and B. Jelavich, *Russia in the East*, pp. 1–10, 20; B. Jelavich, *St. Petersburg and Moscow*, pp. 177–78; and MacKenzie, "Russia's Balkan Policies," pp. 231–33.

120. Gorchakov wrote a note to Bismarck in October 1876, emphasizing Russo-Prussian cooperation on the Balkan crisis because the issue at stake was a "European" one. A. G. Jomini, chief adviser to Gorchakov, also underlined in 1876 that Russian greatness and security were "perfectly in order." What was necessary was "the development of [Russia's] internal life, her productive resources, her prosperity, her culture, her commerce, her industry—all things which require peace. Her foreign policy should thus be purely preventative and defensive." See GARF, f. 678, op. 1, d. 517; and B. Jelavich, *St. Petersburg and Moscow*, p. 173.

121. Narochnitskaia, *Rossiia i natsional'no-osvoboditel'noe dvizhenie*, pp. 50–55; Bushuev, *A. M. Gorchakov*, pp. 103–4; and MacKenzie, "Russia's Balkan Policies," pp. 231–39. The tsar's speech announcing the conference of great powers to avoid the shedding of Russian blood is in S. S. Tatishchev, *Imperator Aleksandr II: Ego zhizn' i tsarstvovanie*, vol. 2 (St. Petersburg: A. S. Suvorin, 1903), pp. 335–36.

122. MacKenzie, "Russia's Balkan Policies," p. 239.

123. *Sochineniia I. S. Aksakova*, pp. 6 and 226. This refrain echoed over and over in panslav rhetoric over the course of decades and was particularly powerful in the 1870s in such publications as Cherniaev's *Russkii mir*, Katkov's papers (especially *Novoe vremia*), and Dostoevskii's *Diary of a Writer* (1875–78). See *Slavianskii sbornik*, p. 9; Nikitin, *Sla-*

vianskie komitety, p. 327; and Thaden, *Russia since 1801*, p. 266. On some of the civic, educational, and religious activities of the Slavic Committees from 1858 to 1872, see GARF, f. 1750, op. 1, d. 72.

124. A Serb source puts this number at only 2,718. See Sumner, *Russia and the Balkans*, p. 187, fn. 1.

125. Peasant soldiers sometimes had to cover 100 *versts*, or over sixty miles, on foot to reach their mobilization depots. They also endured hardships imposed by the blunders of their own commanders. See Fuller, *Strategy and Power*, p. 325; Narochnitskaia, *Rossiia i natsional'no-osvoboditel'noe dvizhenie*, pp. 24–28 and 40–41; Nikitin, *Slavianskie komitety*, p. 320; O. A. Yakovlev, "Russko-turetskaia voina 1877–1878 gg. i russkoe obshchestvo." Avtoreferat dissertatsii (Leningrad: Gos. univ. im. A. A. Zhdanova, 1980), p. 10; RGVIA f. 261 (Monteverde), op. 1, d. 18; and GARF f. 1750, op. 1, d. 82.

126. A. L. Narochnitskii, ed., *Rossiia i natsional'no-osvoboditel'naia bor'ba na Balkanakh 1875–1878* (Moscow: Nauka, 1978), pp. 15–16, 25.

127. *Sochineniia I. S. Aksakova*, p. 216.

128. *Sochineniia I. S. Aksakova*, p. 248; see also pp. 213–63.

129. Nevedenskii, *Katkov i ego vremia*, pp. 362–68; MacKenzie, *Serbs and Russian Panslavism*, pp. 56–57; MacKenzie, *Lion of Tashkent*, pp. 118–50; Nikitin, *Slavianskie komitety*, pp. 272–73; and RGB, Manuscript Division, f. 120, n. 21, kniga 3-ii (letters to Katkov; see especially Aksakov's letter of 27 March 1877).

130. P. Apostol'skii, *Nravstvennye osnovy nastoiashchei voiny* (Moscow: Tip. universitetskaia, 1877), p. 16; P. N. Kadilin, *Griadushchee zavershenie voinoiu 1914 g. istoricheskogo prizvaniia Rossii v roli osvoboditel'nitsey i glavy slavianskogo mira* (Kharkov: Tip. Mirnyi trud, 1914), p. 1; and Robniakova, *Bor'ba iuzhnykh slavian*, pp. 227–28.

131. Narochnitskaia, *Rossiia i natsional'no-osvoboditel'noe dvizhenie*, pp. 37–38.

132. RGVIA, f. 261, op. 1, d. 15; and Narochnitskaia, *Rossiia i natsional'no-osvoboditel'-noe dvizhenie*, p. 29.

133. The blood-red edition of *Novorossiiskii telegraf* reportedly sold twenty thousand copies, significantly higher than the average. See McReynolds, *News under Russia's Old Regime*, pp. 73, 81–84.

134. MacKenzie, *Serbs and Russian Panslavism*, pp. 56–57; Sumner, *Russia and the Balkans*, p. 115; and Narochnitskii, *Rossiia i natsional'no-osvoboditel'naia bor'ba*, pp. 10–11.

135. Slavic Committee activities in 1875–78 included the creation in Paris of an International Committee to Aid the [Slav] Rebels, supervised by G. Veselitskii-Bozhidarovich, a Russian of Herzegovinian origins. Veselitskii gave "eyewitness" lectures to the nobility in Russia to solicit their help for the Slavic cause, while Countess Bludova helped him set up meetings at court. P. A. Monteverde, a Spanish correspondent for *Russkii mir* in the Slavic lands, lobbied the Foreign Ministry to aid the uprisings. See Nikitin, *Slavianskie komitety*, pp. 271–92; and RGVIA, f. 261 (Monteverde), op. 1, d. 15.

136. MacKenzie, "Russia's Balkan Policies," pp. 229–33. Ignatev, on his own initiative, had encouraged two small uprisings in Bulgaria earlier and was never reprimanded by his superiors. See Anderson, *Eastern Question*, pp. 163–66.

137. D. A. Miliutin, *Dnevnik D. A. Miliutina 1873–1875* (Moscow: Tip. Zhurnala "Pogranichnik," 1947–1950), vol. 2, p. 56; and Narochnitskaia, *Rossiia i natsional'no-osvoboditel'noe dvizhenie*, p. 42.

138. M. Domontovich, *Obzor russko-turetskoi voiny 1877–1878 gg. na Balkanskom poluostrove* (St. Petersburg: Gosudarstvennyi tip., 1900), p. 2.

139. See *Slavianskii sbornik*, pp. 10–12, 105–20; MacKenzie, *Serbs and Russian Panslavism*, p. 135; GARF, f. 1750, op. 1, d. 83, d. 107, d. 378, and d. 420; and McReynolds, *News under Russia's Old Regime*, pp. 83–84. For more detail on panslav activity among workers,

peasants, church folk, merchants, and other sectors of the population, see Narochnitskii, *Rossiia i natsional'no-osvoboditel'naia bor'ba*, pp. 62, 78–79, 84, and Izmail M. Grigoriev, "Uchastie narodov srednego Povolzh'ia v natsional'no-osvoboditel'noi bor'be iuzhnykh slavian v period vostochnogo krizisa 1875–1878 gg." Avtoreferat dissertatsii (Kuibyshev: Kuibyshevskii gos. pedagogicheskii institut im. Kuibysheva, 1978), pp. 10–12.

140. In the first ten months of solicitation, the Moscow Committee received only 151,458 rubles in donations. The next four months after that, donations increased to more than 590,000 rubles. The St. Petersburg Committee collected 800, 000 rubles in the same period. *Sochineniia I. S. Aksakova*, pp. 226–27; and Anderson, *Eastern Question*, pp. 186–87. On financial and religious assistance to the Slavs, see GARF, f. 1099 (Filippov, T. I.), op. 1, d. 987–93; and RGVIA, f. 261 (Monteverde), op. 1, d. 15.

141. *Peterburgskaia gazeta*, 11 February 1877, quoted in McReynolds, *News under Russia's Old Regime*, p. 85. A list of fatalities among Russian volunteers is found in GARF, f. 1750, op. 1, d. 125, pp. 2–22.

142. One document records that up to five thousand people came over two days to bid farewell to twenty-five officers who were leaving to join Cherniaev. See RGVIA, f. 261, op. 1, d. 48; Narochnitskii, *Rossiia i natsional'no-osvoboditel'naia bor'ba*, pp. 15–16; Domontovich, *Obzor russko-turetskoi voiny*, p. 3; GARF, f. 1750, op. 1, d. 83; GARF, f. 1750, op. 1, d. 321, pp. 6–7; and Geyer, *Russian Imperialism*, p. 72.

143. Nikitin, *Slavianskie komitety*, pp. 7–8 and 329.

144. MacKenzie, *Serbs and Russian Panslavism*, p. 109; Bushuev, *A. M. Gorchakov*, pp. 99–103; Anderson, *Eastern Question*, pp. 189–93; and Nikitin, *Slavianskie komitety*, p. 296.

145. At this time, the aged Gorchakov had become too incapacitated to thwart Ignatev's influence. See RGB, Manuscript Division, f. 230, k. 4405, ed. 7–9; and C. and B. Jelavich, *Russia in the East*, pp. 4–7.

146. *Rossiiskie samoderzhtsy*, p. 207.

147. RGVIA, f. 261, op. 1, d. 56; and MacKenzie, "Russia's Balkan Policies," pp. 232–33.

148. Miliutin supported war only after he was assured that Great Britain and Austria-Hungary would not fight against Russia. See MacKenzie, *Lion of Tashkent*, pp. 118–50; C. and B. Jelavich, *Russia in the East*, pp. 14–15; A. G. Jomini's notes in GARF, f. 678, op. 1, d. 451; and A. Pidhainy, "Miliutin as War Minister: Reforms and Foreign Policy," in Purves and West, eds., *War and Society*, pp. 147–48.

149. RGVIA, f. 12651, op. 1, d. 1284, pp. 35–39; Geyer, *Russian Imperialism*, p. 73; and Narochnitskii, *Rossiia i natsional'no-osvoboditel'naia bor'ba*, p. 10. Key panslav influences on the empress included her ladies-in-waiting, Countess Bludova, a friend of Pogodin, and A. F. Tiutcheva, daughter of F. Tiutchev and wife of Ivan Aksakov. Other women from the upper nobility were active in Slavic causes, as evident in their membership in the Ladies' Section of the Moscow Slavic Committee. These women boasted names typical of great Russian nobility (Golitsyna, Bariatinskaia, Morozova, Obolenskaia, Naryshkina, Trubetskaia, Cherkasskaia, and Shcherbatova) and the most prestigious addresses in Moscow. The empress and other members of the royal family helped finance some of the educational activities of the Slavic Committees. See GARF, f. 1750, op. 1, d. 6; Ignatev's note to Alexander II in GARF, f. 430, op. 1, d. 538; and Nikitin, *Slavianskie komitety*, pp. 40–42.

150. Nikitin, *Slavianskie komitety*, pp. 295–96.

151. On the irrationality (measured in terms of objective interests) of the Russian decision to go to war in 1877, see Geyer, *Russian Imperialism*, pp. 33–48; and A. Bikash Roy, "Intervention across Bisecting Borders," *Journal of Peace Research* 34 (1997):303–14.

152. K. P. Pobedonostsev, *Pis'ma k Aleksandru III* (Moscow: "Novaia Moskva," 1925), pp. 55–58.

153. Some highlights of Russian intervention on behalf of Slavs and Orthodox subjects of the Porte were (1) a war against Turkey in the period 1768–74, which allowed Russia to gain access to the Black Sea for its trade vessels; (2) Russian assistance to a Serbian uprising against Turkey, and another Russo-Turkish War in 1806–1813—Serbia gained internal autonomy as a result; (3) Russian assistance to the Greek national revolution in the 1820s; (4) a Russo-Turkish War in 1828–29, which helped Greece gain some autonomy; and (5) Russian aid to an anti-Turkish uprising in Herzegovina in 1862. See Anderson, *Eastern Question*, pp. 156–63; Narochnitskaia, *Rossiia i natsional'no-osvoboditel'noe dvizhenie*, pp. 3–10; Robniakova, *Bor'ba iuzhnykh slavian*, pp. 86–93; Pypin, *Panslavizm v proshlom*, p. 75; Nikitin, *Slavianskie komitety*, pp. 25–35; Thaden, *Russia since 1801*, pp. 264–81; MacKenzie, "Russia's Balkan Policies," pp. 222–23; and MacKenzie, *Serbs and Russian Panslavism*, pp. 1–28.

154. Anderson, *Eastern Question*, pp. 164–67; and *Slavianskii sbornik*, p. 8.

155. Hosking, *Russia: People and Empire*, pp. 373–74.

4

Toward the Last Gasp of a Dying Order: Great Power Nationalism, 1905–1914

[The] Slavic question is first and foremost a national question. Interest in the Slavs is interest in nationalism and, thus, interest in our Russian national consciousness. In this context, the growth of Russian interest in the Slavs means the rebirth of Russian national feeling and the rise of Russian patriotism—the decline of which has [led us toward] . . . mental vacillation and the pursuit of cosmopolitan dreams. We see the new emergence of interest toward the Slavs as a sign of the imminent and complete victory of Russian national roots over all those teachings which have splintered our lives and contradicted the very soul and history of the Russian nation.

—P. A. Kulakovskii, 1909

It is high time to recognize that there is only one path toward a Great Russia: we must direct all our energies to that area which is genuinely open to the active influence of Russian culture. That area is the entire Black Sea basin, or all the European and Asian countries bordering on the Black Sea.

—P. B. Struve, 1908

Slavs of all countries, unite!

—A. F. Rittikh, 1908

Everywhere is betrayal and cowardice and lies.

—Tsar Nicholas II, 1917

PERILOUS TIMES IN A WEAKENING STATE

R ussia defeated Turkey in the Russo-Turkish War, but military victory did not
fulfill the dream of a glorious panslav alliance under the imperial wings of the
Russian eagle. Instead, the other European powers—unwilling to sanction Russian dominance in the Balkans—annulled many Russian and Slavic war gains at
the Congress of Berlin in 1878. The conclusion of the war also ended official Russian support for panslavism. Worried by the impact of unprecedented public
mobilization, the government closed down the Moscow Slavic Committee; curtailed the activities of the St. Petersburg, Kiev, and Odessa Committees; and exiled
panslav leader Ivan Aksakov and banned him from publishing in 1878–80.[1]

In 1881, the terrorist campaign of the People's Will (*Narodnaia volia*) succeeded
in its third attempt to assassinate Alexander II. Swearing to end "revolutionary
anarchy" in the country, the new tsar, Alexander III, launched a policy of reaction,
which sought to restore stability in the state. He revived the official principles of
Autocracy, Orthodoxy, and Nationality,[2] and sought national consolidation
through russification rather than panslav adventurism. In 1894, Alexander III
died and his son, twenty-six-year-old Nicholas II, came to the throne. The young
tsar, weak-willed and reluctant to govern,[3] faced numerous challenges to the
authority of his government and, in 1917, was forced to abdicate the throne.
Despite rising internal instability, Russia's last monarch never relinquished belief
in his divine right to rule and the myth of harmonious relations between the
benevolent tsar and his loyal peasant subjects. Dominic Lieven concludes that the
emperor, indeed, "was very far removed from Russian realities and somewhat dis-
inclined to allow mere empirical evidence to spoil his vision of the harmonious
and trusting relationship between the tsar and his people."[4] In contrast to the
tsar's beliefs (which were reinforced by officials devoted to autocratic rule), Russian society was increasingly discontented over political, social, and economic
issues. The educated and urbanized sector demanded greater political participation; peasants clamored for more land; workers struggled for better working conditions; and the landowning nobility insisted on protection of their traditional
status and privileges. Peasant disturbances, workers' strikes, and terrorist acts
became commonplace under Nicholas II, signifying the alarming gap between
ruler and people, and the weakening hold of the state on society.[5]

The year 1905 was a watershed for Nicholas II and Russian autocracy. During
"Bloody Sunday" in January, government troops killed 130 peaceful demonstra-
tors (and bystanders) as they marched to petition the tsar for, among other things,
constitutional reform. Three months later, Russia suffered a major defeat in the
battle of Tsushima Strait, heralding St. Petersburg's ignominious surrender to the
Japanese in the Russo-Japanese War. These events and others intensified internal
and external pressure[6] for political reform to avert a revolution. Capitulating partially, the tsar issued the October Manifesto, granting civil liberties to all Russians,
announcing the creation of a Duma with genuine legislative powers to pass or
reject all proposed laws (for the first time in Russian history!), and promising the
institution of a new order—a constitutional monarchy—in Russia. The manifesto

"set the stage for the open struggle of political concepts and institutions in Russia," particularly issues arising from conflicting principles of the old autocratic order and new ideas of popular sovereignty and political participation.[7]

In the context of national humiliation, occasioned by Russia's defeat in the war with Japan, and internal distress, caused by challenges to the autocratic order, nationalism once again rose to the fore in Russia. Although several variants of nationalism were propagated in the period 1905–14, great power nationalism (with a strong panslav element) eventually became dominant and had an impact on Russia's decision to go to war on behalf of Serbia in 1914. It emphasized ethnic Russian criteria for defining membership in the nation, preached a hegemonic and imperialist self-image, and proposed a threefold national mission: (1) to strengthen and preserve the Russian state, in an imperial and semiliberal form; (2) to shift the focus of Russian foreign policy from the Far East to its historical home—Europe and the Balkans; and (3) to restore Russia's prestige and great power status by assisting Slavs in Turkey and Austria-Hungary in their struggle against imperial rule and by seeking control of the Black Sea straits. The national mission as articulated by great power nationalists had aggressive implications for Russian foreign relations because it was oriented toward changing the international status quo and put Russia in a trajectory of conflict against the powers that ruled over Slavic minorities. Eventually, the ideas of great power nationalists had a direct impact on Russian foreign policy. When international crises confronted Russia in 1914, a domestically weakened regime (experimenting for the first time with mass politics) grasped at great power nationalism as an ideology to bolster unity at home and rejuvenate power abroad. By 1914, proponents of great power nationalism had helped create a "climate of opinion wherein war against Germany and Austria-Hungary [on behalf of brother Slavs] appeared an acceptable and indeed necessary instrument of policy."[8]

Some historians argue that great power nationalism shaped Russian foreign policy because the ruling regime, fearful of losing legitimacy and internal control at home, was compelled to take nationalism into account in its decision making. Nationalism arose primarily from the ranks of "civil society" or a politically articulate public that sought to dilute the power of autocracy and strengthen the voice of the people. Others underline the breakdown of Russia's "united government" (a functioning, semiconstitutional monarchy) in 1907–14 as the prime reason for the impact of nationalism.[9] This chapter supports these views, but highlights international threats and crises as key precipitating factors that pushed nationalism to the forefront of Russian foreign policy.

PANSLAVISM RETREATS, OFFICIAL "NATIONALISM" ADVANCES, 1878–1905

In the three decades after the Russo-Turkish War of 1877–78, no nationalist ideology approximated the phenomenon of panslavism, which briefly united state and society in agreement over the character and purposes of the Russian/Slavic nation. Several domestic and international factors contributed to the decline of panslavism.

Reaction and Russification under Alexander III and Nicholas II, 1881–1905

Alexander III (1881–1894) reasserted autocratic control over Russian domestic and foreign policy decision making, which, under his father, had become diluted with unofficial and societal influences. As tsarevich, Alexander III had shown sympathy for panslavism, but he realized subsequently that the Balkan national liberation movements that preceded the Russo-Turkish War and the assassination of his father were frightening harbingers of potentially fatal dangers to Russian autocracy. National liberation movements could infect the multiethnic subjects of the empire and threaten state disintegration, while political assassinations and other such disturbances could bring closer the demise of the state by revolution. Therefore, after acceding to the throne, the tsar sought to suppress mass politics, terrorism, and revolution. In international affairs, he focused on avoiding foreign entanglements and renewed and strengthened Russian ties with fellow monarchies in Germany and Austria-Hungary.[10]

Alexander III's reactionary rule halted most of the liberal reforms begun by his father and severely restricted the sphere of autonomous civic activity that had facilitated the impact of panslavism. Officials blamed reforms under the previous regime for undermining state authority, cohesion, and order and leading to the chaos, confusion, and terror that culminated in Alexander II's assassination.[11] Through the "Temporary Regulations" of 1881, Alexander III gave broad powers to government officials to control individuals and groups who might, in any way, threaten imperial authority. These powers included summary search, arrest, imprisonment, exile, and trial of persons suspected of subversion. The tsar also launched "counterreforms," including censorship of the liberal and radical press, abolition of university autonomy and the rights of students to form organizations,[12] and curtailment of the powers and autonomy of *zemstvos* or local organs of government.[13]

A second domestic factor contributing to the decline of panslavism was the resurgence of state-sponsored nationalism. Under the tutelage of the reactionary Konstantin Pobedonostsev,[14] Alexander III revived "Autocracy, Orthodoxy, and Nationality" as the basis of the Russian state. Under the principle of Nationality, officials implemented policies to strengthen cohesive governance within the empire, especially cultural russification.[15] Discriminatory measures were taken against non-Russians and non-Orthodox subjects of the tsar, and the political autonomy of regions such as Finland was severely curtailed. The overarching goal of russification was less to create a Russian "nation" in the sense of a homogenized population on whom political authority rested than to facilitate and deepen imperial rule and administration in regions with non-Russian populations.[16] The salience of state-sponsored Nationality and "official" nationalism shrank the space that was formerly available to panslavism as a form of nationalism from below.

Third, Alexander III selected new officials who had little or no sympathy for panslavism. Like the tsar, new ministers and advisers in court rejected panslavism because they saw external entanglements on behalf of "oppressed Slavs" as extremely destabilizing for autocracy. Among these new figures were Pobedonostsev, who advocated strong central authority, eschewed radical change, and favored one religious creed for Russia; Foreign Minister Nikolai Giers, a cautious career diplomat who favored traditional great power diplomacy and the "avoidance of all useless and ill-conceived complications" in foreign policy;[17] and Chief of the General Staff Nikolai Obruchev, who disliked panslavism and its anti-German policy prescriptions.[18] Previously influential panslav officials such as Nikolai Ignatev saw their stars wane. Public opinion condemned Ignatev for Slavic losses at the Congress of Berlin, and the tsar dismissed him as minister of internal affairs in 1882. Ignatev lost practically all influence in public and official circles thereafter.[19]

Russian military and financial weakness after the Russo-Turkish War also made further support of panslavism infeasible and undesirable. Russia's finances were catastrophic in 1878 (when its national debt stood at 4.9 billion rubles) and did not begin to recover until the 1880s. As War Minister Dmitrii Miliutin commented in 1878, Russia had to yield to the conditions imposed by the great powers in Berlin because it could not fight another war—this time probably with Turkey, Great Britain, and Austria-Hungary. He noted, "[our] military forces were so dissipated by war, so weakened, that we could not have hoped for any probability of success."[20]

In the first half (1894–1905) of Nicholas II's reign, panslavism continued to be weak for the same domestic reasons as during his father's reign. Reactionary policies dominated, particularly while Pobedonostsev remained in court, convincing Nicholas II that Russia must preserve autocratic absolutism at any cost. Any concession to mass politics, parliamentarism, or constitutionalism, Pobedonostsev warned, would be a betrayal of the tsar's sacred duties. The government continued to enshrine Official Nationality as the authorized variant of nationalism and to focus on internal stabilization through conservative politics.[21]

The Congress of Berlin and Its Aftermath:
Russia's Foreign Relations, 1878–1905

Russia's foreign relations also contributed to the decline of panslavism. Foremost was the souring of relations between Russia and its Slavic allies after the Russo-Turkish War. The war ended with the Treaty of San Stefano, characterized as the "fullest practical expression ever given in Russian foreign policy to the panslav ideal."[22] The treaty created an enlarged autonomous Bulgarian state tributary to the Turkish sultan; tripled Montenegro's territory; granted formal independence to Serbia, Romania, and Montenegro; outlined reforms in Turkish rule of Bosnia-Herzegovina; and stipulated a huge war indemnity for Turkey to pay (primarily in territorial concessions to Russia). These were substantial gains for panslavism, but they were stripped by the Western powers in

Berlin. The Congress of Berlin and its aftermath deeply disappointed the Slavs, who had counted on Russian ability and willingness to defend their interests. Slavic resentment simmered against Russia and the other European powers who ignored the opinions, interests, and other input of Slavic representatives in Berlin.[23] After Berlin, Russian influence among the Slavs remained chiefly in Bulgaria, whose interests St. Petersburg did defend at the congress. But by 1886, even Bulgaria slipped out of the Russian orbit. A pro-Austrian ruler came to the throne and most of the Bulgarian elite opted for distance from Russia, whose overbearing policies they had come to resent.[24]

The renewal of the Holy Alliance of three empires—Germany, Russia, and Austria-Hungary—in 1881 was also detrimental to panslavism. Partly as a result of this alliance, Vienna and St. Petersburg agreed on a modus vivendi that lasted until 1903, dividing the Balkans into spheres of influence and respecting the status quo in the region. Austria-Hungary's sphere of influence included Serbia, Montenegro, and Bosnia-Herzegovina, while Russia's encompassed Bulgaria and Romania. The other powers cooperated on maintaining the Balkan status quo, thereby avoiding a repetition of regional crises that helped empower panslavism in Russia in 1875–78. While the Balkans were relatively quiescent, imperialist competition heated up in the Far East from the 1890s to the early twentieth century. Russia, like other imperial powers, shifted its expansionist policies to the Far East and, until its defeat in the Russo-Japanese War, St. Petersburg's foreign policy focused on commercial and other imperial opportunities in China, Manchuria, Korea, and indirectly, Japan.[25]

Finally, St. Petersburg's focus on industrial development and economic expansion also drew attention away from the Balkans and panslavism. During the tenure of Finance Minister Serge Witte from 1892 to 1903, in particular, Russia pursued an aggressive policy of tariff protection; monetary stability and financial reform; heavy taxation; and vigorous encouragement of foreign investment, especially from France and Belgium. The Russian economy grew at an average rate of 8 percent annually, and, by 1900, Russia caught up with the other powers (except the United States) in railway construction. The Balkans did not occupy a central place in Russia's foreign relations during this period of intensive economic development. Russian trade with the Balkan Slavs was negligible, no Russian banks operated in the Slavic lands, and Russia did not construct railroads to link it directly with its erstwhile Slavic allies.[26]

WAR, NATIONAL HUMILIATION, AND THE NATIONALIST REACTION

The Russo-Japanese War, 1904–1905

As in 1856, when ignominious defeat in the Crimean War stimulated aggressive nationalist rhetoric in Russia, so defeat by Japan in 1905 provoked a strong nationalist reaction among sectors of the Russian elite. The war began in February 1904 when Japan, after judging that its negotiations with Russia over spheres of influence in Manchuria and Korea would not yield preferred outcomes, attacked an unsuspecting Russian fleet at Port Arthur on the Liaotung Peninsula. Although St. Petersburg had been building up its military forces in the Far East, it was unprepared to resist the Japanese onslaught. Russian forces found themselves in a disastrous war—one in which they suffered defeat after defeat by the Japanese enemy, or the "yellow peril."[27] The Japanese military besieged and captured Port Arthur, pushed the Russian army north into Manchuria, and ultimately destroyed the Russian navy in the Far East. Two particularly humiliating moments for Russia came, first in February and March 1905, when a slightly inferior Japanese army (in numbers of men and guns) took the offensive and defeated a 330,000-strong Russian force south of the city of Mukden. Nearly one hundred thousand Russian soldiers were killed, wounded, or captured, and General A. N. Kuropatkin, commander of the Russian army in the Far East, decided to retreat. The second incident occurred in May 1905, when the Japanese annihilated the Russian Baltic Fleet, which included antique vessels ("self-sinkers") and newer ships that had never properly completed their trials and whose crews were not fully trained to work together. The fleet had traveled for months to get to the Far East and was sunk in the Straits of Tsushima in only two days![28]

Russian humiliation in the Russo-Japanese War stemmed from psychological and tangible causes. It marked the first time that an Asian country, considered a minor power at the time, routed a major European power, causing a psychological shock to Russian society. The articulate public, especially by means of the mass press, expressed shame about Russia's disgraceful conduct of the war. As one eyewitness recorded:

> Impatience, feelings of resentment, indignation—these grew everywhere and became stronger. With each new defeat, with each new retreat to "previously prepared positions" in "accordance with prior plans," indignation grew more intense and there took shape a mood of protest. There was no malicious joy. Oh no! There was a feeling of burning shame and undeserved injury.[29]

The effects of defeat would be felt in the decade after 1905, as the words "Tsushima" and "Mukden" became "terse evocations in public opinion of the state's inability to fulfill even the most basic functions."[30] Time and again, critics of tsarist authority would use these words to denounce the tsar and his cabinet for failing adequately to defend Russian prestige and interests.

Like the Crimean War, the Russo-Japanese War highlighted the incompetence of tsarist authorities. Successive military defeats revealed glaring deficiencies among the Russian higher command and the army itself, and illuminated huge gaps between policies taken at home and realities in the theater of war. Reports of military inadequacies surfaced, including from Russian military officers, and contrasted with reports of superior Japanese performance.[31] Discontent and anger rose among the articulate public, which interpreted Russian defeats as incontestable proof of government incompetence. Many held tsarist authority accountable for the catastrophe in the Far East, and society became increasingly irate and frustrated at the government's conscription of volunteers and its inattention to public opinion and concerns. Never at any point did the war elicit great public enthusiasm or support, and few understood the state's interests in such far-flung territories as Manchuria.[32]

Russia's tangible losses both during the war and after the signing of a peace treaty in Portsmouth, New Hampshire, in August 1905, were another cause of humiliation. Commenting on the treaty, Aleksandr P. Izvolskii, who became foreign minister in April 1906, declared that the

> conditions of peace . . . bore very lightly on Russia; the Japanese renounced all demands of a nature that would affect the vital interests or the dignity of the Russian empire; Russia paid no war indemnity; retained her fleet and lost not an inch of her national territory . . . [save] the southern part of the island of Saghalien [Sakhalin].[33]

Notwithstanding this public posture, and despite the fact that the Portsmouth treaty did include conditions that were more moderate than Japan's original demands, Russia nonetheless suffered significant human, territorial, and economic losses. Four hundred thousand soldiers were either killed or wounded in the war, naval assets worth a quarter of a billion rubles were lost, and two and a half billion rubles were spent to finance the war. St. Petersburg lost its forward positions in Korea and China, and was forced to recognize Japanese dominance in Korea. Russia also had to relinquish leasing rights to the Kwantung Peninsula and yield trading ports and its naval base at Port Arthur; it surrendered southern Sakhalin and all Russian government property on the territory; granted Japan the rights to fish in Russian territorial waters in the Far East; and gave the southern Manchurian railroad to Japan.[34]

Reaction to National Humiliation

Russian defeats in 1904 to 1905 radicalized the moderate liberal opposition to tsarism and inflamed revolutionary fever inside Russia.[35] In October 1904, the Union of Liberation, which grew from the moderate *zemstvo* movement, called for the first time for constitutional rule in Russia. *Zemstvo* leaders also held a congress in November 1904 in St. Petersburg and issued an eleven-point resolution, which openly challenged the tsarist government by calling for broader civil rights, an end to arbitrary arrests, democratization and expansion of local self-government, and an elected national assembly. Merchant groups, the Moscow City Council (Gorodskaia Duma), and other public organizations echoed the call for civil rights and rule of law. Representatives of the revolutionary opposition, specifically, the Social Revolutionaries and their sympathizers from among Russia's national minority groups, met in Paris and called for the overthrow of autocracy and the establishment of representative government. The massacre of "Bloody Sunday" in 1905 prompted bitter comments about how "our brave soldiers could shoot a defenseless crowd with greater accuracy and zeal than they could the Japanese."[36]

Mass protests, agrarian disturbances, workers' strikes, and terrorist acts buffeted the government of Nicholas II during the war with Japan and in the wake of defeat. After Tsushima, in particular, numerous *zemstvo* congresses met in Moscow, intensifying the popular clamor against tsarism and autocracy. Discipline in the military became severely strained, as evidenced by a mutiny of sailors who commandeered the vessel *Potemkin* from the Black Sea Fleet and fled to Romania. A prominent figure in the Ministry of Foreign Affairs recorded in his diary that

> internal confusion has created Herculean proportions of anarchy, and the government's prestige has plummeted lower than at any other time in Russian history. . . . [After Tsushima], disorder and chaos reigned as never before. Nobody knew or understood what went on inside the tsar's head. . . . Prince Lamzdorf said that the sovereign is showing signs of mystical delusion: he believes that matters may be bad now, but they will soon settle down. What can one say to this? Nothing! The Russian people [*narod*] will perish, if it does not soon take matters into its own hands.[37]

In September 1905, a general strike paralyzed large swathes of the economy and prompted the tsar to sign the October Manifesto. This measure failed to assuage public demands or remove the threat of revolutionary chaos. Indeed, after the October Manifesto and into the early part of 1907, civic unrest continued and military units came to the aid of civilian authorities more than eight thousand times.[38]

Besides the new and frequent assertiveness of public opinion and anti-official civic activism, national humiliation in 1905 also elicited nationalist rhetoric emphasizing the restoration of Russian power. Although most of this rhetoric may be more appropriately characterized as assertive than outright aggressive, nonetheless basic ideas were articulated that would later feed a more dangerous variant of great power nationalism. At the forefront were members of the Union of October 17 (the Octobrists), an organization that represented that wing of the liberal movement that had a "traditional, intimate connection with tsarism."[39] The Union had chapters across the empire and was influential among the liberal landowning gentry and the capitalist entrepreneurial class. These sectors carried a sense of self-importance in Russian politics and stability (i.e., constituting a growing civic society) and were shaken by Russia's defeat in the Japanese war and by revolutionary danger at home. They supported government reform for the sake of peace and sought the restoration of Russian national pride and prestige. After 1905, many Octobrists preached a nationalism reasserting Russian imperial might and greatness. In presenting the group's program in 1906, Octobrist leader A. Guchkov noted,

> We cannot relate ourselves negatively to what was created by old Russia. We thought that the greatness of Russia, her glorious name, which had been disgraced in Manchuria, had to be restored, renewed, and carried over to the new Russia.[40]

Joining the Octobrists in articulating a defiant and hegemonic nationalism were Moderate Nationalists and some members of the constitutionalist Kadet party.

Other political elites representing the military, the diplomatic corps, and the tsar himself sought to rise from the Japanese humiliation by preaching that Russia still had a "historic mission and interests" as a great power in Europe, that it still had "sacred obligations" to defend Orthodox peoples and "fellow tribesmen" in the Near East, and that it could fulfill these obligations not by relying on international agreements "but solely by means of the struggle and the presence of well-armed forces." In the meantime, because Russia was militarily weak, it must temporarily retrench from expansionism, rebuild its internal capabilities and, in Foreign Minister Izvolskii's words, be prepared to act when complications arise in Europe "or else . . . be in the position of a half-forgotten Asian power."[41] In the military, some reformers reacted to the 1905 defeat by denying the authority of the tsar, claiming that the highest loyalty of the military should be to the nation, and advocating mass mobilization and mass patriotic indoctrination of the population.[42]

The phenomenon of *ressentiment*, explained in chapter 1, had some bearing on the nationalist reaction of Russian elites to their country's national humiliation. Although Russian elites did not salve their hurt pride by widely demonizing the victorious Japanese, they nonetheless displayed an exaggerated sense of superiority and denial as a means to aggrandize their own status at a time of humiliation. Some argued that Russia could have won the war with Japan if only St. Petersburg had not prematurely decided to end hostilities. In fact, they noted, St. Petersburg ended hostilities just as morale was sinking in the Japanese army and the war was turning in Russia's favor! General Kuropatkin, commander of the Russian army in Manchuria, urged that Russia prepare for a new war that will be fought "not only with the army, but with the whole of a patriotic nation," and urged his compatriots to think beyond defeat:

> Our great nation has issued renewed and strengthened from still heavier trials, and let us not doubt now but that Russia, summoned by the Tsar to a new life, will quickly recover from the temporary blows which she has sustained, and will not fall from her high place among the other nations of the world.[43]

In a similar vein, others denied that Russia's great power status had diminished due to the Japanese defeat. In 1905, for example, V. Doroshevich, a prominent publicist, protested against an Englishman's assertion that Russian power and prestige had been shaken "from the Bosporus to the Pacific Ocean, from the Polar circle to the Himalayas . . . and beyond the Himalayas, in India." Doroshevich argued that just as British colonial defeat at the hands of "some shepherds" in the Boer War did not mean the end of Britain as a great power, neither did Russian defeat at the hands of the Japanese spell the demise of Russian might and prestige.[44] As long as Russia was a geographically large country, it would always be counted among the great powers.

THE RESURGENCE OF NATIONALIST IDEAS: THREE VARIANTS

Although an assertive great power nationalist rhetoric among Russian elites arose in the wake of national humiliation, it was not the only variant of nationalism propagated in 1905–14. At least two other strands of nationalist ideology were discernible: neoslavism[45] and rightist nationalism.

Neoslavism

Neoslavism originated among Czech and Slovak subjects of the Habsburg Empire and became salient in Russia in the years 1908 to 1910.[46] Outside Russia, neoslavism engendered a political movement that, under the leadership of the russophile Czech Karel Kramar, aimed to bring about the unity and predominance of Slavic peoples, particularly within the Austro-Hungarian Empire. Neoslavs deemed this goal realizable only with assistance from Russia.

Neoslavs used race and nationality as the prime criteria for membership in the Slavic nation. Unlike their panslav predecessors in the late nineteenth century, they did not accord religion a central role in determining national identity. In fact, they fully accepted Catholic Poles, Czechs, and Croats as equals with Orthodox Serbs, Russians, and other Slavs.[47] Neoslav criteria for membership in the nation located neoslavism in the camp of ethnic nationalism; however, any aggressive implications of using ethnicity to define insiders and outsiders to the nation were muted by the neoslavs' nonchauvinist, "live-and-let-live" self-image and non-imperial, status quo–oriented definition of the national mission.

The self- and other-image of neoslavs emphasized equality among Slavic peoples and shunned hegemony by any group, particularly the Russians. Neoslavs in Russia declared that the "time of exclusive russophilism had passed"; that the dream of Russian hegemony among the Slavs was unrealizable because Russia "lagged too far [from the position] of a European hegemon"; and that Russians should not assume a "big brother" role.[48] The issues of "freedom, equality, and brotherhood" among all Slavs were so central to neoslavism that one of its erstwhile supporters, Pavel Miliukov, advocated independence for Poland and Russo-Polish rapprochement. Prince G. N. Trubetskoi, at one point a sympathizer of neoslavism, also declared,

> In the name of the feeling of national honor and love of country, we must be full of respect for the Poles and for every other nationality. We must make the Poles citizens of our great empire and grant them the same rights as Russian citizens, the right to be taught and administered in one's own language, the right of local self-government and freedom of religion.[49]

Neoslavs did not reserve equal treatment only for Poles, but for all nationalities within the Russian empire. They were concerned about Russia's internal political, economic, and psychological backwardness and advocated liberal-constitutional principles as a means of modernizing Russia and overcoming its backwardness relative to western Europe.[50] They identified Germany as the chief danger to Slavic aspirations and to the European balance of power. Polish neoslavs, for example, accepted Russo-Polish rapprochement as the only effective way to counter the German threat.[51]

To Russian neoslavs, the national mission[52] included fostering Slavic cultural union and political solidarity in European politics; supporting Slavic aspirations for cultural and political autonomy within the Austro-Hungarian Empire and in Russia; defending Russian national interests, particularly in the Balkans; and maintaining the European balance of power by forging a Slavic alliance against a rising German power. Neoslavs did not preach the need to create one Slavic state led by Russia, neither did they show a strong preference for using military means to carry out the national mission. Domestically, they saw their purpose as creating a constitutional-liberal political order and equal relations among nationalities in the Russian empire. In their view, such changes would modernize Russia and increase its power internationally.[53] The nonexpansionist and inwardly oriented character of the neoslav national mission made this ideology fairly benign for Russian international relations.

Rightist Nationalism

Purveyors of rightist nationalism[54] belonged mainly to the Union of the Russian People (URP or *Soiuz russkogo naroda*), Russia's most politically successful rightist organization. The URP claimed to speak for all "true Russians" and, at the height of its prominence, boasted over one thousand branches and a membership of between two hundred thousand and three hundred thousand. Led by Aleksandr I. Dubrovin, a physician and staunch supporter of monarchy, and V. M. Purishkevich, a landowner, government official, and member of the Duma, URP supporters included representatives of the lower class, the aristocracy, Orthodox clergy, and the intellectual sector. They defined membership in the nation chiefly in ethnic terms—only ethnic Russians were bona fide members of the nation. "True Russians," moreover, were those whose loyalty for "tsar, faith and fatherland," or "Autocracy, Orthodoxy, and Nationality was unwavering."[55]

Rightist nationalists painted the Russian self-image in terms of a united people living harmoniously within the sacred order of autocracy. Echoing slavophile thought, they claimed that the benevolent Russian tsar and his people always lived in mutual affection and trust and in mutual compliance with specific duties and obligations. This internal peace and harmony disintegrated only when Peter the Great introduced Western ideas and Western ways that corrupted Russia's pure traditions and destroyed the harmony between tsar and people. Russia was also the preserver and defender of the true Orthodox faith, suffering more for Christ than any other people. Further, Russia was a benign ruler over other peoples because it allowed non-Russians in the empire to keep their national features (*narodnost'*).

In portraying outsiders, rightist nationalists subscribed to blatantly anti-Western, rabidly anti-Semitic, and unabashedly chauvinistic views. They blamed internal enemies for turmoil and chaos in Russia, particularly revolutionaries, radical constitutionalists (i.e., the Kadets, whom Dubrovin labeled as "bearers of moral leprosy"), and Jews. Among these enemies, rightists hated Jews the most and accused them of conspiratorial designs against Russians and the Russian state. "Jews" encompassed not only concrete people but countless, faceless, unseen "others" who undermined Russian welfare. One member of the URP even described Russia as a battleground between good and evil, with "evil" being personified by Westernized constitutionalists who wanted to undermine autocracy. Lurking behind these constitutionalists were Jewish money (*zhidovskie den'gi*) and traitorous Jews who desired to enslave the Russian people and the world. Rightist animosity toward Jews resulted in forceful methods for dealing with the Jewish "problem." The URP and its armed wing, the Black Hundred, conducted anti-Semitic pogroms, sponsored the assassination of prominent Jewish figures, and promoted widespread demagogic rhetoric that fueled and justified violence against Jews.[56]

Rightist nationalists also castigated other non-Russians in the empire, including Poles, Finns, Muslims, and Armenians, who resisted Russian dominance and who, in the rightists' opinion, were egregiously ungrateful for the benefits they had received from Russian rule. Rightists advocated "Russia for the Russians," and believed that Russians deserved more rights than other nationalities in the empire because they were responsible for creating the state in the first place. They believed that Russia must wage a national struggle against non-Russian traitors, particularly "Pole-papists" on Russian soil. They prescribed russification and Orthodox missionary work as cures for anti-Russian tendencies and particularist aspirations among the empire's ethnic minorities.[57]

Rightist nationalism had clearly aggressive implications for relations between ethnic Russians and non-Russians within the empire and promoted violence among Russia's multinational population. But, in one sense, this ideology was unlikely to bring Russia in direct conflict with other powers and therefore did not have aggressive implications for foreign policy. Specifically, domestic persecution of Jews, Finns, Poles, and other non-Russians was unlikely to lead to military intervention by outside powers. Moreover, the rightists' definition of the national mission included an isolationist foreign policy. They wanted to preserve the Russian empire's territorial integrity, restore internal stability, defend the autocracy, and revive Russian traditions and religious values. To accomplish these goals, they advocated launching a popular crusade on behalf of tsarism and creating an organization to nurture patriotism throughout Russia. Rightists rejected ideas of panslav solidarity and saw Russian intervention on behalf of non-Orthodox Slavs as a self-immolating policy. N. N. Durnovo argued, for example, that Russia should support the Orthodox peoples of the Near East but discard the "chimerical idea of panslavism" because fraternal love was impossible between the Russian Orthodox and Pole-papist, or between the Catholic Croat and Orthodox Serb. Russia must also beware of opportunists and traitors like the Bulgarians, who had proven how panslavism would "gobble the [Russian] national treasure [and] splatter Russian blood," while those whom Russia protected would never deign utter a word in Russia's defense. But in another sense, rightist nationalism did have aggressive implications for Russian international behavior. Its strong xenophobic and chauvinistic content, one can argue, could very easily feed an imperial and militarist foreign policy under certain circumstances.[58]

Great Power Nationalism

The tenets of great power nationalism are best expressed in two sources. One is the writings of Petr B. Struve, a leading Kadet and prominent publicist, especially two articles in the journal *Russkaia mysl'* (Russian thought), which Struve edited from 1907 to 1917.[59] Another is the work of traditional panslavs, published in *Slavianskie izvestiia* (Slavic news), the organ of the St. Petersburg Slavic Committee, and elsewhere.[60] The rudimentary political parties that supported great power nationalism disagreed on many issues of domestic political organization and principles. However, in foreign policy, they concurred on Russia's need to fortify its great power standing, extend its imperial reach, and augment its influence over historical Slavic allies in the Ottoman and Austro-Hungarian Empires. Great power nationalists took an old idea, panslavism, to justify an expansionist and imperialist foreign policy, retargeting the Balkans after Russia's defeat in the Far East.

Struve (who was active in Russian politics until 1908)[61] and his sympathizers supported the institution of constitutional-liberal politics in Russia, coupled with an imperialist foreign policy to bolster Russian state power. They defined the nation in both civic and ethnic terms, including cultural, linguistic, and territorial criteria. The nation included Russians, other Slavs, and national minorities living within the Russian empire. Although Struve favored closer ties among the Slavs, he was more directly concerned with Russian state power than with the creation of a Slavic federation or altruistic assistance to Slavic liberation struggles.

In his formulation of the Russian national self- and other-image, Struve emphasized the idea of *velikaia Rossiia* or an imperial, Great Russia.[62] The nation was inextricably connected with a mighty state; indeed, the state was the expression of the nation, its unifier, and its most powerful ally. Together, state and nation fulfilled man's ineradicable religious need to belong to a body larger and more permanent than himself. Every state had its "own supreme law of existence," and, in Russia's case, that law required Russians to aspire to "free and organic hegemony," "assimilatory growth," and the general pursuit of power.[63] Struve believed that autocracy must be preserved, albeit in a reformed version, because it was the most beneficial type of government for Russia. Any belief that the masses themselves would direct Russian politics in a positive direction was naive and mistaken. State stability required a strong political hierarchy able to pursue external power because without external power, Russia could not survive. The laws of history demanded that weak states, particularly those unable to project power outside their borders, must become victims of their neighbors' appetite for expansion. Thus, for example, in the name of state power and to the dismay of his radical liberal colleagues, Struve in 1904 urged Russian students to rally behind the tsarist army in its war with Japan.[64]

Struve criticized the West, but favored the adoption of moderate Western-style liberal politics, developmental capitalism, and individual initiative. He identified Germany and Austria as threats to Russian and Slavic aspirations, but acknowledged the possibility of coexistence with them. He advocated nonviolent assimilation of non-Russian nationalities within the empire but acknowledged that the territories of Finland and Poland were unlikely ever to be assimilated. Therefore,

Russia should allow Finns and Poles to use their own language in schools, in the courts, and in the *zemstvos*, but rule out political independence because these peoples were "indivisibly connected with the Russian empire."[65] While Struve entertained liberal treatment for Poles and Finns, he took a more chauvinistic stance toward Ukrainians and Jews.[66]

Struve's definition of the national mission had aggressive implications for Russian foreign policy. He emphasized increasing the power of the state through hegemonic and imperial actions, and, unlike those who believed that Russia should shun foreign adventurism to focus on internal order, he believed that imperialism was needed to strengthen cohesion at home. Russia would accomplish its national mission, first, by liberalizing, but not eliminating, the autocratic order. Some measure of reform was needed to strengthen collaboration between state and society. Toward this end, Russia should undertake such policies as improved treatment of its Polish population. This would increase internal cohesion and enhance Russian prestige and credibility among Slavs in Austria-Hungary, who were critical of Russian treatment of its Poles. Russia must reconcile with Poland and grant civil rights to Poles and other nationalities to foster unity within the imperial state. The Russian government also ought to increase the educational level of the masses, protect Russian culture, and emphasize Russian as the linguistic basis of an all-Russian imperial culture. With cohesion strengthened at home, Russia would be prepared to pursue its goals abroad.[67]

Second, Russia must shift its foreign policy focus from the Far East to Europe, and establish cultural, economic, and military hegemony in the Balkans. As Struve argued in 1908,

> Our Far Eastern policy was the logical culmination of the whole foreign policy of Alexander III, when *reactionary* Russia, from lack of true statesmanship turned away from the Near East. The main fallacy of the foreign policy which led us to Tsushima and Portsmouth was that it transferred its center of gravity to a region inaccessible to the real influence of Russian culture. . . . Now it is time to recognize that for the creation of a Great Russia there is only one road: to direct all our forces to the area which is genuinely open to the influence of Russian culture. That area is the *whole Black Sea basin*: that is, all the European and Asian countries bordering on the Black Sea.[68]

Finally, Russia must prevent German and Austro-Hungarian expansion in the Balkans by forging Slavic unity and alliance.

Proponents of panslavism[69] supported Struve's great power nationalism, but they added Orthodoxy as a criterion for membership in the nation. Thus, panslavs continued to malign Poles and other Catholics as traitors to the Slavic cause, and on occasion even asserted that Poles were not members of the Slavic race at all. For instance, the newspaper *Rossiia*, articulating a panslav idea, argued in 1908 that

> except for their language, [Poles] have nothing in common with the other Slavs. . . . They are Slav-speaking foreigners. . . . In the interests of Slavdom the Poles must remain at the mercy of Russia, and anything that Russia does with them in her own interests will be advantageous to [all] Slavdom.[70]

Panslavs, like Struve, portrayed Russia as a hegemonic state and a great power with natural rights to expand territorially and exert "moral, economic, and political influence" abroad. Many no longer spoke of a Slavic federation under Russian rule, but advocated Russian leadership in preserving the Orthodox religion and liberating Slavs who remained under Habsburg or Turkish rule. They also argued for the primacy of the Russian language among all Slavs. In comparing slavdom with the West, they underlined Russian and Slavic spirituality and organic cohesion as qualities superior to Western egotism, materialism, and chaotic pluralism.[71] Finally, they defined the national mission as preserving the unity and great power status of the Russian empire, protecting the rights and privileges of Russians living in the empire's borderlands, and fulfilling Russia's duty to liberate the Balkan Slavs and bring to fruition the "natural" state of Slavic solidarity. Some panslavs acknowledged that their kin in the Balkans, once liberated, might not want to be ruled by Russia but prefer a federation of their own. This was acceptable because, if Russia assisted the birth of such a federation, the Slavs would look to it "with a grateful memory" and be ready to advance Russian interests in return.[72]

FOREIGN POLICYMAKING AND RUSSIAN PUBLIC OPINION

The clearest impact of great power nationalism on Russian foreign policy occurred in 1914. This impact became possible with the backdrop of new mass politics in Russia and continued advances in education and the mass press.

Russia's Experiment in Constitutional Politics, 1905–1914

The tsar's Manifesto of October 1905 marked a fundamental departure from traditional autocratic politics. The creation of a Duma with genuine legislative powers paved the way for the beginning of pluralist politics. Different groups could organize in coalitions, propagate diverse and opposing political ideas, and participate in competitive elections. Although the Duma was not completely representative or democratic (especially the third Duma), it became an important institution for the articulation of Russian public opinion. Between 1906 and 1917, there were four Dumas in Russia. Radical constitutionalists, peasants, and revolutionaries implacably hostile to tsarism dominated the first two Dumas, but these were promptly dissolved by the tsar. The first Duma worked only from April to July of 1906 and the second from February to June of 1907. In 1907, under the tenure of Prime Minister Petr Stolypin,[73] a new electoral law was instituted. Recognized bitterly by tsarism's opponents as a coup d'état because it reasserted the throne's historic rights over the newly promulgated legislative powers of the Duma, this law (known also as the System of 3 June 1907) manipulated eligibility requirements for voting, restructured Russia's electoral districts, and changed other rules to ensure that the majority of elected members of the Duma would be loyal to the government. Stolypin's ploy worked: the third Duma had an absolute majority consisting of Octobrists, Moderate Rights, and Nationalists, illustrating how Russia's engineered electoral rules favored "the propertied and titled . . . Russians and Orthodox over other nationalities and faiths . . . and the more 'trustworthy' elements—the conservative and reactionary."[74] The Octobrists, who represented the majority liberal wing in the third Duma, were reformers who also supported the continuation of tsarist rule in Russia.

The political spectrum in the Duma included extreme Left and Right factions. The extreme Left included Social Democrats and Social Revolutionaries, many of whom were heirs of the terrorist organization People's Will. They supported the propagation of revolutionary ideas, the overthrow of the tsarist regime, and the introduction of a socialist order in Russia.[75] The Right and extreme Right or *pravye*, encompassed "parties, leagues, unions or circles which professed a dedication to the historical principles of Autocracy, Nationality, and Orthodoxy and whose members seemed inspired by the fervent wish to return to the *status quo ante* of a less contentious, less frustrating period of Russian history in which every political impulse had come from above."[76] The *pravye* subscribed to Russian chauvinism and cultural russification, and were hostile to the development of representative government.

At the center of the political spectrum were the Octobrists, Kadets,[77] Moderate Rights, Nationalists, and others. The Octobrists and Kadets favored a constitutional political order in Russia and sought to bind the tsarist regime to its promises of civil rights and freedoms in the October Manifesto. Unlike the Kadets, however, who sought a dissolution of the monarchy, the Octobrists were members of the loyal opposition and were ready to cooperate with the tsarist government led by Stolypin. The Moderate Rights and Nationalists (the latter was a party formed in 1909 by members of the Moderate Rights), like the Octobrists, were allies of the government. Many of them were landowning gentry from Russia's western borderlands. They wanted to use the Duma to strengthen the monarchy and preserve the privileges of native Russians, who were competing against Jews and Poles in the hinterlands.[78]

The Duma became a powerful institution in the development of a public opinion that challenged autocracy's exclusive prerogative of defining the national interest or the ends of Russian foreign policy. The press could report anything that was spoken in Duma sessions, no matter how subversive, "since in effect they were merely passing on what was contained in the official stenographic reports."[79] Together with increasing education and advances in the mass press, public opinion became a strong factor with which tsarist authority had to contend in making its foreign policy.

Mass Press and Mass Education

Advances in mass press and mass education were also an important part of the context within which great power nationalism came to influence Russian foreign policy. These advances made possible the dissemination of great power nationalism and the cultivation of public opinion in its favor. Although Nicholas II's government tried to censor the press, especially when it infringed on foreign policy issues, he nonetheless made concessions beginning in 1905.[80] The press became freer than ever before, becoming an outlet for practically every type of political opinion. Newspapers like I. D. Sytin's *Russkoe slovo*, which aspired to a "truly Russian" voice and sold the most copies on the street, helped increase civic consciousness through their coverage of social and political issues. Other newspapers followed this approach, as evidenced in the amount of space they devoted to political issues. The number of Russian dailies multiplied from 125 in 1900 to 856 in 1913, while the circulation of newspapers with political content also increased. *Russkoe slovo*, for example, increased its circulation from 100,000 in 1906 to one million by 1917.[81]

Progress in mass education continued a process that began in the late nineteenth century. In 1897, the census estimated Russia's educated elite to number approximately 726,000 out of a population of 129 million. Among these were the "active intelligentsia," numbering about 50,000 in the early twentieth century and playing a powerful role in defining the content of social debate in the late imperial period. Further, literacy, the number of institutions of primary and secondary learning, and the number of students in elementary schools all increased dramatically between 1897 and 1914. For example, rural primary schools run by the *zemstvos* increased from 13,129 in 1894 to nearly 45,000 by 1914; similar schools run by the Ministry of Education also increased from 964 in 1894 to nearly 22,000 in 1914. By the early twentieth century, the effects of increased mass education throughout Russia included a new secularization of national identity (i.e., less emphasis on the Orthodox Church as a hallmark of Russianness) and new attitudes challenging traditional authority in the households and villages.[82]

PROPAGATING GREAT POWER NATIONALISM, 1905–1914

The backdrop of constitutional politics, greater literacy, and political journalism facilitated the dissemination of great power nationalism. Yet great power nationalism gained salience in a relatively uneven process in the period 1905–14, with high points coinciding with international crises in 1908–10 and 1912–14. The final and most dramatic impact of great power nationalism was in 1914, when it clearly influenced policymakers' decision to go to war on behalf of Serbia as a Slavic ally.

In 1905–14, great power nationalist ideas, particularly those advocating the merits of panslav activism, circulated in history textbooks, Russian thick journals and newspapers, commemorative books and albums on the Russo-Turkish War of 1877–78, and Slavic conferences and congresses. Some themes emphasized were Russian pride vis-à-vis western Europe, the selfless heroism of Russians who fought for the Slavs in 1877, and the common purpose of Russians and other Slavs.[83] Before 1908, most discussions of panslav ideas were cultural and academic, and panslav gatherings with explicit political purposes were kept secret.[84]

But in May 1908, St. Petersburg hosted "Slavic Week" in preparation for the Prague Slav Congress in the summer of 1908. Czech delegates to "Slavic Week" exchanged political views with members of the tsarist government and the Duma. Other Slavic congresses subsequently transpired, with Russian support and participation, in St. Petersburg in 1909 and Sofia in 1910. But these congresses had no palpable impact on the political advancement of great power nationalism.

Great power nationalists and panslavs also wrote for many publications, including *Novoe vremia, Russkaia mysl', Russkie vedomosti, Moskovskii ezhenedel'nik, Moskovskie vedomosti, Golos Moskvy, Slovo, Okrainy Rossii, Utro Rossii,* and *Russkaia molva. Novoe vremia* was the most influential of these, with a circulation of 150,000 in 1911–14. Among its top publicists was Vasilii V. Rozanov, a philosopher and patriot who preached Russia's predestination to greatness under any and all circumstances. Its editorials emphasized great power policy, patriotism, sacrifice for the state and nation, and moral satisfaction through national prestige. It preached that Russian glory depended on Russian chauvinism within the empire and support for the Slavic cause outside. Nicholas II allegedly read *Novoe vremia* daily, and many in the military called it their favorite publication.[85]

Publications that favored great power nationalism to one extent or other—including *Golos Moskvy* (1906–15); Struve's *Poliarnaia zvezda* (closed in 1906); *Moskovskii ezhenedel'nik* (closed in 1910); *Russkaia mysl'* (especially in 1908–14); P. A. Kulakovskii's *Okrainy Rossii* (1906–12); the Octobrist organ *Slovo* (1905–9); the Progressists' paper, *Utro Rossii* (1909–16); *Slavianskii mir* (1908–11); and *Slavianskie izvestiia* (1903–16)—were not uniformly popular or long-lived. Some closed down due to mediocre public patronage, while others ran afoul of censorship.[86] Public associations also played a role in disseminating great power nationalism. The St. Petersburg Slavic Committee and the Society of Russian Borderlands, for example, sympathized with great power nationalism and helped keep active ties between Russians and Slavs. Other organizations that worked along these lines included the Galicia-Russia Society, the Society for Slavic Culture in Moscow, the Society for Slavic Scholarship in St. Petersburg, the Society for Slavic Mutuality, and discussion groups including a circle led by Struve and financed by wealthy Muscovite merchants.[87] But before 1914, neither these associations nor the mass press could claim an impact on official Russian policy.

Among official institutions, the Duma was where great power nationalism became most prominent. Many legislators were vocal nationalists and panslavs who used the Duma as a pulpit for their ideas. In the first Duma in 1906, for example, academician M. M. Kovalevskii suggested that the legislature should declare its sympathy for the small Slav nations and encourage greater inter-Slavic cooperation. He argued that Russian democracy entailed the duty of protecting all Slavs who had aspirations for freedom. In 1907 and later, Kadet, Octobrist, and Moderate Right newspapers and journals also emphasized the primacy of Russian interests in the Balkans and the Black Sea straits, and many deputies were members and supporters of organizations that favored closer ties between Russians and Slavs. These deputies participated at panslav meetings and congresses. The Russian delegation to the Prague Congress in 1908, for example, was led by V. A.

Bobrinskii (Nationalist), V. A. Maklakov (Kadet), and N. N. Lvov (Progressist). In the 1910 congress in Sofia, most of the Russian delegates came from the St. Petersburg Slavic Committee and the Duma; among them were P. A. Kulakovskii, D. Bergun, V. A. Bobrinskii, G. V. Komarov, and A. Guchkov.[88] During "Slavic Week" in St. Petersburg in May 1908, the Duma also accorded a warm reception to visiting Czech delegates and invited them to a Duma debate to witness how the new political order functioned in Russia. But support in the Duma for great power nationalism did not translate into official policy. In other key institutions—the court, War Ministry, and Finance Ministry—few voices actively supported panslav or aggressive nationalist ideas before 1913. In the military, only a portion of a few hundred politicized officers after 1905 were sympathetic to panslav ideas.[89]

TOWARD 1914: INTERNAL CHAOS, EXTERNAL CRISES

The evolution of great power nationalism before 1914 was uneven and its influence among official circles sporadic and weak. But in 1914, the impact of nationalism became possible, chiefly because a severely weakened government found aggressive nationalism irresistible as an ideology for strengthening state legitimacy and restoring a semblance of national unity in the face of international threats and crises. Russian political discourse, which continued to be steeped in an imperial definition of the state, also contributed to the empowerment of great power nationalist ideas.

Russian Political Discourse: Continued
Affirmation of the Imperial State

The period 1905 to 1914 saw a lively political discourse about domestic reform and Russia's place in the world. Some of the most serious criticism ever of the imperial state—especially of its hegemonic and interventionist foreign policy—emerged. For example, liberal, rightist nationalist and socialist publications including *Russkoe slovo, Grazhdanin, Russkoe znamia, Zemshchina*, and *Russkoe bogatstvo* questioned imperial foreign policy and disparaged costly Russian adventurism on behalf of unworthy Slav allies. V. M. Doroshevich, writing for the popular liberal paper *Russkoe slovo*, characterized the Serbs as children who needed to grow up. When the Balkan Slavs requested Russian assistance in the Balkan League War against Turkey (1912–13), Doroshevich echoed Minister of Finance Witte in saying that "nobody here, no serious thinker, is interested in these vain and restless Balkan peoples who are not really Slavs but badly baptized Turks."[90]

Others asserted that panslav demands for the protection of Slavic rights abroad were unrealistic and hypocritical because the civil rights of Slavs and other minorities were constantly violated within Russia itself. Still others accused panslavs of falsely claiming to speak for society when their positions did not accurately represent the views of the Russian masses. They rejected claims that a "progressive" foreign policy on behalf of persecuted Slavs would increase Russian internal cohesion, and cited the Russo-Turkish War (1877–78) as evidence of panslav activism's failure to bring about unity or progressive measures at home.[91] A few officials sympathized with these views—for example, Baron R. Rosen in the Foreign Ministry in 1912 (former Russian ambassador to the United States) and P. N. Durnovo, minister of internal affairs. Rosen insisted that Russia's mission was not in Europe but in the development of Siberia, and that the idea of a Russian panslav mission would create an unnecessary and dangerous conflict with Austria-Hungary, whose dominance in the western Balkans did not threaten Russian national interests. Durnovo, meanwhile, wrote memoranda to the tsar highlighting the potential dangers of panslav and anti-German policies.[92]

Criticism of the imperial state—especially a few myth-busting arguments against the panslav component of great power nationalism—indicated a new independence and assertiveness in Russian civil society (especially as embodied in the mass press). But despite its advances, civil society did not wield decisive influence in the prevailing structures of Russian politics and decision making.[93] Those who retained the highest authority—the tsar and his government—did not fundamentally question the state's imperial organization or hegemonic foreign policy as the basis of Russian prestige and greatness. The official decision to retrench from foreign activism appeared as but a *temporary* accommodation to *temporary* Russian weakness, not a more permanent reorientation of the supreme value placed on the imperial state.

The guardians of political discourse in Russia did not articulate strong alternatives to imperial Russian foreign policy. In 1907–14, both the liberal and conservative mass press focused a tremendous amount of attention on civil rights, land reform, workers' rights, self-government, and other reforms to diminish the power of autocracy and increase the rights of society. But their coverage attacked only the internal aspect of empire; a similar passion against the external elements of empire was missing. Among political figures, Struve and his supporters advocated prominent changes in the internal empire (e.g., autonomy for the Poles and Finns), but pushed resolutely for a continuation of the external empire lest Russia lose its claim to greatness.[94] The military, an important socializing institution, actively tackled military reform after Russia's defeat in the Far East, and the first independent military newspaper in the Russian empire appeared in 1906. Many voices in the military advocated military and political reform and put forward ideas for improving mass patriotism. Here, too, the predominant issue was not to redefine Russia's greatness as an imperial power, but to revise internal autocratic incompetence in order to rebuild a more effective army.[95] In Russian political discourse as a whole, no effective advocates emerged for a non-imperial foreign policy as a viable and desirable foundation for long-term Russian international relations. Within Russian political discourse, the imperial state and a hegemonic foreign policy remained key pillars of Russian greatness.

Great power nationalism, because it was intimately tied to vivid memories of Russia's role as liberator of the Slavs in the nineteenth century, and especially in the war against Turkey in the 1870s, fit easily with Russia's ongoing imperial state paradigm. It resonated, for example, with the generation that still recalled the unfairness of the Congress of Berlin in 1878, when Russia and its Slavic allies were denied the benefits they felt they had rightly won in war.[96] Great power nationalists used symbols and rhetoric that bolstered the predominant idea of Russia as an imperial state. Describing Darwinian images of struggle between great and small powers, they argued that the great ones would inevitably swallow the small ones. As Stolypin argued in the Duma in 1907, "nations (*narody*) that forget about their national tasks will perish. They will be transformed into dung and fertilizer, which other, stronger peoples will use to grow, expand, and gain even greater strength."[97] Proponents of great power nationalism also emphasized the symbol of Russia as the "Third Rome" and heir to Orthodox Byzantium, whose divine calling required selfless sacrifice. By "saving" the "long-suffering Slavs and opening . . . for them the path to a new life," for example, Russia would fulfill its spiritual calling, preserve its own statehood, and accomplish a mission that was superior to the materialism of the West.[98] Finally, nationalists referred to Russia's mythic wars, including the Russo-Turkish War of 1877, as the basis of Russia's historical position as a great power. The use of war as a symbol of Russian state identity, power, and triumphalism fit well with the continuing positive view of the imperial state and appealed to those who sought a path for Russian victory over humiliation and internal turmoil.[99]

Impending Meltdown: The Erosion of Internal Governance

Weakening and Fragmentation of Political Authority

The period 1905–14 was one of severe erosion of internal governance in Russia, showing just how temporary the stability created by Alexander III's policy of reaction actually was. The concept of popular sovereignty (i.e., that political legitimacy stemmed from the "people" or "nation" [*narod*]) continued to challenge autocracy as the keystone of Russian government. The rift between state and society that had grown in the nineteenth century continued to widen in the early twentieth century. Opposition to tsarism in the first and second Dumas, for example, proved implacable, and even some members of the landed nobility—the conservative mainstay of tsarist support—converted to constitutionalism.[100]

The rift between Russian state and society resulted in large part from Nicholas II's inability to fathom the gravity of changes transpiring in his country. He considered the throne a burden, yet never relinquished the mystical and fervent belief that he, as autocrat, was ordained to be Russia's ruler; that autocracy was best for Russia's welfare; and that the "simple folk" (*prostoi narod*) would remain devoted to their tsar. Even after his October Manifesto, Nicholas II acted as if no major change had occurred in Russian politics. He surrounded himself with conservative-reactionary advisers who reinforced his misperceptions and biases about how Russia should be governed. In addition, he succumbed to the reactionary influence of his wife and the depraved peasant Grigorii Rasputin, who pursued his own personal, lascivious interests while convincing the empress that he could heal her hemophiliac son, tsarevich Aleksei. Rasputin's presence and perceived influence at court contributed to the degradation of autocratic legitimacy in the eyes of society.[101]

The divide between tsar and society widened even more after the 1911 assassination of Stolypin, who, as prime minister, had sought to find an accommodation with Russian public opinion and changing political attitudes. After Stolypin, Nicholas II selected advisers who staunchly reinforced his general unresponsiveness to political demands from below. Not only were the tsar and his closest entourage incompetent in dealing with changes in society, but the tsar himself was so infused with lassitude as a ruler that he often responded to domestic problems by taking longer vacations.[102]

The fragmentation of political authority and political elites after 1905 muddled official policy and decision making, and created opportunities for nationalist public opinion and civic activism to gain a new prominence. The divided nature of political authority was rooted in part in the Fundamental Laws of 1906, which decreed the Council of Ministers, led by the prime minister, as the official center of Russian executive power. The Laws, however, deprived the council of jurisdiction over the ministers of defense and foreign affairs, who continued to answer to the tsar, and over the tsarist court itself. In foreign policy, the tsar handed most of the initiative to Prime Minister Stolypin (whose office did not legally encompass foreign policy) and to Foreign Ministers Izvolskii and Sazonov (1906–11), leading to dual lines of authority and communication. The Fundamental Laws also granted the Duma budgetary powers, but not over the 40 percent of the state budget allocated to the army, navy, state loans, and imperial court. The tsar further sought to emasculate the Duma by revising the role of the State Council, a conservative body in favor of retaining the monarchy. The State Council, half of whose members were elected and half appointed by the tsar, originally had a strictly advisory function; but the tsar transformed it into an upper legislative house with the same powers as the Duma and gave it authority to annul Duma decisions. Besides duplicating the Duma's powers in the State Council, the tsar further diluted legislative authority by granting himself power to announce Duma sessions; disband the Duma (as long as dates for new elections were announced); veto Duma legislation; and, in case of emergency and when the Duma was not in session, issue decrees that would have the status of law. The Fundamental Laws further stipulated that government ministers were to report directly only to the tsar, but the Duma, through its power of interpellation, could also summon ministers for questioning.[103]

Thus, the new Russian "constitutional order" inaugurated in 1906 was rife with confusion of authority and functions.[104] Those who opposed the tsar felt that he had violated the spirit of the October Manifesto, especially because of strictures he imposed on the Duma. The instability of state structures worsened when the tsar dissolved the first two Dumas, even while his own Council of Ministers was in disarray, with three prime ministers succeeding each other in the course of just one year.[105] After Stolypin revamped the electoral laws in June 1907, the third Duma yielded a majority that was more conservative than its predecessors and more willing to work with the government. But though the third and fourth Dumas (1907–14) functioned with some semblance of stability, the underlying problems of amorphous state power and fragmented ruling elites were not resolved.

In the years 1911–14, shortly before and then after Stolypin's death, the highest spheres of official Russian policymaking fractured further. The Stolypin government's alliance with centrists in the Duma failed; the State Council vetoed every Duma legislation that contained even a hint of liberalism, thereby burying all hopes for reform legislation; the Kadet, Octobrist, and Nationalist parties splintered; the Council of Ministers became mired in dissension over policy issues; Nicholas II treated Stolypin's successor, V. N. Kokovtsev, with distance and disdain; and animosity between the Duma and government intensified.[106] The fourth Duma in 1912 was more antigovernmental than its predecessor, with numerous and less manageable political blocs replacing the working majority that had cooperated with Stolypin. By 1913, the Octobrists had split into three factions; many Kadets had turned from Miliukov's leadership and sought a coalition with the Progressists; and even the Nationalists began to take an opposition stance toward the government.[107] Octobrist Mikhail V. Rodzianko captured the deep rift at the highest levels of state when he wrote to the emperor in December 1913:

> Each minister has his own opinion. For the most part, the cabinet is divided into two parties. The State Council forms a third, the Duma a fourth, and of your own opinion the country remains ignorant. This cannot go on, your Majesty, this is not government, it is anarchy.[108]

Amorphous, divided, and unstable state power facilitated the impact of great power nationalism on foreign policy by opening a path for panslavs not only to raise a clamor, but even to pursue unauthorized policies in response to public sentiments in favor of restoring Russian great power status in the Near East. In 1908–14, affairs in the Near East had become salient in Russian public opinion, yet individuals and institutions responsible for foreign policymaking (i.e., the court and Foreign Ministry) failed to provide a clear, decisive, and coherent approach. The court, Council of Ministers, and Foreign Ministry implemented divided and contradictory policies, thereby allowing great power nationalists from the Duma and elsewhere to push their prescriptions to the foreground of policymaking.

From 1906 to 1910, the biggest foreign policy debates in Russia tackled Russian relations with Turkey, Austria-Hungary (and, indirectly, Germany), and the Balkan Slavs. At the outset of Aleksandr P. Izvolskii's appointment as foreign minister, official policy pursued dual and contradictory goals. On one hand, Russian officials wanted to remain friendly with Turkey and Austria in order to avoid foreign policy complications and focus on reconstruction at home; on the other hand, official policy also wanted to restore international prestige by supporting the Balkan Slavs in their struggle against Turkish and Austro-Hungarian and German hegemony. Those who stood behind the official line included the tsar, Izvolskii, Deputy Foreign Minister Charykov, and deputies in the Duma's rightist nationalist camp. In opposition were Octobrists, some Kadets, and Moderate Rights in the Duma and their sympathizers in the tsarist cabinet, who favored an explicitly anti-Austrian and anti-German line and defended Russia's "unequivocal task to unite the Balkan Slavs."[109]

Contradiction in official policy and division between pro- and anti-Austrian camps among Russian political elites were at the root of the crisis over Austria's annexation of Bosnia-Herzegovina (1908–9) and the panslav and great power nationalist fever that seized Russian public opinion. Briefly, Foreign Minister Izvolskii, true to official Russian foreign policy goals, concluded a secret deal with Austrian foreign minister Alois Aehrenthal in 1908 that Russia would not object to Austrian annexation of Bosnia-Herzegovina if Austria would help St. Petersburg attain free passage through the Black Sea straits. Izvolskii did not inform Stolypin or the Duma about the deal, but secured approval and support from the tsar and Deputy Foreign Minister Charykov. In September 1908, Austria annexed Bosnia-Herzegovina, disclosed Izvolskii's affirmation of Russian support, and denied Austrian acquiescence on any quid pro quo involving the straits. A domestic crisis ensued in Russia: Stolypin became highly irate over Izvolskii's secret démarche, and nationalists in the Duma condemned Izvolskii and voiced outrage over Austria's annexation of territory that had a large Slavic (i.e., Serbian) population.

When decisive state authority was needed to resolve Russia's internal crisis over Bosnia, the tsar (who had supreme authority in foreign policy) acted passively. He denied his complicity in the Izvolskii–Aehrenthal deal and refused to support either Stolypin or Izvolskii as tension heightened between the two.[110] The absence of a definitive voice for the state helped the credibility of nationalists and panslavs who loudly condemned Russian indecision and weakness. A huge outcry ensued in the Duma and liberal press, and domestic pressure rapidly accumulated in support of Serbia, which was threatening war against Austria-Hungary. By March 1909, however, both Russia and Serbia ended their belligerence after Germany issued an ultimatum that they must accept Austria's annexation of Bosnia or face the joint forces of Germany and Austria-Hungary.[111]

Fragmented political elites and divided state policy again helped advance great power nationalism in 1910–14. After Russia's humiliation in the crisis of 1908–9, official foreign policy encouraged an alliance among the Balkan Slavs while simultaneously seeking to avoid war with the Turkish government.[112] As in 1907, Russian diplomacy pursued contradictory goals; a Balkan alliance could only be hostile to Turkey and could well draw Russia into a confrontation with the Turks. The absence of strong leadership after Stolypin's death in 1911 further aggravated the situation. Under Stolypin's successor, V. N. Kokovtsev, the Council of Ministers was riven with conflict, particularly between Kokovtsev's supporters and those of War Minister V. A. Sukhomlinov. Kokovtsev and Sukhomlinov quarreled over many issues, including Russian policy in the Balkans. Sukhomlinov, along with Agriculture Minister A. V. Krivoshein,[113] were among the Council's "war party," which supported an aggressive policy to defend Russia's Balkan allies and interests. In 1912, when the Balkan alliance fought Turkey, Sukhomlinov flouted Kokovtsev's authority by ordering partial mobilization of Russian troops on the Austrian border. Nicholas II himself disregarded formal decision making procedures and ignored Kokovtsev's authority by sanctioning the mobilization. Kokovtsev recorded feelings of "isolation" and "full helplessness" in the face of division within the council and lack of support from the tsar.[114]

The lack of clear goals and authority in foreign policy opened the way for great power nationalists to pursue agendas in defiance of official instructions. Two figures were particularly notorious: N. G. Hartwig, Russian representative in Belgrade and a frustrated aspirant for the post of foreign minister, and his counterpart in Sofia, A. Nekliudov. Both exceeded their official instructions on encouraging a Balkan alliance against Turkey in 1911 and 1912. With great zeal, they urged Serbia and Bulgaria not to take official Russian caution seriously because the Russian masses would support the Slavs in any war against Turkey.[115] Hartwig and Nekliudov enjoyed the sympathy of powerful figures at home including the tsaritsa, Grand Duke Nikolai Nikolaevich (whose wife and sister-in-law were daughters of the Montenegrin king),[116] and Prince G. N. Trubetskoi. Trubetskoi was head of the Asiatic department in the Foreign Ministry and a former publicist for *Moskovskii ezhenedel'nik*, a panslav newspaper. The diplomacy of Hartwig and Nekliudov facilitated the birth of the Balkan alliance, which declared war on Turkey in 1912 and sparked nationalist emotions in Russia. Indignation in the press and Duma over government intransigence in protecting Slavic interests again became very pronounced. Panslav initiatives and events flourished: Octobrist leader Guchkov set up field hospitals staffed by Russian volunteers to assist the Balkan Slavs fighting against Turkey; the St. Petersburg Slavic Committee collected donations for the Slavs; the Slavic Philanthropic Society, the Kadet National Club, and other groups met with Duma members to discuss Russian policy; and Duma political parties hosted panslav banquets to condemn official Russian foreign policy and voice their support for the Slavic war against Turkey.[117]

Social Crises

The government's inability to deal effectively with social crises was another sign of weakening political authority in Russia. Terrorism and strikes grew at an intense pace and revealed the tsarist authorities' lack of control. Two earlier waves of terrorism (1878–81 and 1901–5) had claimed such victims as Alexander II, the ministers of internal affairs—D. S. Sipiagin in 1902 and V. K. Plehve in 1904, one minister of education, and Grand Duke Sergei Aleksandrovich. Terrorists from the organization People's Will were largely responsible for the first wave of terror, while Socialist Revolutionaries accounted for the second.

In 1905, terrorist acts claimed the lives of at least 3,611 bureaucrats of all ranks in the Russian empire. In 1906 and 1907, revolutionary terrorism killed approximately 4,500 state officials, including governors, army generals, members of the gendarmerie, and ordinary police in the villages. Prime Minister Stolypin himself suffered a terrorist attack while in his country residence in 1906; he survived, but thirty of his visitors did not. Civilian fatalities from terrorism in the period 1905–7 numbered approximately 2,180. From January 1908 to May 1910, 732 bureaucrats and 3,051 civilians were killed. The lower number of official victims may have been due to the government's harsh response to terrorism; in 1906–9, the government executed 2,825 accused terrorists and in a few months alone in 1907 executed over one thousand people. In addition to lives lost, politically motivated thefts and expropriations led to economic losses throughout the empire.[118]

Such acts created great insecurity in people's daily lives; their effects were particularly vicious in peripheral areas; and regular citizens found minimal solace in the state's ineffective responses.[119] Strikes, which were politically and/or economically motivated, also marred the landscape of Russian autocracy from 1905 to 1907. They were at their most acute during the "revolutionary year of 1905" and waned slightly in 1906–7. They reached their lowest level in 1910, when fewer than fifty thousand workers participated in about two thousand strikes. But during Russia's industrial expansion in 1911–14, strike numbers rose again. By 1914, a new strike wave in Russia, mostly politically driven, reached crisis proportions reminiscent of 1905.[120]

The disturbances of 1914, including strikes and street demonstrations, resulted in large part from an incident that discredited the government, recalling 1905's "Bloody Sunday." In April 1912, police opened fire on thousands of peacefully demonstrating workers at the Lena goldfields in Siberia, killing 147. Reflecting public anger and near-collapse of faith in the government, the Duma called for a complete investigation of the incident and asked the government to outline measures it planned to take to prevent similar occurrences in the future. Government explanations were unsatisfactory and left many with "the distinct feeling that the government was not in control." In 1914, the police again brutally suppressed a meeting of workers convened to support strikers in the Baku oil fields. In response to these actions, in July 1914, a "strike as massive and explosive as any that had erupted among the workers in 1905" swept St. Petersburg. Nearly all factories and commercial establishments in the working class districts of the city ground to a halt, and workers clashed violently with Cossack detachments and police. It was in this setting that the Russian government confronted the Serbian crisis of July 1914.[121]

The Search for Consensus and Political Legitimacy

Division, competition, and strife among state bodies and officials made ideological consensus nearly impossible in Russia from 1907 to 1914. In this context, great power nationalism appeared as a potential cementing factor because its content resonated with Russian tradition and connoted a more stable and powerful Russian state supported by some portion of society. In the early 1900s, the tsarist government first sought support from the Right wing of the Russian political spectrum, including the protofascist Union of Russian People (URP). But this partnership was short-lived because the URP's mass base turned out to be narrower and less reliable than officially presumed, and, by the third Duma in 1907, the extreme Right ceased to be a crucial source of government support.[122] Instead, the tsarist government counted on the new Duma majority of Octobrists, right-wing Kadets, and Moderate Rights/Nationalists who were reformist but loyal to the regime, and many of whom were great power nationalists.

The majority bloc that cooperated with Stolypin in the third Duma was not homogeneous or strongly cohesive at the outset. But after the Bosnia-Herzegovina crisis of 1908–9, they developed a consensus on great power nationalism and panslav activism. This consensus reflected a common desire among forces relatively loyal to the tsar to form a "united government" and avoid further internal strife that weakened the country and prevented it from achieving foreign policy victories. Stolypin himself occasionally encouraged nationalism and Russian chauvinism to rally support for the government. In 1908–12, for example, his government implemented laws (adopted by the Duma) that discriminated against Jews, Poles, Finns, and other non-Russian groups.[123] But Russia's "united government" in the third Duma fractured in 1911. The Octobrists, who supported a reformed monarchy, lost faith in the regime when official complicity became evident in Stolypin's assassination and when the court began to ignore the Duma almost completely—in flagrant violation of the October Manifesto.[124] Although the idea of "united government" eroded, great power activism in the Balkans nonetheless remained popular through the end of the third Duma. In the fourth Duma of 1912, the Progressists, who subscribed to Struve's ideas of great power nationalism, became the most prominent group.

Why were members of the Duma and other political leaders attracted to great power nationalism? Under conditions of mass politics and the weakening legitimacy of autocracy, the political elite sought new foundations for legitimacy. Nationalism appeared particularly attractive because it linked state and society in a communal identity and common purpose. This was important at a time when many people were alienated from the ruling regime and sought ways to establish and strengthen their voice in decisions that affected their lives. Political, rather then material, incentives seemed most compelling for the appeal of great power nationalism among Russian politicians.

Although competition in Russian mass electoral politics in the early twentieth century focused on domestic issues, foreign policy evolved also as an arena of struggle for legitimacy. Nearly all parties after 1905 made claims to speak on behalf of the "people" or "nation" (*narod*) to legitimate their vision of Russian international behavior. The largest contingent of panslav supporters, for example, seeking to distinguish themselves from conservative rightists who shunned international activism, insisted that, unlike rightist nationalists, their mandate came from the nation. This mandate meant not just lip service to Russian great power status but immediate, decisive, and forceful actions to raise Russian prestige abroad.[125] Liberal figures like Miliukov and his Kadet followers, whose Westernized liberalism was "in almost every respect discordant with Russian experience and tradition" (rendering them vulnerable to charges of being unpatriotic), on occasion also expressed support for great power foreign policy to strengthen their link to a "national consensus."[126] Yet others, such as wealthy merchants who created the Progressists Party and were developing their political voice and power for the first time in Russian national politics, also used great power nationalism to establish their credentials as citizens and speakers "not for the government, but for the Russian people." Perhaps the most prominent figure from this group was P. P. Riabushinskii, a supporter of Struve and representative of the "self-affirming merchant class" (*samoutverzhdaiushchee kupechestvo*). In 1912, Riabushinskii declared that it was time for the "Russian merchant to occupy the leading position among Russia's estates, carry with pride the mark of a merchant, and cease to hanker after the mark of the dying nobility." He and his circle fought against the monarchy and those who had compromised Russia's great power status; they argued that Russia's future lay in a "great mission of Slav unification" and in a "healthy militarism" that would restore Russian power and identity in protecting Slavs from their German oppressors.[127]

Great power nationalism was useful not only in the competition for legitimacy among political parties, but also in the struggle for power and authority between Russia's new legislature and old monarchy. Miliukov, for example, argued during the annexation crisis of 1908–9 that the incident betrayed how little consideration the monarchy gave to the Duma and public opinion. He discredited the tsarist government by condemning its weakness in foreign policy and urging war against Austria-Hungary, if necessary.[128] Other cases arose when liberals in the Duma, dismayed by the tsar's obdurate stance against a true constitutional regime, used great power nationalism to challenge tsarist authority, to denigrate the Foreign Ministry for not adequately defending the nation's interests, to advocate reforms in foreign policymaking, and to argue that the Duma and the "people" had a central role to play in foreign policy. Throughout the third Duma, Octobrists and Kadets consistently used great power nationalist ideas to assert legislative authority over the Foreign Ministry. When Foreign Minister Izvolskii made his first statement to the Duma in 1907, Miliukov declared that the government needed "to lean upon public opinion [as represented in the Duma] in its coming diplomatic measures" to "compensate for [Russian] temporary material weakness."[129] Later, in 1908, Guchkov warned the Foreign Ministry that

> the worth of all your diplomatic démarches depends on how much the people's consciousness, the people's will stands behind them. And when . . . you have recourse to ultimata . . . it is to us [the Duma] that you will come for your war credits; you will need our blood and that of our brothers and sons, you will come for money and manpower. . . .[130]

Izvolskii's successor, S. D. Sazonov, was not highly responsive to public opinion at the beginning of his tenure and rarely made presentations to the Duma. But in 1912–13, he became increasingly sensitive to vociferous criticism in the panslav press and Duma regarding Russia's indecisive stance toward Serbia, leader of the Balkan alliance that had declared war on Turkey. Although Sazonov was not eager for Russia to go to war in the Balkans, he nonetheless expressed sympathy for the "Slavic cause" and, by 1914, claimed that the Russian people would never forgive the tsar if he allowed Russia to be humiliated once more (as in 1909).[131] The use of great power nationalism by Duma deputies to strengthen their political authority achieved some results as Sazonov and other officials—including Nicholas II, Stolypin, and Naval Minister Grigorovich—recognized nationalist and panslav public opinion and partially accommodated its proponents.[132]

Material incentives appear weak in motivating elite support for great power nationalism. Although nearly half of Russian exports depended on the goodwill of unreliable powers in the Black Sea straits for transit,[133] nationalist merchants like Riabushinskii did not cite economic arguments in support of their ideology.

The rhetoric and actions of merchants who supported Struve and his nationalist ideas indicated that, as a newly enriched and empowered group, they wanted to play the role of citizens who were effective participants in molding the state and its future. The military's parochial and material interests would also have been well served by great power nationalism. It could justify larger military budgets as well as mobilize the mass population for future wars. Indeed, there were soldiers and retired officers who were preoccupied with great power nationalism and who actively participated in panslav organizations such as the St. Petersburg Slavic Committee and the Society of Russian Borderlands. But the military command never exploited militant nationalism to argue for increased budgetary allocations. Although the army had suffered budget cuts through the 1880s and had not recovered by the early twentieth century, the highest military officials did not exaggerate German or Austro-Hungarian threats or advocate a forceful or immediate Russian response. Many in the military gauged accurately the weakness of the army and favored military reform, patriotic education, and a largely defensive Russian foreign policy. Systematic propagation of panslav or other aggressive nationalist ideas did not take place in the army or navy; neither did commanders push for a strategy of forward action in the Balkans. An exception was War Minister V. A. Sukhomlinov who, in 1912 and 1914, did urge military mobilization on behalf of the Slavs. He professed faith in the "Russian people and their age-old love for the homeland, which was greater than any accidental preparedness or unpreparedness for war."[134] Previously, in the crisis of 1908–9, Sukhomlinov strongly believed that the Russian army was unprepared to go to war against Austria and Germany and did not then argue for Russian military action. But in 1912–14, he came to believe that military inaction would unacceptably damage the prestige of the army and put Russia at a hopeless military disadvantage vis-à-vis an impending and inevitable German rapid mobilization.[135] Sukhomlinov's actions, altogether, appear to have been motivated by considerations of military positioning rather than aggressive nationalism per se.

International Threats and Crises

International threats and crises played the decisive, precipitating role in putting great power nationalism at the forefront of Russian foreign policy in 1914. These threats and crises arose between 1908 and 1914, and their repeated occurrence built momentum in favor of great power nationalist prescriptions.

The gravest threat to Russia's national interest, in terms of great power status and prestige, was rising "German power" in the early 1900s. "German power" meant the joint influence and clout of Germany and Austria-Hungary; in Russian eyes, the latter had effectively become a satellite to the former and, therefore, the influence they exercised in the Balkans was one and the same. Germany had penetrated the Ottoman Empire militarily and economically and supported Austrian expansion in the area (as was the case with Austria's annexation of Bosnia). While German power was growing, Turkey's ability to resist it was weakening. The Ottoman government had become highly unstable, falling in 1908 and 1911, and no longer seemed capable of fending off external powers interested in the spoils of a disintegrating empire. In 1911, after the government fell as a result of war with Italy over Tripoli, the new regime of Said Pasha declared that Turkey could no longer be neutral and must reach an understanding with one or a group of the great powers to protect its vital interests. Russia responded by seeking a Russo-Turkish agreement to open the straits to Russian vessels, but Turkey rejected the proposal; Russian efforts to facilitate the formation of a Slavic confederation that included Turkey also failed to bear fruit.[136] Thus, Russia found itself handicapped in its traditional sphere of influence at the same time that German influence was growing.

The threat of German power, intensified by crises in the period 1908–14, facilitated the impact of great power nationalism. Russia's inability to defend its national interest effectively and the failure of attempts to resolve various crises through international agreement triggered explosions of panslav sentiment and great power nationalism at home. By 1914, nationalist public opinion persuaded a beleaguered government in St. Petersburg that its survival depended on yielding to nationalist influence in its policy abroad. The first of these crises was the 1908 Austrian annexation of Bosnia-Herzegovina.

When Austria announced in January 1908 that it would construct a railway across the Austrian-occupied *sanjak* of Novibazar, thereby linking Austrian territory with Turkey and strengthening Austrian hegemony, the Russian press and Duma reacted negatively. They characterized the move as an incursion of Austrian (and, by implication, German) power "into an area of unique interest to Russia as the Slavic Great Power."[137] Before Austria could implement its railway plan, a Young Turk revolution toppled the Turkish government in July 1908, causing disturbances throughout the Balkans. The Austrian government, anxious not to lose its comparative advantage to Balkan instability, sent a note to Russia declaring that Bosnia-Herzegovina constituted "territories which we have possessed for thirty years, into which we entered by virtue of an international mandate, and which we have conquered by force of arms."[138] If circumstances required, Austria would annex the occupied provinces, and did so in September.

As stated previously, Russian foreign minister Izvolskii believed he had an agreement with his Austrian counterpart that Russia would not object to the annexation if Austria assisted Russia in attaining free passage for its vessels in the Black Sea straits. Once Austria had the upper hand in Bosnia, however, Vienna quickly denied any obligations toward Russia. Izvolskii, caught in a difficult situation and hoping to save face for Russia, urged an international conference to resolve the controversy. He noted that Bosnia's status was governed by the Congress of Berlin, and any change therein required a meeting of Berlin Congress signatories. He also traveled to European great power capitals to seek support for an international conference, but had no success. At home, the press inveighed against an international conference, which *Novoe vremia* declared would only "bring humiliation to Russia" unless Russia could threaten war in the event of failed international diplomacy.[139]

Austria's annexation of Bosnia-Herzegovina triggered and validated great power nationalist opinion in Russia. Invoking memories of Russia's 1905 humiliation by Japan, the press accused the tsarist cabinet of another "diplomatic Tsushima" and "another Mukden." A great debate ensued about Russian foreign policy, and many argued for a forceful response, asserting that Russia had a duty to prevent violence against "fellow tribesmen" in the Balkans. Papers and journals highlighted Austria-Hungary's oppression of Slavs in Bosnia-Herzegovina, warned that Bosnia's fate could befall other Slavic nations, and condemned those in the government who sought to make a deal with Austria at the expense of the non-Russian Slavs. In addition to the explosion of critical opinion in the press, panslav civic activity rose in the wake of the crisis. The Society for Slavic Culture, the Society for Slavic Scholarship, and the Society for Slavic Mutuality convened meetings, and Duma leaders participated actively in many panslav events. The crisis, which Struve called a "national disgrace," also motivated Russian business circles to sponsor panslav publications and activities.[140]

The 1908–9 crisis validated the cry for an assertive response to threats to Russian prestige and core interests. It crystallized the opinion that Austria was determined to humiliate or absorb the Balkan Slavs, that Germany was prepared to grant carte blanche to Austria, and that Russian vacillation could only lead the country to greater humiliation and losses. Nationalists argued that, like Germany and Austria—and even Bulgaria, which exploited the crisis to declare its independence from Turkish rule—Russia should concentrate on its *own* national interest and pursue it without trepidation. The government should have faith in the strength of the *narod* or people to support a policy for reviving Russian honor and prestige. As Octobrist Guchkov argued in *Golos Moskvy*,

> Yes, we are going through new humiliations but let Russia's enemies not hasten to celebrate their victory. . . . It is not the flabby indolence of official Russia, but the indignant patriotism of the whole Russian people, its readiness to lay down its life for its friends, that foreign, and indeed our own diplomats must reckon with. Taking our stand on this disregarded spiritual strength of the Russian people, we may boldly cry in our enemies' faces: "Russia has not yet fallen, she will rise again!"[141]

The Bosnia crisis temporarily forged unity among disparate members of the Russian political spectrum who believed that Russian passivity before Austria-Hungary constituted a shame (*pozor*), that Russia's great power status and aspirations were seriously at risk, that the Balkan states had been insulted, and that Russia should demand compensation for its aggrieved ally, Serbia. The crisis discredited the defensive foreign policy favored by neoslavs and rightist conservatives. At the April and May 1909 Slav meetings in St. Petersburg, for example, support for the neoslav agenda (i.e., equality among all Slavs, rapprochement between Russia and Poland, and Russian solidarity with Slavs in Austria-Hungary) splintered. The Czechs spoke in favor of Austria's annexation, which would have increased Austria-Hungary's already formidable twenty million Slavs (in a population of forty-five million), while Russians pushed for a Russo-Serbian common defense against Austria and Germany.[142] The new salience of great power nationalism terminated the Balkan status quo policy that Russia and Austria-

Hungary had observed since the 1890s. The full impact of this would become evident in the crisis of 1914 and the world war that followed.

The second set of international crises that helped advance great power nationalism occurred during the Balkan wars of 1912–13. In the context of Russia's humiliation in 1908–9, continued internal instability, and increased competition from rival powers,[143] Russian foreign policy in 1910–12 sought to maintain international prestige by encouraging the formation of a Balkan alliance against Turkey (and potentially, also against Austria). Although official Russian policy originally did not push for an alliance to destroy Turkey, it became clear that the Balkan Slavs were moving in that direction. Policymakers in St. Petersburg thus chose to engage in the process rather than be excluded from it. The alliance that formed in 1912 included Serbia, Bulgaria, Greece, and Montenegro. Although Russia urged these states to act cautiously, they ignored Russian advice and declared war on Turkey. In response, Russia cut off military and financial aid to Montenegro, but not to its more important Slavic allies, Serbia and Bulgaria. War began in October 1912 and, to Russia's surprise, ended with a relatively quick and unequivocal Balkan victory.[144] Inside Russia, the war stimulated considerable public enthusiasm and support. The press expressed support for the south Slav cause; many made donations to the Russian Red Cross to assist the Slavs; and others sent telegrams of solidarity to the Serbian, Bulgarian, and Greek kings. In the Duma, attacks rose against extreme rightist deputies, who opposed Russian entanglement in the Balkans.[145]

In December 1912 Turkey signed an armistice with its Balkan opponents, which had practically forced it out of Europe and were poised to make considerable territorial gains. The European powers, however, blocked these gains. At a conference in London, Austria and Italy insisted that the new state of Albania be created out of territory assigned to Serbia by the Balkan alliance. Further, in April 1913, when Montenegro refused to vacate Scutari (an area that was supposed to be part of the new Albanian state), an international naval demonstration and landing force was sent to coerce it to change its mind. The Russian government, unwilling to risk a major confrontation, decided to acquiesce with the great powers' decisions.[146]

Russia's failure to defend the gains of its Balkan protégés roused great indignation in the press and Duma, where critics argued against the injustice of the international solution hammered out by the great powers in London. Prevailing Russian public opinion cried that Russia had been betrayed and its allies deprived of their rightful gains. *Novoe vremia* called the Albanian issue a "terrible blow to Slavdom," an "ignominious retreat," and a "diplomatic Mukden." *Utro Rossii*, the Progressist paper, called the event another push for Austrian power, which scored yet one more "bloodless victory over Russian diplomacy." *Utro Rossii* attacked the "German element" (i.e., ethnic Germans in Russian officialdom) for "paralyzing [Russian] political will and . . . national energy," and preventing the full realization of ties between Russia and the south Slavs. Public ire also greeted the Scutari issue, with crowds breaking into the Austrian embassy in St. Petersburg, a panslav

demonstration attracting some forty thousand people, and Slavic banquets condemning the Russian government's betrayal of slavdom. One representative of the
military declared that Russian official behavior exhibited "an insulting lack of
faith in the strength of the Russian people and the Russian army."[147] Foreign Minister Sazonov suffered the brunt of many attacks, including insinuations of high
treason. Officials in the highest rungs of power felt acutely the pressure of public
opinion, and the tsar approved Sukhomlinov's request for a partial mobilization
of troops in military districts bordering Austria-Hungary.

Another crisis in 1913 highlighted the German threat and generated support for
aggressive nationalism. In November, Germany assigned General Liman von
Sanders to be in charge of the Turkish army and take command at Constantinople.
This was in response to a Turkish request for a German military mission to help
reorganize Turkey's armed forces after the Balkan wars of 1912–13. Having learned
from bitter experience about the domestic consequences of Russian passivity on
Balkan issues, Foreign Minister Sazonov reacted strongly this time to German
incursion in a sensitive area of Russian foreign policy. He told Berlin of Russian
concerns, and sought French and British support for joint actions to let the Turkish government know of the Triple Entente's (i.e., the alliance of Russia, France,
and Great Britain) objections. The French and British did not immediately support
Sazonov's appeal because a British admiral had also just been assigned to head a
naval training squadron in Turkey, in much the same capacity as von Sanders. But,
in his memoirs, Sazonov explained that Germany's action made Russia feel "if not
exactly under direct threat from a neighboring empire . . . nonetheless under
threat from the possibility that . . . the last remnants of Turkish control over the
straits will be swept away,"[148] thereby benefiting German power. The crisis dissipated in January 1914, when Germany found a face-saving solution by promoting
von Sanders to the higher rank of honorary field marshal, thereby eliminating his
role as active commander of the Turkish army.

Although the Liman von Sanders crisis was short-lived, it precipitated more
controversy and a hardening of Russian foreign policy positions. The crisis
sparked new accusations in the press about the failure of Russian diplomacy and
the futility of delusions that Germany could be Russia's friend. It led Sazonov to
initiate a plan for forceful action if the affair was not resolved satisfactorily. After
the crisis, Naval Minister Grigorovich approached Sazonov and Prime Minister
Kokovtsev for support in enlarging Russia's Black Sea fleet in response to antici-
pated growth in the Turkish Black Sea squadron. Grigorovich noted international
and domestic policy considerations for his request, especially his fear of the
domestic consequences of a "moral impression of our fleet's defeat, inflicted upon
us, it would seem, by a long shattered Turkey."[149] Thus, a shift toward greater
assertiveness occurred in Russian foreign policy, ending the cautious approach of
the Stolypin era. Great Britain and France's reaction also convinced Russian policymakers to consolidate the Triple Entente as never before because Russia needed
Entente support in order to implement a victorious and assertive Balkan policy.

The final crisis that catapulted great power nationalism to the forefront of
Russian foreign policy had to do with Serbia, Russia's most important Slavic ally

since the end of the second Balkan war of 1913.[150] Extremist Serbian patriots assassinated Franz Ferdinand, heir to the Habsburg throne, in Sarajevo on June 28, 1914. The Austrian government subsequently issued a crushing ultimatum to Serbia. As in 1908–9 and 1912–13, Russian efforts failed to resolve the crisis through an international agreement. Not only did the dynamics of the crisis move too fast for negotiation among the great powers, but the international alliance system in Europe at the time was set up to discourage compromise.[151] Austria did not even bother to answer Sazonov's request for negotiations, and Nicholas II's own entreaty to Wilhelm II of Germany not to "go too far for the sake of our old friendship" failed to change the dynamics of crisis.[152] But, unlike in 1908–9 and 1912–13, Russian policymakers, though well aware of their state's weakness, were no longer willing to act passively and risk another humiliation in the Balkans. They openly contemplated the option of assertive mobilization that great power nationalists had advocated for years and acted on the belief that Russia could face the crisis head-on because the strength of its people or nation (*narod*) would sustain it in fulfilling its historic mission.

GREAT POWER NATIONALISM AND ITS IMPACT ON RUSSIA'S ENTRY INTO WORLD WAR I

Dominic Lieven notes that the crisis of July 1914, which precipitated World War I, humiliated Russia because the Central Powers communicated Germanic racial superiority toward the Slavs and implicitly denied the "Russian people's own dignity and . . . their equality with the other races of Europe."[153] As a reaction to crisis and humiliation, aggressive nationalist ideas and panslav agitation became salient in Russian politics. Although nationalism, by itself, did not cause Russia to go to war in 1914,[154] it nonetheless had a demonstrable impact on Russian decision making.

First, the rhetoric of great power nationalism constantly advocated an assertive Russian policy in the Balkans—up to and including war. Thus, over the years it helped to condition Russian policymakers and the public to support the choice of war on behalf of Slavic allies. This conditioning worked in part because Russian intervention on behalf of the Slavs had a long history in Russian foreign policy. Second, great power nationalism roused public or civic activity that pressured the government to carry out an aggressive policy on behalf of the Slavs. And third, Russian nationalists encouraged the Slavs themselves to go to war, forcing Russian officials to take a stand on Russia's historical commitment to defend its Slavic allies.

Beginning in 1908, nationalist rhetoric regularly cited war as a positive option in Russian foreign policy. Prince G. N. Trubetskoi argued, for example, that Russia must be willing to go to war to prove to the Balkan Slavs that it could defend their interests. Otherwise, Russia's Slavic allies would constantly be targeted for territorial division and humiliation, and Russia would be unable to stop German domination in the Balkans and might lose Constantinople, whose fate was of "vast historical and strategic importance."[155] Great power nationalists and panslavs in the Duma, while acknowledging Russian weakness vis-à-vis Austria and Germany in 1909, nonetheless encouraged the Serbs to prepare for a future war under more propitious circumstances, when Austria would be made to "pay dearly for Russia's humiliation."[156]

During and after the Balkan wars of 1912–13, proponents and sympathizers of great power nationalism stoked anti-German sentiment among the Russian public and agitated for war on behalf of the Slavs. In a Duma debate in 1913, V. A. Bobrinskii identified Germany as the culprit behind Austrian maneuvers to deny Serbia its territorial gains from war. He argued that it was impossible to preserve peace while Austria persecuted peoples of Slavic culture and Orthodox religion,[157] and he and others insisted that the Balkan alliance would not have splintered after its victory against Turkey had Russia only shown more commitment to its Slav allies. The Octobrists Guchkov and Rodzianko also urged Nicholas II to go to war in 1913 to protect Russian interests. They argued that "the [Black Sea] straits must be ours [and that a] war will be joyfully welcomed [in Russia] and will raise the government's prestige."[158] Guchkov in 1912 also encouraged the Serbs to launch a war against Turkey.

Proponents of great power nationalism insisted that Russia must assert its cultural and political role in Europe, where its fate lay. Publicist A. A. Kireev, for example, expressed a sentiment, to be repeated in 1912 by Foreign Minister Sazonov, that increased possessions in Asia could not substitute for Russia's European role. Only by asserting influence in the Balkans could Russia preserve its greatness; otherwise, it risked becoming "a tolerated but inferior outrunner of Western culture."[159] In the military, the events of 1912–13 spurred panslav sympathizers in the officers' corps to express their loathing for Austria and their dismay at Russia's military weakness since 1905. Officers participated in public demonstrations on behalf of the Slavs. For example, the garrison commander of the Peter and Paul fortress and his entire staff attended a memorial in April 1913 for the allied dead in the Balkan war against Turkey. Retired generals and active officers also joined in public demonstrations against tsarist passivity in the Balkans, and advocated a reassertion of Russian power to force Austria to retreat from its demands.

In 1914, actions and arguments by great power nationalists fueled passions for war between Russia and Austria-Hungary. Six months before the war, *Novoe vremia* and the Russo-Galician Society in St. Petersburg engaged in anti-Austrian activities by highlighting Austrian abuse of Slavs in Ruthenia. Not only were these activities hypocritical given Russia's abuse of its own Slavic subjects, but they were also potentially damaging to Russian economic interests[160] and intensified Austria's animosity toward Russia. Although cautious voices arose among Russian leaders and Duma opinion makers in the few months preceding World War I,[161] those who favored aggressive nationalism had the dominant voice during the July 1914 crisis. Meetings in the Council of Ministers and between the tsar and the council on July 24 and 25, 1914, were particularly important. Agriculture Minister Krivoshein, War Minister Sukhomlinov, Navy Minister Grigorovich, and Foreign Minister Sazonov were key participants at these meetings. Krivoshein held to his vision of the strength and loyalty of the *narod* in support of Russia's historic mission among the Slavs. In remarks that made a "profound impression" on the cabinet, Krivoshein warned that the greatest threat to Russia was in *not* acting to defend its great power status. He argued that while war was undesirable because of its potential domestic consequences, "public and parliamentary opinion would fail to understand why, at this critical moment involving Russia's vital interests, the Imperial Government was reluctant to act boldly."[162]

Sazonov supported Krivoshein and declared that further concessions from Russia, as in 1908–9 and 1912–13, would only feed German aggression. He declared that the "moment had come when Russia, faced with the annihilation of Serbia, would lose all her authority if she did not declare herself the defender of a Slavonic nation threatened by powerful neighbors. . . . If Russia failed to fulfill her historic mission she would be considered a decadent State and would henceforth have to take second place among the powers."[163] Sukhomlinov and Grigorovich certified Russian military readiness and called for general mobilization. These ministers believed that war with Germany was unavoidable and Russia, therefore, could not afford to delay its military preparations.[164]

During the crisis of 1914, Russian leaders, including the tsar, became convinced to one extent or another of the validity of great power nationalist arguments. In late July 1914, they converged on a basic inversion of past thinking on Russian foreign policy, which under Stolypin had emphasized the avoidance of international conflict and adventurism to nurture reforms at home and prevent a revolutionary upheaval. Krivoshein and his co-thinkers argued that Russia had largely been rebuilt, that domestic governance no longer hinged on caution but assertiveness in foreign policy, and that Russia must abandon the supine diplomacy it had practiced since 1908. Sazonov declared that another Russian capitulation to Berlin's demands would constitute an act "for which Russia would never forgive the Sovereign, and which would cover the good name of the Russian people in shame."[165] Thus, in the July 1914 crisis, the Tsar and Sazonov began seriously to consider war as an option. Sazonov, who had become highly sensitive to public criticism since the crisis of 1908–9, and tsar Nicholas II, who believed the myth that the people would unequivocally support him in wartime, argued that mobilization for war was imperative to defend Russia's great power authority and bolster its internal social and political cohesion.[166] In one historian's words,

> [The] traditional formula connecting war and revolution had been completely inverted by the summer of 1914. Not only was there no spokesman for restraint in the council [of ministers], but because of the empire's pitiful diplomatic career since 1908, statesmen felt a threat from the prospect of society's response to inaction. . . . To capitulate yet again [in the July 1914 crisis] could [further] damage the state's own authority at home while casting into doubt its international claims to Great Power status.[167]

In July 1914 the disposition toward war was more prevalent than ever before among Russian policymakers. But, recognizing Russian internal weakness, Russian diplomats did attempt to avoid war. Even after Austria had declared war on

Serbia and Russia itself had ordered partial mobilization, Nicholas II took pains to inform Wilhelm II that St. Petersburg did not plan offensive action against Germany and delayed orders for general mobilization until the last minute.[168]

But last-minute diplomacy failed and, on the eve of World War I, panslavism became Russia's rallying cry. *Novoe vremia* decried the "onslaught of the Germanic tribes against the Slavs" and called for "unity, strength of spirit, and a firm stance against the foe" in the war "for the very foundations of our fatherland." Struve wrote that war was "called upon to complete the external expansion of the Russian empire, realizing her imperial tasks and Slav mission."[169] Sazonov spoke to the Duma about Russia's duty to the Serbs, who were of common history, descent, and faith. And the tsar himself, in declaring Russia's entry into the war, noted that Russia had never been indifferent to the fate of its Slavic brethren.

CONCLUSION

In 1914, great power nationalist ideas triumphed over a realistic assessment of Russia's geopolitical position and internal strength to sustain a war effort, and contributed to a revolution that, in 1917, swept away the autocratic order and the reign of the tsars. Clearly, before 1914 positive changes occurred in Russian politics, including the development of fairly strong civic identity and a sense of citizenship among members of the nobility, educated class, business elite, publishers, and others. The experiment with representative government through the Duma was also to be welcomed, even after Stolypin's manipulation of electoral rules. The third Duma showed the potential of gradualism in rearranging relations between state and society, and the possibility of cooperation between government and people.

But two (arguably fatal) problems blocked the further peaceful evolution of Russian politics. First, the majority of liberals and moderate conservatives who held the "center" of Russian politics (e.g., the majority in the Stolypin Duma) did not give up the idea of Russian greatness as an imperial state. They failed to realize that reform at home would be impossible without also giving up hegemonic and imperial policies abroad. An imperial state with a mission to assert international hegemony continued to be a supreme value among many who prevailed in Russian political discourse. Second, the tsar and others around him failed to realize that many of the prerogatives of autocratic power had to be given up for the Russian state to survive. The tsar sabotaged his own (begrudgingly given) liberal reforms, did not work with the Duma to develop a more robust law-based society, and persisted in the superstitious belief of harmony between tsar and people at a time when many in society no longer supported autocratic rule. Tsarist government was divided and political authority fragmented, making the regime vulnerable to pressure from great power nationalism when international threats and crises arose and intensified in the years 1908–14.

In 1914, international threats and crises pushed Russian policymakers into a position where they saw no other viable options but those prescribed by great power nationalists to preserve Russian prestige abroad and restore unity at home. Aggressive nationalism became most resonant during years of international crises: 1908–9, 1912–13, and 1914. In contrast, during the period 1910–12, when the Balkans were quiescent, mass support for nationalism (and, consequently, pressure on the tsarist regime to act forcefully in the Balkans) also waned. During these years, for example, at least three nationalist and panslav publications (*Moskovskii ezhenedel'nik, Okrainy Rossii,* and *Slavianskie izvestiia*) closed down for lack of a receptive audience.[170]

Besides threats and crises, two other international factors facilitated the impact of great power nationalism. One was the intensification of nationalism among Slavs and other minorities in the Balkans and the weakening of the Ottoman and Habsburg Empires, and another was the consolidation of the Triple Entente. The intensification of nationalism among Slavs and other minorities in the Balkans was a process long in the making. By 1900, Serbia, Bulgaria, Romania, and Greece had obtained independent or autonomous status from the Porte, although all of them still had diasporas living under foreign rule. Serbia and Bulgaria were also increasing in power; their populations were becoming more cohesive, better educated, and economically competitive. At the same time, Serbian and Bulgarian leaders were effectively using nationalist rhetoric to mobilize their populations. In Austria-Hungary, nationalism among Czechs and Slovaks was also intensifying, especially after universal suffrage became law in the Austrian half of the Habsburg Empire in 1907 and a Slavic majority came to the Vienna Reichstag. Despite this gain, Czechs and Slovaks continued to suffer linguistic and economic discrimination. Thus, they turned their eyes toward Russia for potential assistance in their struggle for independence. Russophile leaders, though not always a durable element of the Balkan political landscape, were prominent in the early twentieth century.[171]

Strong Balkan nationalism threatened the integrity of the Ottoman and Habsburg Empires, both of which were undergoing internal decay. Turkey, in particular, was increasingly losing control of its subject Christian populations; by implementing repressive policies of centralized power and Ottomanization of its Slavic and Orthodox subjects, the Turkish government fueled nationalist resentment among its subject populations. The "sick man of Europe," Turkey was clearly in its last years of being a European power, and other great powers were jockeying for the most advantageous position in anticipation of its fall.[172]

Rising Slavic nationalism and the weakening of Turkey and Austria-Hungary encouraged Russian aspirations to turn to the Balkans as the proving ground for great power politics after 1905. Responding in part to calls from the Slavic nations, deputies in the newly formed Duma in 1906 expressed sympathy for Slavic struggles against their rulers and argued for policies to protect the Slavs. Second, nationalism among the Balkan Slavs motivated the formation of the Balkan alliance of 1912. Serbia, in particular, vigorously sought the alliance as a vehicle for pursuing its territorial ambitions against the Habsburg and Ottoman Empires, and to repay Austria-Hungary for past actions against Serbia, including the annexation of Bosnia-Herzegovina.[173] It conducted secret negotiations with Bulgaria in 1911, while seeking Russian support to help overcome Serbo-Bulgarian differences. Russia had only a minimal role in the drafting of the Serbo-Bulgarian treaty that was signed in March 1912, and an even less important role in subsequent treaties signed between Bulgaria and Greece, and Montenegro and Bulgaria. Notwithstanding their secondary role in the Balkan alliance, Sazonov and his colleagues deemed it crucial to be involved in the Balkan negotiations because, at the very least, their presence might help deter developments detrimental to Russian interests. Moreover, as "protector" of the Slavs, Russia would damage its international prestige by abstaining from the formation of a key Balkan alliance.[174] Third, extremist Serbian nationalism led to the assassination of Franz Ferdinand and the crisis that ensued in July 1914. Austria's refusal to give Russia and its Serbian ally any face-saving way out of the crisis contributed to a situation that worked in favor of aggressive nationalist arguments in Russia.[175]

The consolidation of the Triple Entente also helped great power nationalism become a factor in Russian foreign policy. Russia sought to consolidate this alliance as never before in the wake of the Liman von Sanders affair in 1913. During the July 1914 crisis, Russia sought, and gained, assurance that France would aid Russia if attacked by Germany or by Austria-Hungary with German help. The French government confirmed its "unconditional support" to Sazonov verbally and in writing by July 27, 1914. At the same time, Russia also received supportive communications from Great Britain.[176] This situation contrasted sharply with 1908–9 and 1912–13, when Russia was too weak to fight a war over its Balkan interests and could not count on assistance from its international allies (though Russia certainly asked).[177] Consolidation of the Entente by 1914 constituted an "opportunity" for Russia to consider war without fear of having to face its potentially dire consequences alone.

Even though an arguably aggressive form of nationalism had an impact on Russian foreign policy in 1877–78 and 1914, the foreign policy that actually resulted tended very much to fall within traditional Russian "great power" politics (i.e., asserting influence in a traditional area of interest). Russian actions did not amount to extreme militarism or relentless expansion to aggrandize the "nation." The historical and sentimental element of Russian interest in the Balkans involved Russia's role for over two hundred years as ally of the Slavic and Orthodox peoples of Turkey and Austria-Hungary. Traditionally, even other powers had recognized the Near East as a Russian sphere of influence. Strategically, Russia also had a legitimate interest in restoring passage for its vessels through the Black Sea straits; as the war with Japan illustrated, such passage was crucial for Russia's naval mobility. In a larger sense, control of the straits was important to guarantee Russian defense against attacks along the Black Sea coast.[178] Russian actions, though informed by nationalism at home, were largely consistent with prevalent "great power" ideas based on imperial competition. In the late nineteenth and early twentieth centuries, such competition was a norm guiding relations between Russia and other leading European powers.

The dark side—perhaps one might call it tragedy—of cases of Russian nationalism and foreign policy described in this chapter and the previous one was how briefly state and society held together in a consensus over national identity and purposes. In 1914, as in 1878, the prominence of nationalism did not lead to a more enduring unity of government and people in Russia. Although great power nationalism proved a potent ideological instrument for furthering the aims of the imperial state, reality soon revealed its weakness and limitation in forging nation-state cohesion. The words of V. Miakotin in *Russkoe bogatstvo* in 1908 were prescient: Russia was living through a time when "our immense country, up to its very last corner, is caught in convulsions of despair and suffocating under the unprecedented weight of arbitrariness and violence"; yet, great power nationalists and panslavs dared to fantasize that "not only can we live under these circumstances, but we can even experience a 'national renaissance.'"[179] Indeed, sympathizers of great power nationalism suffered from severe delusions. Only three years after their ideas demonstrably influenced Russian foreign policy, Russia would be engulfed in a revolution, revealing an unbridgeable divide between state and society, and heralding the end of the old order and the beginning of over seventy years of travail under Soviet communism.

NOTES

1. Aksakov received permission to publish again in the 1880s and did so with his conservative nationalist newspaper, *Rus'*. See David MacKenzie, *The Serbs and Russian Panslavism 1875–1878* (Ithaca: Cornell University Press, 1967), pp. 332–33; Stephen Lukashevich, *Ivan Aksakov 1823–1886: A Study in Russian Thought and Politics* (Cambridge: Harvard University Press, 1965), pp. 141–42; and Edward C. Thaden (with Marianna Forster Thaden), *Interpreting History: Collective Essays on Russia's Relations with Europe* (Boulder: Social Science Monographs, 1990), p. 208.

2. These "sacred" principles, first declared by Minister of Education Sergei Uvarov in 1833, constituted official government ideology during the reign of Nicholas I in 1825–1855. Uvarov characterized "Autocracy, Orthodoxy, and Nationality" as "the principles which form the distinctive character of Russia, and which belong only to Russia . . . and without which [Russia] cannot prosper, gain in strength, live." The official principle of Autocracy meant subjection to the tsar, on whom all political and legal authority ultimately rested. Orthodoxy meant adherence to the dogma of the state-supported church, and Nationality connoted belief in the superiority of Russian language and culture and renewed russification of the non-Russian regions of the empire. See Nicholas V. Riasanovsky, *Nicholas I and Official Nationality in Russia 1825–1855* (Berkeley: University of California Press, 1969), pp. 73–75.

3. Nicholas II's personality was well suited for a family man—a loving husband and doting father—but not for a leader of an enormous empire on the verge of imploding. The Russian throne was a burden to the young tsar, who, in his scrupulously kept diaries, wrote daily about the weather, family gatherings, outings, and receptions, but made no substantive assessments of the political events and challenges of his time. See *Rossiiskie samoderzhtsy 1801–1917*, 2nd ed. (Moscow: Mezhdunarodnye otnosheniia, 1994), pp. 323–24.

4. Dominic Lieven, *Russia's Rulers under the Old Regime* (New Haven: Yale University Press, 1989), p. 280.

5. Richard Charques, *The Twilight of Imperial Russia* (London: Oxford University Press, 1958), pp. 11–47; and Terence Emmons, *The Formation of Political Parties and the First National Elections in Russia* (Cambridge: Harvard University Press, 1983), pp. 1–17.

6. After "Bloody Sunday," for example, French financial circles, to whom Russia was indebted, issued a warning that no more loans would be forthcoming in the absence of Russian domestic political reform. Emmons, *Formation of Political Parties*, p. 9.

7. Emmons, *Formation of Political Parties*, p. 17.

8. Geoffrey A. Hosking, *The Russian Constitutional Experiment, Government and Duma, 1907–1914* (London: Cambridge University Press, 1973), p. 215.

9. See Dominic Lieven, *Russia and the Origins of the First World War* (New York: St. Martin's, 1983); I. V. Bestuzhev, *Bor'ba v Rossii po voprosam vneshnei politiki 1906–1910* (Moscow: Nauka, 1961); Dietrich Geyer, *Russian Imperialism: The Interaction of Domestic and Foreign Policy 1860–1914*, trans. Bruce Little (New Haven: Yale University Press, 1987); David M. McDonald, *United Government and Foreign Policy in Russia 1900–1914* (Cambridge: Harvard University Press, 1992); and David M. McDonald, "A Lever without a Fulcrum: Domestic Factors and Russian Foreign Policy, 1905–1914," in Hugh Ragsdale, ed. and trans., *Imperial Russian Foreign Policy* (Cambridge, UK: Cambridge University Press, 1993), pp. 268–311.

10. I. S. Rybachenok, "Brak po raschetu. N. K. Giers i zakliuchenie russko-frantsuzskogo soiuza," in *Rossiiskaia diplomatiia v portretakh* (Moscow: Mezhdunarodnye otnosheniia, 1992), pp. 256–59.

11. Shortly after Alexander III's accession to power, the tsar allowed liberal and conservative circles to struggle for control of the government. However, by late 1881, it was clear that conservative and reactionary forces had triumphed. On this point and others elucidating the triumph of reaction from 1878 to 1882, see Peter A. Zaionchkovsky, *The Russian Autocracy in Crisis 1878–1882*, trans. Gary M. Hamburg (Gulf Breeze, Fla.: Academic International Press, 1979).

12. The reactionary approach to university education was evident in an 1887 note to Alexander III from one of his most influential advisers, V. P. Meshcherskii, who advised the tsar to "clean out" all the students of St. Petersburg University and allow only the worthy ones to reregister. Such a measure, Meshcherskii argued, would improve student life, rid the university of dangerous ideas, and strengthen the moral foundations of young people. See Gosudarstvennyi arkhiv Rossiiskoi Federatsii (State Archive of the Russian Federation; hereafter, GARF), f. 677, op. 1, d. 588.

13. Zaionchkovsky, *Russian Autocracy in Crisis*, pp. 90–91; James H. Billington, *The Icon and the Axe: An Interpretive History of Russian Culture* (New York: Vintage, 1970), p. 449; and a letter from Prince V. A. Dolgorukov to Minister of Internal Affairs D. A. Tolstoy in 1883, arguing that the *zemstvos* were dangerously gaining too much autonomy from government control, in Russkaia gosudarstvennaia biblioteka (Russian State Library or the former Lenin Library; hereafter, RGB), Manuscript Division, f. 120, k. 18, ed. 48. The *zemstvos* were established in 1864 in thirty-four provinces and had authority over education, sanitation, agronomy, medical care, road-building, and local judicial administration. They lost many of their powers under Alexander III. See Alexander V. Zenkovsky, *Stolypin: Russia's Last Great Reformer* (Princeton: Kingston Press, 1986), pp. 84–86. Richard Pipes argues that Alexander III's "Temporary Regulations" "codified and systematized . . . repressive legislation" and established "all the elements of the police state . . . in imperial Russia by the 1880s," in *Russia under the Old Regime* (New York: Scribner, 1974), pp. 305–12.

14. Pobedonostsev was also Procurator of the Holy Synod or lay head of the Russian Orthodox Church from 1880 to 1905. He later became chief adviser to both Alexander III and Nicholas II. He believed in the state as the representation of truth and the national will, and argued that all instruments—including the office of the autocrat, the press, the law and judicial system, education, family life, and the Orthodox Church—must be put in the serv-

ice of the state. He condemned Western rationalism and constitutionalism and urged Russia to pursue its own path of "organic" development based on the immutable laws of the land and history. See Konstantin P. Pobedonostsev, *Reflections of a Russian Statesman* (Ann Arbor: University of Michigan Press, c. 1965) and Robert F. Byrnes, "Pobedonostsev on the Instruments of Russian Government," in Ernest J. Simmons, ed., *Continuity and Change in Russian and Soviet Thought* (Cambridge: Harvard University Press, 1955), pp. 115–26.

15. Before Alexander III, voluntary and administrative rather than cultural russification were the norms in the Russian empire. Voluntary russification referred to the unplanned assimilation of particular groups (e.g., Ukrainians, Tatars, Chuvashes, Belorussians, and others) who naturally adopted Russian language, customs, and culture as a result of serving in the Russian army or bureaucracy, living in Russian areas, or marrying Russians. Administrative russification referred to the state's efforts to unify the borderlands with the center through the "*gradual* introduction of Russian institutions and laws and extension of the use of Russian in the local bureaucracy and as a subject of instruction in the schools." Cultural russification, which dominated at the end of the nineteenth and the beginning of the twentieth century, aimed not only at political and administrative unification of the Russian borderlands with the center, but also at more coercive linguistic, religious, and cultural assimilation of non-Russians. It was no longer sufficient for subjects of the empire to be loyal to the tsars; they must also accept and internalize Russian language, values, and culture. See Edward C. Thaden, ed., *Russification in the Baltic Provinces and Finland 1855–1914* (Princeton: Princeton University Press, 1981), pp. 8–9; Hugh Seton-Watson, *The New Imperialism* (Chester Springs, Penn.: Dufour Editions, 1961), pp. 30–31; and Seymour Becker, "Contributions to a National Ideology: Histories of Russia in the First Half of the Nineteenth Century," *Russian History* 13 (Winter 1986):331–32.

16. The approach to russification taken by the tsarist government very much depended on the region and ethnic and national group in question. Thus, there were different russification decrees and policies for Poland, Finland, Bessarabia, Turkestan, and so on. See Iu. I. Semenov, ed., *Natsional'naia politika v imperatorskoi Rossii: Tsivilizovannye okrainy* (Moscow: Staryi sad, 1997), pp. 67–97.

17. See Rybachenok, "Brak po raschetu," pp. 257–58; and Charles and Barbara Jelavich, eds., *The Education of a Russian Statesman: The Memoirs of Nicholas Karlovich Giers* (Berkeley: University of California Press, 1962).

18. M. S. Anderson, *The Eastern Question 1774–1923* (New York: St. Martin's, 1966), pp. 221, 234–39; and Nicholas Riasanovsky, *A History of Russia*, 4th ed. (New York: Oxford University Press, 1984), p. 399.

19. Ignatev's tenure in the Ministry of Internal Affairs was brief (1881–82). The tsar dismissed him after he proposed broad public political participation through the revival of the seventeenth-century *zemskii sobor*, an assembly of officials, clergy, and elected representatives of peasants, merchants, and nobles from all over Russia. Ignatev died largely a forgotten man in Russia in 1908. See Geoffrey Hosking, *Russia: People and Empire 1552–1917* (Cambridge: Harvard University Press, 1997), pp. 373–74; and V. M. Khevrolina, "San Stefano: Venets i zavershenie diplomaticheskoi kar'ery N. P. Ignat'eva," in *Rossiiskaia diplomatiia v portretakh*, pp. 238–55.

20. D. A. Miliutin, *Dnevnik D. A. Miliutina 1873–1875*, vol. 3 (Moscow: Tip. Zhurnala "Pogranichnik," 1950), p. 68. See also T. H. Von Laue, *Serge Witte and the Industrialization of Russia* (New York: Columbia University Press, 1963), pp. 17–18; and William C. Fuller, Jr., *Strategy and Power in Russia 1600–1914* (New York: Free Press, 1992), pp. 338–41.

21. The St. Petersburg Slavic Committee conducted some activities in the late 1890s including an evening to honor the panslav general, Mikhail Cherniaev, and a competition

for the best history of the Balkan uprisings and the Russo-Turkish War. These activities and their sponsors, however, had no real political impact. See GARF, f. 1099, op. 1, d. 1052, pp. 1–2; and GARF, f. 1099, op. 1, d. 1051, pp. 2–3, 25–39, and 163–67.

22. Anderson, *Eastern Question*, p. 203.

23. For example, Bulgaria was not represented in Berlin even though twenty-two of the fifty-four articles discussed at the congress concerned its interests. Serbia, Montenegro, and Romania were also not admitted, and the Serbs were particularly disappointed because Russia minimized their territorial gains in favor of Bulgaria. A representative from Bosnia-Herzegovina went to Berlin, but the great power delegates ignored him, consigning Bosnia-Herzegovina to Austrian occupation. The Balkan Slavs understood that Russia was going to act chiefly in its own interest, at the cost of discriminating against some Slavs and sacrificing panslav "solidarity." Russian foreign minister Giers informed the Serbian representative in St. Petersburg in 1878 that Russian interests came first, then Bulgaria's, then Serbia's. On the souring of relations between Russia and the Slavs, see Alexander Joseph Michaels, *Neoslavism and Its Attempt at Russo-Polish Rapprochement 1908–1910*, Master's Thesis, American University, 1956, pp. 1–26; Anderson, *Eastern Question*, pp. 210–16; and Charles Jelavich, *Tsarist Russia and Balkan Nationalism* (Berkeley: University of California Press, 1958), pp. 12–13. On domestic criticism of Russian policy at the Congress of Berlin, see V. I. Ado, "Berlinskii Kongress 1878 g. i pomeshcheche-burzhuaznoe obshchestvennoe mnenie Rossii," *Istoricheskie zapiski* 69 (1961):101–41.

24. Anderson, *Eastern Question*, pp. 227–78; C. Jelavich, *Tsarist Russia and Balkan Nationalism*, pp. 12–13; and L. Martov, P. Maslov, and A. Potresov, eds., *Obshchestvennoe dvizhenie v Rossii v nachale XX–ogo veka* (St. Petersburg: Tip. t-va "Obshchestvennaia pol'za," 1911), vol. 4, part 1, pp. 260–66.

25. Andrew Malozemoff, *Russian Far Eastern Policy 1881–1904: With Special Emphasis on the Causes of the Russo-Japanese War* (New York: Octagon, 1977), pp. 41–253; Rybachenok, "Brak po raschetu," pp. 257–58; Fuller, *Strategy and Power*, pp. 368–72; Bestuzhev, *Bor'ba v Rossii po voprosam vneshnei politiki 1906–1910*, p. 179; and Anderson, *Eastern Question*, pp. 236, 250, 261. On agreements between Russia and Austria to preserve the status quo in the Balkans, see Martov, et al., eds., *Obshchestvennoe dvizhenie*, vol. 4, part 1, pp. 260–66.

26. The bulk of external financing for Russia's economic boom of the late 1880s to 1900 came from France and Belgium. By 1900, out of 269 foreign companies in Russia (all founded since 1888), 162 were Belgian, fifty-four French, thirty German, and nineteen British. See Hugh Seton-Watson, *Decline of Imperial Russia 1855–1914* (London: Methuen, 1952), pp. 109–20; M. E. Falkus, *The Industrialization of Russia 1700–1914* (London: Macmillan, 1972), pp. 51–57; and A. J. P. Taylor, *The Struggle for Mastery in Europe 1848–1918* (Oxford: Clarendon, 1954), p. 484.

27. Historians generally point to a racist element in Russian perceptions of Japan and cite Nicholas II's phrase referring to the Japanese as "yellow monkeys." But, while conceding that racism and racial slurs did play a role in Russian jingoistic literature, Louise McReynolds asserts that the major Russian newspapers themselves did not denigrate the Japanese racially. In reading hundreds of Russian newspaper articles on the war, she did not once find reference to the Japanese as "monkeys." See her *The News under Russia's Old Regime: The Development of a Mass Circulation Press* (Princeton: Princeton University Press, 1991), pp. 191–97.

28. Fuller, *Strategy and Power*, p. 401; J. N. Westwood, *Russia against Japan, 1904–1905: A New Look at the Russo-Japanese War* (London: Macmillan: 1986), pp. 116–53; V. A. Zolotarev and I. A. Kozlov, *Russko-iaponskaia voina 1904–1905 gg: Bor'ba na more*

(Moscow: Nauka, 1990), pp. 165–92; Evgenii Politovskii, *From Libau to Tsushima* (New York: Dutton, 1908); and Don C. Rawson, *Russian Rightists and the Revolution of 1905* (Cambridge, UK: Cambridge University Press, 1995), pp. 10–11, 40.

29. Quoted in Abraham Ascher, *The Revolution of 1905: Russia in Disarray* (Stanford: Stanford University Press, 1988), p. 43. My thanks to Brian D. Taylor for this citation.

30. McDonald, *United Government,* p. 74.

31. J. N. Westwood, *Endurance and Endeavor: Russian History 1812–1980,* 2nd ed. (New York: Oxford University Press, 1981), p. 142 (see also pp. 141–43 for examples of Russian military blunders in the war); and McReynolds, *News under Russia's Old Regime,* pp. 190–92.

32. "Politika Rossii 1905–1907 godov. Iz dnevnika F. F. Martensa," *Mezhdunarodnaia zhizn'* 1 (1996):99–107 (my thanks to Mark Kramer for this source); Westwood, *Russia against Japan,* pp. 152–53; Ben-Cion Pinchuk, *The Octobrists in the Third Duma 1907–1912* (Seattle: University of Washington Press), pp. 5–7; Zolotarev and Kozlov, *Russko-iaponskaia voina,* pp. 181–85; and P. A. Buryshkin, *Moskva kupecheskaia* (New York: Izd. M. Chekhova, 1954), pp. 308–15.

33. A. Iswolsky, *The Memoirs of Alexander Iswolsky* (Gulf Breeze, Fla.: Academic Press International, 1974), p. 129.

34. A. V. Ignatev and Iu. F. Subbotin, "Pod grom pushek. S. Iu. Witte i dogovory 1904 i 1905 godov s Germaniei i s Iaponiei," in *Rossiiskaia diplomatiia v portretakh,* pp. 333–35; Martov, et al., eds., *Obshchestvennoe dvizhenie,* vol. 2, pt. 1, pp. 30–32; and K. F. Shatsillo, *Rossiia pered pervoi mirovoi voiny (vooruzhennye sily tsarizma v 1905–1914 gg.)* (Moscow, 1974), pp. 13–14.

35. Worker and peasant discontent, roused by the state's failure to alleviate the misery of the masses, had already expressed itself in strikes and uprisings before 1905. In 1902, peasant riots erupted in several Russian provinces, with peasants burning noble estates and looting livestock and equipment. In the years 1900–1904, numerous strikes occurred annually, ranging from a low of sixty-eight to a high of 550 in 1903. In 1903, a strike among oil workers in Baku spread to several other major cities and illustrated the potentially paralyzing impact of mass actions on the Russian economy. See Rawson, *Russian Rightists,* pp. 4–7; and Martov, et al., eds., *Obshchestvennoe dvizhenie,* vol. 2, pp. 224–25.

36. "Politika Rossii 1905–1907 godov. Iz dnevnika F. F. Martensa," p. 100.

37. "Politika Rossii 1905–1907 godov. Iz dnevnika F. F. Martensa," pp. 105, 107.

38. Pinchuk, *Octobrists,* pp. 4–7; Rawson, *Russian Rightists,* pp. 4–18; Martov, et al., eds., *Obshchestvennoe dvizhenie,* vol. 2, pp. 213–14, 224–25; A. V. Ignatev, "K voprosu o vliianii russko-iaponskoi voiny na revoliutsionnye sobytiia 1905 goda v Rossii," in S. L. Tikhvinskii, ed., *Vneshniaia politika Rossii (istoriografiia): Sbornik statei* (Moscow: Nauka, 1988), pp. 74–102; Buryshkin, *Moskva kupecheskaia,* pp. 310–15; A. A. Kizevetter, *Na rubezhe dvukh stoletii (vospominaniia 1881–1914)* (Prague: Izd. "Orbis": 1929), pp. 372–73, 384–85; and Fuller, *Strategy and Power,* p. 407.

39. Pinchuk, *Octobrists,* p. 10.

40. Pinchuk, *Octobrists,* p. 14.

41. The preceding quotes are from McDonald, *United Government,* pp. 108–113, 123, 141; N. A. Fedorova, ed., *Istoriia SSSR, XIX i nachalo XX–ogo veka,* pp. 351–52; Geyer, *Russian Imperialism,* pp. 250–55; Avrekh, *Stolypin i tret'ia Duma,* p. 31; and P. A. Zabolotskii, *Vozrozhdenie idei slavianskoi vzaimnosti i novye izucheniia slavianstva* (Nezhin: Tip. V. K. Melenevskogo, 1912), pp. 7–9.

42. Fuller, *Strategy and Power,* p. 395.

43. Aleksei Kuropatkin, *The Russian Army and the Japanese War* (New York: Dutton, 1909), p. 203.

44. V. Doroshevich, *Vostok i voina* (Moscow: Tip. I. D. Sytina, 1905), pp. 181–95.

45. Some scholars use the term neoslavism to refer to the revival of traditional panslavism in the early twentieth century in Russia. Because there are stark differences between neoslavism and panslavism, I do not conflate these two terms and use them to refer to two distinct schools of nationalist thought. At different points in time and in an inconsistent manner, neoslav proponents in Russia included Kadet Miliukov, Octobrist Guchkov, Kadet P. B. Struve, and liberal Nationalists D. A. Vergun and V. A. Bobrinskii. See Michaels, *Neoslavism*, p. 58.

46. On the rise of neoslavism in 1905–8, see Paul Vyšný, *Neo-Slavism and the Czechs, 1898–1914* (Cambridge, UK: Cambridge University Press, 1977), pp. 55–90.

47. Michaels, *Neoslavism*, pp. 1–4.

48. P. Pertsov', *Panrussizm ili panslavizm?* (Moscow: Tip. A. I. Mamontova, 1913), pp. 2–3, 6–7, 66.

49. Hosking, *Russian Constitutional Experiment*, pp. 222–23. See also Vyšný, *Neo-Slavism and the Czechs*, p. 62; and William C. Fuller, Jr., *Civil–Military Conflict in Imperial Russia 1881–1914* (Princeton: Princeton University Press, 1985), p. 205.

50. A neoslav commentator noted that in Russia, one could strongly sense "backwardness, grayness, [and] provincialism." See Pertsov', *Panrussizm*, p. 25; and Lieven, *Russia and Origins of First World War*, pp. 91–101.

51. Vyšný, *Neo-Slavism and the Czechs*, pp. 84–86; and Hosking, *Russian Constitutional Experiment*, pp. 222–23.

52. The original Czech neoslavs formulated the Slavic national mission as "the promotion of greater understanding among the Slav nationalities" and the elimination of existing inter-Slav conflicts within and outside the Habsburg Empire. Slav unity and understanding would help Austro-Hungarian Slavs assert more effectively their political rights vis-à-vis the predominant German and Magyar nationalities in the Habsburg Empire. The Czechs and their neoslav compatriots hoped to transform Austria-Hungary into a genuine federation with equal rights for all nationalities and to shift the Dual Monarchy's foreign policy from closeness with Germany to a new rapprochement with Russia. Vyšný, *Neo-Slavism and the Czechs*, p. 248.

53. Lieven, *Russia and Origins of First World War*, pp. 91–101.

54. The term "rightist" refers generally to political groups that supported Russia's floundering autocracy in the early twentieth century, including the Russian Monarchist Party, the Union of Russian Men (*Soiuz russkikh liudei*), the Union of Russian People (*Soiuz russkogo naroda*), the Russian Assembly (*Russkoe sobranie*), the Russian Borderlands Society, and the Council of United Nobility (*Sovet ob"edinennykh dvorianskikh obshchestv*). In this book, "rightist" refers more exclusively to the extreme end of the pro-autocracy spectrum, especially as represented by the Union of Russian People.

55. Walter Laqueur, *Black Hundred: The Rise of the Extreme Right in Russia* (New York: HarperCollins , 1993), pp. 18–20; and Rawson, *Russian Rightists*, pp. 56–62.

56. Rawson, *Russian Rightists*, pp. 68–71, 127–41; G. V. Butmi-de-Katsman, *Konstitutsiia i politicheskaia svoboda*, 2nd ed. (St. Petersburg: Tip. Uchilishche glukhonemykh, 1906); N. N. Durnovo, *Russkaia panslavistskaia politika na pravoslavnom vostoke i v Rossii* (Moscow: Russkaia pechatnia, 1908), pp. 59–62, 87; Hosking, *Constitutional Experiment*, p. 220; Hans Rogger, "Was There a Russian Fascism? The Union of Russian People," *Journal of Modern History* 36 (December 1964):398–415; V. Ostretsov, *Chernaia sotnia i krasnaia sotnia* (Moscow: Voenno-patrioticheskoe literaturnoe ob"edinenie "Otechestvo," 1991), *passim*; Stephen J. Carter, *Russian Nationalism: Yesterday, Today, and Tomorrow* (New York: St. Martin's, 1990), pp. 36–42; and Laqueur, *Black Hundred*, pp. 18–28, 249–51.

57. Durnovo, *Russkaia panslavistskaia politika*, pp. 13, 38, 59–62; and Rawson, *Russian Rightists*, pp. 67–68. Some rightists, like N. N. Durnovo, had reservations, however, about the coercive nature of russification in areas like Georgia and Moldavia and urged that Russians learn first the language of these people in order to russify them more effectively.

58. V. Ivanovich, *Rossiiskie partii, soiuzy i ligi* (St. Petersburg, 1906), pp. 110–17; Durnovo, *Russkaia panslavistskaia politika*, pp. 63–69, 116–18, 126–27; Alfred Levin, *The Third Duma: Election and Profile* (Hamden, Conn.: Archon, 1973), pp. 141–48; Laqueur, *Black Hundred*, p. 26; and Rawson, *Russian Rightists*, p. 59.

59. Struve first made his mark in Russian politics as an advocate of "legal Marxism" or the correctness of Marxist economic and sociological axioms. Unlike many Russian Marxists, however, he did not favor revolution. See Billington, *Icon and the Axe*, pp. 462–63; Andrzej Walicki, *A History of Russian Thought: From the Enlightenment to Marxism* (Stanford: Stanford University Press, 1979), pp. 435–43; and S. L. Frank, *Biografiia P. B. Struve* (New York: Chekhov, 1956), pp. 1–24. For more on Struve's life, see Richard Pipes, *Struve: Liberal on the Left 1870–1905* (Cambridge: Harvard University Press, 1970) and *Struve: Liberal on the Right 1905–1944* (Cambridge: Harvard University Press, 1980).

60. The St. Petersburg Slavic Committee published the weekly *Slavianskie izvestiia* (1883–91). The journal was re-titled *Slavianskoe obozrenie* (1892–1902) and was renamed yet again, *Izvestiia Sankt Peterburgskogo slavianskogo blagotvoritel'nogo komiteta* (1902–4). In the period 1903–16, the journal reverted to its original title and was not published in 1911. This information is from the card catalog of the RGB in Moscow and from *Russkaia periodicheskaia pechat' 1702–1894* (Moscow: Gos. izd. politicheskoi literatury, 1959), pp. 696, 722.

61. Struve retired to Sosnovka near St. Petersburg in 1908 to work as a teacher. However, he continued to write on political issues in Russia. See Pipes, *Struve: Liberal on Right*, p. 180; Avrekh, *Stolypin i tret'ia Duma*, p. 457; and Philip Boobbyer, "Russian Liberal Conservatism," in Geoffrey Hosking and Robert Service, eds., *Russian Nationalism Past and Present* (London: Macmillan, 1998), pp. 35–45.

62. "Great Russia" was the title of Struve's best-known nationalist treatise. He took this title from a speech by Stolypin, which declared that revolutionaries wanted "great upheavals" but "we [nonrevolutionaries] want a Great Russia." See Frank, *Struve*, pp. 72–75; and P. B. Struve, "Velikaia Rossiia," *Russkaia mysl'* 29, no. 1 (1908):143–57 and an abbreviated translation of this article in "A Great Russia," *Russian Review* 11 (1913):11–30.

63. Pipes, *Struve: Liberal on Right*, p. 90; and Hosking, *Russian Constitutional Experiment*, p. 220.

64. Lieven, *Russia and Origins of First World War*, pp. 125–27; Frank, *Struve*, pp. 41–42, 75–77; and Avrekh, *Stolypin i tret'ia Duma*, pp. 456–57.

65. Frank, *Struve*, pp. 211–12; P. Struve, "Politika vnutrenniaia i politika vneshniaia," *Russkaia mysl'* 2 (1910):143; and Avrekh, *Stolypin i tret'ia Duma*, p. 33.

66. Frank, *Struve*, pp. 96–98, 220–23.

67. Vyšný, *Neo-Slavism and the Czechs*, pp. 75–76; Pipes, *Struve: Liberal on Right*, pp. 169–70; Frank, *Struve*, pp. 220–23; and Lieven, *Russia and Origins of First World War*, pp. 125–27.

68. Avrekh, *Stolypin i tret'ia Duma*, p. 31; and Pipes, *Struve: Liberal on Right*, pp. 88–92.

69. Some prominent panslavs in the early 1900s were General A. A. Kireev, a publicist and courtier with strong ties to the tsarist family and whose brother died in the Russo-Turkish War of 1877–78; P. A. Kulakovskii, professor of Slavic studies, editor of the journal *Okrainy Rossii* (*Russian Borderlands*), and member of the St. Petersburg Slavic Committee; and General A. F. Rittikh, also a member of the St. Petersburg Committee.

70. Vyšný, *Neo-Slavism and the Czechs*, p. 79.

71. Lieven, *Russia and Origins of First World War*, pp. 21–22; and A. F. Rittikh, *Ob"edinennoe slavianstvo* (St. Petersburg: Tip. V. D. Smirnova, 1908), pp. 14–25. For more on the self-image and other-image of Russian panslavs and the revival of ideas of such nineteenth-century panslavs as N. Danilevskii, L. Štur, and V. Lamanskii, see L. Lobov, "Slavianstvo kak mir budushchego," *Slavianskie izvestiia* 6 (1909):733–41. Panslavs were also critical of neoslavism; see, e.g., "Razocharovanie v neoslavianakh," *Slavianskie izvestiia* 6 (1909):835–36.

72. Rittikh, *Ob"edinennoe slavianstvo*, pp. 17–25; Lieven, *Russia and Origins of First World War*, pp. 21–22; and the preamble to *Okrainy Rossii* as described in Joseph L. Wieczynski, ed., *The Modern Encyclopedia of Russian and Soviet History* (Gulf Breeze, Fla.: Academic International Press, 1977), vol. 18, p. 150. In 1914, shortly before World War I, some panslavs returned to near-exact nineteenth-century assertions about Russia's role as leader of the Slav world against the Romano-Germanic world; Russia's right to rule Constantinople; and Russia's calling to create and lead a Slavic federation. See, for example, P. Kadilin, *Griadushchee zavershenie voinoiu 1914 g. istoricheskogo prizvaniia Rossii v roli osvoboditel'nitsy i glavy slavianskogo mira* (Kharkov: Tip. Mirnyi trud, 1914), pp. 4–27.

73. On the life and activities of Stolypin, see Alfred Levin, "Peter Arkadevich Stolypin: A Political Appraisal," *Journal of Modern History* 37 (December 1965):445–63; and Edward Chmielewski, "Stolypin's Last Crisis," *California Slavic Studies* 3 (1964):95–126.

74. Alfred Levin, "The Russian Voter in the Elections to the Third Duma," *Slavic Review* 4 (December 1962):676; Charques, *Twilight of Imperial Russia*, p. 172; and Hosking, *Russian Constitutional Experiment*, pp. 46–50. Stolypin's electoral law decreased the number of Duma deputies from 524 to 442; for its full impact, see Samuel N. Harper, *The New Electoral Law for the Russian Duma* (Chicago: University of Chicago Press, 1908), p. 55; Levin, *Third Duma*, pp. 112–39; Martov, et al., eds., *Obshchestvennoe dvizhenie*, vol. 4, pt. 2, pp. 143–48; and C. J. Smith, "The Russian Third State Duma: An Analytical Profile," *Russian Review* 17 (1958):201–210. For the 3 June System's discriminatory effects against the peasantry, see Leopold H. Haimson, "Conclusion: Observations on the Politics of the Russian Countryside (1905–14)," pp. 286–87, in Leopold Haimson, ed., *The Politics of Rural Russia 1905–1914* (Bloomington: Indiana University Press, 1979). The new electoral rules' discriminatory effect against non-Russians was evident in the decrease of Polish seats from forty-six in the second Duma to fourteen in the third. See Michaels, *Neoslavism*, p. 61.

75. Lenin and the Bolsheviks were a splinter from the Social Democrats. For information on the Left spectrum and its role in Duma politics, see Levin, *Second Duma*, pp. 35–50; and *Gosudarstvennaia duma v Rossii v dokumentakh i materialakh* (Introduction by F. I. Kalinychev) (Moscow: Gos. izd. iuridicheskoi literatury, 1957).

76. Emphasis in original. See Hans Rogger, "The Formation of the Russian Right 1900–1906," *California Slavic Studies* 3 (1964):66.

77. Many of the Kadets, including their nominal leader, Pavel Miliukov, were maximalist in their demands for a constitutional regime and utter rejection of the tsarist monarchy. However, they fit in the centrist category because they did not advocate violence to implement their political agenda. On Kadet maximalism, see V. A. Maklakov, *The First State Duma*, trans. Mary Belkin (Bloomington: Indiana University Press, 1964), pp. 1–5; and Levin, *Third Duma*, pp. 26–34.

78. Robert Edelman, *Gentry Politics on the Eve of the Russian Revolution* (New Brunswick: Rutgers University Press, 1980), pp. 49–51; and Hosking, *Russian Constitutional Experiment*, pp. 22–23.

79. Hosking, *Russia: People and Empire*, p. 444.

80. See Charques, *Twilight of Imperial Russia*, pp. 203–204, 207–208; Robert Thurston, "The Concerns of State, 'Society,' and People in Moscow 1906–1914," *Russian History* 11 (1984):60–82; and Michael Melançon, "The Socialist Revolutionaries from 1902 to 1907," *Russian History* 12 (Spring 1985):2–47.

81. McReynolds, *News under Russia's Old Regime*, pp. 170–77, 239, and her appendixes on content analysis of top Russian newspapers in the years 1907–13; and Louise McReynolds, "V. M. Doroshevich: The Newspaper Journalist and the Development of Public Opinion in Civil Society," in Edith W. Clowes, et al., eds., *Between Tsar and People: Educated Society and the Quest for Public Identity in Late Imperial Russia* (Princeton: Princeton University Press, 1991), pp. 233–47.

82. Emmons, *Formation of Political Parties*, pp. 2–3. For Russian literacy rates from 1897 to 1920, see I. M. Bogdanov, *Gramotnost' i obrazovanie v dorevoliutsionnoi Rossii i v SSSR* (Moscow: Izd. "Statistika," 1964), pp. 5, 65–82. See also Lieven, *Russia and Origins of First World War*, pp. 15 and 119; Christopher Read, *Religion, Revolution, and the Russian Intelligentsia 1900–1912* (London: Macmillan, 1979), pp. 6–7; and Jeffrey Brooks, *When Russia Learned to Read: Literacy and Popular Literature, 1861–1917* (Princeton: Princeton University Press, 1985), pp. 38–58. Pupils in Russian primary schools increased from over four million in 1899 to 6,629,978 in 1911; see I. Z. Kaganovich, *Ocherk razvitiia statistiki shkol'nogo obrazovaniia v SSSR* (Moscow: Gos. statisticheskoe izd., 1957).

83. See, for example, such officially sanctioned books for youth and family reading as *Sem'ia Aksakovykh* (St. Petersburg: Tip. M. Akinfieva i I. Leonteva, 1904) and E. N. Tikhomirova, *Za svobodu brat'ev-slavian* (Moscow: Tip. K. L. Men'shova, 1911). The former praised the Aksakov family's Russian roots and values, Ivan Aksakov's unswerving loyalty to Russian panslavism, and his devotion to the Russian motherland. The book admonished its young readers to emulate the example of Ivan and his slavophile brother Konstantin. The second book extolled Russia's selfless heroism in fighting to liberate "Slavs, who are our brothers by blood and faith" in 1877. In 1902, for the twenty-fifth anniversary of the Russo-Turkish War, commemorative albums with panslav content were also published. See, e.g., *Dvadtsatipiatiletie velikoi osvoboditel'noi voiny 1877–1902* (Moscow: Tip. T–va I. D. Sytina, 1902) and *Voina za osvobozhdenie slavian 1877–1878* (St. Petersburg: Voennaia tip., 1902). Proceeds from sales of the first album went toward support for Slavic students studying in Moscow. Ludovit Štur's famous panslav treatise was also republished in Russia in 1909 (*Slavianstvo i mir budushchego* [St. Petersburg, 1909]). Other panslav writings were Zabolotskii, *Vozrozhdenie idei slavianskoi vzaimnosti* and parts of the 1912 "Russian thinkers" (*russkie mysliteli*) series of the publishing house, Put'. See Pertsov, *Panrussizm*, p. 58.

84. Thus, for example, a November 1904 congress of Slavic nationalities in Paris, at which Russian delegates participated, was kept secret. See Michaels, *Neoslavism*, p. 39.

85. See Arseni Gulyga, "The 'Anguish of Being Russian': A Note on the Life and Works of Vasili Rozanov," *Glas* 6 (1993):185, 192–93, 197; *Russkaia periodicheskaia pechat' (1702–1914)* (Moscow: Gos. izd. politicheskoi literatury, 1959), pp. 509–11; Lieven, *Russia and Origins of First World War*, pp. 96–100, 129–32; Avrekh, *Stolypin i tret'ia Duma*, p. 457; and Durnovo, *Russkaia panslavistskaia politika*, p. 112. From 1912 to 1917 *Novoe vremia* was edited by the "Association of A. S. Suvorin," which also published other panslav literature. See Wieczynski, *Modern Encyclopedia*, pp. 109–10.

86. *Slovo*, *Moskovskii ezhenedel'nik*, and *Okrainy Rossii* closed down for lack of public support, while *Poliarnaia zvezda* ran afoul of censorship in its short life. *Russkaia mysl'* was a successful slavophile journal in the 1880s (with a peak circulation of 13,000 to 14,000),

but its subscribers by the period 1907–9 had dropped to 2,522. Struve edited the journal in 1910 and enlivened its content by opening new sections called "Russia and Foreign Lands" and "History of Russian Literature and Culture." *Golos Moskvy,* the Octobrists' paper funded by conservative merchants, never attracted a very wide readership. See *Bibliografiia periodicheskikh izdanii Rossii,* vol. 3 (Leningrad: Ministerstvo kul'tury RSFSR, 1960), pp. 241, 517; Pipes, *Struve: Liberal on Right,* pp. 169–70; *Russkaia periodicheskaia pechat' 1895–oktiabr' 1917* (Moscow: Gos. izd. politicheskoi literatury, 1957), p. 61; Frank, *Struve,* pp. 40–75; McReynolds, *News under Russia's Old Regime,* p. 211; and Lieven, *Russia and Origins of First World War,* pp. 96–100, 114–16.

87. V. A. Bobrinskii of the Nationalist party and his colleague A. I. Savenko led the Galicia-Russia Society, whose goal was to protect the rights of Slavs living in Galicia, a region under Austrian control. In 1913, the society had approximately 250 to 300 members in St. Petersburg. The Society for Slavic Culture and the Society for Slavic Scholarship were founded by Miliukov, Struve, and Maklakov from the Kadets; N. N. Lvov, M. A. Stakhovich, M. M. Fedorov, and D. N. Shipov from the Progressists in the Third Duma; and Guchkov, N. A. Khomiakov, and Kapustin from the Octobrists. These organizations' goal was to enhance inter-Slavic cultural, literary, and scholarly exchanges so that Slavs could appreciate better the richness of their common traditions. See Hosking, *Russian Constitutional Experiment,* pp. 224–25; Edelman, *Gentry Politics,* pp. 191–96; and V. Miakotin, "Nabroski sovremennosti," *Russkoe bogatstvo* 11 (1908):202.

88. Vyšný, *Neo-Slavism and the Czechs,* pp. 187–90; and Hosking, *Russian Constitutional Experiment,* pp. 224–25.

89. Fuller, *Civil–Military Conflict,* pp. 205–7.

90. Quoted in Hans Kohn, *Panslavism: Its History and Ideology* (Notre Dame: University of Notre Dame Press, 1953), p. 205.

91. The extreme Right in the Duma was skeptical that panslavism could even be progressive at all. They argued that panslavism was only an excuse for Russia to seize power abroad and introduce Russian dominion in the Balkans. See Miakotin, "Nabroski sovremennosti," pp. 204–13; Bestuzhev, *Bor'ba v Rossii,* p. 350; Hosking, *Russian Constitutional Experiment,* p. 229; and Pipes, *Struve: Liberal on Right,* p. 92.

92. Lieven, *Russia and Origins of First World War,* p. 90; and McDonald, *United Government,* pp. 199–201.

93. The fragmentation of social groups whose members comprised civil society was a dominant feature of Russian society in the early twentieth century. The landowning nobility, commercial–industrial class, peasantry, bourgeoisie, clergy, and intelligentsia were all divided by social and psychological differences. Further, historians have documented the divisions that existed within each group. The nobility, for example, had five political parties representing it in 1905, and the 1910 congress of the United Nobility recognized the primacy of regional differences among Russian nobles. See Alfred Rieber's remarks in "Diskussiia po dokladam," in *Reformy ili revoliutsiia? Rossiia 1861–1917: Materialy kollokviuma istorikov* (St. Petersburg: Nauka, 1992), pp. 264–68; and Leopold Haimson, "The Problem of Social Stability in Urban Russia, 1905–1917," *Slavic Review* 23, no. 4 (1964):619–24 and 24, no. 1 (1965):1–22.

94. McReynolds, *Russia's News under the Old Regime,* pp. 239–52; and Boobbyer, "Russian Liberal Conservatism," p. 45.

95. Fuller, *Civil–Military Conflict,* pp. 196–207.

96. Geyer, *Russian Imperialism,* pp. 281, 312–13.

97. Durnovo, *Russkaia panslavistskaia politika,* pp. 61–62; Lieven, *Russia and Origins of First World War,* pp. 125–27; and Charques, *Twilight of Imperial Russia,* pp. 182–85.

98. See, e.g., Kadilin, *Griadushchee zavershenie voinoiu,* esp. pp. 2–23; and *Voina za osvobozhdenie slavian,* pp. 1–5.

99. Russia's alleged four greatest wars, which defined the state's historical role as a great power, were the 1612 land war, Peter the Great's war against Sweden, the war against Napoleon, and the Russo-Turkish War (1877–78). One writer characterized the Russo-Turkish War as a "gigantic and heroic effort to resolve . . . Russia's historical fate." See I. V. Preobrazhenskii, *Za brat'ev slavian: Po povodu 25-letiia sviashchennoi voiny 1877–1878* (St. Petersburg: Izd. P. P. Soikina, 1903), p. 3.

100. But in the years 1907–10 many of the landed nobility returned to their traditional loyalty to the state, and their ranks in the third Duma (i.e., the Moderate Rights/Nationalists) pursued largely cooperative relations with the Stolypin government. See Haimson, "Conclusion," in Haimson, ed., *Politics of Rural Russia,* pp. 65–75.

101. *Rossiiskie samoderzhtsy,* pp. 310–16, 320–37, 351–53; Lieven, *Russia's Rulers under the Old Regime,* chapter 9; Pipes, *Struve: Liberal on Right,* pp. 23–27, 30–31; McDonald, *United Government,* p. 188. In 1911, Stolypin confronted the tsar with information gathered by the Chief of Gendarmes, which warned about Rasputin's suspicious character and his corrosive impact on public respect for the throne. Nicholas II responded that the information on Rasputin might well be true but, he continued, "I ask you never again to speak to me about Rasputin; after all, there is nothing I can do." See *Rossiiskie samoderzhtsy,* p. 357; and M. V. Rodzianko, *The Reign of Rasputin: An Empire's Collapse,* trans. Catherine Zvegintzoff (Gulf Breeze, Fla.: Academic International Press, 1973).

102. The tsar's advisers included Prince V. P. Meshcherskii, editor of *Grazhdanin,* and Minister of Internal Affairs P. N. Durnovo. On the views and activities of Durnovo, see Lieven, *Russia's Rulers under the Old Regime,* pp. 207–230. See also Hans Rogger, *Russia in the Age of Modernisation and Revolution 1881–1917* (New York: Longman, 1983), pp. 20–29.

103. The State Council's elected members included fifty-six high-propertied deputies from the provincial *zemstvos,* eighteen from the gentry, twelve from commerce and industry, six from the clergy, six from the Academy of Sciences and the universities, and two from the Finnish Diet. See Riasanovsky, *History of Russia,* pp. 408–9; and Lieven, *Russia's Rulers under the Old Regime,* pp. 27–83.

104. Hosking notes that Russia was undergoing transition from autocracy to constitutionalism at a time of "deep social conflict." During such transition, disputes about the nature of authority and uncertainty about the location of power create severe instability in the political system. Hosking, *Russian Constitutional Experiment,* p. 12.

105. Serge Witte was prime minister for six months; I. L. Goremykin for three; and, finally, in July 1906, P. A. Stolypin became prime minister. Stolypin was to stay in this post until 1911.

106. The tsar dismissed Kokovtsev in January 1914 and replaced him with the geriatric I. L. Goremykin (who had been prime minister for a few months in 1906). Many saw Goremykin's appointment as "the placing of a figurehead at the helm of a moribund United Government." Foreign Minister Sazonov described Goremykin as "an old man who had long since lost not only the ability to be interested in any matter except for his personal tranquility and well-being, but simply even to reckon with the surrounding reality." See McDonald, *United Government,* p. 198; and S. D. Sazonov, *Vospominaniia* (Moscow: Mezhdunarodnye otnosheniia, 1991), p. 94. In 1914, some members of the Council of Ministers campaigned for an end to Duma deputies' freedom of speech at the rostrum and immunity from prosecution. Edelman, *Gentry Politics,* pp. 196–98.

107. Hosking, *Russian Constitutional Experiment,* pp. 182–214; Avrekh, *Stolypin i tret'ia Duma,* pp. 407–57; McDonald, *United Government,* pp. 177–86; and V. S. Diakin, *Russkaia burzhuaziia i tsarizm v gody pervoi mirovoi voiny 1914–1917* (Leningrad: Nauka, 1967).

108. Quoted in Hosking, *Russian Constitutional Experiment,* p. 213.

109. Bestuzhev, *Bor'ba v Rossii,* pp. 186, 181–87; and A. V. Ignatev, *Vneshniaia politika Rossii v 1905–1907 gg.* (Moscow: Nauka, 1986), pp. 107–9.

110. Bestuzhev, *Bor'ba v Rossii,* pp. 215–18; and McDonald, *United Government,* pp. 127–37.

111. B. Jelavich, *St. Petersburg and Moscow,* pp. 264–70.

112. Vyšný, *Neo-Slavism and the Czechs,* pp. 141–43; and Edward C. Thaden, *Russia and the Balkan Alliance of 1912* (University Park: Pennsylvania State University Press, 1965), pp. 9–10.

113. Krivoshein argued that Russia should defend its vital interests in the Balkans and go to war if necessary. His differences with Kokovtsev led him to spearhead an effort to unseat the prime minister in 1913. McDonald, *United Government,* pp. 184–85, 197, 204–5.

114. McDonald, *United Government,* pp. 177–87.

115. Hartwig was a well-known slavophile and once led the Foreign Ministry's Asiatic department. The Russo-Turkish War (1877–78) impressed him deeply as a young adult, and he advocated Russian help for "brother Slavs" throughout his career. As Russia's ambassador to Serbia, he engaged constantly in anti-Austrian agitation. His actions and those of Nekliudov recall the excesses of Nikolai Ignatev, the notorious panslav diplomat. Thaden, *Russia and Balkan Alliance,* pp. 58–98; Taylor, *Struggle for Mastery,* p. 484; and Andrew Rossos, *Russia and the Balkans: Inter-Balkan Rivalries and Russian Foreign Policy 1908–1914* (Toronto: University of Toronto Press, 1981), pp. 26–27.

116. Nikolai Nikolaevich was a close relative of the tsar and led the St. Petersburg military district. He allegedly lobbied the tsar on behalf of panslavism. See *Rossiiskie samoderzhtsy,* p. 341; Lieven, *Russia and Origins of First World War,* chap. 4; and McDonald, *United Government,* pp. 183–84.

117. Bestuzhev, *Bor'ba v Rossii,* pp. 336–54; Hosking, *Russian Constitutional Experiment,* pp. 233–37; Thaden, *Russia and Balkan Alliance,* p. 112; and McDonald, *United Government,* pp. 182, 188–89.

118. *Rossiiskie samoderzhtsy,* p. 322; Charques, *Twilight of Imperial Russia,* p. 161, Zenkovsky, *Stolypin,* p. 5; Anna Geifman, "Ubii!" *Rodina,* no. 1 (1994):25–26; and Anna Geifman, *Thou Shalt Kill: Revolutionary Terrorism in Russia 1894–1917* (Princeton: Princeton University Press, 1993).

119. Geifman, "Ubii!" p. 26. People could barely trust the government's competence to fight terrorism when it could not even protect its own ranks. For example, evidence of police connivance in the assassination of Stolypin emerged—this when Stolypin was not only prime minister but also minister of internal affairs! Hosking, *Russian Constitutional Experiment,* pp. 147–48.

120. Levin, *Second Duma,* pp. 366–67. According to Levin, there were 6,164 strikes in 1906, 2,545 of which were economically motivated. In 1907, strikes totaled 3,573; 973 of these were mainly for economic reasons. There were about seven hundred thousand workers on strike in Russia in 1912; nine hundred thousand in 1913; and over 1.5 million in the first seven months of 1914. Charques, *Twilight of Imperial Russia,* pp. 111–39, 200; and Edelman, *Gentry Politics,* pp. 199–200.

121. Pinchuk, *Octobrists,* pp. 182–83; see also Charques, *Twilight of Imperial Russia,* p. 192; Seton-Watson, *Decline of Imperial Russia,* p. 291; McDonald, *United Government,* p. 207; and Haimson, "The Problem of Social Stability in Urban Russia," pp. 627–40.

122. Tsarist support for rightist groups, especially the URP, never amounted to a full-fledged partnership because the chauvinism at the core of these groups' ideology was a threat to the multiethnic empire. Stolypin himself was wary of the tsar's support for extremists like the URP, and his government subsidized other, more moderate Right

groups. For example, moderate nationalists led by P. N. Balashev received financing for over a year from Stolypin's government for their local activities. See Avrekh, *Stolypin i tret'ia Duma*, pp. 414–15; Levin, *Third Duma*, p. 148; G. Yurskii, *Pravye v tretei Gosudarstvennoi Dume* (Kharkov: Izd. Tsentral'nogo predvybornogo komiteta ob"edinnenykh russkikh liudei, 1912), pp. 91–125; Rogger, "Formation of the Russian Right," pp. 66–94; and Laqueur, *Black Hundred*, pp. 23–24, 27.

123. These included (1) the Kholm bill, which removed the Kholm territory from Poland and transferred it to Russia because many residents on the territory were Russian; (2) the Finland bill, which removed much of Finland's autonomy and made imperial laws supreme on Finnish territory; (3) the western *zemstvo* bill, which changed the suffrage to ensure a Russian (as opposed to Polish) majority in the *zemstvos* of nine provinces; and (4) other bills that discriminated against Jews, Muslims, and other minorities. See *Tret'ia gosudarstvennaia Duma: Materialy dlia otsenki ee deiatel'nosti* (St. Petersburg: Trud, 1912), pp. 139–50, 372–77; Yurskii, *Pravye v tretei Gosudarstvennoi Dume*, pp. 1–5, 91–120; and Zenkovsky, *Stolypin*, pp. 15–27.

124. The Duma majority that supported the government splintered over domestic policies, including Great Russian chauvinism; cohesiveness also weakened as Stolypin's own political favor with the tsar waned in 1911. The individual parties themselves had leadership and other internal disputes, which created new configurations of party lines and new groupings. See Avrekh, *Stolypin i tret'ia Duma*, pp. 407–56; Pipes, *Struve: Liberal on Right*, p. 93; *Tret'ia gosudarstvennaia Duma*, pp. 135–37, 359–71; and Pinchuk, *Octobrists*, pp. 161–68, 182–83.

125. Hosking, *Constitutional Experiment*, pp. 241–42, 245, 215–16; and E. Uribes, "Praviashchie krugi Rossii i Balkanskii krizis 1911g." *Istoricheskie zapiski* 105 (1980):88–94.

126. See Miliukov, *Balkanskii krizis*, pp. 55–56, 133–51; Charques, *Twilight of Imperial Russia*, pp. 104–5, 153; and Geyer, *Russian Imperialism*, pp. 295–97.

127. The quotes by Riabushinskii are from Diakin, *Russkaia burzhuaziia i tsarizm v gody pervoi mirovoi voiny*, pp. 33–34; V. P. Riabushinskii, ed., *Velikaia Rossia: Sbornik stat'ei po voennym i obshchestvennym voprosam*, book 2 (Moscow: Tip. Riabushkina, 1911), p. 5; James L. West, "The Riabushinsky Circle: *Burzhuaziia* and *Obshchestvennost'* in Late Imperial Russia," in Clowes, et al., eds., *Between Tsar and People*, p. 49; and I. F. Grindin, ed., "Kistorii kontserna br. Riabushinskikh," in *Materialy po istorii SSSR*, vol. 6 (Moscow: Izd. Akademii Nauk SSSR, 1959), pp. 603–40.

128. Bestuzhev, *Bor'ba v Rossii*, pp. 237–39; and Michaels, *Neoslavism*, p. 39.

129. Avrekh, *Stolypin i tret'ia Duma*, pp. 424–25.

130. See *Tret'ia gosudarstvennaia duma*, pp. 282–90. Guchkov was personally very interested in military and naval affairs and used his leadership of the Duma's defense committee to advance his personal authority on these issues. On army and navy issues, the Duma was empowered to consider legislation when new appropriations were required. The army and navy, however, managed to hide many appropriations from the Duma, and deputies occasionally resorted to novel ways to control these appropriations with the clandestine help of some officers. Hosking, *Russian Constitutional Experiment*, pp. 227, 230; see also Carter, *Russian Nationalism*, pp. 34–37; and Anton I. Denikin, *The Career of a Tsarist Officer: Memoirs, 1872–1916*, trans. Margaret Patoski (Minneapolis: University of Minnesota Press, 1975), pp. 218–20.

131. McDonald, *United Government*, pp. 183–89, 205–7; *Tret'ia gosudarstvennaia Duma*, p. 291; and Thaden, *Russia and Balkan Alliance*, pp. 134–35.

132. Nicholas II, for example, asked the publisher of *Novoe vremia* in 1909 to assist Russian foreign policy and help prevent a war for which Russia was not prepared by ter-

minating publication of anti-German articles. Other high officials undertook similar non-coercive measures to ask public opinion leaders to quell their panslav agitation in 1908–9. See Bestuzhev, *Bor'ba v Rossii*, pp. 283–84, 290; see also Fiona Hill, "Domestic Anxiety and International Humiliation: Russian National Interest, Public Opinion, and the Annexation of Bosnia-Herzegovina 1908–1909," xerox ms., pp. 6–10; and McDonald, *United Government*, p. 196 on Grigorovich's arguments in 1913 for a more aggressive posture in the Black Sea as a response to the demands of public opinion.

133. Pipes, *Struve: Liberal on Right*, pp. 174–82. Some merchants did fear enemy control of the straits, which materialized during World War I. Turkey closed off the straits, and, as a consequence, allied forces had great difficulty supplying Russia with arms and munitions for its army and raw materials for its economic production. Edward C. Thaden, *Russia since 1801* (New York: Wiley, 1971), p. 410.

134. V. N. Kokovtsov, *Iz moego proshlogo: Vospominaniia 1903–1914*, vol. 2 (Moscow: Nauka, 1992), p. 128. Even if military commanders had wanted to instigate aggressive nationalist education in the military, their chances for success would have been impeded by the low levels of literacy among peasant recruits who made up the bulk of the army. In 1902, the army was 80 percent peasant and had a dismal literacy rate. Denikin, *Career of a Tsarist Officer*, pp. 80–84, 209–10; Lieven, *Russia and Origins of First World War*, pp. 96–116; Fuller, *Strategy and Power*, pp. 338–50, 377–84; and Fuller, *Civil–Military Relations in Imperial Russia*, pp. 205–7. Examples of military publications supporting panslavism are Rittikh, *Ob"edinennoe slavianstvo* and *Voina za osvobozhdenie slavian*.

135. Geyer, *Russian Imperialism*, pp. 281, 312–13.

136. Thaden, *Russia and Balkan Alliance*, pp. 47, 56–57, 83; and Rossos, *Russia and the Balkans*, pp. 8–33.

137. McDonald, *United Government*, p. 147. Publications that joined the chorus against Austria's railway plan included *Novoe vremia*, *Rus'*, *Slovo*, *Rech'*, *Sankt Peterburgskie vedomosti*, and *Birzhevye vedomosti*. See Martov, et al., eds., *Obshchestvennoe dvizhenie*, vol. 4, pt. 1, pp. 268–69.

138. Quoted in McDonald, *United Government*, p. 129. See also Bestuzhev, *Bor'ba v Rossii*, pp. 202–3 for Austrian motivations leading to the annexation.

139. McDonald, *United Government*, pp. 135–39; and Bestuzhev, *Bor'ba v Rossii*, pp. 225, 249–50.

140. P. Lavrov, "Anneksiia Bosnii i Gertsegoviny: Otnoshenie k nei Slavianstva," *Vestnik Evropy* (3 March 1909):30–50; Bestuzhev, *Bor'ba v Rossii*, pp. 222–29; Miliukov, *Balkanskii krizis*, p. 133; Martov, et al., eds., *Obshchestvennoe dvizhenie*, vol. 4, pt. 1, pp. 271–74; Geyer, *Russian Imperialism*, pp. 301–2; Pipes, *Struve: Liberal on Right*, pp. 178–82; Michaels, *Neoslavism*, pp. 43–62, 68–70.

141. *Golos Moskvy*, 17 March 1909, as quoted in Hosking, *Russian Constitutional Experiment*, pp. 232–33. Some, including the moderate Miliukov and his Kadet followers, took a more favorable view of war as an option in Russia's policy vis-à-vis rival powers in the Balkans. See Bestuzhev, *Bor'ba v Rossii*, pp. 225, 265–66.

142. Vyšný, *Neo-Slavism and the Czechs*, pp. 2, 142–44; Lavrov, "Anneksiia Bosnii i Gertsegoviny," pp. 30–50; and Miakotin, "Nabroski sovremennosti," p. 200.

143. By 1911, for example, Turkey was considering plans for naval expansion in the Black Sea, Italy had invaded Tripoli, and France had made territorial gains in Morocco. See Thaden, *Russia and Balkan Alliance*, pp. 9–11.

144. The Balkan victors marred this victory by disagreeing over the division of territorial gains. As a result, a second Balkan war broke out in June 1913—this time between Bulgaria, on one hand, and Serbia, Greece, Romania, and Turkey on the other. Bulgaria suf-

fered a resounding defeat and had to yield much of the territory it had gained in the first Balkan war; Serbia and Greece, in the meantime, gained much of Macedonian territory and an extra million and a half subjects each. See Thaden, *Russia and Balkan Alliance*, p. 131; B. Jelavich, *St. Petersburg and Moscow*, pp. 270–71; and Taylor, *Struggle for Mastery*, pp. 497–98.

145. Edelman, *Gentry Politics*, pp. 194–96; and Bobykin, *Ocherki istorii*, p. 121.

146. Hosking, *Russian Constitutional Experiment*, pp. 235–36; and Uribes, "Praviashchie krugi Rossii," pp. 84–98.

147. Quotes in this paragraph are from Hosking, *Russian Constitutional Experiment*, pp. 235–36; Sazonov, *Vospominaniia*, p. 87; McDonald, "A Lever Without a Fulcrum," pp. 299–302; and McDonald, *United Government*, pp. 185–86.

148. Sazonov, *Vospominaniia*, pp. 137–50; and Taylor, *Struggle for Mastery*, pp. 508–9.

149. McDonald, *United Government*, pp. 190–97; Taylor, *Struggle for Mastery*, pp. 508–9; and G. P. Gooch and H. N. Temperley, eds., *British Documents on the Origins of the War*, vol. X/1 (London: H. M. Stationery Office, 1927–38), p. 397 on a detailed description of the Russian public response to the Liman affair.

150. After the second Balkan war in 1913, Bulgaria collapsed militarily and left Russia's sphere of influence, while the Balkan alliance itself disintegrated. At this point, Serbia became Russia's sole reliable ally in the Near East. See B. Jelavich, *Russia's Balkan Entanglements*, pp. 234–35.

151. On one hand, a powerful Germany stood behind Austria-Hungary and was committed to go to war in defense of the latter's interests. On the other hand, France stood behind Russia, and Great Britain behind France. These opposing alliances were set up to act almost automatically once a member of one side launched hostilities against any member of the other side. In July 1914 Russia made an attempt to negotiate a way out of the crisis and avoid war, but failed. Austria itself miscalculated that Russia, as in 1909, could be bullied into doing nothing when its interests in the Balkans were threatened. See Fuller, *Strategy and Power*, pp. 445–48.

152. Bobykin, *Ocherki istorii*, pp. 155–56.

153. Lieven, *Russia and Origins of First World War*, p. 37.

154. See, e.g., Anderson, *Eastern Question*, p. 307.

155. Trubetskoi was known for his lengthy pieces on international relations and Russian foreign policy in 1906–12. A well-known slavophile descended from old Russian nobility (the Trubetskois and Lopukhins), he subscribed to Struve's great power nationalism. He and his brother co-edited *Moskovskii ezhenedel'nik*, which supported panslav ideas, and they also participated in the activities of the Struve and Riabushinskii circles. Lieven, *Russia and Origins of First World War*, pp. 91–101; and Bestuzhev, *Bor'ba v Rossii*, pp. 225, 265–66.

156. Bestuzhev, *Bor'ba v Rossii*, p. 289.

157. Hosking, *Russian Constitutional Experiment*, pp. 238–39.

158. Lieven, *Russia and Origins of First World War*, p. 129.

159. Lieven, *Russia and Origins of First World War*, pp. 90–91, 116.

160. In 1913, 43 percent of Russia's exports went to Germany, Austria's ally, while Russia took 47 percent of German exports. Lieven, *Russia and Origins of First World War*, pp. 132–34; and Edelman, *Gentry Politics*, pp. 144, 191–96.

161. P. N. Durnovo wrote a lengthy memorandum to the tsar in early 1914 urging reconciliation with Germany to protect Russian interests in the straits and to prevent conflict that could lead to revolution. Former Finance Minister Witte shared Durnovo's opinion, but they did not prevail on Nicholas II. Others like the Nationalist leader Savenko and

Kadet leader Miliukov also urged caution a few weeks before war broke out, but Miliukov changed his position at the Duma session of July 26, when everyone but the Social Democrats agreed on national unity and support for the government in its struggle to free Europe and slavdom from German domination. See McDonald, *United Government*, pp. 199–201; Hosking, *Russian Constitutional Experiment*, p. 240; Edelman, *Gentry Politics*, p. 195; and Lieven, *Russia and Origins of First World War*, pp. 78–79, 89–90, 123–25.

162. McDonald, *United Government*, pp. 197, 204–5.

163. McDonald, *United Government*, p. 204.

164. Fuller, *Strategy and Power*, p. 447; and Lieven, *Russia and Origins of First World War*, pp. 108–12.

165. McDonald, *United Government*, pp. 205–7; Sazonov, *Vospominaniia*, p. 247; and Lieven, *Russia and Origins of First World War*, pp. 139–43.

166. McDonald, *United Government*, pp. 206–7; and Fuller, *Strategy and Power*, pp. 446–47.

167. McDonald, *United Government*, pp. 205–6.

168. Bobykin, *Ocherki istorii*, pp. 153–58.

169. *Novoe vremia*, 20 July 1914; Hosking, *Russian Constitutional Experiment*, p. 240; Pipes, *Struve: Liberal on Right*, p. 209; and Kohn, *Panslavism*, p. 205.

170. Avrekh, *Stolypin i tret'ia Duma*, pp. 410–11; and Pipes, *Struve: Liberal on Right*, p. 180.

171. This included the Young Czechs, led by Karel Kramar, in Austria and the Karadjordjevic dynasty, which came to power in Serbia in 1903. On the rise of Balkan nationalism, see B. Jelavich, *St. Petersburg and Moscow*, pp. 258–65; Thaden, *Russia and Balkan Alliance*, pp. 58–98; Vyšný, *Neo-Slavism and the Czechs*, pp. 1–54; and Hosking, *Russian Constitutional Experiment*, p. 224.

172. B. Jelavich, *St. Petersburg and Moscow*, pp. 258–60, 264–65; Lieven, *Russia and Origins of First World War*, pp. 38–39, 43–46; Uribes, "Praviashchie krugi Rossii," p. 93; and Rossos, *Russia and the Balkans*, pp. 15, 32. On the demise of Turkish power in Europe from 1894 to 1913, see B. Jelavich, *Russia's Balkan Entanglements*, pp. 210–35; and Thaden, *Russia and Balkan Alliance*, pp. 29–37.

173. Serbia intensely pursued its own self-interest in negotiating the Balkan alliance. It invented, for example, a "Macedo-Slav" nationality in Macedonia to convince Bulgaria to grant it the northern strip of Macedonia. Serbia also claimed Turkish territory on the Adriatic Sea that was not inhabited by Serbs but by Albanians. Rossos, *Russia and the Balkans*, pp. 16–17; and Taylor, *Struggle for Mastery*, pp. 485–86.

174. Thaden, *Russia and Balkan Alliance*, pp. 9–11, 75–77, 93–109; and Uribes, "Praviashchie krugi Rossii," pp. 78–93.

175. Austria's ultimatum to Belgrade in late July 1914 asked for a formal abandonment by the Serbian government of south Slav irredentist claims and the dismantlement of the *Narodna Obrana* (National Defense), a Serbian nationalist society that had been operating in Serbia and Bosnia before 1914. Serbia responded with a conciliatory note, which Austria promptly rejected. See Anderson, *Eastern Question*, pp. 305, 308.

176. Bobykin, *Ocherki istorii*, pp. 155–56; McDonald, *United Government*, p. 204; and Fuller, *Strategy and Power*, p. 488. Russia shifted its alliance from Germany to France in the 1890s and early twentieth century because it feared German power and expansion. From its earliest days, the Russo-French alliance had presumed war against Germany, and French funds had helped build railways on Russia's western frontier for precisely this purpose. Rogger, *Russia in Age of Modernisation*, pp. 168–72; and Lieven, *Russia and Origins of First World War*, pp. 24–27.

177. Great Britain and France both indicated that they would not support Russia if it went to war over Balkan issues in 1908–9 and 1912–13. See Bestuzhev, *Bor'ba v Rossii*, pp. 281–82; Fuller, *Strategy and Power*, pp. 418–23; and Thaden, *Russia and Balkan Alliance*, pp. 112–13.

178. Bestuzhev, *Bor'ba v Rossii*, p. 200; Sazonov, *Vospominaniia*, pp. 57–58; and Alfred J. Rieber, "Persistent Factors in Russian Foreign Policy: An Interpretive Essay," in Ragsdale, ed., *Imperial Russian Foreign Policy*, p. 325.

179. Miakotin, "Nabroski sovremennosti," p. 216.

5

Recreating Russia: Soviet Demise, Humiliation, and the Rise of Nationalisms, 1989–1998

We have . . . [put an] end to the Cold War, the arms race and the insane militarization of our country, which crippled our economy, distorted our thinking and undermined our morals. . . . We . . . renounced interference in the affairs of others and the use of troops beyond our borders. . . . The peoples and nations of this country have acquired genuine freedom to choose their own way towards self-determination.

—Mikhail Gorbachev, 1991

In the past, the mere mention of [the great Russians'] name used to destroy the walls of impregnable fortresses. Now they are defeated by Lilliputians. . . . We have lost our identity; "Russians"—this word has become an empty sound without any meaning.

—Aleksandr Kazintsev, 1992

Russia must become a great power because it is good for her, and good for the world.

—Natalia Narochnitskaia, 1993

[W]hy was this country called great. . . . Why did this country, in particular, give birth to [great] literature of the nineteenth century? Why did great philosophical thought arise here? Why do we possess great scientific potential? Why did we win wars?

—Nikita Mikhalkov, 1999

NATIONALISM IN POST-SOVIET RUSSIA

Nationalism, articulated in different variants, has become the most prominent ideological force in Russia since the collapse of the Soviet Union (USSR) in 1991. It resonates broadly and deeply among many segments of Russian society and colors the rhetoric of nearly all elites in the Russian political spectrum—from liberal reformers to fascist patriots.[1] In the wake of the destruction of a great state (the USSR), the politically articulate Russian public has turned its attention to the questions: What is Russia? Where are its borders and what kind of political authority should rule it? Who is a Russian? How can state and society be wedded in a common national identity (*natsional'naia identichnost'*)? How should Russia conduct its relations with newly independent neighbors who, for centuries, were part of the old Russian and Soviet empires and who house millions of ethnic Russians on their territory? What is the role of a diminished Russia in the evolving world order, and how should it interact with the United States and other Western powers? In the context of present travails, how should Russia rebuild its dwindling prestige and resources, and reassert itself as a great power?

This chapter describes nationalist ideas that emerged in the late- and post-Soviet periods, largely in response to the above questions and to the weakening and demise of the once feared and powerful Soviet state. Some of these ideas meet the definition of aggressive nationalism and have been propagated widely in post-Soviet Russia. Aggressive nationalism has proven to be a constant source of pressure on state authorities, but it has been an ineffective determinant of Russian foreign policy. It has not become a rallying cause for mobilization of the majority of the Russian public, and extreme nationalist tenets have not evolved into a blueprint for the state's international behavior.

This chapter, like the two previous chapters, links the rise of aggressive nationalism in post-Soviet Russia with national humiliation. Humiliation resulted from the disintegration of the Soviet Union, a state whose self-image was steeped in "great power" (even "superpower") myths. The Soviet Union's collapse occurred rapidly, creating profound political, military, territorial, economic, and social shocks and losses for Russians, who found themselves in a much shrunken new state. Aggressive nationalist rhetoric helped cause the initially pro-Western government of Boris Yeltsin and Andrei Kozyrev to shift its rhetoric in a more assertive nationalist direction, particularly in foreign affairs, beginning in late 1992 and 1993. Yeltsin and members of his government employed more nationalism in their rhetoric, sponsored various projects to formulate an official "national idea," and occasionally opposed Western positions on foreign policy matters perceived to be of core interest to Russia.[2] But these developments, taken together, did not amount to official support for aggressive nationalism. Although aggressive nationalists widely propagandized their ideas and successfully cultivated support from some portion of the Russian public, they failed to mobilize a critical mass of the population or garner sufficient support from Russian policymakers to implement their ideas. As of the end of 1998, Russian state authorities had not gone to war with Russia's neighbors on behalf of extreme nationalist causes; neither had they pursued violent hegemony or imperial restoration in the name of nationalism. This was the case despite assertions about the prevalence of nationalist-inspired Russian neoimperialism in the post-Soviet period.[3]

This chapter describes five competing strands of nationalism in post-Soviet Russia: Westernizing nationalism, nativism, moderate statism, aggressive statism, and national patriotism. Of these, moderate statism has so far been most dominant. It (1) defines membership in the nation in terms of ethnicity and language (i.e., Russians and Russian speakers), but also acknowledges the rights of non-Russians in the Russian Federation; (2) emphasizes a strong and unitary Russian state with great power status in the international system; and (3) advocates a hegemonic role in the former Soviet space and a more independent foreign policy vis-à-vis the West, especially the United States. Moderate statism prescribes an assertive Russian foreign policy, but does not particularly favor warfare to advance national chauvinism, ethnic unification, or an expansionist and imperial national mission. It employs a rhetoric of national greatness to mitigate perceptual damage to the Russian self-image caused by national humiliation, but keeps Russian foreign policy options largely within the confines of predictable or normal behavior for a much weakened, erstwhile superpower state. While moderate statism is not the most benign form of nationalist ideology, its highly resonant components stand in stark contrast to more ethnic exclusivist, militarist, and fascist variants of Russian nationalism.

To understand the evolution of post-Soviet Russian nationalism, it is helpful to review the Soviet past. Chapter 2 chronicled the communist regime's policies to build a supranational Soviet nation while simultaneously institutionalizing nations on an ethnic basis. This chapter highlights the survival of Russian nationalism in the context of Soviet supranationalism and internationalism and describes the legacy that the Soviet Union bequeathed to Russia in terms of nationalist ideas. It also briefly explores Joseph Stalin's use of Russian nationalism to preserve the state during World War II and, finally, assesses the impact of Gorbachev's *glasnost'* and *perestroika* on the rise of nationalism.

UNEASY COEXISTENCE: RUSSIAN NATIONALISM AND COMMUNIST POLITICS

From Lenin to Brezhnev: The Persistence of Nationalism[4]

The relationship between Russian nationalism and communism before Gorbachev was one of uneasy coexistence. First, communist ideology was fundamentally antithetical to nationalism in general and Russian nationalism in particular. However, the inherent antagonism between communism and nationalism did not spell the demise of Russian nationalist ideas; in fact, these ideas persisted throughout communist rule. Third, nationalist ideas persisted in various forms in the Soviet Union, including nativist, statist, and national patriotic variants. Moreover, communist rulers at times exploited nationalist ideology to serve state purposes, but nationalism never became predominant over communist ideology.

The Bolshevik revolution swept into power an ideology that, at its core, was antagonistic to nationalism. Communist thought emphasized internationalism and class ideology as the central and guiding principles of the Bolshevik-ruled state. Although V. I. Lenin and Stalin, for example, accepted nations as real and objective entities, they also preached that the preservation and development of national languages and cultures were but temporary and requisite phases toward the time when all peoples would ultimately join the "universal culture, revolution, and communism."[5] Early Bolshevik thinking and policy also deemphasized and maligned Russian nationalism, which, Lenin argued, was the nationalism of the "oppressor nation" and an impediment to the realization of a socialist state that would transcend national differences. By the time of the Tenth Party Congress in 1921, the Bolshevik government had defined the "nationality" question in terms of

> neat opposition between "Great Russians" and "non-Great Russians" [nonethnic Russians]. The Great Russians belonged to an advanced, formerly dominant nation possessed of a secure tradition of national statehood and frequently guilty of ethnic arrogance and insensitivity known as "great power chauvinism." All the other nationalities . . . were victims of tsarist-imposed statelessness, backwardness and "culturelessness" . . . which made it difficult for them to take advantage of new revolutionary opportunities and sometimes tempted them to engage in "local nationalism."[6]

For the eventual triumph of socialism, Lenin underscored the need to eliminate Russian chauvinist nationalism and cultivate Russian "internationalism." The Bolshevik government decreed that ethnic Russians should accept not only the "formal equality of nations, but also . . . the kind of inequality at the expense of the big oppressor nation that would compensate for the de facto inequality that exists in life."[7] Thus, under Lenin, a federal plan emerged, emphasizing equal rights for Russians and non-Russians, including the right of self-determination. Bolshevik leaders gave non-Russian groups opportunities to promote their indigenous cultures and languages, and created political administrative units rooted in ethnic particularism.[8]

Official communist ideological and political antagonism toward nationalism did not end the propagation of Russian nationalist ideas. From Lenin to Leonid Brezhnev, state authorities occasionally retreated on tenets of communist ideology, and revived and co-opted nationalist ideas while maintaining adherence to communism. At other times, they suppressed Russian nationalism, but it survived underground to resurface at later times.

The clearest example of the Soviet state's co-optation of Russian nationalism occurred during Stalin's regime, particularly in the 1930s and through the end of World War II. During this period, nationalism coexisted with the excesses of Stalinist communism and proved indispensable to the defense of the Soviet state when confronted with potential destruction by Hitler's war machine. On one hand, Stalin's nation-destroying policies of forced collectivization, industrialization and mass purges, mass deportation, and the institutionalization of the cultural straitjacket of "socialist realism" decimated Russian and non-Russian groups in the Soviet Union—all for the ostensibly greater purpose of moving the state closer to communism.[9] On the other hand, Stalin, more than any other Soviet leader, expounded Russian nationalist rhetoric, adopted chauvinist policies, and relied on Russian nationalist ideas to mobilize the population during World War II. As early as 1924, Stalin's russocentrism was evident, lending credence to Lenin's reproach that he was among those who erred on the side of "Great Russian chauvinism." In speaking about "socialism in one country" (an idea originally raised by Nikolai Bukharin), Stalin attacked Leon Trotsky and others whose internationalist beliefs, in his view, belied their "lack of faith in the revolutionary potentialities of the [Russian] peasant movement . . . and proletariat in Russia."[10] By the late 1930s, official policies included national glorification of the Russian past, cultural and linguistic russification of non-Russians, anti-Semitism, and strains of xenophobia. Stalin declared Russia the most sovereign and most revolutionary of the Soviet nations, and when the Russian Soviet Federated Socialist Republic (RSFSR) adopted a republican version of the Soviet constitution in 1937, a *Pravda* editorial rhapsodized,

> Russian culture enriches the culture of other peoples. The Russian language has become the language of world revolution. Lenin wrote in Russian. Stalin writes in Russian. Russian culture has become international, for it is the most advanced, the most humane. Leninism is its offspring, the Stalin Constitution its expression.[11]

Stalin's regime curbed Soviet revolutionary historiography and approved new textbooks that extolled the "progressive" aspects, virtues, and accomplishments of the tsarist past. Historians began to depict the benign quality of tsarist imperialism, which, they argued, brought progress and civilization to backward peoples. They also portrayed Russian imperial rule over other nations as a lesser evil compared to domination by more despotic powers such as Persia, Turkey, or even Poland. State authorities commissioned monuments to Russian heroes, resurrected Russian folklore (with characters in some folkloric songs resembling Lenin and Stalin), and elevated Russia to "hero-nation" status and "first among equals" in the Soviet Union. In the second half of the 1930s, songs of the "motherland" (*rodina*) replaced songs about the Comintern (Communist International), and patriotic education intensified, focused on the idea of ancient Rus' as unifier of all peoples of the motherland. Books and films propagandizing the glory of the motherland featured Russian, Ukrainian, and Georgian heroes; but notwithstanding this diverse ethnic tapestry, the idea of patriotism centered on Russia and the Russian state. Political power became highly centralized in Moscow, and Russians replaced local ethnic leaders in non-Russian republics.[12]

Stalin's Russian nationalist revival reached its apogee during World War II, when he invoked images of an imperiled "Mother Russia" to urge and inspire Russians to fight against Nazi aggression. In November 1941, at a critical and difficult moment for the Soviet state, Stalin spoke about the singular role of the "great Russian nation, the nation of Plekhanov and Lenin, Belinsky and Chernyshevsky,

Pushkin and Tolstoy, Glinka and Tchaikovsky, Gorky and Chekhov . . . Repin and Surikov, Suvorov and Kutuzov."[13] In extolling the "courage of [Soviet] ancestors," Stalin named only ethnic Russian military figures of the past. In addition, during the war years, state officials emphasized symbols of the Orthodox Church along with those of the Communist Party; named military academies after imperial Russian military heroes; and popularized traditional Russian military insignia. At the end of what came to be known as the Great Patriotic War or the Fatherland War, Stalin made his famous toast to the Russian nation—"the leading nation of the USSR," "the guide for the whole Union," "intelligent, persevering, and patient."[14] Yet, at the same time, he did not cease to emphasize the importance and contributions of the communist revolution and the centrality of socialism as the goal of the Soviet Union. In 1944, he declared, "The socialist order, made possible by the October revolution, gave our people and our army great and insuperable strength."[15]

Under Nikita Khrushchev, Stalin's successor, state authorities emphasized *Soviet* patriotism while suppressing the most visible expressions of Russian nationalist ideology and cultural hegemony. In his famous denunciation of Stalin at the 1956 Twentieth Party Congress and on other occasions, Khrushchev condemned Stalin's crimes against the Soviet Union's non-Russian nations,[16] the excessive centralization of power, and policies of russification and Russian ethnic hegemony. He reemphasized non-Russian cultural rights and traditions; restored national histories; and diluted the political power of the Russian ethnic group through indigenization, or the appointment of indigenous cadres at every level of the communist hierarchy in the 1950s. He also authorized the closing and/or razing of thousands of Russian Orthodox churches from 1959 to 1964. He emphasized internationalism and announced at the Twenty-Second Party Congress in 1961 that economic and cultural progress had produced the "rapprochement" of nations. He further noted that the Leninist national policy of 1922 had been fulfilled: "the development of the nations and egalitarianism had created the conditions necessary to transcend prejudice and strong nationalist feelings" in the Soviet Union.[17]

Khrushchev's regime, while suppressing ethnic Russian nationalism, nonetheless allowed nationalist expression in publications such as *Novyi mir*. *Novyi mir* was the foremost Soviet literary journal, and among its authors were those who called for sociopolitical reform and criticized Stalin's legacy in the countryside and among the Russian peasantry. Various *Novyi mir* writers focused on rural Russia, and their prose became known as village prose (*derevenskaia proza*). Village prose recalled some ideas of the slavophiles of the nineteenth century, including religious values, idealization of the peasantry, and the equation of Russian national identity with traditional peasant identity and culture.[18]

Under Brezhnev, official suppression of nationalism continued, but the regime also tolerated expressions of Russian nationalism. These came out either through officially approved organizations and publications, or clandestinely via *samizdat* or underground publications. In the 1960s and 1970s, several organizations and publications with nationalist leanings became active in Soviet political life. These included the All-Russian Social–Christian Union for the Liberation of the People (VSKhSON); the officially sponsored All-Russian Society for the Preservation of Historical and Cultural Monuments (VOOPIiK); and the journals *Nash sovremennik, Molodaia gvardiia,* and *Novyi mir.* VSKhSON published in *samizdat* a rough blueprint for post-Soviet society, ruled by a Russian Orthodox theocratic state. On a more open front, writers in *Molodaia gvardiia,* the organ of the Central Committee of the Komsomol or Soviet youth organization, emphasized ecological concerns, the preservation of prerevolutionary Russian architecture and churches, and traditional peasant values and way of life. They rejected and attacked what, in their view, was a pro-Western reform outlook among writers in *Novyi mir.* But the most important nationalist publication in the 1970s and until the early 1980s was *Nash sovremennik,* which published village prose writers as well as nationalist historians and literary critics. The journal was popular among official and public circles, won numerous official awards, and increased in circulation from 60,000 in 1968 to 336,000 by 1981. Yet other nationalist writing flourished in *Veche,* a *samizdat* journal devoted to discussion and debate among Russian nationalist thinkers.[19]

In the early 1970s, two other documents, associated with Russia's most prominent writer of the time, Aleksandr Solzhenitsyn, reflected a resurgence of nationalist thought. These were the *samizdat* publication *From under the Rubble* (including essays by Solzhenitsyn and others) and Solzhenitsyn's *Letter to the Soviet Leaders.* These publications deplored the social, demographic, environmental, political, and spiritual ills of Soviet-ruled Russia and recommended possible solutions.

Russian nationalist ideas always coexisted with communism and flourished when blessed officially by the state. From Lenin to Brezhnev, articulators of Russian nationalism did not subscribe to a monolithic nationalist ideology, but propagated different ideas. One was nativism, which emphasized the traditions of rural and Orthodox Russia and which was most evident in village prose writings and in the work of Solzhenitsyn. For the most part, nativism was an "underground" strand of nationalism, whose adherents articulated a form of protest against communism and Soviet policies. A second type of Russian nationalism was national patriotism, whose content was chauvinistic, anti-Semitic, xenophobic, and imperialistic. National patriotism was present during Stalin's rule and also in some of the underground nationalist literature of the Brezhnev era, but, like nativism, this brand of nationalism was neither consistently prominent nor officially popular.[20] A third and most important nationalist strand was statism, prevalent under Stalin and emphasizing power and greatness as the most essential attributes of the state. Statism preached the primacy of Russian language and culture and celebrated Russia's imperialist past as both benign and valuable. Under the Brezhnev regime, the state also tolerated statist nationalist ideas. As long as proponents of these ideas supported a strong Soviet state and accepted the Soviet incarnation of the former Russian empire, they managed to avoid official opprobrium and punishment.[21] Although statist nationalism never supplanted communist ideology, it enjoyed the greatest legitimacy and broadest room for expression throughout the Soviet period. Russian nationalists supported statism in part because it accorded the Russian ethnic group a privileged place. Moscow was the center of power, and Russians dominated the highest echelons of the Communist Party, the military officers corps, and other Union institutions. The officers corps, for example, was approximately 61 percent Russian in the late 1980s. These arrangements justified the absence of separate Russian republican institutions within the Soviet Union.[22]

The survival of Russian nationalism during the Soviet period, especially its prominence during Stalin's rule, was consistent with the practice of nation-building in imperial Russia (as described in chapter 2). Specifically, nation-building was distorted in favor of service to the state. It helped to preserve and strengthen the state, and bolstered rule by the communists. State officials manipulated Russian ethnic symbols to enhance their own legitimacy and to mobilize the population to defend the state. But they did not facilitate the development of society as a more autonomous actor vis-à-vis the state, failed to give genuine political rights to the people (but granted bogus rights such as ritual voting), and crushed large numbers of people under the weight of the imperial Soviet political and military machine. Marxism-Leninism, the state's official ideology, continued to outweigh nationalism.[23] In the end, the Russian "nation" remained a stunted entity in the Soviet Union, and nationalism did not function to cement state–society relations in a permanent way.

Glasnost', Perestroika, and the Rebirth of Nationalism

Russian nationalism traversed a rough and uneven path in the first six decades of communist rule. One version of it, focused on Russian greatness and flavored with chauvinism, reached an apex under Stalin. After Stalin, no particular variant of nationalism became officially prominent again, despite alleged sympathy and support in high places in the late 1960s and early 1970s.[24] Official elites and the broader public also did not debate or discuss nationalism openly or widely because of Soviet ideological restrictions.[25] This changed drastically after Gorbachev came to power in 1985. His policies of *glasnost'* (openness) and *perestroika* (restructuring) created a new opening for nationalist ideas to occupy a central place on the Soviet political landscape. Russian nationalists took advantage of political liberalization not only to propagate their ideas, but also to compete for political power in Russian elections. These nationalists, in the first years of *glasnost'*, concentrated on preserving Russia's historical and cultural monuments, protecting the environment (e.g., the fate of Siberian rivers, which Soviet authorities wanted to divert to Central Asia), addressing social problems (e.g., alcoholism and high mortality rates), and revealing the truth about the Stalinist past.[26] But other nationalists propagandized a more alarming set of ideas, including anti-Semitic scapegoating, chauvinism, anti-Westernism, and antimoderniza-tion. They used *Nash sovremennik* as their platform, and organized such extremist groups as *Pamiat'*.[27]

Three developments in the Gorbachev period stand out. First, *glasnost'* stimulated a revival of nationalist ideas. Previously unavailable works of nineteenth-century conservative nationalist thinkers including Nikolai Karamzin, Konstantin

Leontev, Nikolai Danilevskii, Ivan Il'in, and Dmitrii Ilovaiskii were republished in Moscow.[28] Russian intellectuals and publicists wrote a barrage of patriotic articles in the popular media and in Russian thick journals, criticizing the Soviet system, the legacies of Marxism-Leninism, and Gorbachev's *perestroika* itself. In *Novyi mir*, for example, numerous articles from 1987 to 1989 countered Marxist tenets; denounced the "anti-people" and "anti-Russian" policies of communism and Bolshevism; and advocated greater Russian national self-awareness and other ideas for a non-violent, Russian national revival.[29]

Second, concessions by the state to nationalist demands and aspirations, first in the non-Russian republics and later in Russia itself, helped to legitimate nationalism. Contravening previous communist policy, Gorbachev allowed thousands of Orthodox churches to reopen, announced his own baptism, and blessed his wife's participation in the millennial celebration of Russia's conversion to Orthodoxy. He also granted (or, at least, failed to oppose) demands for Russia to have its own republican institutions within the Soviet Union, including a Russian Academy of Sciences, a Russian Communist Party, and even a Russian Foreign Ministry.[30] Official accommodation of, and indecision toward, centrifugal nationalisms in Russia and other former Soviet republics further loosened the already weakening moorings of the Soviet state away from multiethnic federation toward nationally constituted states. Gorbachev's government did not explore nationalist alternatives that might help keep the multiethnic Soviet state together. Officials, for example, barely paid attention to arguments for developing a civic variant of Russian (*rossiiskii*) nationalism that might arrest the process of Soviet collapse and prevent future problems for minorities in newly constituted ethnic states.[31] Instead, they persisted in defining the Soviet Union's problems as one of communist system reform rather than stunted or distorted nation-building.

Third, new political institutions and processes created opportunities for Russian nationalists to compete in the political arena and enhanced the rising political viability of nationalism as an alternative ideology to Soviet communism. Elections to the USSR Supreme Soviet in 1989 and to the Russian Federation Supreme Soviet in 1990 were particularly important. Although most members of the nationalist bloc lost in both elections, they nonetheless gained the political experience and public exposure necessary for future political battles. Defeat energized some groups—e.g., the United Workers Front—into creating formal organizations for future political work. In 1990–93, those nationalists who did win seats in the Soviet legislature joined forces with communists in organizations like *Soiuz* and the National Salvation Front to form an active and outspoken opposition to their Western-oriented, liberal democratic colleagues. More importantly, elections in 1989, 1990, and 1991 gave Boris Yeltsin, ousted Politburo member, a chance to run for political office—first for the Russian Supreme Soviet and subsequently for Russian president. Yeltsin campaigned on a platform of populism and social justice ("land to the peasants"), Russian sovereignty from the Soviet Union ("all peoples of the USSR must have de facto economic, political, and cultural independence"), and some form of democratic government. Until the autumn of 1989, Yeltsin had not exploited the nationalist themes of Russian humiliation, pride, and sovereignty. But elections turned him into a patriot, and, in May 1990, he declared that the "issue of primary importance is the spiritual, national, and economic rebirth of Russia, which has been for long decades an appendage of the center and which, in many respects, has lost its independence."[32] Yeltsin co-opted symbols used by nationalists, including the Russian tricolor flag; at his inauguration as president, he invited the head of the Orthodox Church to speak and played Glinka's "A Life for the Tsar" as the national anthem. Yeltsin's rise to political power after being expelled from the Communist Party hierarchy illustrated the challenge nationalism posed to the dominance of communist ideology and authority in Gorbachev's Soviet Union.

During *perestroika*, individuals and groups identified with conservative, authoritarian, chauvinist, and imperialist strands of nationalist thought became the loudest voices for Russian nationalism, although their impact on actual policy was much less than the decibel level of their propaganda. These groups promoted a strong, hegemonic Russian nation; the preservation of the Soviet imperial state; discipline and order; and defense of Russian national interests from assaults by traitorous Westerners, Jews, Georgians, and other non-Russians. They identified themselves as true defenders of Russia and attacked Gorbachev and his cohort of "democrats" who had surrendered Russia's welfare to the West, emphasized deceptive "all-human values" over Russian distinctiveness, and created chaos in Russia's social and economic life. A few Russian liberals in the USSR Supreme Soviet attempted in early 1990 to discredit the authority of conservative and extremist nationalists to speak "in the name of the Russian people [and] Russia," but with little success.[33] Further, the disintegration of the Soviet Union in December 1991 seemed to prove the correctness of nationalists who had argued that liberal-democratic notions of the Russian nation and its mission would destroy the state and end Russia's historical great power status.

SOVIET DISINTEGRATION, NATIONAL HUMILIATION, AND THE RISE OF AGGRESSIVE NATIONALISM

National humiliation and aggressive nationalist reaction to it were particularly salient phenomena in the late Soviet and early post-Soviet periods. The next two sections focus on the period 1989–95, chronicle the extent and depth of Russian national humiliation, and describe the (mostly, but not exclusively) aggressive nationalist rhetoric that accompanied humiliation.

Depth and Extent of Russian National Humiliation

National humiliation in the former Soviet Union occurred in a society that was, during nearly seventy-five years of communist rule, steeped in myths of national greatness and great power status. The Soviet Union was one of the world's two nuclear superpowers and had become an industrialized and formidable state, whose internal and external empire included constituents of the tsarist state, eastern Europe, and client regimes in many parts of the developing world. During the Cold War, the Soviet Union's alter ego was the United States; both were superpowers with competing ideological and political systems, each pretending to a position of correctness and dominance in international affairs.

The chronicle of Russian national humiliation leading to, and after, the breakup of the Soviet state is stark. In 1987–91, the Russian great power image crumbled when *glasnost*' allowed scholars, the press, and ordinary citizens to document and discuss the reality "that seventy years of communist overlordship had left [Russia] in abject poverty and spiritual and intellectual confusion."[34] Statistics were released for the first time revealing the realities of environmental degradation, alcoholism, crime, delinquency, Aeroflot crashes, and substandard health services. Scholars underlined that since 1917, the Russian ethnic group had steadily lost ground per capita to other nationalities in higher education, housing and social infrastructure, agricultural investment, and overall economic development. The Russian republic also subsidized consumer goods for other Soviet republics, and lost billions in rubles of revenue in the process. Policies of "bleeding the Russian heartland," some concluded, had caused a catastrophic decline in the Russian population, making Russia the only Soviet republic, besides Latvia and Estonia, "to have suffered a decrease in the percentage of the titular nationality." One study showed that in the years 1979–87 alone, Russia's rural population declined by four million, equivalent to the dying out of two to three thousand villages annually. The Russian demographic situation was so dire that observers predicted that the Russian population could decrease by half in just two generations.[35]

Revelations about the dark side of Soviet history added to Russian humiliation by revealing the shame, incompetence, cruelty, and treachery of a regime that many Russians deemed superior and in which they took pride. The film *Repentance*, the novel *Children of the Arbat*, national hearings on the Molotov–Ribbentrop Pact, Soviet troop withdrawal from Afghanistan and the release of information on damages suffered there, the Chernobyl disaster, and numerous revelations about Stalin's murderous policies abraded Russians' esteem of themselves and their supposed great state. The Communist Party, a former quasi-sacred institution of truth and authority (even for those who were not believers, the Party still represented authority and minimum well-being), became instead for many a symbol of incompetence, lies, torment, and injustice.[36]

By the end of 1991, Russia's national humiliation reached new depths. First, the Soviet Union's defeat in the decades-old superpower Cold War with the United States became clear. The USSR was no longer able or willing to continue intense competition either in the nuclear arms race or in the race for client states and influence in the developing world. Second, the Soviet state disintegrated, with concomitant territorial, political, economic, and social losses for Russia. What was formerly a successor entity to the centuries-old Russian empire, encompassing thirteen million square miles and a population of over 260 million people by the end of the 1980s, suddenly crumbled, without a shot being fired, on December 31, 1991. Although in preceding years Soviet power had been on the wane—with the withdrawal of troops from Afghanistan; the reunification of Germany and the loss of Soviet satellite states in Eastern Europe; the disintegration of the Warsaw Treaty Organization; the withdrawal from Soviet client states in Asia, Africa, and Latin America; the signing of arms control treaties that entailed the destruction of significant parts of the Soviet nuclear arsenal and the dismantling of Soviet conventional force superiority in Europe—the complete disintegration of the state nevertheless shocked many ethnic Russians and russified elites. For the first time in over three hundred years, Russia was detached from its imperial conquests and lost such traditional "Russian" lands as the Crimea, Belarus, and eastern Ukraine. Indeed, Russia had shrunk to a size smaller than it was when Peter the Great died in 1725![37]

Territorial losses not only reduced Russia's geographic stature, but also eliminated access to natural resources, including rich agricultural lands in Kazakhstan and Ukraine, cotton in Uzbekistan, oil and gas in Azerbaijan and Central Asia, and fabulous resorts on the Black Sea coast in Georgia. Key transportation and communication routes by sea and rail also disappeared. In addition, the amputation of territories long in the Russian tsarist, then Soviet imperial, domain created thirty million displaced persons, twenty-five million of whom were Russians who suddenly found themselves at risk of expulsion or becoming second-class citizens in alien states. In addition, military-strategic losses resulted from the breakup of the gargantuan Soviet army into new national units; the loss of defense enterprises, bases, and other military installations outside the Russian republic; and the division of nuclear and conventional weapons with other former Soviet republics. The shrinking of Russian economic weight to half that of the Soviet Union also implied a dearth of resources to maintain what had been one of the world's most formidable military machines.[38]

The process of national humiliation continued into the first three years of Russia's independent existence, when the new state experienced challenges to its territorial integrity from such constituent parts as Tatarstan, Bashkortostan, Yakutia, and, most seriously, Chechnya. Although Moscow succeeded in thwarting these challenges, its first war in Chechnya (1994–96) revealed to the world the Russian army's ineptitude, repeated official mishandling of the crisis, and implicit complicity with the Chechen "outlaws." Besides Chechnya, other sources of intensified humiliation arose from such social phenomena as soaring violent crime rates, open impoverishment of those segments of the population that failed to adjust to new economic realities, and widespread social malaise and depression. Internationally, Russian prestige also suffered. Some opinion makers in Russia felt that their state had been left out of major diplomatic initiatives such as the drawing of a Middle East peace agreement, while others emphasized that Russia yielded to the West all that it wanted without receiving appropriate compensation. Russia suffered such ignominy as yielding to Western pressures to cancel agreements on a nuclear reactor deal with India, a long-standing Soviet and Russian ally.[39] By the early 1990s (and before NATO expansion to states formerly in the Soviet Union's orbit), there was sufficient national humiliation to provoke aggressive nationalist rhetoric among certain sectors of Russian public opinion.

Aggressive Nationalist Reaction

Public consciousness of national humiliation became a salient theme in Russian political discourse in the late Soviet period and intensified after the Soviet Union's collapse in the period 1991–95. Referring to the demise of the Soviet state, representatives of practically all major strands of political ideology used a vocabulary connoting wounded feelings, a sense of injustice, and sentiments of betrayal and victimization, particularly by the "West." Representatives of liberal, conservative, moderate, and radical political opinion in Russia commonly used the words "humiliated," "wounded," "destroyed," "dying," "raped," "genocide," "catastrophe," "bloodied," "losers," "beggars," "ashamed," "nonhumans," "mutants," "hapless," "semicolonial," "hated," "poor and paltry," "insulted," "spat upon," and "despised" to refer to the fate of their great state, the Russian people, and Western characterizations of the Russian nation.[40] This graphic language of humiliation appeared in the late 1980s and remained in the 1990s in the mass media, thick journals, public speeches, and other fora. Those who used the language of humiliation often followed their references with assertive expressions such as "Great Russia," "great power," "glory," "strong," "salvation," "rich," "mighty," "noble," "spiritual and blameless," "warrior," "correct, righteous people," "genetically great," and "worthy of respect" to refer to their hopes for Russia's future and to describe the true qualities of the Russian nation. In one instance that captured the language of humiliation, an extreme nationalist article poignantly described television coverage of the deaths and dislocation of ethnic Russians in Moldova, a newly independent former Soviet republic. The author wrote that after showing the corpses of three hundred Russians who were killed, the program brazenly shifted to a commercial for Vidal Sassoon shampoo. He concluded that the message was that Russians could be annihilated by others, and "the world would not even blink."[41]

Expressions of humiliation came from elites who used to occupy positions of privilege and power in the Soviet Union and suddenly found themselves floundering in a sea of uncertainty after 1991. The rules of economic, social, and political power in their society changed in ways that disadvantaged them. Some of these elites became assertive, if not extreme, nationalists. Former KGB general Aleksandr Sterligov, who leads the Russian National Assembly, for example, pithily remarked to this author that he, a former "general with great connections," could not buy regular medication for his granddaughter. Aleksandr Kazintsev, an extremist nationalist with the journal *Nash sovremennik*, observed how offensive it was for one of his friends to be unable to pay for a needed operation.[42]

Elite reaction to national humiliation included gradations of assertive nationalism, not purely extremist positions. In the early 1990s, moderate figures who originally subscribed to nativist ideas emphasizing religion and rural values shifted to positions centered on the primacy of a strong and hegemonic Russian state and an oppositionist attitude toward the West. Viktor Aksiuchits, for example, who led the Russian Christian Democratic Movement and who originally espoused a slavophile, spiritual nationalism, allied himself with the anti-Western

Govorukhin Bloc by the December 1995 Duma elections. Others who represented Westernizing liberal views in the early post-Soviet period—e.g., Yeltsin, Kozyrev, Sergei Stankevich, and Vladimir Lukin—all came to espouse a language of patriotism and nationalism. Valery Zorkin, first chief of the Russian Constitutional Court and an early sympathizer with Western-style democracy, later came to associate himself with extreme nationalists.[43]

The larger Russian public also expressed feelings of national humiliation, coupled with nationalist assertions, in letters to national newspapers, responses to polls, regional publications, and mass demonstrations. For example, letters to some of the most vitriolic nationalist papers decried the treatment of war veterans who risked their lives for Russia and came to doubt the value of their previously sacred war medals. These letters argued that Russian society, since the demise of the Soviet Union, had become one of "monstrous lawlessness and outrage upon the memory of those who died" for the motherland (*chudovishchnoe bezzakonie i nadrugatel'stvo nad pamiat'iu pogibshykh*). Others claimed that Russian society had become focused on the "dollar" and lost its "human face," Russian brains had been turned into a cheap commodity for Western buyers, and "democracy" was pushing mothers to murder their children and kill themselves. In placards at demonstrations and in vandals' slogans, it was common to find expressions of outrage at Western entities and Western treatment of Russia. Poll results also showed nostalgia for the old days of Soviet superpower status; consternation about the humiliating and deplorable treatment of Russians and their cultural symbols in the "near abroad"; drastic disillusionment with ideas and people from the West; a belief that the West deliberately caused many of Russia's woes; and a deep desire to restore respect for Russian national history, culture, and values. Further, regional publications printed articles excoriating those responsible for the breakup of the Soviet Union—calling them "occupants" and "moral degenerates" who had committed crimes against the "great Russian state and Russian people" and had succumbed naively to the false "altruism of international financial capital" and the dubious munificence of the "Judeo-masonic American order."[44]

The linkage between national humiliation and aggressive variants of nationalism may be explained—at least at the elite level—by *ressentiment*. *Ressentiment* is evident in extreme nationalist comments about Russian superiority and corresponding Western inferiority, scorn and hatred for the West, emphasis on Western perfidy, and disdain for Western assistance.[45] For example, Stanislav Kuniaev, long a rabid patriot, compared Russia with the United States thus:

I hate America. . . . I have traveled all over the United States . . . and spent two months there. At first I was amazed and surprised by everything. Then I began to figure things out, I began to think, and realized that this society was very unpleasant—despite all its wealth and interesting features. . . . American propaganda and the mass media are horrible. I watched American television and had to laugh. If television were the expression of the essence of the American people, then that essence is horrible and shameful. And now when our own television is becoming more and more American, I begin to hate America even more. I think American TV is an example of totalitarian thinking. It shows a civilized country in a state of primitive barbarism . . . Whenever we [Russians] ended our isolation towards America, we have only exposed ourselves to the worst part of it. This is a tragedy.[46]

CONTENDING VARIANTS OF RUSSIAN NATIONALISM

After the Soviet Union's collapse, Russian politicians faced the task of rebuilding the state within new boundaries. The task of state-building under conditions of severe and extensive national humiliation stimulated nearly all significant political groups and figures to don some form of nationalist mantle in order to establish their legitimacy as leaders and politicians. This behavior is consistent with the idea noted in chapter 1: nationalism is an ideology with powerful legitimating effects; by anchoring political power in the "nation" (a malleable concept), nationalism confers legitimacy on elites who successfully claim to represent the nation's inter-ests and project a credible commitment to defending and fulfilling the national mission. In Russia, where the state must be rebuilt, official and unofficial elites have found themselves competing for the legitimacy conferred by nationalism. Because of national humiliation and the requirements of state-building, all politics in Rus-sia essentially became nationalist politics. Indeed, even politicians who were not nationalists in the period 1989–91 came to adopt one variant or other of national-ist ideology in the ensuing years.[47]

Below is a typology of nationalist ideas that have been, and continue to be, propagated in Russia in the late and post-Soviet contexts.[48] This typology seeks to capture key tenets on membership in the nation, self- and other-image, and the national mission. This categorization reflects overlapping ideological lines among Russian nationalists but tries to highlight key differences from one strand of thought to another. The categories also tend more to represent ideological posi-tions than particular groupings of nationalist individuals (although some groups are mentioned as supporters of particular ideas). Many individual proponents of nationalism in post-Soviet Russia have tended to adopt different nationalist posi-tions at different times. They have also changed political affiliation as required by political exigencies, and those with seemingly contradictory convictions have sometimes come together in political coalitions.

Westernizing Nationalism

At a November 1998 seminar at Harvard University, former Russian deputy min-ister of defense Andrei Kokoshin introduced himself as a "Russian nationalist" who believed that it was in Russia's national interest to stay allied with the West for a "healthy, wealthy future."[49] Kokoshin's remarks were in the spirit of ideas articulated by Yeltsin, Kozyrev, Valerii Tishkov, the late Galina Starovoitova, and others who, especially in the early 1990s, subscribed to a Westernizing brand of nationalism. This type of nationalism was officially important in 1991–92, but has weakened considerably. Westernizing nationalism defines the nation primarily in civic terms—i.e., Russia includes all citizens within Russia's territorial boundaries (hence, Yeltsin's frequent use of the civic and multiethnic *rossiiane* and *rossiiskii*—as opposed to the ethnic term, *russkii*—to refer to Russians). A corollary to the civic definition of the nation are liberal and flexible policies of autonomy for non-Russians within the Russian Federation. Religious and ethnic differences matter less than common adherence to rules that govern the interaction of citizens and their relations with the state.[50] The civic definition of the nation does not, however, preclude recognition of ethnic Russians and Russian speakers in the former Soviet republics or "near abroad" as rightful affiliates of the nation. The nation must defend their interests by relying on negotiations and international legal norms and institutions, with force to be considered only under truly extreme circumstances.[51]

Westernizing nationalism views the legacy of Marxism-Leninism and the Soviet system as the cause of many of Russia's problems. The national self-image highlights Russia as a non-imperial power; a cooperative member of the international system; and a state whose immense potentials could be realized through democracy, market reform, and international integration and participation. Integration in the international, "civilized" community is of such high priority that in 1991–92, Yeltsin, Kozyrev, and others pledged active participation in UN peacekeeping and hinted at facilitating Eastern European incorporation into such Western organizations as the European Community and even NATO! Kozyrev declared in 1991 that Russian failure to integrate into "the democratic community of states . . . would amount to a betrayal of the nation and Russia's final slide toward the category of third-rate states."[52]

Westernizing nationalists reject categorical assertions of Russian uniqueness, and view Russia's sociocultural heritage to be within the family of western European nations. Although Russia has its particularities of history and culture, it is nonetheless part of an interdependent community that adheres to universal values and standards. In rare cases, recalling the rhetoric of the original nineteenth-century Westernizer Petr Chaadaev, some Westernizing nationalists juxtapose Russia's fundamental striving and orientation to become European with a self-debasing assessment of Russian culture as fundamentally despotic and marked by failure (at the individual and collective levels) to understand the difference between freedom and will (*svoboda* and *volia*).[53] Most Westernizing nationalists reject claims to restore the Russian or Soviet empire, but welcome non-coercive, mutually beneficial processes of integration among former constituents of the Soviet Union. They acknowledge that Russia does not face major aggressors to its security in the near-term. They also view the West as a partner, but concede instances when Russian and Western interests diverge. In the late 1990s, Westernizing nationalists condemned NATO expansion as "profoundly unfair in the military and political sense" and "a move aimed against Russia as a civilization."[54]

The national mission of Westernizing nationalists, consistent with their self- and other-image, implies generally benign actions toward the outside world. This includes preserving Russia's territorial status quo, protecting Russian citizens within and outside Russia by recourse to international norms, modernizing the economy through market reforms and a vibrant state sector, achieving an internationally sanctioned role as peacekeeper in the former Soviet Union, and attaining full integration into key international institutions. Russia is to be a strong and powerful state, but one that rejects its imperialist past. Westernizing nationalists also express support for promoting a state-supported, healthy, nonchauvinistic brand of patriotism that would aid Russia's progress toward a national consensus and a more stable democratic state.[55]

Nativism

Different voices have articulated strands of nativist nationalism in post-Soviet Russia, but there is no unified nativist ideology or a coherent, organized nativist nationalist movement. These voices include the late cultural historian Dmitrii Likhachev, writer Aleksandr Solzhenitsyn, village prose writers, diplomat and political scientist Sergei Kortunov, and philosopher and sociologist Igor' Chubais (brother of Anatolii Chubais).[56] Nativists disagree on many issues, but they share a focus on Russian tradition and history, issues of morality and spirituality, and the survival and national welfare of the Russian ethnic group. Nativism (per Solzhenitsyn) defines the Russian nation as an ancient ethnic, linguistic, and territorial entity encompassing Great Russians (Russia proper), Little Russians (Ukraine), and White Russians (Belarus). Solzhenitsyn advocates the reunification of "traditional" Russian lands including the present Russian Federation, Ukraine, Belarus, and northern Kazakhstan, but rules out unification by violent means. He disavows Russian imperialism, arguing that Russia should not expend its strength on unnecessary territorial expansion or wars for imperial glory. Before the Soviet Union collapsed, Solzhenitsyn argued that republics in the USSR's periphery should be allowed to leave, and even republics like Belarus and Ukraine should be able to separate from the union if their peoples voted such an option. Hence, he is willing to limit Russia to the post-Soviet boundaries of the Russian Federation.[57]

Echoing nineteenth-century slavophilism, nativist thought promotes a Russian self-image rooted in the Christian Orthodox faith, an abiding belief in social justice and "constrained autocracy,"[58] and a deep appreciation of Russia's cultural and natural inheritance. Nativism rejects Marxism-Leninism as an alien ideology imposed on Russia and condemns Soviet tyranny as a product of that ideology rather than an expression of the "Russian character." It sees a return to idealized native peasant values, such as *sobornost'* or communalism, and Russian Orthodoxy as the key to Russian renewal. Both in the pre- and post-Gorbachev eras, nativist thinkers have condemned Soviet policies that destroyed Russian religion, nature, and culture and have sought steps for restoration and preservation.[59] Some nativists see monarchy as the system of government best suited for Russia, but this idea is considerably weak. Others advocate enlightened authoritarian rule or forms of democracy that resonate with Russia's cultural and historical experience. Nativist thought underscores the danger of blindly copying the Western model or thoughtlessly embracing Western values of liberalism, materialism, and consumerism. The Western model has weaknesses and features that make it

unsuitable for the Russian context, and the type of government that will ultimately work best for Russia is one that takes its tradition into account.[60]

The nativist self-image tends to be inclusive of other peoples and cultures and
advocates the flourishing of languages and cultures of all national groups in the
Russian Federation. The writings of Likhachev, for example, stress the greatness of
ancient Russia and the ability of bearers of Russian culture to produce works of
distinctive aesthetic value that have enriched the world. At the same time, they
emphasize that Russian culture has itself been remarkably open to, and been
enriched by, outside influences. Like Likhachev, Solzhenitsyn advocates the cultural advancement of all peoples of Russia, but adamantly opposes political
autonomy for minorities because of the potential threat to the Russian unitary
state.[61] Although nativism is generally inclusive, some of its adherents display a
deep aversion to foreign—especially Western—ideas and styles. They claim innate
Russian superiority to the West and predict that Western superiority over Russia
is temporary; Russia will eventually flourish and surpass the West in moral and
spiritual development. Some nativists also express anti-Semitism and hostility to
minorities in their rhetoric, leading some analysts to conclude that Russian
nationalism as defined by someone like Solzhenitsyn could lead to authoritarian
nationalism or fascism.[62]

A final component of the nativist self-image is the depiction of the Russian
nation as a victim or persecuted group, both during the Soviet regime, when
Stalin annihilated millions in his purges and in war, and in the post-Soviet period,
when millions of Russians suddenly found themselves stranded in "foreign countries." Michael Confino argues that the mentality of victimhood, which divests
Russians of responsibility for their suffering and historical tragedies, could lead to
scapegoating of other groups and justify violence against them. While this argument has some merit, it must be balanced against valid nativist concerns about the
fate of Russian refugees and the treatment of ethnic Russians in the "near abroad."
Further, not all nativists subscribe to a mentality of victimhood; Likhachev's and
Igor' Chubais's writings, for example, point to the Russian government as a guilty
party in the suffering of Russians and highlight Russian responsibility for dealing
with the past and not repeating tragic mistakes.[63]

Russia's mission in nativist thought is primarily defensive and inward-looking
and implies nonviolent international relations. It reflects the chief aspiration of
dissidents and *derevenshchiki* in the Soviet period: to restore and defend the physical and spiritual well-being of the land and people. This means arresting the
degradation of the environment; lowering Russian mortality rates; increasing the
Russian birth rate; giving land to the peasants; reeducating the youth in moral and
spiritual values; preserving Russia's cultural and historical legacies; rebuilding a
strong state (without imperial coercion) that would institute basic political freedoms at home; protecting the human rights of Russians in the former Soviet
Union; and fending off Western economic, political, or cultural exploitation. On
defending the rights of Russians in the "near abroad," some nativists favor incorporating majority Russian regions into Russia if the people vote for such an outcome in popular referenda. At minimum, they advocate national-cultural auton-

omy for Russians living in the former Soviet republics.[64] But all eschew force as a means to achieve these ends.

Nativist thought advocates the revival of Russian national consciousness as a healthy phenomenon and a prerequisite to the resolution of current crises that confront Russian state and society. In the words of Arsenii Gulyga, "There is nothing to be feared from the growth of the Russian . . . national consciousness. . . . Only nations with a developed sense of self-esteem can be friends with other nations. Faceless mobs are capable only of oppressing each other."[65] Russians must end their self-flagellation in the post-Soviet period, examine in a sober and realistic way the good and ill in their history, discuss broadly and actively the Russian past, renounce imperial expansion, and create an active civil society to mediate between state and people.[66] Ultimately, at least in the opinion of Sergei Kortunov, Russia has a larger mission of creating and preserving a world-class culture that would help unify humanity, impart to it a spiritual dimension, and return it to a path of "genuinely human values."[67]

Moderate Statism and Aggressive Statism

There are ideas common to all statist nationalists, but the moderate and aggressive camps differ significantly in their prescriptions. In fact, the prescriptions of aggressive statists tend to bring them more in line with extremist national patriots, whose ideology will be described in the next section. Key representatives of statist ideology include Vladimir Putin, Evgenii Primakov, Vladimir Lukin, Yurii Luzhkov, Gennadii Zyuganov, and General Aleksandr Lebed. To some extent, the rhetoric of Vladimir Zhirinovsky and the program of his Liberal-Democratic Party of Russia (LDPR) also contain statist nationalism,[68] but Zhirinovsky belongs more in the camp of extremist national patriots. Individual statists disagree on many issues, but share the priorities of creating and preserving a strong state with a unified territory, one language, and a shared high culture.[69] They seek the revival of Russia as a great power, but differ in advocating *moderate or aggressive* methods to fulfill Russia's national mission.

Statism includes in the nation ethnic Russians, Russian speakers, others assimilated into Russian culture and devoted to the Russian motherland, and all law-abiding citizens of Russia, regardless of ethnic origin. Thus, for example, Lebed's erstwhile political base, the Congress of Russian Communities,[70] declared in 1995 that "Russians are not defined by ethnic characteristics but by their whole relation with . . . language, culture, tradition, and faith." Similarly, the platform of Zhirinovsky's Liberal Democratic Party claims that "[in] a multinational country such as Russia, one must avoid a narrow, ethnocentric conception of national identity and approach the concept of 'nation' in terms of citizenship in a unified and indivisible Fatherland."[71] The nation, in statist thought, is a "superethnos" of sorts—a combination of ethnic groups sharing a high culture and uniformly engaged in building and maintaining a strong, unified state. At the same time, some statist thinkers highlight a more Slavic core to the Russian nation (i.e., Russians, Ukrainians, and Belorussians), or single out the Russian ethnic group's status. Thus, Zyuganov declares that there should be no shame in identifying the ethnic Russian people's role as "preserver, chief bearer, and protector of great Russian (*Rossiiskii*) statehood."[72]

Statists do not accept the post-Soviet borders of the Russian Federation. They want to include at least Ukraine and Belarus in the Russian state and, at most, all the "historical" borders of the old Soviet Union and the tsarist empire. In Zyuganov's words, the borders of a new post-Soviet union "will not be substantively different from the borders of the USSR."[73] Statists also portray a Russian self-image infused with "great power" history and ideas. They emphasize that Russia is only temporarily demoralized, and will inevitably regain its natural position as a world power and as a "cement" uniting the numerous peoples of the former Russian and Soviet empires. Adherence to the "great power" idea—involving a strong and disciplined state, military and economic power, a hegemonic role in the former Soviet region, and prestige in the larger international community—is the strongest thread binding statist nationalists. This idea is rooted in the concept of "Eurasia," which posits that Russia is a unique entity positioned between East and West, whose empire emerged partly as a result of conquest and partly because of Russia's natural attraction as a "superethnos" to other ethnoses. The original Eurasianists in the early twentieth century concluded that a new cultural and civilizational entity had emerged in Russia, which was neither Asian nor European. This entity was, in essence, a nation fused from peoples of different ethnic origins. Russia, thus, is a "nation of nations" that could potentially gather again its former units in a closely integrated structure.[74] Statists emphasize Russian hegemony on the territory of the former USSR and call for a Russian equivalent of the Monroe Doctrine. In the early 1990s, in particular, many argued that Russia should be the guarantor of political and military stability in the former Soviet space and should have a military presence, where possible, on the territory of newly independent neighbors. Unless Russia takes charge, its own sovereignty and security may be jeopardized by intervention from such international bodies as NATO or the Organization for Security and Cooperation in Europe.[75]

Statists divide into moderate and aggressive camps in assessing democracy; economic development; the communist past; and perceptions of the "other," especially the United States and the collective West. Moderates argue that Russia should continue to develop along essentially democratic and market-oriented lines, but without mindlessly copying the Western model. Some concede that "transitory" authoritarian rule might be necessary.[76] This camp rejects the communist past, condemns the excesses of communism and its deadening effect on independent thought, and seeks to reconcile democracy with strong patriotism. Its members believe that Russia should maintain its multiethnic character and pursue cooperative relations with the West, while renouncing naive ideas of full-fledged partnership or alliance with the United States and other European powers. Russia must go its own way in spheres where it has unique, historical, and traditional ties and interests, such as in Serbia or in developing countries like India, where the Soviet Union nurtured relations for years. Moscow should cultivate friends wherever they may be found, as long as these relations serve Russian national interests and do not cause serious conflict between Russia and the international community. Lukin, for example, shortly after being appointed ambassador to Washington, immediately highlighted the need for Russia to diminish its intensive focus on the West. Finally, moderate statists feel betrayed by the Western decision to expand NATO, yet they conclude that the West has not entirely abandoned Russia and can remain a collaborative partner in many areas. Russia must also acknowledge that its own weakness and inconsistency in foreign policy obstruct relations with Western countries, and, in the final count, the most severe threats to Russian security do not stem from outsiders but from Russia's internal social, political, and economic problems.[77]

Aggressive statist thinkers, unlike moderate statists, are deeply ambivalent or outright hostile to democracy, especially the kind they believe has been imposed on them by internal traitors abetted by Western powers. They equate Russian democratization with conspiracies to destroy the state:

> In time of grave sociopolitical or economic crisis, parliamentary debates and conciliatory commissions are *suicidal for any society.* . . . The slogan of democracy at any price is not so very harmless. It . . . is backed by all those who for years have wanted to destroy Russia and now want a Russia floundering in endless factional bickering . . . a Russia incapable of any positive, constructive effort for the good of the nation. . . . The entire history of Russia, its existence as a sociopolitical system is incontrovertible proof that *as a polity, Russia has always been held together by a strong system of state power.* [emphasis in original][78]

Others, such as Zyuganov and the Communist Party of the Russian Federation (CPRF), see *narodovlastie* or rule by the majority of the working masses (via local "soviets") as the ideal political system. Although Western democracy may not be the appropriate organizational principle for Russian statehood, they argue that the state will not last if it opposes the interests of society and harms the well-being of the people. Lebed, along these lines, argues that liberal values from the West may not be suited to the Russian temperament, but, nonetheless, he supports a political program that includes rule of law and other democratic standards.[79] As for economic development, the aggressive statist camp favors a mixed economy, which includes both the private sector and a highly active state sector. Some, especially leaders of the CPRF, pay rhetorical homage to private property while asserting that capitalism "does not fit the flesh and blood, the customs or the psychology of our society. . . . Once already it caused a civil war. It is not taking root now, and it will never take root."[80] Others, like Moscow mayor Yurii Luzhkov, favor a form of capitalism that flourishes through tight connections between political and economic power—a model that has been called "prosperous authoritarianism."[81]

Zyuganov and other aggressive statists do not reject the communist past but acknowledge the contributions to Russian history of communism and communist leaders, including Stalin. They highlight the nationalist aspect of the communist past, and point to the Communist Party of "Sholokhov and Korolev, Zhukov and Gagarin, Kurchatov and Stakhanov."[82] They stress the Communist Party's role and Stalin's leadership in the Soviet Union's valiant defense against Nazism and the "victory of the people" in catching up with industrialization during Stalin's rule. Lebed, in a similar vein, has expressed admiration for Stalin's adept use of nationalism to unite the Russian people in the face of great external threat.[83] As for perceptions of the "other," especially the West, aggressive statists articulate dangerous ideas including xenophobia, anti-Semitism, and excessive anti-Westernism. Lebed, for example, excoriates the influence on Russia of Western religions (calling American Mormons "scum and mold" at one point), pop culture, and capitalism. Zyuganov and Zhirinovsky have also pronounced invectives against Jews, accusing them of conspiratorial motives and actions against Russia. Zhirinovsky once argued that when the Jewish population of a country reached a certain level, that country went to war, while Zyuganov has condemned "cosmopolitans" who have ruled Russia since Stalin and were responsible for destroying Russian statehood. Finally, aggressive statists see the West, especially the United States, as Russia's foe, aspiring to political, military, and economic dictatorship over the world. They blame the West for conspiring to destroy Russia and "colonize" it by transforming it into a source of raw materials. They emphasize Russophobia (accurately in some instances) in the attitudes of Western politicians toward Russia, and argue that the West aims for "the maximal weakening of Russia's position and influence" in Russia's own backyard.[84]

Statist nationalism argues that the Russian national mission is, first and foremost, to restore great power status, prevent the further weakening and potential disintegration of the state, and protect ethnic Russians in the "near abroad" using both international norms and force if necessary. Russia should aspire to regional hegemony and integrate the former Soviet republics by voluntary means. State leaders must create a unifying idea to consolidate support for the state and revive discipline, authority, order, and spiritual values. Russia must have a strong army because, in the world, the strong have been, and always will be, respected. Leaders should reject foreign policy that favors Western goals while hurting Russian national interests and harness more effectively the patriotic, intellectual, and spiritual resources of the country. Statists diverge on the importance of cooperation with the West to fulfill Russia's national mission. Moderate statists openly advocate close ties and pragmatic cooperation with the West, and do not advocate behavior that would make Russia an international pariah. Moreover, some downplay altogether the external component of Russia's mission and argue that Russia must focus its energies on internal stability and welfare. The best foreign policy is one that does not seek haphazard "integration" with former Soviet republics or forced restoration of the USSR, but one that allows Russia the stable space it needs to solve its domestic problems. Only an economically robust and politically stable Russia could become a force to attract its neighbors in an integrative relationship.[85]

Aggressive statists favor a more isolationist approach vis-à-vis the West, exhorting Russians to cultivate and live by "national egoism."[86] Zyuganov has expressed his preference for a self-sufficient Russia, one with fewer ties to Western countries and international institutions that "erode the sovereignty of the Russian state." Some aggressive statists also show little aversion to violence as a means of fulfilling the national mission. Lebed, for example, in touting Chilean General Pinochet as an example of a great leader, has glibly noted that Pinochet killed only 3,500 people but restored his country's economy and allowed his people to live in a "civilized, flourishing country." Aleksandr Rutskoi, too, while verbally denouncing violence, has simultaneously expressed his fascination with theories on violent crowd behavior and his belief that the majority always follows the stronger leader. Further, his leading role in the bloodshed in Moscow in October 1993 proved his willingness to incite violent action. And Aleksei Mitrofanov, Zhirinovsky's colleague and head of the Committee on Geopolitics of the Russian Duma, advocates forms of economic strangulation of Russia's neighbors, "divide and conquer" policies (e.g., supporting Armenia against its neighbors), and assertive territorial claims against other states on Russia's periphery.[87]

Extremist National Patriotism[88]

"National patriotism" is the general label used in self-reference by Russia's most extreme nationalists. Their ideas trace a line back to the Black Hundred movement in early twentieth-century Russia and the diaspora Russian fascist movement from 1925 to 1945,[89] and include chauvinism, anti-Semitism, and a propensity for violence. National patriots include some of Russia's most vocal and notorious nationalists: Zhirinovsky (who fits both the aggressive statist and national patriotic camps); Aleksandr Barkashov, leader of Russian National Unity; Aleksandr Prokhanov, former editor of the newspaper *Den'* (now called *Zavtra*); Dmitrii Vasiliev, head of *Pamiat'*; General Aleksandr Sterligov, leader of the Russian National Assembly and former KGB general; Stanislav Terekhov of the unofficial Russian Officers' Union; Viktor Anpilov, leader of the Russian Communist Workers Party; General Albert Makashov, leader of the All-Russian Officers Assembly; Nikolai Lysenko, head of the National Republican Party of Russia; and editors of *Molodaia gvardiia* and *Nash sovremennik*. National patriots define the nation primarily in ethnic and racial terms, though some pay verbal homage to civic and more inclusive definitions of the nation. This author interviewed prominent national patriots, and only one openly expressed his racial views. Others initially claimed that the Russian nation was not exclusively ethnic, but subsequently referred to ethnicity, blood, and language as key criteria for membership and, particularly, *leadership*, in the nation. These national patriots indicated that they would disenfranchise Jews in Russia, if given the opportunity. When pressed about how they might determine if someone's blood was purely Russian, two answered that they would simply "know." In publications, national patriots accuse Jews—whom they characterize as members of the "transnational financial oligarchy" based in the United States—as guilty of destroying Russia and seeking to establish world rule. A few also advance the idea of "integral nationalism," favoring the elimination of "incomplete types" (*nepolnotsennye*) such as gypsies, homosexuals, and the handicapped, and the creation in Russia of "a new type of white man, traditional in blood and new in spirit."[90]

Some national patriots reject Marxism-Leninism and implicate the communist revolution in genocide against the Russian nation, but a greater number subscribe to the "single stream" view of history: the Soviet Union was fully legitimate because it was simply a continuation of the great Russian state. Further, some insist that the years of Stalinist rule, 1937–53, were golden years when Russians were able truly to live by Russian rules. Zhirinovsky, among others in the national patriotic camp, has expressed admiration for Stalin's ability to understand the "psychology of power."[91] Russia's status as a great power is a supreme value to national patriots, as it is to statists; however, the former are more vitriolic in their chauvinism, violent proclivities, and desire for imperial restoration and new expansion (even going beyond the borders of the former USSR). The National Salvation Front and Zhirinovsky's LDPR, for example, include in their doctrine ideas of a "new empire" that expands beyond the 1990 borders of the USSR. National patriots view the Russian self-image chiefly as a great, imperial power, and argue that Russia is a unique empire because it was not artificially, but organically created. Russian imperialism is benign because Russian rule is benevolent compared to rule by others, like the Mongols or Chinese. In Barkashov's words:

> History has dictated that the Russian People, because of its profound spirituality, density and military might, culture and economy, and most of all its fairness, became that magnetic nucleus around which a grand multinational empire-state formed in the course of centuries. . . . It was not internationalism or any kind of all-human values—but the [essence and] national character of the Russian People that was the chief attracting and strengthening force at the core of the state.[92]

National patriots also support the use of force to restore the former Russian/Soviet empire and to defend the interests of ethnic Russians outside the Russian Federation. They equate Russia's loss of territory to a fulfillment of the dreams of such historical foes as Carl XII of Sweden, Napoleon Bonaparte, and Adolf Hitler. To them, there is no Russia without the borders of empire. As an article in *Literaturnaia Rossiia* argues, "where are the boundaries of that country for which Russian citizens shed their blood, and the blood of their enemies. . . . [If] these boundaries no longer exist, then there is no Russia."[93]

In terms of the ideal state organization, national patriots contend that Russia flourishes only under a strong, centralized, and authoritarian state, and Russians must make the requirements of the state their highest priority. Because of these beliefs, national patriots openly reject the Western democratic model and see themselves in irreconcilable opposition to the post-Soviet Russian government. They characterize Russian democrats—from Gorbachev to Yeltsin—as traitorous, criminal, antinational, "totalitarian-comprador," "an alien people," and even "cannibalistic." Democrats and reformers have allowed foreign capital to rob Russia blind, and national patriots claim that Russia must incorporate its unique history and culture in the development of a new economic system. While Russia should not return to its communist past, the state should nonetheless be the "source and guarantor of [economic] rules of the game" and should even restore non-hard currency trading with former partners in the developing world, eastern Europe, and the "near abroad."[94]

Many ideas that dominate the national patriotic self-image reflect an extreme interpretation of Eurasianism.[95] National patriots portray Russia as a unique, organic, and self-sufficient geographic and cultural entity, with "natural," imperial borders. Russia embodies both East and West, but resembles the former more in terms of communal values, spirituality, and striving for social justice. It has a historic, divine, and inevitable calling to be a great power, and any attempts to hinder the fulfillment of this calling are bound to fail. Russia must keep its unique, God-given identity and resist any attempts at Europeanization or Westernization, especially in the political sphere, because these would bring only ills and shame, such as what happened in the aftermath of the Bolshevik, Western-inspired revolution of 1917.[96] The national patriotic journal *Elementy*, touting the "Eurasian worldview" of national patriots, condemns the evil of globalism; extols extreme rightists in Europe; justifies Soviet expansionism; highlights Western "conspiracies" and other Western evils; expounds fascist ideology; proclaims the supremacy of geopolitics above all other approaches to international relations; praises Stalin's brilliant geopolitical moves for the Soviet Union; condemns Gorbachev for destroying the Soviet "heartland" state; and heralds the virtues of strong will, action, and militarism.[97] *Elementy* and national patriotic organizations such as Barkashov's Russian National Unity also use symbols of fascism, especially the swastika. These symbols and other national patriotic propaganda constitute an effort to promote siege mentality, xenophobia, racism, and militarism.

Military power features prominently in the national patriots' self-image, and national patriotic organizations such as the Officers' Union, Russian National Unity, *Pamiat'*, Russian National Union (*Nikolai Vorobev*), and the National-Republican Party of Russia (*Nikolai Lysenko*) are paramilitary in nature. Various national patriotic organizations also use war anthems to rally the faithful, and have engaged in pogrom-type actions against religious and national minorities.[98] For national patriots, a strong military is the key to Russian greatness in the past and future. The armed forces are the "savior of the Fatherland" in its critical moments; as Aleksandr Prokhanov has declared, the Soviet army "connected the past and the present, the old and the young, and guaranteed stability and sovereignty." War is better than peace because people become weak and demoralized when all is in order. War reinvigorates the nation and tightens discipline in the army.[99] Similarly, Barkashov has declared the army the "last hope of the Russian Nation." He has argued that "at all times, the Army has been the symbol of Russian power, independence, and the guarantor of peaceful, creative labor. The Army has been an inalienable part of the Russian Nation because its members are [ethnic] Russians."[100] National patriots argue that it is the sacred duty of the state to provide for the needs of the army and restore the Russian military to its former strength and glory. Moreover, where national interests are at stake, the state should not hesitate to use armed force. National patriots want to see Russian youth inculcated with military-patriotic values or the "warrior spirit." Karem

Rash, a propagandist for the military, favors military intervention in politics because soldiers are better human beings than civilians and they "don't wear a thread of foreign-made clothes."[101] Altogether, for national patriots the military represents an invaluable resource for resuscitating heroic vitalism needed for the rebirth of the Russian nation.

An image of victimization is common in national patriotic thought. Russia is cast as the victim of other former Soviet republics that prospered at its expense. National patriots blame a "Zionist conspiracy" or "Jews hiding behind Russian surnames" for Bolshevik abuses and the destruction of the Russian state and environment. They blame Russian "democrats" for committing genocide against their own people and selling Russian resources wholesale and at a discount to criminals, particularly from the West. They see ethnic Russians in the "near abroad" humiliated and persecuted while the Western world stands idly by. They view the West and its leaders as having deliberately orchestrated the downfall of the Soviet Union and the emasculation of the Russian state. The West, and especially the United States, always will be a threat to Russian culture and statehood, an exploiter of Russia's natural resources, a spiritually hollow and inegalitarian society, promoter of an anti-Christian universal world order, home of "civilized barbarism," and the relentless antagonist of a blameless Russia.[102]

Russia's mission, according to national patriots, is to restore the great Russian imperial state under ethnic Russian leadership (preferably, for some, a monarchy) and to spread the national-patriotic world view as a means to save Russia. Russians should seek to fulfill their national mission with minimal, if any, concern for the opinion and norms of their neighbors and the West. Loyal members of the nation should advocate protection for Russians abroad; overthrow the Western-oriented, "slavish" government of Yeltsin; block arms control agreements that weaken Russia; restore Russian military power and prestige; correct negative social trends in the Russian family and society; seek a "third path" toward economic prosperity, neither capitalist nor communist; and establish authority, law, and order in domestic politics. Because Russia's historical position as a great state was taken away by "artificial and violent means . . . Russia should resort to similar means to take back all that was taken from it."[103] For some, Russia's mission has a Stalinist and fascist flavor. Mikhail Antonov, leader of the Union for the Spiritual Revival of the Fatherland, has suggested a full-fledged attack on the "rootless and cosmopolitan" intelligentsia (i.e., Jews). Others call for purging cities like St. Petersburg of all non-Russians; dismissing leaders who are not ethnic Russians; and supporting armed action against non-Russians, especially "Caucasians" (e.g., the Chechens), who threaten the integrity of the Russian state. They also believe that sympathizers with minorities, including those who have fought for Chechen human rights, are traitors and should be punished by the state.[104]

The table below summarizes key ideas among contending variants of Russian nationalism.

Table 5.1   Contending Strands of Nationalism in Russia

	Membership in Nation	*Self- and Other-Image*	*National Mission*
WESTERNIZING NATIONALISM	• civic: all residents within the territory of Russia are members of the nation • ethnic and linguistic Russians outside Russia are rightful affiliates of nation • territorially, Russia is the Russian Federation	• communism is not integral to Russian character • Russia is great power, but non-imperial and democratic • Russia part of larger international community • outside world, especially West, can be Russian partner • greatest threats to Russia come from inside	• preserve territorial status quo • modernize economy • protect Russians in "near abroad" using international norms and by establishing harmonious relations with neighbors • attain integration in international institutions. • cooperate with western countries on problems of transnational security
NATIVISM	• ethnic: members of nation share ethnic, territorial, and linguistic features; included are Great Russians, Little Russians (Ukrainians) and White Russians (Belorussians) • territorially, Russia should include at minimum Russian Fed., Belarus, E. Ukraine, and northern Kazakhstan	• communism is alien to Russian character; Soviet rule victimized Russian nation • Russian true values are *sobornost'* (communalism), Orthodox Christianity, culture and nature • Russia has contributed to other cultures and vice-versa • Russia is spiritually superior to West • democracy compatible with Russia but must be nativized	• preserve environment • halt demographic catastrophe among Russians • make Orthodoxy strong influence in nation • educate youth in moral and spiritual values and in healthy patriotism • preserve Russian culture • build strong state that is able to defend against exploitation by outsiders and meet needs of its people

Table 5.1   Contending Strands of Nationalism in Russia *(continued)*

	Membership in Nation	Self- and Other-Image	National Mission
			• defend rights of Russians abroad and support Slavic integration by nonviolent means
MODERATE STATISM	• civic: members of nation include ethnic Russians, native Russian speakers and others assimilated into Russian culture; • territorially, Russia at minimum includes all Slavic lands	• divided opinion on communism; some believe Soviet Union legitimate because it preserved empire and great power status • Russia is destined to be great power • Russia is unique because of position between Europe and Asia • Russian empire not so bad; much of it formed voluntarily and naturally • Russia should be regional leader or hegemon • democracy is suitable for Russia, with transitional authoritarian govt. if necessary • West can be partner but its interests do not always coincide with Russia's	• return Russia to great power status • defend interests of Russians abroad using international norms and force in extreme cases • maintain territorial integrity of Russian Federation • exercise hegemonic (but non-coercive) role in FSU and lead voluntary regional integration • unify state, society, army and revive discipline via patriotism • reject foreign policy that caters to Western interests to detriment of Russian national interest
AGGRESSIVE STATISM	• same as above, though argue special role in Russian state for ethnic Russians • tendency to equate	• communism contributed to Russian progress • favor authoritarian government • West cannot be	• same as above; force is a preferred option for fulfilling national mission • Russia can fulfill national goals by

Table 5.1   **Contending Strands of Nationalism in Russia** *(continued)*

	Membership in Nation	*Self- and Other- Image*	*National Mission*
	Russia with all of the FSU	trusted; it seeks Russia's downfall	relying chiefly on own resources, intellect, values, and patriotism (no need for cooperation with Western states)
NATIONAL PATRIOTISM	• ethnic: members of nation are ethnic Russians; pure Russians exist; outsiders, esp. Jews, not worthy to be members of nation; Russians should rule Russia • territorially, Russia is equivalent to FSU	• many believe Soviet rule legitimate because it preserved empire and great power status • Russia is a unique nation and superior to others • Russian imperialism is benign • strong, centralized authoritarian rule is best for Russia • military is source of Russian greatness • Russian "democrats" are traitors and slaves of West; most of them are Jews • militarism, heroism, decisive actions are supreme values • West is anti-Christian foe that orchestrated Russia's downfall	• restore Russian imperial state under Russian leadership; overthrow govt. of "democrats" and "reformers" • maintain Russian territorial integrity and defend national interest with unapologetic use of force • restore discipline in country, arrest negative demographic trends • protect Russians abroad using coercive means if necessary; end subsidized trade to all neighbors • cease catering to Western states • block arms control agreements, restore Russian military might, educate youth in military and heroic values • seek unique path of development for Russia, no need to seek integration with international community

WEAKNESS OF AGGRESSIVE NATIONALISM 1989–1998

The most virulent nationalist ideas—embodied in aggressive statism and national patriotism—had limited impact on Russian politics in the period 1989–98. These ideas failed to mobilize the majority of Russia's politically articulate public, and, as a result, the most extreme nationalists remained on the periphery of Russian political power.

Institutional Support

Among key institutions in Russian politics in 1989–98, only the leadership of the former Russian Supreme Soviet, a section of the Russian Duma, a few former high-ranking military officers, and a few individuals in the Russian Orthodox Church expressed support for extreme nationalism. National-patriotic leaders like Sterligov, Makashov, and Prokhanov did not come to power, and their occasional supporters like Rutskoi, Ruslan Khasbulatov (former speaker of the Supreme Soviet), and Zorkin of the Constitutional Court have been marginalized in politics. Rutskoi, for example, while having made a political comeback as governor of Kursk, cooperated with the moderate Yeltsin government and spoke the language of market capitalism to try and bring Western investment to Kursk.[105] In the executive branch, leaders until 1998 pursued primarily a moderate statist nationalism. This was true of Yeltsin, and former Prime Ministers Viktor Chernomyrdin and Evgenii Primakov, all of whom, in general, refrained from the rhetoric of national patriotic paranoia and chauvinism. Chernomyrdin, for example, negotiated openly with the Chechens in the Budennovsk hostage crisis in June 1995, showing respect for, and positing dignity in, the Chechens, whom national patriots had characterized as subhuman. Yeltsin, more problematically, used a highly strident tone against the Chechens, labeling them "bandits" and "terrorists." But this racist tone was the exception rather than the rule in Yeltsin's rhetoric. In presidential elections in 1996 and on many other occasions, he generally articulated a moderate statist nationalism emphasizing national pride. His government also gave its blessing to history writing that highlighted positive aspects of Russia's past and its people; current national accomplishments; and national honor, duty, and consolidation.[106] Yeltsin's numerous personnel changes in his cabinet brought into government mainly moderate statist nationalists, rather than extremist nationalists. Thus, he proved wrong overwrought Western warnings of, for example, "a return to the tough policies of the Brezhnev years."[107] Aleksandr Lebed, the most abrasive nationalist figure to join Yeltsin's team, lasted but a few months in his position.

The Russian Duma was the main institution where aggressive nationalism was most often heard. Some deputies spouted xenophobic rhetoric; the Duma passed a 1997 law giving the Russian Orthodox Church a privileged position vis-à-vis other religions; a majority of deputies passed a resolution in 1996 declaring the 1991 dissolution of the Soviet Union null and void; and communist leaders in the Duma participated in rallies and congresses with extremist

national patriots. But the Duma, in 1993–98, also developed genuine parliamentary politics and eschewed violent confrontation with the executive,
thereby rejecting the confrontational and radical methods of extreme nationalists. Duma speaker (since 1995) Gennadii Seleznev has been a moderate
leader, and groups like Zhirinovsky's LDPR, while spouting aggressive nationalism, actually cooperated consistently with the policies of the Yeltsin government, prevented Yeltsin's impeachment, and even supported Yeltsin's controversial 1998 nomination of the Westernized liberal Sergei Kiriyenko to the post
of prime minister.[108]

The Russian army and the Orthodox Church in 1989–98 did not support
extreme national patriotism. While former defense minister Pavel Grachev occasionally espoused nationalist rhetoric, asserting, for example, that he would "not
allow the honor and dignity of Russians to be insulted on the territory of any
state," neither he nor his successors preached racist or militarist nationalism.
Grachev and former chief of the general staff Mikhail Kolesnikov also opposed the
rhetorical excesses of nationalists in the Duma. Those military men who became
leaders in extremist nationalist organizations (e.g., Rutskoi, Filatov, Makashov,
Achalov, Viktor Alksnis, and Terekhov) had to resign their commissions to pursue
their political activities.[109] Other military officials who chose to pursue politics
allied with more moderate ideologies. For example, Lieutenant General Viktor
Ustinov, Zhirinovsky's erstwhile military adviser, left the LDPR to join the statist
Our Home is Russia. The late General Lev Rokhlin, like other political figures
from the military, argued for greater attention and resources to the beleaguered
Russian army, but did not propagate extreme nationalism to advance his cause.
Many of the rank and file of the army also continued to be apolitical; they did not
support military involvement in domestic political battles but were loyal to their
professional duty of protecting the state from external threats.[110] As for the Orthodox Church, a few individual priests preached extreme nationalism, and national
patriots such as Barkashov and his Russian National Unity sought to claim
authority from Russia's Orthodox heritage. But the church leadership did not
propagate extremist nationalism. Patriarch Aleksii II met with political figures
representing liberal to nationalist credentials, refused official status for Orthodoxy, and "unofficially" endorsed Yeltsin in the 1996 elections.[111]

Extremist Nationalism and Mass Mobilization

In 1989–98, national patriotism was a weak and fragmented force for public mobilization, as evidenced by attendance at mass demonstrations, electoral results, and
responses to poll questions. In 1990–93, there was some public enthusiasm for mass
demonstrations in support of national patriotism. Attendance at rallies in Moscow,
for example, grew from approximately a few hundred in 1991 to tens of thousands
by late 1992 and early 1993.[112] But these demonstrations lost momentum in
1994–95, and mass participation in rallies since 1993 was not very high. The unofficial, alternative national patriotic rally to celebrate the fiftieth anniversary of Soviet
victory over Nazi Germany in May 1995 did draw as many as thirty thousand peo-

ple, but this was most likely due to the resonance of the fiftieth anniversary itself rather than a sign of the renewed strength or more permanent appeal of extreme nationalism. Other aggressive nationalist rallies drew few participants: a May 1, 1994, rally attracted ten thousand, and another later in the same month drew five thousand. In August 1995, only one thousand people showed up at the extreme nationalists' commemoration of the 1991 failed coup against Gorbachev. In 1997, no more than several thousand people attended a communist-nationalist rally to mark the anniversary of Yeltsin's bloody crackdown on the Supreme Soviet in 1993. And, in 1998, despite nationalist and communist predictions of a turnout in the hundreds of thousands, only five thousand showed up in Moscow to celebrate the anniversary of the October Revolution, while another ten thousand marched in St. Petersburg. The celebration itself created a scandal because of the virulent anti-Semitic remarks pronounced by national patriot General Makashov, a member of the Duma faction led by the CPRF, and the communists' subsequent reticence to condemn Makashov's provocative and dangerous rhetoric.[113]

On the electoral front, the most virulent national patriots fared poorly in the 1989 elections to the USSR Supreme Soviet, the 1991 elections to the Russian Supreme Soviet, and the 1993 and 1995 elections to the Russian Duma. Some, like Sergei Baburin's Russian National Union, did not even manage to collect the requisite number of signatures to qualify for elections in 1993. In 1995, another group, the Union of Patriots, led by General Sterligov and General Achalov, suffered an early death by failing to collect 200,000 signatures to put their party on the ballot—this after they conceded having paid for the signatures they did collect! In addition, groups like *Pamiat'*, the National Salvation Front, and the National Republican Party of Russia became completely marginalized in politics. The most aggressive nationalist camp to do well in elections was Zhirinovsky's LDPR. The LDPR received almost a quarter of party votes in 1993, but in the 1995 Duma elections, it garnered only 11 percent of party list votes (less than half of what it won in 1993) and lost at least thirteen seats in the new Duma. It also won only one dismal seat in single-mandate voting. LDPR leaders attributed their poorer performance in 1995 to the fact that most nationalistic parties and candidates were vying for the nationalist mandate, and therefore each got a smaller portion of the total vote. Zhirinovsky's own popular rating plummeted from 22 percent in 1993 to 6 percent in 1996, and evidence shows that the LDPR's impressive electoral gains in 1993 may have been partly the result of falsification.[114] The party also suffered regional electoral setbacks in 1995, prodding an LDPR leader to comment that election results were like a "cold shower" for his group.[115]

Zyuganov and the CPRF, touting aggressive statism, had some success in elections. The party performed well in the 1993 Duma elections and did even better in 1995. Once a leader in the extremist National Salvation Front, Zyuganov in 1995 focused on a more socially progressive and moderate statist nationalist platform. His party program combined social welfare policies (thus addressing Russian social and economic discontent) and highlighted such Russian/Soviet "folkloric" heroes as Il'ia Muromets (epic hero), Yurii Gagarin (first man in space), Marshal Georgii Zhukov (World War II hero), and Aleksei Stakhanov (legendary worker). The CPRF trumpeted "greatness" in Russian history, egalitarianism in Russian communal life, Russian traditions and Orthodoxy, and the achievements of the Soviet regime. Zyuganov, while emphasizing Russia's great power status, eschewed violent confrontation in 1995 and cited his nonviolent record during the forceful confrontation between Yeltsin and the Supreme Soviet in October 1993. In the December 1995 elections, the CPRF won 22.31 percent of party list votes and a large percentage of single-member constituency votes, increasing its Duma seats from 45 to 158 (roughly one-third of the entire legislature). But the limits of communist nationalism were evident in Zyuganov's loss to Yeltsin in the 1996 presidential elections; nationalism proved insufficient to overcome public fears that Zyuganov, a communist, would orchestrate a return to the Soviet past.[116]

Other nationalist groups that ran in the 1995 Duma elections fared poorly. Lebed's Congress of Russian Communities garnered 4.31 percent of party votes. Rutskoi's *Derzhava* or Great Power movement, launched in 1995 with a promise to restore the Soviet Union, clean up all crime and corruption, and bring a day of accounting for the "criminal and illegal" regime of Boris Yeltsin, received only 2.57 percent of party votes. Other nationalist groups such as the Govorukhin Bloc, Communists–Labor Russia, My Fatherland, the Christian Democratic Union, and the National Republican Party received only between 0.28 percent to 4.5 percent of party votes, thus failing to cross the 5 percent barrier for gaining party seats in the Duma.[117]

In gubernatorial elections that followed presidential elections in 1996, again, extreme nationalism did not triumph. Of forty-five new governors, only one was backed by the LDPR (in Pskov); twenty-four ostensibly were supported by the CPRF; and two were linked to backers of Lebed. But in the year after gubernatorial elections, communist-backed governors proved less loyal to the CPRF, opting instead for pragmatic cooperation with the government led by Chernomyrdin. Local legislative elections in December 1997 in Novosibirsk, Tambov, Tomsk, Smolensk, and Krasnoyarsk yielded a mix of victorious communist as well as business-oriented candidates.[118] One can generalize from electoral results of the 1990s (gubernatorial, Duma, and presidential) that a form of aggressive nationalism (i.e., a combination of the LDPR and CPRF votes) can mobilize a sector of the Russian population, but not enough to dominate Russian politics. There *is* a nationalist constituency in Russia that veers toward some aggressive ideas, but certainly not the most aggressive forms of nationalism. Indeed, the CPRF and LDPR, representing the nationalist core in electoral politics, turned out to be relatively more moderate in rhetoric (the CPRF in the 1995 elections) and action (the LDPR, because of its cooperative record with the Yeltsin government) than their national patriotic counterparts. Moreover, Yeltsin's presidential victory over Zyuganov in 1996 implied in part that Russians were not ready to vote for nationalism where real power was at stake (i.e., the presidency).

Public opinion data in 1989–98 provide further evidence of the weak resonance of extreme nationalist ideas, especially zealous and violence-oriented claims to restore the Soviet empire, subjugate non-Russians, create an authoritarian regime, or forcefully defend the interests of Russians abroad. In a joint Western–Russian poll in August 1995, only 12 percent expressed support for a military regime, and over 83 percent rejected the use of force to protect Russians living in the former Soviet Union. Again in 1996, taking into account Russia's tragic experience in Chechnya, 93 percent of Russians in a poll favored negotiations with the former Soviet republics to resolve problems related to the Russian diaspora, 60 percent favored economic sanctions, and only 19 percent supported military action. While polls indicated widespread nostalgia about the past and what many perceive as better social welfare and less corruption in the Soviet Union, very few wanted a restoration of the Soviet state. After the August 1998 market collapse in Russia, an Interfax poll showed 34 percent favoring a form of dictatorship to solve Russia's problems, while 45 percent disagreed that dictatorship was a proper solution. Poll numbers supporting "dictatorship" contradicted other poll results indicating strong support for human rights and basic freedoms, and may indicate less of a desire for the authoritarianism favored by extreme nationalists than a rejection of the chaotic and ineffective government of post-Soviet Russia. This is consistent with other poll results showing that most respondents who regretted the breakup of the Soviet Union felt that way because of their fear of the breakdown of economic ties and of violent conflict between former Soviet republics.[119] Racist, anti-Semitic, and xenophobic ideas were unpopular, with very few Russians expressing support for the existence of a "pure Russian nation" or a state only for ethnic Russians or Orthodox believers. Many Russians in 1989–98 avoided nationalist hysteria and strongly condemned Moscow's abuses against Chechens in the 1994–96 war in Chechnya; in fact, up to one million people signed an antiwar petition led by Nizhnyi-Novgorod governor Boris Nemtsov. And in the wake of the August 1998 financial collapse, most Russians polled blamed Yeltsin (57 percent) and his government, while only 6 percent blamed foreign banks. Finally, in 1995 and 1996, polls showed that 75 percent of the general Russian public thought it was important to cooperate with the United States and western European countries, while 92 percent of the elite held the same opinion.[120]

Electoral and poll results in 1989–98 indicated that the mobilizing power of extreme Russian nationalism was limited. Whether or not this situation will hold into the future is unclear. What happens if an extremist group such as the LDPR joins forces with other national patriotic groups in future elections? Will their mobilizing power prove stronger together rather than apart? Will the CPRF, whose leaders consistently flirt with national patriotism, eventually discard signs of moderation and adopt a more violent ideology? If the central government runs out of resources to offer to regional leaders, will these leaders turn into a more cohesive base for nationalist-communist opposition against the government in Moscow? In the aftermath of Yeltsin's resignation in 1999 and Moscow's second war in Chechnya, will the mobilizing power of extreme nationalists increase? Some of these issues will be addressed in the concluding chapter.

Fissiparous Nationalism and Hurdles in Mass Media and Financing

The weakness of malignant Russian nationalism in 1989–98 was evident in other areas, including the absence of an effective and cohesive extremist national patriotic organization; limited support in the mass media; and unsteady sources of financing. Numerous national-patriotic coalitions failed in 1989–98, and constant fragmentation marked the political activity of nationalists in general. The most recent coalition with an aggressive nationalist flavor, the Popular Patriotic Union of Russia, organized in August 1996 and headed by Zyuganov, quickly lost the support of some national patriots. In addition, the coalition encountered problems in sustaining ties with fascist types like Makashov.[121] Membership in extreme nationalist parties was also limited. A study in 1996 showed eight organizations with members of one thousand or more; fifteen with at least one hundred members; and eighteen with less than one hundred members.[122]

In the mass media, extreme nationalists were a weak force. In 1993, such newspapers as *Den'*, *Sovetskaia Rossiia*, *Rabochaia tribuna*, *Pravda*, *Literaturnaia Rossiia*; the journals *Molodaia gvardiia*, *Nash sovremennik*, and *Elementy*; and the television show *600 sekund*, seemed to be flourishing and helped create "an atmosphere of chauvinism, the emergence of an explosive combination of feelings."[123] But the accelerated pace of extreme nationalist propaganda abated in 1993, especially after the violent clash between Yeltsin's government and leaders of the Supreme Soviet. October 1993 dealt a setback to national patriotic propaganda; extremist nationalist leaders landed in jail, while newspapers sympathetic to their views suffered sanctions. The government closed down *Den'* and *Sovetskaia Rossiia*, and ordered *Pravda* to change its editorial staff. *Den'* subsequently republished under a new name, *Zavtra*, and *Sovetskaia Rossiia* won a court case against the government.

Although national patriotic publications had a respectable level of circulation in Russia, their subscribers, as of late 1995, were heavily outnumbered by those for more moderate and liberal newspapers. *Moskovskii komsomolets*, for example, which ranked third in popularity in Russia, had a critically uncompromising stand against national patriotic ideas.[124] Drastic drops in mass circulation of newspapers in 1995–98 also affected the nationalist press, and publications like *Zavtra*, which continued to claim a circulation of 100,000 in 1998 (unchanged since 1995), were likely exaggerating their figures.[125] Market and political pressures curtailed the breadth and effectiveness of extreme nationalist mobilization in newspapers and on television (the most powerful medium in Russia), and the roster of individuals who controlled post-Soviet Russia's "media empires" in the late 1990s did not include supporters of national patriotism.[126] It is difficult to account exactly for the sources of financing for national patriotic groups in 1989–98, but one study notes that financing for extremist nationalist activities tended to come from entrepreneurs and from the commercial activities of the groups themselves. Evidence also suggests that aggressive nationalists raised money through criminal activities. For example, at the end of 1993, Interpol arrested a member of a group—which later joined forces with the extremist National Republican Party of Russia—for trying to negotiate the sale of Russian fissile material. Groups like the LDPR were able to raise money from private companies and banks (raising more money for the 1995 Duma elections than the liberal Yabloko party, for example), but the influence of national patriotism among key financial circles in Russia was limited.[127] Indeed, in the 1996 presidential elections, major financial powers supported Yeltsin rather than Zyuganov, and in return, they received lucrative deals from the government.

Why was aggressive nationalism a weak force in post-Soviet Russian politics until 1998? If, in the past, eroded governance, imperial discourse, and crises in a hostile international environment helped to empower aggressive nationalism, what role did these factors play in the evolution of nationalism in the post-Soviet period? The next chapter addresses these questions and examines critical areas of Russian foreign policy—the "near abroad" and the former Yugoslavia—to illustrate the weak influence of aggressive nationalism on Russian foreign policy.

NOTES

1. David Filippov, "Nationalism Moves into the Mainstream," *Moscow Times*, 29 July 1994, pp. 1–2; "Artistic Freedom Brings Difficult Choices for the New Guard of Russian Filmmakers," *Christian Science Monitor*, 26 April 1995, p. 11; "Russians Vie for Votes, and Anything Goes," *New York Times*, 16 November 1995, pp. A1, A10; A. I. Vdovin, *Rossiiskaia natsiia* (Moscow: Izd-vo Roman-gazeta, 1996), chapter 1; interviews by the author with Russian politicians and intellectuals in Moscow, Berlin, and New York from 1993 to 1998; and "Hostility to the U.S. Is Now Popular with Russians," *New York Times*, 12 April 1999, pp. A1, A9.

2. Russian nationalist rhetoric has been strong under the new president, Vladimir Putin, but the use and impact of nationalism under his rule are beyond the scope of this book.

3. See Walter Russell Mead, "Don't Panic, Panic First," *Esquire*, October 1998, pp. 92–97, 162–63; John P. Hannah, "The (Russian) Empire Strikes Back," *New York Times*, 27 October 1993, p. A23; Yuri N. Afanasev, "Russian Reform Is Dead," *Foreign Affairs* 73 (March/April 1994):21-27; Zbigniew Brzezinski, "The Premature Partnership," *Foreign Affairs* 73 (March/April 1994):67–82; Fiona Hill and Pamela Jewett, "*Back in the USSR*": *Russia's Intervention in the Internal Affairs of the Former Soviet Republics and the Implications for United States Policy toward Russia,* Strengthening Democratic Institutions Project, Harvard University, 1994. The only war that the Russian government launched between 1991 and 1998 was the war against Chechnya. Because Chechnya cannot be classified as a case of foreign policy, this chapter does not discuss it in great detail. I would note, however, that the first war in Chechnya illustrated the weakness of aggressive nationalism. First, Yeltsin's use of nationalist rhetoric to mobilize ethnic Russians against Chechens failed. Second, the war hurt large numbers of ethnic Russians—both civilian and military—and provoked intense public condemnation of the government's authoritarianism. Third, mass public opinion against the war led to actions of protest, including a no-confidence vote in the Duma against the government, condemnation in the press of abuses committed by the Russian military, and legal and political actions by civic groups to defend human rights in Chechnya. See Kronid Liubarskii, "Pust' Gosduma zaplatit mne rubl'," *Novoe vremia* 37 (1995):19–20; interview with Anatoly Shabad (member of Russian Duma, human rights activist, and critic of the war in Chechnya), New York, 6 February 1995; and *Zhurnalistika i voina* (Moscow: Russian American Press Information Center, 1995), 76 pp.

4. For a fuller account see John B. Dunlop, *The Contemporary Faces of Russian Nationalism* (Princeton: Princeton University Press, 1983), pp. 38–63; Hélène Carrère d'Encausse, *The End of the Soviet Empire* (New York: Basic, 1993), pp. 171–95; and Edward Allworth,

ed., *Ethnic Russia in the USSR* (New York: Pergamon, 1980), esp. chapters by John Dunlop, Frederick Barghoorn, Dimitry Pospielovsky, Ruslan Rasiak, and Bogdan Denitch.

5. Quoted in Yuri Slezkine, "The USSR as a Communal Apartment, or How a Socialist State Promoted Ethnic Particularism," *Slavic Review* 53 (Summer 1994):420.

6. Slezkine, "USSR as a Communal Apartment," p. 423; see also *Desiatyi s"ezd Rossiiskoi Kommunisticheskoi Partii: Stenograficheskii otchet* (Moscow: Gosudarstvennoe izd., 1921), p. 101.

7. Slezkine, "USSR as a Communal Apartment," p. 425.

8. This issue is developed at length in chapter 2. See also Hélène Carrère d'Encausse, *Decline of An Empire* (New York: Harper and Row, 1979), pp. 13–46; Vladimir Ilyich Lenin, "The Right of Nations to Self-Determination," in Omar Dahbour and Micheline R. Ishay, eds., *The Nationalism Reader* (Atlantic Highlands, N.J.: Humanities Press, 1995), pp. 208–14; Ronald Grigor Suny, *The Revenge of the Past: Nationalism, Revolution, and the Collapse of the Soviet Union* (Stanford: Stanford University Press, 1993); and Bohdan Nahaylo and Victor Swoboda, *Soviet Disunion: A History of the Nationalities Problem in the USSR* (New York: Free Press, 1989), pp. 19–60. The historical record indicates that the Bolsheviks took ethnic identity as a primordial given. By creating ethnoterritorial units within the Soviet federation, they sought to nurture ethnonational "form" (i.e., language and culture) while also maintaining the "substance" of communist ideology, which would eventually supersede ethnic distinctions and sentiments.

9. The famine that resulted from collectivization killed an estimated five million, while millions more died in Stalin's deportations, executions, and concentration camps. See Robert C. Tucker, "Stalinism as Revolution from Above," in Robert C. Tucker, ed., *Stalinism: Essays in Historical Interpretation* (New York: Norton, 1977), pp. 82–87, 88, 92. On socialist realism as a policy intended to create a uniform socialist truth in literature and the arts, see Edward J. Brown, *Russian Literature since the Revolution* (Cambridge: Harvard University Press, 1982), pp. 15–16.

10. Tucker, "Stalinism as Revolution," pp. 94, 104; and Robert V. Daniels, ed., *A Documentary History of Communism*, updated and rev. ed., vol. 1 (Hanover, N.H.: University Press of New England, 1984), pp. 172–75.

11. Robert C. Tucker, *Stalin in Power: The Revolution from Above 1928–1941* (New York: Norton, 1990), p. 568.

12. Tens of thousands of indigenous leaders were expelled or arrested from the Communist Parties of Ukraine, Belorussia, and others in the late 1930s. See Tucker, "Stalinism as Revolution," pp. 94–104; Tucker, *Stalin in Power*, pp. 482–91, 504–5, 568–72; Iu. Poliakov, "O massovom soznanii v gody voiny," *Svobodnaia mysl'* 11 (1994):62–76; Walter Laqueur, *Black Hundred: The Rise of the Extreme Right in Russia* (New York: HarperCollins, 1993), pp. 61–65; Frederick Barghoorn, *Soviet Russian Nationalism* (New York: Oxford University Press, 1956), p. 216; and Nahaylo and Swoboda, *Soviet Disunion*, pp. 60–80. On some of Stalin's most inhumane policies against the non-Russian nationalities, see Aleksandr M. Nekrich, *The Punished Peoples: The Deportation and Fate of Soviet Minorities at the End of the Second World War* (New York: Norton, 1978).

13. I. Stalin, *O velikoi otechestvennoi voine Sovetskogo Soiuza* (Moscow: Gos. izd-vo politicheskoi literatury, 1950), p. 30.

14. *Pravda*, 25 May 1945; and Carrère d'Encausse, *Decline of an Empire*, pp. 33–36; Roman Szporluk, "History and Russian Nationalism," *Survey* 24 (Summer 1979):1-6; S. Enders Wimbush, "The Russian Nationalist Backlash," *Survey* 24 (Summer 1979):36-41; Tucker, "Stalinism as Revolution," pp. 105–6; and Leonard Schapiro, "Epilogue: Some

Reflections on Lenin, Stalin and Russia," in G. R. Urban, ed., *Stalinism* (Cambridge: Harvard University Press, 1986), pp. 423–24.

15. Stalin, *O velikoi otechestvennoi voine*, p. 144.

16. Khrushchev rehabilitated five nationalities that were deported under Stalin: the Balkars, Chechens, Ingush, Karachais, and Kalmyks. Three other groups—the Crimean Tatars, Volga Germans, and Meshkhetian Turks—were not rehabilitated, however. See I. Kreindler, "The Soviet Deported Nationalities: A Summary and an Update," *Soviet Studies* 38 (1986):387–405.

17. Khrushchev elaborated that "fusion" (*sliianie*) or a true merging of peoples in one communist entity was the ultimate goal. But in the near term, he focused on the less-ambitious idea of *sblizhenie* or drawing together of the distinct nations of the Soviet Union into the "Soviet people" (*sovetskii narod*), a united entity based on brotherly tolerance and directed by the Communist Party. See Carrère d'Encausse, *Decline of an Empire*, pp. 13–46; Darrell P. Hammer, "Alternative Visions of the Russian Future: Religious and Nationalist Alternatives," *Studies in Comparative Communism* 20 (Autumn/Winter 1987):266–68; and Graham Smith, "Nationalities Policy from Lenin to Gorbachev," in Graham Smith, ed., *The Nationalities Question in the Soviet Union* (London: Longman, 1990), pp. 7–8.

18. On village prose, see Philippa Lewis, "Peasant Nostalgia in Contemporary Soviet Literature," *Soviet Studies* 3 (1976):548–69; Gleb Zekulin, "The Contemporary Countryside in Soviet Literature: A Search for New Values," in James R. Millar, ed., *The Soviet Rural Community* (Urbana: University of Illinois Press, 1971), pp. 376–404; and Brown, *Russian Literature*, pp. 292–312. The village prose or *derevenshchiki* movement began in the 1950s. Its most prominent representatives included Fedor Abramov, Valentin Rasputin, Vasilii Shukshin, Vasilii Belov, and Sergei Zalygin. Rasputin and Belov have become active promoters of nationalism in post-Soviet Russia.

19. The KGB suppressed *Veche* in 1974. On VSKhSON, see John B. Dunlop, *The New Russian Revolutionaries* (Belmont, Mass.: Nordland, 1976) and Hammer, "Alternative Visions," pp. 269–70. On *Novyi mir, Molodaia gvardiia*, and *Nash sovremennik*, see Yitzhak M. Brudny, "The Heralds of Opposition to Perestroyka," in Ed A. Hewett and Victor H. Winston, eds., *Milestones in Glasnost and Perestroyka: Politics and People* (Washington, D.C.: Brookings, 1991), pp. 153–59.

20. Alexander Yanov describes the ideas of extremist national patriots in *The Russian Challenge and the Year 2000* (Oxford: Blackwell, 1987); see also Dunlop, *Contemporary Faces* and Laqueur, *Black Hundred*, passim.

21. "National Bolsheviks" is the term many use to refer to adherents of Russian nationalism who simultaneously supported Marxism-Leninism and communism as ideologies that saved and preserved the great Russian imperial state. In the Gorbachev years, these people rallied for the preservation of communism as the sole hope of keeping the Soviet state intact. See Laqueur, *Black Hundred*, pp. 65–66; and John B. Dunlop, *The Rise of Russia and the Fall of the Soviet Empire* (Princeton: Princeton University Press, 1993), pp. 128–29.

22. See Michael Rywkin, "The Russia-Wide Soviet Federated Socialist Republic (RSFSR):Privileged or Underprivileged?" in Allworth, ed., *Ethnic Russia in the USSR*, pp. 184–86; and Brian D. Taylor, "Red Army Blues: The Future of Military Power in the Former Soviet Union," *Breakthroughs* 2 (Spring 1992):3.

23. On the preceding points, see also E. A. Rees, "Stalin and Russian Nationalism," in Geoffrey Hosking and Robert Service, eds., *Russian Nationalism Past and Present* (New York: St. Martin's, 1998), pp. 100–102.

24. See Aleksandr Solzhenitsyn, *Pis'mo vozhdiam Sovetskogo Soiuza* (Paris: YMCA Press, 1974); John B. Dunlop, "The Many Faces of Contemporary Russian Nationalism," *Survey*

24 (Summer 1979):18–35; Alexander Yanov, *The Russian New Right* (Berkeley: Institute of International Studies, 1978), *passim*; and Walter Laqueur, *The Long Road to Freedom* (New York: Macmillan, 1989), chap. 6.

25. On the secrecy surrounding discussions of nationalism and nationality policy during communism, see Eduard Bagramov, "Kak delalas' natsional'naia politika," *Nezavisimaia gazeta*, 24 January 1992, p. 5.

26. Geoffrey Hosking, "The Russian National Revival," *Radio Free Europe/Radio Liberty Report on the USSR* (hereafter, *RFE/RL Report on the USSR*), 1 November 1991, pp. 5–8; Hammer, "Alternative Visions of the Russian Future," pp. 233–90; and Dunlop, "Many Faces," pp. 18–35.

27. See Stephen Carter, *Russian Nationalism Yesterday, Today, Tomorrow* (New York: St. Martin's Press, 1990), pp. 103–118; and Brudny, "Heralds of Opposition," pp. 159–61. Western observers originally thought *Pamiat'* would be a major force in Russian politics, but by 1993 it had fragmented and lost its prominence.

28. This author lived in Russia for almost two years from 1990 to 1992 and visited again for one-week to three-month periods in 1994–98 and saw the proliferation of these works in street kiosks and other booksellers. On the ideas of some of these thinkers, see Andrzej Walicki, *A History of Russian Thought: From the Enlightenment to Marxism* (Stanford: Stanford University Press, 1979), pp. 52–57, 291–309; Richard Pipes, *Karamzin's Memoir on Ancient and Modern Russia: A Translation and Analysis* (New York: Atheneum, 1974); Laqueur, *Black Hundred*, pp. 8–13, 298–302; and D. Ilovaiskii, "Kratkie ocherki russkoi istorii," in *Uchebniki dorevoliutsionnoi Rossii* (Moskva: Prosveshchenie, 1993), pp. 181–384. There has, of course, been an overall renaissance of prerevolutionary Russian thought as part of the Russians' search for useable ideas and a unifying identity in the post-Soviet period.

29. Vladislav Krasnov, *Russia beyond Communism: A Chronicle of National Rebirth* (Boulder: Westview, 1991), chaps. 2 and 3.

30. Intellectuals—among them the writers Rasputin and Belov—led the crusade for Russia to have its own institutions. At a session of the USSR Congress of People's Deputies, Belov decried the lack of Russian institutions, which incited russophobia because it led other republics to equate Russia with the Soviet center. Rasputin followed with a statement that Russia should even consider seceding from the Soviet Union if its demands for separate institutions were not met. See Hélène Carrère d'Encausse, "Videt' real'nuiu opasnost'," *Moskovskie novosti*, 23 July 1989; Sergei Grigoriants, "Imperiia ili soiuz," *Russkaia mysl'*, 4 September 1987; and the Central Committee position paper on nationalities in "'A Strong Center and Strong Republics': The CPSU's Draft 'Platform' on Nationalities Policy," *RFE/RL Report on the USSR*, 1 Sept. 1989, pp. 1–4.

31. See, for example, Valerii Tishkov, "Narody i gosudarstvo," *Kommunist* 1 (January 1989):49–59. Tishkov has been a consistent proponent of civic nationalism in the former Soviet Union and in post-Soviet Russia.

32. Roman Laba, "How Yeltsin's Exploitation of Ethnic Nationalism Brought Down an Empire," *Transition*, 12 January 1996, pp. 8, 5–13; Dunlop, *Rise of Russia*, pp. 38–62; and John Morrison, *Boris Yeltsin: From Bolshevik to Democrat* (New York: Dutton, 1991), pp. 142–43.

33. "Deklaratsiia dvizheniia 'Grazhdanskoe deistvie,'" *Ogonek* 8 (February 1990):5.

34. Nicolai N. Petro, *The Rebirth of Russian Democracy* (Cambridge: Harvard University Press, 1995), p. 101.

35. Petro, *Rebirth of Russian Democracy*, pp. 100–101; and Galina Litvinova, "Starshii ili ravnyi?" *Nash sovremennik* 6 (June 1989):10–20.

36. On how *glasnost'* undermined Communist Party authority and swept away the fragile posts of societal stability in the Soviet Union, see chapters by Joel M. Ostrow and

Walter D. Connor in Mark Kramer, ed., *The Collapse of the Soviet Union* (Boulder: Westview, 2000).

37. Zhores Medvedev, "Yeltsin and His 'Little' Russia: Why is Moscow Cheering a Historic Loss?" *Washington Post*, 12 January 1992, p. C1.

38. For figures that delineate the extent of Russia's military-strategic losses, see Stephen M. Meyer, "The Devolution of Russian Military Power," *Current History* (October 1995):322–28; and Tomas Ries, "Russia's Military Inheritance," *International Defense Review* 3 (1992):223–26.

39. See Konstantin Pleshakov, "Vizit v ravnodushnuiu Ameriku," *Moskovskie novosti*, 5 September 1993, p. 7. See also a series of articles on Chechnya by Emil Payin and Arkadii Popov, all in *Izvestiia*: "Da zdravstvuet revoliutsiia!" 7 February 1995, p. 4; "Kriminal'nyi rezhim," 8 February 1995, p. 4; "Diplomatiia pod kovrom," 9 February 1995, p. 4; and "Vlast' i obshchestvo na barrikadakh," 10 February 1995, p. 4; interview with Aleksandr Piskunov (deputy chair of Duma Defense Committee), Moscow, 29 September 1995; Medvedev, "Yeltsin and His 'Little' Russia," p. C1; Meyer, "Devolution of Russian Military Power," p. 322; Michael Specter, "Russians Pounding Rebels Who Hold 100 Hostages," *New York Times*, 16 January 1996, pp. A1, A8 and "Strife in Chechnya Embroils a Neighboring People," *New York Times*, 14 January 1996, p. 3. On social malaise, alcoholism and rising Russian mortality rates, and suicides in Russia, see "Demograficheskoe polozhenie Rossii," *Svobodnaia mysl'* 3 (1993):96–105; and Penny Morvant, "Alarm over Falling Life Expectancy," *Transition*, 20 October 1995, pp. 40–45, 72.

40. The Russian words used, in different variations, are *unizhenie, umalenie, razrushenie, iznasilovali, chuvstvo uiazvimosti, vymiranie, bezpravie, nishchaia i nichtozhnaia zhizn', polukolonial'noe, necheloveki, nashu krov' ne tseniat, genotsid, mutant chelovechestva, stesniat'sia,* and so on.

41. See S. Kara-Murza, "Unichtozhenie Rossii," *Nash sovremmenik* 1 (1993):136. See also interviews with Stanislav Govorukhin, Moscow, 29 September 1995; Gennadii Seleznev (speaker of the Russian Duma, leading member of the Communist Party of the Russian Federation, and former editor of *Pravda*), Moscow, 29 September 1995; Stanislav Kuniaev (editor of *Nash sovremennik*), Moscow, 14 October 1993; General Viktor Filatov (former editor of *Voenno-istoricheskii zhurnal*), Moscow, 15 October 1993; General Aleksandr Sterligov (former KGB general), Moscow, 15 October 1993; Alla Latynina (liberal critic), Moscow, 31 May 1994; Dmitrii Rogozin (leader of Congress of Russian Communities), Moscow, 11 October 1993; Vladimir Lukin (former Russian ambassador to the United States and former chair of Duma Foreign Affairs Committee), Moscow, 3 June 1994; Galina Starovoitova, New York, 16 November 1992; Aleksandr Rutskoi, Moscow, 8 June 1994; and remarks by members of the Russian Duma at a conference in Madrid, Spain, 30 May–4 June 1995, author's notes. See also Vladimir Beliaev, "Rossiia kak ob"ekt agressii," *Literaturnaia Rossiia*, 5 March 1993, p. 4; "Natsional'no-osvoboditel'noe dvizhenie otvechaet na voprosy 'Chto delat'? I kto vinovat'?" *Russkoe delo* 1 (1993):1; Petr Vykhodtsev, "Genotsid russkogo naroda: Unichtozhenie Rossii!," *Molodaia gvardiia* 2 (1993):177–97; Fatei Shipunov, "Put' spaseniia Rossii," *Molodaia gvardiia* 1 (1993):206–25; Stanislav Govorukhin, *Velikaia kriminal'naia revoliutsiia* (Moscow: Izd. Andreevskii flag, 1993), pp. 122–23; Aleksandr Kazintsev, "Russkaia krov'," *Den'*, 9–15 August 1992, p. 5; Viktor Aksiuchits, "Tribuna oppozitsii: Sformirovat' sil'niuiu natsional'nuiu vlast'," *Russkii sobor*, 2 February 1993, p. 6; Iu. V. Chesheva, "Kto nashi deputaty: Narodnye predstavitely ili narodnye predateli?" *Russkii vostok* 4 (1993):1; Michael Shuster, interview with Dmitrii Vasiliev of Pamiat', National Public Radio, October 1992, xeroxed transcript; Sergei Stankevich, "Razdelit' sfery vliianiia," *We/My* 19, no. 39 (September 1993):5; *Kongress russkikh obshchin*

(Party Program of the Congress of Russian Communities), pamphlet, Moscow, 1995; *Programma Kommunisticheskoi partii Rossiiskoi Federatsii* (Moscow: Informpechat', 1995), pp. 4–5; and Boris Fedorov, *Patriotizm i demokratiia*, pamphlet of the "Vpered, Rossiia!" movement, 1995, pp. 3–5.

42. Interviews with Sterligov, Moscow, 15 October 1993; and Aleksandr Kazintsev, Moscow, 13 October 1993. Natalia Narochnitskaia, an intellectual who has promoted aggressive nationalism and at one point teamed up with Yeltsin's former vice president Aleksandr Rutskoi in the movement Derzhava (Great Power), is the daughter of one of the most distinguished historians in Soviet times. Dmitrii Rogozin informed this author that he came from a privileged family, his father being a general in the Soviet General Staff. Govorukhin, whose language is steeped in national humiliation, has complained about the death of his career as a filmmaker in the new post-Soviet Russia. Interview with Govorukhin, Moscow, 29 September 1995.

43. While running the Moscow office of the Harvard Project on Strengthening Democratic Institutions in 1990–92, I personally knew Stankevich, Lukin, and Zorkin, and observed the evolution of their nationalist rhetoric. See also "Russia and the West: Nag, Nag," *Economist*, 8 April 1995, pp. 44–45; and an example of Viktor Aksiuchits's early moderate thought in "Zapadniki i pochvenniki segodnia," *Rossiia i Evropa: Opyt sobornogo analiza* (Moscow: Nasledia, 1992), pp. 533–44.

44. In a poll conducted by VTsIOM (All-Russian Center for the Study of Public Opinion), 66 percent of those polled in 1995 (as opposed to 50 percent in 1992) positively assessed the Soviet Union; 71 percent opposed the idealization of the Western way of life; and 81 percent condemned the denigration of Russian national tradition and patriotic history (e.g., the deemphasis of Russian victory in World War II). A majority of respondents also indicated nostalgia for great power rulers like Peter the Great and Stalin, expressed dislike for democracy, indicated a belief that the West wants to transform Russia into a Third World country, and asserted that the greatest priority of their country should be to restore Russian greatness and its great power role in the world because, like the Soviet Union, Russia must check American ambition for world dominance. See VTsIOM Survey Results, 11 August 1995, xeroxed copies received by author; interview with Latynina, Moscow, 14 May 1994; "Pis'ma v gazetu *Den*'," *Den*', 9–15 August 1992, p. 3; letters to various newspapers reprinted in "Demokraticheskoe igo," *Molodaia gvardiia* 1 (1993):225–30; "Zhenshchiny protiv uproshcheniia rossiiskoi istorii," *Rossiiskie vesti*, 7 May 1994, p. 1; Lukin's comments in Stephen Sestanovich, ed., *Rethinking Russia's National Interest* (Washington, D.C.: Center for Strategic and International Studies, 1994), pp. 106–11; "Hard Times Help Russians to See Soviet Era in a New Light," *Financial Times*, 17 August 1995, p. 2; Michael Specter, "The Great Russia Will Live Again," *New York Times Magazine*, 19 June 1994, pp. 26–33, 44–45, 52, 56; and Chesheva, "Kto nashi deputaty," p. 1.

45. See also comments by Mikhail Lapshin, head of the Agrarian Party, on being "humiliated" when attending meetings in the West, in *Prism* (electronic version), 20 October 1995, part 2. Letters to the newspaper *Den*' scoffed at U.S. humanitarian aid and crassly referred to members of the U.S. Peace Corps in Russia as "snout-faced mugs" (*mordovoroty*) who will likely become informers for the CIA. See "Pis'ma v gazetu *Den*'," p. 3.

46. Interview with Kuniaev, Moscow, 14 October 1995. Govorukhin echoed these same sentiments in interview with Govorukhin, Moscow, 29 September 1995.

47. The use of nationalism as a legitimating instrument in politics has been common to all elites engaged in state-building in the former Soviet Union. In Uzbekistan, for example, President Islam Karimov replaced Karl Marx's statue at the central square in Tashkent with a statue of Tamerlane, conqueror and ruler of Central Asia and the Transcaucasus in the

fourteenth century. Although Tamerlane was not Uzbek, Uzbek elites claimed him as a symbol to help develop "national pride and love of the motherland" among the youth and all citizens of Uzbekistan. See "Move Over, Marx," *Transition*, 9 February 1996, p. 3.

48. For other categorizations of nationalists, see Roman Szporluk, "Dilemmas of Russian Nationalism," *Problems of Communism* (July/August 1989):15–35; V. Muntian, "Nekotorye problemy russkogo natsional'nogo dvizheniia," in B. Churbanov, et al., *Neformaly: Kto oni? Kuda zovut?* (Moscow: Izd. politicheskoi literatury, 1990), pp. 111–33; V. Solovei, "Sovremennyi russkii natsionalizm: Ideino-politicheskaia klassifikatsiia," *Obshchestvennye nauki* 2 (1992):119–29; Evgenii Krasnikov, "Neprimirimaia oppozitsiia," *Vek XX i mir* (October 1993):64–68; and Margot Light, "Foreign Policy Thinking," in Neil Malcolm, et al., eds., *Internal Factors in Russian Foreign Policy* (Oxford: Oxford University Press, 1996), pp. 33–100.

49. Author's personal notes, 5 November 1998.

50. Valerii Tishkov, "Smertel'nyi gambit natsional'noi politiki," *Nezavisimaia gazeta*, 7 February 1992, p. 5 and his *Ethnicity, Nationalism and Conflict in and after the Soviet Union: The Mind Aflame* (London: Sage, 1997), chapter 12.

51. See Kozyrev's interview in *Kuranty*, 16 April 1993, p. 6; Boris Yeltsin, "Russia is Strong in Intellect, Resources, and Culture," *Rossiiskie vesti*, 21 April 1993, pp. 1–2; and Yegor V. Bykovsky, "New Russian Hawk," *Moscow News* (English ed.), 21–27 April 1995, p. 2. In 1995, Kozyrev added the use of force as an option in light of aggressive nationalist attacks against his allegedly overly "pro-Western" orientation.

52. Andrei Kozyrev, "Preobrazhenie ili kafkianskaia metamorfoza: Demokraticheskaia vneshniaia politika Rossii i ee prioritety," *Nezavisimaia gazeta*, 20 August 1992, pp. 1, 4.

53. See, e.g., Vladimir Kantor, "Rossiiskoe 'svoeobrazie': Genezis i problemy," *Svobodnaia mysl'* 10 (1994):78–85.

54. Andrei A. Kokoshin, *Reflections on Russia's Past, Present, and Future*, Harvard University, Project on Strengthening Democratic Institutions, 1997, pp. 36, 18-50; "There Is No Europe Without Russia" (President Boris Yeltsin's Remarks at the Council of Europe Summit, 10 October 1997), *Rossiiskie vesti*, 14 October 1997; Andrei Kozyrev's "Russia: A Chance for Survival," *Foreign Affairs* 71 (Spring 1992):1–16; "Rossiia obrechena byt' velikoi derzhavoi," *Novoe vremia* 3 (1992):20–24; and "Ne trebuite pirozhkov na dorogu," *Literaturnaia gazeta*, 16 October 1991, p. 3. See also Yeltsin's speech to the UN Security Council in "Gotovy k prodolzheniiu partnerstva," *Rossiiskaia gazeta*, 3 February 1992, p. 1; and Sergei Blagovolin, "O vneshnei i voennoi politike Rossii," *Svobodnaia mysl'* 18 (1992):3–15.

55. Kokoshin, *Reflections on Russia's Past*, pp. 22–50; "Kozyrev Presents Overview of Foreign Policy Tasks," *Rossiiskie vesti*, 3 December 1992, p. 2; "Foreign Ministry Document Outlines Foreign Policy," *Interfax*, 1 December 1992; "Russian Diplomacy Reborn," *International Affairs* (Moscow) 3 (March 1991):120–34; Aleksei Kiva, "A Superpower Which Ruined Itself," *International Affairs* (Moscow) 2 (February 1992):13–22; Vadim Zagladin, "Russia at World Crossroads," *Novoe vremia* 48 (1992):23–26; "Russia Calls for CIS Integration," *RFE/RL News Briefs*, 15–19 March 1993, p. 5; "U federal'noi partii 'DemRossii' budut blagonadezhnye chleny," *Segodnia*, 26 May 1994, p. 2; and Kozyrev, "Preobrazhenie ili kafkianskaia metamorfoza," pp. 1, 4.

56. Other nativists include Stanislav Govorukhin, the filmmaker, and Viktor Aksiuchits. Govorukhin's films, *Tak zhit' nel'zia* (We Cannot Live This Way) and *Rossiia, kotoruiu my poteriali* (Our Lost Russia), played a significant role in expressing and strengthening popular disdain for the communist system in the days of *glasnost'*. Aksiuchits, head of the Russian Christian Democratic Party, left the Communist Party in 1978, was a member of Democratic Russia and a nativist who has occasionally joined forces with more aggressive nationalist groups. See Aleksandr Verkhovskii, et al., *Politicheskii ekstremizm v Rossii*

(Moscow: Panorama, 1996), *passim;* and Govorukhin, *Velikaia kriminal'naia revoliutsiia;* *100 partiinykh liderov Rossii* (Moscow: RAU-Korporatsiia, 1993), pp. 10–11, 14–15; "Rossiiskoe Khristianskoe Demokraticheskoe Dvizhenie (RKhDD)," *Dvizheniia. Partii. Assotsiatsii. Soiuzy. Kluby. Sbornik materialov i dokumentov* [vol. no. missing] (Moscow: RAU-Press, 1992), pp. 7–117. (All cites from the latter source are in the author's possession).

57. See Aleksandr Solzhenitsyn, *Kak nam obustroit' Rossiiu* (Paris: YMCA Press, 1990) and Eduard Volodin, "Novaia Rossiia v meniaiushchemsia mire," *Literaturnaia Rossiia,* 26 January 1990, pp. 3–4.

58. Constrained autocracy refers to an alternative strand of Russian political culture that accepts rule by a prince or autocrat, so long as that rule ensures "domestic tranquility and good government" that is accountable to the popular will and to the values of the Church. If the autocrat fails in his duty, the people deserve the right to "establish a new governmental compact." See Petro, *Rebirth of Russian Democracy,* pp. 31, 28–59.

59. On the tragic loss of faith and the destruction of the Russian Orthodox Church under communism, see Natalia Gladshchikova, "Aleksandr Panchenko: Rossiia ne umerla, slava Bogu! Khotia, konechno, oslabela," *Segodnia,* 9 November 1993, p. 10; and Igumen Innokentii (Pavlov), "Tragediia russkoi tserkvi: v chem ona?" *Segodnia* 23 July 1993, p. 13.

60. Sergei Kortunov, *Russia's National Identity in a New Era,* ed. and trans. Richard Weitz, Harvard University, Strengthening Democratic Institutions Project, September 1998, pp. 29–32 (a fuller version of Kortunov's ideas are in Sergei Kortunov, *Rossiia: Natsional'naia identichnost' na rubezhe vekov* [Moscow: Moskovskii obshchestvennyi nauchnyi fond, 1997]); Igor' Chubais, "Chto takoe ideinyi krizis, ili kak Rossiia vosstanovit svoiu identichnost'," *Izvestiia,* 17 June 1998, p. 4; Solzhenitsyn, *Pis'mo vozhdiam,* chap. 7; "Akademik D. Likhachev: Russkie veriat v skazki o russkikh," *Komsomol'skaia pravda,* 12 January 1994, p. 3; and Igor' Shafarevich, "Rossiia i mirovaia katastrofa," *Nash sovremennik* 1 (1993):100–129.

61. See Dmitrii S. Likhachev, "Rossiia," *Literaturnaia gazeta,* 12 December 1988, pp. 5–6; *Reflections on Russia,* ed. Nicolai N. Petro, trans. Christina Sever (Boulder: Westview, 1991); and David G. Rowley, "Aleksandr Solzhenitsyn and Russian Nationalism," *Journal of Contemporary History* 32 (1997):334–36.

62. See, e.g., Yanov, *The Russian New Right,* p. 7; and Michael Confino, "Solzhenitsyn, the West, and the New Russian Nationalism," *Journal of Contemporary History* 26 (1991):611–36.

63. Igor' Chubais, *Ot Russkoi idei—k idee Novoi Rossii* (Moscow: Izd. dom "Sotsial'naia zashchita," 1997), pp. 52–75; V. Kozlov, "Russkii vopros: istoriia, sovremennost'," *Vesti gorodov iuga Rossii, Krasnodarskie izvestiia* [joint issue], 27 February 1993, p. 17; Igor' Shafarevich, *Russofobiia* (Munich: Rossiiskoe natsional'noe ob"edinenie, 1989); Confino, "Solzhenitsyn, the West and the New Russian Nationalism," pp. 631–32; and "Akademik D. Likhachev: Russkie veriat," p. 3.

64. Nativist thought as described in this section is elaborated in Dmitrii Likhachev, *The National Nature of Russian History* (2nd Annual W. Averell Harriman Lecture, Columbia University, 13 November 1990), pp. 11–18; "Ot pokaianiia k deistviiu," *Literaturnaia gazeta,* no. 37, 1987; "A chto ostanetsia Rossii?" *Den',* no. 3 (83), 1993, p. 8; "O russkoi intelligentsii," *Novyi mir,* 2 (1993): 3–9; Solzhenitsyn, *Kak nam obustroit' Rossiiu* and *Pis'mo vozhdiam;* Kozlov, "Russkii vopros," p. 17; Krasnov, *Russia beyond Communism,* pp. 1–39; Szporluk, "Dilemmas of Russian Nationalism," pp. 15–35; Dimitry Pospielovsky, "Russian Nationalism: An Update," *RFE/RL Report on the USSR,* 9 February 1990, pp. 8–17; Dunlop, *Contemporary Faces,* pp. 144–200; Roman Solchanyk, "Ukraine, Russia, and the National Question: An Interview with Aleksandr Tsipko," *RFE/RL Report on the USSR,* 17 August

1990, pp. 19–24; and "Esli natsiia ne ponimaet tsennosti gosudarstva, ona opasno bol'na," *Komosomol'skaia pravda*, 14 January 1992, p. 3.

65. Arsenii Gulyga, "O russkoi dushe," *Moskovskie novosti*, no. 22, 1988, p. 3.

66. Igor' Chubais is a major proponent of these ideas. See his "Chto takoe ideinyi krizis," p. 4; John Thornhill, "Chubais: A Crisis of Ideas Is the Real Trouble," *Financial Times*, 3 October 1998; and Kortunov, *Russia's National Identity*, pp. 11–32. Alla Latynina, like many nativists, argues that "national consciousness is . . . creative. . . . I have hope in Russia's future because I don't see its [prerevolutionary] past in shades of black." See Alla Latynina, "Kolokol'nyi zvon—ne molitva," *Novyi mir*, no. 8 (1988), 232–44; "Kliuch k chemu?" *Literaturnaia gazeta*, no. 15, 1989; and Sergei Alekseev, "Vybor Rossii. . . . V chem zhe on?" *Nezavisimaia gazeta*, 13 November 1993, pp. 1, 3.

67. Kortunov, *Russia's New National Identity*, p. 9.

68. On the complexity of Zhirinovsky's rhetoric, which includes "nationalist, non-nationalist, and even anti-nationalist ideas," see Robert Service, "Zhirinovskii: Ideas in Search of an Audience," in Hosking and Service, eds., *Russian Nationalism Past and Present*, pp. 179–97.

69. See, e.g., *Chto takoe "Dukhovnoe Nasledie"* (Moscow: Obozrevatel', 1996), pp. 12–37, which repeatedly notes weak statehood as the root of Russian ills and the restoration of *derzhavnost'* (great powerness) as the key to resolving Russian problems. *Dukhovnoe Nasledie* is a nationalist organization allied with Zyuganov's Communist Party and run by Aleksei Podberezkin, considered by many as chief ideologue of the CPRF. See also Aleksandr Dreiling, "Patrioty i natsionalisty v sovremennom politicheskom prostranstve Rossii," *Politicheskii monitoring*, no. 12 (59), pp. 1–2 (published by Mezhdunarodnyi institut gumanitarno-politicheskikh issledovanii, Moscow).

70. The Congress of Russian Communities (or KRO, in its Russian acronym) was, in 1995, the bloc that General Aleksandr Lebed joined in the run-up toward the 1995 Duma elections.

71. The KRO and LDPR platform quotes are from Dreiling, "Patrioty i natsionalisty," p. 2.

72. Gennadii Zyuganov, *Derzhava* (Moscow: Informpechat', 1994), p. 69.

73. Zyuganov, *Derzhava*, p. 67. Statists seem unable to perceive a Russia that is bereft of Ukraine, for example. See interviews with Boris Fedorov, Berlin, Germany, 24 August 1994, and Rogozin, Moscow, 11 October 1993. See also "General i ego armiia," *Novoe vremia* 37 (1995):19–20. Arkadii Volsky once stated that the "Soviet people" are genetically the same; therefore they naturally belong in an imperial union. See *RFE/RL Post–Soviet/East European Report*, 6 October 1992, p. 5.

74. The original Eurasianists included the linguist N. S. Trubetskoi; the geographer P. N. Savitskii; the legal scholars V. N. Il'in and N. N. Alekseev; the historians M. M. Shakhmatov and G. V. Vernadskii; and the philosophers G. V. Florovskii and L. P. Karsavin. Their ideas are elaborated in P. N. Savitskii, *Iskhod k vostoku* (Exodus to the East) (Sofia: Rossiisko-Bulgarskoe knigoizd., 1921). For an overview on Eurasianism, see Dmitry V. Shlapentokh, "Eurasianism Past and Present," *Communist and Post-Communist Studies* 30 (1997):129–51.

75. Igor' Malashenko, "Russia: The Earth's Heartland," *International Affairs* (Moscow):46–54; Valentin Larionov, "Geostrategiia nas obiazyvaet," *Krasnaia zvezda*, 4 December 1992, pp. 2–3; A. Migranian, "Real and Illusory Guidelines in Foreign Policy," *Rossiiskaia gazeta*, 28 March 1992, in *Current Digest of the Post–Soviet Press* (CDPSP) 44 (9 September 1992):1–4; and statements by Sergei Stepashin, former head of the Russian Federal Security Service (successor to the KGB), in "Russia Criticizes New Ukrainian Security Concept," *RFE/RL News Briefs*, 24–28 May 1993, p. 2.

76. See "Strategiia Rossii v XXI veke: Analiz situatsii i nekotorye predlozheniia (Strategiia-3), Tezisy Soveta po vneshnei i oboronnoi politike," *Nezavisimaia gazeta*, 18 June 1998, p.1; "Soviet Chaos Stymies Aid, Reform in Moscow," *Washington Post*, 7 October 1991, p. A1; and Fedorov, *Patriotizm i demokratiia.*

77. *Kontseptsiia natsional'noi bezopasnosti Rossiiskoi Federatsii, ukazom Prezidenta Rossiiskoi Federatsii ot 17 dekabria 1997 g.*, no. 1300, 37 pp.; Anatolii Utkin and Vladimir Batiuk, *Sovremennaia sistema mezhdunarodnykh otnoshenii i Rossiia* (Moscow: Institut SShA i Kanady Rossiiskoi Akademii Nauk, 1996); Viacheslav Ushakov, "Velikaia natsiia," *Nezavisimaia gazeta*, 3 June 1994, p. 6; Anatolii Utkin, *Rossiia i zapad: Problemy vospriiatiia i perspektivyi stroitel'stva otnoshenii* (Moscow: Rossiiskii nauchnyi fond, 1995); "Strategiia Rossii v XXI veke," p.1; Yuli M. Vorontsov, "One Thing All Russians Agree On," *Washington Post*, 10 March 1998; Sergei Parkhomenko, "Pervyi rossiiskii posol, naznachennyi lichno El'tsinym," *Nezavisimaia gazeta*, 3 March 1992, p. 4; and Tamara Zamyatina, "Yabloko's Hopes," *Prism* (electronic version), part 4, 1 December 1995.

78. Elgiz Pozdnyakov, "Russia Today and Tomorrow," *International Affairs* 2 (February 1993):29–30.

79. Zyuganov, *Derzhava*, pp. 67–68; *Chto takoe "Dukhovnoe Nasledie,"* pp. 28–29; "Vyderzhki iz vystupleniia secretaria Soveta bezopasnosti, pomoshchnika prezidenta Rossii Aleksandra Lebedia na II konferentsii 'Soiuza patrioticheskikh i natsional'nykh organizatsii Rossii,'" Moscow, *Natsional'naia sluzhba novostei* (electronic version), 27 June 1996; and Bill Keller, "Will the Real Lebed Please Stand Up?" *New York Times Book Review*, 12 December 1997, p. 12.

80. Zyuganov, quoted in Alessandra Stanley, "The Hacks Are Back," *New York Times Magazine*, 26 May 1996, p. 32.

81. "Curious Hybrid of West and East," *Financial Times*, Russia Annual Country Report, 30 April 1999, p. VI; Andrey Fadin, "The Political Potential of the Mayor of Moscow," *Transition*, 21 February 1997, p. 34; David Hoffman, "In Moscow, Business and Politics Mix," *Washington Post*, 19 December 1997, p. A1; and "Economic Lessons from Moscow," *Economist*, 31 October 1998, p. 55.

82. Interestingly, Zyuganov's rhetoric recalls that of Stalin, who justified Soviet ties with imperial Russia because it was the Russia of "Pushkin and Tolstoy, Glinka and Tchaikovsky, Gorky and Chekhov." See Stalin, *O velikoi otechestvennoi voine*, p. 30.

83. Zyuganov, *Derzhava*, p. 66; Sven Gunnar Simonsen, "Still Favoring the Power of the Workers," *Transitions* 4 (December 1997):52–56; and "Lebed Tells Yeltsin to Remember What Stalin Said," Reuters (Moscow), 8 July 1998.

84. Anna Dolgov, "Communist Anti-Semitism," Associated Press, Moscow, 26 December 1998; Renfrey Clarke, "Russian 'Communists' Bend to Anti-Semitism," *Johnson's Russia List* (JRL No. 2481; electronic source), 17 November 1998; *Voennaia reforma: Vooruzhennye sily Rossiiskoi Federatsii* (Moscow: Dukhovnoe nasledie, 1998), p. 9; Sergei Glaz'ev, "Russofobiia," *Nezavisimaia gazeta*, 18 November 1997; Anatol Lieven, *Chechnya: Tombstone of Russian Power* (New Haven: Yale University Press, 1998), introduction (where he cites racialist Western commentary on Russia and Russians); interview with Aleksei Mitrofanov, Russian Duma, Moscow, 9 April 1998; Adrian Karatnycky, "The Real Zyuganov," *New York Times*, 5 March 1996, p. A23; "Vyderzhki iz vystupleniia sekretaria Soveta bezopasnosti"; Zyuganov, *Derzhava*, pp. 85–88; Aleksandr Rutskoi, "V zashchite Rossii," *Pravda*, 30 January 1992, pp. 1, 3; Viktor Gushin, "Byt' li Rossii imperskoi: Chem skoree eto sluchitsia, tem luchshe," *Nezavisimaia gazeta*, 23 July 1993, p. 5; *Programma kommunisticheskoi partii*, pp. 19–20; Aleksandr Tsipko and Maryanne Ozernoy, "The New Communist Patriotic Ideology," *Prism*, pt. 1, 22 Decem-

ber 1995; Aleksei Pushkov, "Russia and America: The Honeymoon Is Over," *Foreign Policy* 93 (Winter 93/94):78–82.

85. In the words of a report by the statist Council for Foreign and Defense Policy, a "policy aimed primarily at the restoration of the USSR would inevitably compromise Russia's well-being, and could not be carried out without great bloodshed. . . . The pace of [any] new integration will depend most decisively on the success of economic reforms and political stabilization in Russia." See *Will the Union Be Reborn? The Future of the Post–Soviet Region*, Harvard University, Strengthening Democratic Institutions Project, June 1997, pp. 13–14; *Chto takoe "Dukhovnoe Nasledie*," pp. 7–14; "Aleksandr Lebed': Ocherednoi voiny Rossiia ne perezhivet," *Argumenty i fakty*, no. 22, June 1994, p. 6; "Strategiia Rossii v XXI veke"; *Russia and the Outside World: A New Agenda for the Twenty-First Century* (An International Conference Organized by the Council on Foreign and Defense Policy), Harvard University, Project on Strengthening Democratic Institutions, September 1998, 25 pp.; *Kontseptsiia natsional'noi bezopasnosti*, 37 pp.; Stankevich, "Razdelit' sfery vliianiia," p. 19; "Civic Union Discusses Foreign Policy Concept," *RFE/RL News Briefs*, 18–22 January 1993, p. 3; interview with Rogozin, Moscow, 11 October 1993; "Communist Party: From Monolith to Open House," *Moscow Times*, 30 September 1995, pp. 1–2; and V. I. Krivokhizha, "Rossiia v novoi strukture mezhdunarodnykh otnoshenii," *Polis* 3 (1995):9–22.

86. Aleksei Mitrofanov, *Russia's New Geopolitics*, Harvard University, Strengthening Democratic Institutions Project, July 1998, pp. 9–13. In numerous personal conversations with this author, Mitrofanov has downplayed his viewpoints, insisting that they were just a way to attract attention. See also "Yeltsin, Rival Differ on Ties to the West," *Washington Post*, 30 May 1996, p. A1.

87. See Mitrofanov, *Russia's New Geopolitic*, pp. 9–13; PBS, *Russia Betrayed? Voices of the Opposition*, 12 December 1995. In my interview with Rutskoi, he spoke at length about his admiration for Gustave Le Bon, the French philosopher who wrote on the psychology of the crowd and violent collective action. He also said the Nazis had a "great philosophy" but they corrupted it in practice. See Interview with Rutskoi, Moscow, 8 June 1994; and Gustave Le Bon, *The World in Revolt*, trans. Bernard Miall (London: Unwin, 1921).

88. An excellent general guide to extremist national-patriotic figures and organizations in Russia is Verkhovskii, et al., *Politicheskii ekstremizm v Rossii*.

89. The Black Hundred was the armed wing of the Union of Russian People, formed in 1905 as a response to liberal and revolutionary challenges to tsarist autocracy. The Black Hundred were militant, anti-Semitic, demagogic, and xenophobic. See Laqueur, *Black Hundred*, pp. 290–92; and John J. Stephan, *The Russian Fascists: Tragedy and Farce in Exile 1925–45* (New York: Harper and Row, 1978), pp. 1–18.

90. See Vladimir Avdeev, "Integral'nyi natsionalizm," in Soiuz Vozrozhdeniia Rossii, *Russkii stroi* (Moscow: Intellekt, 1997), pp. 243–60. Of the national patriots interviewed for this book, only General Viktor Filatov acknowledged openly his racial views. See interviews with Filatov, Moscow, 15 October 1993; Sterligov, Moscow, 15 October 1993; Kuniaev, Moscow, 14 October 1993; and Vladimir Zhirinovsky, Moscow, 14 October 1993. See also "Armiia—nadezhda Rossii!" in V. Likhachev and V. Pribylovskii, eds., *Russkoe Natsional'noe Edinstvo: Istoriia, politika, ideologiia* (Moscow: Panorama, 1997), pp. 77–78.

91. The implication is that Stalin got rid of Jews and was a true Russian nationalist. See interview with Filatov, Moscow, 15 October 1993; interview with Mitrofanov, 9 April 1998; A. Barkashov, "Printsipy russkogo natsional'nogo edinstva," in Likhachev and Pribylovskii, eds., *Russkoe Natsional'noe Edinstvo*, p. 86; "'Russkaia partiia' v KPSS prosushchestvovala do nachala perestroiki," *Den'*, 28 February–6 March 1993, p. 3; "Natsional'no-osvoboditel'noe

dvizhenie otvechaet," p. 1; and Wendy Slater, "Russian Communists Seek Salvation in Nationalist Alliance," *RFE/RL Research Report,* 26 March 1993, pp. 8–13.

92. Barkashov, "Printsipy russkogo natsional'nogo edinstva," p. 86; see also Verkhovskii, et al., *Politicheskii ekstremizm,* pp. 48–51; and Vladimir Zhirinovsky, *Poslednii brosok na iug* (Moscow: Liberal Democratic Party of Russia, 1993). On chauvinism, General Filatov exclaims, "We [Russians] have always helped other peoples. Who were the Chechens one hundred years ago? They were mountain people who knew nothing except horses! Who were the Kazakhs? Just people chasing sheep and camels. But we have turned them into civilized nations!" Interview with Filatov, Moscow, 15 October 1993.

93. In a similar vein, Baburin has said, "Russia is the former Soviet Union. . . . It is politicians, not the people, who want national states." See Vladimir Beliaev, "Rossiia kak ob"ekt agressii novogo tipa. Sud'bonosnoe vremia," *Literaturnaia Rossiia,* 5 March 1993, p. 4; and Marina Shakina, "The Discreet Charm of a Russian Nationalist," *New Times* 47 (1992):10–13.

94. "Pod znamenami patriotov," *Sovetskaia Rossiia,* 12 May 1994, pp. 1, 3; Chesheva, "Kto nashi deputaty," p. 1; Shamil' Sultanov, "Vyzov imperii," *Den',* no. 33, 1992; Beliaev, "Rossiia kak ob"ekt agressii," p. 4; "Rezoliutsiia fronta natsional'nogo spaseniia," *Russkii vostok,* no. 4 (1993), p. 4; Evgenii Troitskii, ed., *Russkii put' v razvitii ekonomiki* (Moscow: Tip. Mosmetrostroia, 1993), p. 38 and *passim*; and Verkhovskii, et al., *Politicheskii ekstremizm,* p. 268.

95. Extremist versions of Eurasianism appeared in 1989, first through the newspaper *Poslednii polius,* which closed after two issues. The more successful newspaper *Den'* then took up the Eurasianist idea, and a biweekly journal dedicated to Eurasianism, *Elementy,* appeared in 1992 and published six issues as of July 1995. See Verkhovskii, et al., *Politicheskii ekstremizm,* p. 219; and Solovei, "Sovremennyi russkii natsionalizm," p. 125. Eurasianism has fueled widespread interest and debate in Russia, and is discussed in many moderate formats. See, e.g., *Vestnik Evrazii. Acta Eurasica* 1 (1995); *Global'nye problemy i perspektivy tsivilizatsii (fenomen evraziistva)* (Moscow: Russian Academy of Sciences, 1993); and *Panorama-Forum* (a journal published by the Tatarstan Academy of Sciences; special issue on Eurasianism, pro and con) 1 (1997).

96. Interview with Kuniaev, Moscow, 14 October 1993; Shipunov, "Put' spaseniia Rossii," pp. 219–20; Igor' Isaev, "Evraziistvo: Mif ili traditsiia?" *Kommunist* 12 (1991):106–18; Lidiia Novikova and Irina Sizemskaia, "Dva lika Evraziistva," *Svobodnaia mysl'* 7 (1992):100–110; a reprint of a 1927 article by Nikolai Trubetskoi, "Obshcheevraziiskii natsionalizm," in *Svobodnaia mysl'* 7 (1992):111–16; "Evraziiskoe soprotivlenie," *Den'* no. 2 (30), pp. 2-3; and a six-part series by Dmitrii Balashov called "Eshche raz o velikoi Rossii," *Den',* no. 4 (23), 1991; no. 4 (25), 1991; no. 1 (29), 1992; 26 Jan.–1 Feb. 1992; no. 5 (33), 1992; and 5-11 April 1992.

97. See, e.g., "Liudi dlinnoi voli," pp. 1–3, "Pravoslavnaia revoliutsiia protiv sovremennogo mira," pp. 18–19, "Rossiia i prostrantsvo," pp. 31–34, and "Stalin kak geopolitik," pp. 36–37, all in *Elementy* 4 (1993); "Temnaia taina rynka," pp. 12–13 and "Teoreticheskaia panorama geopolitiki," pp. 1–8 in *Elementy* 1 (1992); and "Mondializm i taina Rossii," *Elementy* 2 (1992):26–27.

98. See, e.g., "I vnov' prodolzhaetsia boi," *Nezavisimaia gazeta,* 5 May 1994; and Robert Orttung, "A Politically Timed Fight against Extremism," *Transition,* 23 June 1995, pp. 2–6.

99. Prokhanov urges Russians not to be sentimental about violence and bloodshed because they have shed blood throughout their history. They should take American general Norman Schwarzkopf as a model because he did not flinch when giving the command for carpet bombing of Iraq. Referring to Afghanistan, Prokhanov called the struggle a

fight for "space equilibrium"; this is reminiscent of the Nazi wars for *lebensraum* or living space. See Michael Shuster, interviews with Aleksandr Prokhanov and Colonel Viktor Alksnis, National Public Radio, October 1992, xeroxed transcripts; "Afganistan: Ispytanie ognem," *Literaturnaia gazeta,* 29 April 1987, p. 6; Sergei Khovanskii, "Afghanistan: The Bleeding Wound," *Detente* 6 (Spring 1986), pp. 2–4; "Rezoliutsiia fronta natsional'nogo spaseniia," p. 4; and Vera Tolz and Elizabeth Teague, "Prokhanov Warns of Collapse of Soviet Empire," *RFE/RL Report on the USSR,* 9 February 1990, pp. 1–3.

100. "Armiia—nadezhda Rossii!," pp. 77, 79.

101. General Makashov has suggested that military experience should be mandatory for future Russian leaders. The theme song of the National Salvation Front, a coalition of national patriots, is " Sviashchennaia voina" (Holy War), a World War II anthem. See Valerii Vyzhutovich, "Kommunisty i patrioty, shag vpered!" *Izvestiia,* 26 October 1992, p. 2; Stephen Foye, "Military Hardliner Condemns 'New Thinking' in Security Policy," *RFE/RL Report on the USSR,* 13 July 1990, pp. 4–6; and Mikhail Tsypkin, "Karem Rash: An Ideologue of Military Power," *RFE/RL Report on the USSR,* 3 August 1990, pp. 8–11. In line with the idealization of military power, some national patriotic publications have featured ideas and leaders of Nazi Germany. See, for example, "Ideologiia," *Elementy* 1 (1992):49–56.

102. National patriots never seem to identify Russian causes for Russian problems, but always see outsiders, especially Jews, as the culprits. Nikolai Lysenko, leader of the National Republican Party of Russia, accuses Jews of bringing catastrophe to Russia and surviving at the expense of the Russian nation. In a similar vein, when asked about the nuclear arms race, Prokhanov declares, "[M]y people are not guilty. Guilty are the black imperialist forces [led by the United States]." See "Nasha tsel'—sozdanie velikoi imperii," *Nash sovremennik* 9 (1992):122–30; interviews with Filatov, Moscow, 15 October 1993; Kuniaev, Moscow, 14 October 1993; and Govorukhin, Moscow, 29 September 1995. Stephen Shenfield, "Making Sense of Prokhanov," *Detente* 5 (1987):28–29, 51; Shipunov, "Put' spaseniia Rossii," pp. 206–25; Kara-Murza, "Unichtozhenie Rossii," pp. 130–40; Vykhodtsev, "Genotsid russkogo naroda," pp. 177–97; Walter Laqueur, "Foreign Policy Concepts of the Right," *New Times* 38 (1992):12–14; S. V. Kurginian, et al., *Postperestroika* (Moscow: Izd. politicheskoi literatury, 1990); I. S. Kulikova, et al., *Fenomen Zhirinovskogo* (Moscow: Kontrolling, 1992); "Chto s soiuzom?" *Den'* no. 3 (83), 1993, p. 7; Aleksandr Barkashov, "Era Rossii," *Den',* no. 20 (48), 1992, p. 5 and no. 21 (49), 1992, p. 5; and V. Ushkuinik, *Pamiatka russkomu cheloveku* (Moscow: Russkii natsional'nyi sobor, 1993).

103. Barkashov, "Printsipy russkogo natsional'nogo edinstva," p. 86.

104. Antonov subscribed to Russian chauvinism as far back as the 1960s, and authored a popular piece in *samizdat* entitled "Uchenie slavianofilov—vyshii vzlet samosoznaniia v Rossii v doleninskii period" [The Teachings of the Slavophiles—The Highest Flight of Russian Consciousness in the Pre-Lenin Period], *Veche* 1 (1971). See also a speech by Barkashov in February 1997 and the 1997 program of Russian National Unity in Likhachev and Pribylovskii, eds., *Russkoe natsional'noe edinstvo,* pp. 153–57; "Rezoliutsiia front natsional'nogo spaseniia," p. 4; "Dokumenty vsearmeiskogo ofitserskogo sobraniia," *Den',* 28 Feb.–6 Mar. 1993):1; "Obrashchenie k chitateliu," *Nash marsh* (a fascist newspaper that uses a swastika-like symbol), no. 2 (1993), p. 2; Douglas Smith, "Formation of New Russian Nationalist Group Announced," *RFE/RL Report on the USSR,* 7 July 1989, pp. 5–8; "Anpilov Wants Khasbulatov Replaced by a Russian," in *RFE/RL News Briefs,* 3–7 May 1993, p. 2; Adi Ignatius, "Mayor of Moscow? Spider the Metalhead is Ready to Serve," *Wall Street Journal,* 18 Feb. 1993, pp. A1, A13; Celestine Bohlen, "Irate Russians Demonize Traders from Caucasus," *New York Times,* 20 October 1992, p. 3; Zhirinovsky, *Poslednii brosok na iug;* A. N. Sterligov, *Nam nuzhno chisto russkoe reshenie* (Moscow: No publisher, 1993); Troitskii,

Russkii put' v razvitii ekonomiki; Liubarskii, "Pust' Gosduma zaplatit mne rubl'," pp. 19–20; and Vadim Belotserkovsky, "Who is Discrediting Russia?" *Moscow News* (English ed.) 28 April–4 May 1995, p. 2.

105. "Reformed Rutskoi Courts U.S. Investors," *Moscow Times,* 9 April 1998, pp. 1–2; and Rutskoi's comments at the first Russian Investment Symposium, Kennedy School of Government, Harvard University, January 1997.

106. Interestingly, the Yeltsin government emphasized such accomplishments of the people as the new generation of ICBM missiles (Topol M) launched in 1998 and the record grain harvest of the year. This was reminiscent of Soviet-style propaganda, but is far distant from aggressive national patriotism. See Valerii Kucher, "1998: Hopes and Sources of Support," *Rossiiskie vesti,* 6 January 1998; "Yeltsin Hits Campaign Trail, Telling Voters to Forget Past," *New York Times,* 6 April 1996, pp. A1, A5; and "Yeltsin Wants to Stay Out of Warfare in Yugoslavia," *New York Times,* 31 March 1999, p. A12.

107. Amos Perlmutter issued this warning in the context of Primakov's appointment to replace Kozyrev as Russian foreign minister; see *Washington Post,* 14 January 1996; Wendy Sloane, "Upstaged in Crisis, Yeltsin Gets Catcall for Failing to Lead," *Christian Science Monitor,* 21 June 1995, p. 1. Yeltsin's government, until late 1998, had a majority contingent of liberal reformists. But after the August 1998 financial crisis, Yeltsin appointed more communist-nationalists to work in the government, leaving Finance Minister Mikhail Zadornov as the only person with genuine liberal credentials in the government. Again, despite dire predictions among Western observers, this group of leaders did not shift Russian policy in an aggressive nationalist direction.

108. Interview with Mitrofanov, Moscow, 9 April 1998; "Shopping, Zhirinovsky Style," *Washington Post,* 26 August 1997, p. A10; former Duma deputy Viacheslav Nikonov's comments in *Nezavisimaia gazeta,* 24 May 1994, as summarized in *Politica Weekly,* 22–28 May 1994 (electronic version); and Robert Sharlet, *Russian Politics on the Eve of the Parliamentary Campaign,* Center for Strategic and International Studies, vol. III, no. 9 (September 1995), 4 pp.

109. Stephen Foye, "Post–Soviet Russia: Politics and the New Russian Army," *RFE/RL Research Report,* 21 August 1992, pp. 5–12.

110. The situation in Russia has been unlike that in Weimar Germany, where military insubordination and politicization played a more important role in advancing malevolent nationalism. See Woodruff Smith, *The Ideological Origins of Nazi Imperialism* (New York: Oxford University Press, 1986), pp. 211–16; and Gordon A. Craig, *Germany 1866–1945* (New York: Oxford University Press, 1978), pp. 426–28. See also interview with Colonel Aleksandr Sirotkin (deputy head for Russian peacekeeping in the General Staff), Moscow, 30 September 1995; Andrei Tarakanov, "The Rise of Russia's 'Military Opposition,'" *Transition,* 9 August 1996, pp. 6–10; Deborah Yarsike Ball, "How Reliable Are Russia's Officers?" *Jane's Intelligence Review,* May 1996, pp. 204–7; "Pravda strashnee bomby," *Sovetskaia Rossiia,* 26 June 1997, p. 2; and "Ex-General Warns 'Extinction' Is Destiny of Russia's Nuclear Forces," *Washington Post,* 26 June 1997, p. A27. Support among the military for Zhirinovsky in 1993 mirrored his percentage of support among the population at large. See James H. Brusstar and Ellen Jones, "Attitudes within the Russian Officers Corps," *Strategic Forum* 15 (January 1994): 4 pp.

111. Patriarch Aleksii, visiting Serbia in April 1999, also suggested that Russia's Serbian Orthodox brethren shared the blame for the 1999 conflict in Kosovo. See "Russia Seeks to Mediate Kosovo Crisis," *New York Times,* 21 April 1999, p. A12; Albert Shatrov, "Karaiushchii namestnik boga," *Nezavisimaia gazeta,* 15 April 1998, p. 6; "Church Leans toward Yeltsin in Russian Vote," *New York Times,* 30 May 1996, pp. A1, A3; Elena Chinyaeva,

"Russian Orthodox Church Forges a New Role," *Transition*, 5 April 1996, pp. 14–23. The most outspoken extremist from the church hierarchy, Metropolitan Ioann of St. Petersburg, died in 1995. Other problems including internal schism, religious competition from abroad, past links with the KGB, and a populace that is not as religiously inclined as the church would like hamper prospects for the church to become an effective purveyor of extreme nationalism. A 1995 survey of almost three thousand respondents from thirteen regions showed only 3.8 percent claiming that religion played a fundamental role in their lives and 50.3 percent claiming that it played an insignificant or practically zero role in their lives. See Marian Leighton, "From KGB to MFA: Primakov Becomes Russian Foreign Minister," *Post–Soviet Prospects* IV, no. 2 (February 1996): 4 pp.; VTsIOM Survey Results, 11 August 1995, xeroxed copies; and Oksana Antic, "Patriarch Aleksii II: A Political Portrait," *RFE/RL Report on the USSR*, 8 November 1991, pp. 16–18.

112. In 1990–92, this author lived in Moscow and witnessed the sparse attendance at several "red-brown" demonstrations in the city. In February 1993, a demonstration organized by the extremist National Salvation Front and the Russian Communist Party to celebrate Defenders of the Fatherland Day drew twenty to forty thousand people. Another demonstration for May Day (May 1, 1993) drew as many as one hundred thousand participants. See Slater, "Russian Communists Seek Salvation," p. 13.

113. "Thousands Mark Anniversary of Attack on Russian Parliament," *Wall Street Journal Interactive Edition*, 4 October 1997; "Alternative Rally in Moscow," *Open Media Research Institute* (hereafter, *OMRI*) *Daily Digest* (electronic version), 10 May 1995, pt. I; "Opposition Garners 5,000," *Moscow Times*, 14 May 1994, p. 2; and "Coup Anniversary Marked," *OMRI Daily Digest*, 21 August 1995.

114. Interview with Mitrofanov, Moscow, 9 April 1998; Boris Kagarlitsky, "Russia Chooses—And Loses," *Current History* (October 1996): 307; Sergei Grigoriev and Matthew Lantz, "Lessons of the 1995 State Duma Elections," *Demokratizatsiya* 4 (Spring 1996):159–63; "The Devil They Don't Know," *Economist*, 23 Dec.–5 Jan. 1996, p. 59; "Union of Patriots Declares Solidarity with *Derzhava*," *OMRI Special Report: Russian Election Survey*, 3 November 1995; "Thirteen Parties Qualify for Russian Ballot," *New York Times*, 11 November 1993, p. A12; interview with Aleksei Mitrofanov, Madrid, Spain, 2 June 1995; and "Nationalist's Big Appeal: Promise of a Better Life," *New York Times*, 16 December 1993, p. A10. Without falsification, one study concludes that the LDPR would have come in second place in the 1993 elections, with only thirty-six instead of fifty-nine mandates by party list. See A. A. Sobianin and V. G. Sukhovol'skii, *Demokratiia, ogranichennaia fal'sifikatsiiami* (Moscow: Proektnaia gruppa po pravam cheloveka, 1995), pp. 77–99.

115. "Moscow Region Votes for a Communist," *Moscow News* (English ed.), 19–25 May 1995, pp. 1, 3.

116. In October 1993, Zyuganov went on record for a peaceful resolution to the standoff between Yeltsin and the Supreme Soviet. See interview with Zyuganov, October 1994; Tsipko and Ozernoy, "New Communist Patriotic Ideology"; and Aleksandr S. Tsipko, "Why Gennady Zyuganov's Communist Party Finished First," *Demokratizatsiya* 4 (Spring 1996):185–99.

117. Robert W. Orttung, "Duma Elections Bolster Leftist Opposition," *Transition*, 23 February 1996, pp. 6–11; M. McFaul and N. Petrov, eds., *Politicheskii almanakh Rossii 1995* (Moscow: Moskovskii tsentr Karnegi, 1995), p. 111; Evgenii Krasnikov, "Outsiders Playing in Kremlin's Hands," *Moscow News*, no. 87, 1995 in *Politica Weekly Press Summary* (hereafter, *Politica Weekly*; electronic version), 23 Dec.–12 Jan. 1996; "Union of Patriots Declares Solidarity," *OMRI Daily Digest*, 3 November 1995; "Natsional'no-patrioticheskaia ideia: moda ili potrebnost'?" p. 11; Soiuz Vozrozhdeniia Rossii, *Istoricheskaia spravka*, xeroxed

ms.; and "Russkie obshchiny gotovy vziat' vlast' v strane," *Nezavisimaia gazeta*, 22–28 April 1995, p. 3.

118. Laura Belin, "All Sides Claim Victory in 1996 Gubernatorial Elections," *Transition*, 21 February 1997, pp. 24–27; "Governors Prefer 'Party of Power' to Opposition," *IEWS Regional Report* (electronic version), 8 May 1997; and "Election Roundup," *IEWS Russian Regional Report*, 8 January 1998, p. 5.

119. "Russian Voters 'Disillusioned,'" *Financial Times*, 1 August 1995, p. 2; "Russia Poll: Bring On Dictatorship," Associated Press, 23 September 1998; "Russians Experience Growing Nostalgia for Former USSR," Interfax in English, 22 January 1997; L. D. Gudkov, "Russkii neotraditsionalizm," *Informatsionnyi biulleten' monitoringa* 2 (March/April 1997):25–32; L. A. Sedov, "SSSR i SNG v obshchestvennom mnenii Rossii," *Informatsionnyi biulleten' monitoringa* 1 (January/February 1997):13; and Leonid Sedov, "Russian Government Not Legitimate, People Say," *Obshchaia gazeta*, 23 July 1998.

120. At the time of writing of this book, the Kosovo crisis of 1999 had led to a rise in anti-Westernism in Russian public opinion. To illustrate, in 1997–98, only 5 percent of Russians polled thought NATO expansion qualified as a "main event of the year" (in contrast to 34 percent who thought Princess Diana's death was a "main event" and 28 percent who cited "accidents, terrorist and ecological catastrophes"). In April 1999, in the context of the NATO bombing of Serbia over the Kosovo conflict, VTsIOM polled 1,600 Russians; only 39 percent felt positive toward the United States (in contrast to 67 percent three months earlier), while 49 percent noted that they viewed America as "mainly bad" or "very bad" (up from 23 percent). See R. G. Ianovskii, "Vostok-zapad: Sotsial'nye izmeneniia i dinamika geopoliticheskoi situatsii," *Sotsis* 7 (1998):10; "Hostility to U.S. Is Now Popular with Russians," *New York Times*, 12 April 1999, pp. A1, A9; "Most Russians Approve Primakov as PM, poll finds," Moscow, Reuters, 23 September 1998; "Poll: 41 Percent Says Invasion of Chechnya a 'Mistake,'" Mayak Radio Network, 2 December 1997 (in this survey 40 percent also indicated the decision was not "thought through" and 11 percent thought it was the correct step to take); T. Kutkovets and I. Kliamkin, *Russkie idei* (based on a polling project called *Osobyi put' Rossii*) (Moscow, 1997), p. 2; "Yeltsin's Vietnam?" *Economist*, 10 February 1996, pp. 51–52; Dmitrii Balburov, "Samashki Massacre Shows Grim Reality of War," *Moscow News* (English ed.), 21–27 April 1995, pp. 1–2; VTsIOM Survey Results, 11 August 1995, xeroxed copies; and "Losses Rise as Russian Grip Tightens on Grozny," *Financial Times*, 9 January 1995, pp. 1, 12.

121. The Russian Communist Workers' Party, formerly led by Anpilov, left the Popular Patriotic Union of Russia and joined forces with Terekhov's Officers Union. On fragmentation among nationalist organizations, see Dreiling, "Natsional-patrioticheskaia oppozitsiia," pp. 1–10; Jeremy Lester, "Overdosing on Nationalism: Gennadii Zyuganov and the Communist Party of the Russian Federation," *New Left Review* 37 (January/February 1997):48–51; Sergei Baburin, "Oppozitsiiu ne dolzhny vozglavliat' kommunisty," *Nezavisimaia gazeta*, 14 August 1996, p. 5; Clarke, "Russian 'Communists' Bend to Anti-Semitism"; and "In Election Fallout, Hardline Russian Communist Is Ousted," *New York Times*, 23 July 1996, p. 4.

122. Verkhovskii, et al., *Politicheskii ekstremizm*, pp. 55–57.

123. Yurii Afanasev, et al., *God posle avgusta: Gorech' i vybor* (Moscow: Literatura i politika, 1992), p. 121. The national patriotic show of Aleksandr Nevzorov, *600 Sekund*, was extremely popular on Russian television in the early 1990s. Authorities tried to close down the show, but failed because of mass protests on Nevzorov's behalf. After October 1993, the show was effectively cancelled, but Nevzorov returned to Russian television soon thereafter. In 1993, subscriptions to national patriotic papers like *Den'* were increasing. In 1992, *Den'*

had approximately twenty thousand subscribers; by August 1993, this number was up to fifty-seven thousand. See phone interview with *Den'* editorial offices, Moscow, 3 and 11 August 1992; and "The Russian Media after *Glasnost*," *RFE/RL Post–Soviet/East European Report*, 20 October 1992, pp. 1, 6.

124. Late 1995 subscription figures were 100,000 for *Zavtra* and 250,000 for *Sovetskaia Rossiia*. Compare these with figures for pro-government newspapers (likely to take a cosmopolitan statist line) or liberal and moderate publications: *Argumenty i fakty* (three million), *Moskovskii komsomolets* (one million), *Komsomol'skaia pravda* (1.2 million), *Izvestiia* (600,000), *Rossiiskaia gazeta* (495,000), *Moscow News* (175,000), *Kommersant-Daily* (100,000), and *Segodnia* (100,000). See Laura Belin, "Wrestling Political and Financial Repression," *Transition* 1 (6 October 1995), pp. 59–63, 88.

125. Comparative 1998 circulation given by the newspapers themselves were: *Komsomolskaia pravda* (71,000), *Zavtra* (100,000), *Nezavisimaia gazeta* (48,000–51,000), *Sovetskaia Rossiia* (300,000), *Moscow News* (25,000), *Izvestiia* (406,840), and *Segodnia* (51,600).

126. "Russian Media Empires," Radio Free Europe/Radio Liberty (electronic version), September 1997; "Gazprom May Buy Pravda," *Financial Times*, 23 December 1996, p. 16; Belin, "Wrestling Political and Financial Repression," pp. 59–63, 88; and conversation with Aleksei Pushkov (deputy director of ORT channel), Moscow, 28 September 1995.

127. Verkhovskii, et al., *Politicheskii ekstremizm*, p. 57; various conversations with Aleksei Mitrofanov of LDPR; and "Political Parties and Blocs Electoral Funds," *Politika Weekly* (electronic version), 2–8 December 1995. Commercial activity by political parties and movements was a normal aspect of Russian political life in the 1990s. For example, *Dukhovnoe nasledie*, the key source of ideological support for the CPRF, ran a bookstore for profit. Literature for sale included not only nationalist literature, but numerous other publications on business and other subjects. See author's personal notes from a visit to *Dukhovnoe nasledie* headquarters, Moscow, 14 April 1998.

6

The Weakness of Aggressive Nationalism: Russian Policy in the Near Abroad and in Former Yugoslavia, 1989–1998

We [Russians] have always helped other peoples. Who were the Chechens one hundred years ago? They were mountain people who knew nothing except horses. Who were the Kazakhs? Just people chasing sheep and camels. But we have turned them into civilized nations!

—General Viktor Filatov, 1993

The Russian empire was never a classical empire of the colonial type. . . . "Empire" in the Russian language . . . is the equivalent of the word "imperium." We are talking about a conciliar (and spiritual) community of peoples. . . . Russia is a unique civilization, a unique world with its own values and interests, and especially, its own philosophical space. It fulfills its own unique, essential, and civilizing role in the world.

—Sergei Kortunov, 1997

[A] policy aimed primarily at the restoration of the USSR would inevitably compromise Russia's well-being, and could not be carried out without much bloodshed. . . . The pace of [any] new integration will depend most decisively on the success of economic reform and political stability in Russia.

—Council on Foreign and Defense
Policy, Moscow, 1997

ADDRESSING A PUZZLE: THE FEEBLE FORCE OF EXTREMIST NATIONALISM

Western observers who warn about "Weimar Russia" have implied that Russia, like Weimar Germany, may succumb to extremist nationalist ideas. In the words of one observer, "Russia today is a land awaiting a master. Russia today looks ominously like Weimar Germany."[1] Yet, toward the end of the 1990s, extremist nationalism had not fired the imagination of most of the Russian public or guided the actions of policymakers. Of the three factors that helped empower aggressive Russian nationalism in the past, as discussed in previous chapters, only one—the severe erosion of governance—was helpful to the promotion of aggressive nationalism in 1989 to 1998. Two others, the prevalent political discourse and international threats and crises, weakly contributed to the empowerment of extreme nationalism. This chapter will discuss these factors and then examine Russian policy in the "near abroad" and in the former Yugoslavia to illustrate the weakness of aggressive nationalism in Russian foreign policy under Boris Yeltsin.

Erosion of Governance

The erosion of governance in Russia, until 1998, was evident in the political, economic, and social spheres and contributed to public cynicism, anger, and discontent toward the ruling regime. Because aggressive nationalists were vehemently critical of Yeltsin's government, eroded governance should have helped bolster the credibility and attractiveness of their ideas. But though domestic conditions deteriorated harshly in Russia in the years 1991–98, they proved insufficient to mobilize mass support for extremist nationalism. Other factors also offset the potential effect of eroded governance on enhancing the attractiveness of aggressive nationalism.

Governance eroded, first, in the political sphere, where public confidence in Russia's "reformist" and "democratic" government has plummeted consistently since 1991. In repeated polls in 1994–96, 78 to 84 percent of Russians (representing the elite as well as general public) "somewhat agreed" or "completely agreed" with the statement that their officials did not care about the people's opinions. Only one-fifth to one-third of those polled expressed confidence in any government institutions and in individual leaders such as Yeltsin or Viktor Chernomyrdin. In addition, allegations of bribery, corruption, and other scandals and salacious revelations plagued members of Yeltsin's government, Yeltsin himself, and his closest entourage.[2] The public became deeply cynical of repeated government announcements on economic recovery and stabilization, and exhibited little trust in the political authorities' intent or ability to clean up corruption in the economy.[3] Russia's financial market collapse and ruble devaluation in August 1998, which hurt ordinary citizens more than wealthy bankers and business elites (who were able to siphon dollars abroad before devaluation), further increased public perception of the government's contempt for public welfare.[4]

Besides the low public credibility of the government and the discrediting of "democratic reform," the weak ability of Russian officialdom to function cohesively or effectively also eroded governance. In October 1993, for example, opposition between the former Supreme Soviet and Yeltsin resulted in a crisis of state that was resolved only through violent confrontation. Violence and use of the armed forces[5] by the executive branch lengthened Yeltsin's political life, but also destroyed Yeltsin's democratic-liberal coalition and led to diminished public confidence in Yeltsin personally, and in his government collectively. Yeltsin's subsequent illnesses also led to calls for him to resign as president. In addition, since 1991 Russian regions have challenged central authority in Moscow. Constituent parts of the Russian Federation have threatened secession or asserted "sovereignty" (e.g., Chechnya, Tatarstan, Bashkortostan, and Yakutia), while others have sought to dilute Moscow's control over economic, military, and other resources on their territory. Moscow's 1994–96 war in Chechnya, where between thirty thousand and one hundred thousand citizens died, was particularly illustrative of Moscow's ineffective ability to rule. Largely because of the war, Yeltsin's approval rating plummeted to the single digits in 1995, and public comments of disgust and distrust in the ruling regime and in Russian politicians became widespread.[6] Since the war, hundreds of parents have filed suit against the Russian government for the alleged illegality that surrounded decision making on Chechnya. In the words of one of the mothers of soldiers who died in the war, "We want . . . the whole story to be told. We want Russians to understand how their children were treated, what they were forced to do and how."[7]

Eroded governance in 1991–98 was evident as well in the economy, where the government failed to create the prosperity it had promised for years—and the people had been expecting—as a result of "market reform." Since Russian independence in 1991, Russians have experienced severe economic realities that were practically absent during the days of Soviet cradle-to-grave welfare. These included hyperinflation (with many losing their life's savings overnight), unpredictable monetary reform, unemployment, enterprise shutdowns, chronic nonpayment of wages by the government and state enterprises, and sharp and highly visible economic inequality among new sectors of "haves" and "have-nots." From late 1990 to 1995, nominal prices increased 279,942 percent while real income fell 39 percent. The numbers of the poor increased, with anywhere from 24 to 35 percent (thirty-five million to fifty-two million) of the population estimated to be living below the poverty line in 1996–99. While the richest 10 percent earned only 5.4 times what the bottom 10 percent earned in 1992, this ratio increased to fourteen times by 1995. Official unemployment rose from 367,500 in October 1992 to one million in August 1993 to two million in 1995, and independent experts estimated that many millions more might be actually unemployed.[8]

From 1996 to the early part of 1998, some improvements did occur in the Russian economy. With International Monetary Fund (IMF) assistance, the government managed to curb inflation, and Russians enjoyed price and exchange rate stability for nearly three years. In 1997, Russia's gross domestic product inched up 0.4 percent after a decade of continuous slump, industrial production climbed 1.9 percent, consumer confidence increased, and unemployment fell. But problems remained in terms of the government's inability to curb spending and collect taxes, attract more direct investment, curb capital flight, end the rapacious habits of Russia's wealthiest elite, eliminate high bureaucratic and other hurdles for small businesses, and create a more sustainable way to finance its budget. The government accumulated $50 billion of new debt (added to $100 billion of Soviet-era debt) and, in August 1998, devalued the ruble and defaulted on its domestic debt. The Russian financial market collapsed as a result, new fears of hyperinflation arose, and by the end of the year the Russian economy had shrunk by 4.8 percent. While the worst economic scenarios did not materialize after August 1998, what became clear was that Russian economic growth and prosperity had been delayed once again and could not be taken for granted in the future.[9]

In the social sphere, eroded governance was evident in statistics on crime, drugs, bombings, assassinations, refugee inflows, and disastrous demographic trends. In the first half of the 1990s, many Russians defined crime as the greatest threat in their lives. Ordinary citizens were alarmed by statistics on the near doubling of the crime rate from 1985 to 1992, with a total number of 2,799,600 reported criminal cases in 1993. Many crimes in Russia were violent, and in 1992–93, a 195 percent increase occurred in attacks using explosives, while a 250 percent increase was reported in firearm offenses. Sixteen bombings were reported in 1993, and 116 in the first six months of 1994. Five hundred contract killings occurred in Moscow in 1994, and murders continued "to climb precipitously" in 1995. High-profile murders were particularly alarming, with several dozen Russian bankers, for example, killed in Mafia-style killings in 1995 and a few more killed in 1996–97.[10] In late 1997, former Russian Interior Minister Anatolii Kulikov reported that there were 12,000 organized Russian crime groups. He also noted that economic crimes had risen 50 percent, organized crime by over 10 percent, and drug-related crimes by a shocking 80 percent (to 131,000 cases) in the first nine months of 1997. On the positive side, reported crime in Russia in 1997 fell 8.4 percent from 1996 levels. Although crime declined overall, especially in Moscow (where the crime rate fell 20 percent in 1997), nonetheless Russia's problems with criminal activity continued. In 1998, in particular, the cold-blooded murder of Duma member Galina Starovoitova in St. Petersburg shocked Russians and the rest of the world.[11]

Demographic trends and refugee problems also manifested the effects of eroded governance. Between 1992 and 1996, more than three million Russian men between the ages of twenty-three and forty died, the equivalent of 550,000 per year. These numbers dwarfed fatalities in wars in Chechnya and Afghanistan, and were the result of alcoholism, suicide, homicide, disease, and a failing health-care system. Russia's death rate outstripped its birthrate, and its mortality rate of 15.1 deaths per one thousand became one of the worst among the countries of Asia, Europe, and America. Although demographers noted that the worst decline of the population had been arrested since 1995, nonetheless there were few encouraging signs at the close of the decade. In 1999, a report by the United Nations Development Program underlined the high rates of suicide and declining life expectancies among men in Russia as part of a "human crisis of monumental proportions."[12] Extreme nationalists seized upon Russia's dire demographic trends in the 1990s as a rallying point and condemned Yeltsin's government for genocide against its own people.[13]

Refugees also caused internal instability in Russia, especially in 1991–94. Many returnees to Russia were residents of non-Slavic republics of the former Soviet

Union, who did not feel politically or economically secure in their new states of residence. Between 1991 and 1996, nearly 2.5 million ethnic Russians returned to Russia, with another million plus non-Russian refugees and internally displaced people from the Commonwealth of Independent States (CIS) joining them. This inflow of population taxed Russian government resources. But the direst forecasts of many more millions of refugees flowing into Russia did not come true. Indeed, beginning in 1994, the refugee flow diminished as a result of the abatement of ethnic conflicts in neighboring states and the improvement of living conditions for ethnic Russians in places like the Baltic states.[14]

The erosion of governance in Russia was severe up until 1998. But, at the close of the 1990s, it was insufficient to cause the downfall of the government and the political victory of extremist nationalist opposition forces. Some mitigating factors help explain why. First, despite repeated conflict and disagreements between executive and legislative powers in Russia, there was no repetition of the kind of impasse that led to the violent confrontation of October 1993. Yeltsin's government engaged in pragmatic relations with nationalists and communists in the Duma, and both branches of government—even at times of crisis—abided by the provisions of the constitution adopted in 1993, which gave overwhelming power to the president.[15] Yeltsin also signed a civic accord document with most Duma factions in 1994, and made adjustments in his cabinet partly to quell strong nationalist criticism from the Duma. Elections also gave the Russian public opportunities (other than the violent change preferred by extreme nationalists) to vent their grievances; 63 percent of the electorate voted in Duma elections in 1995 and 70 percent in the presidential contest in 1996.[16]

Second, improvements in crime control and the lesser inflow of refugees alleviated domestic insecurity and diminished social pressures inside Russia. In the economic sphere, monetary stabilization from 1996 to early 1998 also increased the well-being of many. While some scholars question the overall wisdom of IMF-supported policies of macroeconomic stabilization, nonetheless, such stabilization did bring increased consumption and a degree of predictability to Russian economic life.[17] The coping abilities of many in the population also proved indispensable in the context of zigzagging economic developments. Many Russians coped by growing their own food, working longer hours, working at multiple jobs, becoming entrepreneurs, and sharing resources among family and other social networks. One survey showed, for example, that the average number of hours people spent "moonlighting" was 20 per week, and the maximum was 120! In another survey, 40 percent of respondents claimed to have made adjustments to changes in their economic life that make or have made a return to the Soviet past highly unlikely. The growth of the entrepreneurial spirit and capitalist skills also helped many Russians, while other sectors found sustenance in the belief that legendary "Russian patience and endurance" would save the country.[18] Those from the younger generation who became relatively prosperous under Russia's new economic conditions helped older relatives adjust to new realities. In a comparison of two generations in two families, for example, the younger members, who planned to shun extreme nationalists and vote for Westernizing democrats in the December 1995 Duma elections, commented,

> Life is better than three years ago. . . . There is more money and more optimism for the future . . . [For] us, like many of our friends, our lives have improved, and we've learned a lot about how to manage this new economy . . . You have to rely on your-self in the first place, and not wait for the state . . . We still have the chance to con-struct our own lives as we want to live them.[19]

Russian economic difficulties should not be trivialized, and it is uncertain how long Russian coping strategies will continue to work. But, until 1998, these diffi-culties were insufficient to lead to aggressive nationalist mobilization.

Wane (and Wax?) of Imperial Discourse

Traditional Russian political discourse has emphasized the value of the imperial organization of the state—a sprawling, multinational entity ruled by strong, central authority. It has tended as well to equate Russian national greatness with imperial maintenance, expansion, or projection of military power abroad. As previous chapters in this book have argued, these discursive biases toward empire have, in the past, facilitated the impact of aggressive nationalist ideas. But this discourse changed in significant ways in 1989–98. Although certain areas of Russian discourse remained steeped in imperialist thinking, there also were changes from the traditional emphasis on the state as imperial power. Important individuals and institutions that act as guardians of collective Rus-sian memory and discourse offered alternative ways to define Russian state power and the basis of national greatness. Most important, they advocated internal welfare and stability over the forceful restoration of the former Soviet empire as the supreme value for Russia as a state and Russians as a nation. It is premature to judge if the shift toward an anti-imperial or non-imperial dis-course will be long lasting. Nonetheless, the fact that this discourse emanated from both Russian elite and general public opinion contributed to creating an environment that was not receptive to extreme nationalism.

The shift toward an anti-imperial political discourse began under Mikhail Gorbachev. Early on, Gorbachev expressed concern about "bifurcated conscious-ness" (*razdvoinoe soznanie*) in society, and urged intellectuals and others to study the past to elucidate lessons that might help "unite and mobilize people" and "render more cohesive the actions of the party [i.e., the state] and the people."[20] In an unprecedented way, Russians began to deal with "blank spots" in their his-tory and brought to light the mistakes, miscalculations, and abuses of the impe-rial state. Public voices attacked Joseph Stalin's murderous treatment of Russians and other peoples of the Soviet Union, and condemned the communist regime's lack of accountability to the people as it pursued goals to strengthen the imperial state. Two cases were particularly outstanding under Gorbachev: hearings in the Congress of People's Deputies that brought to light the perfidious Molotov–Ribbentrop Pact of 1939 and hearings on the Soviet decision to fight a war in Afghanistan in 1979. In both instances, state authorities initially hesitated to acknowledge imperial mistakes and excesses. But a mobilized civil society—working through the new institutions of the Supreme Soviet and Congress of People's Deputies and taking advantage of new freedoms of political expression—successfully pushed the regime to acknowledge the mistakes of the past, render judgment on these responsible, and commit to steps to recompense victims and prevent similar abuses in the future.

Gorbachev's legacy in the sphere of political discourse was twofold: (1) his rule removed the shackles of ideology from political discourse, eliminating the stultifying language of Soviet politics and allowing for more effective communication between state and people,[21] and (2) his policies allowed a specifically anti-imperial discourse to develop. This discourse condemned the monopoly of the Communist Party on power, exposed the lies and lawless behavior of state authorities, accused the Soviet regime of destroying independent states (i.e., the Baltics), and asked state authorities to account for the suffering inflicted on society by such secret official decisions as the war in Afghanistan. Anti-imperial discourse under Gorbachev permeated the top echelons of state power and society at large. Gorbachev, speaking at the Twenty-Seventh Congress of the Communist Party, called Afghanistan a "bleeding wound" inflicted by "counterrevolutionaries and imperialists." Further, the Supreme Soviet commission assigned to assess the Molotov–Ribbentrop Pact condemned its secret protocols, which led to the forced integration of the Baltic states into the Soviet Union. The Supreme Soviet commission declared the protocols "at variance with the sovereignty and independence of . . . countries" whose fates were decided by Hitler's Germany and Stalin's Soviet Union. Without doubt, the anti-imperial discourse that developed under Gorbachev deeply undermined the Soviet state and contributed to its destruction in 1991.[22]

In the post-Soviet period until 1998, many individuals and groups continued to argue for the restoration of some form of the imperial state.[23] But, at the same time, many others sharply criticized imperial ideas and articulated alternative, non-imperial definitions of the state. Powerful voices in Russia—including liberals who were prominent in the Yeltsin government, scholars and publicists, and moderate statists whose ideas were described in the previous chapter—highlighted the dangers posed to Russian national interests by any return to imperialism. Others eschewed all extremist orientations, underlined the absurdity of Western conspiracy theories against Russia, debunked extreme nationalist promises to the masses, and began actively to redefine concepts like "Eurasia" and "great power" in order to discredit myths propagated by imperial-minded nationalists. They asserted, for example, that Russia was unique, but had a mutually enriching relationship with many of the world's great cultures. Russia should be a great power, but it should influence its neighbors through its own internal prosperity and without resort to force and coercion. Russia could be a great power again only if it was willing to learn from its neighbors, including ways to strengthen democratic rule, and if it managed to overcome its socioeconomic difficulties.[24]

Some analysts labeled post-Soviet Russian political discourse as "moderate" or "realist"[25] because it deemphasized imperial claims and ambitions and emphasized pragmatic policies in line with more limited definitions of the national interest. Congruent with this assessment, many Russian scholarly writings in the 1990s articulated a civic, non-imperial nationalism for Russia; highlighted Russian historical and philosophical traditions in support of civic nationalism; and argued that democracy and nationalism could and should be combined as core principles of the Russian state.[26] Individuals and groups in the "establishment"—specifically, those with access to the highest government officials and whose views were widely covered by the Russian press—also advocated non-imperial views. They favored pragmatic cooperation with neighbors in the "near" and "far" abroad and emphasized internal problems and public welfare as the central priorities of the state. Their arguments appeared in such official documents as Russia's National Security Concept (December 1997), which highlighted economic reform and social stability as the highest priorities of the state, and the Concept on the State Nationalities Policy (June 1996), which emphasized the Eurasian idea of equality of cultures and commonality of values inside a multiethnic Russia.[27] Although these "establishment" groups became increasingly frustrated with the United States and other Western powers, especially in the context of NATO expansion in 1998–99, nonetheless they did not adopt an imperial nationalist rhetoric.[28]

Russia's evolving non-imperial political discourse was a countervailing element against aggressive nationalist ideas in the 1990s. Support for this discourse among both elites and the larger public connoted the existence of a partial foundation on which longer-term consensus between state and society on a non-imperial national identity and national priorities might become possible.[29] An encouraging development in this regard was elite and mass condemnation of Moscow's war in Chechnya in 1994–96 (the war echoed past imperial thinking), which contributed to the Yeltsin government's decision to sign a peace agreement at the end of 1996.[30] In addition, polls of politicians, intellectuals, journalists, experts, and the larger public showed majority support for the idea of Russia as a great power that defended its own interests without embarking on imperial actions or forceful attempts to reconquer territories that were part of the old Russian empire.[31] These poll results were in line with government policy in the 1990s[32] and indicated the incipient overlap of interests between state and society.

But it is too early to judge final outcomes. How robust is Russia's non-imperial or anti-imperial discourse? How easily might internal and external events shift this discourse back to old imperial patterns? A growing perception of threats in the international environment is one factor that could clearly lead to a reversal of non-imperial Russian political discourse. This factor is discussed at length in the next section. But in addition, specific domestic factors also warn of the fragility of non-imperial discourse. First, there is residual ambiguity in the minds of many Russians as to where exactly the borders of the Russian state lie. Even those who openly disavow imperial ideas have difficulty accepting the borders of the Russian Federation, given that these borders were set arbitrarily by Soviet authorities.[33] And powerful politicians such as Moscow mayor Yurii Luzhkov have repeatedly made claims that territory such as Sevastopol should be returned to Russia. In coming years, the institutionalization of post-Soviet borders through treaties, combined with the relatively free movement of Russian and CIS citizens on the territory of the former Soviet Union, should limit the success of nationalist politicians seeking to exploit the issue of Russian territorial claims. But in the near term, the uncertain nature of Russia's borders will be a factor that heightens the risk of revival of an imperial discourse.

Second, the continued independence and competence of the Russian mass media will also be key. Russia's anti-imperial discourse became possible in the Gorbachev years in large part because of the dismantling of ideological strictures imposed on the mass media. In the post-Soviet period, the press and other mass media have continued to present diverse viewpoints and have functioned as a useful forum for debating imperial and non-imperial conceptions of Russian state power and national identity. They played an especially commendable role in advancing anti-imperial discourse during the 1994–96 war in Chechnya. However, recent warning signs have appeared regarding the competence and independence of the mass media. Russian journalists, for example, were reluctant to cover the fate of Kosovar Albanians expelled by Serbian authorities from their homes during the Kosovo crisis in 1999. Instead of more balanced and accurate coverage, the media largely joined a bandwagon of pro-Serbian, anti-NATO and anti-Western coverage. Although criticism of NATO's policy was warranted, it was unfortunate that the Russian media did not cover more fully the damage caused by the Serbian government's policy of ethnic cleansing.[34] The sometimes heavy hand of state and oligarchical owners of powerful Russian media may also impede the independence and effectiveness of the press in the future, and could restrict open debate of imperial thinking and policy.

Third, norms and laws against extremist and hate speech, and Russian reassessment of the past, will also have an impact on the future of non-imperial political discourse. In the area of laws and norms, the Russian government has not yet fully formulated and implemented an uncompromising approach against extremist groups propagating hate speech. These groups tend to be empire-promoters, and legal sanctions against their extreme propaganda and violent activities should curb the future promotion of imperial discourse. A presidential decree to combat extremism does exist, but has not been implemented consistently. On a more positive note, some local and federal authorities have taken steps to discredit or punish extremist groups.[35] Finally, the strength of non-imperial political discourse will depend very much on how Russians continue to assess the past and its implications for the present. The writing of new history textbooks and the teaching of history in Russian schools will play particularly important roles in shaping the values and ideas of young Russians. Problems exist in terms of meager resources to revamp Soviet-era books, the popularity of conservative and imperial-minded nineteenth-century historians, and the lack of willingness to adopt better textbooks if they are available. There is also evidence that post-Soviet Russian history textbooks have made little progress in rethinking and rejecting imperial principles and policies that characterized the Soviet past.[36]

A Relatively Benign—But Increasingly
Uncertain—International Environment

In Russia, radical nationalists in the 1990s consistently conjured threats to the nation and advocated forceful nationalist mobilization to safeguard Russian independence and security. Objective factors such as the instability of borders and armed conflicts in the former Soviet space helped make the "threats" touted by extreme nationalists more credible. Overall, however, threats from the international system, which involved military, economic, and prestige elements, proved manageable and did not favor an aggressive nationalist agenda. At the end of 1998, there had been no international crises to spur Russian policymakers to use aggressive nationalism for mass mobilization. Russia, moreover, utilized international institutional resources to mitigate its economic and security problems.

The "near abroad" or newly independent states of the former Soviet Union were the first source of threats to Russian security. These threats had some basis in reality, but were exaggerated by aggressive nationalists. They argued, for example, that the second-class status of Russians and Russian-speakers in the "near abroad" threatened Russian prestige and authority and could lead to military crisis in the event of violent clashes between Russians and their host populations. There were legitimate reasons for Russians abroad to feel threatened and discriminated against. For example, ethnic Russians were unable to gain full rights in the former Soviet republics, especially Estonia and Latvia, where citizenship and language laws worked against Russians who were born in, or immigrated to, the area after 1940. These laws did not violate international standards of human rights, but did infringe on standards of humanitarian behavior and threatened political and economic disenfranchisement of large numbers of Russian speakers. In parts of Ukraine and Kazakhstan, sizeable Russian populations complained about job discrimination, limitations on mass media and educational materials in the Russian language, and other treatment that relegated them to what they felt as "second-class citizen" categories. They also complained about new textbooks that presented Russians in a negative light and created a hostile environment for their children. In Kazakhstan, high levels of insecurity caused as many as one million Russians to flee in 1991–93.[37]

Extreme nationalists portrayed the plight of "Russians abroad" in exaggerated terms. In the early 1990s, newspapers like *Den'* and television programs like Aleksandr Nevzorov's *600 Sekund* sensationalized the hardships of Russians. In one television report on Nevzorov's program in early 1991, Russians in Estonia were shown making public claims that the Estonian government treated them like prisoners. Dramatic shots of Russian refugees appeared, with ominous music in the background and a voice declaring, "They [the enemies of Russia] are getting ready." Rutskoi and other leaders in the Russian Supreme Soviet in 1991–93 exploited the Russian diaspora issue to support secessionism by Russian-dominated regions in the "near abroad" and their unification with Russia.[38]

Another threat from the "near abroad" involved the outbreak of ethnic and other conflicts, which killed from tens to hundreds of thousands of former Soviet citizens, including an indeterminate number of Russians. Particularly in the Caucasus and Central Asia (Armenia, Azerbaijan, Georgia, and Tajikistan), where deadly wars raged in the early 1990s, Russian populations had to flee for their lives. Those who remained, including Russian border guards and "peacekeeping" troops, lost many lives and felt deeply insecure. Conflicts in Central Asia and the Caucasus, as of 1994, accounted for approximately 80 percent of all immigration to Russia, causing tremendous social, economic, and political strain on the country. The potential outbreak of other conflicts and the escalation of ongoing ones further heightened Russian perceptions of external threat.[39] Yet one more problem from the "near abroad" was the rise of new military powers on Russia's borders. Relations with Ukraine, for example, were contentious, and tensions erupted over such issues as ownership of the Black Sea Fleet, control of the Crimea, and U.S.–Ukrainian military exercises based on scenarios that Russians found offensive.[40]

Besides the "near abroad," the West—especially its policy of NATO expansion to countries that were formerly Soviet satellites—was another source of threat to Russia. Even before NATO expansion was a fact, extremist nationalists accented the threat of NATO aggression as manifested, for example, in the bombing of Serbian positions in Bosnia. They characterized NATO as an unwelcome meddler in areas of central interest to Russia and called NATO actions in Bosnia-Herzegovina a mockery of any Western "partnership" with Moscow. By 1995, continued NATO use of force in Bosnia motivated nearly all members of the Russian political spectrum, not only national patriots, to express alarm at, and condemnation of, the alliance's actions, labeling them a "blow to Russian prestige." Prominent leaders, including Yeltsin, suggested that NATO expansion would bring the world back to a tense and confrontational situation between two armed camps, and General Lebed warned that NATO expansion eastward could cause a third world war. Between 1995 and 1998, Russian elites expressed anger, dismay, and a sense of betrayal by the West over NATO expansion. Although the Russian mass public was less agitated than the elites by the NATO issue, nonetheless a U.S. Information Agency poll in 1997 showed that seven in ten Russians believed that the United States was "using Russia's current weakness to reduce it to a second-rate power." Moreover, 60 percent of those polled said they did not trust NATO.[41] Besides NATO expansion and NATO bombings, the threat of new geopolitical rivalry in the former Soviet space also emerged among Russia, the United States, Turkey, and others who staked a claim to economic interests in the region, especially oil in the Caspian.[42]

By the end of 1998, however, most threats to Russia had diminished—except for NATO expansion and NATO's military role in areas where Russia had strong historical and geopolitical interest. In terms of "Russians abroad," the worst scenarios of abuse of ethnic Russians did not materialize. The Central Asian states, for example—wary of the damage to their economies that could result from further migration of skilled Slavic professionals—offered Russians dual citizenship (Turkmenistan and Tajikistan), facilitated citizenship change (Kazakhstan), or made Russian an official language (Kyrgyzstan). In the Baltics, many ethnic Russians became willing to live with citizenship restrictions rather than return to Russia, where they felt their standard of living would worsen. And Latvia and Estonia, which had numerous quarrels with Russia over their citizenship laws, passed a package of amendments in 1998 to make it easier for ethnic Russians to become citizens in both states.[43] Some of the most thorny citizenship issues in the Baltics were also resolved with assistance and pressure from international organizations, including the Organization for Security and Cooperation in Europe (OSCE) and the European Union (EU). Further, the most violent conflicts on Russia's periphery diminished in intensity, many of them due to forceful intervention either by Moscow-dominated peacekeeping forces or by remnants of the Russian army still in place in the former Soviet republics (e.g., Tajikistan, Georgia, and Moldova). The risks of other violent conflicts near Russia's borders decreased overall, and interstate borders became more stable with the institution of strong presidential rule (except in Ukraine and Moldova) and incipient economic progress in neighboring states. The denuclearization of Russia's neighbors, with assistance from the United States, further reduced threats to Russian security. In addition, international organizations helped lessen Russian insecurity; the United Nations approved Russian peacekeeping in Georgia and sent a special envoy to facilitate the peace process in Tajikistan, and the OSCE assisted in drawing up a peace plan for Nagorno-Karabakh and worked actively with all parties, including Russia, to implement it.[44]

NATO expansion, by the end of 1998, continued to be an unpleasant and threatening development for Russia.[45] However, early steps taken by the United States and NATO member governments to assuage Russian concerns were helpful, including active engagement with Russia via NATO's Partnership for Peace Program, special arrangements for Russian troops in NATO-led operations in Bosnia, and the signing of the "Founding Act" to govern Russian cooperation with an expanded NATO. These steps provided the Russian government a degree of "inclusion" in the most prestigious security club of the world. In addition, the United States and western European governments proved lenient and helpful in other military and economic aspects of Russian security. They supported Russian inclusion in such international institutions as the Council of Europe, the Group of Seven (which became the "Summit of the Eight" in 1997), Asia-Pacific Economic Cooperation Council (APEC), and the Paris Club. Russia also concluded an agreement on restructuring Soviet-era debt with the London and Paris Clubs and signed agreements on partnership and cooperation with the European Union and the Organization for Economic Cooperation and Development (OECD). U.S.–Russian cooperation in many areas proceeded as well via the mechanism of the Gore–Chernomyrdin (and successor) commissions. Most important, the international financial institutions (i.e., the IMF and the World Bank), prodded by the United States in particular, granted billions in loans and other support to Russia, largely for political reasons and without holding Russia to the same stringent requirements that rank-and-file countries have had to observe.[46] All these steps notwithstanding, the humiliation and threats associated with NATO expansion did not entirely disappear. To most Russian elites, the expansion of a Western

Cold War institution to Russian borders remained a serious affront. NATO's bombing of Serbia over Kosovo in 1999, in particular, gave credence to some of the worst fears articulated by Russians: Russian exclusion from key international security decisions, NATO military intervention in areas of importance to Russia, and potential intervention by the Western alliance in Russia itself or on former Soviet territory.

As for geopolitical competition in the former Soviet space, an October 1995 decision by the multinational Azerbaijan International Operating Company to export Caspian Sea oil via two pipelines—one through Russia and another through Georgia—showed that international actors took Russian interests in the Caspian seriously and wished to avoid hostile confrontation over resources on Russia's periphery. Russia toned down its claims on the Caspian Sea and signed an agreement with Kazakhstan in 1998, largely accepting the position of other Caspian littoral states on how to divide the Caspian Sea and its resources.[47] Western political leaders, on other fronts, contributed to creating a relatively benign international environment for Russia by tolerating Russian military and other interventions in the "near abroad," helping Moscow save face by not condemning the 1994–96 war in Chechnya, announcing support for Moscow-led "integration" in the former Soviet Union as long as it is done on a "voluntary" basis, reacting sympathetically to Russian concerns about revising such treaties as the Conventional Forces in Europe Treaty (CFE), and honoring Russian history and sacrifices by joining in Moscow's May 1995 landmark celebration of the fiftieth anniversary of Russian victory over fascism.[48] Until the end of 1998, a relatively benign international environment enabled moderate nationalists in Russia to argue against the claims of extremists. For example, Yeltsin cited Russian membership in international institutions as proof that Russia was not so humiliated and continued to be a great world power, without whose cooperation "acute international problems" could not be resolved.[49] But NATO's plans for further expansion and NATO actions in the Kosovo crisis in 1999 have made the international environment more uncertain for Russian interests. This uncertainty, coupled with ongoing Russian weakness, will likely increase Russian perceptions of international threat. The implications of this for Russian nationalism and foreign policy will be discussed in the concluding chapter.

THE WEAKNESS OF AGGRESSIVE NATIONALISM IN RUSSIAN FOREIGN POLICY

Russian foreign policy since the breakup of the Soviet Union tended to be inconsistent. This was understandable, given the unsettled nature of Russian ideology, politics, and economy, and the unsettled character of the international system itself. Beginning in 1992–93, the Yeltsin–Kozyrev leadership's initially very pro-Western foreign policy rhetoric shifted to a more nationalistic tone. But this nationalism was largely of the moderate statist variety and excluded the more violent and imperial ideas of extremist nationalists.

The rest of this chapter will examine test cases of Russian foreign policy to illustrate the weak influence of aggressive nationalism in the 1990s. These cases cover Russian actions in three areas: (1) the fate of Russian minorities in the "near abroad," (2) violent conflicts in the "near abroad," and (3) the conflict in Bosnia. These three areas are critical because they deal with Russian national identity, pride, and power and influence. The issues of Russian minorities and conflicts in the "near abroad" challenged Russian policymakers to define who were members of the Russian nation, what the state should do on their behalf, and how far Russia should go in exercising leverage and power over former imperial territories. The Bosnia conflict, on the other hand, brought to the fore Russia's "great power" claims and the meaning of those claims at a time of Russian weakness and low international prestige. Western states challenged traditional Russian influence in Bosnia, and Western military force came in direct confrontation with Russia's historical, Orthodox Serbian allies. If aggressive Russian nationalism were to manifest itself in Russian actions, these areas would certainly have been on top of the agenda.

It has been fairly common to find arguments that a dangerous nationalism (i.e., one steeped in imperial thinking) was at the center of post-Soviet Russian foreign policy. But a close examination of Russian foreign policy in the 1990s indicates the weak influence of extreme nationalism. For example, Moscow authorities never implemented a maximalist or forceful policy to protect Russian minorities in the "near abroad." Neither did they marshal the state's resources toward reasserting control over the new sovereignty of former Soviet republics. While there was evidence of Russian military intervention in conflicts in the former Soviet space, this intervention was geared toward preserving *some* influence in Russia's immediate periphery rather than ending the independence of neighboring states. Russia's posture as the de facto major power in the region may be characterized as the normal reaction of a historical great power dealing with the aftermath of imperial collapse. The policy pursued by Yeltsin's government emphasized the primacy of the "near abroad" in Russian foreign affairs and sought to preserve legitimate Russian strategic, economic, and humanitarian (i.e., the welfare of Russian minorities) interests under largely adverse circumstances. This could hardly be characterized as a policy of extreme nationalism. In the former Yugoslavia as well, Russian policymakers were unwilling to compromise and jeopardize their cooperative relations with Western countries and international institutions for the sake of aggressive nationalist sentiments and arguments. Although there was some sharp rhetoric against Western policy in the Balkans, official Russian actions ultimately tended to be pragmatic and cognizant of Russian weakness.

Russians Abroad: Crimea/Ukraine, Kazakhstan, and the Baltics

The fate of an estimated twenty-five million[50] Russians living outside the Russian Federation was a highly sensitive issue in Russian politics in 1991–98. At times, the rhetoric of Russian officials, and Western analyses of actions emanating from Moscow, pointed to aggressive nationalism in Russia's approach to the Russian diaspora. In 1994, for example, shortly after the victory of Zhirinovsky in the Russian parliament, Kozyrev declared that it would be dangerous for Russian troops to withdraw completely from former Soviet lands and unwise to "ignore historic ties, and what has been achieved over centuries . . . in [the former Soviet] space sealed by the common history and culture of the multimillion Russian-speaking population." Months later, in declaring war on Chechnya, Yeltsin justified Russian violence on the grounds of protecting the security of Russian "citizens not only in Chechnya, but also beyond." This led one commentator to write that Chechnya might only be the beginning of the "Kremlin's radical turn from isolationism to neoimperialism."[51] But was official Russian behavior on behalf of "Russians abroad" truly guided by nationalist neoimperialism? Did authorities in Moscow encourage and support Russian groups to secede from their new states and join Russia?

Crimea/Ukraine

The Crimean Peninsula had been part of Russia since 1783, but in 1954 Nikita Khrushchev presented it as a gift to the Ukrainian republic. Crimea was the only region in Ukraine with a clear Russian majority—67 percent of the population— and with political elites that had openly favored reunification with Russia. Crimea was also the location of the port of Sevastopol, home of the former Soviet Black Sea Fleet and, until 1997, a disputed possession between Russia and Ukraine. Immediately after the breakup of the Soviet Union, nationalist-minded members of the Russian parliament raised the issue of reexamining the Soviet decision to bestow Crimea on Ukraine. In a provocative step, parliamentarians led by Sergei Baburin visited Crimea in early 1992, called for the "third defense of Sevastopol," and asked for Russian intervention in defense of the "honor of the Russian people." In July 1993, the Russian Supreme Soviet's confrontational tone over Crimea intensified when the legislature unanimously passed a declaration on Sevastopol as a constituent part of Russia. These developments drowned out more moderate voices, which warned about avoiding conflict with Ukraine and noted the lack of political and military resources to implement drastic steps favored by aggressive nationalists.[52]

From 1991 to 1994, pro-Russian parties were active in Crimea, including the Republican movement and the Russian Party, which advocated separatism from Ukraine and a Slavic union of Russia, Belarus, and Ukraine. In 1992, these groups announced Crimean independence and passed a constitution that annulled Kiev's authority. Tensions with Kiev worsened when, in the 1994 Crimean elections, leaders of the movement to reunify Crimea with Russia won both the presidency and the majority of seats in parliament. A crisis arose in March 1994, when the Crimean parliament voted to restore its 1992 pro-independence constitution (which Kiev had earlier canceled). But infighting among Crimean separatists and Crimea's financial dependence weakened the separatists' position vis-à-vis Kiev, and by March 1995, the Ukrainian central government managed to impose measures that reined in Crimean separatism and installed leaders in both parliament and the cabinet who were more accommodating of Ukrainian authority. By the end of 1995, it was clear that Kiev had regained control of Crimea and also avoided severe conflict with Russia.[53]

Some members of the Russian political elite eagerly supported the Russian separatist movement in Crimea. They took such provocative steps as an offer of dual citizenship to Russians in Crimea; a Supreme Soviet declaration on Sevastopol as Russian territory; inflammatory rhetoric by Supreme Soviet deputies and leaders like Aleksandr Rutskoi and Oleg Rumiantsev who visited Crimea; and declarations of support for Crimean separatists from the extremist National Salvation Front, *Pravda*, and others.[54] These moves generated pressure against Kiev, but did not constitute a neoimperial nationalist policy. The majority of these confrontational measures were undertaken by critics of the Yeltsin government, while the government itself pursued a moderate approach. Executive power in Moscow used rhetoric in support of the Russian population in Crimea largely to appease the nationalist sector of Russian public opinion. But the Kremlin did not supply weapons or money to Crimean separatists, and Yeltsin and Kozyrev consistently characterized Crimea as a Ukrainian *domestic* problem. In March 1994, when the Crimean parliament restored its 1992 independence constitution and caused a crisis with Kiev, Kozyrev warned that the "Yugoslav drama should not be repeated in Crimea. . . . There the [war] started with demands of sovereignty and ultimatums to back up state integrity." During the worst quarrels between Kiev and Crimea in 1995, the new Russian Duma and the cabinet basically ignored numerous missions and appeals for economic and political assistance by Crimean separatist leaders. Given Ukraine's dependence on Russia for energy (90 percent of Ukrainian fuel came from Russia), Moscow could have tightened the noose on Kiev on behalf of the Russian diaspora, but it did not. By late 1995, as Kiev continued to clamp down on Russian communities in Crimea, Moscow remained largely silent and Crimean separatists acknowledged that their cause must be shelved, at least for the moment.[55]

Moscow's policies toward the Russian population in Crimea largely followed the 1994 government decree on "State Policy of the Russian Federation with Respect to Compatriots Residing Abroad" and the 1995 "Russia's Strategic Course with Countries That are Participants of the CIS." These documents codified Russia's policy in three prongs: to promote the voluntary integration of "Russians abroad" into the political, economic, and social life of their new states of residence; to preserve Russian culture; and to use trade sanctions if the rights of Russians were violated.[56] Positive developments in 1995–98 in Russian–Ukrainian relations further confirmed the moderate line of Moscow officials. Yeltsin signed a treaty with Ukraine in 1997, recognizing Ukraine's territorial integrity and renouncing all border claims against Kiev. In return, Ukraine agreed to allow Russia's Black Sea Fleet to keep its base in Sevastopol for another twenty years. Since the signing of the treaty, military and economic cooperation has continued between the two countries. The problem of the Russian diaspora in Crimea and elsewhere in Ukraine is far from resolved, however. Russians complain about the closing of Russian schools, the termination of Russian mass media programs, and the exclusively negative portrayal of Russians in Ukrainian textbooks. But the record in the 1990s shows that Russian authorities were cooperative on most issues and did not yield to coercive measures advocated by neoimperial nationalists.[57]

Kazakhstan

Kazakhstan in the 1990s was another test case of the weak impact of extremist nationalism on Russian policy. Of the former Soviet republics, Kazakhstan was the sole republic where the titular nationality, the Kazakhs, constituted a minority population. In 1989, 40 percent of Kazakhstan's 16.5 million population were Kazakhs, 38 percent Russians, and the rest a mix of other nationalities. Most of the Russian population in Kazakhstan was concentrated in the north and east, mostly in industrial cities or "virgin lands" settled under Khrushchev. Those in the north lived within a day's drive of Russia's 3,000-mile border with Kazakhstan. Kazakhstan was rich in natural resources, especially oil and gas, and represented potential lucrative gains for Moscow should it succeed in controlling Kazakhstan, in part by playing the ethnic Russian card.

Although Kazakh president Nursultan Nazarbaev tried to strike a balance between Kazakh and Russian nationalisms, he failed to protect his country's Russian population from discrimination. In 1991–95, Russians in Kazakhstan complained about increasing job discrimination, particularly in the government sphere, where most employment was concentrated. Ethnic Kazakhs replaced Russians and other Slavs in political and industrial leadership positions; this included the replacement of Slavic prime minister Sergei Tereshchenko by a Kazakh, Akezhan Kazhegeldin, in 1994. In the 1994 Supreme Soviet elections, Russians also complained about unfair procedures that disqualified many Russian candidates, resulting in only 128 Russians running out of 750 parliamentary candidates. Russians witnessed as well the narrowing of their educational opportunities, and those with families felt deeply discouraged about their children's future prospects in the country. In addition, moderate Russian activists were persecuted and arrested. For example, the Russian writer Boris Suprunyuk was arrested in 1994 after writing about Kazakh discrimination against Russians and arguing in favor of the legalization of Russian social and cultural organizations, dual citizenship, and Russian as a second state language (Kazakh is currently the state language, and Russian the language for "interethnic communication"). Some Russian publications were also banned and official recognition denied to organizations wishing to represent the interests of Russians and other Slavic peoples. These developments led many Russians to feel that they had become second-class citizens. As a result, more than a million Russians fled Kazakhstan by 1995, nearly four hundred thousand more returned to Russia in 1996 and 1997, and many of those left behind remained deeply demoralized.[58]

Officially, Moscow reacted to the plight of Russians in Kazakhstan in a moderate manner, even though extreme nationalists argued for drastic measures. Ethnic Russians who stayed in Kazakhstan (with the exception of Cossack groups in the north) themselves expressed a desire to avoid violent confrontation. There was no evidence in Moscow of official support for militant Cossacks or other Russian groups intent on undermining the territorial integrity of Kazakhstan. To the contrary, Russian official policies disregarded outright the welfare of the Russian population in Kazakhstan; for example, taking Kazakhstan out of the ruble zone in the early 1990s hurt ethnic Russians the most because they were dependent on Russian-linked industrial production. Moscow did not compensate ethnic Russians and did not pressure Kazakhstan to do so after claiming that responsibility was in the hands of the Kazakh government. Moscow officials did lobby for dual citizenship—a measure widely supported by Russians in Kazakhstan. But Kazakh officials offered Russia only an agreement on simplified procedures for Russians to gain Kazakhstani citizenship. Russian officials could have pressed more aggressively for dual citizenship because that right was already constitutionally granted to ethnic Kazakhs, who could also hold Chinese or other citizenship, but they did not. By late 1995, leaders of the most active Russian social and cultural organization, LAD (Russian Rebirth Society), gave up on assistance from Moscow, claiming that Russian leaders liked to brandish their concern for "Russians abroad" but ultimately did nothing effective on their behalf.[59]

Baltics: Estonia and Latvia

When the Soviet Union disintegrated, roughly one-third of Estonia's 1.6 million inhabitants were either ethnic Russian or native Russian speakers, with areas like Narva in Estonia being almost completely Russian. In Latvia, approximately 40 percent of the over 2.5 million population was Russian, including approximately fifty thousand retired military officers and their families. This demographic balance was largely the result of Russian migration and resettlement in the Baltics between 1935 and 1989. During the days of *glasnost'* and *perestroika*, Baltic activists persistently lobbied and demonstrated for independence from the Soviet Union. Many Russian residents and even Yeltsin supported these bids for independence, but discovered shortly after 1991 that the consequences had negative effects on Russian interests.

In 1991–95, Russians in Latvia and Estonia complained about discrimination in Baltic citizenship and language laws. Many were particularly resentful about being excluded from political and economic rights when they had lived most of their lives in the Baltics and had their children and grandchildren born there. They were also deeply unhappy about being branded as "occupiers," and complained that they should not have to "answer for Stalin and the Soviet Union"; after all, "many Estonians served the regime . . . and [did not] bear any responsibility." Many who were, or had been, associated with the Soviet military and security services were specifically penalized in the process of citizenship acquisition. Other nonmilitary professionals experienced what they felt were unfair practices in the administration of language examinations and saw threats to their job security.[60]

Some Russian officials and other commentators proclaimed over and over again that the "human rights" of Russians in the Baltics were being massively violated. Several motivations likely underpinned this rhetoric, including legitimate concerns over the fate of ethnic kin and the desire to prevent the massive influx of Russian refugees from the Baltics to Russia. At the same time, imperial motivations may have been present as well: by maligning Baltic policy, Moscow officials could more easily justify retaining troops in Estonia and Latvia or maintaining access to military-strategic sites in the area. Yeltsin's government did exert pressure on the governments of Estonia and Latvia to reexamine their language and citizenship policies. In June 1993, Russia halted deliveries of natural gas to Estonia. In October 1992 the Russian government halted the pull-out of troops from the Baltics and the Russian Defense Ministry threatened to do so again in 1994. The Russian Supreme Soviet also expressed support for a referendum on autonomy in Narva, thereby posing a threat to Estonia's territorial integrity, and called for economic sanctions against the Baltic states. Ultimately, however, Moscow's bark proved worse than its bite. Such measures as the halting of gas supplies to Estonia, for example, lasted no more than a week, and Moscow completed the withdrawal of all Russian troops from Estonia and Latvia by September 1994 (after a year's delay).[61] Although Russian relations with Estonia and Latvia were not entirely harmonious in the years 1996–98, nonetheless positive developments occurred. These included Latvia's and Estonia's amendments to liberalize their citizenship laws, the preparation of a treaty on borders between Estonia and Russia (Lithuania and Russia signed such a treaty in 1997), and softened official Russian rhetoric toward the Baltics.[62] Overall, Russian policy on the Russian diaspora in the Baltics was occasionally assertive and stern, but did not amount to a policy of nationalist, neoimperial restoration.

Will Russia's relatively moderate and restrained policy on Russians in the "near abroad" likely continue in the future? Three brief points lead to an affirmative answer. First, the Russian government does not have the financial resources to implement a more coherent and effective policy of support for ethnic Russian populations abroad. Therefore, Russians in the CIS and the Baltics will likely focus more on negotiating positive conditions of residence and citizenship in their new states than on soliciting official assistance from Russia. Second, Moscow's reliance on the CIS as a multilateral institution within which to resolve problems related to "Russians abroad" serves as a further restraint on aggressive measures on behalf of its diaspora population. Finally, Russians themselves in the former republics of the Soviet Union are not sufficiently organized to become a strong, mobilized force pushing for union with Russia or otherwise supporting coercive Russian policies toward their host governments. A study by David Laitin contends that Russians in Kazakhstan, Estonia, Latvia, and Ukraine are developing a distinct (if embryonic) "Russian-speaking" national identity. They favor a strong CIS over a strong Russia, and exhibit "a clear poverty in identification with Russia."[63] The single most important factor that can turn Russian policy in an aggressive direction would be pogroms and other violent actions against ethnic Russians in the "near abroad." But this did not happen in the 1990s and is unlikely to occur in the future.

Russian Intervention in Zones of Conflict:
Georgia, Moldova, and Tajikistan[64]

Did Russian intervention in zones of conflict in the "near abroad" manifest nationalist-inspired neoimperialism? Did Moscow cause specific conflicts that it could
exploit to restore control over its newly independent neighbors? Did it rely primarily on force to pursue its own interests, and did its intervention ultimately have a
destructive or constructive impact? This section does not render a full history of
conflicts in the former Soviet space, but seeks to answer the preceding questions
by looking at Russian actions in the Georgia–Abkhazia conflict, the Transdnestr–Moldova dispute, and the civil war in Tajikistan. Russian policy in these
conflicts in the 1990s amounted to opportunism to retain some influence in the
"near abroad." It also reflected military challenges associated with the collapse of
the Soviet Union and new statehood among the former Soviet republics.[65] In sum,
Russian policy showed more the limits on hegemonic Russian power projection
than the beginnings of an imperialist policy favored by extreme nationalists.

Georgia

Moscow did not create the conflict between separatist Abkhazia and the central
government in Georgia; in fact, this conflict had roots that extended to the Soviet
period. Abkhazia, a sizable region on Georgia's western Black Sea Coast, became
part of the Georgian Soviet Socialist Republic in December 1921, but retained its
Union republic status, granted by the Bolsheviks in March 1921, until the early
1930s. Tensions were always thick between Georgians and Abkhazians. Georgians,
who for decades constituted a majority in Abkhazia (46–48 percent), resented the
fact that Abkhazians, whose proportion of the population in the Abkhaz republic
never exceeded 25 percent and had decreased to 18 percent by the early 1990s,
held practically all positions of power. The Abkhazians, in turn, resented their loss
of Union republic status and sought, unsuccessfully, to have it restored in 1978
and 1989. They also attempted to unite with the Russian Federation and supported the preservation of the USSR in the 1991 Soviet referendum, which Georgia itself boycotted.[66]

Tensions flared in 1992 when, under the leadership of Vladislav Ardzinba, new
electoral rules further skewed the proportionality of Abkhaz–Georgian representation in the Abkhaz republic's Supreme Soviet (allotting twenty-eight of sixty-
five seats to Abkhazians). Violence broke out in August 1992 when, most likely in
response to Abkhazia's renunciation of the Georgian constitution and the restoration of its 1925 independence constitution, Georgian forces attacked the Abkhaz
capital of Sukhumi. The Abkhazians were not entirely unprepared because
Ardzinba had by then created his own National Guard. Fighting continued until
1993, with Moscow brokering at least two cease-fires in September 1992 and July
1993, both of which were broken by the Abkhazians. The war with Abkhazia, coupled with Tbilisi's battles against forces loyal to deposed Georgian ex-president
Zviad Gamsakhurdia, created a state crisis for Georgia and almost led to the state's
dismemberment and military collapse in 1993. By July of that year, President

Eduard Shevardnadze of Georgia turned to Russia for assistance and accepted membership in the CIS as the price for Russian intervention. Moscow officials then brokered a cease-fire in December. In June 1994, Russia deployed three thousand Russian peacekeeping forces in the region. The United Nations endorsed this operation in October 1994 and sent its own observers.[67]

Moscow exploited the conflict between Georgia and Abkhazia to further its own interests, which were to bring Georgia into the CIS and keep Russian bases on Georgian soil. Moscow achieved both of these by exploiting Georgian political and military vulnerability. First, Russian officials did nothing to discipline Russian military officers and mercenaries who were helping Abkhazian separatists. Russian friends of Ardzinba gave military-technical assistance to Abkhaz fighters, and some fought directly on behalf of Abkhazia. For example, jet fighters and fighter bombers downed by Georgian forces had Russian military markings and were piloted by Russians. Some analysts claimed that Russian mercenaries received direct orders from Moscow, but the extent to which Moscow officials authorized military actions on behalf of Abkhazia against Georgia remained unclear. In any case, Russian official support for Abkhazia stopped well short of favoring Abkhazian independence or absorption into the Russian Federation. Second, Moscow did nothing to discipline the Abkhazians after they unilaterally violated two cease-fires mediated by Yeltsin in 1992–93. These violations facilitated the Abkhaz army's policy of "ethnic cleansing" against Georgians. In September 1993, for example, after the Abkhazians retook the city of Sukhumi, over two hundred thousand Georgian refugees were forced to flee through the Caucasus mountains, and hundreds died. Third, Russian officials ignored volunteer troops and other military assistance to Abkhazia from the Confederation of Mountain Peoples (Chechnya, Ossetia, Kabardino-Balkaria, and Adygei). The message was that Russia would not do much toward a peaceful resolution of the conflict until Georgian officials made clear that they would take steps favorable to Russian strategic interests. Thus, in 1992 Shevardnadze blamed Russia for siding with Abkhazia and remarked that "we were let down, treacherously deceived. . . . It's very bitter that, in some measure, representatives of Russia took part in this dirty affair."[68]

Russian intervention in Georgia certainly reflected what might be called opportunistic hegemony, but did not amount to an attempt to dismember Georgia and restore Russian imperial control. Although Moscow officials either closed their eyes or tacitly approved Russian military assistance to Abkhazia, they did not allow the buildup of overwhelming force that could have allowed Abkhazia to dismember Georgia. Once Georgia had turned to Moscow, Russian officials including Yeltsin and then-defense minister Pavel Grachev kept their side of the bargain and pushed Georgian–Abkhaz negotiations forward when they stalled. Russian officials also made clear to Ardzinba, a noxious ethnic cleanser, that he could no longer count on favors from Moscow. Russia imposed a blockade on Abkhazia and closed all cross-border trade with the republic in 1995.[69] Moscow's intervention, regardless of its unevenness, did stop the bloodshed in Georgia at a time when, despite Shevardnadze's pleas, no other power or international organization was willing to intervene in any effective manner.[70]

At the end of 1998, Georgia and Abkhazia continued to be in a state of "no war, no peace," with occasional low-intensity conflict occurring in the zone dividing their jurisdictions. Russian troops remained the chief "peacekeepers" between the warring sides, but had difficulty preventing provocations and violations of the peace by the disputants and their guerrilla supporters. Russia's policy in the area focused on maintaining its peacekeeping force and cooperating with various international bodies, including a UN Observer Force, to maintain Georgian–Abkhaz negotiations. Moscow officials were unwilling to put maximum pressure on Ardzinba to make him commit to a Georgian–Abkhaz settlement, and it was doubtful if he and his supporters would yield to such pressure if it were forthcoming. The Russian government, after the 1994–96 war in Chechnya, was unwilling to be involved in large-scale hostilities, and pressures at home and meager resources limited, and will continue to limit, the role that Russia could play in Georgia.[71] Overall, Russian policy in Georgia was a reflection of Russian weakness and the opportunism of a waning power, rather than the ascendant overlordship of an imperial, nationalist regime.

Moldova

The Moldavian Soviet Socialist Republic was a creation of the Bolshevik government. It combined Bessarabia (which once belonged to the Russian empire but was part of Romania until the USSR regained it via the Molotov–Ribbentrop Pact of 1939) and the east bank of the Dnestr River (which used to be part of Ukraine). When Moldovan officials, in the context of a disintegrating Soviet Union, declared intentions to reunite with Romania, officials in the Transdnestr region (on the left bank of the Dnestr) protested and announced their own intent to secede from Moldova. They created the "Dnestr Moldovan Republic" (PMR, in its Russian acronym), which had a population of approximately seven hundred thousand, 60 percent of whom were Russians and Ukrainians. More important than the ethnic composition of the republic, however, (70 percent of Russians in Moldova lived quite contently outside the PMR) were several other facts: Transdnestr was home to numerous retired Soviet military personnel; it was the headquarters of the Fourteenth Army of the Soviet Union; 40 percent of its factories served the Soviet military-industrial complex; and it was led by mostly hard-line, pro-empire figures from the Soviet era.[72] These facts help explain why the region, including its ethnic Moldovan population, did not support reunification with Romania. The PMR population preferred to stay within the Soviet Union because their interests and security were best served in the Soviet context. The Soviet legacy also helps explain why, in 1992, members of the Russian military joined the conflict in support of the PMR. After all, PMR authorities supported military personnel and their families, who did not have other clear and viable options of support after the demise of the Soviet state.

Violence broke out between Moldovan forces and PMR military formations in the summer of 1992. The Moldovan army, however, did not prevail against PMR forces, which were supported by soldiers from the former Soviet Fourteenth

Army, stationed in Transdnestr. In July 1992, Moldovan leaders agreed to negotiate with their Russian counterparts in Moscow; a cease-fire agreement was subsequently signed by officials from Moscow, Chisinau (capital of Moldova), and Tiraspol (capital of PMR). CIS peacekeeping forces were then deployed, consisting of troops from the Soviet Fourteenth Army, Moldova, and the PMR. These developments notwithstanding, at the end of 1998 there was yet no lasting solution to the status of the PMR within Moldova. Transdnestr authorities refused offers by Moldovan officials for autonomy, even in the context of much dampened pro-Romanian nationalism in Moldova. The Fourteenth Army, as of November 1998, remained partially in Transdnestr despite an October 1994 withdrawal agreement between Russia and Moldova.[73]

Moscow authorities did not provoke the Transdnestr conflict, which had roots in Moldovan radical nationalism, Soviet political and military legacies, and the fever of secessionism that hit the Soviet Union in its last years. Russian officials, however, exacerbated and exploited the conflict to regain some influence in Moldova. In particular, Moscow wanted Moldova to join the CIS and allow Russia to maintain military facilities in Moldova. Obstructive and destructive actions emanating from Moscow included, first, declarations by the Supreme Soviet that "genocide" was being conducted against Russians in Moldova and calls for Russia to use the Fourteenth Army "to defend our countrymen in the Transdnestr region." This rhetoric, along with visits to the PMR by prominent political figures like Rutskoi and Sergei Stankevich in the early 1990s, encouraged radical leaders of the PMR to pursue a violent course against Moldovan authorities. Second, officials in Moscow, especially Yeltsin and his ministers, permitted the Fourteenth Army to act as a partisan force on behalf of PMR secessionists. Army personnel gave weapons and ammunition to the "Dnestr Women's Defense Committee," and fought actively in PMR operations. Further, the Fourteenth Army drafted local Moldovan-Dnestr residents into its ranks, thereby blurring distinctions between the Russian military and military forces of the secessionist Transdnestr republic.[74] Third, Russia did not use its political, military, and economic leverage to pressure recalcitrant PMR authorities to accept reasonable Moldovan offers of autonomy; a move in this direction would most likely have promoted a lasting settlement to the conflict and stabilized Moldovan politics. Moscow officials' slowness in withdrawing the Fourteenth Army (which has been renamed the Operational Group of Russian Forces) from Moldova also hindered the peace process, creating the appearance that Russian officials wanted to use Russian military presence as a point of leverage to obtain a more permanent military base in Moldova.[75]

Many of Moscow's actions in the PMR conflict were destructive, but did not amount to a program of nationalist neoimperialism. Instead, Russian policy reflected a more limited interest—maintaining a presence and some influence in what was former Soviet territory. This behavior was fairly predictable in the context of a collapsed imperial power. Moscow officials took advantage of factors that worked in their favor—such as local discontent against Moldova's pro-Romanian nationalism and the presence of the Fourteenth Army in Transdnestr. On the positive side, actions by Russian authorities did have some mitigating effect on the conflict, and intervention by the Fourteenth Army effectively prevented full-scale civil war.[76] Only Moscow had the will and resources to tackle the conflict in Transdnestr in 1992; efforts by such international organizations as the OSCE failed to prevent war, and the OSCE later refused a Moldovan request for peacekeeping forces. Moscow did not rely chiefly on force, but also worked with Moldovan leaders: for example, to guarantee jointly the peace agreement signed in 1992. Russian officials never declared support for Moldovan dismemberment; neither did they recognize the PMR as an independent state.[77]

Russia's actions in Moldova were largely opportunistic. Moscow authorities exploited (and were themselves exploited by) a population that supported Russian influence in the "near abroad." As of March 1995, well over 90 percent of Transdnestr voters still welcomed Russian intervention and opted in a referendum to keep the Fourteenth Army in Moldova. Moscow's inability to control the Fourteenth Army was not an expression of aggressive nationalism, but a result of the overall erosion of military discipline since the breakup of the Soviet Union. By the time the Fourteenth Army was officially transferred to Russian jurisdiction, General Lebed reported that 2,041 units of small arms had already been stolen from military warehouses in Transdnestr. Moreover, Moscow could not be blamed for actions taken in the Soviet era, such as the Soviet Ministry of Defense's offer of support to Cossack volunteers who came to the defense of Transdnestr in December 1991.[78] As of 1998, the conflict in Transdnestr remained unresolved, with PMR authorities continuing to be defiant about independence. Moscow officials continued to play a mediation role, along with Ukraine and international organizations such as the OSCE. Although Moldovan and Transdnestrian authorities signed various agreements and memoranda, they disagreed on what these documents meant and how they should be implemented. Some analysts argued that Russian "peacekeepers" in Transdnestr allowed unreconstructed secessionists to harden and fortify the boundary between the PMR and the rest of Moldova. Members of the Russian Duma did broach the official recognition of the Transdnestr Republic as an independent state, and refused to ratify the 1994 agreement on withdrawing the Fourteenth Army. Nonetheless, as Moldovan President Petru Lucinschi emphasized, Russian authorities did not exert undue pressure on Moldova, and the attitude of a group of Duma deputies did not embody official Russian foreign policy. Russia did not strangle Moldova's energy supply and continued supplying Moldova with much-needed fuel in return for food and produce in the 1990s.[79]

Tajikistan

The seeds of civil war in Tajikistan, a country of five million people, were not planted by Russian foreign policy. Numerous analysts have traced the origins of the war to interclan rivalry for power in the context of imminent Soviet disintegration and in the period thereafter.[80] In fact, in 1991–92, four ruling groups succeeded each other in Tajikistan, with the last group led by Imomali Rakhmonov managing to hold on to power chiefly because of Russian military and economic backing. Fighting among Tajik groups—governmental neocommunists, on one hand, and opposition democratic and Islamic groups, on the other—turned extremely bloody in 1992, with an estimated twenty thousand to fifty thousand people killed and hundreds of thousands of people displaced. The 201st Russian Motorized Rifle Division, stationed in Tajikistan, tried to maintain neutrality in the conflict, but their neutral pose quickly ended when Tajik opposition forces, assisted by Afghan mujahedins, brutally attacked Russian border guards in July 1993. Shortly thereafter, Russia widened its military presence in Tajikistan, took control of the Tajik–Afghan border, and staffed the Tajik Defense Ministry with Russian officials. By the end of 1995, an estimated twenty-five thousand Russian peacekeeping troops were in Tajikistan.[81]

Russian intervention in Tajikistan had some objectionable aspects, but did not constitute a policy of nationalist neoimperialism. Russians were not mobilized en masse to restore imperial control of Tajikistan. In fact, there was little enthusiasm in Russia for the Tajik operation. A September 1993 poll showed 60 percent of Russians opposed to troop deployment in Tajikistan, while elites also criticized Moscow's military involvement.[82] Those who objected to Russian actions criticized Moscow's backing of Tajikistan's authoritarian government, ignoring or perhaps even approving acts of aggression by Russian soldiers against Tajik and Afghan civilians, and allowing Russian troops to participate in military operations against Tajik opposition forces on the territory of Tajikistan (thus playing a partisan role in a civil war).[83] These criticisms must be qualified. It would have been impossible for Russian forces to maintain neutrality in the Tajik civil war when their central task, especially that of the border guards, was to prevent unauthorized incursions from Afghan territory. By accepting a role to protect Tajikistan's borders (borders that the Tajiks themselves could not protect), troop actions automatically became biased toward the ruling regime. The breakdown of military discipline, especially in the observance of human rights, was in part a predictable consequence of the breakup of the Soviet state and army, and a problem that new civilian authorities in Moscow could not resolve immediately or fully. Soviet troops in Tajikistan were mostly Russians who had lived practically all their lives in Central Asia and had minimal chances of continuing their service in Russia. With an insecure future as the Soviet Union disintegrated, some of them chose to desert the army and fight for one side or other in the civil war.[84]

Although Russian behavior did not amount to aggressive nationalism, there were some dangerous signs of demonizing rhetoric against Muslims in the early 1990s. Relatively respectable Russian newspapers like *Nezavisimaia gazeta* and the military's *Krasnaia zvezda* published articles that colored the wars in Chechnya and Tajikistan with the antagonistic hue of "Islamic jihad against Russia." Some Russian elites also carelessly spread anti-Islamic rhetoric.[85] Fortunately, the wholesale extremist characterization of Islam did not persist, and a rhetoric defining Muslims as Russia's enemies did not develop.

On the positive side, Russian forces in Tajikistan did help restore order after a bloody civil war, end the most serious human rights abuses that followed, and make possible the return of over six hundred thousand displaced persons and refugees to their homes.[86] Moscow also sought nonviolent solutions to the Tajik dilemma; its intervention in Tajikistan, after all, had been very costly militarily and economically.[87] Beginning in 1994, Yeltsin and his top aides supported UN-mediated talks among the warring Tajik parties, supported the UN Observer Mission in Tajikistan, urged the Tajik government to come to the negotiating table, and sought the assistance and participation of other Central Asian states and Iran and Pakistan in the peace process. These efforts, in part, led to a cease-fire mediated by the United Nations, Russia, and Iran in September 1994. But warring factions in Tajikistan continued to engage in violence. In early 1995, both sides took turns breaking the UN-brokered cease-fire. As of late 1998, Russian troops remained in Tajikistan, working with the Tajik military to prepare against potential threats from Taliban-governed Afghanistan.[88]

Russia's actions in Tajikistan illustrated the normal reaction of a former great power to some of the dilemmas of postimperial collapse. Moscow officials intervened to stop a bloody civil war in their state's traditional sphere of influence, and did so to protect legitimate interests. Russian interests in the conflict included protecting Tajikistan's borders from Afghan incursions and preventing the influence of Islamic fundamentalism in the former Soviet space (a task the new Tajik state could not fulfill). Moscow authorities were also concerned about the estimated two hundred thousand Russians still living in Tajikistan as of autumn 1993 (down from four hundred thousand two years earlier). At the end of 1995, no resources or support were forthcoming to meet opposition demands for UN peacekeeping and UN-monitored elections to end the war, and Moscow was the only actor able and willing to get involved in the Tajik disaster.

Conflict in Bosnia

In the war among Muslims, Catholic Croats, and Orthodox Serbs in Bosnia, Russia initially took a position that supported the West and the international community, even if it meant standing behind measures—such as economic sanctions—that hurt Russia's traditional Serbian allies. In 1992 Russia also joined the UN Protection Force (UNPROFOR) to underline its solidarity with the collective policies of the international community. Nationalists in Russia opposed Moscow's initial policies and deplored what they characterized as "one-sided" international sanctions against Serbia. Some tried to depict Serbia as a victim of international "intervention" not only against Serbs in particular, but Slavs[89] and Orthodox believers in general. They argued that, in the future, Russians in Ukraine and Belarus might well find themselves in a position similar to that of their embattled Serbian kin, who had been held hostage by Westernizing Croats and Slovenians. In that case, the international community would intervene to prevent Russia from justifiably aiding its citizens abroad, just as it was preventing aid to Serbia.[90]

In 1992–93, criticism by nationalists of Russian cooperation with the West in the Balkans proliferated and intensified. Criticism was especially sharp in the former Supreme Soviet, some of whose members engaged in their own shuttle diplomacy with Belgrade in 1993 and returned to Moscow with comments and recommendations opposing the Foreign Ministry and chiding Foreign Minister Kozyrev for his servility toward the West. The Supreme Soviet passed a resolution calling on Russia to support sanctions against all sides in the Yugoslav war, not just Serbia, and to oppose "military interference" in the conflict. Efforts to discredit Kozyrev's Foreign Ministry increased when the nationalist newspaper *Den'* published a classified memorandum written by the Russian ambassador to the United Nations, Yulii Vorontsov. In reference to further sanctions against Yugoslavia, the memorandum argued, "it is very important not to oppose . . . the western countries and the U.S., where public opinion is strong against [Serb leader] Milosevic."[91] This leak ignited an explosion in the Supreme Soviet, leading some deputies to question the legality of Russian actions in the United Nations. Pressure from the Supreme Soviet and extreme nationalists in the media prompted Kozyrev to deemphasize Russian solidarity with Western policy, and, in April 1993, Russia abstained from a UN vote on additional sanctions against rump Yugoslavia.[92]

Between late 1993 and the fall of 1995, Russian and Western policies in the Balkans increasingly diverged or, at least, did not move in a synchronous manner. In February 1994, for example, after refusing to send its blue helmet troops in Croatia to Sarajevo to help police a UN-brokered military agreement, Russian authorities suddenly dispatched their battalion of airborne troops from Croatia into Sarajevo to help implement the UN agreement to place Serb heavy weapons under the control of UNPROFOR. Russia's action had a net positive impact on Serb compliance, but some Western diplomats felt that the Russian–Western relationship was near breaking point.[93] Russians also bristled at NATO bombing of Serbian positions after Serbian troops refused to stop their assaults on UN-protected "safe havens." Zhirinovsky declared the bombings tantamount to a "declaration of war on Russia," while other officials, including the defense minister, similarly condemned NATO actions. Public opinion supported this position, with 77 percent of 4,800 people polled by the Center for International Sociological Research expressing agreement with Zhirinovsky.[94] In late summer 1995, Moscow and Washington engaged in competitive diplomatic initiatives in the Balkans. Yeltsin condemned renewed Croatian aggression, while U.S. officials highlighted and criticized Serbian atrocities. In September 1995, in response to a Serb attack on a Sarajevo marketplace, NATO once again launched airstrikes against Serb positions. This prompted another barrage of bitter and angry comments from Moscow, including Yeltsin's denunciation of "the cruel bombardment and shelling" of the Serbs. The Russian Duma demanded Kozyrev's resignation because of "multiple serious mistakes that [had] led to the humiliating failure of Russia's Balkans policy," and an end to Russian participation in UN economic sanctions against Serbia.[95]

Although by late 1995 a crisis was brewing in Russian relations with the West, and the United States in particular, over the war in Bosnia, moderate Russian policies ultimately emerged. First, Kozyrev met with U.S. Deputy Secretary of State Strobe Talbott in September 1995 and subsequently issued a conciliatory tone reaffirming "partnership" with the West and Russian cooperation with NATO in the search for a peaceful settlement in Bosnia. Second, Yeltsin and U.S. President Bill Clinton met in New York a month later and agreed on Russian military participation in peacekeeping forces in Bosnia. Although this agreement was beset by difficult details regarding the command of Russian troops under a NATO operation, a deal acceptable to Moscow was eventually concluded. Although the deal did not give Russia its maximum goal of gaining a veto over NATO decisions, then-Russian Defense Minister Grachev declared that it was sufficient for Moscow to be "gradually . . . introduced into NATO's political kitchen" and to have a "consultative voice." Third, Russian officials snubbed the foreign minister of the self-declared Serb republic of Bosnia when he visited Moscow in September, and prominent deputies in the Duma conceded finally that Russia was too weak economically to impose its preferences in the Balkans or to expect to block NATO.[96] Thus, despite its occasional harsh rhetoric and opposition to NATO actions in Bosnia, the Russian government pursued a moderate policy that recognized Russia's weakness and put a high premium on cooperation with the West. Contrary to what an aggressive nationalist policy might dictate, Russian troops did not fight on behalf of Serbian allies, massive Russian volunteers did not join Serb forces in a "Slavic" or "Orthodox" struggle against Western powers, and Moscow did not undertake actions to sabotage Western policies in Bosnia.

The signing of the Dayton peace accord in 1995 and its subsequent implementation created a new framework for practical cooperation between Russia and Western powers led by the United States. Russia sent 1,400 of its troops to participate in the NATO-led peacekeeping force of 31,000 in Bosnia. Within the limits of its resources, Russia became an active and constructive participant in the Dayton settlement.[97] At times, however, Russian policy clearly opposed measures supported by Western countries—e.g., Russian objections in 1997 to Western efforts to prevent extremist Serbian nationalists, led by indicted war crimes suspect Radovan Karadzic, from manipulating elections. This led some diplomats to conclude that Russia remained a staunch supporter of extremist Yugoslav President Slobodan Milosevic.[98] But the devotion of Russian officials to Milosevic should not be overestimated. In the context of NATO expansion and Russia's utterly reduced stature in Europe, it is predictable that Russian officials—still remembering the days when their country was a superpower—should cling to their last "friend" and allies in Europe: Yugoslavia and the Serbs. Lord David Owen, former co-chair of the Steering Committee of the International Conference on the Former Yugoslavia, captured sharply the motivation of Russians in the Bosnian conflict:

> The Russian-Serbian relationship is one of declining sentiment, not one of vital interest. But it did become the symbolic measure of whether Russians were being treated as genuine partners by the [United States] and Europe: slights were too often interpreted as being of far greater significance than was ever intended. . . . Whenever Russia had to choose between its vital interests, usually involving keeping on good terms with the US, and its sentimental attachments . . . it came down on the side of interest. Russia will never be treated as an inferior partner . . . and whenever that prospect emerged the Russians became difficult.[99]

CONCLUSION

This chapter has shown that, as of late 1998, aggressive variants of nationalism did not guide Russian foreign policy. Russian policymakers were largely averse to extremist nationalism and shunned the prohibitively high and unacceptable risks and costs that would result from implementing aggressive nationalist policies, especially those that argued for a restoration of the old Soviet empire and for Russian military dominance beyond its borders. Although most of Russia's neighbors were relatively weak, the costs to Moscow of reconquering or coercively (and even peacefully!) swallowing them would be enormous. Thus, even a Belarus that sought union with Russia was shunned by Russian policymakers, and the union agreement signed by Belarus and Russia in 1997 was not implemented meaningfully. Russia's enthusiasm for reunification with Belarus might grow in the context of an international environment in which Russians feel increasingly isolated. But such a reunification—carried out voluntarily and peacefully—could not be labeled the product of nationalist neoimperialism. The CIS itself has not become Russia's new imperial domain, where dreams of a nationalist restoration of empire might be realized. Russian officials in the 1990s did not devote time and resources to making the CIS a coherent entity; they did not mobilize the CIS as an organization by which to impose their will on newly sovereign neighbors; and the hundreds of documents and agreements signed under CIS auspices have become largely meaningless.[100] Beyond the "near abroad," Russian officials sought a meaningful role in international peacekeeping in Bosnia. But they did not follow extreme nationalist prescriptions to support the Serbs or Russia's "Slavic brothers" at the expense of cooperative relations with Western powers.

In the post-Soviet period, until 1998, a relatively moderate version of nationalism has proven more ascendant than extremist variants. But the last words on Russian nationalism have not yet been said. The pragmatism and moderate statist nationalism of most Russian political elites has been a hopeful sign, but one that is not guaranteed to determine Russian ideology, goals, and actions in the long term. The moderate statist goals of national honor, dignity, welfare, and great power status are legitimate, and they resonate deeply and widely with most Russian elites and the public at large. In contrast, chauvinism, imperialism, and militarism as core elements of the Russian national identity and as guiding principles for the Russian state and its foreign policy have found minimal resonance.

Important questions remain. To what extent will Russian national humiliation continue in the future? Will Russia become a modern entity where state and society are bonded by a largely benign nationalist ideology? What dangers might obstruct the long-term consolidation of moderate statist nationalism? If nationalism is an ideology thickly intertwined with comparisons and relations of the self with the outside world, what actions by other states—especially the United States—will influence the further evolution of aggressive or benign Russian nationalism? What does the aftermath of NATO's war with Serbia over Kosovo in 1999 imply for Russian nationalism and foreign policy? What policy implications for the United States and other Western powers arise from this analysis? These are themes that will be discussed in the next and final chapter.

NOTES

1. Walter Russell Mead, "Don't Panic, Panic First," *Esquire*, October 1998, p. 165.

2. Richard B. Dobson, *Is Russia Turning the Corner? Changing Russian Public Opinion, 1991–1996*, (Washington, D.C.: U.S. Information Agency, September 1996, pp. 5–6, 39; "Yeltsin's Opposition Delays Impeachment Vote," *New York Times*, 12 April 1999, p. A5; "Chubais Ally Sacked in Book Scandal," *Financial Times*, 15 November 1997; and Aleksandr Korzhakov, *Boris El'tsyn: Ot rassveta do zakata* (Moscow: Interbuk, 1997).

3. In 1997, only 37 percent of Russians polled by VTsIOM believed that a new decree to fight corruption would make a difference. The decree was Yeltsin's sixth declaration since 1992 to launch a "war on corruption." See "Another Battle in Russia's Phony War on Corruption," *Washington Post*, 29 June 1997, p. C2; "Russian Privatisations Face Crime Probe," *Financial Times*, 6 February 1996, p. 2; "Yeltsin Declares Economic Decline Has Been Stopped," *New York Times*, 5 July 1997, p. 1; and "Russia: Chubais Says It Has 'Weathered Storm,'" *Financial Times*, 16 December 1997.

4. Russian bankers and business elites were able to protect their assets, thanks in part to a $4.8 billion infusion from the IMF. See "Russia Spent $4.8bn of IMF Fund to Defend Ruble," *Financial Times*, 20 August 1998, p. 1; and David E. Sanger, "In House Testimony, Rubin Admits Loans to Russia May Have Been Used 'Improperly,'" *New York Times*, 19 March 1999, p. A10.

5. "Vse o chernom oktiabre," *Komsomol'skaia pravda*, 4 October 1993, special ed.

6. "Lebed Calls for Yeltsin to Transfer His Powers," *New York Times*, 29 September 1996, p. A9; Robert W. Orttung, "Regional Power Grab: Russian Center-Periphery Relations during Crisis," American Association for the Advancement of Slavic Studies Annual Meeting, September 1998 (xeroxed ms.); Elizabeth Fuller and Scott Parrish, "Chechen Conflict Ends with Shaky Peace," *Transition*, 7 February 1997, pp. 74–75; "'Komanda' reformatorov raskololas' pered vyborami potomu, chto nikogda ne byla monolitnoi," *Izvestiia*, 26 October 1993, p. 2; "Friends of Boris," *Economist*, 1 April 1995, pp. 42–43; "The More Voters Come to the Polls, the Higher Reformers' Chances Would Be," *Izvestiia*, 20 October 1995, p. 2; Chrystia Freeland, "Russian 'Criminal' List Put up for Election," *Financial Times*, 26 October 1995, p. 2; and Vladimir Shlapentokh, "Russian Elections: Hatred of 'Ins' versus Fear of 'Outs,'" *Christian Science Monitor*, 27 September 1995, p. 19.

7. "Soldiers' Parents Wage New Chechen Battle," *Washington Post*, 18 January 1998, p. A27.

8. "Fewer Russians Live under the Bread Line," *Moscow Times*, 27 September 1997, p. 4; *Ekonomika Rossii (ianvar'–mai 1996 g.)*, Moscow, Goskomstat, 1996; "Denezhnaia reforma—sobytie sugubo politicheskoe: Denznak peremen," *Moskovskie novosti*, 1 August 1993, p. 1; Sheila Marnie, "How Prepared Is Russia for Unemployment?" *RFE/RL Research Report*, 4 December 1992, pp. 44–50; "Russia Opens Up Market but Few Have the Money," *New York Times*, 18 November 1993, p. A3; "Soaring Unemployment Is Spreading Fear in Russia," *New York Times*, 8 May 1994, p. 3; John Lloyd, "Russians Harvesting the Bitter Fruits of Reform," *Financial Times*, 3 October 1995, p. 2; "Rich Debate Rages over Russian Poverty," *Financial Times*, 19 April 1995, p. 3.

9. See Nick Wadhams, "Study: 1/3 of Russians in Poverty," Associated Press, Moscow, 20 July 1999; John Thornhill, "Russia: Head Off Famine or Pay Creditors?" *Financial Times*, 15 October 1998; David Hoffman, "Only Elite Benefit in 'People's Capitalism,'" *Guardian*

Weekly, 25 January 1998; Economist Intelligence Unit, Country Risk Report, *Russia*, 25 February 1998; Mark Kramer, "The Changing Economic Complexion of Eastern Europe and Russia: Results and Lessons of the 1990s," xeroxed ms., April 1999; Patrick Lannin, "New 'Soviet-Style' Russia Plan Seen as Flop," Reuters (Moscow), 1 October 1998; and "Reforms On Hold Until after the Election," *Financial Times*, Russia Annual Country Report, 30 April 1999, p. II.

10. Stephen Handelman, *Comrade Criminal* (New Haven: Yale University Press, 1995); John Lloyd, "Anti-Crime Measures Split Russians," *Financial Times*, 27 June 1994, p. 3; "The High Price of Freeing Markets," *Economist*, 19 February 1994, pp. 57–58; Lee Hockstader, "A System in Which Everything Favors the Bad Guys," *Washington Post National Weekly Ed.*, 20–26 March, 1995, pp. 8–9; "Muscovites Polled on Those Holding Power in Moscow," *Politica Weekly*, 9–22 December 1995; and "Russia's Organised Crime Networks," *Strategic Comments*, International Institute for Strategic Studies, 1997.

11. "A Leading Russian Lawmaker Is Shot Dead," *New York Times*, 21 November 1998, p. A3; "Suspects Sought in Bombing in Southern Russia That Killed 53," *New York Times*, 21 March 1999, p. 15; "Another Trolley Bombing in Moscow Leaves 30 Hurt," *New York Times*, 13 July 1996, p. 4; Michael Specter, "AIDS Onrush Sends Russia to the Edge of an Epidemic," *New York Times*, 18 March 1997, pp. A1, A12; Michael Specter, "A Drug Plague Boils Out of Russia's Kitchens," *New York Times*, 9 November 1997, p. 5 (Week in Review); Peter Henderson, "Mafia Warnings Aim to Scare Investors—Russia," Reuters, Moscow, 10 October 1997; Pavel Anokhin, "Crime Rate Checked," *Rossiiskie vesti*, 28 January 1998; and John Thornhill, "Russia: Moscow's Recorded Crime Rate Falls 20 Percent," *Financial Times*, 6 January 1998.

12. "UN: Former Soviets Hardest Hit," Associated Press, 29 July 1999. In Moscow, where the economy has been better than in the rest of the country, there have been reports of a baby boom. See Michael Specter, "In Moscow Baby Boom, a Vote for the Future," *New York Times*, 26 August 1997; see also Julie DaVanzo and David Adamson, *Russia's Demographic "Crisis": How Real Is It?* RAND Issue Paper, July 1997; Michael Specter, "Deep in the Russian Soul, a Lethal Darkness," *New York Times*, 8 June 1997, p. 1; and "In One's Earthly Life One Must Be Born, Get Married, and Die," *Nezavisimaia gazeta*, 14 January 1998.

13. See, e.g., "Resisting Extinction," *Sovetskaia Rossiia*, 11 February 1997.

14. *CIS Migration Report* (Geneva: International Organization for Migration, 1997), pp. 87–97; "Ethnic Russian Influx Forecast," *Financial Times*, 16 August 1995, p. 2; "Bezhentsy: Dolgoe vremia mucheniia," *Izvestiia*, 20 May 1994, p. 1; "Russia Prepares for Millions of Refugees," *RFE/RL News Briefs*, 14–18 June 1993, p. 1; and interviews with leaders of LAD (Russian Rebirth Society, a Russian cultural and human rights organization in Kazakhstan), Almaty, Kazakhstan, 9 October 1995.

15. In April 1998, when the Kremlin was considering the potential dissolution of the Duma if it failed to approve Kiriyenko as prime minister, one of Yeltsin's senior advisers stressed to this author that everybody, including those in the Kremlin, was abiding with the law (i.e., the 1993 constitution). See notes from conversation with Mikhail Komissar, deputy chief of the presidential administration, the Kremlin, Moscow, 14 April 1998.

16. Robert W. Orttung and Scott Parrish, "From Confrontation to Cooperation in Russia," *Transition*, 13 December 1996, pp. 16–20; and Laura Belin and Robert W. Orttung, "Electing a Fragile Political Stability," *Transition*, 7 February 1997, pp. 67–70.

17. See, e.g., Stephen E. Hanson and Jeffrey S. Kopstein, "The Weimar/Russia Comparison," *Post–Soviet Affairs* 13 (1997):252–83. Clearly, macroeconomic stabilization at any cost should not be the policy in Russia, but Russian policymakers must find an effective way to undertake difficult economic reform while maintaining a social safety net for the most vul-

nerable sectors of the population. See "Bleak Future for the Poor," *Financial Times*, 30 April 1999, Russia Annual Country Report, p. V.

18. VTsIOM Survey Results, 11 August 1995, xeroxed copies; "Russians Find Capitalism in the Genes," *Financial Times*, 3 November 1995, p. 3; and "Sladkaia zhizn' dorogo stoit," *Novoe vremia*, 38 (1995):21. The 1998 financial market collapse in Russia did not lead to deep pessimism among Russians; sentiments of doom and gloom seemed more prevalent among Western investors, who lost billions in the Russian stock and bond markets.

19. Steven Erlanger, "Russian Generations Out of Tune: Listen In," *New York Times*, 7 December 1995, pp. A1, A18.

20. "Ubezhdennost'—opora perestroiki: Vstrecha v TsK KPSS," *Pravda*, 14 February 1987, p. 1.

21. For rules that governed political and historical discourse in the Soviet Union, see Nancy Whittier-Heer, *Politics and History in the Soviet Union* (Cambridge: MIT Press, 1971); on changes in the style of post-Soviet political discourse, see Richard D. Anderson, Jr., Valery V. Chervyakov, and Pavel B. Parshin, "Political Speech and the Emergence of Participatory Attitudes in Russia," American Political Science Association Annual Meeting, Washington, D.C., August 1997.

22. See Gorbachev's political report to the CPSU (Communist Party of the Soviet Union) Twenty-Seventh Congress in *Pravda*, 26 February 1986, pp. 2–10; "On the Legal and Political Assessment of the Soviet–German Nonaggression Treaty of 1939," *Izvestiia*, 27 December 1989, pp. 1–2; *Names That Have Returned* (Moscow: Novosti Press Agency Publishing House, 1989); and Astrid S. Tuminez, "Soviet Politics in Transition: Two Case Studies," Second Year Paper, Political Science Department, Massachusetts Institute of Technology, Spring 1990.

23. Many of these arguments have been described above in the ideologies of nationalists, especially statists and national patriots. An interesting book that sustains the pro-imperial discourse is *Russkii stroi*, sponsored by Soiuz Vozrozhdeniia Rossii, an umbrella nationalist organization that includes the Congress of Russian Communities, the Russian Christian Democratic Movement, the Constitutional Democratic Party, the Party of People's Freedom, and the Social Democratic Party of Russia. The book's numerous authors advocate Russian imperialism and even fascist ideology, but they included one author—ostensibly to preserve the appearance of debate—who explicitly contradicted Russian pretensions for empire and great power status. See V. B. Avdeev, eds., *Russkii stroi* (Moscow: Intellekt, 1997).

24. Vladimir Shlapentokh, "Creating 'the Russian Dream' after Chechnya," *Transition*, 21 February 1997, pp. 28–32; Sergei Kurginian, "Esli khotim zhit'," *Den'*, no. 1 (81) 1993, p. 2; Aleksandr Prokhanov, "Esli khotim pobedit'," *Den'*, no. 1 (81) 1993, p. 3; Sergei Kurginyan, "Kapkan dlia Rossii, ili igra v dve ruki," *Nash sovremennik* 2 (1993):141–58; "Russian Reformer Takes On Popular Ultranationalist," *Christian Science Monitor*, 15 June 1994, p. 4; Egor Gaidar, "Stavka na negodiaev: Ot natsional-patriotov iskhodit samaia bol'shaia opasnost' dlia Rossii," *Izvestiia*, 17 May 1994, p. 5; *Acta Eurasica* (entire issue) 1 (1995); Russian Academy of Sciences, Institute of Philosophy, *Rossiia mezhdu Evropoi i Aziei: Evraziiskii soblazn'* (Moscow: Nauka, 1993); N. Arkhangel'skaia, "It Is Expensive to Be a Great Power," *Kommersant Daily*, 17 October 1995, p. 4; A. A. Galkin, *Zapadnia: Rasskaz o tom, chto prines nemetskim rabochim natsional-sotsializm* (Moscow: Russko-Amerikanskii fond profsoiuznykh issledovanii i obucheniia, 1995); V. I. Krivokhizha, "Rossiia v novoi strukture mezhdunarodnykh otnoshenii," *Polis* 3 (1995):9–22; D. Furman, "Ukraina i my: Natsional'noe samosoznanie i politicheskoe razvitie," *Svobodnaia mysl'* 1 (1994):69–83; Mikhail Leontiev, "Den' osvobozhdeniia ot psikhopatii," *Segodnia*, 15 June 1994, p. 2; and Orlov, "Vosstanie protiv razuma," p. 9.

25. Shlapentokh, "Creating 'the Russian Dream'," pp. 28–32; and Andrei P. Tsygankov, "From International Institutionalism to Revolutionary Expansionism: The Foreign Policy Discourse of Contemporary Russia," *Mershon International Studies Review* 41 (November 1997):247–68.

26. See, e.g., Igor' Chubais, *Ot russkoi idei—k idee Novoi Rossii* (Moscow: Izd. dom "Sot-sial'naia zashchita," 1997); A. I. Vdovin, *Rossiiskaia natsiia* (Moscow: Izd-vo Roman-gazeta, 1996); Tat'iana Solovei, "Russkoe i sovetskoe v sovremennom samosoznanii russkikh," in Martha Brill Olcott, et al., eds., *Identichnost' i konflikt v postsovetskikh gosudarstvakh* (Moscow: Moskovskii Tsentr Karnegi, 1997), pp. 346–58; *Za realizm, sozdanie, i gumanizm* (Moscow: Klub "Realisty," 1995); and *Russkaia ideia: Demokraticheskoe razvitie Rossii* (Moscow, 1996); and Iurii Poliakov, "Rossiiskie prostory: Blago ili prokliat'e?" *Svobodnaia mysl'* 12 (1992):17–22.

27. Elena Chinyaeva, "A Eurasianist Model of Interethnic Relations Could Help Russia Find Harmony," *Transition*, 1 November 1996; and "Kontseptsiia natsional'noi bezopas-nosti Rossiiskoi Federatsii," *Rossiiskaia gazeta*, 26 December 1997, pp. 4–5. A key example of "establishment" groups referred to here is Sergei Karaganov's Center for Foreign and Defense Policy, whose various reports have been cited in this book.

28. Conversation with Viacheslav Nikonov (former Duma member and director of Politika Foundation), Moscow, 14 April 1998.

29. This is discussed in chapter 2. See also Simon Dixon, "The Past in the Present: Contemporary Nationalism in Historical Perspective," in Geoffrey Hosking and Robert Service, eds., *Russian Nationalism Past and Present* (New York: St. Martin's, 1998), pp. 158–59.

30. The war was "imperial" in that it once again exhibited state authorities' cruelty toward the people and the absence of official accountability in decision making that led to the war. Interview with Anatoly Shabad (former Duma member and critic of Yeltsin's human rights policy), New York, 6 February 1995.

31. Aleksei Pushkov, "Russia and America: The Honeymoon Is Over," *Foreign Policy* 93 (Winter 93/94):81–83; VTsIOM Survey Results, August 1995, xeroxed copies; Anatole Shub, *Russian Elites Discuss Russia's Place in the World*, United States Information Agency, December 1996; and Dobson, *Is Russia Turning the Corner?*, pp. 5–39.

32. Henry E. Hale, "The Rise of Russian Anti-Imperialism," *Orbis* (Winter 1999):1–16.

33. A focus group of seventy-three elite and educated Russians in four cities in 1996 indicated that a majority believed Russia's borders were larger than those of the Russian Federation. See Shub, *Russian Elites Discuss*, pp. 15–16.

34. See, e.g., coverage of the Kosovo crisis in *Nezavisimaia gazeta* between March 25 and April 6, 1999. *Nezavisimaia gazeta* is reputed to be one of Russia's more reliable and respectable newspapers.

35. Steven Erlanger, "Russia Court Calls 'Protocols' Anti-Semitic Forgery," *New York Times*, 27 November 1993, p. 6; "Fascists Sentenced in Yaroslavl," OMRI Daily Digest (electronic version), 14 March 1996; "Russia Police Detain 10 Neo-Nazis," Moscow, Associated Press, 8 February 1999; "Courts Stand for Press Freedom," *RFE/RL News Briefs*, 14–21 May 1993, p. 3; "Confrontation Again," *Economist*, 5 March 1994, p. 58; "Anti-Semitic Newspaper Back after One Year Ban," *Moscow Times*, 30 September 1995, p. 3; "Vecher zhurnala Ele-menty," *Sovetskaia Rossiia*, 7 June 1994, p. 2; and "Pisateli trebuiut ot pravitel'stva reshitel'nykh deistvii," *Izvestiia*, 5 October 1993, p. 3.

36. Elizabeth Kridl Valkenier, "Teaching History in Post-Communist Russia," Harriman Institute Forum, Columbia University, April 1993; John Varoli, "Russia Prefers to Forget," *Transitions*, July 1997, pp. 35–41; and Alessandra Stanley, "Lest Russians Forget, a Museum of the Gulag," *New York Times*, 29 October 1997, pp. A1, A8. A dissertation on Russian his-

258 Chapter Six

tory textbooks preliminarily concludes that a large amount of pernicious, imperial discourse is still taught in Russian schools. See David Mendeloff, "Making History: Truth-Telling, Myth-Making and National Self-Image in Post-Soviet Russia," Massachusetts Institute of Technology, Political Science Department, 1999–2000.

37. Yushin, "Russian Bridge," *Nezavisimaia gazeta*, 7 February 1996, p. 3; Paul Castleman, "Discrimination against Latvia's Russian Minority," *Christian Science Monitor*, 21 May 1991, p. 19; Steven Erlanger, "In the Baltics, There May Be No Home for Russians," *New York Times*, 22 November 1992, pp. A1, A12; "Latvia's Worry: What to Do with All Its Russians," *New York Times*, 1 March 1994, p. A3; "Empire Lost, Russian People Stream Out of Central Asia," *Christian Science Monitor*, 19 September 1995, p. 6; interview with members of LAD, Almaty, 9 October 1995; and "Russia Will Not be Russia Without a Navy," *Moskovskaia pravda*, 18 October 1995, p. 2.

38. In April 1992, the Congress of People's Deputies adopted a resolution in support of secessionist Russians in Transdnestr in Moldova. See Eduard Kondratev, "Vizit Rutskogo v Pridnestrov'e," *Izvestiia*, 6 April 1992, p. 1; personal notes from Russian television Channel One, 1991.

39. Fighting in Tajikistan alone produced 10,000 fatalities and half a million refugees in one year. See Steven Erlanger, "Moscow Fears for Troops in Tajikistan," *New York Times*, 30 September 1992, p. A12; "Conflicts in the Caucasus," *CIS Conference on Refugees and Migrants*, United Nations High Commissioner on Refugees, 30–31 May 1996, p. 14; *Gosudarstvennaia politika Rossii v konfliktnykh zonakh*, Center for Ethnopolitical Studies, Foreign Policy Association, Moscow, 1994, pp. 29–31; Gabriel Schoenfeld, "Outer Limits," *Post-Soviet Prospects* 17 (January 1993).

40. Carol J. Williams, "Marines Alter Maneuvers after Russians Oppose Scenario," *Los Angeles Times*, 30 August 1997, p. A23.

41. John Helmer, "Russia Enemy No. 1: America," *Journal of Commerce*, 15 October 1997; Michael R. Gordon, "The Anatomy of a Misunderstanding," *New York Times*, 25 May 1997, p. E3; "Mikhail Gorbachev vystupil v Kongresse SShA, podverg rezkoi kritike plany rasshireniia NATO," Itar-TASS, Washington, 16 April 1997; Aleksei Mitrofanov, *AntiNATO: Novaia ideia Rossiiskoi geopolitiki* (Moscow, undated brochure); "The NATO Distraction" (comments by Grigorii Yavlinskii), *Transition*, 21 March 1997, pp. 32–34; Yuli M. Vorontsov, "One Thing All Russians Agree On," *Washington Post*, 10 March 1998; "Vmeshatel'stvo: Bespretsedentnaia voennaia aktsiia NATO na Balkanakh," *Pravda*, 6 April 1993, p. 3; Lieutenant General Leonid Ivashov, "Strong CIS Means Strong Russia," *Nezavisimaia gazeta*, 20 October 1995, p. 2, in *CIS Weekly Press Summary* (electronic version), 21–27 October 1995; "NATO Airstrikes Seen through Russian Eyes," *Christian Science Monitor*, 25 September 1995, p. 19.

42. See, e.g., "U.S. Stakes Its Claim in Central Asia," *Financial Times*, 4 May 1995, p. 4; and *The Caucasus and the Caspian*, vol. II, Harvard University, Strengthening Democratic Institutions Project, 1997.

43. "Moscow Welcomes Estonian Citizenship Law Changes," Radio Free Europe/Radio Liberty Newsline, 14 December 1998; Martinsh Gravitis, "Latvian Ex-PM Leads Vote, Citizenship Law on Track," Riga, Reuters, 4 October 1998; "Yeltsin Threatens Sanctions on Latvia," *Moscow Times*, 9 April 1998, pp. 1–2; "Vynuzhdennye migranty iz stran SNG i Baltii," *Sotsis* 6 (1998):56; Michael Specter, "Estonians Cast a Wary Eye on Russian Election," *New York Times*, 26 May 1996, p. A3; and "Orphans of the USSR," in *CIS Conference on Refugees and Migrants*.

44. Gravitis, "Latvian ex-PM Leads Vote," 4 October 1998; Text of the Kazakhstan–Russian agreement on citizenship in Foreign Broadcast Information Service (FBIS-SOV),

26 January 1995, pp. 67–68; Text of the dual citizenship agreement between Russia and Turkmenistan, FBIS-SOV, 27 December 1993, p. 78; Interview with Col. Sirotkin, Moscow, 30 September 1995; U.S. Department of Defense, *Cooperative Threat Reduction*, April 1995; "Less Poor, Less Democratic," *Economist*, 22 April 1995, p. 56; "Our Diplomacy Pursues Russian Interests," *Nezavisimaia gazeta*, 19 October 1995, pp. 1–2; and Foundation for Interethnic Relations, *Bibliography on the OSCE High Commissioner on National Minorities*, 2nd ed., August 1995, pp. 10, 12.

45. In a 1999 poll of 1,600 Russians, 31 percent of those aged eighteen to thirty-nine felt that NATO posed a threat to Russia, while 41 percent of those forty and older felt the same. Elites, on the other hand, continued to be anxious about NATO. As Viacheslav Nikonov told this author, the clearest message of NATO expansion was that Russian opinion did not matter to the Western powers, which regarded Russia—liberal or authoritarian—as a threat. See Conversation with Nikonov, Moscow, 14 April 1998; and Michael R. Gordon, "Russia Remains Uneasy over NATO's Expansion," *New York Times*, 14 March 1999, pp. 1, 12. For many Russians, NATO's bombing of Serbia over the Kosovo crisis in 1999 fulfilled their worst fears of NATO's aggressive and hegemonic intent.

46. Kramer, "Changing Economic Complexion of Eastern Europe and Russia," pp. 13–29; Nigel Gould-Davies and Ngaire Woods, "Russia and the IMF," *International Affairs* (London) 75 (January 1999):1–22; David Hoffman, "For Yeltsin, Business Prospects Outweighed NATO Threat," *Washington Post*, 27 May 1997, p. A1; Michael Dobbs, "Christopher Pursues Political Objectives by Economic Means," *Washington Post*, 12 February 1996, p. A14; Conversation with IMF official in Moscow, April 1998; "Plan for a G8 Including Russia," *Financial Times*, 5 February 1996, p. 2; "Russia Assures US Reform Goes On: Chernomyrdin Hopes to Win $9.5 bn IMF Loan," *The Guardian*, 30 January 1996, p. 9.

47. "Russians, Kazakhs Agree on Caspian," *Moscow Times*, 10 April 1998, p. 13; and "The Politics of Caspian Oil," *Strategic Comments*, International Institute for Strategic Studies, 13 December 1995, 2 pp. See also Hale, "Rise of Russian Anti-Imperialism," pp. 11–12.

48. One should note, though, that Western governments have also slighted Russia diplomatically—for example, in failing to invite Russian officials to the fiftieth anniversary of D-Day in 1994. My thanks to Stephen Hanson for pointing this out. See also William Odom and Peter Reddaway, "Yeltsin's False Truce," *New York Times*, 3 April 1996, p. A15. "Victory in the Capital and in a Village on the Volga," *Moscow News* (English ed.), 12–18 May 1995, p. 3; "Why Europe Is Careful Not to Scold the Bear," *New York Times*, 2 January 1995, p. 6; "World Leaders Pay Tribute to Triumph over Nazis," *New York Times*, 10 May 1995, p. A1, 16; and Dmitrii Gornostaev, "Pickering Is Dropping Hints," *Nezavisimaia gazeta*, 26 April 1995, p. 2.

49. " The Guidelines of State Policy: From the Address of the President of the Russian Federation Boris Yeltsin to the Federal Assembly of the Russian Federation on February 17, 1998," *Military News Bulletin* 7 (March 1998).

50. This figure is from the last Soviet census of 1989, and has not been changed since.

51. "Nationalist Vote Toughens Russian Foreign Policy," *New York Times*, 25 January 1994, p. A6; "Russian Impasse Sets Off a Ruble Panic," *New York Times*, 19 January 1994, p. A6; and comments by Yeltsin and Vitalii Tret'iakov in *Zhurnalistika i voina* (Moscow: Russian American Press Information Center, Moscow, 1995), pp. 28 and 30.

52. "Chernyi peredel' territorii byvshego soiuza?" *Nezavisimaia gazeta*, 24 January 1992, p. 1; "Parlament Rossii prizyvaet ukrainskikh kolleg vernut'sia k voprosu o Kryme i flote," *Izvestiia*, 24 January 1992, p. 1; "The Crimea in February 1992," *Moscow News* (English ed.), 9–16 February 1992, p. 9; and Fiona Hill and Pamela Jewett, *Back in the USSR: Russia's Intervention in the Internal Affairs of the Former Soviet Republics and the Implications for*

United States Policy toward Russia, Strengthening Democratic Institutions Project, Harvard University, 1994, p. 78.

53. "Crimea Votes for Greater Freedom from Ukraine," *Christian Science Monitor*, 23 May 1994, p. 4; "Separatist Winning Crimea Presidency," *New York Times*, 31 January 1994, p. A8; *Gosudarstvennaia politika Rossii*, pp. 85–86; and Tor Bukkvoll, "A Fall from Grace for Crimean Separatists," *Transition*, 17 November 1995, pp. 46–49.

54. Hill and Jewett, *Back in the USSR*, pp. 70–85.

55. "Crimea Votes for Greater Freedom," p. 4; Bukkvoll, "A Fall from Grace," pp. 46–49; Hill and Jewett, *Back in the USSR*, p. 71; and "Russian Community of Sevastopol Accused of Instigating National and Racial Hostility," *Segodnia*, 1 November 1995, p. 9, in *CIS Weekly* (electronic version), 28 October–3 November 1995. Some have also argued that Russia's preoccupation with the war in Chechnya, which Moscow justified in terms of preserving Russian territorial integrity, was a significant factor in constraining Russian reaction to developments in Crimea. See "Rossiia pozitsii v Krymu ne sdala," *Nezavisimaia gazeta*, 22–28 April 1995, p. 3.

56. For an interpretation of the 1995 document on the CIS as "a comprehensive plan of action for the forced reconstruction of Russian dominance within the CIS," see Stephen Foye, "Russia and the 'Near Abroad,'" *Post-Soviet Prospects* 3, no. 12 (December 1995):1. This author disagrees strongly with Foye's interpretation.

57. John Thornhill, "Russians Protest at Crimea Accord," *Financial Times*, 2 June 1997, p. 2; "Russia and Ukraine," *Washington Post*, 4 June 1997, p. A22; "Compatriots Seek Contacts with Their Homeland," *Rossiiskaia gazeta*, 6 December 1997; "Russia, Ukraine Start Exercises," *Moscow Times*, 15 April 1998, p. 4; "Ukraine to Remain Top Consumer of Russian Natural Gas in 1998," Kiev, Dow Jones Newswires, 11 September 1997; Andrei Kapustin, "Slav Extremists, Unite," *Nezavisimaia gazeta*, 24 February 1996, p. 3; and "Strategicheskii kurs Rossii s gosudarstvami-uchastnikami Sodruzhestva Nezavisimykh Gosudarstv," *Rossiiskaia gazeta*, 23 September 1995.

58. The Russian Orthodox Church in Kazakhstan reported an increase in the number of requests for services for suicide-related deaths among Russians. See "Vynuzhdennye migranty iz stran SNG," p. 56; "Empire Lost, Russian People Stream Out," p. 6; "Ethnic Russians Realize Kazakhs 'Are Bosses Now,'" *Christian Science Monitor*, 7 March 1994, p. 4; "Kazakhs Arrest Writer, Raising Ethnic Tension," *Christian Science Monitor*, 19 April 1994, p. 7; Bess A. Brown, "Overriding Economics," *Transition*, 15 February 1995, pp. 53-54; "Russian Rumblings," *Economist*, 12 March 1994, p. 42; and interview with Nurbulat Masanov, Almaty, 4 October 1995.

59. The two documents on citizenship signed between Russia and Kazakhstan are in *Rossiiskaia gazeta*, 25 February 1995. See also "Russian Rumblings," p. 42; *Sociopolitical Situation in the Post–Soviet World* (Moscow: Ethnopolitical Studies Center, Foreign Policy Association, February 1993), p. 25; *Gosudarstvennaia politika Rossii*, pp. 56–58; and interview with leaders of LAD, Almaty, October 1995. For a perspective that interprets Moscow's policies in Kazakhstan to be more sinister, see Hill and Jewett, *Back in the USSR*, pp. 30–38.

60. "In the Baltics, There May Be No Home for Russians," pp. A1, A12; for a history and overview of citizenship issues in the Baltics, see *Citizenship and Alien Law Controversies in Estonia and Latvia*, Harvard University, Strengthening Democratic Institutions Project, April 1994, pp. 1–41.

61. Ann Sheehy, "The Estonian Law on Aliens," *RFE/RL Research Report*, 24 September 1993, p. 10; Hill and Jewett, *Back in the USSR*, pp. 18–20; John Lloyd, "Estonian Mouse Determined to Find Way to Get Russian Bear Off Its Back," *Financial Times*, 25 July 1994, p. 2; and *Citizenship and Alien Law Controversies*, p. 23.

62. "Latvia Approves Citizenship Change," *Moscow Times*, 23 June 1998, p. 2; Maura Reynolds, "Yeltsin Pledges to Protect Baltics," Moscow, Associated Press, 24 October 1997; and John Thornhill, "Baltic: NATO Aspirants Freeze Out Moscow," *Financial Times*, 6 September 1997. Language controversies in the Baltics have not ended, however. In July 1999, for example, the Latvian parliament passed a measure that would effectively end the use of Russian in public life. See Anatol Lieven, "No Russian Spoken Here," *New York Times*, 16 July 1999, p. A19.

63. David D. Laitin, *Identity in Formation: The Russian-Speaking Populations in the Near Abroad* (Ithaca: Cornell University Press, 1998), p. 320 and chapters 10 and 11; and Igor Zevelev, "Russia and the Russian Diasporas," *Post-Soviet Affairs* 12 (1996):265–84.

64. This section does not cover in detail the conflict between Armenia and Azerbaijan over Nagorno-Karabakh, but the author believes that most of the arguments below on Russian postimperial opportunism apply as well to Nagorno-Karabakh. Russian authorities have sided more with Armenia because of historical ties between the two and clearly because the Armenian side wants Russian support against Azerbaijan. In the meantime, in the context of NATO expansion and Azeri calls for U.S. or NATO bases to be built in Azerbaijan, it is understandable that Russia would pursue a pro-Armenian policy. The totality of Russian actions in this conflict, as in others, does not indicate the influence of extremist nationalism. For more on Nagorno-Karabakh, see Edward W. Walker, *No Peace, No War in the Caucasus: Secessionist Conflicts in Chechnya, Abkhazia and Nagorno-Karabakh*, Harvard University, Strengthening Democratic Institutions Project, February 1998, pp. 26–45; Elizabeth Fuller, "Transcaucasus—Doomed to Strategic Partnership," *Transition*, 15 November 1996, pp. 29–31; Emil Danielyan, "No War, No Peace in Nagorno-Karabakh," *Transitions*, August 1997, pp. 44–49; Natalia Airapetova, "Sochuvstvie russkogo obshchestva reshaet vopros o budushchem Armenii," *Nezavisimaia gazeta*, 15 April 1998, p. 6; and "Azerbaijan Says NATO Bases Sole Defense against Russia," Radio Free Europe/Radio Liberty Newsline, 2 March 1999.

65. As Sherman Garnett has argued, there has been a "gravitational pull" on Russian armed forces to participate in conflicts whether or not Moscow officials ordered it. See Sherman W. Garnett, *The Impact of the New Borderlands on the Russian Military*, Occasional Paper 9, International Security Studies Program, American Academy of Arts and Sciences, August 1995. The former Soviet (now Russian) military was scattered on the territory of the former empire; military officers possessed weapons that parties in conflict wanted; and soldiers sought to defend parochial interests (such as finding alternative means to provide for their families when Moscow could not pay military wages). These circumstances, along with weakening civilian authority in the wake of imperial collapse, help explain Russian military intervention in conflicts in the former Soviet Union.

66. *Gosudarstvennaia politika Rossii*, pp. 77–78; and "Abkhazia: A Bloody New Chapter in a Long History of Ethnic Conflict," *RFE/RL Post-Soviet/Eastern European Report*, 15 September 1992, pp. 3–4.

67. *Gosudarstvennaia politika Rossii*, pp. 77–78; Kevin O'Prey, *Keeping the Peace in the Borderlands of Russia* (Washington, D.C.: Henry L. Stimson Center Occasional Paper 23, July 1995), pp. 23–24; and Elizabeth Fuller, "Between Anarchy and Despotism," *Transition*, 15 January 1995, pt. 2, pp. 64–65.

68. Irakli Zurab Kabakadze, "Russian Troops in Abkhazia: Peacekeeping, or Keeping Both Pieces?" *Perspectives on Central Asia*, Center for Political and Strategic Studies 2, no. 6 (September 1997); *Gosudarstvennaia politika Rossii*, p. 78; the following from the *New York Times*: "Georgian Regional Capital under Aerial Attack," 21 September 1993, p. A7; "Looming Confrontation in Georgia Threatens," 5 October 1992, p. A3; "An Old Georgian

Story: Dancing with the Devil," 24 October 1993, p. E3; and Hill and Jewett, *Back in the USSR*, pp. 47–52.

69. "Russian Naval Blockade of Sukhumi Explained," *Jamestown Monitor*, 30 October 1995; "How to Make Enemies and Influence People," *Economist*, 19 August 1995, p. 46; and Aleksandr Pel'ts and Petr Karapetian, "Rossiia, pokhozhe, uvodit Gruziiu i Abkhaziiu ot novogo voennogo protivostoianiia," *Krasnaia zvezda*, 20 September 1994, p. 1. On Ardzinba's ethnic cleansing record, see "Georgian Talks of New War with Separatists," *New York Times*, 19 November 1993, p. A11.

70. "Georgian Asks U.S. to Back Peace Force," *New York Times*, 8 March 1994.

71. Walker, *No Peace, No War*, pp. 11–25; and the following from Radio Free Europe/Radio Liberty Newsline: "Coordinating Council Discusses Abkhaz Repatriation," 12 February 1999; "Georgian, Russian Officials Discuss Abkhazia," 18 June 1998; "Georgian President Discloses Details of Abkhaz Settlement," 30 April 1998; and "Georgia Accuses Russia of Obstructing Abkhaz Settlement," 2 February 1998.

72. Julian Duplain, "Chisinau's and Tiraspol's Faltering Quest for Accord," *Transition*, 20 October 1995, pp. 12–13.

73. "Moldovan Premier Ends Moscow Visit," Radio Free Europe/Radio Liberty Newsline, 2 November 1998; "Economic Difficulties Blunt Nationalist Drive in Moldova," *New York Times*, 27 December 1993, p. A8; and Mihai Gribincea, "Challenging Moscow's Doctrine on Military Bases," *Transition*, 20 October 1995, pp. 4–8.

74. Yeltsin himself acknowledged the role of the Fourteenth Army in Moldova and stated in 1992 that "there are supporters of the Dnestr region among the Fourteenth Army's officer corps, and they are beginning to switch over, sometimes with equipment, to the side of the Dnestr people." See Vladimir Socor, "Russia's Fourteenth Army and the Insurgency in Eastern Moldova," *RFE/RL Research Report*, 11 September 1992, p. 45; O'Prey, *Keeping the Peace*, pp. 41–46; Hill and Jewett, *Back in the USSR*, pp. 61–62; and Svetlana Gamova, "Aleksandr Lebed': Sama zhizn' zastavliaet generalov zanimat'sia politikoi," *Izvestiia*, 20 July 1994, pp. 1, 4.

75. Moldovan authorities have opposed a permanent Russian base in Moldova. See Gribincea, "Challenging Moscow's Doctrine," pp. 4–8.

76. The assignment of Lieutenant General Lebed to lead the Fourteenth Army in 1992 restored some discipline to the military. President Snegur of Moldova commented in 1995 that Lebed was "a man who can strictly control the arms stores and prevent distribution of arms to local formations—features his predecessor didn't possess. . . . My opinion of him is good." Duplain, "Chisinau's and Tiraspol's Faltering Quest," p. 12.

77. *Gosudarstvennaia politika Rossii*, p. 81; and O'Prey, *Keeping the Peace*, p. 44.

78. Gribincea, "Challenging Moscow's Doctrine," p. 7.

79. "Lucinschi on Relations with Russia, NATO," Radio Free Europe/Radio Liberty Newsline, 9 March 1998; Mihai Gribincea, "Rejecting a New Role for the Former Fourteenth Russian Army," *Transition*, 22 March 1996, pp. 38–40; and Gottfried Hanne, "Playing Two Different Tunes, as Usual, in Moldova," *Transitions*, December 1997, pp. 68–71.

80. See, e.g., Nassim Jawad and Shahrbanou Tadjbakhsh, *Tajikistan: A Forgotten Civil War* (London: Minority Rights Group, 1995) and Olivier Roy, *The Civil War in Tajikistan: Causes and Implications* (Washington, D.C.: U.S. Institute of Peace, 1993).

81. Martha Brill Olcott, "Sovereignty and the 'Near Abroad'," *Orbis* 39 (Summer 1995):361; "Refugees Fleeing Tajikistan Strife," *New York Times*, 14 January 1993, p. A12; *Gosudarstvennaia politika Rossii*, pp. 59–60; and O'Prey, *Keeping the Peace*, pp. 34–35.

82. Sergei Gretzky, "Civil War in Tajikistan: Causes, Developments, and Prospects for Peace," in Susan Eisenhower and Roald Z. Sagdeev, eds., *Central Asia: Conflict, Resolution,*

and Change (Washington, D.C.: Center for Post-Soviet Studies, 1995), p. 241; and conversation with Aleksei Arbatov, Istanbul, 26 August 1995.

83. Works that censure Moscow's role in Tajikistan are Hill and Jewett, *Back in the USSR*, pp. 40–44; and Helsinki Watch, *War or Peace? Human Rights and Russian Military Intervention in the "Near Abroad,"* 5, no. 22 (December 1993):12. A perspective that notes Russia's constructive role is O'Prey, *Keeping the Peace*, pp. 34–36.

84. "Moscow Fears for Troops in Tajikistan," *New York Times*, 30 September 1992, p. A12.

85. Gretzky, "Civil War in Tajikistan," pp. 240, 244–45.

86. Daniel Sneider, "Russian Bear Roams in Battered Tajikistan," *Christian Science Monitor*, 12 May 1994, p. 7; Gillian Tett, "Mourners for the Soviet Empire," *Financial Times*, 27 November 1995, p. 14; and "Central Asia on the Move," *CIS Conference on Refugees and Migrants*, pp. 8–9.

87. Moscow at one point subsidized up to 70 percent of the Tajik national budget. See Jawad and Tadjbakhsh, *Tajikistan*, p. 22.

88. See the following from Radio Free Europe/Radio Liberty Newsline: "Joint Military Exercises in Tajikistan," 3 September 1998 and "Rybkin's Whirlwind Tour of Central Asia," 17 April 1998; Brown, "Overriding Economics," pp. 55–56; Gretzky, "Civil War in Tajikistan," pp. 224–41; Elizabeth Fuller, "Tajik Cease-Fire Agreement Reached," *RFE/RL Daily Report*, 19 September 1994; Sharam Akbarzadeh, "Striving for Unity over Regional and Ethnic Division," *Transition*, 20 May 1995, p. 55.

89. These extremists conveniently denied that Serbia's opponents in former Yugoslavia were themselves Slavic peoples.

90. See the collective appeal of nationalist leaders in "Brat'ia-Slaviane," *Den'*, no. 3 (83) 1993, p. 5; the analysis of the Eurasianist Center for Metastrategic Research in "Geopolitika Iugoslavskogo konflikta," *Elementy* 2 (1992):2–5; and "Mnenie obozrevatelia," *Pravda*, 2 June 1992, p. 3, which includes this warning: "Punishment [for Serbia] is now being arranged under the UN flag. But what will happen tomorrow? If one day Russia stands up in earnest for a Russian-speaking population somewhere in the CIS, they will punish us, too."

91. Interfax, 3 June 1992.

92. Kozyrev maintained that he felt "sick at heart" for this decision, which was taken because of pressure from nationalists. See "Kozyrev Regrets Abstaining on UN Vote," *RFE/RL News Briefs*, 26–30 April 1993, p. 3; see also Suzanne Crow, "Russia Adopts a More Active Policy," *RFE/RL Research Report*, 19 March 1993, p. 4; and "Decree of the Russian Federation Supreme Soviet 'On the Russian Federation's Approach to the Yugoslav Conflict,'" in FBIS-SOV, 4 January 1993, p. 34.

93. Author's correspondence with Lord David Owen, 27 August 1996; and David Owen, *Balkan Odyssey* (New York: Harcourt Brace, 1995), pp. 63–67.

94. James Sherr, "Doomed to Remain a Great Power," *The World Today*, Royal Institute of International Affairs, January 1996, p. 9; and "Pax Russiana?" *Economist*, 19 February 1994, p. 57.

95. See the following reports from the *Financial Times*: "U.S. and Russia Divided on Bosnia," 14 August 1995, p. 1; "Yeltsin Condemns 'Cruel Bombardment,'" 31 August 1995, p. 2; "Anger in Russian Parliament over Bosnia Strikes," 7 September 1995, p. 2; and "Yeltsin Gesture to Bosnia as Rift with U.S. Widens," 11 August 1995, p. 1.

96. "Russia Drops Strident Line over NATO's Air Strikes," *Financial Times*, 16–17 September 1995, p. 2; "Stalemate Ends over Russia's Role in Bosnia," *New York Times*, 28 October 1995, p. 5; "Moscow Accepts NATO Troop Plans," p. 28; "Poderzhka budet moral'noi," *Moskovskie novosti*, 24 Sept.–1 Oct. 1995, p. 17; "Pas'ians na bochke s porokhom," *Narodnaia Duma*, October 1995, p. 6; "Moscow Soothed by U.S. Deal, At Least Until

Details Emerge," *Christian Science Monitor*, 25 October 1995, p. 8; and Sherr, "Doomed to Remain," p. 12.

97. Because of its own economic troubles, Russia has not been a strong player in Bosnia's economic reconstruction. See, e.g., Raimo Vayrynen, "Economic Incentives and the Bosnian Peace Process," in David Cortright, ed., *The Price of Peace: Incentives and International Conflict Prevention* (Lanham, Md.: Rowman & Littlefield, 1997), pp. 155–80.

98. Guy Dinmore, "Bosnia: West Accuses Russians of Obstruction," *Financial Times*, 22 August 1997; and William Drozdiak, "Moscow Warns NATO on Bosnia," *Washington Post*, 12 September 1997, p. A27.

99. Owen, *Balkan Odyssey*, pp. 358–59.

100. Supporting this point is Hale, "Rise of Russian Anti-Imperialism."

7

Through a Glass, Darkly: Russian Nationalism and Russia's Future

It is a bitter thing for a Russian not to have a nation, and to terminate everything in the Sovereign alone.

—P. G. Kakhovskii (Decembrist), 1825

There is nothing to be feared from the growth of the Russian . . . national consciousness. . . . Only nations with a developed sense of self-esteem can be friends with other nations. Faceless mobs are capable only of oppressing each other.

—Arsenii Gulyga, 1988

[The] breakup of the USSR . . . was not simply bad, it was catastrophic. . . . [But] it is now an inexorable reality and, therefore, one must begin with the inevitable fact of Russia's existence in its present form. A colossal change—one that we have not yet fully understood—has occurred. . . . A shift in the entire conception of our country's historical development will be inevitable. The change in Russia's status and Russia's borders, in the end, should change the very way we define ourselves as Russians.

—Iurii Poliakov, 1992

Paranoia in Russia feeds on itself, seeking and finding confirmation in everything that happens—emphatically including the recent Western decision to expand NATO up to the very borders of the former Soviet Union. . . . I know no Russian, regardless of political orientation, who favors it. To the contrary, NATO's projected expansion plays directly into the hands of the nationalists who exploit fears of the West to argue that Russia must reconstruct the empire and rebuild the military in order to hold its own in an unfriendly world.

—Richard Pipes, 1996

RUSSIAN NATIONALISM: THE TRODDEN PATH

This book contends that nationalism—a political ideology that defines membership in the nation, its self-image, and mission and is tied to the premise that a nation or people is the repository of legitimate political authority—has never effectively bonded state and society in Russia. This is in contrast to western European states, where nationalism was used effectively to bond state and people, especially in the nineteenth century, and became a means for fostering political stability and cohesion in modern nation-states. In Russia, nationalism tended to be a fragmented force. The fragmented nature of nationalism is evident in contending variants of Russian nationalist ideology in the past century and a half, and in the evanescent quality of support for nationalism by either Russian state elites or the mass public, or both. Russian state authorities in the tsarist and Soviet periods did not engage sufficiently or effectively in the project of nation-building—either in the ethnic or civic sense—thus creating a weak foundation for nationalism as a long-term cementing and mobilizing ideology. Russian state and society have not, in a sustained manner, united in a common conception of Russia's identity and purposes as a nation and have not had stable consensus on rules and arrangements that should govern their relations.

Focused on parochial interests and committed to a predominantly imperial and authoritarian conception of state power, Russian state authorities did not tap the power of nationalism as a political ideology to strengthen and legitimize the state in an enduring way. Unlike western Europe, where states mobilized their resources to transcend differences within populations and create relatively homogeneous nations with a common frame of political and cultural reference, in Russia national identity fragmented along ethnic, socioeconomic (i.e., Europeanized nobility and intelligentsia versus "Russian" peasantry), and political (i.e., authoritarian and imperial state versus repressed society) lines. Russia's rulers also failed to allow or facilitate the development of society as an autonomous actor and as a source of largely voluntary support for the state. Instead, in Russia the state tended to keep society in its iron grip, coerce support from the people, and punish signs of independent societal movement. In this context, Hans Rogger's conclusion rings true:

> [In the West] the transition from the dynastic to the national state, the dissolution of old loyalties and allegiances had, by the nineteenth century, made nationalism a major factor of political loyalty and social integration. Nationalist sentiments, ideologies and movements had helped to throw bridges across conflicts of class and religion, had created common bonds between individuals and groups and had reconciled society and its members to the state to a surprising degree. . . . Nationalism had become more than a vague sentiment or an intellectual abstraction. It had become the expression of a substantial degree of agreement about the arrangements by which the society lived. . . . It had come not only to accept but to affirm the state.[1]

When nationalism has manifested itself strongly in Russia, two features have been outstanding. One is that nationalism served ultimately and predominantly to strengthen the state and uphold its imperial purposes. That aspect of national-ism which emphasized the people or nation as the repository of legitimate politi-cal authority, and the concomitant practice of balancing rights and duties between state and people, did not take root. Both in cases where nationalism was limited to a small sector of elites (e.g., nationalism as a factor in Russian expansion in Central Asia in the second half of the nineteenth century) and in cases where elites and the broader public converged on particular nationalist concepts and goals (e.g., nationalism under Joseph Stalin, panslavism in the 1870s, and great power nationalism prior to World War I), the end result was the same: the state grew stronger while society did not gain political space and concessions from the state. State authorities tended to support and promote nationalism only for brief inter-ludes, either to advance imperial state-building or to respond to acute challenges to their legitimacy and power.

The people, on the other hand, when mobilized by nationalism, rallied to obey orders of the state, made sacrifices that preserved various ruling regimes, and defended the state and its borders from external threat. But, in the aftermath of nationalist mobilization, the mass of Russians always found themselves at the los-ing end, with their status and concerns remaining deeply subordinated to those of the state. There were, to be sure, moments when many in Russian society believed that the state might surrender some of its prerogatives to the people and empower the nation by providing autonomous political space, effective mechanisms for political participation, and greater room for social and economic initiative. These moments included the aftermath of the Russian victory over Napoleon in 1812, the period of Great Reforms under Alexander II in the 1860s, and the signing of the October Manifesto in 1905. The state did indeed grant some concessions to society during these periods, but taken in totality, reversals to a traditional subju-gation of the people by the imperial state tended to overwhelm moments of movement toward a more balanced relationship. The transition to a modern nation-state—one in which state and society more or less agreed on the common civic and/or ethnic contours of the nation, the rules by which state and society should carry on their affairs, and the ultimate goals of the nation—simply did not happen. Nationalism itself, when supported by either state or people, or both, did not help integrate state and society or become the basis of a stable and lasting domestic arrangement.

Elements of nationalist consciousness did play a role in the longevity of the Russian imperial state, but it was largely the state's coercive power that was key to its long existence. This was true in the Russian empire, when autocratic rule, Orthodoxy, and popular belief in the sanctity of tsarist authority combined to sus-tain the state. And in the Soviet period, a mix of Russian great power nationalism, communist ideology, modernizing policies, and authoritarian rule kept the state intact for over seven decades. The use of nationalist ideas notwithstanding, Rus-sia (in tsarist and Soviet times) could not be described as having completed the transition to modern state–society relations with nationalism as a pillar. In the post-Soviet period, Russia continues to deal with this legacy. Post-Soviet rulers and citizens still grapple with the long-standing issue of integrating state and society through consensual arrangements that reflect shared beliefs about the Russian nation and Russian values, aspirations, and rules to live by.

A second prominent feature of Russian nationalism is that in cases where it briefly bonded state and society (e.g., in 1876–78 and in 1914), the sentiments that motivated nationalist fervor were mainly national humiliation and defiance in the face of external threats, crises, and the prospect of further humiliation. The third and fourth chapters in this book illustrate this. During the periods studied, an aggressive form of nationalism became widespread, mobilized large numbers of people, and influenced Russian foreign policy, particularly decisions to go to war. The impact of nationalism occurred during moments when both Russian state authorities and the articulate public believed that their state had been deeply humiliated, was facing further humiliation, and must respond decisively to external threats and challenges. Chapters 3 and 4 showed that Russian nationalism, when it manifested itself (however briefly) as an integrative force, was the product *not* of pride, victory, prosperity, or state-sponsored socioeconomic development or nation-building, but the result of shame and a desire to compensate for humiliation and weakness in an unfriendly world.[2]

In the post-Soviet period, the rise of nationalist discourse has itself been the product of new humiliation and Russian loss and shame. However, as chapter 6 pointed out, such mitigating factors as weaker imperial discourse and a relatively benign international environment have held aggressive nationalism in check in Russia until 1998. How can the impact of national humiliation be further minimized? Can a strong but benign nationalism develop in Russia—a nationalism that articulates primarily a civic definition of the nation; emphasizes a nonchauvinistic self-image and celebrates the interpenetration of Russian and other cultures; and argues for a national purpose focused on internal prosperity, preservation of cultural achievements, and a balancing of political rights and duties between state and society? Can Russia consolidate state–society relations on the basis of nationalism that is not the product of humiliation and resentment against the outside world?

The importance of nationalism to the construction of the post-Soviet Russian state and the definition of its domestic and foreign policy priorities cannot be underestimated. Beginning in the late 1980s and intensifying after the breakup of the Soviet Union in 1991, Russians have been asking, "Who are we? Where are we going? What is our place in the world?" This dynamic is not unique to Russia. Other states and civil communities, in the aftermath of destruction of an established order, have searched for what one scholar has called a "new basis of personal and collective self-respect."[3] In the nineteenth and twentieth centuries, such self-respect has often been rooted in nationalism.

The present period in Russia is one of promise and peril. The promise holds that Russia will evolve into a modern, stable, and participatory political entity, where a benign nationalism welds state and society in a common purpose, secures the state, and benefits the people by making state authorities accountable to the nation. This promise implies that nationalism will be a force with propitious effects on Russian political stability, economic development, and collective welfare—becoming, in essence, "an inevitable concomitant of social life and of many generous human impulses."[4] The fulfillment of this promise would mean that Russia in the twenty-first century could evolve into a state that is internally stable and prosperous, with a foreign policy that will likely be predictable, nonaggressive, and oriented toward the status quo. The peril or portent, on the other hand, is that Russia will return to old patterns of imperial discourse and behavior. Specifically, in the face of ongoing internal political rifts, economic hardship, and an increasingly hostile external environment, Russians may find renewed attraction to imperial discourse and support for imperial state power. In this case, the type of nationalism that will consolidate relations between state and society will likely contain chauvinism and imperialism, and will favor proving by forceful means that Russia is still a great power. An authoritarian, militarist state might emerge, flouting the welfare and political prerogatives of society and maintaining a level of legitimacy largely by wielding military power abroad. This kind of Russia will likely witness bloodshed and instability within its own borders and cause conflict in neighboring states (especially the former Soviet space), and even farther abroad.[5] What factors point to the likelihood of either Russia's promise or peril? What actions by external actors might catalyze one outcome or the other?

BREAKING WITH THE PAST? PROMISE AND PERIL IN POST-SOVIET RUSSIA

Recasting the Purposes of State, or Breaking Decisively with Empire

Proposition: The more successful the guardians of discourse are in defining the state, its purposes, and the source of its greatness in non-imperial terms, the less likely that aggressive nationalism will become resonant and the more likely that a benign nationalism will consolidate in Russia.

The chapters in this book dealing with Russian panslavism in 1856–78 and Russian great power nationalism in 1905–14 show that the prevalence of an imperial discourse was one of three factors that helped to empower briefly an aggressive form of nationalism. This discourse highlighted and sustained the idea that Russia had a "special mission," that the state as empire was an ideal organization, and that external power projection was a pillar without which the "greatness" of the Russian state would be rendered meaningless. In both cases, many of those who served as guardians of Russian collective memory and arbiters of political discourse strongly defined state power and legitimacy in imperial terms. They argued that Russia must not only maintain its imperial domains, but fight beyond its borders on behalf of Slavic and Orthodox kin in order to preserve its authority and status as a great power. This discourse provided a hospitable environment for the claims of panslavs and great power nationalists, whose ideas influenced Russian foreign policy during periods of internal instability, heightened perceptions of external threat, and international crises.

In the post-Soviet period, imperial discourse has remained a staple in some sectors of the Russian political spectrum. However, as chapters 5 and 6 argued, this discourse has become weaker than in the past. Although some Western political observers insist on an imperial trend in Russian political rhetoric and foreign policy in the 1990s,[6] nonetheless ideas of empire, imperial restoration, or imperial expansion have become less legitimate, been questioned widely, and proven weakly resonant among Russia's articulate public. Such ideas have also not underpinned Russian foreign policy decisions. This is amply demonstrated by Russia's anemic and ineffective attempts to protect or reincorporate ethnic Russians and Russian speakers in the "near abroad," and by the absence of dedicated effort by state leaders to integrate former Soviet republics back into Russia.[7] Prominent political figures, political analysts and commentators, scholars, and cultural leaders have highlighted the perils of imperial discourse. They have also offered alternative, non-imperial ways to define Russia's purposes as a state, norms that should govern state–society relations, and supreme values that the nation should hold. This non-imperial and anti-imperial trend began under Mikhail Gorbachev and has contributed to the evolution of a moderate, statist Russian nationalism. But the robust quality of Russia's non-imperial discourse cannot be taken for granted, and, as chapter 6 argued, a great risk remains that under conditions of internal political division and continued external humiliation, Russians might well be attracted again to traditional imperial values and assertions. It thus becomes extremely important for Russian intellectual, political, religious, and cultural leaders to make strong and sustained efforts to curb imperial discourse and highlight the perils of the imperial state. If they do so, it is likely that the impact of national humiliation will become muted because it will no longer be juxtaposed against a Russian self-image steeped in imperial, "great power" thought. The broader the consensus that the legitimacy and greatness of the state do not hinge on the exercise of imperial power or the fulfillment of messianic purposes, the less sting will result from national humiliation and the less likely the advance of an aggressive form of nationalism. Instead, the likelihood increases that state and society will focus their attention and energy on internal welfare, stability and cohesion, and on cultural or socioeconomic aspects of "greatness" rather than notions of external hegemony and power projection.

The weakening of Russian imperial discourse in the post-Soviet period may also be linked to the idea, advanced by Rogers Brubaker, that nationhood or nationness could sometimes be the result of events—discrete moments that lead to "sudden fluctuations in the 'nationness' of groups and relational settings."[8] Of central significance are the colossal events of 1991—when the Soviet Union collapsed, Russia's borders shrank to a size smaller than they were nearly three centuries ago, and the Russian population for the first time had an 80 percent ethnic Russian majority. Although the Soviet collapse led to national humiliation and stimulated an aggressive nationalist rhetoric, paradoxically and at the same time the *actual* breakup of the Soviet/Russian empire also presented Russians with a reality that forced them to delink Russian nationhood from the huge, sprawling, authoritarian, and deceased multiethnic empire. In a sense, this event may have constituted an effective form of "anti-imperial shock therapy" for Russian state and society. It made non-imperial thinking no longer a hypothetical proposition to be debated, but a necessary means for Russians to make sense of reality. As a shrunken and liberalizing Russia began and continued to build itself as a state—and as its newly independent neighbors proceeded to do likewise—many Russians adjusted to Russia's new geopolitical reality. Those who had been the strongest purveyors of imperial definitions of state power and an imperial identity for the nation enjoyed only occasional and partial public support. Many—perhaps most—Russians, while still confused about the nature and borders of their state, seem to have adjusted to Russia's new geopolitical reality, as evidenced by widespread unwillingness to support imperial ideas or pay the costs of imperial action.

The collapse of the Soviet Union, as an anti-imperial event contributing to new and evolving Russian nationhood, produced two specific outcomes that could help the advance of a benign Russian nationalism. First, the collapse dramatically reduced the scale of Russia's ethnic kaleidoscope, thereby mitigating one of the major impediments to Russian nation-building in the past. Russia's 80 percent ethnic Russian population can—more realistically than ever before—form the core around which an "imagined community" or nation might emerge. But the challenge remains of incorporating non-Russian minorities into the Russian nation. This precludes the use of an exclusively ethnic definition of the nation, especially in the context of ascendant ethnic identity among Chechens, Tatars, Bashkirs, and other groups.[9] To avoid ethnic unrest, it is important for a civic definition of the nation to prevail, for all ethnic groups in the Russian Federation to be granted full political rights, and for minorities to be given cultural and other forms of autonomy. Civic nationalism is a realistic option and can be facilitated by the fact that Russia's current population already shares the attributes of a common language and a common high culture (made possible by decades of Soviet education and modernization). In other words, a foundation exists for Russia to become a cohesive nation—one that is based on combined attributes of culture and citizenship, and is non-imperial.[10]

A second effect of the Soviet collapse that could be helpful to the development of a benign Russian nationalism is that it made the Russian "nation-state" a geographic reality (i.e., the Russian Federation), thereby validating "nation-state" organization as an alternative to empire-state organization. "Nation-state" organization as an alternative to empire was never a consideration during the tsarist regime. Neither was it a strong alternative during the Soviet period. But, as noted in chapter 2, the Soviet government institutionalized quasi–"nation-states" through the formation of ethnoterritorial administrative units and the implementation of various ethnically determined policies. Soviet rule paradoxically created and strengthened nations, while professing adherence to an internationalist and even antinationalist ideology. When the regime collapsed, the default borders of its successor states became primarily those ethnoterritorial lines that Soviet power had drawn and maintained for over seven decades. Although many Russians remain confused or dissatisfied with their state's new post-Soviet borders, nonetheless in almost a decade of independence, the idea of "nation-state" organization—specifically, Russia without its extensive, contiguous, imperial domains—has become viable. Public and elite confusion and/or dissatisfaction over Russia's shrunken borders have not intensified since 1991 and have not led to political, military, or other mobilization to change those borders. In the meantime, some of the thorniest postimperial territorial issues for Russia—for example, the status of Sevastopol in Crimea—have been resolved in the medium term through leasing arrangements and formal Russian recognition of the borders of Ukraine.

Imperial discourse still exists in Russia, but its legitimacy has been frail and its influence muted. Will it remain so in the long term? A positive response will depend in large part on how Russians handle several hurdles. First, Russian intellectuals, political elites, and other guardians of discourse must continue to grapple with the imperial past. They must sustain a critical examination and discussion of history and highlight the high costs of empire and the dangers of a revived imperial discourse. Sadly, critical views of history that prevailed during Gorbachev's *glasnost'* and in the early post-Soviet years have been replaced in many instances by clichéd assertions about Russian great power status and Soviet-style bravado about, for example, new weapon systems as a sign of Russian greatness.[11] Igor' Chubais, who passionately argues for Russian "historicism" or a full appraisal of Russian history as sine qua non for the growth of healthy nationalism, states that the imperialism and expansionism of the past must be fully studied, understood, and disavowed. In his words:

> In reclaiming our [national] ideological roots, [we] must seek to understand what kind of crisis shook Russia a century ago [and led to the Bolshevik revolution], and how it could have been overcome. One of the most important and organic components of the Russian idea in the past five centuries has been the gathering of lands or growth and expansion. It is precisely this idea which became outmoded. . . . Russia [in the mid-nineteenth century] began a slow transition . . . from quantitative to qualitative growth. Western European states experienced this phase back in the sixteenth to eighteenth centuries, but Russia began this transition only after it had become the largest state on earth. Nothing but tragedy followed those European states which occasionally returned to the old model of expansion (e.g., Napoleon and Hitler). The Bolsheviks, too, tried to fuel a global fire and world revolution instead of finally focusing on building a fire in their own hearth and cleaning their own yard. This, too, led to nothing but tragedy.[12]

Chubais's argument is an important one. As scholars have shown, self-serving, biased, and chauvinist approaches to history in such states as Germany and Japan were factors that fed aggressive nationalism and imperialism in these states.[13] The challenge in Russia is to sustain an open, wide-ranging, and critical examination of the past in order to draw lessons that will help focus Russian thinking and actions on problems at home rather than on power projection abroad or the restoration of old imperial domains. This critical examination of the past must also be disseminated widely, especially among the youth who will someday become leaders, decision makers and fully participating citizens in Russian politics. Impediments to a critical discourse on the past include rising public disinterest in exhuming evidence of past crimes and excesses by the imperial state; elite concerns that Russian self-flagellation about the past will create self-hatred; and official limitation since 1995 of access to state archives, particularly those containing key documents on the communist regime.[14]

Second, Russian government officials must play a more active and effective role in promoting anti-imperial discourse as part of post-Soviet Russian state-building and nation-building. Boris Yeltsin's government deserved credit for writing a constitution that is nonchauvinistic and for promoting a largely non-imperial moderate statist discourse; but its record also had blemishes. For example, officials under Yeltsin were guilty of using wholesale references to Chechens and other Caucasians as "bandits." While state authorities clearly had to condemn crimes committed by particular groups or individuals, their use of language that criminalized entire peoples and whitewashed Russia's own guilt did not bode well for moderate nationalism. Governmental discussion of Chechnya, in particular, has been marked by the absence of official acknowledgement of Russia's complex historical relations with Chechnya, persistent Chechen resistance against Russian domination, and extremely cruel methods used by the state (including deportation by Stalin) to subdue the Chechen population.[15] Official—as well as unofficial—discourse that brands certain groups as "murderers, terrorists, and bandits" can lead to their dehumanization and creates the risk that imperial aggression against them will occur or recur. Acts of violence could potentially be justified not only against minorities within the state, but also against other groups outside Russia's borders. In the case of Chechnya, the Russian people largely resisted the rhetoric of their leaders during the Chechen war of 1994–96. As human rights leader Sergei Kovalev argues, enough citizens were mobilized to force their government to end the war.[16] But there can be no room for complacency. State authorities play a key role in setting the tone and determining the content of political discourse, and their role is crucial in expunging language that promotes the revival of imperial and chauvinist thought.

State authorities can also play a more constructive role in the symbolic[17] and legal aspects of discourse. The Yeltsin government did well to use an inclusive, civic definition of the Russian nation. It also removed the infamous "fifth point," which delineated nationality in Russian internal passports and underpinned discrimination in both tsarist and Soviet Russia. But the government, less constructively, redeployed other imperial symbols—e.g., the double-headed eagle, which adorns the new post-Soviet Russian internal passports. It also gave favored treatment to the Russian Orthodox Church, and chose a national anthem, "A Life for the Tsar," which connotes devotion to the ruler of state rather than the people or nation. In Moscow itself, new symbols in the post-Soviet period (commissioned by mayor Yurii Luzhkov) have also been imperial in flavor. Perhaps most flagrant is the mammoth Zurab Tsereteli sculpture of Peter the Great that looms over part of the Moscow River a short distance from the Kremlin.

The task of creating and disseminating new non-imperial symbols will be an important one in the future. Valerii Tishkov, former head of the Russian State Committee on Nationalities, has noted that the Russian White House (*Belyi dom*) could have been a new and important civic and non-imperial symbol of post-Soviet Russia, but this symbol has been tainted by Yeltsin's bombing of it in 1993 and the violent disbanding of parliament. Another symbol that can, and perhaps should, be emphasized is the Russian Federation's tricolor flag, which was officially adopted on August 21, 1991. Influenced by the flag of the Netherlands, Peter the Great used this symbol as the civil ensign on Russian ships, and it was first used on land in 1883. The Bolsheviks repressed the flag, but it resurfaced in 1990. Though not a perfect symbol, Yeltsin waved the flag from a tank during a heroic moment of "democratic" opposition against leaders of the 1991 coup against Gorbachev. The flag could thus be used to connote Russian ties with the West and opposition to tyranny, and could become an important symbol of a non-imperial Russia.[18]

Other positive and non-imperial national symbols might be figures from Russia's shared high culture, which could help underline the idea that Russia's greatness is not based on imperialism but on the genius of its many and multiethnic writers, musicians, and artists, who have contributed immensely to world culture. The multitudinous, deep-felt, and even extravagant remembrances of Aleksandr Pushkin, father of Russian literature, on the occasion of his two hundredth birthday in 1999, was a welcome sign in this regard. As the late Dmitrii Likhachev argued, Russia must remain a great power not only because of its size and population, but also because of its great culture:

> If we can preserve our culture and all that enables it to develop—libraries, museums, archives, schools, universities, and periodicals . . . if we can preserve unspoiled our rich language, literature, musical education, scientific institutes, then we will indisputably occupy first place in Northern Europe and Asia.[19]

Unfortunately, many of Russia's cultural and scientific resources have become severely eroded in the post-Soviet period, and many Russian cultural figures have left Russia for new lives abroad. Nonetheless, there remains a colossal cultural heritage on which Russians could partly build and define their nation. The consolidation of a benign Russian nationalism in the future will depend in part on the government's ability to engage political, business, and intellectual forces to generate and promote symbols that depict non-imperial values of state and society, emphasize Russia as a society whose culture is open to both East and West, and connote no special mission for Russia other than to take care of itself and advance the welfare of its people. These types of symbols could help dampen remnants of enthusiasm for empire and help strengthen the cohesion of the Russian nation in its post-Soviet incarnation.

Russian political authorities could also do more to constrain the rise of imperial discourse by strengthening legal sanctions against extremist nationalism. Extremist groups in Russia that openly preach Russian racial superiority and advocate violence and terrorism against racial or religious minorities create an atmosphere that fosters imperial ideas and sentiments. Their acts of vandalism and terrorism contribute to internal fear and instability, increase societal polarization, and create rifts that will obstruct the development of a benign Russian nationalism. If left uncontrolled, this atmosphere of fear and hatred will help justify demands for a strong imperial state that curtails the rights of citizens at home (especially nonethnic Russians) while imposing its will on neighbors abroad.

While extremist groups clearly have the right to free speech, and their members generally cannot be arrested unless evidence shows that they have violated laws (particularly Article 74 of the Russian Criminal Code or the law against inciting ethnic hatred), nonetheless, Russian leaders should censure these groups publicly. Censure should be accompanied by unequivocal confirmation of the rights of all individual Russians, whatever their ethnic background or religious persuasion. The Russian government should also avoid vigilantly the use of exclusivist ethnic or religious markers as determinants of social, political, and economic power. The law against inciting ethnic hatred in the Criminal Code should be defined more clearly, publicized more broadly, and applied more consistently. In the late 1990s, repeated incidents of hate speech (especially, anti-Semitic) by political figures went uncensured. Examples in 1998 included repeated anti-Semitic comments by Nikolai Kondratenko, governor of Krasnodar; the November 1998 anti-Semitic speech of Albert Makashov at a communist rally in Moscow; and anti-Semitic remarks by Viktor Ilyukhin, member of the Duma. The weakness of official sanctions against hate speech has been discouraging and is an area where the Russian record could be improved.

Besides hate speech, repeated bombings and vandalism of Jewish property, beating of dark-skinned people (including a U.S. Marine in 1998, Gypsies, and approximately fifteen black students a month in Moscow, according to one report), and open fascist rallies in Moscow in the late 1990s signaled the need to strengthen Russia's legal framework to counteract extremism. On the positive side, authorities in cities such as Moscow and Yaroslavl' did ban neofascist rallies and arrested and imprisoned neo-Nazis for violations of Article 74 of the Criminal Code. More actions like these are needed to strengthen the norm against racism, fascism, and other forms of extremism.[20]

More critical and honest approaches to the Russian past must also be cultivated, including the writing and use of textbooks that acknowledge the dangers and excesses of imperialism under both tsarism and communism. Russian officials should consider greater access to communist archives, acknowledgment of past wrongdoings, and a more vigorous debate on traditions of the past that should be preserved and those that should be discarded. The ideological battle on how to define Russian national "greatness" is not over, and tendencies by political and other elites to emphasize the imperial aspect of Russia as a historical "great power" could only hurt the evolution of a benign Russian nationalism. As for archival access, it would be helpful if the Russian government convened an independent commission of respected authorities to decide what materials genuinely qualify as "state secrets" that must be kept from public view for the safety of the country. Otherwise, most archives of the communist era should be made publicly available. The greater the public attention to the abuses of the communist past, the deeper will be the remembrance of the tragedies caused by imperial authority at home and abroad, and the less likely a return to old imperial thought and action.

Imperial discourse in post-Soviet Russia has not yet fully become a thing of the past, and anti-imperial discourse remains a relatively new and fragile development. The scholar Ilya Prizel contends that it was only in the 1960s that Russian nativists and nationalists "began to question the burdens of empire on Russia and attempted to devise a paradigm with Russia's distinct needs and interests at its center. Until then, Russian intellectuals, whether nationalist Slavophiles or liberal Westernizers, believed in the permanence of the imperial structure."[21] Russians—especially elites who play an important role in the formation of collective memory—must vigilantly deemphasize the messianic, civilizational, and great power/militarist components of their national self-image. This is not an insuperable task. Perhaps Russians can learn from the Poles, whose elites have traditionally embraced a view of the nation that was imperial and, for centuries, envisioned Poland as a great military power with a civilizing mission and a racially superior ruling class. These elites were out of touch with Polish society. Only after the dismemberment of the Polish Commonwealth at the end of the eighteenth century, the partitioning of Poland and disastrous uprisings in the nineteenth century, and the tragedies of the twentieth century did Polish nationalism complete its transition from a universal-civilizational to a "narrow" approach—one that is focused on national welfare and "realistic assessments of current realities and of the future."[22] Modernization processes and critical assessments of the past, including Polish anti-Semitism, have helped to consolidate a healthier version of nationalism in Poland—one that seems genuinely to bond masses and elites and serves broad rather than narrow interests.

Searching for Internal Stability, Grappling with Recurrent Crises

Proposition: The continued erosion of internal governance in Russia, leading to political, economic, and social instability, could obstruct the development of benign nationalism. By undermining public confidence in the state, it may lead divided and weakened state elites to support aggressive nationalism as a means to secure and enhance their legitimacy and position.

Two of the chapters in this book showed that deep erosion in Russian internal governance, manifested in political, economic, and social deterioration, facilitated the impact of aggressive nationalism. Under conditions of eroded internal governance, the ruling regime became increasingly vulnerable to accusations from below, especially from aggressive nationalist groups, that it was incompetent, corrupt, and unfit to rule and must, therefore, be replaced. Pressure from below intensified especially under conditions of liberalizing reform or when the Russian government allowed some form of political participation and created opportunities for the expression of public opinion. The two instances described in this book when Russia's ruling authorities yielded to aggressive nationalist pressure occurred during periods of liberalizing reform in Russian politics: in 1856–78, and in 1905–14. At the end of these periods, state officials—whose legitimacy hinged on some popular support—upheld aggressive nationalism in part to regain support from society and to prevent what some perceived to be the impending destruction of the state's ruling system.

The erosion of internal governance, however, is an insufficient factor for the triumph of aggressive nationalism. The post-Soviet period (until 1998) illustrates this. Although political, economic, and social problems had been persistent since 1991, the government of Boris Yeltsin not only survived, but aggressive nationalist ideas neither captured the minds and hearts of most Russians, nor became a blueprint for Russian international behavior. Nobody expects democratic political stability and economic prosperity in Russia in the near term. On all fronts—political, economic, and social—major fluctuations and uncertainty will likely reign. Russia had five prime ministers between March 1998 and August 1999, highlighting the diffused, confused, and irresponsible nature of political power. Yeltsin in May 1999 ousted Prime Minister Primakov, who had the highest level of popular support among Russian politicians, and then three months later ousted Primakov's replacement. As head of state, Yeltsin himself veered between long periods of inactivity and sickness to brief moments of vigor (usually employed to fire another government). Economically, the government's chief accomplishment of reining in inflation and maintaining a stable exchange rate was deeply undermined by the financial crisis of August 1998. As this book goes to press, it remains to be seen if the new government of Vladimir Putin will take effective measures to make the economy more productive, transparent (i.e., governed by law to a significant degree), and prosperous.

The specifics of Russian political and economic restructuring are beyond the scope of this book. Based on past experience, the processes and outcomes of such restructuring will likely be uneven for a long time, and the end goals of a mature market economy or a consolidated democracy cannot be taken for granted. However, a few signposts in Russia's ongoing evolution will help or hinder the development of a benign nationalism. On the political front, an uncontrolled escalation of political infighting and a deeper fragmentation of political authority could help the cause of aggressive nationalists who preach order and promise to rule Russia with an iron hand. On the other hand, the continued development (however bumpy) of democratic processes and institutions could help align the ideology and interests of the state with those of the people and will benefit the consolidation of a benign nationalism. These processes and institutions include elections, free speech, civil associations, political parties, and a representative legislature. Progress in democratization can strengthen national cohesion because it entails an active interplay of input by both state and society in decision making on issues that affect the lives of most Russians. This process can help correct what scholars have variously labeled "dual Russia," a "gap between the governors and the governed," and a "crisis of coherence." All these phrases refer to the same persistent phenomenon: the lack of integration between state and society. In imperial Russia, and in the Soviet Union, this lack of integration resulted in the "state's [incapacity] to bring consistency to disparate behaviors and attitudes, to prevent the transfer of citizens' affection and effort to alternate structures, and to exercise collective wit."[23] State authorities tended to lag in understanding issues that ailed society at large, and because society did not possess autonomous and effective means to make its voice heard, its interests tended to be neglected or abused by the state.[24]

In the 1990s, Russian efforts to democratize suffered setbacks, particularly during Yeltsin's bombing of the old Supreme Soviet in 1993 and the government's secret decision to launch a war in Chechnya in 1994. Notwithstanding these setbacks, elections on local, regional, and national levels took place peacefully in 1993, 1995, 1996, and 1999. In the case of Chechnya, public pressure—especially in the context of the 1996 presidential elections—played an important role in the regime's decision to end the war in 1996. And in 1993–99, both executive and legislative branches maintained adherence to the 1993 constitution. These events and processes signal the growth of a participatory culture, incipient rule-of-law, and mediation between state and people. But these positive developments are fragile, and problems in Russia are legion. The state, in many ways, has failed to act as an autonomous and effective institution that formulates and implements policies to the benefit of most members of society. Especially under Yeltsin, the state was captured by narrow groupings, leading most citizens to be highly cynical and distrustful of their government. Even though a majority of Russians have participated in elections, a 1997 poll showed as many as 60 percent believing that there were no effective ways to influence their public authorities. Other polls, repeated in 1993, 1994, 1995, and 1996, showed between 90 and 93 percent believing that the government did a "fairly poor" or "very poor" job in maintaining order. Similar opinions prevailed in 1993–96 among 83 to 89 percent of those polled about the government's ability to provide social protection. Other polls repeated in 1993, 1996, and 1997 showed, respectively, 51, 54, and 66 percent believing that the situation in the country had gone out of the government's control. Finally, in a 1998 poll, 63 percent said they thought their government was criminal and corrupt, and 41 percent agreed with the assessment that the Yeltsin government was "alien to the people."[25]

Deep public distrust and cynicism toward the government does not bode well for the consolidation of benign nationalism. When public trust is low in the government's intentions and capabilities, the alignment of beliefs, values, and interests between state and society becomes difficult. People will look instead to alternative groups and forces to represent their interests, including aggressive nationalists. In the future, the extent to which Russia's government can improve its record on political, economic, and social governance will help determine the public resonance of various nationalist alternatives. The better the government's performance, the less likely that people will support aggressive nationalist ideas and programs. As internal governance strengthens and domestic stability increases, the chances that nationalist demagoguery will be an effective tool to win elections will likely diminish.

On the economic and social fronts, the formation in the post-Yeltsin period of a government that is united on an economic reform program and is able and willing to work with public opinion to generate support for further economic change will be critical. This will not be easy, given the intense competition among narrow and powerful groups for control over the country's wealth, resources, and productive capacity and the past influence of these groups on the government. Yeltsin and his revolving array of top officials presided over growing societal inequality, the nearly free transfer of the state's choicest economic assets to cronies and various bankers and oligarchs, corruption, and fiscal irresponsibility. This lends a gloomy pall to Russia's economic future and presents a difficult legacy to overcome. The government's mode of operation must change, but change will not occur overnight, nor can it address all problems at once. The formation of a stronger and more united government is a first and very important step, and time will tell if the presidency of Vladimir Putin will be such a government.

Second, post-Yeltsin leaders must more honestly explain their programs to the Russian people and desist from unrealistic and contemptuous promises.[26] Honesty and an appeal to the deep love of most Russians for their homeland (*rodina*) would serve the government better than dubious promises, and may even generate support for measures that will inevitably cause pain (e.g., bankruptcies of unproductive enterprises). A new government should also find means to break free from the grip of narrow and rapacious groups that have been the chief beneficiaries of past Russian market reform. The practice of market "reform" without public support is not tenable, and could lead only to further internal division and conflict. Anatolii Chubais, a chief architect of Russian marketization, has proudly proclaimed that his style was "Bolshevik"—that is, he conducted privatization without public support and in the fastest time possible. Such flagrant contempt for the people spotlights a problematic tradition of governance that harks back not only to the Bolsheviks but also to the tsarist empire. This tradition sparked internal crises that brought the state to the brink of, and then to actual, disintegration.

Third, a new government should use its resources (including available assistance from abroad) to target those who are most vulnerable, instead of bailing out corrupt bankers and businessmen or continuing policies of blanket subsidies.[27] If these changes can take place, there will be a greater likelihood that Russians will see more common cause and values with their government, and subscribe to a nationalism that is focused on internal unity and welfare.

Responding to a More Hostile International Environment: Kosovo and Beyond

Proposition: Perceptions by the Russian public and leaders of an increasingly hostile international environment, coupled with the occurrence of crises that portend further Russian national humiliation, will obstruct the development of a benign Russian nationalism and could lead to the empowerment of an aggressive nationalism.

Aggressive nationalists in Russia have characterized Russia's relationship with the United States as that between "slave and master." They have portrayed the United States as a power seeking to bend Russia to its will in the economic, political, and military spheres. In their opinion, the West is an ill-intentioned adversary, and Russian survival depends not on cooperation with the West but on the revival of military power and economic self-sufficiency.[28] These ideas have not had a major impact on Russian behavior in the 1990s, but they highlight the importance of the international environment as a key factor in the evolution of Russian nationalism and foreign policy.

This book argues that the international system was a determining factor in the rise and impact of aggressive nationalism in Russia in the past. The chapters on 1856–78 and 1905–14 showed that rising Russian perceptions of threat to vital and traditional interests in the "Near East," coupled with international crises and fears of irreparable national humiliation, assisted the spread of aggressive nationalist ideas and made possible their impact on foreign policy. During most of the 1990s, the international system was relatively benign to Russian interests. But NATO expansion to areas formerly in the Soviet/Russian sphere of influence and further expansion to countries that were part of the USSR have substantively augmented Russian elite perceptions of external threat. These elites, representing all parts of the political spectrum, have articulated the view that NATO expansion is directed against Russia and that NATO intends to become the sole arbiter of global security, excluding Russia from any meaningful role.

Although the most negative reactions to NATO expansion have come mainly from Russian political elites, NATO's bombing campaign in Yugoslavia over the Kosovo crisis in 1999 drew a much more widespread negative reaction from all sectors of Russian society. Unlike at any other point in the post-Soviet period, Russian elites and the mass public united in expressions of anti-Western sentiment and passionate condemnation of the Western alliance. Former Prime Minister Evgenii Primakov, en route to Washington as NATO's bombs began falling on Serbia, turned his plane around in a sign of protest. Poll results showed as many as 90 percent believing that NATO did not have the right to attack Yugoslavia without a UN mandate, 52 percent feeling indignation at the attack, and 64 percent believing that the Kosovar Albanians' plight was an internal Yugoslav matter. The Russian consensus that Kosovo was not an issue for NATO to resolve had long been expressed in the Duma, where, as of March 1999, at least forty-five declarations and resolutions in this regard had been passed by both liberal and conservative legislators.[29]

The intensely negative Russian reaction to NATO bombing of Yugoslavia (which various individuals and groups labeled "barbaric," "genocidal" and "Hitlerite") had several explanations. First, there was a genuine populist sympathy for fellow Orthodox Slavs who became victims of NATO bombs. This sympathy was based on historical, cultural, and religious ties and memories, though it contrasted certainly with the more problematic and sometimes turbulent official relations between Serbia and Russia in the tsarist period, Yugoslavia and the USSR in the Soviet period, and Serbia and Russia in the post-Soviet period.[30] In the Kosovo conflict, Russian sympathy for the Serb side was strong also because the Russian mass media inadequately covered the heinous ethnic cleansing perpetrated by Slobodan Milosevic's government and army against the Kosovar Albanians. Instead, the media highlighted the destruction of Serbia and innocent civilian victims of NATO bombs. The strength of popular sympathy for Serbians who were defiant of NATO was evident in the desire of many Russians (67 percent in one poll) to do something personally to help Serbia. Although massive Russian voluntarism to fight on behalf of the Serbian army did not occur, nonetheless, a few Russian volunteers, both medical and military, did go to Yugoslavia, and at least one Russian officer died in Kosovo.[31] This public mobilization, even at a very low level, was remarkable because since 1991, foreign policy issues had been of secondary importance to ordinary Russians. It indicated a strong emotional aspect to the Serbian issue that was not evident on other foreign policy matters and crises that had confronted Russia since the collapse of the Soviet Union.

Second, Russian opposition to NATO bombing was also due to mass and elite perceptions of danger to Russia itself. In the context of decaying Russian military power and nonexistent economic might, Russians felt no comfort as the world's most potent military machine bombed an ally close to their borders and in utter disregard of their objections. NATO's bombing conjured the sentiment that Russia had become entirely insignificant in international affairs, and Western powers could do as they pleased without serious consideration of Russian preferences, interests, and objections. Ordinary Russians as well as official figures compared Kosovo with Russia's own secessionist Chechnya and raised the specter of potential NATO intervention in future Russian internal conflicts. Although many in the West might think it fantastic for Russians to worry about a direct NATO attack over ethnic and secessionist disputes on their territory or in the "near abroad," nonetheless the sentiment has been widespread. It cannot be dismissed as the rambling of those on the extreme fringes of Russian politics—indeed, it has been repeated by those perceived in the West to be among some of the more sophisticated, Westernized Russian crowd. For example, Boris Fedorov, former finance minister and a banker, once asserted that the bombing of Kosovo was nothing more than "preparation for a NATO raid on Russia."[32]

The ambiguity of geographic and substantive limits to NATO "out of area" operations, and NATO's willingness to act without a UN mandate on Kosovo, has given Russians reason to believe that the alliance and the West as a whole intends to prevent Russia's revival as a strong power. In the words of one journalist, it was as if the West wanted to rub "Moscow's nose in its new second-tier status."[33] Thus, the vehement Russian opposition to NATO bombing was a form of backlash against Western actions that spotlighted and intensified Russia's humiliating helplessness. It was this very helplessness that was echoed in the paranoid comments and hazardous policy recommendations of nationalist politicians during the conflict. Communist leader Gennadii Zyuganov and others, for example, argued that Russia should send arms to the Serbs; renew ties with rogue states such as Iran, Libya, and Iraq; send volunteers to defend Serbia; form a new federation with Yugoslavia and Belarus; and station nuclear weapons on Belarusian territory.[34]

Representatives of the Russian government and opinion leaders in the press took a strident tone on Kosovo, and Russian policy exhibited some muscle-flexing during and after the conflict. A Russian reconnaissance ship was sent to the Adriatic Sea during the conflict, Russian military representatives were withdrawn from NATO headquarters, and Duma Speaker Gennadii Seleznev announced that h and Yeltsin had discussed the possibility of targeting strategic warheads on NATO countries.[35] After the bombing, Russian troops dashed ahead of NATO soldiers into Kosovo and occupied the airport in Pristina, causing a diplomatic uproar. Afterward, the Russian military conducted a major military maneuver called Zapad-99 or West-99, in which the enemy clearly was NATO. During the exercise, four strategic bombers were sent on mock bombing missions to the United States, the first time in over a decade that such a maneuver was practiced in Russia.

But ultimately, Russian policy on Kosovo and its aftermath did not spell the triumph of aggressive nationalism. During the conflict itself, official (as well as unofficial) rhetoric contained elements of moderation. For example, while Yeltsin and others criticized NATO's bombing of Serbia, they also warned that Russia must not be involved in the war. Some prominent journalists and analysts drew attention to Milosevic's "compromised" regime, Russian weakness, and the folly of such rash actions as encouraging volunteers to fight for Serbia or withdrawing Russian ambassadors from NATO countries. Others argued that Russia could not pretend to great power status until it solved its problems at home, including, in the words of political commentator Aleksei Pushkov, "rotten regimes, a half-dead military industry and army."[36] Statements and positions from such official figures as Viktor Chernomyrdin, Russian special envoy on Kosovo, and the semiofficial Council for Defense and Security Policy, were also reasonable in tone. They argued for independent Russian input to the resolution of the Kosovo conflict (e.g., peacekeepers should be deployed from countries that were not involved in bombing Yugoslavia) and reminded the United States to pay attention to setbacks in U.S.–Russian relations created by NATO bombing of Yugoslavia.[37] The bottom line in these statements was that Russia would not be treated as a junior partner that simply blessed the preferences of NATO and the West. This position was neither extremist nor unreasonable, and rightly reminded Western countries of their own security interests involving Russia. The issue of not being taken for granted as a junior partner was not new and has been highly apparent in previous Russian–Western negotiations on Bosnia.[38]

It is beyond this book's scope to foretell the ultimate impact of the Kosovo conflict. In its immediate aftermath Russian official policy largely continued to affirm the importance of cooperative ties with the West. On the economic front, negotiations with the International Monetary Fund (IMF) resumed, and Russian cooperation on Kosovo may have been a facilitating factor in the IMF's approval of a new $4.5 billion loan. The loan kept Russia from defaulting on its debt to the IMF and unlocked other official assistance (e.g., from Japan and the World Bank). In the sphere of security, the Russian government renewed its collaboration with the United States on denuclearization via the Nunn–Lugar Cooperative Threat Reduction program and resumed arms control talks, including on the ABM (Anti-Ballistic Missile) Treaty and START (Strategic Arms Reductions Talks) III. Russian troops also became full participants in the NATO-led Kosovo Peacekeeping Force (KFOR). Although Kosovo ultimately proved the weak appeal of extremist nationalist ideas, nonetheless the story of Russian perceptions of external threat and resentment against the West is not over. How international diplomats and policymakers continue to manage the rather delicate relations between Russia and the United States, and between Russia and NATO, will continue to influence the evolution of Russian nationalism. If further and deeper Russian humiliation (similar to Kosovo) results from other crises yet to come, then ammunition will be added to the arsenal of aggressive Russian nationalists. Their arguments about Western perfidy, Western conspiracy to prevent Russia's great power renaissance, and the need to rebuild and exercise Russian military power abroad will gain greater credibility. This does not mean that aggressive nationalism will inevitably prevail in Russia if Western policies appear hostile to basic Russian interests; but in the stream of contingent events, the empowerment of such nationalism could become a more real potential outcome than might otherwise be the case.

RUSSIA AND THE WEST: WHAT ACTIONS WILL MATTER?

The type of nationalism that will help consolidate the statehood of post-Soviet Russia will depend in large part on internal Russian political discourse and choices that Russian politicians and society will make. However, the international environment will influence how these choices are framed and made, and what constraints and pressures Russian citizens and decision makers will face. The potential impact of the international environment is particularly important in Russia, where centuries of imperial history have created strong myths and expectations regarding the respect and prestige that should be Russia's due on the world stage. These myths and expectations are highly at odds with Russia's present state of weakness, but nonetheless they exist and help explain Russian sensitivity to humiliation in international affairs. Given the importance of the international environment, what actions can international actors take to mitigate pressures that will likely help the rise and empowerment of aggressive Russian nationalism?

Three general policy-relevant principles arise from this book's analysis. One is that Western actors should, as much as possible, give Russia "breathing space" as its people seek to redefine their national identity and national priorities at a pivotal point in their history. This "breathing space" might be provided best by avoiding actions that intensify Russian humiliation and feed Russian paranoia. Western actors need to be sensitive to the fact that cataclysmic changes have deeply undermined Russians' traditional view of themselves as belonging to a mighty, "great power" state. A pithy and intense process is ongoing to redefine the Russian "nation," its relationship to the state, and priorities that should guide both nation and state. If outside actors cause further Russian humiliation and if international crises arise as a result, Russians will likely be distracted from the task of consolidating a more benign national identity and may succumb to the enticement and promises (however unrealistic) of imperialist and aggressive nationalism.

A second policy-relevant principle is that Western actors should continue engage Russia as a partner or collaborator on many fronts, even while und standing that such engagement may not always mean full cooperation, dictability, or delivery on Russia's part. The risk of unpredictable results is worth taking, however, in light of what is at stake: Russia's evolution as a stable and confident partner of Western states. The importance of continued interaction and collaboration arises from the argument that a benign nationalism in Russia can develop over time only as Russians gain pride and confidence in their ability to hold their own with Western interlocutors. In the long term, Russians should develop a fuller appreciation of their own distinction as a people, while recognizing interests, traits, and priorities shared with Westerners. As this happens, Russia will be able to normalize its relations with the West. Feelings of resentment and humiliation will be minimized, and a Russia with the potential to be an equal partner with the West can emerge. If, on the contrary, Western engagement is terminated, the resulting Russian isolation could intensify nationalist resentment and stimulate belligerence against the outside world.

Third, Western policymakers should be keenly aware of the delicate balancing act they must keep toward Russia. On one hand, it is important to avoid humiliating Russia and to create an international environment where Russians feel that they can be valued participants. On the other hand, Western policy should not tolerate or justify Russian actions that clearly encourage imperial thought and behavior and therefore help provide fertile ground for aggressive nationalism. For example, while the mild Western reaction to Moscow's first Chechnya war in 1994–96 may have contributed to creating a relatively benign international environment for Russia, it doubtless also made easier the Russian decision to launch a second brutal war in Chechnya in 1999. A key challenge to Western policy—and an area in which the Western record has not been stellar—is to convey clearly that human rights and democracy are issues that Western states care most deeply about and are core standards by which the outside world will judge Russia. It is difficult to do this consistently and effectively, but greater awareness and effort toward this end could have propitious effects on Russia's evolution.

Other policy implications from this book's analysis are set forth below.

1. Geopolitics and the "Near Abroad"

Western policy can help minimize Russian humiliation by facilitating Russian integration into Western political and security systems. Such integration will likely enhance Russian perceptions of a benign international environment, and will also make a material difference in bringing internal Russian policies more in line with international standards. For example, all death sentences in Russia have been commuted, chiefly because Russian authorities have wanted to comply with standards set by the Council on Europe, where Russia became a member in 1996.[39] Unfortunately, Western policy has not always focused on Russian integration. The closing of NATO's doors to Russia, in particular, isolates Russia from the central security and political-military organization in post–Cold War Europe. Although NATO expansion cannot be undone, policymakers belonging to the alliance should consider having NATO adopt a stance that opens the door to Russian membership if and when Russia is able to comply to standards that all other

NATO members are required to meet. This would convey the message that outsiders truly consider Russia a potential member of the community of Western democracies and are willing to give it time to attain standards required by NATO and its member-states. A NATO that is more open to Russia could also expect greater transparency from Russia and could potentially have greater influence on the development of a cooperative and predictable Russian security policy. It would also be prudent to postpone indefinitely a second round of NATO expansion, especially if it involves states that were formerly part of the Soviet Union. A second expansion involving the Baltics or Ukraine,[40] for example, would undoubtedly intensify Russian humiliation. NATO decision makers must weigh carefully the impact on European and global security of adding more new members versus causing a simmering and potentially long-lasting Russian resentment against the alliance and its individual members. NATO member-states should also consider that a Russia with nuclear weapons, a crumbling military, and a dysfunctional government is likely to pose a greater threat when it is resentful of the outside world than a Russia that sees outsiders harboring benign interests and seeking to avoid Russian humiliation and exclusion.

As for the "near abroad," it would be advisable for Western states and institutions to use their political and economic leverage to encourage Russia's newly independent neighbors to integrate their Russian minorities and cultivate their loyalty to the states where they live. Western efforts in this area have already proven constructive. For example, Western states, the Council on Europe, and the Organization for Security and Cooperation in Europe (OSCE) together worked to help improve citizenship laws that formerly discriminated against Russians in the Baltic states. The more Russian minorities are integrated, the greater loyalty they will have toward their new governments and the more stable the newly independent states themselves will become. In this setting, there will be less pretext for aggressive Russian nationalists to argue for forceful policies on behalf of stranded kin abroad; and even if they make such arguments, they will be unlikely to succeed in mobilizing the population inside Russia itself.

Western assistance policies should also be used, where possible, to facilitate cooperative ties between Russia and its newly independent neighbors. Such ties could contribute to a benign international environment, which, in turn, would diminish the appeal of aggressive Russian nationalism. This may be easier said than done, however, because the interests of specific actors who are either donors or targets of assistance often do not coincide. But if the United States and its allies want a relatively stable environment in the former Soviet Union, then the effort is worthwhile to find ways to structure assistance to enhance regional cooperation and mitigate regional tensions. An outstanding example of external assistance that catalyzed cooperation between Russia and its neighbors is the Cooperative Threat Reduction Program or Nunn–Lugar program. Passed by the U.S. Congress in 1991, the program deployed U.S. assistance to hasten and facilitate cooperation among Russia, Ukraine, Kazakhstan, and Belarus on denuclearization, dismantlement of nuclear weapon systems, and strengthening of measures against the proliferation of weapons of mass destruction. The program was highly instru-

in convincing Ukraine, Kazakhstan, and Belarus to become nonnuclear powers and to surrender their nuclear warheads to Russia for destruction. Overall, the program is a powerful example of the constructive regional leverage that could result from Western assistance programs.[41]

Western or multilateral assistance and engagement might also be used to encourage regional cooperation in the economic sphere. In the Caucasus, for example, regional competition over energy resources in the Caspian Sea could lead to conflict in the future among post-Soviet states that lay claim to these resources: Russia, Azerbaijan, Kazakhstan, and Turkmenistan.[42] While the politics of Caspian Sea oil and pipelines are too complicated to be discussed at length here, one scholar concludes that the inclusion of Russian firms in oil exploration projects in the Caspian has had a judicious effect in mitigating residual imperialist impulses in Russia. Such inclusion has helped dampen strands of aggressive nationalism and helped create a domestic lobby for a moderate Russian foreign policy in the region.[43]

The United States is an important player in the politics of Caspian Sea oil. Its own interests include assistance to American oil companies that want to take part in any oil boom; the diversification of future U.S. energy sources; and the isolation of Iran, which borders the Caspian Sea and has claims to its resources. It would be unrealistic to expect the United States to set aside these interests and altruistically make regional cooperation the centerpiece of policy. At the same time, U.S. policymakers should carefully address the relationship between American interests and regional stability; clearly, severe instability would jeopardize any long-term pursuit of U.S. interests. Thus far, the U.S. role has been mixed: on one hand, U.S. policymakers should be commended for statements encouraging Russian inclusion in Caspian Sea oil and gas deals, and for ignoring such provocative proposals as those made by Azerbaijani officials to build U.S. military bases in Azerbaijan. On the other hand, U.S. policy has tilted clearly toward Azerbaijan, Kazakhstan, and Turkmenistan, creating tensions with Russia while lending support to authoritarian regimes and ignoring environmental concerns in the Caspian. Perhaps the United States is not the best actor to take the lead in fostering cooperative outcomes in the Caspian. The World Bank, the IMF, and the United Nations (through its environmental program) are involved in the region as well, and these multilateral entities may be the more appropriate actors to provide incentives for regional economic cooperation.[44]

2. Foreign Direct Investment and Russian Market Reform

The August 1998 financial meltdown in Russia led to widespread criticism of the role of international financial institutions (IFIs)—especially the IMF—and other Western actors in Russian market reform. Revelations and allegations subsequent August 1998 help to bolster this criticism. A common and specific accusation is the IMF supplied Russia with loans even when Russian policymakers repeatfailed to deliver on their economic obligations and promises. In addition, tions such as the U.S. Agency for International Development (USAID) facilitated large-scale mass privatization—a process marked by widespread corruption and cronyism. This model of privatization failed to bring market discipline to the Russian economy and intensified the looting of Russian assets and resources.[45]

The role of Western states and institutions in Russia's economic transition will likely be controversial for a long time. But should Western actors disengage from Russian market reform? The answer is no. Russian stability in the coming years will depend very much on the building of a more functional market economy—one with rules and structures that will make it easier for the majority of Russians to provide for their material welfare and thus feel greater economic security. Toward this end, it would be advisable for Western economic assistance to focus on strengthening the infrastructure that would help attract foreign investment to Russia and also convince domestic capital to stay inside Russia. The litany on this infrastructure is well known: tax reform, international accounting standards, transparency and corporate governance, banking reform, and accountability to donors. While none of these issues can be resolved quickly, incremental progress in each area might be possible under a more disciplined and politically stable post-Yeltsin government. Genuine improvement in the economy in the future could only add to the stability that is important for a more benign type of nationalism to develop in Russia.

3. Social and Cultural Spheres

Western states, nongovernmental organizations (NGOs), and multilateral institutions have been very active in rendering assistance in the social and cultural spheres in Russia in the past decade. Indeed, one might argue that never before in Russian history has there been such a massive inflow of Western ideas and actors into Russia and, at the same time, a massive outflow of Russians to study and observe Western social and cultural ideas and practices. Western assistance and activity in the social and cultural spheres have addressed a wide range of policy areas: education, history-writing, environmental preservation, cultural legacy, legal reform, health, science, mass media, philanthropy, women's rights, conflict prevention, and many others.[46]

It is difficult to pin down or quantify the efficacy of Western social and cultural assistance activities in Russia, although some institutions (e.g., USAID) try to do so.[47] The impact of many of these endeavors is unlikely to be obvious immediately, but will appear only in the medium and long term. The more important point is that, however imperfect, these activities tend to contribute to the development of a civil society in Russia, defined as "an overlapping network of civic associations that binds a population into a society autonomous of the state."[48] This purpose is extremely important, given the historical weakness of Russian society vis-à-vis state power (a theme emphasized in this book). If numerous and robust mechanisms and institutions develop to articulate society's interests to state authorities and bring pressure to bear on behalf of those interests, then it i̇ likely that future Russian national priorities will become oriented toward servi the well-being of the people. Such an outcome would definitely contribute to consolidation of a benign Russian nationalism.

It would be advisable in the future for Western actors to continue and even increase their social and cultural assistance programs in Russia. These programs will be vital in the long term to the normalization of Russian relations with the international community and to Russia's integration with Western states. There is no room here to critique in detail the range of Western projects involving Russian social and cultural policies, but a few recommendations are in order. First, funders of these projects should solicit independent and regular evaluation of their programs and implement corrections when and where necessary. In addition, assistance programs should give the bulk of resources (with appropriate oversight) to Russians rather than expensive Western consultants or advisers. Russians have the greatest stake in their country's fate, and they should have the opportunity to design and manage projects that would be most appropriate to their particular dilemmas and concerns. The role of Russians is particularly important in projects that aim to direct Russian discourse away from its imperial past. Support should be forthcoming especially for individuals and groups who are engaged in creating a useable but non-imperial past, and who can skillfully weave from Russia's rich historical, cultural, and philosophical legacy a vision of a civic, pluralistic, and confident Russian nation.[49] Third, where considerable synergies exist, outside donors and activists should encourage Russians to collaborate with other CIS and Western organizations—for example, on environmental or history-writing projects. Such collaborative efforts could help diminish animosities, facilitate mutual learning, and create social networks to counteract chauvinism, xenophobia, and other elements of extreme nationalism.[50]

WITHOUT A CRYSTAL BALL: WHITHER RUSSIA?

The West must not take present Russian weakness as a guarantee of Russian inaction on major foreign policy issues in the long term. As this book shows, weakness alone has not stopped Russian policymakers in the past from behaving forcefully and yielding to aggressive nationalist recommendations in foreign policy. Critical factors that pushed Russia over the brink in the past included perceptions of threat, international crises, and the portent of further and unacceptable humiliation. In 1875–78 and 1914, Russian policymakers gambled on nationalist mobilization in a desperate attempt to bolster their shaky hold on power and to prove that Russia could still be a significant player in the international arena. The present period is one of tremendous uncertainty for Russia. Potential positive outcomes—especially Russia's evolution into a viable, modern, unified state—will be more likely if international actors refrain from further humiliating what was once a great power. Russia once again finds itself needing time and space to focus on internal reform. This time around, a chance exists for Russia to transform itself, ⊃ shape a post-Soviet, non-imperial national identity and institutionalize a state ɑt is more responsive and accountable to society. Having gotten rid of commu-ɴ and jettisoned the old empire, Russians have the chance to join what they selves have called the community of "normal, civilized nations."

This book was completed nearly a decade after the breakup of the Soviet Union and the birth of Russia as a new state. The euphoria that marked the early period after the breakup of Soviet communism has yielded to pessimism and even dire predictions among Western observers and analysts. Some use the phrase "Weimar Russia" to refer to what they believe is a likely future scenario—a Russia with an aggressive nationalist ideology, authoritarian domestic politics, and a dangerous foreign policy. Few are genuinely optimistic about Russia's early transformation to a stable, pluralistic political system based on the rule of law, and those with any optimism at all quip in a hardly reassuring way that Russia after all is a "land of miracles."[51]

Russia today is in fact a weak and humiliated state whose people have not completely discarded the belief that there was a "great" past based on imperial power. The central question for the coming decades is whether or not Russian state and society will fully reject the imperial tradition and make a choice to follow a benign variant of the nation-state: one whose people and government are united by a civic national identity, non-imperial definitions of state power and greatness, and internally directed national goals. Gorbachev, however ambivalent and confused his policies may have been, deserved credit for launching, intentionally or unintentionally, the greatest and most courageous experiment of redirecting Russia from a past marked by authoritarian and imperial government. As the historian Alfred Rieber argues, Gorbachev set out on a gargantuan task to solve the paradox of power in Russia by ending "the contradiction of a powerful superstructure resting on a weak socioeconomic base; [to] offer a third choice lying between monolithic state control and civil war; and to [remake] a great power confident of its stability and security."[52] In other words, Gorbachev hoped to be a truly modernizing leader, seeking to make state–society relations more coherent and less rooted in fear and coercion.

The denouement of Gorbachev's brave experiment, unfortunately, was the disintegration of the Soviet state. Although his successors in post-Soviet Russia no longer have to deal with the complex ethnic mosaic of the dimension of the Soviet Union, nonetheless they too face the challenge of consolidating a new Russian national identity and establishing cohesion between state and society. Some factors might help make their task slightly simpler than Gorbachev's. First, Russia as it exists now does have a seventy-year geographic past as the Russian Federation (RSFSR) in the Soviet Union. This might mitigate the artificiality of its new borders and diminish resistance to the idea of a smaller, non-imperial Russia. Second, Russia today is more ethnically homogeneous than ever before in its history and is unencumbered by massive, contiguous imperial domains. The debate has been lively and energetic on what kind of nation Russia should become and what its purposes should be. An awesome responsibility rests on those who are now making a new Russian history, particularly the liberal camp in Russian politics. Liberal-minded politicians cannot let communists, fascists, and extremists take the lead in formulating and propagating definitions of the Russian "nation." must be at the forefront of the struggle to nurture pride and love in Rus they must emphasize a Russia defined in non-imperial terms, a Russia state answers to the people, and a Russia that shuns the ways of the old bloated state and emaciated society. Unfortunately, the divisiveness of Russian liberals has hindered the formation of a more united language focused on national pride and identity. Liberals have become vulnerable to charges of fawning over the West while neglecting Russian interests. It is a complex task for Russian liberals to adopt the language of nationalism. But given that the "nation" is a malleable category, they must do more to articulate their own positive version of who belongs to the Russian nation, the basis of Russian greatness, and the causes worthy of people's commitment and sacrifice.

The political philosopher Igor' Chubais has declared that the post-Soviet period may be "Russia's last chance to understand itself, to make the transition from expansion to domestic reconstruction, to gather stones and not throw away stones."[53] Russians as a people must choose and recreate a national identity (and even a nationalist ideology—in the sense of defining their preferred social order as a people and the path toward it). At a time of great dislocation, particular nationalist ideas could help serve as motors of well-being at home and peaceful relations abroad. The past gives much reason for pessimism, as do recent worrisome developments in Russia's international environment and seemingly intractable internal political, economic, and social problems. Will Russians be able to overcome their problems by exercising collective wit? Will leaders be found with greater integrity, professionalism, and national devotion than those who have been at the center of Russian politics since 1991? Will external actors play a more constructive role in the evolution of Russian statehood and nationhood? All good things do not come together. But in the Russian case, the overthrow of communism, the partial erosion of imperial discourse, and the absence of mass support for extremist nationalism until 1998 are a few signs of the reservoir of patience, reasoning, and desire for a better life of the Russian people. This creates the main foundation of hope for the future: Russians as a people and a nation in the making—who more or less understand what their most important choices are—have learned from their past, and will choose actions appropriate for their own welfare and prosperity.

NOTES

1. Hans Rogger, "Nationalism and the State: A Russian Dilemma," *Comparative Studies of Society and History* 4 (1962):253. Similarly, Richard Pipes recently accentuated what he calls the absence of a "well-developed sense of nationhood and statehood" among Russians. See Richard Pipes, "Introduction," in Heyward Isham, ed., *Remaking Russia: Voices from Within* (Armonk, N.Y.: Sharpe, 1995) p. 4.

2. An exception might be the late 1930s and early 1940s, when socialist-spurred socio10omic development did create a sense of national pride among Russians and facilitated nalist mobilization during World War II. The author thanks Donald L. M. Blackmer ing this point.

nhard Bendix, *Nation-Building and Citizenship: Studies of our Changing Social* keley: University of California Press, 1977), p. xii.

4. Leonard W. Doob, *Patriotism and Nationalism: Their Psychological Foundations* (New Haven: Yale University Press, 1964), p. 263.

5. These scenarios are unlikely to materialize fully or occur in an instant and be sustainable. They are described here as general, interpretive guides to Russia's future. In the next decade, there will likely be intermediate outcomes to lend credence to the argument that one type of scenario is unfolding as opposed to another. The negative scenario, if it occurs soon, will likely be unsustainable given Russia's extreme economic weakness. Without economic power, Russia will be unable to sustain an aggressive foreign policy. But in the short term, it can certainly cause instability of great magnitude both in its periphery and in more far-flung areas.

6. See, for example, Uri Ra'anan and Kate Martin, eds., *Russia: A Return to Imperialism?* (New York: St. Martin's, 1996).

7. As Henry Hale cogently summarizes in a research article, Russia "has not, in fact, invested much effort in 'reintegrating' the former Soviet space. Instead, powerful market-oriented political forces have consistently led Russia to torpedo every good chance it has had to reunify some of the newly independent states (NIS). . . . What is most striking about these foreign policy trends is that these patterns of behavior have been *structural* and have persisted despite many changes in top government personnel and political atmosphere." See Henry E. Hale, "The Rise of Russian Anti-Imperialism," *Orbis* (Winter 1999):1–16.

8. Rogers Brubaker, *Nationalism Reframed: Nationhood and the National Question in the New Europe* (Cambridge, UK: Cambridge University Press, 1996), p. 20.

9. Tatarstan's intellectual and political leaders have been assertive about their own identity, their rights vis-à-vis Moscow authorities, and their people's old and great culture and history. See, for example, the content of a journal published in Tatarstan, *Panorama-Forum* 1 (1997), with articles by Tatarstan president Mintimer Shaimiev and one of his top political advisers, Rafael' Khakimov. In 1998, protests by Tatarstan and Bashkortostan led the Russian government to amend its law on citizenship to allow Russians to include retroactively their ethnicity or nationality on their birth certificates. The Russian government originally wanted to remove all references to ethnicity from both birth certificates and internal passports of Russian citizens.

10. Chechnya poses perhaps the most difficult challenge to Russian interethnic cohesion—even on civic nationalist terms. The republic's de facto independence from the Russian government, its near-absence of governance and cohesive authority, and the war and destruction wrought by the Russian central government in its war in Chechnya in 1994–96 and in 1999 will make the reintegration of this republic into the Russian Federation extremely difficult. One very slim hope is that the Russian economy will recover and the central government will be able to fund incentives for Chechens to want to reintegrate politically and economically with Russia. The difficulty of finding common ground between Moscow and Chechen authorities was apparent in face-to-face discussions at The Hague attended by this author in 1997. See personal notes, Peace Palace, The Hague, April 22–24, 1997. See also *The Search for Peace in Chechnya: A Sourcebook 1994–1996* (Produced by Diane Curran, Fiona Hill, and Elena Kostritsyna), Project on Strengthening Democratic Institutions, Harvard University, March 1997.

11. For example, a review of a government-sponsored book on Russian history from the ninth to the twentieth centuries highlights the Topol M, Russia's newest intercontinent ballistic missile, as a key manifestation of Russian power and glory and something t' Russians can "hold on to" and "be grateful for." See Valerii Kucher, "1998: Hopes Sources of Support," *Rossiiskie vesti*, 6 January 1998. See also a forthcoming dissertat'

Russian history textbooks by David Mendeloff, Political Science Department, Massachusetts Institute of Technology, 2000.

12. Igor' Chubais, "Chto takoe ideinyi krizis, ili kak Rossii vosstanovit' svoiu identichnost'," *Izvestiia*, 17 June 1998, p. 4.

13. See the text and extensive footnotes in Stephen Van Evera, "Hypotheses on Nationalism and War," in Michael E. Brown, et al., eds., *Nationalism and Ethnic Conflict* (Cambridge: MIT Press, 1996–97), pp. 48–52.

14. See, for example, John Varoli, "Russia Prefers to Forget," *Transitions*, 4 July 1997, pp. 35–41; Mark Kramer, "Backward to the Future," *Washington Post*, 1 December 1996, pp. C1–2; and Sergei Kortunov, *Rossiia: Natsional'naia identichnost' na rubezhe vekov* (Moscow: Moskovskii obshchestvennyi nauchnyi fond, 1997), pp. 33–43. Kortunov pithily asks, "is it not time for us to stop repenting [of the past]?"

15. See, for example, the extensive compilation of government statements and documents on Chechnya in *The Search for Peace in Chechnya*, March 1997; and Sergei Kovalev, "Russia after Chechnya," *New York Review of Books*, 17 July 1997, pp. 27–31. Another worrisome development, in May 1999, was the glossing over by "reform" elites such as Anatolii Chubais of the record of then newly confirmed prime minister Sergei Stepashin in instigating the war in Chechnya and violating human rights and democratic norms in that war. See "Chubais on Stepashin and the 'Irreversibility' of Russian Reform" (Summary by Elizabeth Reisch of Chubais's comments at the Carnegie Endowment for International Peace) in *Johnson's Russia List*, electronic version, No. 3294, 20 May 1999.

16. Kovalev concludes that the "Chechen crisis was the first serious battle for democracy in Russia. It would be going too far to say that our newborn, weak, sickly, uncertain civil society won this battle. But at least it didn't lose. Peace in the North Caucasus is probably all we are capable of today. And this is of course much less than is needed in order to win the future for Russia." See Kovalev, "Russia after Chechnya," p. 31.

17. The importance of symbols in the development of nationalism is a central theme in Paul R. Brass, *Ethnicity and Nationalism: Theory and Comparison* (New Delhi: Sage, 1991).

18. See Valery Tishkov, *Ethnicity, Nationalism, and Conflict in and after the Soviet Union: The Mind Aflame* (London: Sage, 1997), p. 266; and David Hoffman, "Russia's New Internal Passport Drops Nationality, Drawing Praise and Protests," *Washington Post*, 25 October 1997, p. A20. My thanks to Steven Solnick and Eduard Ponarin for pointing me to information on the origins of the tricolor flag; see http: www.fotw.net/flags/ru.html.

19. Dmitrii Likhachev, "I Object: What Constitutes the Tragedy of Russian History," in Isham, ed., *Remaking Russia*, p. 63.

20. The information in the previous two paragraphs has been culled from numerous reports by the Jewish Telegraphic Agency, the Union of Councils for Soviet Jews, and Radio Free Europe/Radio Liberty. See also United States, Department of State, *Country Report on Human Rights Practices*, 1997 and 1998; "Russia Police Detain 19 Neo-Nazis," Associated Press, 8 February 1999; and "Fascists Sentenced in Yaroslavl," OMRI (Open Media Research Institute) Daily Digest, 14 March 1996. The role of Moscow mayor Yurii Luzhkov in combating extremism has been interesting. Although Luzhkov many times has made provocative nationalist claims such as the return of Sevastopol to Russia or the sending of Russian troops to fight on behalf of Serbian troops against NATO, nonetheless, he has also been at the forefront in combating neo-Nazism in Moscow. Thus, he has provoked the ire of anti-mitic groups that, in May 1999, distributed leaflets portraying him wearing a yarmulke falsely claiming that he was a Jew.

. Ilya Prizel, *National Identity and Foreign Policy: Nationalism and Leadership in 1, Russia and Ukraine* (Cambridge, UK: Cambridge University Press, 1998), p. 154.

22. Prizel, *National Identity and Foreign Policy*, p. 108. See also pp. 38–152 for a full treatment of the evolution of Polish nationalism.

23. Timothy J. Colton, "Gorbachev and the Politics of System Renewal," in Seweryn Bialer and Michael Mandelbaum, eds., *Gorbachev's Russia and American Foreign Policy* (Boulder: Westview, 1988), pp. 153–54; and Erik P. Hoffmann, "The Dynamics of State–Society Relations in Post-Soviet Russia," in Harry Eckstein, et al., eds., *Can Democracy Take Root in Post-Soviet Russia?* (Lanham, Md.: Rowman & Littlefield, 1998), p. 95.

24. Robert Tucker quotes the late Evgenii Gnedin, who, in 1978, remarked that the "state or state apparatus [in the Soviet Union], on the one hand, and society, on the other, are evolving in separate directions." See Robert C. Tucker, *Political Culture and Leadership in Soviet Russia* (New York: Norton, 1987), pp. 162–71.

25. L. D. Gudkov, "Russkii neotraditsionalizm," *Informatsionnyi biulleten' monitoringa*, 2 (March/April 1997), p. 26; Richard B. Dobson, *Is Russia Turning the Corner? Changing Russian Public Opinion 1991–1996* (Washington, D.C.: United States Information Agency, September 1996), p. 38; and Leonid Sedov, "Russian Government Not Legitimate, People Say," *Obshchaia gazeta*, 23 July 1998 (translation by RIA Novosti).

26. For example, Russian leaders and their Western advisers have been known to promise that the end to economic hardship was just around the corner.

27. For example, social subsidies are currently not well targeted in Russia. They are given to approximately 1,100 categories of people and cover more than 60 percent of the total population. See Andrew Jack, "Bleak Future for the Poor," *Financial Times*, Russia Annual Country Report, 30 April 1999, p. v. For further elaboration of some of the points made in this paragraph, see Pauline Jones Luong, "The Current Economic Crisis in Russia is Neither," Program on New Approaches to Russian Security, Policy Memo No. 35, Harvard University, November 1998.

28. See, for example, Sergei Glaziev, "Russofobiia: Chtoby vyzhit', nam nado perestat' nadeiat'sia na drugikh," *Nezavisimaia gazeta*, 18 November 1997; "Zhul'nichestvo XX veka: Zachem Rossiia kormit' Zapad?" *Sovetskaia Rossiia*, 2 June 1994, p. 1; and Tat'iana Koshkareva and Rustam Narzikulov, "Istinnaia tsena milliardov MVF neizvestna, poskol'ku sut' kreditnykh dogovorennostei derzhitsia v glubokoi taine," *Nezavisimaia gazeta*, 15 July 1998.

29. "Russian Public Opposes NATO Actions in Yugoslavia, Poll Shows," Moscow, Bloomberg, 13 April 1999; Michael Wines, "Hostility to U.S. Is Now Popular with Russians: Bombing of Yugoslavia Shifts Public Feeling," *New York Times*, 12 April 1999, pp. A1, A9; and Ekaterina A. Stepanova, *Explaining Russia's Dissension on Kosovo*, Program on New Approaches to Russian Security, Policy Memo No. 57, Harvard University, March 1999, p. 2.

30. Serbia has never been a passive and compliant ally to Moscow, often using Moscow to strengthen its own state-building project (in the nineteenth and early twentieth centuries), but rejecting Moscow's official policy line and advice when their interests diverged. In the Soviet period, Yugoslavia under Josip Broz Tito was considered to have the greatest independence of the Eastern European satellite states. On Russian–Serbian tensions after Kosovo in 1999, see, for example, Chris Hedges, "Angry Serbs Hear a New Explanation: It's All Russia's Fault," *New York Times*, 16 July 1999, p. A9.

31. Oksana Yablokova, "Russian Doctors Fly to Aid of Yugoslavs," *Moscow Times*, 11 1999; "Russians in Novi Sad as NATO Bombs Oil Refinery," Agence France Presse, 5 1999; and Irina Borogan and Aleksandr Krylov, "Volunteers Are Going to Fight Balkan War," *Segodnia*, 24 May 1999, pp. 1–2.

32. John Lloyd, "The Russian Devolution," *The New York Times Magazine*, 1999, p. 61.

33. Wines, "Hostility to U.S. Is Now Popular with Russians," p. A9; Stepanova, *Explaining Russia's Dissension*, pp. 1–3; and "NATO Is Creating an International Precedent: The 'Kosovo Scenario' Could Be Played Out on the Territory of Any Country Including Russia," *Krasnaia zvezda*, 26 June 1998.

34. Gennadii Zyuganov, "Stop the Aggression!" *Zavtra*, March–April 1999, No. 13 (278), p. 1; and "A Toothless Growl," *The Economist*, 1 May 1999, p. 48.

35. Seleznev's spokesman later claimed that his boss's words had been misinterpreted. See Greg Myre, "Yeltsin Discussed Targeting NATO," Associated Press, 9 April 1999.

36. See Aleksei Pushkov, "Disgust" and Vitaly Tretiakov, "In Anticipation of a Split," *Nezavisimaia gazeta*, 26 March 1999, pp. 1 and 3; Vitaly Tretiakov, "Two Unambiguous Answers," *Nezavisimaia gazeta*, 1 April 1999, p. 1; Aleksandr Bovin, "Prestige Is Worth More Than Money," *Izvestiia*, 25 March 1999, p. 4; Maksim Yusin, "The Russian Echo of the Balkan War," *Izvestiia*, 26 March 1999, p. 1; and Michael R. Gordon, "Moscow Opposes Air Raids, but Is Miffed at Serbs," *New York Times*, 23 March 1999, p. A11.

37. "O konturakh plana prekrashcheniia agressii protiv Iugoslavii," Zaiavleniie Soveta po vneshnei i oboronnoi politike, *Nezavisimaia gazeta*, 19 May 1999; and Viktor Chernomyrdin, "Impossible to Talk Peace with Bombs Falling," *Washington Post*, 27 May 1999.

38. See chapter 5.

39. See "Russia and the Death Penalty—A Fact Sheet," Human Rights Watch website (http://www.hrw.org), June 1999.

40. Of the former Soviet republics that have expressed an interest in joining NATO, the Baltic states have received the warmest response. In July 1999, for example, Deputy Secretary of State Strobe Talbott declared at a State Department meeting that "The Baltic states are not only eligible for [NATO] membership but desirable. [Despite Russian objections] I [reiterate] our strong position that no state should be excluded from NATO membership on grounds of history or geography." See "Baltic States Determined to Move on NATO Enlargement," DPA, Washington, D.C., 16 July 1999.

41. For specifics on the Cooperative Threat Reduction Program, see Craig Cerniello, "U.S. Security Assistance to the Former Soviet Union," *Arms Control Today* (September 1996):25–26; and William J. Perry, *Report of the Secretary of Defense to the President and the Congress* (Washington, D.C.: U.S. Government Printing Office, 1996), pp. 63–70.

42. Iran, while not a post-Soviet state, also has claims to energy resources in the Caspian.

43. Henry Hale explores this idea more fully in his "The Rise of Russian Anti-Imperialism," pp. 1–16.

44. The problems related to the exploitation of Caspian Sea resources seem best suited for multilateral solutions that international organizations can facilitate. See, e.g., the analysis in Douglas Blum, "Sustainable Development and the New Oil Boom: Cooperative and Competitive Outcomes in the Caspian Sea," Harvard University, Program on New Approaches to Russian Security, Working Paper No. 4, May 1998. For an overview of international organizations and the issues they address through assistance programs in Azerbaijan (and these issues seem suited for regional collaboration), see "IMF Approves Third Annual ESAF Loan for Azerbaijan and Financing under the CCFF and EFF," Press Release 99/5, International Monetary Fund, 26 January 1999.

See, for example, Catherine Belton, "Zadornov Admits Russia Lied to IMF," *Moscow* August 1999; "Boldyrev Says Foreign Loans 'Senselessly Squandered,'" *Jamestown Monitor*, 2 August 1999; and Mark Kramer, "U.S. Policy and Russia's Economic

Plight: Lessons from the Meltdown," Harvard University, Project on New Approaches to Russian Security, Policy Memo No. 37, November 1998.

46. The author was a program officer at Carnegie Corporation from 1994 to 1998 and had firsthand involvement and familiarity with many types of assistance projects to Russia and the Newly Independent States (NIS).

47. USAID uses a grading scale of 1 to 7 to measure the degree of NGO sustainability. The 1998 version of the NGO Sustainability Index covers twenty-three countries in the former Soviet Union and eastern and central Europe.

48. James Richter, "Promoting Activism or Professionalism in Russia's Civil Society?" Harvard University, Project on New Approaches to Russian Security, Policy Memo No. 51, November 1998.

49. Aileen Kelly highlights a minority countertradition in Russian literature and philosophy that emphasizes pluralism, integrity, critical thought, and moral autonomy. Emphasizing this type of legacy can help the evolution of benign Russian nationalist ideology and, in Kelly's words, help Russia become "part of the West on its own terms." See Aileen M. Kelly, *Views from the Other Shore: Essays on Herzen, Chekhov, and Bakhtin* (New Haven, Conn.: Yale University Press, 1999).

50. This author, for example, while working as a foundation program officer, helped secure funding for a series of conferences and publications in Russia involving Russian, CIS, and Western scholars. The CIS scholars represented numerous ethnic groups and their goal was to discuss and analyze the concept of "Eurasia." In what ways did Russia influence the culture of other peoples of the former Soviet Union, and how did these peoples influence Russian culture in return? The program was designed to foster dialogue on mutual influences among the peoples of the former Soviet Union (as opposed to chauvinism by any particular group) and to contribute to renewing scholarly ties among scholars in the CIS.

51. John Thornhill, "The Voice of Modern Liberalism," *Financial Times*, 30 April 1999, Russia Annual Country Report, p. iv.

52. Alfred J. Rieber, "Persistent Factors in Russian Foreign Policy: An Interpretive Essay," in Hugh Ragsdale, ed. *Imperial Russian Foreign Policy* (Cambridge, UK: Cambridge University Press, 1993), p. 358.

53. Chubais, "Chto takoe ideinyi krizis," p. 4.

Postscript

As this book goes to press, Vladimir Putin recently won Russia's presidential elections. In the relatively brief time that Putin has been at the center of Russian politics, it has become clear that nationalism will be an important feature of his leadership. Putin has emphasized time and again the importance of patriotism, which he has defined as "a feeling of pride in the fatherland, its history and achievements. If we lose patriotism and national pride, we will deteriorate as a people; we will no longer have the capacity for great deeds."[1] He has also focused on the need for social consensus and underlined the restoration of a strong state as the key to Russian renaissance. In his words, "A strong state for Russia is not an anomaly . . . but on the contrary is the source and guarantor of order, the initiator and main driving force of all change." Although he has confirmed that Russia is a European state whose "isolation from Europe and . . . the civilized world" was unimaginable, he also has declared that Russia is not like the United States or Great Britain, where "liberal values have deep historic roots."[2]

Overall, Putin's rhetoric may be characterized as belonging to the moderate statist nationalism described in this book. His view of Russia as a nation that combines traditional Russian values and universal human values, emphasis on a "worthy life" (*dostoinaia zhizn'*) for all Russian citizens, and focus on the "supremacy of internal goals over external ones"[3] create the impression that his nationalism is largely benign. However, there are several attributes of Putin's leadership that also connote a more worrisome type of nationalism. First, Putin's popularity in Russia (and, hence, the near- consensus around his leadership) grew so fast only because he ruthlessly prosecuted a brutal war in Chechnya, causing untold destruction. Although he has not employed ethnic Russian chauvinist arguments, he has nonetheless systematically dehumanized the Chechens as "bandits," "terrorists," "scum," and "dark forces" and disparaged Chechnya as a "world of banditry" or "fortress" of terrorist In describing the captured and disfigured Chechen commander Salman Raduv Putin said: "[Raduyev was] one of those who terrorized . . . Great Russia" and "some kind of animal. . . . [We] will bring all of them to this condition." rhetoric contributes to a revival of Russian imperial discourse and the whi ing of Russian oppression and crimes against another ethnic group. Put

tures against criticism and open press coverage of government policy in Chechnya also cloud the future of competent and open debate in Russia regarding the role of the state and its accountability to its citizens.[5] Second, the excessive use of force, scorched-earth tactics, and numerous reports of torture in the war in Chechnya underscore a blatant disregard for human and individual rights. The government's ultimatum for all residents to flee the Chechen capital, Grozny, by December 11, 1999, or "be viewed as terrorists and bandits . . . [and] be destroyed"[6] was particularly odious (but, fortunately, was not carried out after vigorous protest by Western states and international organizations). One implication of Putin's record on human rights is that he may well not be the kind of leader who can cultivate and deepen the civic space necessary for benign nationalism (one that acknowledges the people as the repository of political authority) to flourish.[7] Third, Putin's official acts returning former KGB chief Yurii Andropov's bust to its place at the KGB headquarters in Moscow, restoring military training in secondary schools, and strengthening the role of the former KGB in the armed forces[8] connote an atmosphere where, as in the past, the power of the state and its repressive organs could become overwhelming. Putin has yet to prove what his ultimate intentions are, but his reliance on the KGB as a symbol and institution of governance belies a lack of imagination on ideas and actions that might help Russia move away from its traditional history of the state growing "fat" while the people grew "thin."[9]

Surely Russia's new president deserves the benefit of the doubt in the near future. But a danger lies in the fact that Putin's domestic economic tasks will likely continue to be highly challenging, thus leading to domestic instability, while simultaneously the international environment may not prove benign for Russian interests if NATO expands further, the United States builds a national missile defense system, and Russia is edged out of such spheres of influence as the Caspian Sea. Add to these conditions a weakening anti-imperial discourse inside Russia, as evidenced by the war in Chechnya (whose resolution will be long in coming), and Putin's moderate statist nationalism could well slide down the slippery slope to a more aggressive variety of nationalist ideology.

NOTES

1. See "Vladimir Putin: Rossiia na rubezhe tysiacheletiia," *Rossiiskaia gazeta*, 31 December 1999, p. 4.

2. *BBC News Online*, 5 March 2000; and "Vladimir Putin: Rossiia na rubezhe tysiacheletiia," p. 4.

3. See "Vladimir Putin's Open Letter to Russian Voters," *Russia Today* (electronic version), 1 March 2000.

4. "Raduyev Maintains He Was Only Obeying Orders," *Moscow Times*, 18 March 2000.

5. On this point, see Andrei Piontkovsky, "Russia Goes Nuclear over Chechnya," *Prism* (electronic version), no. 17, part 3, September 1999; and Daniel Williams, "Freed Reporter Beatings by Russians," *International Herald Tribune*, 1 March 2000, p. 4.

6. "Russia Politics: Chechens the Pawns in Yeltsin's Game," *Economist Intelligence Unit Limited*, 7 December 1999.

7. On human rights and Chechnya, see Patrick E. Tyler, "At Russian Camp, 2 Views of Chechen Prisoners," *New York Times*, 1 March 2000, p. 10; Celestine Bohlen, "Russian Liberals Start to Rethink Their Support for Putin," *International Herald Tribune*, 3 March 2000, p. 5; and Physicians for Human Rights, Press Release, "Random Survey Conducted by U.S. Medical Group of Displaced Chechens Finds Widespread Killings," 26 February 2000.

8. On Putin's early official acts, see Masha Gessen, "Russian Society Regresses to a Military Mind-Set," *International Herald Tribune*, 1 March 2000, p. 11; and Michael Wines, "Putin Steering to Reform, But with a Soviet Discipline," *New York Times*, 20 February 2000, pp. 1, 14.

9. This phraseology refers to a quote by Vasilii Kliuchevskii, cited on p. 29.

Bibliography

BOOKS AND MONOGRAPHS

English

Allworth, Edward, ed. *Ethnic Russia in the USSR*. New York: Pergamon, 1980.

Anderson, Benedict. *Imagined Communities: Reflections on the Origins and Spread of Nationalism*. London: Verso, 1983.

Anderson, James, ed. *The Rise of the Modern State*. Brighton, Sussex, UK: Wheatsheaf, 1986.

Anderson, M. S. *The Eastern Question 1774–1923*. New York: St. Martin's, 1966.

Armstrong, John. *Nations before Nationalism*. Chapel Hill: University of North Carolina Press, 1982.

Ascher, Abraham. *The Revolution of 1905: Russia in Disarray*. Stanford: Stanford University Press, 1988.

Barghoorn, Frederick. *Soviet Russian Nationalism*. New York: Oxford University Press, 1956.

Barkey, Karen, and Mark Von Hagen, eds. *After Empire: Multiethnic Societies and Nation-Building*. Boulder: Westview, 1997.

Bendix, Reinhard. *Kings or People: Power and the Mandate to Rule*. New Brunswick, N.J.: Transaction, 1996.

———. *Kings or People: Power and the Mandate to Rule*. Berkeley: University of California Press, 1978.

———. *Nation-Building and Citizenship: Studies of Our Changing Social Order*. Berkeley: University of California Press, 1977.

Berghahn, V. R. *Germany and the Approach of War in 1914*. New York: St. Martin's, 1973.

Berlin, Isaiah. *Russian Thinkers*. New York: Penguin, 1978.

Bessel, Richard. *Germany after the First World War*. New York: Oxford University Press, 1993.

Betts, Richard. *Soldiers, Statesmen and Cold War Crises*. Cambridge: Harvard University Press, 1977.

Bialer, Seweryn. *Stalin's Successors: Leadership, Stability, and Change in the Soviet Un ̀ Cambridge, UK: Cambridge University Press, 1980.

———, ed. *Politics, Society, and Nationality inside Gorbachev's Russia*. Boulder: We 1989.

———. *The Domestic Context of Soviet Foreign Policy*. Boulder: Westview, 1981.

Bialer, Seweryn, and Michael Mandelbaum, eds., *Gorbachev's Russia and American Foreign Policy*. Boulder: Westview.

Bibliography on the OSCE High Commissioner on National Minorities, 2nd ed. The Hague: Foundation for Interethnic Relations, August 1995.

Billington, James H. *The Icon and the Axe: An Interpretive History of Russian Culture*. New York: Vintage, 1970.

Black, C. E. *The Dynamics of Modernization: A Study in Comparative History*. New York: Harper and Row, 1966.

Black, J. L. *Nicholas Karamzin and Russian Society in the Nineteenth Century*. Toronto: University of Toronto Press, 1975.

Brass, Paul R. *Ethnicity and Nationalism: Theory and Comparison*. New Delhi, India: Sage, 1991.

Breuilly, John. *Nationalism and the State*. 2nd ed. Chicago: University of Chicago Press, 1994.

——. *Nationalism and the State*. Manchester, UK: Manchester University Press, 1982.

Brooks, Jeffrey. *When Russia Learned to Read: Literacy and Popular Literature, 1861–1917*. Princeton: Princeton University Press, 1985.

Brown, Edward J. *Russian Literature since the Revolution*. Cambridge: Harvard University Press, 1982.

Brown, Michael, et al., eds. *Nationalism and Ethnic Conflict*. Cambridge: MIT Press, 1996–97.

Brubaker, Rogers. *Nationalism Reframed: Nationhood and the National Question in the New Europe*. Cambridge, UK: Cambridge University Press, 1996.

Brzezinski, Zbigniew. *The Grand Chessboard*. New York: Basic Books, 1996.

Carlton, Eric. *War and Ideology*. London: Routledge, 1990.

Carrère d'Encausse, Hélène. *The End of the Soviet Empire*. New York: Basic, 1993.

——. *Decline of an Empire*. New York: Harper and Row, 1979.

Carter, Stephen J. *Russian Nationalism Yesterday, Today, Tomorrow*. New York: St. Martin's, 1990.

The Caucasus and the Caspian, Vol. II. Harvard University, Strengthening Democratic Institutions Project, 1997.

Chaadaev, P. *Philosophical Letters and Apology of a Madman*. Translated by Mary-Barbara Zeldin. Knoxville: University of Tennessee Press, 1969.

Chadwick, Munro. *The Nationalities of Europe and the Growth of National Ideologies*. New York: Cooper Square, 1973; reprint of 1945 edition.

Charques, Richard. *The Twilight of Imperial Russia*. London: Oxford University Press, 1958.

Cherniavsky, Michael. *Tsar and People: Studies in Russian Myths*. New Haven: Yale University Press, 1961.

Christian, David. *Living Water: Vodka and Russian Society on the Eve of Emancipation*. Oxford: Clarendon, 1990.

Christoff, P. *An Introduction to Nineteenth-Century Russian Slavophilism: A Study in Ideas*. Vols. 1 and 2. The Hague: Mouton, 1961 and 1972.

CIS Migration Report. Geneva: International Organization for Migration, 1997.

Citizenship and Alien Law Controversies in Estonia and Latvia. Harvard University, Strengthening Democratic Institutions Project, April 1994.

wes, Edith W., et al., eds. *Between Tsar and People: Educated Society and the Quest for blic Identity in Late Imperial Russia*. Princeton: Princeton University Press, 1991.

r, Walker. *Ethnonationalism*. Princeton: Princeton University Press, 1994.

Conquest, Robert. *The Harvest of Sorrow: Soviet Collectivization and the Terror-Famine.* London: Hutchinson, 1986.

——, ed. *The Last Empire: Nationality and the Soviet Future.* Stanford: Hoover Institution Press, 1986.

Cortright, David, ed. *The Price of Peace: Incentives and International Conflict Prevention.* Lanham, Md.: Rowman & Littlefield, 1997.

Cracraft, James. *The Church Reform of Peter the Great.* London: Macmillan, 1971.

——, ed. *Major Problems in the History of Imperial Russia.* Lexington, Mass.: Heath, 1994.

Craig, Gordon A. *Germany 1866–1945.* New York: Oxford University Press, 1978.

Curtiss, John Shelton. *Russia's Crimean War.* Durham: Duke University Press, 1979.

Dahbour, Omar, and Micheline R. Ishay, eds. *The Nationalism Reader.* Atlantic Highlands, N.J.: Humanities Press, 1995.

Dallin, Alexander, and Gail W. Lapidus. *The Soviet System in Crisis.* Boulder: Westview, 1991.

Daniels, Robert V., ed. *A Documentary History of Communism.* Updated and rev. ed., vol. 1. Hanover, N.H.: University Press of New England, 1984.

DaVanzo, Julie, and David Adamson. *Russia's Demographic "Crisis": How Real Is It?* RAND Issue Paper, July 1997.

Dawisha, Karen, and Bruce Parrott. *Russia and the New States of Eurasia: The Politics of Upheaval.* Cambridge, UK: Cambridge University Press, 1994.

——, eds. *The End of Empire? The Transformation of the USSR in Comparative Perspective.* Armonk, N.Y.: Sharpe, 1997.

Deng, Francis, and William Zartman, eds. *Conflict Resolution in Africa.* Washington, D.C.: Brookings, 1991.

Denikin, Anton I. *The Career of a Tsarist Officer: Memoirs, 1872–1916.* Translated by Margaret Patoski. Minneapolis: University of Minnesota Press, 1975.

Deutsch, Karl W. *Nationalism and Social Communication: An Inquiry into the Foundations of Nationality.* 2nd ed. Cambridge: MIT Press, 1966.

Deutscher, Isaac. *Stalin: A Political Biography.* 2nd ed. New York: Oxford University Press, 1949.

DiMaggio, Paul J., and Walter W. Powell, eds. *The New Institutionalism in Organizational Analysis.* Chicago: University of Chicago Press, 1991.

Dobson, Richard B. *Is Russia Turning the Corner? Changing Russian Public Opinion, 1991–1996.* Washington, D.C.: U.S. Information Agency, September 1996.

Doob, Leonard. *Patriotism and Nationalism: Their Psychological Foundations.* New Haven: Yale University Press, 1964.

Dowler, Wayne. *Dostoevsky, Grigor'ev, and Native Soil Conservatism.* Toronto: University of Toronto Press, 1982.

Doyle, Michael. *Empires.* Ithaca: Cornell University Press, 1986.

Dunlop, John B. *The Rise of Russia and the Fall of the Soviet Empire.* Princeton: Princeton University Press, 1993.

——. *The New Russian Nationalism.* New York: Praeger, 1985.

——. *The Contemporary Faces of Russian Nationalism.* Princeton: Princeton University Press, 1983.

——. *The New Russian Revolutionaries.* Belmont, Mass.: Nordland, 1976.

Durman, Karel. *The Time of the Thunderer: Mikhail Katkov, Russian National Extremism and the Failure of the Bismarckian System, 1871–1887.* Boulder: East European Monographs, 1988.

Dyker, D. A. *The Process of Investment in the Soviet Union.* Cambridge, UK: Cambridge University Press, 1983.

Eckstein, Harry, et al. *Can Democracy Take Root in Post-Soviet Russia?* Lanham, Md.: Rowman & Littlefield, 1998.

Edelman, Robert. *Gentry Politics on the Eve of the Russian Revolution.* New Brunswick: Rutgers University Press, 1980.

Eisenhower, Susan, and Roald Z. Sagdeev, eds. *Central Asia: Conflict, Resolution, and Change.* Washington, D.C.: Center for Post-Soviet Studies, 1995.

Eklof, Ben. *Russian Peasant Schools: Officialdom, Village Culture, and Popular Pedagogy, 1861–1914.* Berkeley: University of California Press, 1986.

——, John Bushnell, and Larissa Zakharova, eds. *Russia's Great Reforms, 1855–1881.* Bloomington: Indiana University Press, 1994.

Eklof, Ben, and Stephen Frank, eds. *The World of the Russian Peasant: Post-Emancipation Culture and Society.* Boston: Unwin Hyman, 1990.

Emerson, Rupert. *From Empire to Nation: The Rise to Self-Assertion of Asian and African Peoples.* Boston: Beacon, 1960.

Emmons, Terence. *The Formation of Political Parties and the First National Elections in Russia.* Cambridge: Harvard University Press, 1983.

Evans, John L., ed. and trans. *Mission of N. P. Ignat'ev to Khiva and Bukhara in 1858.* Newtonville, Mass.: Oriental Research Partners, 1984.

Fadner, Frank J. *Seventy Years of Pan-Slavism in Russia: Karazin to Danilevsky 1800–1870.* Washington, D.C.: Georgetown University Press, 1962.

Falkus, M. E. *The Industrialization of Russia 1700–1914.* London: Macmillan, 1972.

Feuchtwanger, E. J. *From Weimar to Hitler: Germany, 1918–33.* London: Macmillan, 1993.

Fowkes, Ben. *The Disintegration of the Soviet Union: The Triumph of Nationalism.* London: Macmillan, 1997.

Fullbrook, Mary. *Germany, 1918–1990: The Divided Nation.* London: Fontana, 1991.

Fuller, Jr., William C. *Strategy and Power in Russia 1600–1914.* New York: Free Press, 1992.

Fuller, Jr., William C. *Civil–Military Conflict in Imperial Russia 1881–1914.* Princeton: Princeton University Press, 1985.

Garnett, Sherman W. *The Impact of the New Borderlands on the Russian Military.* Occasional Paper 9, International Security Studies Program, American Academy of Arts and Sciences, August 1995.

Geifman, Anna. *Thou Shalt Kill: Revolutionary Terrorism in Russia 1894–1917.* Princeton: Princeton University Press, 1993.

Gellner, Ernest. *Nations and Nationalism.* Ithaca: Cornell University Press, 1983.

Gerschenkron, Alexander. *Economic Backwardness in Historical Perspective.* Cambridge: Harvard University Press, 1962.

Geyer, Dietrich. *Russian Imperialism: The Interaction of Domestic and Foreign Policy in Russia 1860–1914.* Translated by Bruce Little. New Haven: Yale University Press, 1987.

Gleason, Abbott. *European and Muscovite: Ivan Kireevsky and the Origins of Slavophilism.* Cambridge: Harvard University Press, 1972.

Goldfrank, David M. *The Origins of the Crimean War.* New York: Longman, 1994.

Goldstein, Judith, and Robert O. Keohane, eds. *Ideas and Foreign Policy: Beliefs, Institutions, and Political Change.* Ithaca: Cornell University Press, 1993.

Gooch, G. P., and H. N. Temperley, eds. *British Documents on the Origins of the War.* Vol. X/1. London: H. M. Stationery Office, 1927–38.

Gourevitch, Philip. *We Wish to Inform You That Tomorrow We Will Be Killed with Our Families: Stories from Rwanda.* New York: Farrar, Straus, and Giroux, 1998.

Greenberg, Louis. *The Jews in Russia: The Struggle for Emancipation.* Vol. 2. New York: Schocken, 1976.

Greenfeld, Liah. *Nationalism: Five Roads to Modernity.* Cambridge: Harvard University Press, 1992.

Gurian, Waldemar, ed. *Soviet Imperialism: Its Origins and Tactics.* Notre Dame: University of Notre Dame Press, 1953.

Gurr, Ted, ed. *Handbook of Political Conflict.* New York: Free Press, 1980.

Haimson, Leopold, ed. *The Politics of Rural Russia 1905–1914.* Bloomington: Indiana University Press, 1979.

Hajda, Lubomyr, and Mark Beissinger, eds. *The Nationalities Factor in Soviet Politics and Society.* Boulder: Westview, 1990.

Hall, Peter. *The Political Power of Economic Ideas: Keynesianism across Nations.* Princeton: Princeton University Press, 1989.

Handelman, Stephen. *Comrade Criminal.* New Haven: Yale University Press, 1995.

Hanrieder, Wolfram F., ed. *Comparative Foreign Policy: Theoretical Essays.* New York: David McKay, 1971.

Harper, Samuel N. *The New Electoral Law for the Russian Duma.* Chicago: University of Chicago Press, 1908.

Hayes, C. J. H. *Essays on Nationalism.* New York: Russell and Russell, 1966.

———. *France: A Nation of Patriots.* New York: Columbia University Press, 1930.

Hellie, Richard. *Enserfment and Military Change in Muscovy.* Chicago: University of Chicago Press, 1971.

Helsinki Watch. *War or Peace? Human Rights and Russian Military Intervention in the "Near Abroad."* December 1993.

Hermann, Charles, et al., eds. *New Directions in the Study of Foreign Policy.* Boston: Allen and Unwin, 1987.

Hewett, Ed A., and Victor H. Winston, eds. *Milestones in Glasnost and Perestroyka: Politics and People.* Washington, D.C.: Brookings, 1991.

Hill, Fiona. "In Search of Great Russia: Elites, Ideas, Power, the State, and the Pre-Revolutionary Past in the New Russia, 1991–1996." Doctoral Thesis, History Department, Harvard University, 1998.

———, and Pamela Jewett. *"Back in the USSR." Russia's Intervention in the Internal Affairs of the Former Soviet Republics and the Implications for United States Policy toward Russia.* Strengthening Democratic Institutions Project, Harvard University, 1994.

Hobsbawm, Eric J. *Nations and Nationalism since 1780.* Cambridge, UK: Cambridge University Press, 1990.

———, and Terence Ranger, eds. *The Invention of Tradition.* Cambridge, UK: Cambridge University Press, 1983.

Holsti, Kalevi J. *Peace and War: Armed Conflicts and International Order 1648–1989.* New York: Cambridge University Press, 1991.

Hosking, Geoffrey. *Russia: People and Empire 1552–1917.* Cambridge: Harvard University Press, 1997.

———, and Robert Service, eds. *Russian Nationalism Past and Present.* New York: Martin's, 1998.

Hosking, Geoffrey A. *The Russian Constitutional Experiment, Government and 1907–1914.* Cambridge, UK: Cambridge University Press, 1973.

Hroch, Miroslav. *Social Conditions of National Revival in Europe.* Translated by Cambridge, UK: Cambridge University Press, 1985.

Hunczak, Taras, ed. *Russian Imperialism from Ivan the Great to the Revolution.* New Brunswick: Rutgers University Press, 1974.

Ikenberry, G. John, et al., eds. *The State and American Foreign Economic Policy.* Ithaca: Cornell University Press, 1988.

Isham, Heyward, ed. *Remaking Russia: Voices from Within.* Armonk, N.Y.: Sharpe, 1995.

Iswolsky, A. *The Memoirs of Alexander Iswolsky.* Gulf Breeze, Fla.: Academic International Press, 1974.

Jawad, Nassim, and Tadjbakhsh, Shahrbanou. *Tajikistan: A Forgotten Civil War.* London: Minority Rights Group, 1995.

Jelavich, Barbara. *Russia's Balkan Entanglements 1806–1914.* New York: Cambridge University Press, 1991.

———. *History of the Balkans: Eighteenth and Nineteenth Centuries.* Vol. 1. Cambridge, UK: Cambridge University Press, 1983.

———. *St. Petersburg and Moscow: Tsarist and Soviet Foreign Policy 1814–1974.* Bloomington: Indiana University Press, 1983.

Jelavich, Barbara, and Charles Jelavich. *Russia in the East 1876–1880.* Leiden, Netherlands: Brill, 1959.

———, eds. *The Education of a Russian Statesman: The Memoirs of Nicholas Karlovich Giers.* Berkeley: University of California Press, 1962.

Jelavich, Charles. *Tsarist Russia and Balkan Nationalism.* Berkeley: University of California Press, 1958.

Jervis, Robert. *Perception and Misperception in International Politics.* Princeton: Princeton University Press, 1976.

Jones, Gareth W. *Nikolay Novikov, Enlightener of Russia.* Cambridge, UK: Cambridge University Press, 1984.

Kagan, Donald. *On the Origins of War and the Preservation of Peace.* New York: Doubleday, 1995.

Kaiser, Robert J. *The Geography of Nationalism in Russia and the USSR.* Princeton: Princeton University Press, 1994.

Kamenskii, Aleksandr B. *The Russian Empire in the Eighteenth Century: Searching for a Place in the World.* Translated and edited by David Griffiths. Armonk, N.Y.: Sharpe, 1997.

Karnow, Stanley. *In Our Image: America's Empire in the Philippines.* New York: Ballantine, 1989.

Katz, Martin. *Mikhail N. Katkov: A Political Biography 1818–1887.* The Hague: Mouton, 1966.

Keep, John. *Soldiers and the Tsar: Army and Society in Russia 1462–1874.* Oxford: Clarendon, 1985.

Kellas, James G. *The Politics of Nationalism and Ethnicity.* New York: St. Martin's, 1991.

Kelly, Aileen M. *Views from the Other Shore. Essays on Herzen, Chekhov, and Bakhtin.* New Haven: Yale University Press, 1999.

Keohane, Robert, and Joseph Nye. *Power and Interdependence.* Glenview, Ill.: Scott, Foresman, 1989.

——hane, Robert, ed. *Neorealism and Its Critics.* New York: Columbia University Press, 1986.

—, Mohammad Anwar. *England, Russia, and Central Asia (A Study in Diplomacy)* ⁷–1878. Khyber Bazar-Peshawar: University Book Agency, 1963.

—ans. *The Mind of Modern Russia.* New Brunswick: Rutgers University Press, 1955.

—slavism: Its History and Ideology.* Notre Dame: University of Notre Dame Press,

—a of Nationalism.* New York: Collier, 1944.

Kokoshin, Andrei A. *Reflections on Russia's Past, Present, and Future.* Harvard University, Strengthening Democratic Institutions Project, 1997.

Kortunov, Sergei. *Russia's National Identity in a New Era.* Edited and translated by Richard Weitz. Cambridge: Harvard University, Strengthening Democratic Institutions Project, September 1998.

Kramer, Mark, ed. *The Collapse of the Soviet Union.* Boulder: Westview, 2000.

Krasnov, Vladislav. *Russia beyond Communism: A Chronicle of National Rebirth.* Boulder: Westview, 1991.

Kupchan, Charles A., ed. *Nationalism and Nationalities in the New Europe.* Ithaca: Cornell University Press, 1995.

Kuropatkin, Aleksei. *The Russian Army and the Japanese War.* New York: Dutton, 1909.

Laitin, David D. *Identity in Formation: The Russian-Speaking Populations in the Near Abroad.* Ithaca: Cornell University Press, 1998.

Landsberger, H. A., ed. *Rural Protest: Peasant Movements and Social Change.* London: Macmillan, 1974.

Lanin, E. B. *Russian Characteristics.* London: Chapman and Hall, 1892.

Lapidus, Gail, ed., *The New Russia: Troubled Transformation* (Boulder: Westview Press, 1995).

Lapidus, Gail, et al., eds. *From Union to Commonwealth: Nationalism and Separatism in the Soviet Republics.* Cambridge, UK: Cambridge University Press, 1992.

Laqueur, Walter. *Black Hundred: The Rise of the Extreme Right in Russia.* New York: Harper-Collins, 1993.

———. *The Long Road to Freedom.* New York: Macmillan, 1989.

Lauren, Paul, ed. *Diplomacy: New Approaches in History, Theory and Policy.* New York: Free Press, 1979.

Lavrin, Janko. *Russia, Slavdom, and the Western World.* London: Geoffrey Bles, 1969.

Layton, Susan. *Russian Literature and Empire: Conquest of Caucasus from Pushkin to Tolstoy.* New York: Cambridge University Press, 1994.

Le Bon, Gustave. *The World in Revolt.* Translated by Bernard Miall. London: Unwin, 1921.

Lederer, Ivo J., ed. *Russian Foreign Policy: Essays in Historical Perspective.* New Haven: Yale University Press, 1962.

Levin, Alfred. *The Third Duma, Election and Profile.* Hamden, Conn.: Archon, 1973.

———. *The Second Duma. A Study of the Social-Democratic Party and the Russian Constitutional Experiment.* 2nd ed. Hamden, Conn.: Archon, 1966.

Lewin, Moshe. *The Gorbachev Phenomenon: A Historical Interpretation.* Berkeley: University of California Press, 1989.

Lieven, Anatol. *Chechnya: Tombstone of Russian Power.* New Haven: Yale University Press, 1998.

Lieven, Dominic. *Russia's Rulers under the Old Regime.* New Haven: Yale University Press, 1989.

———. *Russia and the Origins of the First World War.* New York: St. Martin's, 1983.

Lubin, Nancy, and Monica Ware. *Aid to the Former Soviet Union: When Less Is More.* Washington, D.C.: Project on the Newly Independent States, 1996.

Lukashevich, Stephen. *Ivan Aksakov 1823–1886: A Study in Russian Thought and Politics.* Cambridge: Harvard University Press, 1965.

MacKenzie, David. *The Lion of Tashkent: The Career of General M. G. Cherniaev.* Athens: University of Georgia Press, 1974.

———. *The Serbs and Russian Panslavism 1875–1878.* Ithaca: Cornell University Press, 1967.

MacMaster, Robert E. *Danilevsky: A Russian Totalitarian Philosopher.* Cambridge: Harvard University Press, 1967.

Maklakov, V. A. *The First State Duma.* Translated by Mary Belkin. Bloomington: Indiana University Press, 1964.

Malcolm, Neil, et al. *Internal Factors in Russian Foreign Policy.* Oxford: Oxford University Press, 1996.

Malozemoff, Andrew. *Russian Far Eastern Policy 1881–1904: With Special Emphasis on the Causes of the Russo-Japanese War.* New York: Octagon, 1977.

Mandelbaum, Michael, ed. *The Rise of Nations in the Soviet Union.* New York: Council on Foreign Relations, 1991.

Maresca, John J. *The End of the Cold War Is Also Over.* Edited by Gail W. Lapidus and Renee de Nevers. Stanford, Calif.: Center for International Security and Arms Control, April 1995.

May, Ernest. *American Imperialism: A Speculative Essay.* New York: Atheneum, 1968.

Mayall, James. *Nationalism and International Society.* Cambridge, UK: Cambridge University Press, 1990.

McCarter, Joan, and Holt Ruffin. *Channels: A Guide to Third Sector Projects, Organizations, and Opportunities in the New Independent States.* Seattle: Center for Civil Society International, 1995.

McCauley, Martin, and Peter Waldron. *The Emergence of the Modern Russian State, 1855–1881.* London: Macmillan, 1988.

McConnell, Allen. *A Russian Philosophe: Alexander Radishchev, 1749–1802.* The Hague: Nijhoff, 1964.

McDaniel, Tim. *The Agony of the Russian Idea.* Princeton: Princeton University Press, 1996.

McDonald, David M. *United Government and Foreign Policy in Russia 1900–1914.* Cambridge: Harvard University Press, 1992.

McFaul, Michael. *Domestic Politics of NATO Expansion in Russia: Implications for American Foreign Policy.* Harvard University, Program on New Approaches to Russian Security, Policy Memo No. 5, October 1997.

———. *Russia between Elections: What the December 1995 Results Really Mean.* Washington, D.C.: Carnegie Endowment for International Peace, 1996.

McKim, Robert, and Jeff McMahan, eds. *The Morality of Nationalism.* New York: Oxford University Press, 1997.

McReynolds, Louise. *The News under Russia's Old Regime: The Development of a Mass Circulation Press.* Princeton: Princeton University Press, 1991.

Meininger, Thomas. *Ignatev and the Establishment of the Bulgarian Exarchate 1864–1872: A Study in Personal Diplomacy.* Madison: University of Wisconsin Dept. of History, 1970.

Mercer, Jonathan L. *Reputation and International Politics.* Ithaca: Cornell University Press, 1995.

Michaels, Alexander Joseph. "Neoslavism and Its Attempt at Russo-Polish Rapprochement 1908–1910." Master's Thesis, American University, 1956.

Millar, James R., ed. *The Soviet Rural Community.* Urbana: University of Illinois Press, 1971.

Miller, Wright. *Russians as People.* New York: Dutton, 1960.

Mitrofanov, Aleksei. *Russia's New Geopolitics,* Harvard University Project on Strengthening Democratic Institutions, July 1998.

Morris, Warren. *The Weimar Republic and Nazi Germany.* Chicago: Nelson-Hall, 1982.

Morrison, John. *Boris Yeltsin: From Bolshevik to Democrat.* New York: Dutton, 1991.

Mosse, W. E. *Alexander II and the Modernization of Russia.* Revised ed. New York: Collier, 1962.

Motyl, Alexander J., ed. *The Post-Soviet Nations.* New York: Columbia University Press, 1992.

Nahaylo, Bohdan, and Victor Swoboda. *Soviet Disunion: A History of the Nationalities Problem in the USSR.* New York: Free Press, 1989.

Nekrich, Aleksandr M. *The Punished Peoples*: The Deportation and Fate of Soviet Minorities at the End of the Second World War. New York: Norton, 1978.

Nicholls, A. J. *Weimar and the Rise of Hitler,* 2nd ed. New York: St. Martin's, 1979.

Olcott, Martha Brill, ed. *The Soviet Multinational State: Readings and Documents.* Armonk, N.Y.: Sharpe, 1990.

O'Prey, Kevin. *A Farewell to Arms? Russia's Struggle with Defense Conversion.* Washington, D.C.: Twentieth Century Fund, 1995.

———. *Keeping the Peace in the Borderlands of Russia,* Washington, D.C.: Henry L. Stimson Center Occasional Paper 23, July 1995.

Owen, David. *Balkan Odyssey.* New York: Harcourt Brace, 1995.

Perry, William J. *Report of the Secretary of Defense to the President and the Congress.* Washington, D.C.: US Government Printing Office, 1996.

Petro, Nicolai N. *The Rebirth of Russian Democracy.* Cambridge: Harvard University Press, 1995.

———, ed. *Reflections on Russia.* Translated by Christina Sever. Boulder: Westview, 1991.

Petrovich, Michael Boro. *The Emergence of Russian Panslavism 1856–1870.* Westport, Conn.: Greenwood, 1956.

Pinchuk, Ben-Cion. *The Octobrists in the Third Duma 1907–1912.* Seattle: University of Washington Press, 1974.

Pipes, Richard. *The Russian Revolution.* New York: Knopf, 1990.

———. *Survival Is Not Enough.* New York: Simon and Schuster, 1984.

———. *Struve: Liberal on the Right 1905–1944.* Cambridge: Harvard University Press, 1980.

———. *Russia under the Old Regime.* New York: Scribner,1974.

———. *Struve: Liberal on the Left 1870–1905.* Cambridge: Harvard University Press, 1970.

———. *The Formation of the Soviet Union.* Rev. ed. Cambridge: Harvard University Press, 1964.

———, trans. *Karamzin's Memoir on Ancient and Modern Russia: A Translation and Analysis.* New York: Atheneum, 1974.

———, trans. *Karamzin's Memoir on Ancient and Modern Russia: A Translation and Analysis.* Cambridge, Mass.: Harvard University Press, 1959.

Pobedonostsev, Konstantin P. *Reflections of a Russian Statesman.* Ann Arbor: University of Michigan Press, c. 1965.

Poggi, Gianfranco. *The State: Its Nature, Development, and Prospects.* Cambridge, UK: Polity, 1990.

Politovskii, Evgenii. *From Libau to Tsushima.* New York: Dutton, 1908.

Prizel, Ilya. *National Identity and Foreign Policy: Nationalism and Leadership in Poland, Russia, and Ukraine.* Cambridge, UK: Cambridge University Press, 1998.

Pulzer, Peter. *The Rise of Political Anti-Semitism in Germany and Austria.* Rev. ed. Cambridge: Harvard University Press, 1964.

Purves, J. G., and D. A. West, eds. *War and Society in the Nineteenth-Century Russian Empire.* Toronto: New Review Books, 1972.

Ra'anan, Uri and Kate Martin, eds. *Russia: A Return to Imperialism?* New York: St. Martin's Press, 1996.

Raeff, Marc. *Understanding Imperial Russia: State and Society in the Old Regime.* New York: Columbia University Press, 1984.

———. *Michael Speransky, Statesman of Imperial Russia, 1772–1839.* 2nd ed. The Ha Nijhoff, 1969.

Ragsdale, Hugh. *The Russian Tragedy: The Burden of History.* Armonk, N.Y.: Sharpe

———, ed. and trans. *Imperial Russian Foreign Policy.* Cambridge, UK: Cambridge sity Press, 1993.

Rawson, Don C. *Russian Rightists and the Revolution of 1905.* Cambridge, UK: Cambridge University Press, 1995.

Read, Christopher. *Religion, Revolution, and the Russian Intelligentsia 1900–1912.* London: Macmillan, 1979.

Riasanovsky, Nicholas V. *A History of Russia.* 4th ed. New York: Oxford University Press, 1984.

———. *Nicholas I and Official Nationality in Russia 1825–1855.* Berkeley: University of California Press, 1969.

———. *Russia and the West in the Teachings of the Slavophiles.* Gloucester, Mass.: Peter Smith, 1965.

Richardson, James L. *Crisis Diplomacy: The Great Powers Since the Mid-Nineteenth Century.* Cambridge, UK: Cambridge University Press, 1994.

Rieber, Alfred J. *The Politics of Autocracy: Letters of Alexander II to Prince A. I. Bariatinskii 1857–1864.* The Hague: Mouton, 1966.

Rodzianko, M. V. *The Reign of Rasputin: An Empire's Collapse.* Translated by Catherine Zvegintzoff. Gulf Breeze, Fla.: Academic International Press, 1973.

Rogger, Hans. *Russia in the Age of Modernisation and Revolution 1881–1917.* New York: Longman, 1983.

———. *National Consciousness in Eighteenth-Century Russia.* Cambridge: Harvard University Press, 1960.

Rossos, Andrew. *Russia and the Balkans: Inter-Balkan Rivalries and Russian Foreign Policy 1908–1914.* Toronto: University of Toronto Press, 1981.

Roy, Olivier. *The Civil War in Tajikistan: Causes and Implications.* Washington, D.C.: U.S. Institute of Peace, 1993.

Schapiro, Leonard. *Rationalism and Nationalism.* New Haven: Yale University Press, 1967.

The Search for Peace in Chechnya: A Sourcebook 1994-96. Produced by Dianne Curran, Fiona Hill and Elena Kostritsyna, Harvard University Project on Strengthening Democratic Institutions, March 1997.

Sestanovich, Stephen, ed. *Rethinking Russia's National Interest.* Washington, D.C.: Center for Strategic and International Studies, 1994.

Seton-Watson, Hugh. *Nations and States.* Boulder: Westview, 1977.

———. *The Russian Empire 1801–1917.* Oxford: Clarendon, 1967.

———. *The New Imperialism.* Chester Springs, Penn.: Dufour, 1961.

———. *The Decline of Imperial Russia 1855–1914.* London: Methuen, 1952.

Shafer, Boyd C. *Nationalism: Its Nature and Interpreters.* Washington, D.C.: American Historical Association, 1976.

———. *Faces of Nationalism: New Realities and Old Myths.* New York: Harcourt Brace Jovanovich, 1972.

Shub, Anatole. *Russian Elites Discuss Russia's Place in the World.* Washington, D.C.: U.S. Information Agency, December 1996.

Sikkink, Kathryn. *Ideas and Institutions: Developmentalism in Brazil and Argentina.* Ithaca: Cornell University Press, 1991.

Simmons, Ernest J., ed. *Continuity and Change in Russian and Soviet Thought.* Cambridge: Harvard University Press, 1955.

th, Anthony. *Theories of Nationalism.* 2nd ed. London: Duckworth, 1983.

, Anthony D. *The Ethnic Origins of Nations.* Oxford: Blackwell, 1986.

Graham, ed. *The Nationalities Question in the Soviet Union.* London: Longman, 1990.

oodruff. *The Ideological Origins of Nazi Imperialism.* New York: Oxford University ?86.

Snyder, Louis L. *Encyclopedia of Nationalism.* New York: Paragon, 1990.

———. *Roots of German Nationalism.* Bloomington: Indiana University Press, 1978.

———. *German Nationalism: The Tragedy of a People.* Harrisburg, Penn.: Telegraph Press, 1952.

Sociopolitical Situation in the Post-Soviet World. Moscow: Ethnopolitical Studies Center, Foreign Policy Association, February 1993.

Sorel, Albert. *The Eastern Question in the Eighteenth Century.* New York: Howard Fertig, 1969.

Stark, Gary D. *Entrepreneurs of Ideology.* Chapel Hill: University of North Carolina Press, 1981.

Starr, Frederick S., ed. *The Legacy of History in Russia and the New States of Eurasia.* Armonk, N.Y.: Sharpe, 1994.

Stephan, John J. *The Russian Fascists: Tragedy and Farce in Exile 1925–45.* New York: Harper and Row, 1978.

Stern, Fritz. *Dreams and Delusions.* New York: Knopf, 1987.

Sumner, B. H. *Russia and the Balkans 1870–1880.* London: Archon, 1962.

Suny, Ronald Grigor. *Looking toward Ararat: Armenia in Modern History.* Bloomington: Indiana University Press, 1993.

———. *The Revenge of the Past: Nationalism, Revolution, and the Collapse of the Soviet Union.* Stanford: Stanford University Press, 1993.

———. *The Making of the Georgian Nation.* Bloomington: Indiana University Press, 1989.

Taranovski, Theodore, ed. and trans. *Reform in Modern Russian History.* New York: Cambridge University Press, 1995.

Taylor, A. J. P. *The Struggle for Mastery in Europe 1848–1918.* Oxford: Clarendon, 1954.

Tetlock, Philip, et al., eds. *Behavior, Society and Nuclear War.* Vol. 2. New York: Oxford University Press, 1991.

Thaden, Edward C. (with Marianna Forster Thaden). *Interpreting History: Collective Essays on Russia's Relations with Europe.* Boulder: Social Science Monographs, 1990, p. 208.

Thaden, Edward C. *Russia's Western Borderlands 1710–1870.* Princeton: Princeton University Press, 1984.

———. *Russia since 1801.* New York: Wiley, 1971.

———. *Russia and the Balkan Alliance of 1912.* University Park: Pennsylvania State University Press, 1965.

———, ed. *Russification in the Baltic Provinces and Finland, 1855–1914.* Princeton: Princeton University Press, 1981.

Tilly, Charles. *Coercion, Capital, and European States AD 990–1992.* Cambridge, UK: Blackwell, c. 1992.

———, ed. *The Formation of National States in Western Europe.* Princeton: Princeton University Press, 1975.

Tishkov, Valery. *Ethnicity, Nationalism and Conflict in and after the Soviet Union: The Mind Aflame.* London: Sage, 1997.

Tuchman, Barbara. *The Proud Tower.* New York: Macmillan, 1966.

Tucker, Robert C. *Stalin in Power: The Revolution from Above 1928–1941.* New York: Norton, 1990.

Tucker, Robert C. *Political Culture and Leadership in Soviet Russia.* New York: Norton, 1987, pp. 162–71.

———, ed. *Stalinism: Essays in Historical Interpretation.* New York: Norton, 1977.

Ulam, Adam. *Expansion and Coexistence.* New York: Holt, Rinehart, and Winston, 1974.

United States Department of Defense. *Cooperative Threat Reduction.* April 1995.

Urban, G. R., ed. *Stalinism*. Cambridge: Harvard University Press, 1986.

Von Laue, T. H. *Serge Witte and the Industrialization of Russia*. New York: Columbia University Press, 1963.

Vyšný, Paul. *Neo-Slavism and the Czechs 1898–1914*. Cambridge, UK: Cambridge University Press, 1977.

Walicki, Andrzej. *A History of Russian Thought: From the Enlightenment to Marxism*. Stanford: Stanford University Press, 1979.

Walker, Edward W. *No Peace, No War in the Caucasus: Secessionist Conflicts in Chechnya, Abkhazia and Nagorno-Karabakh*. Cambridge: Harvard University, Strengthening Democratic Institutions Project, February 1998.

Wallander, Celeste, ed. *The Sources of Russian Foreign Policy after the Cold War*. Boulder: Westview, 1996.

Weber, Eugen J. *Peasants into Frenchmen: The Modernization of Rural France, 1870–1914*. London: Chatto and Windus, 1979.

Weber, Max. *Economy and Society: An Outline of Interpretive Sociology*. Edited by Guenther Roth and Claus Wittich. New York: Bedminster, 1968.

Weeks, Theodore R. *Nation and State in Late Imperial Russia: Nationalism and Russification on the Western Frontier, 1863–1914*. DeKalb: Northern Illinois University Press, 1996.

Westwood, J. N. *Endurance and Endeavor: Russian History 1812–1980*. 2nd ed. New York: Oxford University Press, 1981.

Westwood, N. *Russia against Japan, 1904–1905. A New Look at the Russo-Japanese War*. London: Macmillan, 1986.

Wetzel, David. *The Crimean War: A Diplomatic History*. Boulder: East European Monographs, 1983.

Whittier-Heer, Nancy. *Politics and History in the Soviet Union*. Cambridge: MIT Press, 1971.

Wieczynski, Joseph L., ed. *The Modern Encyclopedia of Russian and Soviet History*. Vol. 18. Gulf Breeze, Fla.: Academic International Press, 1977.

Will the Union Be Reborn? The Future of the Post-Soviet Region. Harvard University, Strengthening Democratic Institutions Project, June 1997.

Yanov, Alexander. *The Russian Challenge and the Year 2000*. Oxford: Blackwell, 1987.

———. *The Russian New Right*. Berkeley, Calif.: Institute of International Studies, 1978.

Zaionchkovsky, Peter A. *The Russian Autocracy in Crisis 1878–1882*. Translated by Gary M. Hamburg. Gulf Breeze, Fla.: Academic International Press, 1979.

Zenkovsky, Alexander V. *Stolypin: Russia's Last Great Reformer*. Princeton: Kingston Press, 1986.

Russian and French

Afanasev, Yurii, et al. *God posle avgusta: Gorech' i vybor*. Moscow: Literatura i politika, 1992.

Aksakov, Ivan Sergeevich. *Sochineniia: Slavianskii vopros 1860–1886*. Moscow: Tip. M. G. Volchaninova, 1886.

Aksakov, Konstantin. *Polnoe sobranie sochinenii*. Moscow: Tip. P. Bakhmeteva, 1861.

Aleksandr II: Ego lichnost', intimnaia zhizn' i pravlenie. Moscow: Galaktika, 1991.

Apostol'skii, P. *Nravstvennye osnovy nastoiashchei voiny*. Moscow: Tip. universitetskaia, 1877.

Avdeev, V. B. *Russkii stroi*. Moscow: Intellekt, 1997.

Avrekh, A. Ia. *Stolypin i tret'ia Duma*. Moscow: Nauka, 1968.

Barsov, Nikolai P. *Slavianskii vopros i ego otnoshenie k Rossii*. Vilnius: Tip. A. Syrkina, 1867.

Barsukov, Nikolai. *Zhizn' i trudy M. P. Pogodina*. St. Petersburg: Tip. M. M. Stasiulevicha, 1888.

———, ed. *Pis'ma M. P. Pogodina, S. P. Shevyreva i M. A. Maksimovicha k Kniaz'iu P. A. Viazemskomu 1825–1874 gg.* St. Petersburg: Tip. M. Stasiulevicha, 1901.

Berkov, E. A. *Krymskaia kampaniia.* Moscow: Moskovskii rabochii, 1939.

Bestuzhev, I. S. *Krymskaia voina 1853–1856 gg.* Moscow: Izd. Akademiia Nauk SSSR, 1956.

Bestuzhev, I. V. *Bor'ba v Rossii po voprosam vneshnei politiki 1906–1910.* Moscow: Nauka, 1961.

Bibliografiia periodicheskikh izdanii Rossii. Vol. 3. Leningrad: Ministerstvo kul'tury RSFSR, 1960.

Bobykin, V. I. *Ocherki istorii vneshnei politiki Rossii.* Moscow: Gosud. Uchebno-pedagogicheskoe izd. Min. Prosveshcheniia RSFSR, 1960.

Bogdanov, I. M. *Gramotnost' i obrazovanie v dorevoliutsionnoi Rossii i v SSSR.* Moscow: Izd. "Statistika," 1964.

Buryshkin, P. A. *Moskva kupecheskaia.* New York: Izd. M. Chekhova, 1954.

Bushuev, S. K. *A. M. Gorchakov.* Moscow: Mezhdunarodnye otnosheniia, 1961.

———. *Krymskaia voina.* Moscow: Izd. Akademiia Nauk SSSR, 1940.

Butmi-de-Katsman, G. V. *Konstitutsiia i politicheskaia svoboda.* 2nd ed. St. Petersburg: Tip. Uchilishche glukhonemykh, 1906.

Cheshko, S. V. *Raspad Sovetskogo Soiuza.* Moscow: Rossiiskaia Akademiia Nauk, 1996.

Chikhachev, P. A. *Velikie derzhavy i vostochnyi vopros.* Moscow: Nauka, 1970.

Chto takoe "Dukhovnoe Nasledie." Moscow: Obozrevatel', 1996.

Chubais, Igor'. *Ot russkoi idei—k idee Novoi Rossii.* Moscow: Izd. dom "Sotsial'naia zashchita," 1997.

Churbanov, B., et al. *Neformaly. Kto oni? Kuda zovut?* Moscow: Izd. politicheskoi literatury, 1990.

Danilevskii, N. Ia. *Rossiia i Evropa. Vzgliad na kul'turnye i politicheskie otnosheniia slavianskogo mira k germanskomu.* 4th ed. St. Petersburg: Izd. V. V. Kashpireva, 1869.

Desiatyi s"ezd' Rossiiskoi Kommunisticheskoi Partii: Stenograficheskii otchet. Moscow: Gosudarstvennoe izd., 1921.

Diakin, V. S. *Russkaia burzhuaziia i tsarizm v gody pervoi mirovoi voiny 1914–1917.* Leningrad: Nauka, 1967.

Domontovich, M. *Obzor russko-turetskoi voiny 1877–1878 gg. na Balkanskom poluostrove.* St. Petersburg: Gosudarstvennyi tip., 1900.

Doroshevich, V. *Vostok i voina.* Moscow: Tip. I. D. Sytina, 1905.

Dostoian, I. S. *Russkaia obshchestvennaia mysl' i balkanskie narody: Ot Radishcheva do Dekabristov.* Moscow: Nauka, 1980.

Dubrovin, N. E. *Istoriia Krymskoi voiny i oborony Sevastopolia.* St. Petersburg: Tip. Tovarishchestva "Obshchestvennaia pol'za," 1900.

Durnovo, N. N. *Russkaia panslavistskaia politika na pravoslavnom vostoke i v Rossii.* Moscow: Tip. Russkaia pechatnia, 1908.

Dvadtsatipiatiletie velikoi osvoboditel'noi voiny 1877–1902. Moscow: Tip. T-va I. D. Sytina, 1902.

Dvizheniia. Partii. Assotsiatsii. Soiuzy. Kluby. Sbornik materialov i dokumentov [vol. no. missing]. Moscow: RAU-Press, 1992.

Ekonomika Rossii (ianvar'–mai 1996 g.). Moscow: Goskomstat, 1996.

Fadeev, Rostislav. *Mnenie o vostochnom voprose.* St. Petersburg: Tip. departamenta Udalova, 1870.

———. *Russkoe obshchestvo v nastoiashchem i budushchem (Chem nam byt'?).* St. Petersburg: Tip. "Obshchestvennaia pol'za," 1874.

———. *Shestdesiat' let kavkazkoi voiny.* Tiflis: Voenno-pokhodnaia tip. Glavnogo Shtaba, 1860

Fedorov, Boris. *Patriotizm i demokratiia.* Pamphlet of the "Vpered, Rossiia!" Movement, Moscow, 1995.

Fedosova, I. A., ed. *Istoriia SSSR, XIX i nachalo XX–ogo veka.* Moscow: Vysshaia shkola, 1981.

Frank, S. L. *Biografiia P. B. Struve.* New York: Chekhov, 1956.

Galkin, A. A. *Zapadnia. Rasskaz o tom, chto prines nemetskim rabochim natsional-sotsializm.* Moscow: Russko-Amerikanskii Fond Profsoiuznykh issledovanii i obucheniia, 1995.

Gdlian, T. and N. Ivanov. *Kremlevskoe delo.* Moscow: Gramota, 1996.

Global'nye problemy i perspektivy tsivilizatsii (fenomen evraziistva). Moscow: Russian Academy of Sciences, 1993.

Gosudarstvennaia duma, stenograficheskie otchety, sessiia 1. Vol. 1. St. Petersburg, 1906.

Gosudarstvennaia duma v Rossii v dokumentakh i materialakh. Introduction by F. I. Kalinychev. Moscow: Gos. izd. iuridicheskoi literatury, 1957.

Govorukhin, Stanislav. *Velikaia kriminal'naia revoliutsiia.* Moscow: Izd. Andreevskii flag, 1993.

Graf Nikolai Pavlovich Ignatev. Biograficheskii ocherk s portretom. St. Petersburg: Tip. S. Dobrodeeva, 1880.

Grigoriev, Izmail M. "Uchastie narodov srednego Povolzh'ia v natsional'no-osvoboditel'noi bor'be iuzhnykh slavian v period vostochnogo krizisa 1875–1878 gg." Avtoreferat dissertatsii. Kuibyshev: Kuibyshevskii gos. pedagogicheskii institut im. Kuibysheva, 1978.

Ignatev, A. V. *Vneshniaia politika Rossii v 1905–1907 gg.* Moscow: Nauka, 1986.

Institut Otkrytoe Obschestvo. *V poiskakh svoego puti: Rossiia mezhdu Evropoi i Aziei.* Moscow: Logos, 1997.

Ivanovich, V. *Rossiiskie partii, soiuzy i ligi.* St. Petersburg, 1906.

Kadilin, P. N. *Griadushchee zavershenie voinoiu 1914 g. istoricheskogo prizvaniia Rossii v roli osvoboditel'nitsy i glavy slavianskogo mira.* Kharkov: Tip. Mirnyi trud, 1914.

Kaganovich, I. Z. *Ocherk razvitiia statistiki shkol'nogo obrazovaniia v SSSR.* Moscow: Gos. statisticheskoe izd., 1957.

Katkov, Mikhail. *O samoderzhavii i konstitutsii.* Moscow: Pechatnia A. I. Snegirovoi, 1905.

Kizevetter, A. A. *Na rubezhe dvukh stoletii (vospominaniia 1881–1914).* Prague: Izd. "Orbis," 1929.

Kokovtsov, V. N. *Iz moego proshlogo: Vospominaniia 1903–1914.* Moscow: Nauka, 1992.

Kortunov, Sergei. *Rossiia: Natsional'naia identichnost' na rubezhe vekov.* Moscow: Moskovskii obshchestvennyi nauchnyi fond, 1997.

Korzhakov, Aleksandr. *Boris El'tsyn: Ot rassveta do zakata.* Moscow: Interbuk, 1997.

Kotov, N. I., and A. A. Tsyganov. *Voennye Rossii.* Moscow: RAU Press, 1992.

Kulikova, I. S., et al. *Fenomen Zhirinovskogo.* Moscow: Kontrolling, 1992.

Kurginian, S. V., et al. *Postperestroika.* Moscow: Izd. politicheskoi literatury, 1990.

Kutkovets, T., and I. Kliamkin. *Russkie idei* [based on a polling project called Osobyi put' Rossii]. Moscow, 1997.

Lamanskii, V. *Chego nam osobenno zhelat' i chto nam nuzhnee delat' v zapadno-slavianskikh zemliakh.* St. Petersburg: Tip. E. Evdokhimova, 1885.

Likhachev, V., and V. Pribylovskii, eds. *Russkoe Natsional'noe Edinstvo: Istoriia, politika, ideologiia.* Moscow: Panorama, 1997.

Luciani, Georges. *La société des slaves unis 1823–25.* France: Univérsité de Bordeaux, 1963.

Martov, L., P. Maslov, and A. Potresov, eds. *Obshchestvennoe dvizhenie v Rossii v nachale XX– ogo veka.* St. Petersburg: Tip. t-va "Obshchestvennaia pol'za," 1911.

McFaul, M., and N. Petrov, eds. *Politicheskii almanakh Rossii 1995.* Moscow: Moskovskii Tsentr Karnegi, 1995.

Miketov, Ia. *Chto sdelalo narodnoe predstavitel'stvo tret'ego sozyva.* St. Petersburg: Tip. P. A. Suvorina, 1912.

Miliukov, P. *Balkanskii krizis i politika A. P. Izvolskago.* St. Petersburg: Tip. "Obshchestvennaia Pol'za," 1910.

Miliutin, D. A. *Dnevnik D. A. Miliutina 1873–1875.* Moscow: Tip. Zhurnala "Pogranichnik," 1947–1950.

Mitrofanov, Aleksei. *AntiNATO: Novaia ideia Rossiiskoi geopolitiki.* Moscow, undated brochure.

Names That Have Returned. Moscow: Novosti Press Agency Publishing House, 1989.

Narochnitskaia, L. I. *Rossiia i natsional'no-osvoboditel'noe dvizhenie na Balkanakh 1875–1878.* Moscow: Nauka, 1979.

Narochnitskii, A. L., ed. *Rossiia i natsional'no-osvoboditel'naia bor'ba na Balkanakh 1875–1878.* Moscow: Nauka, 1978.

Nechkina, M. V. *Obshchestvo soedinennykh slavian.* Moscow: Gosudarstvennoe izd., 1927.

Nevedenskii, S. *Katkov i ego vremia.* St. Petersburg: Tip. A. S. Suvorina, 1888.

Nikitin, S. A. *Slavianskie komitety v Rossii v 1858–1876 godakh.* Moscow: Izd. Moskovskogo universiteta, 1960.

Olcott, Martha Brill, et al., eds. *Identichnost' i konflikt v postsovetskikh gosudarstvakh.* Moscow: Moskovskii Tsentr Karnegi, 1997.

Ostretsov, V. *Chernaia sotnia i krasnaia sotnia.* Moscow: Voenno-patrioticheskoe literaturnoe ob"edinenie "Otechestvo," 1991.

Pertsov', P. *Panrussizm ili panslavizm?* Moscow: Tip. A. I. Mamontova, 1913.

Pobedonostsev, K. P. *Pis'ma k Aleksandru III.* Moscow: "Novaia Moskva," 1925.

Pogodin, M. P. *Istoriko-politicheskie pis'ma i zapiski v prodolzhenii krymskoi voiny, 1853–1856.* Moscow: V. M. Frish', 1874.

Pogrebinskii, A. P. *Ocherki istorii finansov dorevoliutsionnoi Rossii.* Moscow: Gosfinizdat. 1954.

Politologiia na rossiiskom fone. Moscow: Luch, 1993.

Preobrazhenskii, I. V. *Za brat'ev slavian: Po povodu 25–letiia sviashchennoi voiny 1877–1878.* St. Petersburg: Izd. P. P. Soikina, 1903.

Programma Kommunisticheskoi partii Rossiiskoi Federatsii. Moscow: Informpechat', 1995.

Pypin, A. N. *Panslavizm v proshlom i nastoiashchem.* St. Petersburg: Knigo-izd. "Kolos," 1913.

Riabushinskii, V. P., ed. *Velikaia Rossia: Sbornik stat'ei po voennym i obshchestvennym voprosam.* Book 2. Moscow: Tip. Riabushkina, 1911.

Rittikh, A. F. *Ob"edinennoe slavianstvo.* St. Petersburg: Tip. V. D. Smirnova, 1908.

Robniakova, L. I. *Bor'ba iuzhnykh slavian za svobodu i russkaia periodicheskaia pechat'.* Leningrad: Nauka, 1986.

Rodzianko, M. V. *Krushenie imperii.* New York: Multilingual Typesetting, 1986.

Rossiia i Evropa: Opyt sobornogo analiza. Moscow: Nasledia, 1992.

Rossiia mezhdu Evropoi i Aziei: Evraziiskii soblazn'. Moscow: Nauka, 1993.

Rossiiskaia diplomatiia v portretakh. Moscow: Mezhdunarodnye otnosheniia, 1992.

Rossiiskie samoderzhtsy 1801–1917. 2nd ed. Moscow: Mezhdunarodnye otnosheniia, 1994.

Russkaia ideia: Demokraticheskoe razvitie Rossii. Moscow: Rossiiskii Nauchnyi Fond, Moskovskoe otdelenie, seriia Nauchnye doklady, vol. 31, 1996.

Russkaia periodicheskaia pechat' 1702–1894. Moscow: Gos. izd. politicheskoi literatury, 1959.

Russkaia periodicheskaia pechat' 1702–1914. Moscow: Gos. izd. politicheskoi literatury, 1959.

Russkaia periodicheskaia pechat' 1895–oktiabr' 1917. Moscow: Gos. izd. politicheskoi literatury, 1957.

Russkaia politicheskaia mysl' vtoroi poloviny XIX v. Moscow: Akademiia Nauk, 1989.

Russkii put' v razvitii ekonomiki. Moscow: Mosmetrostroia, 1993.

Sakulin, P. N. *Iz istorii russkogo idealizma. Kniaz' V. F. Odoevskii. Myslitel', pisatel'.* Vol. 1. Moscow: Izd. M. i S. Sabashnikovykh, 1913.

Samarin,Y. F. *Stat'i, vospominaniia, pis'ma.* Moscow: Terra, 1997.

Savitskii, P. N. *Iskhod k vostoku.* Sofia: Rossiisko-Bulgarskoe knigoizd., 1921.

Sazonov, S. D. *Vospominaniia.* Moscow: Mezhdunarodnye otnosheniia, 1991.

Sbornik dogovorov Rossii s drugimi gosudarstvami 1856–1917. Moscow: Gos. izd. politicheskoi literatury, 1956.

Semenov, Iu. I., ed. *Natsional'naia politika v imperatorskoi Rossii: Tsivilizovannye okrainy.* Moscow: Staryi sad, 1997.

Sementkovskii, R. I. *M. N. Katkov: Ego zhizn' i literaturnaia deiatel'nost'.* St. Petersburg: Izd. F. Pavlenkova, 1892.

Sem'ia Aksakovykh. St. Petersburg: Tip. M. Akinfieva i I. Leonteva, 1904.

Shafarevich, Igor. *Russofobiia.* Munich: Rossiiskoe natsional'noe ob"edinenie, 1989.

Shatsillo, K. F. *Rossiia pered pervoi mirovoi voiny (vooruzhennye sily tsarizma v 1905–1914 gg.)* Moscow, 1974.

Shelest, P. E. *Dnevnik P. E. Shelesta.* Rossiiskii Tsentr Khraneniia i Izucheniia Dokumentov Noveishei Istorii, Fond 666, Delo 2, listy 333–48.

Shtur, L. *Slavianstvo i mir budushchego* (foreword by V. I. Lamanskii). Moscow: Imperskoe obshchestvo istorii i drevnosti Rossii pri Mosk. universitete, 1867.

Slaviane i Rossiia. Moscow: Nauka, 1972.

Slavianskii sbornik: Slavianskii vopros i russkoe obshchestvo v 1867–1878 godakh. Moscow: Biblioteka SSSR im. V. I. Lenina, 1948.

Sobianin, A. A., and V. G. Sukhovol'skii. *Demokratiia, ogranichennaia fal'sifikatsiiami.* Moscow: Proektnaia gruppa po pravam cheloveka, 1995.

Soiuz Vozrozhdeniia Rossii. *Istoricheskaia spravka.* Xeroxed ms.

Solovev, V. S. *Sobranie sochinenii.* Vol. 5. St. Petersburg: Izd. Tov. "Obshchestvennaia pol'za," 1901.

Solzhenitsyn, Aleksandr. *Kak nam obustroit' Rossiiu.* Paris: YMCA Press, 1990.

————. *Pis'mo vozhdiam Sovetskogo Soiuza.* Paris: YMCA Press, 1974.

Sotsial'no-politicheskaia situatsiia v postsovetskom mire. Moscow: Ethnopolitical Studies Center, Foreign Policy Association, April 1993.

Sovetskaia istoricheskaia entsiklopediia. Moscow: Sovetskaia entsiklopediia, 1967.

Stalin, I. *O velikoi otechestvennoi voine Sovetskogo Soiuza.* Moscow: Gos. izd-vo polit. lit-ry, 1950.

Sterligov, A. N. *Nam nuzhno chisto russkoe reshenie.* Moscow: No publisher, 1993.

100 partiinykh liderov Rossii. Moscow: RAU-Korporatsiia, 1993.

Takhotskii, L. *Gospodin Petr Struve v politike.* St. Petersburg: Knigoizd. 'Novyi mir,' 1906.

Tatishchev, S. S. *Imperator Aleksandr II: Ego zhizn' i tsarstvovanie.* Vol. 2. St. Petersburg: A. S. Suvorin, 1903.

Tereshchenko, V. K. "M. P. Pogodin v obshchestvenno-ideinoi bor'be 30–50kh godov XIX stoletiia." Avtoreferat dissertatsii. Moscow: Gos. universitet im. Lomonosova, 1975.

Tikhomirova, E. N. *Za svobodu brat'ev-slavian.* Moscow: Tip. K. L. Men'shova, 1911.

Tikhvinskii, S. L., ed. *Vneshniaia politika Rossii (istoriografiia): Sbornik statei.* Moscow: Nauka, 1988.

Tret'ia gosudarstvennaia Duma: Materialy dlia otsenki ee deiatel'nosti. St. Petersburg: Trud, 1912.

Troitskii, Evgenii, ed. *Russkii put' v razvitii ekonomiki.* Moscow: Tip. Mosmetrostroia, 1993.

Troitskii, S. M. *Finansovaia politika russkogo absoliutizma v xviii veke.* Moscow: Nauka, 1966.

Uchebniki dorevoliutsionnoi Rossii. Moskva: Prosveshchenie, 1993.

Ushkuinik, V. *Pamiatka russkomu cheloveku.* Moscow: Russkii natsional'nyi sobor, 1993.

Utkin, Anatolii. *Rossiia i zapad: Problemy vospriiatiia i perspektivyi stroitel'stva otnoshenii.* Moscow: Rossiiskii nauchnyi fond, 1995.

———, and Vladimir Batiuk. *Sovremennaia sistema mezhdunarodnykh otnoshenii i Rossiia.* Moscow: Institute SShA i Kanady Rossiiskoi Akademii Nauk, 1996.

Valuev, P. A. *Dnevnik P. A. Valueva.* Moscow: Akademiia Nauk, 1961.

Vdovin, A. I. *Rossiiskaia natsiia.* Moscow: Izd-vo Roman-gazeta, 1996.

Verkhovskii, Aleksandr, et al. *Politicheskii ekstremizm v Rossii.* Moscow: Panorama, 1996.

Voennaia reforma: Vooruzhennye sily Rossiiskoi Federatsii. Moscow: Dukhovnoe nasledie, 1998.

Voina za osvobozhdenie slavian 1877–1878. St. Petersburg: Voennaia tip., 1902.

Yakovlev, O. A. "Russko-turetskaia voina 1877–1878 gg. i russkoe obshchestvo." Avtoreferat dissertatsii. Leningrad: Gos. univ. im. A. A. Zhdanova, 1980.

Yanov, Alexander. *Posle El'tsina. "Veimurskaia" Rossiia.* Moscow: Moskovskaia gorodskaia tip. A. S. Pushkina, 1995.

Yurskii, G. *Pravye v tretei Gosudarstvennoi Dume.* Kharkov: Izd. Tsentral'nogo predvybornogo komiteta ob'edinnenykh russkikh liudei, 1912.

Zabolotskii, P. A. *Vozrozhdenie idei slavianskoi vzaimnosti i novye izucheniia slavianstva.* Nezhin: Tip. V. K. Melenevskogo, 1912.

Za realizm, sozidanie, i gumanizm. Moscow: Klub "Realisty," 1995.

Zhirinovsky, Vladimir. *Poslednii brosok na iug.* Moscow: Liberal Democratic Party of Russia, 1993.

Zhurnalistika i voina. Moscow: Russian American Press Information Center, 1995.

Zolotarev, V. A., and I. A. Kozlov. *Russko-iaponskaia voina 1904–1905 gg: Bor'ba na more.* Moscow: Nauka, 1990.

Zyuganov, Gennadii. *Derzhava.* Moscow: Informpechat', 1994.

JOURNAL ARTICLES AND UNPUBLISHED MANUSCRIPTS

Acta Eurasica (entire issue) 1 (1995).

Ado, V. I. "Berlinskii Kongress 1878 g. i pomeshcheche-burzhuaznoe obshchestvennoe mnenie Rossii." *Istoricheskie zapiski* 69 (1961):101–41.

Afanasev, Yuri N. "Russian Reform Is Dead." *Foreign Affairs* 73 (March/April 1994):21–27.

Akbarzadeh, Sharam. "Striving for Unity over Regional and Ethnic Division." *Transition,* 20 May 1995, pp. 53–56.

Aksiuchits, Viktor. "Tribuna oppozitsii: Sformirovat' sil'niuiu natsional'nuiu vlast'." *Russkii sobor* (2 February 1993):6.

"Alternative Visions of the Soviet Future." *Studies in Comparative Communism* 20 (Autumn/Winter 1987):233–90.

Amin, Tahir. "Nationalism and Internationalism in Three Communitarian Traditions: Liberalism, Marxism and Islam." Xerox ms. (26 March 1986), 68 pp.

Ball, Deborah Yarsike. "How Reliable Are Russia's Officers?" *Jane's Intelligence Review* (May 1996):204–7.

Becker, Seymour. "Contributions to a National Ideology: Histories of Russia in the First Half of the Nineteenth Century." *Russian History* 13 (Winter 1986):331–32.

Belin, Laura. "All Sides Claim Victory in 1996 Gubernatorial Elections." *Transition,* 21 February 1997, pp. 24–27.

———. "Wrestling Political and Financial Repression." *Transition* 1, 6 October 1995, pp. 59–63, 88.

———, and Robert W. Orttung. "Electing a Fragile Political Stability." *Transition,* 7 February 1997, pp. 67–70.

Blagovolin, Sergei. "O vneshnei i voennoi politike Rossii." *Svobodnaia mysl'* 18 (1992):3–15.

Boyce, James K., and Manuel Pastor, Jr. "Aid for Peace: Can International Financial Institutions Help Prevent Conflict?" *World Policy Journal* (Summer 1998):42–49.

Brown, Bess A. "Overriding Economics." *Transition*, 15 February 1995, pp. 53–56.

Brubaker, Rogers. "Nationhood and the National Question in the Soviet Union and Post-Soviet Eurasia." *Theory and Society* 23 (1994):47–78.

———. "Rethinking Nationhood: Nation as Institutionalized Form, Practical Category, Contingent Event." *Contention* 4 (Fall 1994):3–19.

Brusstar, James H., and Ellen Jones. "Attitudes within the Russian Officer Corps." *Strategic Forum* 15 (January 1994): 4.

Brzezinski, Zbigniew. "The Premature Partnership." *Foreign Affairs* 73 (March/April 1994):67–82.

Bukkvoll, Tor. "A Fall from Grace for Crimean Separatists." *Transition*, 17 November 1995, pp. 46–49.

Calhoun, Craig. "Nationalism and Ethnicity." *Annual Review of Sociology* 19 (1993):222–24.

Cherniavsky, Michael. "'Holy Russia': A Study in the History of an Idea." *American Historical Review* 63 (April 1958):617–37.

Chesheva, Iu. V. "Kto nashi deputaty: Narodnye predstavitely ili narodnye predateli?" *Russkii vostok* 4 (1993).

Chinyaeva, Elena. "A Eurasianist Model of Interethnic Relations Could Help Russia Find Harmony." *Transition*, 1 November 1996, pp. 30–38.

———. "Russian Orthodox Church Forges a New Role." *Transition*, 5 April 1996, pp. 14–23.

Chmielewski, Edward. "Stolypin's Last Crisis." *California Slavic Studies* 3 (1964): 95–126.

Confino, Michael. "Solzhenitsyn, the West, and the New Russian Nationalism." *Journal of Contemporary History* 26 (1991):611–36.

Conversi, Daniele. "Reassessing Current Theories of Nationalism: Nationalism as Boundary Maintenance and Creation." *Nationalism and Ethnic Politics* 1 (Spring 1995):72–85.

Danielyan, Emil. "No War, No Peace in Nagorno-Karabakh." Transition, August 1997, pp. 44–49.

Dawson, Jane I. "Ethnicity, Ideology, and Geopolitics in Crimea." *Communist and Post-Communist Studies* 30, no. 4 (December 1997):427–44.

"Decree of the Russian Federation Supreme Soviet 'On the Russian Federation's Approach to the Yugoslav Conflict.'" *FBIS-SOV* (4 January 1993):34.

"Demograficheskoe polozhenie Rossii." *Svobodnaia mysl'* 3 (1993):96–105.

"Demokraticheskoe igo." *Molodaia gvardiia* 1 (1993):225–30.

Dreiling, Aleksandr. "Patrioty i natsionalisty v sovremennom politicheskom prostranstve Rossii." *Politicheskii monitoring* 12, no. 59.

Dunlop, John B. "The 'Party of War' and Russian Imperial Nationalism." *Problems of Post-Communism* (March/April 1996):29–34.

———. "The Many Faces of Contemporary Russian Nationalism." *Survey* 24 (Summer 1979):18–35.

Duplain, Julian. "Chisinau's and Tiraspol's Faltering Quest for Accord." *Transition*, 20 October 1995, pp. 10–13.

Evangelista, Matthew. "The Paradox of State Strength: Transnational Relations, Domestic Structures, and Security Policy in Russia and the Soviet Union." *International Organization* 49 (Winter 1995):1–38.

Fadin, Andrey. "The Political Potential of the Mayor of Moscow." *Transition*, 21 February 1997, p. 34.

Foye, Stephen. "Russia and the 'Near Abroad.'" *Post–Soviet Prospects* 3, no. 12 (December 1995).

Fuller, Elizabeth. "Transcaucasus—Doomed to Strategic Partnership." *Transition*, 15 November 1996, pp. 29–31.

———. "Between Anarchy and Despotism." *Transition*, 15 January 1995, pp. 64–65.

———, and Scott Parrish. "Chechen Conflict Ends with Shaky Peace." *Transition*, 7 February 1997, pp. 74–75.

Furman, D. "Ukraina i my: Natsional'noe samosoznanie i politicheskoe razvitie." *Svobodnaia mysl'* 1 (1994):69–83.

Gagnon, V. P., Jr. "Ethnic Nationalism and International Conflict: The Case of Serbia." *International Security* 19 (Winter 1994/95):13–66.

Geifman, Anna. "Ubii!" *Rodina* 1 (1994): 25–26.

Goldanskii, Vitalii. "Russia's Red-Brown Hawks." *Bulletin of the Atomic Scientists* 49 (June 1993):24–27.

Gould-Davies, Nigel, and Ngaire Woods. "Russia and the IMF." *International Affairs* (London) 75 (January 1999):1–22.

Greenfeld, Liah. "The Formation of the Russian National Identity: The Role of Status Insecurity and Ressentiment." *Comparative Study of Society and History* (July 1990):552–70.

Gribincea, Mihai. "Rejecting a New Role for the Former Fourteenth Russian Army." *Transition*, 22 March 1996, pp. 38–40.

———. "Challenging Moscow's Doctrine on Military Bases." *Transition*, 20 October 1995, pp. 4–8.

Grigoriev, Sergei, and Matthew Lantz. "Lessons of the 1995 State Duma Elections." *Demokratizatsiya* 4 (Spring 1996):159–63.

Grindin, I. F., ed. "K istorii kontserna br. Riabushinskikh." *Materialy po istorii SSSR*. Vol. 6. Moscow: Izd. Akademii Nauk, 1959.

Gudkov, L. D. "Russkii neotraditsionalizm." *Informatsionnyi biuletten' monitoringa* 2 (March/ April 1997):25–32.

"The Guidelines of State Policy: From the Address of the President of the Russian Federation Boris Yeltsin to the Federal Assembly of the Russian Federation on February 17, 1998." *Military News Bulletin* 7 (March 1998).

Gulyga, Arseni. "The 'Anguish of Being Russian': A Note on the Life and Works of Vasili Rozanov." *Glas* 6 (1993):185–97.

Haimson, Leopold. "The Problem of Social Stability in Urban Russia, 1905–1907." *Slavic Review* 23, no. 4 (December 1964):627–40.

Hale, Henry E. "The Rise of Russian Anti-Imperialism." *Orbis* (Winter 1999):1–16.

Hammer, Darrell P. "Alternative Visions of the Russian Future: Religious and Nationalist Alternatives." *Studies in Comparative Communism* 20 (Autumn/Winter 1987):265–76.

Hanne, Gottfried. "Playing Two Different Tunes, as Usual, in Moldova." *Transition*, December 1997, pp. 68–71.

Hanson, Stephen E., and Jeffrey S. Kopstein. "The Weimar/Russia Comparison." *Post-Soviet Affairs* 13 (1997):252–83.

Helmer, John. "Russia Enemy No. 1: America." *Journal of Commerce* (15 October 1997).

Hill, Fiona. "Domestic Anxiety and International Humiliation: Russian National Interest, Public Opinion, and the Annexation of Bosnia-Herzegovina 1908–1909." Xeroxed ms.

Hosking, Geoffrey. "The Russian National Revival." *Radio Free Europe/Radio Liberty Report on the USSR* (1 November 1991):5–8.

Ianovskii, R. G. "Vostok-zapad: Sotsial'nye izmeneniia i dinamika geopoliticheskoi situatsii." *Sotsis* 7 (1998):10.

Intenberg, B. S. "Nachalo massovogo 'khozhdenia v narod.'" *Istoricheskie zapiski* 69 (1961):142–48.

James, Patrick, and John R. Oneal. "The Influence of Domestic and International Politics on the President's Use of Force." *Journal of Conflict Resolution* 35 (June 1991): 307–32.

Jervis, Robert. "Cooperation under the Security Dilemma." *World Politics* 2 (1978):167–213.

"Johann Gottfried von Herder." *Encyclopedia of Philosophy*. Vols. 3 and 4. New York: Macmillan, 1967.

Jones, Lynne. "Nationalism and the Self." *Peace and Democracy News* 6, no. 2 (Winter 1992/93):20–28.

Kabakadze, Irakli Zurab. "Russian Troops in Abkhazia: Peacekeeping, or Keeping Both Pieces?" *Perspectives on Central Asia, Center for Political and Strategic Studies* 2, no. 6 (September 1997).

Kagarlitsky, Boris. "Russia Chooses—And Loses." *Current History* (October 1996):307.

Kantor, Vladimir. "Rossiiskoe 'svoeobrazie': Genezis i problemy." *Svobodnaia mysl'* 10 (1994):78–85.

Kara-Murza, S. "Unichtozhenie Rossii." *Nash sovremmenik* 1 (1993):130–40.

Kartsov, Iu. S. " Za kulisami diplomatii." *Russkaia starina* 133 (January 1908).

Katkov, Mikhail. "Chto nam delat' s Pol'shei?" *Russkii vestnik* (March 1863):469–76.

Khovanskii, Serge. "Afghanistan: The Bleeding Wound." *Détente* 6 (Spring 1986):2–4.

Kier, Elizabeth. "Culture and Military Doctrine: France between the Wars." *International Security* 19 (Spring 1995):65–93.

Kimball, Stanley Buchholz. "The Prague 'Slav Congress' of 1868." *Journal of Central European Affairs* 22 (1962): 179–80.

Kiva, Aleksei. "A Superpower Which Ruined Itself." *International Affairs* (Moscow) 2 (February 1992):13–22.

Kohn, Hans. "Herder, Johann Gottfried (1744-1803)." *The Encyclopedia of Philosophy*, vol. 3. New York: MacMillan, 1967.

Kongress russkikh obshchin [Party Program of the Congress of Russian Communities]. Moscow, 1995.

Kotchoubey, Boris I. "The Russian or the Soviet Mentality: Which One Will Be Integrated into Europe?" *Mind and Human Interaction* 3, no. 2 (January 1992):47–48.

Kozyrev, Andrei. "Russia: A Chance for Survival." *Foreign Affairs* 71 (Spring 1992):1–16.

Kramer, Mark. "The Changing Economic Complexion of Eastern Europe and Russia: Results and Lessons of the 1990s." Xeroxed ms., April 1999.

Krasnikov, Evgenii. "Neprimirimaia oppozitsiia." *Vek XX i mir* (October 1993):64–68.

Kreindler, I. "The Soviet Deported Nationalities: A Summary and an Update." *Soviet Studies* 38 (1986):387–405.

Krivokhizha, V. I. "Rossiia v novoi strukture mezhdunarodnykh otnoshenii." *Polis* 3 (1995):9–22.

Kulakovskii, P. A. "Vozniknovenie slavianskikh obshchestv v Rossii i znachenie ikh pervogo s"ezda v Peterburge." *Slavianskie izvestiia* 5 (1909):621–35.

Kurginian, Sergei. "Kapkan dlia Rossii, ili igra v dve ruki." *Nash sovremennik* 2 (1993):141–58.

Laba, Roman. "How Yeltsin's Exploitation of Ethnic Nationalism Brought Down an Empire." *Transition*, 12 January 1996, pp. 5–13.

Lapshin, Arkadii. "From the Russian Point of View." *International Affairs* (Moscow) 10 (October 1991):79–81.

Laqueur, Walter. "Foreign Policy Concepts of the Right." *New Times* 38 (1992):12–14.

————. "Russian Nationalism." *Foreign Affairs* (Winter 1992/93):102–16.

Lavrov, P. "Anneksiia Bosnii i Gertsegoviny: Otnoshenie k nei Slavianstva." *Vestnik Evropy* (3 March 1909):27–52.

Lednicki, W. "Poland and the Slavophil Idea." *Slavonic Review* 7 (March 1929).

Leighton, Marian. "From KGB to MFA: Primakov Becomes Russian Foreign Minister." *Post–Soviet Prospects* IV, no. 2 (February 1996): 4 pp.

Leikina-Svirskaia, V. P. "Formirovanie raznochinskoi intelligentsii v 40–kh godakh XIX v." *Istoriia SSSR* 1 (1958):83–104.

Lester, Jeremy. "Overdosing on Nationalism: Gennadii Zyuganov and the Communist Party of the Russian Federation." *New Left Review* 37 (January/February 1997):48–51.

Levin, Alfred. "Peter Arkadevich Stolypin: A Political Appraisal." *Journal of Modern History* 37 (December 1965):445–63.

————. "The Russian Voter in the Elections to the Third Duma." *Slavic Review* 4 (December 1962):660–77.

Lewis, Philippa. "Peasant Nostalgia in Contemporary Soviet Literature." *Soviet Studies* 3 (1976):548–69.

Liberman, Peter. "The Spoils of Conquest." *International Security* 18 (Fall 1993):125–53.

Lind, Michael. "In Defense of Liberal Nationalism." *Foreign Affairs* 73 (May/June 1994):87–99.

Litvinova, Galina. "Starshii ili ravnyi?" *Nash sovremennik* 6 (June 1989).

Liubarskii, Kronid. "Pust' Gosduma zaplatit mne rubl'." *Novoe vremia* 37 (1995):19–20.

Lobov, L. "Slavianstvo kak mir budushchego." *Slavianskie izvestiia* 6 (1909):733–41.

MacKenzie, David. "Panslavism in Practice: Cherniaev in Serbia (1876)." *Journal of Modern History* 36 (September 1964):279–97.

Malashenko, Igor.' "Russia: The Earth's Heartland." *International Affairs* (Moscow):46–54.

March, James G., and Johan P. Olsen. "The New Institutionalism: Organizational Factors in Political Life." *American Political Science Review* 78 (September 1984).

Melançon, Michael. "The Socialist Revolutionaries from 1902 to 1907." *Russian History* 12 (Spring 1985):2–47.

Mendeloff, David. "Making History: Truth-Telling, Myth-Making and National Self-Image in Post-Soviet Russia." Massachusetts Institute of Technology, Political Science Department, 1999–2000.

Meyer, Stephen M. "The Devolution of Russian Military Power." *Current History* (October 1995):322–28.

Miakotin, V. "Nabroski sovremennosti." *Russkoe bogatstvo* 11 (1908):198–208.

Migranian, A. "Real and Illusory Guidelines in Foreign Policy." *Current Digest of the Post-Soviet Press* (CDPSP) 44 (9 September 1992):1–4.

Morvant, Penny. "Alarm Over Falling Life Expectancy." *Transition*, 20 October 1995, pp. 40–45, 72.

"Move Over, Marx." *Transition*, 9 February 1996.

"Nasha tsel'-sozdanie velikoi imperii." *Nash sovremennik* 9 (1992):122–30.

"Natsional'no-osvoboditel'noe dvizhenie otvechaet na voprosy 'Chto delat'? i Kto vinovat?'" *Russkoe delo* 1 (1993): 206–25.

Novikova, Lidiia, and Irina Sizemskaia. "Dva lika Evraziistva." *Svobodnaia mysl'* 7 (1992):100–110.

O'Brien, Conor Cruise. "The Wrath of Ages." *Foreign Affairs* 72 (November/December 1993):142–49.

Olcott, Martha Brill. "Sovereignty and the 'Near Abroad.'" *Orbis* 39 (Summer 1995):353–67.

Orttung, Robert. "A Politically Timed Fight against Extremism." *Transition*, 23 June 1995, pp. 2–6.

Orttung, Robert W. "Duma Elections Bolster Leftist Opposition." *Transition*, 23 February 1996, pp. 6–11.

——, and Scott Parrish. "From Confrontation to Cooperation in Russia." *Transition*, 13 December 1996, pp. 16–20.

"O russkoi intelligentsii." *Novyi mir* 2 (1993):3–9.

"Osnovy voennoi doktriny Rossii." *Voennaia mysl'* (Special ed., 1992).

Panorama-Forum [a journal published by the Tatarstan Academy of Sciences; special issue on Eurasianism, pro and con] 1 (1997).

Papmehl, K. A. "The Empress and 'Un Fanatique': A Review of the Circumstances Leading to the Government Action against Novikov in 1792." *Slavonic and East European Review* 68 (1990):665–91.

Petro, Nicolai N. "Toward a New Russian Federation." *The Wilson Quarterly* (Summer 1990):114–22.

——. "'The Project of the Century': A Case Study of Russian Nationalist Dissent." *Studies in Comparative Communism* 20 (Autumn/Winter 1987):235–52.

Poliakov, Iu. "O massovom soznanii v gody voiny." *Svobodnaia mysl'* 11 (1994):62–76.

Poliakov, Iurii. "Rossiiskie prostory: Blago ili prokliat'e?" *Svobodnaia mysl'* 12 (1992):17–22.

"The Politics of Caspian Oil." *Strategic Comments*. London: International Institute for Strategic Studies (13 December 1995).

"Politika Rossii 1905–1907 godov. Iz dnevnika F. F. Martensa." *Mezhdunarodnaia zhizn'* 1 (1996):99–107.

Pollard, Alan P. "The Russian Intelligentsia: The Mind of Russia." *California Slavic Studies* 3 (December 1962).

"Populism, Nationalism, and Marxism: The Origins of Revolutionary Parties among the Armenians of the Caucasus." *Armenian Review* 32 (June 1979):134–51.

Porter, Bruce. "The Coming Resurgence of Russia." *The National Interest* (Spring 1991):14–23.

Posen, Barry. "The Security Dilemma and Ethnic Conflict." *Survival* 35 (Spring 1993):27–47.

Pozdnyakov, Elgiz. "Russia Today and Tomorrow." International Affairs 2 (February 1993).

Pushkov, Aleksei. "Russia and America: The Honeymoon Is Over." *Foreign Policy* 93 (Winter 93/94):76–90.

Rakhmatullin, M. A. "Voiny Rossii v Krymskoi kampanii." *Voprosy istorii* 8 (1972):94–118.

Rapoport, Semon. "The Russian Slavophiles and the Polish Question." *Polish Review* 1 (April 1917).

"Razocharovanie v neoslavianakh." *Slavianskie izvestiia* 6 (1909):835–38.

Ries, Tomas. "Russia's Military Inheritance." *International Defense Review* 3 (1992):223–26.

"Rising Nationalism." *CQ Researcher* (22 May 1998):474–75.

Robert, Cyprien. "Les deux panslavismes: Situation actuelle des peuples slaves vis-à-vis de la Russia." *Revue des deux mondes* (1 November 1846):453–83.

Roeder, Philip G. "Soviet Federalism and Ethnic Mobilization." *World Politics* 43 (January 1991):196–232.

Rogger, Hans. "The Skobelev Phenomenon." *Oxford Slavonic Papers* 9 (1976):46–78.

——. "The Formation of the Russian Right 1900–1906." *California Slavic Studies* 3 (1964): 66–94.

——. "Was There a Russian Fascism? The Union of Russian People." *Journal of Modern History* 36 (December 1964):398–415.

———. "Nationalism and the State: A Russian Dilemma." *Comparative Studies in Society and History* 4 (1962):253–62.

Rosen, Stephen Peter. "Military Effectiveness. Why Society Matters." *International Security* 19 (Spring 1995):5–31.

Rowley, David G. "Aleksandr Solzhenitsyn and Russian Nationalism." *Journal of Contemporary History* 32 (1997):334–36.

———. "Russian Nationalism and the Cold War." *American Historical Review* 99 (February 1994).

Roy, A. Bikash. "Intervention across Bisecting Borders." *Journal of Peace Research* 34 (1997):303–14.

"Russian Diplomacy Reborn." *International Affairs* (Moscow) 3 (March 1991):120–34.

"Russia's Organised Crime Networks." *Strategic Comments*, London: International Institute for Strategic Studies, 1997.

Ryavec, Karl W. "Weimar Russia?" *Demokratizatsiya* (Fall 1998).

Schoenfeld, Gabriel. "Outer Limits." *Post–Soviet Prospects* 17 (January 1993), 4 pp.

Sedov, L. A. "SSSR I SNG v obshchestvennom mnenii Rossii." *Informatsionnyi biulleten' monitoringa* 1 (January/February 1997):13.

Shafarevich, Igor'. "Rossiia i mirovaia katastrofa." *Nash sovremennik* 1 (1993):100–129.

Sharlet, Robert. "Russian Politics on the Eve of the Parliamentary Campaign." *Post-Soviet Prospects* III, no. 9 (September 1995):4.

Shchetinina, G. I. "Universitety i obshchestvennoe dvizhenie v Rossii v poreformennyi period." *Istoricheskie zapiski* 84 (1969):164–215.

Shenfield, Stephen. "Making Sense of Prokhanov." *Detente* 5 (1987):28–29, 51.

Sherr, James. "Doomed to Remain a Great Power." *The World Today*. Royal Institute of International Affairs, January 1996.

Shipunov, Fatei. "Put' spaseniia Rossii." *Molodaia gvardiia* 1 (1993):206–25.

Shlapentokh, Dmitry V. "Eurasianism Past and Present." *Communist and Post-Communist Studies* 30 (1997):129–51.

Shlapentokh, Vladimir. "Creating 'the Russian Dream' after Chechnya." *Transition*, 21 February 1997, pp. 28–32.

Simes, Dimitri. "Russia Reborn." *Foreign Policy* 85 (Winter 1991/92):41–62.

Simonsen, Sven Gunnar. "Still Favoring the Power of the Workers." *Transitions*, 4 December 1997, pp. 52–56.

Sinyavsky, Andrei. "Russian Nationalism." *Massachusetts Review* 31 (Winter 1990).

Slezkine, Yuri. "The USSR as a Communal Apartment, or How a Socialist State Promoted Ethnic Particularism." *Slavic Review* 53 (Summer 1994):414–52.

Smith, Anthony D. "The Ethnic Sources of Nationalism." *Survival* 35 (Spring 1993):48–62.

Smith, C. J. "The Russian Third State Duma: An Analytical Profile." *Russian Review* 17 (1958):201–10.

Snyder, Jack. "Nationalism and the Crisis of the Post–Soviet State." *Survival* 35 (Spring 1993):5–26.

———. "Gorbachev and the Waning of Soviet Expansionism." *International Security* 12 (Winter 1987/88):93–131.

Solovei, V. "Sovremennyi russkii natsionalizm: Ideino-politicheskaia klassifikatsiia." *Obshchestvennye nauki* 2 (1992):119–29.

Struve, P. B. "Politika vnutrenniaia i politika vneshniaia." *Russkaia mysl'* 2 (1910).

———. "Velikaia Rossiia." *Russkaia mysl'* 29, no. 1 (1908):143–57.

Szporluk, Roman. "Dilemmas of Russian Nationalism." *Problems of Communism* (July/August 1989):15–35.

———. "History and Russian Nationalism." *Survey* 24 (Summer 1979):1–6.

Tarakanov, Andrei. "The Rise of Russia's 'Military Opposition.'" *Transition,* 9 August 1996, pp. 6–10.

Taylor, Brian D. "Russian Civil–Military Relations after the October Uprising." *Survival* 36 (Spring 1994):3–29.

———. "Red Army Blues: The Future of Military Power in the Former Soviet Union." *Breakthroughs* 2 (Spring 1992):1–8.

Text of the Dual Citizenship Agreement between Russia and Turkmenistan. Foreign Broadcast Information Service (FBIS-SOV), 27 December 1993, p. 78.

Text of the Kazakhstan–Russian Agreement on Citizenship. FBIS-SOV, 26 January 1995, pp. 67–68.

Thurston, Robert. "The Concerns of State, 'Society,' and People in Moscow 1906–1914." *Russian History* 11 (1984):60–82.

Tishkov, Valerii. "Narody i gosudarstvo." *Kommunist* 1 (January 1989):49–59.

Tolz, Vera. "Moscow and Russia's Ethnic Republics in the Wake of Chechnya." *Post-Soviet Prospects* 3, no. 10 (October 1995), 4 pp.

Trubetskoi, Nikolai. "Obshcheevraziiskii natsionalizm." *Svobodnaia mysl'* 7 (1992):111–16.

Tsipko, Aleksandr S. "Why Gennady Zyuganov's Communist Party Finished First." *Demokratizatsiya* 4 (Spring 1996):185–99.

Tsygankov, Andrei P. "From International Institutionalism to Revolutionary Expansionism: The Foreign Policy Discourse of Contemporary Russia." *Mershon International Studies Review* 41 (November 1997):247–68.

Tuminez, Astrid S. "Soviet Politics in Transition: Two Case Studies." Second Year Paper, Political Science Department, Massachusetts Institute of Technology (Spring 1990).

Urban, Michael. "The Politics of Identity in Russia's Postcommunist Transition: The Nation against Itself." *Slavic Review* 53 (Fall 1994):740.

Uribes, E. "Praviashchie krugi Rossii i Balkanskii krizis 1911 g." *Istoricheskie zapiski* 105 (1980):72–104.

Van Evera, Stephen. "Hypotheses on Nationalism and War." *International Security* 18 (Spring 1994):5–39.

Varoli, John. "Russia Prefers to Forget." *Transitions,* July 1997, pp. 35–41.

Verdery, Katherine. "Whither 'Nation' and 'Nationalism'?" *Daedalus* 122 (Summer 1993):37–46.

Vestnik Evrazii. *Acta Eurasica* 1 (1995) [entire issue].

Vykhodtsev, Petr. "Genotsid russkogo naroda. Unichtozhenie Rossii!" *Molodaia gvardiia* 2 (1993):177–97.

"Vynuzhdennye migranty iz stran SNG i Baltii." *Sotsis* 6 (1998):56.

"War or Peace? Human Rights and Russian Military Intervention in the "Near Abroad." *Helsinki Watch* 5, no. 22 (December 1993):12.

Weiner, Myron. "Peoples and States in a New World Order." *Third World Quarterly* 13 (1992):317–32.

———. "The Macedonian Syndrome." *World Politics* 23 (July 1971):65–83.

Wimbush, S. Enders. "The Russian Nationalist Backlash." *Survey* 24 (Summer 1979):36–41.

Wortman, Richard. "Koshelev, Samarin, and Cherkassky and the Fate of Liberal Slavophilism." *Slavic Review* 2 (June 1962):261–79.

Yavlinskii, Grigorii. "The NATO Distraction." *Transition,* 21 March 1997, pp. 32–34.

Zagladin, Vadim. "Russia at World Crossroads." *Novoe vremia* 48 (1992):23–26.

Zevelev, Igor. "Russia and the Russian Diasporas." *Post-Soviet Affairs* 12 (1996):265–84.

PAPERS PRESENTED AT CONFERENCES AND SYMPOSIUMS

Anderson, Richard D. Jr., Valery V. Chervyakov, and Pavel B. Parshin. "Political Speech and the Emergence of Participatory Attitudes in Russia." American Political Science Association Annual Meeting. Washington, D.C., August 1997.
Greenfeld, Liah. "The Viability of the Concept of Nation-State." A paper presented to the American Sociological Association. Pittsburgh, August 1992.
Likhachev, Dmitrii. "The National Nature of Russian History." 2nd Annual W. Averell Harriman Lecture. Columbia University, 13 November 1990.
Messick, David M. "Nationalism as Ethnocentrism: A Social Psychological View." A summary prepared for the Workshop on Nationalism and International Conflict. National Academy of Sciences. Washington, D.C., 6–7 December 1988.
Orttung, Robert W. "Regional Power Grab: Russian Center–Periphery Relations during Crisis." American Association for the Advancement of Slavic Studies Annual Meeting. September 1998 (xeroxed ms.).
"Russia and the Outside World: A New Agenda for the Twentieth Century." An International Conference Organized by the Council on Foreign and Defense Policy. Harvard University, Strengthening Democratic Institutions Project, September 1998.
Valkenier, Elizabeth Kridl. "Teaching History in Post-Communist Russia." Harriman Institute Forum. Columbia University, April 1993.

NEWSPAPERS AND MAGAZINES

English

Agence France Press
Associated Press
Boston Globe
Business Review (Moscow)
Christian Science Monitor
Current Digest of the Post-Soviet Press
Dow Jones Newswires
Economist
Economist Intelligence Unit Country Report & Country Risk Report
Esquire
Financial Times
Guardian
International Herald Tribune
Los Angeles Times
Moscow News
Moscow Times
Newsday
Newsweek
New York Review of Books
New York Times
New York Times Magazine

New Yorker
Radio Free Europe/Radio Liberty News Briefs
Radio Free Europe/Radio Liberty Research Report
Reuters
Time
US News and World Report
Wall Street Journal
Washington Post

Russian

Argumenty i Fakty
Den'/Zavtra
Elementy
Interfax
Itar-TASS
Izvestiia
Kommersant-Daily
Kommunist
Komsomolskaia pravda
Krasnaia zvezda
Krasnodarskie izvestiia
Kuranty
Literaturnaia gazeta
Literaturnaia Rossiia
Megapolis-Express
Moskovskaia pravda
Moskovskie novosti
Moskovskii komsomolets
Narodnaia Duma
Nash marsh
Nezavisimaia gazeta
Novoe vremia
Obshchaia gazeta
Ogonek
Pravda
Rossiiskaia gazeta
Rossiiskie vesti
Russkaia mysl'
Russkii vostok
Russkoe delo
Segodnia
Sovetskaia Rossiia
Vesti gorodov iuga Rossii
We/My

ELECTRONIC SOURCES

CIS Weekly Press Summary
Economica Weekly Press Summary
IEWS Regional Report
Johnson's Russia List
Monitor (Jamestown Foundation)
National Public Radio
Open Media Research Institute Daily Digest
Politica Weekly Press Summary
Prism
Radio Ekho Moskvy
Radio Free Europe/Radio Liberty
Radio Mayak

ARCHIVAL SOURCES

Gosudarstvennyi arkhiv Rossiiskoi Federatsii (GARF)
Rossiiskaia gosudarstvennaia biblioteka, Otdel rukopisei (RGB)
Rossiiskii gosudarstvennyi voenno-istoricheskii arkhiv (RGVIA)

INTERVIEWS

Arbatov, Aleksei
Blagovolin, Sergei
Filatov, Viktor
Govorukhin, Stanislav
Kazintsev, Aleksandr
Komissar, Mikhail
Kuniaev, Stanislav
LAD [Russian Rebirth Society] members
Latynina, Alla
Lukin, Vladimir
Mitrofanov, Alexei
Nikonov, Viacheslav
Owen, David
Petrov, Sergei
Piskunov, Aleksandr
Prokhanov, Aleksandr
Pushkov, Alexei
Rogozin, Dmitrii

Rutskoi, Aleksandr
Satarov, Georgii
Seleznev, Gennadii
Shabad, Anatolii
Sirotkin, Aleksandr
Starovoitova, Galina
Sterligov, Aleksandr
Torbakov, Igor
Zhirinovsky, Vladimir
Zorkin, Valerii
Zyuganov, Gennadii

Index

Abkhazia, 244–46
aggressive nationalism, 58–59, 202–8, 230, 232, 253, 269, 272–73, 282, 285–86; in Crimea and Ukraine, 239–41; and elections, 204–5, 229; elite, fragmentation of, influence of on, 276, 277; and foreign policy, 6, 7, 23n58, 238, 253, 280, 288; governance, erosion and breakdown of, 13–15, 226, 229, 276, 277, 278; incentives for, 14–15; international environment, influence of on, 234–37, 283–84; Kazakhstan, 241–42; legal sanctions against, 274–75; and national humiliation, 174, 268, 280, 283–84, 288; national patriotic coalitions, 206–7; NATO expansion, influence of on, 235, 236–37; and newly independent states, 285–86; post-Soviet Russia, 174–75, 202–8; and Russian diaspora, 238–39, 243; state security, influence of on, 234; threats and crises, influence of on, 15–16, 234, 279, 280, 281–82; weakness of, 202–8, 208n3, 237–54; and Western policies, 283–88. *See also* great power nationalism; nationalism; Russian nationalism
aggressive statism, 175, 193–95
Aksakov, Ivan, 70, 72, 73, 74–75, 76, 81, 91, 92–93, 94, 116
Aksakov, Konstantin, 63, 64
Albania, 147
Alexander I, 37–38
Alexander II, 34, 37, 38, 68, 79, 88, 93, 116, 118

Alexander III, 38, 50n27, 116, 118–19, 136, 156n12
Andrassy Note (1875), 90
anti-Semitism, 126–27, 177, 179, 180, 194, 195, 198, 220n102, 275
Antokolskii, Mark, 93
Ardzinba, Vladislav, 244
Armenia, 41, 235, 261n64
assistance, Western, 285–86
associations (nationalist), 133, 146, 164n87, 178–79
Austro-Hungarian Empire, 90, 125, 145–47
austroslavism, 59
autocracy, Russian, 36–38, 86–88; constrained, 189, 215n58; great power nationalism on, 128, 129; October Manifesto of 1905, 34, 116–17, 123, 130, 137, 142; and political legitimacy, 85; slavophilism on, 64–65. *See also* tsarist monarchy
Azerbaijan, 235, 261n64

Balkans, 89–94, 95–97, 146, 147–49, 153–54; foreign policy in, 138, 139, 140; great power nationalism in, 145–46, 147, 149–52. *See also* Ottoman Empire; Russo-Turkish War; Serbia; Turkey, wars with
Belarus, 253
benign nationalism, 5, 268, 269, 271, 274–75, 276, 277, 278, 279
Berlin, Congress of. *See* Congress of Berlin
Berlin Memorandum (1876), 90

329

mission, national, 74–75; and foreign policy, 9–10, 125–26, 127, 129; and nationalism, 117, 188–89, 190–91, 194, 195,
198, 199, 200, 201
moderate statism, 175, 192–93, 200, 202,
253, 270, 297
Moldova, 236, 244, 246–48
monarchy (Russian). *See* tsarist monarchy
Montenegro, 90, 91
Moscow Slavic Benevolent Committee, 82,
89, 90, 116. *See also* committees, Slavic;
congresses, Slavic
"movement to the people" (1874), 86

Nagorno-Karabakh, 261n64
nation, 4, 39, 187–88, 189; definitions of, 2,
3, 18n7, 19n15, 25–26, 31, 191–92, 195,
271; membership in, criteria of, 8–9,
70–71, 117, 125, 126, 129, 175, 191, 192,
195, 199, 200, 201, 238; Russian, 30, 31,
33–34, 35–36. *See also* nation-building;
nation-state; nationalism; Russian
nationalism
nation-building, 26–27, 266, 274; liberal
politicians, role of in, 289–90; non-
imperial and anti-imperial discourse,
273, 289–90; in Russian state, 30, 31,
33–34, 35–36, 38, 39, 46, 266, 271, 273;
in Soviet Union, 42–45, 180
nation-state, 1, 13, 26–27, 28–29, 36, 267,
271–72, 289–90
national patriotism, 175, 179, 195–98, 201,
203, 204
nationalism, 14, 99, 175, 194, 266; benefits
of, 268–69; benign, 5, 268, 269, 271,
274–75, 276, 277, 278, 279; civic, 8–9,
232, 271; definition of, 1, 2, 17n3, 266;
and elite, 3, 4–5, 185–86, 266, 267; ethnic, 8, 13, 125, 126; evolution of, 2,
26–27, 28, 48n8; and foreign policy, 2,
4, 19n16, 237; hegemonic (Russian), 59,
70–71, 74, 125, 127; and historical
scholarship, 272–73; and humiliation,
national, 6–7, 10–12, 21n40, 123–24,
186, 288; as ideology, 2, 4, 5, 15, 16, 25;
malevolent effects of, 1–2, 5; and
national mission, 9–10, 117, 125–26,
127, 129, 160n52, 188–89, 190–91, 194,
195, 198, 199, 200, 201; political aspect

of, 2–3, 28; and ressentiment, 10–11,
124; self-image, national, 9, 125, 126,
128, 188, 189, 190, 192, 196, 197, 198,
199, 200–201, 276; Soviet patriotism vs.
Russian patriotism, 178; in Soviet
Union, 45, 175–80, 181, 213n47; varieties of, 5, 59; and violence, 8, 9, 195.
See also aggressive nationalism; ethnic
conflicts; great power nationalism;
nation; panslavism; Russian nationalism
nativism, 175, 179, 189–91, 199–200
neoslavism, 59, 125–26, 146, 160n45,
160n52
newly independent states. *See* Soviet
republics, former
Nicholas I, 34, 66, 79
Nicholas II, 38, 50n27, 116, 119, 136–37,
139, 155n3, 165n101
North Atlantic Treaty Organization
(NATO), 235, 236–37, 251–52, 259n45,
280, 281, 282, 284–85, 294n40

October 17, Union of (Octobrists), 123,
131, 138, 142
October Manifesto of 1905, 34, 116–17,
123, 130, 137, 142
opposition (in Russia), 34, 37–38, 116–17,
122, 123, 140–41, 159n35, 166n120. *See
also* political movements (in Russia)
Orthodox Church, 63, 64, 65, 71, 85, 90,
118, 181, 189, 202, 203. *See also* religion
other-image: aggressive statism on, 194;
great power nationalism on, 128–29;
national patriotism on, 195–96, 198,
201; nativism on, 199; neoslavs on, 125;
panslavism on, 71, 73–74; rightist
nationalists on, 126; statism on,
200–201; Westernizing nationalism on,
188, 199
Ottoman Empire, 58, 59, 66, 90; weakening
of, 98–99, 144–45, 153. *See also*
Balkans; Russo-Turkish War; Serbia;
Turkey, wars with

panslavism, 6, 20n31, 70, 74, 100n4,
101n12, 127, 130, 140, 267, 269; and
aggressive nationalism, 58–59; and
Balkan crises, 89–94, 146, 147–48; and

About the Author

Astrid S. Tuminez is associate director of research for Alternative Investments Group at AIG Global Investment Corp. She is an adjunct fellow at the Council on Foreign Relations and was a former program officer at Carnegie Corporation of New York and a consultant to the World Bank. She holds a master's degree in Soviet studies from Harvard University and a doctorate in political science from the Massachusetts Institute of Technology.

DATE DUE

			Printed in USA

HIGHSMITH #45230